The Civic World of Early Renaissance Florence

THE
CIVIC WORLD
OF
EARLY
RENAISSANCE
FLORENCE

∽

BY GENE BRUCKER

PRINCETON UNIVERSITY PRESS
PRINCETON, NEW JERSEY

Library of Congress Cataloging in Publication Data will
be found on the last printed page of this book

This book has been composed in Linotype Janson

Printed in the United States of America
by Princeton University Press, Princeton, New Jersey

For Marion

Acknowledgments

I began work on this book in 1960, when a sabbatical leave from the University of California at Berkeley and a fellowship from the Guggenheim Foundation allowed me to spend a year in Florence. That pattern was repeated four years later, when the American Council of Learned Societies awarded me a fellowship to continue my research in Florence. While enjoying the hospitality of the Institute for Advanced Study at Princeton in 1968–1969, I completed the transcription of microfilmed documents and began to write the first chapters of the book. In 1973–1974, I was awarded a grant from Berkeley's Humanities Institute, which gave me free time to complete the manuscript. To all these institutions, their administrators, and their staffs, I express my gratitude. I would also like to thank the personnel of the state archives in Florence, Prato, and Siena, the Biblioteca Nazionale *and the* Biblioteca Mediceo-Laurenziana *in Florence, and the Vatican archives in Rome for their help in providing me with the archival material on which this book is based.*

I owe a particular debt to my friend Dottore Gino Corti, who has discovered and deciphered important documents for me, and whose scrutiny of my transcriptions has saved me from countless errors. I also thank Carolyn Dewald who patiently checked my Latin references in the footnotes. I am very grateful to my editors, Lewis Bateman and Marjorie Sherwood, for their help in preparing the manuscript for publication. F. W. Kent of Monash University and Dale Kent of La Trobe University, Australia, kindly allowed me to read their manuscripts and to utilize their material prior to its publication. I would like to thank Ronald Witt of Duke University for permitting me to read a draft of his article, "Florentine Politics and the Ruling Class, 1382–1407," and Lionel Rothkrug of Concordia University, Montreal, for sending me a copy of his manuscript, "Popular Religion and Holy Shrines." I have received good counsel and criticism from amici who have read parts or all of this study: F. W. and Dale Kent, Ronald Witt, Richard Trexler, Lauro Martines, William Bouwsma, Irwin Scheiner, Randolph Starn. I thank Antonio Calabria for helping me compile the index.

My wife Marion, to whom I dedicate this book, has helped me to persevere in an enterprise that at times seemed to have no end. I am deeply grateful to her and to my children, who have given me so much support and encouragement.

G. B.

Abbreviations

ACP	*Atti del Capitano del Popolo*
AEOG	*Atti dell' Esecutore degli Ordinamenti della Giustizia*
AP	*Atti del Podestà*
APG	*Archivio di Parte Guelfa*
Ashb.	*Biblioteca Mediceo-Laurenziana, Florence; MS Ashburnham*
ASI	*Archivio storico italiano*
BNF	*Biblioteca Nazionale di Firenze*
Conc.	*Archivio di Stato, Siena; Concistoro*
CP	*Consulte e Pratiche*
CRS	*Corporazioni Religiose Soppresse*
Datini	*Archivio di Stato, Prato; Archivio Datini*
DBCMLC	*Dieci di Balìa, Carteggi, Missive: Legazioni e Commissarie*
DBRA	*Dieci di Balìa, Relazioni di Ambasciatori*
Delizie	*Delizie degli eruditi toscani,* ed. Ildefonso di San Luigi (Florence, 1770–1789)
DSCOA	*Deliberazioni dei Signori e Collegi, Ordinaria Autorità*
Flor. Studies	*Florentine Studies. Politics and Society in Renaissance Florence,* ed. N. Rubinstein (London, 1968)
GA	*Giudice degli Appelli*
Lana	*Arte della Lana*
LF	*Libri Fabarum*
Magl.	*Magliabechiana*
MAP	*Mediceo Avanti il Principato*
Merc.	*Tribunale di Mercanzia*
Minerbetti	*Cronica volgare di anonimo fiorentino già attribuita a Piero di Giovanni Minerbetti,* ed. E. Bellondi, *Rerum Italicarum Scriptores,* new ed., xxvii, part 2 (Città di Castello, 1915–1918)
Panc.	*Fondo Panciatichiano*
Pres.	*Archivio delle Prestanze*
Prov.	*Registri delle Provvisioni*
RRIISS	*Rerum Italicarum Scriptores*
SCMC	*Signori, Carteggi, Missive, I Cancelleria*
SCMLC	*Signori, Carteggi, Missive, Legazioni e Commissarie*
SCRRO	*Signori, Carteggi, Rapporti e Relazioni di Oratori*

Stefani   *Cronica fiorentina di Marchionne di Coppo Stefani*, ed. N. Rodolico, *Rerum Italicarum Scriptores*, new ed., xxx, part 1 (Città di Castello, 1903–1955)

Strozz.   *Carte Strozziane*

Note: Unless otherwise indicated, archival references are to the *Archivio di Stato*, Florence. All dates cited are New Style.

Contents

Acknowledgments   vii

Abbreviations   ix

Introduction: The Historiography of Early Renaissance Florence   3

I. Corporate Values and the Aristocratic Ethos in Trecento Florence

Social Aggregations   14
Corporatism and the Aristocratic Spirit   30
The Ciompi Revolution   39
The Guild Regime of 1378–1382   46

II. Domestic Politics, 1382–1400

The Early Years of the New Regime   60
The Defeat of the Alberti   75
The Crisis of 1393   90

III. Foreign Affairs: 1382–1402

Florentine Imperialism, 1382–1388   102
The First Visconti War   125
The Beleaguered Republic, 1392–1398   144
The Final Confrontation, 1398–1402   165

IV. Florentine State-Building

The Liquidation of the Visconti Empire   187
Problems of Territorial Government   208
Challenges to the Florentine State: Ladislaus and Genoa   225

V. The Florentine *Reggimento* in 1411

The Social Composition of the Regime   248
The Political Elite   262
The New Style of Politics   283
Civic Values   302

VI. Crisis, 1411–1414

The Four Horsemen   319
The Genoese War   340
The Polarization of the Regime   352
The Second War with Ladislaus   368

VII. The Ordeal of Peace and the Ordeal of War: 1414–1426

    Peace Without Prosperity   396
    Peacetime Problems and Anxieties   406
    The Regime's Recovery   425
    War   447

VIII. The Regime's Climacteric, 1426–1430

    The Revival of the Factions   472
    Disintegration   481
    The Balance Sheet   500

Index   509

The Civic World of Early Renaissance Florence

The Historiography of Early Renaissance Florence

FLORENCE, the premier city of the Renaissance, has long been a subject of scrutiny by her own prideful citizens, by other Italians, and by admiring foreigners. Most students of the city's past have felt, with Voltaire, that Florence occupies a central place in the history of Renaissance Italy, of Renaissance Europe, indeed of Western civilization. They have traced the lines of her evolution from a small provincial town in the eleventh century to a city that, by 1300, was one of Europe's largest and richest. They have studied, too, the political developments that paralleled this demographic and economic growth: the rise of the autonomous commune, the vicissitudes of republican government, the establishment of a princely dynasty. They have been attracted by the reputations of her famous sons: Dante and Boccaccio, the galaxy of artists from Giotto to Michelangelo, Medici bankers and statesmen, the Ferrarese friar Savonarola who adopted the city and there experienced martyrdom. Nourishing this interest in Florence's past is a reservoir of source material that, for richness and variety, is unmatched by that for any other European community. In the documentation that has survived from the Renaissance centuries can be found information for every taste and temperament, illuminating every facet of human experience. The extraordinary size and quality of Florence's historical patrimony is due partly to the intellectual curiosity of her population, and partly to her good fortune in escaping many (though not all) of the perils that have afflicted other parts of Europe in modern times: war, revolution, social upheaval, natural disasters.

Since the end of World War II, the study of Florentine history has developed into a large-scale enterprise. No other European city in the pre-industrial age has been explored so intensively. To a remarkable degree, this massive scholarly enterprise has been unstructured and uncoordinated, without the guidance of an established tradition. Contributing to this situation has been the predominance of foreign scholars in the field, and the absence of any local institutional structure to promote and guide research.[1] Methods and perspectives imported from abroad (positivism, Marxism, *Geistesgeschichte*, struc-

---

[1] R. Starn, "Florentine Renaissance Studies," *Bibliothèque d'humanisme et Renaissance*, XXXII (1970), 678.

turalism) have left traces in the scholarship, but none has become so deeply entrenched as to establish a school of Florentine studies. There has been little agreement on method, or on the assignment of priorities to research problems. Critics have often noted that Florentine historians tend to explore their own bailiwicks, with scant reference to the work of their colleagues, and with slight interest in the study of similar problems elsewhere.[2] Thus Florentine history is characteristically parochial and non-comparative. It is no accident that Florentine scholars have not joined together—as their counterparts in Milan, Venice, and Rome have done—to write a collective history of the city.[3] The spirit of individualism (some might say of anarchy) is too strong for such collaborative effort.

There are, however, discernible patterns and trends in this untidy and heterogeneous body of historical writing: concentrations of research on specific periods and problems. The decades after the Black Death have been more intensively studied by the current generation of scholars than the medieval centuries, which had been the primary concern of prewar historians: Davidsohn, Salvemini, Ottokar, Sapori. And within the time-span of the Florentine Renaissance, from the mid-fourteenth to the mid-sixteenth century, scholars have focused upon particular moments of crisis, when the city's experience changed (or appeared to change) sharply and decisively.[4] One conjuncture, particularly favored by demographic and economic historians, is the decade of the 1340s, when Florence's pattern of growth was abruptly reversed by famine, plague, and economic dislocation. The beginning of the fifteenth century is another turning-point, from a "medieval" to a "Renaissance" age, most clearly marked in the plastic arts and in education, but with shifts and realignments in other spheres. The third crisis is most precisely and dramatically marked by the French invasion of 1494, and the subsequent efforts of Florentines—and other Italians—to preserve their civilization from the onslaught of the ultramontane barbarians.

The schemes of periodization that are built around these "crises"

---

[2] A rare exception is Lauro Martines' comparative analysis of Florentine and Milanese governments in his *Lawyers and Statecraft in Renaissance Florence* (Princeton, 1968), ch. 11. Cf. the comparative treatment of Tuscan fiscal systems by William Bowsky, *The Finance of the Commune of Siena 1287-1355* (Oxford, 1970), ch. 11.

[3] Starn, 678-79. Starn's review of *Florentine Studies* edited by Nicolai Rubinstein (London, 1968), is an excellent if brief analysis of recent Florentine historiography.

[4] On the current predilection of historians for "crises," see Starn's suggestive analysis in *Past and Present*, no. 52 (Aug. 1971) 3-22.

have not gained the universal acceptance of Florentine historians, who disagree sharply about their significance. Illustrating these discordant viewpoints are the writings of David Herlihy and Philip Jones, both specialists in the economic history of late medieval Tuscany. Herlihy has formulated a model of economic development characterized by distinct phases and clearly defined turning-points.[5] He insists that the demographic reversal of the 1340s was a critical moment in Tuscan history, signifying the end of three centuries of growth and the beginning of a long period of economic stagnation followed by a gradual recovery. He stresses the differences between the old agrarian regime—characterized by high rents and interest rates, rising grain prices, and an exploited peasantry on the bare edge of subsistence—and the new order of the *mezzadria* that, he argues, brought prosperity and stability to the Tuscan countryside. In Herlihy's view, the Renaissance was a distinct phase in Florentine (and Tuscan) history, marked by a modest demographic and economic recovery, the reallocation of wealth in both country and town (the aristocracy richer, merchants and artisans poorer), and significant changes in life styles and mentalities. Jones examines the agrarian history of Tuscany from a different point of view and arrives at different conclusions. His recent article on the disintegration of the Tuscan manor is a dense, massively documented study that stresses the complexity and eccentricity of medieval agrarian developments, in which he sees no clear trends and no sharp, decisive breaks.[6] He places greater stress on continuity, and on variety and vicissitude, than does Herlihy, and he is less inclined to see the *mezzadria* as the panacea for rural Tuscany's ills. Jones' skepticism about the concept of Renaissance is most clearly expressed in his essay on communes and despots, where he argues that political structures and attitudes did not change significantly from the eleventh to the eighteenth century. In Italy, he writes, "the 'Renaissance state' is a fiction to be banned from the books."[7]

Most Florentine historians would dispute Jones' assertion that the Renaissance, as a periodizing concept, has neither validity nor utility. The majority would probably accept Denys Hay's dictum that "there was a Renaissance," though some might question his statement that the evidence for its reality was "overwhelming."[8] Within this area

[5] In his article on S. Maria Impruneta, *Flor. Studies*, 242–76, and his *Medieval and Renaissance Pistoia* (New Haven, 1967).

[6] *Flor. Studies*, 193–241.

[7] *Transactions of the Royal Historical Society*, 5th ser., xv (1965), 95.

[8] *The Italian Renaissance in its Historical Background* (Cambridge, 1966), 1.

of rough consensus, however, there are disagreements over defining these concepts, medieval and Renaissance, and over locating them on Florence's temporal grid. Students of the plastic arts—and more generally, of Florentine culture—are most strongly persuaded that the changes they observe in their special fields signify a radical transition from one age to another. George Holmes, for example, perceives the Renaissance as a Florentine creation, an intellectual movement "of rather extreme and sudden secularization of ideas, under the auspices of the classics, over a broad spectrum of interests . . . and a sudden blossoming of highly original attitudes in a transitory movement."[9] To students of population and productivity, of social and political structures, the transformations are not so abrupt nor so dramatic. But change there was, from *trecento* to *quattrocento*, in the material environment as well as in the realms of thought and sensibility.[10]

In recent studies of Florentine politics in the early Renaissance (which I shall define arbitrarily as the period from the Ciompi Revolution in 1378 to the advent of the Medici in 1434), three themes have received particular emphasis. First, scholars have noted the contraction of the social base of politics, and the concentration of power in the hands of an oligarchy, after the collapse of the guild regime in 1382. Paralleling this change in the social foundations of political power was the transformation of the structure, and also the spirit, of government: the disintegration of the medieval commune and the rise of a territorial state, characterized by the centralization of authority and the establishment of a bureaucratic administration. A third important issue is the emergence of an intense civic spirit, which transformed the parochial and partisan loyalties of the medieval commune into a patriotic commitment to the institutions and values of a secular, republican community. Each of these themes has a history: an initial formulation, a critical evaluation of varying degrees of intensity, and, after reservations and qualifications, integration into the historiographical tradition. The most venerable (and probably the most widely accepted) is the elitist hypothesis, which can be traced back to Machiavelli and other sixteenth-century historians, and which has reappeared in the nineteenth-century syntheses of Capponi and Perrens, and in the twentieth-century interpretations of Schevill, Martines, and Tenenti.[11] More controversial is the statist theory formulated in

[9] *The Florentine Enlightenment 1400–50* (London, 1969), xix.

[10] Cf. Starn, "Florentine Renaissance Studies," *op. cit.*, 683.

[11] See A. Molho, "The Florentine Oligarchy and the *Balìe* of the Late Trecento," *Speculum*, XLIII (1968), 23–25.

its most extreme form by Marvin Becker. The intensity of the debate over this hypothesis testifies to its significance for the history of Renaissance Italy, and indeed for all Europe. The "civic" thesis is the creation of Hans Baron, whose seminal work, *The Crisis of the Early Italian Renaissance* (1955; second edition, 1966), has stimulated a flood of laudatory and critical comment.[12] The scholarly controversies arising from this book have been quite as spirited as those over the territorial state; they constitute a staple element in recent Florentine historiography.

Ever since Gaetano Salvemini published his classic study on the struggle between magnates and *popolani* in the late thirteenth century, students of Florentine history have been sensitized to the problems of class conflict, and to the impact of these tensions upon politics, religion, and culture.[13] This materialist focus is most pronounced in the writings of Alberto Tenenti and Lauro Martines. These scholars have argued that the most significant development in Florentine history during the late fourteenth century was the achievement of total control of the state by Florence's entrepreneurial class. This process, Tenenti asserts, was the consequence of changes in the Florentine economy and, specifically, the trend toward a greater concentration of wealth and a more centralized control over economic activity by that mercantile elite. Tenenti insists that a genuinely popular government in Florence was never possible, and that some form of oligarchic government was inevitable, given the economic conditions of the second half of the *trecento*. Camouflaging the stark realities of a class ruling exclusively for its own benefit was an antiquated constitutional structure that, in its operations and its ideology, perpetuated the myth (widely accepted and cherished in Florence) of a regime based upon the whole guild community. Some progress was made by the oligarchy in reorganizing the administrative structure to insure more rational and efficient government, and thus more effective control over the city and its territory. The ruling elite thus began, though it did not complete, the process of transforming the medieval commune into a modern bureaucratic state.[14]

---

[12] N. Rubinstein, in *Flor. Studies*, 10–11. For bibliographical references to a contrary viewpoint, see L. Martines, "Political Conflict in the Italian City States," *Government and Opposition*, III (1968), 73–74.

[13] This perspective also predominates in Peter Herde's analysis; see his "Politische Verhaltensweisen der Florentiner Oligarchie 1382–1402," in *Geschichte und Verfassungsgefüge: Frankfurter Festgabe für Walter Schlesinger* (Wiesbaden, 1973), 156–249.

[14] *Florence à l'époque . . . Medicis: de la cité à l'état* (Paris, 1968).

Like Tenenti, Martines focuses his attention upon those wealthy Florentines who constituted the city's ruling class and who exercised control over every aspect of life. Their regime was unequivocally oligarchic: "By oligarchy I mean government where only the few have a voice and where among these the rich tend to hold the most authoritative positions."[15] Although economic and social conditions in the late *trecento* promoted this oligarchic trend, the basic impulse came from the aristocratic families whose members resisted the pressures for a more broadly constituted regime, pressures that were particularly intense during the Ciompi revolution and its troubled aftermath. "From the 1380's," Martines writes, "the upper-class families moved to reverse things, partly by fostering the concentration of power in certain offices." He emphasizes the dynamism of this ruling class, which enlisted the services and the loyalties of the professional groups in Florentine society, the humanists and the lawyers, whose knowledge and expertise were exploited for the benefit of the oligarchy. In his study of Florentine statecraft in the fifteenth century, Martines develops the concept of an inner oligarchy of 400–700 citizens that "constituted the effective ruling class," and the Florentine perception of the state as the personal possession of the men who controlled it.

Tenenti and Martines view the centralization and rationalization of authority as a consequence of the drive by the Florentine mercantile aristocracy to strengthen its control over the state, and thus over the territory (and its inhabitants) governed by the state. The prime mover in this process is the energy and will of a ruling elite. Both trends, oligarchic and statist, are gradual, but the critical stages occur in the years after 1382. Marvin Becker moves the critical moment back a half-century, to the 1340s; that decade marks, in his analysis, the transition from a loosely organized and tolerant regime to a polity that was hostile to privilege and immunity, and austere and puritanical in spirit. The social group that accomplished this transformation was not the aristocracy, but the guildsmen from the middle strata of society, who demanded government that was strict, impartial, and efficient. Though Becker incorporates all facets of Florentine experience —the emotional and the aesthetic as well as the tangible and the concrete—into his conceptual vision, his scheme is based upon material foundations. and specifically upon the fiscal system. The fisc was the ligament uniting public and private interests; in a very real sense, the ruling class owned the state through its investment in the funded debt. These "owners" pursued a statist policy designed primarily to increase

---

[15] *Lawyers and Statecraft*, 387. For his general argument, 387–404, 467–76.

revenues and thus to promote the solvency of the regime and protect the investments of the shareholders in this public enterprise.[16]

Becker connects the intensification of civic feeling in Florence in the late fourteenth century to the breakdown of the corporate order; citizens gave their allegiance increasingly to the state because the older collectivities had become too weak to command loyalty. Hans Baron attributes this civic revival to the effect of external events and, specifically, to the Visconti threat to the republic's independence that reached its climax in the summer of 1402. It is this peril, Baron argues, that transformed Leonardo Bruni into a passionate defender of the Florentine republic and of the political and moral values that he associated with republicanism. Born of a diplomatic and military crisis, civic humanism became the quasi-official culture of the Florentine ruling class. Its point of view was secular; its program included a justification of the active life, and of mundane concerns generally; and the formulation of a new historical outlook that described Florence's experience—the experience of a dynamic, independent republic—in very positive terms.[17]

Before these themes—elitism, statism, and civism—can be fully integrated into a coherent interpretation of Florentine politics in the early Renaissance, they should be reexamined in the light of recent criticism, and of new evidence. They do not fit neatly together, either logically or chronologically. Several scholars have noted, for example, the anomaly of an intensified civic spirit emerging at a time when the social base of Florentine government was contracting, when fewer citizens were participating in political life.[18] Becker has argued that the statist trend intensified after the 1340s; Tenenti and Martines view this development as a phenomenon of the fifteenth century. Most fundamental are the disagreements over what might be called the priorities of causation. Baron sees external stimuli as the key catalyst

---

[16] Becker's thesis is developed in the two volumes of his *Florence in Transition* (Baltimore, 1967-68), but is most succinctly formulated in "The Florentine Territorial State and Civic Humanism in the Early Renaissance," *Flor. Studies*, 109-39. Cf. the critiques of Becker's analysis by L. Martines, P. Jones, R. Starn and P. Herde, in *Speculum*, XLIII (1968), 689-92; *English Historical Review*, LXXXV (1968), 410-13; *Bibliothèque d'humanisme et Renaissance*, XXX (1968), 624-27; and *Historische Zeitschrift*, CCX (1970), 745-47.

[17] Some positive appraisals of Baron's thesis are in *Renaissance Studies in Honor of Hans Baron*, ed. A. Molho and J. Tedeschi (Dekalb, Ill., 1971), xi-lxx; for critical reviews, see P. Jones in *History*, LIII (1968), 410-13; A. Tenenti in *Annales*, XXV (1970), 1396-98; and P. Herde in *Historisches Jahrbuch*, XC (1970), 385-87.

[18] Jones, in *History*, LIII, 412; Molho, *Speculum*, XLIII, 24; D. Hay, in *Renaissance Studies in Honor of Hans Baron*, xxvii-xxviii.

in changing Florentine ideas and values; for Martines and Herde, the dynamic element in Florentine history is the entrepreneurial class. Underlying each of these interpretations is a set of assumptions about the historical process that is rarely articulated by their authors, and not always exposed by their critics. Historical relationships, Geoffrey Barraclough has written recently, "are never direct or obvious; there is always something mysterious and intangible about the way things relate."[19] Florentine historians have been no more successful in clarifying these mysteries than their brethren in other fields.

Clarity and precision of terminology, and analytical rigor, have not been distinctive trademarks of Florentine historians, who have been criticized for relying too heavily upon subjective impressions, and for neglecting to examine and classify data carefully.[20] It is doubtless true, as Daniel Waley has written, that "a great deal more counting will have to be done before Florentine economic and social—and even ecclesiastical—history can be given convincing analytical treatment."[21] But the ideal of a Florentine *histoire totale*, with its roots in statistical analysis and its goal the study of all dimensions of human experience over the *longue durée*, may not be feasible, at least for the fourteenth and fifteenth centuries. The fragmentary nature of the evidence limits our ability to answer some elementary questions about population size, birth and death rates, immigration and emigration, and prices of foodstuffs, raw materials, and industrial products before the sixteenth century.[22] Though some of this evidence is buried in notarial records and *Mercanzia* volumes, and the account books and correspondence of individuals, business companies, and ecclesiastical foundations, it may not be adequate for this kind of analysis.[23]

[19] *The New York Review of Books* (4 June 1970), 55.

[20] See, e.g., Jones' criticism of Becker's methodology; *Eng. Hist. Review*, LXXV, 565–66. Such terms as "aristocracy," "patriciate," "oligarchy," "bourgeoisie," "gente nuova," and "family" have rarely been defined with precision by Florentine historians; cf. R. Goldthwaite's comments on "family" in *Private Wealth in Renaissance Florence* (Princeton, 1968), 260–61. The most precise terminology concerning families is employed by F. W. Kent, in *Family Worlds in Renaissance Florence* (Princeton, 1977), 3–17.

[21] *Eng. Hist. Review*, LXXXV (1970), 836.

[22] For a sanguine view of the possibilities for quantitative history in late medieval and early Renaissance Tuscany, see D. Herlihy, "The Tuscan Town in the Quattrocento: A Demographic Profile," *Medievalia et Humanistica*, new ser., no. 1 (1970), 81–84. On the state of our knowledge of Florentine economic history, see Goldthwaite, *Private Wealth*, 235–36.

[23] When the scholarly enterprises of Elio Conti, Charles de la Roncière, and David Herlihy are eventually completed, a comprehensive analysis of Florence's material foundations in these centuries may be feasible. Conti has published two

With so much that we do not know (and perhaps cannot know) about Florence's material foundations in these decades, we may need another viewpoint to comprehend the transition from a medieval to a Renaissance city, and to relate those developments—the triumph of oligarchy, statism, an intensely civic ethos—to other facets of Florentine experience. The key to that understanding, I shall argue in this book, is the changing social order: the transformation of the forms of association that underlay politics. I agree with those scholars who have argued that the corporate foundations of the commune grew weaker in the fourteenth century; the historical significance of the Ciompi revolution was its revelation of that erosion.[24] But these collectivities never withered away entirely: indeed, they displayed a remarkable capacity for survival, and for influencing the political process on behalf of their social constituencies. The history of Florentine politics after 1378 is the story of this community's efforts to sustain a polity that was firmly anchored in the past, institutionally and psychologically, but that could adapt to changes in the social and economic order, as well as to discrete events. Florence's constitution remained quite static in these decades, because her citizens were extremely conservative and reluctant to sanction any significant alteration of their institutions. But in very important ways the political system had been transformed. Those who governed the republic in 1427 came from the same social groups as their counterparts of 1382, but they wielded power differently. Moreover, their perception of politics had changed, to one that Machiavelli would have found familiar. To chart these innovations in Florence's political style, and to relate them to changes in the economy, the social order, and the culture, is a primary goal of this study.

The book's main thesis is the transformation of Florentine politics from corporate to elitist: from a polity controlled and guided by corporate interests to one governed by a cadre of statesmen—experienced, skilled, professional. The restructuring of the political system was certainly stimulated by events—by internal challenges to those who governed, as well as by foreign threats—but it was also, and

---

volumes of his *La formazione della struttura agraria moderna nel contado fiorentino* (Rome, 1965–1966). For Herlihy's enterprise, see his "Tuscan Town." R. Goldthwaite has recently published an article on Florentine grain prices, using data from the records of the hospital of S. Maria Nuova and a manuscript in the *Conventi Soppressi*; "I prezzi del grano a Firenze dal XIV al XVI secolo," *Quaderni storici*, x (1975), 5–36.

[24] A point of view that I did not emphasize sufficiently in my article on the Ciompi; *Flor. Studies*, 314–56.

perhaps more fundamentally, a response to social change. In the first chapter, I shall attempt to show how the corporate entities that constituted the traditional social order had lost cohesiveness and vitality in the years after the Black Death.[25] Corporate politics did not disappear with the Ciompi revolution, but that crisis revealed the flaws in the old order and the need to alter the political system. The process of adjustment began during the tenure of the guild regime of 1378–1382 and continued throughout the 1380s and 1390s. The internal history of these realignments is described in the second chapter, the impact of foreign affairs in the third. By the first decade of the fifteenth century, an elitist regime had developed from the old corporate chrysalis. Its distinctive features emerged during the crisis years of the Visconti wars (1389–1402); its vitality was demonstrated by its aggressive campaign to expand Florentine territory in the years following the death of Giangaleazzo Visconti (chapter IV). I have selected the year 1411, when this regime might be said to have achieved maturity, to identify the elite's membership, and to describe its style. There followed three years of crisis (1411–1414) when the regime's capacity for survival was severely tested (chapter VI). Having emerged from that ordeal, the republic enjoyed a respite from war for nearly seven years, when another constellation of troubles— economic, political, military—again threatened its existence (chapter VII). The year 1427 was the regime's climacteric: the moment when its fortunes turned downward until, seven years later, it fell.[26] The final chapter analyzes the process of disintegration and the leadership's inability to shore up the tottering regime.

The sources for this study are now quite familiar. They have been cited in the published work of Florentine scholars who have diligently explored the documents, public and private, that have survived for these decades. Perhaps the best guide to the official records is Lauro Martines' recent study on lawyers, which also contains valuable references to the private *fondi*—letters, diaries, memorials—that add much to our knowledge of Florentine politics after 1380.[27] One particular

[25] I have discussed this phenomenon briefly in my *Renaissance Florence* (New York, 1969), 97–101; it is an important theme in Becker's analysis; *Flor. Studies*, 110–16.

[26] The political development of these years is described by Dale Kent; *The Rise of the Medici: Faction in Florence 1426–1434*, to be published by the Clarendon Press. The problems of the fisc are discussed by A. Molho, *Florentine Public Finances*, ch. 5–7.

[27] *Lawyers and Statecraft*, 57–61, 112–15, 215–19. Fewer chronicles were written (or have survived) after 1380 than before; L. Green, *Chronicle into History* (Cambridge, 1972), *passim*. But private sources are incomparably richer for the

source has been fundamental to this analysis: the *Consulte e Pratiche*, the record of Florentine political deliberations. Though known and exploited by scholars for more than a century,[28] these debates have not been systematically studied, nor their historical value fully appreciated. They constitute the most complete record of the political thought of any European community—urban, regional, national—prior to the English Civil War.[29] For the years between 1382 and 1434, that record is comprehensive, with only a few lacunae.[30] These records identify the leading statesmen of the regime: the men whose opinions and judgments were most frequently solicited and heard in the palace of the Signoria. They also reveal the problems confronting the republic —the significance attached to them, the controversies they provoked, their solutions. Finally, they register change: in the balance of power, in the methods of exercising authority and making decisions, in the ways that Florentine politicians perceived reality—how they saw themselves and their world.

---

later period; G. Brucker, ed., *Two Memoirs of Renaissance Florence: the Diaries of Buonaccorso Pitti and Gregorio Dati*, trans. Julia Martines (New York, 1967), 9–12.

[28] Cesare Guasti published selections from this source in his edition of the *Commissioni di Rinaldo degli Albizzi*, 3 vols. (Florence, 1867–1873).

[29] Brucker, *Florentine Politics and Society, 1343–1378* (Princeton, 1962), ix. Felix Gilbert used the *Consulte e Pratiche* very extensively in his "Florentine Political Assumptions in the Period of Savonarola and Soderini," *Journal of the Warburg and Courtauld Institutes*, xx (1957), 187–214. For a perceptive evaluation of the historical value of these protocols, see Herde, "Politische Verhaltensweisen," 175–77.

[30] The inventory of the *Consulte e Pratiche* is printed in D. Marzi, *La Cancelleria della Repubblica fiorentina* (Rocca S. Casciano, 1910), 515–16.

CHAPTER I

Corporate Values and the Aristocratic Ethos in Trecento Florence

SOCIAL AGGREGATIONS

FROM the beginnings of their documented past, medieval Florentines (like other Italian city-dwellers) had displayed a strong and persistent impulse to band together into associations, and to invest those bodies with a corporate character. They drafted constitutions specifying the rights and obligations of membership; they exacted oaths of fealty; they convened assemblies; they levied dues and services. These organizations gave their members a measure of security in a turbulent world where public authority was weak, and where survival depended upon cooperation and mutual assistance. In addition to providing support, both material and psychic, they performed an important social function by resolving conflicts and restraining violence among their members. As Florence grew in size, and her society and polity became more complex, new associations were formed in response to changing needs. A citizen of Dante's generation (*c.* 1300) would customarily belong to several of these societies: a guild, a confraternity, the Parte Guelfa, the commune.[1]

The commune of the *trecento* was a composite of these collectivities, and the institutional embodiment of the corporate spirit. Its legislative councils, of the *Popolo* and the Commune, were the organs of political associations that had been formed in the past. Membership in the commune was restricted to citizens who were matriculated into one or more of the city's twenty-one guilds. Comprising the supreme executive, the Signoria, were eight priors chosen as representatives of the guild community, and the standard-bearer of justice. Among the groups which advised the Signoria on policy, and voted on legislation, were agents of corporations that had been integrated into the communal structure: the Sixteen standard-bearers of the militia companies who represented the city's neighborhoods; the captains of the Parte Guelfa; the guild consuls. Every magistracy—from the Signoria to the officials charged with collecting gabelles at the city gates or

---

[1] Of the vast literature on this subject, four recent works may be cited: P. J. Jones, "Communes and Despots," *op. cit.*, 71–96, and esp. 85; D. Waley, *The Italian City-Republics* (London, 1969), ch. 5; J. K. Hyde, *Society and Politics in Medieval Italy* (London, 1973), ch. 4, 5; and *Violence and Civil Disorder in Italian Cities, 1200–1500*, ed. L. Martines (Berkeley and Los Angeles, 1972).

those responsible for internal security—functioned collegially: debating issues, promulgating edicts, levying fines.[2]

The corporate ethos was fundamentally egalitarian. Members of a guild, political society (*parte*), or militia company (*gonfalone*) were assumed to possess equal rights and privileges, and to bear equal obligations to the society and their fellows. "If any one of us is offended or outraged by any person," so read a clause in the charter of a fourteenth-century Guelf association, "each and every one is obligated to help, defend and avenge him with his life and property, and to respond to that quarrel as though it were his own person."[3] By joining a corporation, the Florentine acquired "brothers" who, individually and collectively, could make claims upon him that he had sworn an oath to acknowledge. These obligations took no account of differences in wealth, social status, or personal qualities. "Members of late medieval confraternities and *corpora mystica*," Lionel Rothkrug has written, "were compelled by oath of entry to treat every other person in the community according to a whole set of reciprocal rights and duties without regard to personal choice."[4] In theory if not always in practice, that principle applied to every corporate society in Florence, whether religious or secular.

This corporate spirit was revealed most graphically during the celebrations honoring Florence's patron, John the Baptist. Every year, on the day before the saint's feast (24 June), the guilds displayed the finest examples of their wares and skills: in cloth-making and leatherwork, in gold ornaments and woodcarving. Competing for the public's attention were members of religious confraternities, "who assemble [Gregorio Dati reported] at the place where their meetings are held, dressed as angels, and with musical instruments of every kind and marvelous singing. They stage the most beautiful representations of the saints, and of those relics in whose honor they perform."[5] Later that day, representatives from each of the city's sixteen electoral districts (*gonfaloni*) brought candles to the Baptistery, as offerings to their patron saint. On the feast day itself, a more formal procession moved through the streets, headed by the captains of the Parte Guelfa,

---

[2] F. Gilbert, *Machiavelli and Guicciardini* (Princeton, 1965), 12–14. Good examples of this collegiate mentality are the accounts of the deliberations of the cathedral *operai*; C. Guasti, *Santa Maria del Fiore* (Florence, 1887).

[3] C. Guasti, ed., *Le Carte Strozziane del R. Archivio di Stato di Firenze* (Florence, 1884–1899), I, 99; trans. in Brucker, *The Society of Renaissance Florence* (New York, 1971), 85.

[4] In his unpublished manuscript, "Popular Religion and Holy Shrines," part II, iv.

[5] This account in G. Dati, *Istoria di Firenze dall'anno MCCCLXXXX all'anno MCCCCV* (Florence, 1735), 84–89, partly trans. in Brucker, *Society of Renaissance Florence*, 75–78.

their standard carried by a page on horseback. Behind the captains were representatives of the towns in Florence's dominion, and the nobles of the *contado* and district, required by the terms of their submission to the republic to bring their insignias and candles to the Baptistery. Then came the Signoria, accompanied by their collegiate associates, the Twelve *buonuomini* and the Sixteen. Preceding the priors in the procession was the great flag of justice, the symbol of the commune's authority, which left the palace of the Signoria only on these formal occasions, or when civic turmoil threatened the regime's security.

During those times of crisis, armed citizens rushed to join those associations which appeared to offer the greatest security, and for which they felt the strongest affinity. For many, the family was the cornerstone of their world, and the palace of the family's patriarch, or its loggia, the place of assembly. Others banded together with neighbors into militia companies, to protect their district from riots, and, if summoned by the priors, to march to the palace of the Signoria. During the Ciompi revolution (July–August 1378) and again in January 1382, the guilds formed the most important blocs in the street battles that were fought in the square in front of the palace of the Signoria. On 31 August 1378, armed guildsmen led by the butchers defeated the cloth-workers, the Ciompi, recently organized into their own guild, and overthrew the popular republic that had governed Florence for six weeks.[6] The regime established after the Ciompi revolution was itself overthrown three years later, when members of the cloth manufacturers' guild defeated contingents from the lower guilds led, once again, by the butchers.[7] In each of these disorders, the flags of the guilds, the commune, and the Parte Guelfa played a prominent role: as assembly points for their members, as symbols of legitimacy. These banners were used to bolster allegiance to the existing regime; they were also employed by dissidents to rally support for corporate values and institutions that (so the rebels argued) had been suppressed by those in power. "Long live the *popolo* and the guilds!": that cry reverberated through the city during every political crisis from the 1370s to the end of the century and beyond.

The armed guildsmen mobilized around their standards had deter-

---

[6] Brucker, "Ciompi," *Flor. Studies*, 315–16, 326, 329, 347–51.

[7] See below, 60; Brucker, *Society of Renaissance Florence*, 78–80. But families and their dependents also played an important role in political strategy and consciousness. In April 1382, Simone Capponi offered to the Signoria the services of himself, "et omnes habiles de domo de Caponibus, et centum famulos et quinquentos florenos"; *Diario d'anonimo*, 441.

mined Florence's destiny in the summer of 1378; thereafter, the power of the guild community waned rapidly. Its impotence was dramatized by a putative rebellion in October 1393, the last moment in Florentine history when guild loyalties and aspirations played an important if ultimately unsuccessful role in a political crisis. The revolt began when a debtor, seeking to avoid capture by the police, shouted: "Long live the *popolo* and the guilds!" Upon hearing this clamor, artisans and shopkeepers seized their arms and rushed to the piazza della Signoria. A goldsmith named Giovanni Ottinelli left his shop and ran through the streets urging his colleagues to "close down your shops . . . for this is the day that we shall be free!" A dyer, Leonardo di Niccolò, assumed the leadership of the rebellious artisans; he and his followers invaded the palace of the captain, seized that official and mounted him on a horse with a banner displaying the arms of the *popolo*. Defending the regime against this mob were citizens identified by the chroniclers as "good Guelfs," together with contingents of the civic militia and mercenaries in the commune's service.[8] If the testimony of a certain Starmine di Amideo can be believed, two rival youth gangs, called the *Berta* and the *Magrone*, took advantage of this imbroglio to attack each other.[9] In the fighting between the rebels and the regime's supporters, Sandro di Niccolò was killed; the banner of the *popolo* was seized from the artisans by Messer Michele de' Medici and carried to the palace of the Signoria. One artisan later confessed that he had urged Michele "to raise that banner and hold it upright . . . and the artisans will follow and defend you."[10] But Michele declined this opportunity to become a hero of the lower guildsmen. Demoralized by the death of their leader and the seizure of the flag, the artisans fled from the square in disorder. That evening two

[8] These details from *BNF*, *Panc.*, 158, ff.174v–175r; and from the convictions of the participants; *ACP*, 1988, ff.5r–15r, 90r–91r.

[9] From Starmine's petition for absolution in Oct. 1422; *Prov.*, 122, ff.166v–168r: "Ipse Starnina cum multis aliis fuit criminatus et causa fuit non ea que fuit inserta, sed pro eo quia fiebant certe pugne manibus vacuiis inter cives in maxima copia pro qualibet parte, quarum una vulgo dicebantur 'L'Aberta,' reliqua, 'E Magroni.' Et quod ipse ut iuvenis aptus ad similia partem cum multis sequacibus tenebat della Berta intantum quod multi ex alia qui eum hodie habuerunt ipsum penes rectorem inculpaverunt pro dicto tractatu, sperantes ipsum ponere in manibus rectoris. . . ." For other details on the role of these gangs in this uprising, see *Acquisti e Doni*, 140 (7), no. 56.

[10] "O domine Michael! Erigatis istam banderiam et teneatis eam rectam, nec teneatis aliquid, quia ista est banderia cum armis populi; artifices vos sequentur et deffendent"; *ACP*, 1988, ff.14v–15r. Minerbetti wrote in his chronicle that the artisans appealed to Messer Vieri de' Medici to lead them; Minerbetti, *anno* 1393, ch. 22.

prominent citizens, Messer Rinaldo Gianfigliazzi and Messer Donato Acciaiuoli, carried the banners of the *popolo* and the Parte Guelfa around the square, followed by a large crowd shouting: "Long live the *popolo* and the Parte Guelfa!"[11]

The failure of the guilds to sustain their political authority has led some historians to minimize their role in the political and social life of early Renaissance Florence.[12] But evidence does exist to suggest that the corporate spirit was not moribund, and that the commune had not become the sole respository of the allegiances that these associations had once inspired. Lauro Martines has noted how strongly and aggressively the guilds defended their privileges, even against the commune.[13] Although the guilds may have suffered some diminution of their autonomy in the late *trecento*, they continued to exercise substantial control over their members: forcing them to abide by the rules regulating their crafts, adjudicating disputes, levying assessments, requiring their presence at the funerals of fellow guildsmen.[14] Confraternities proliferated in the decades after the Black Death, a trend which suggests that the religious sodality became increasingly important in the lives of the Florentines.[15] The only corporate body to experience a permanent loss of its authority and prestige, and its capacity to attract recruits in these years, was the Parte Guelfa.[16]

To perceive the family, the lineage, as a corporate unit in a social order formed by collectivities is to grasp an important truth about this urban community. Though the family had no charter or constitution, nor formal rules and regulations, it was—and remained—the most cohesive force in Florentine society through the Renaissance and beyond.[17] Lineages were held together by *fidei commissum*; by jointly

[11] *Panc.*, 158, f.174v.

[12] That theme is fundamental to Becker's interpretation of Florentine history in these years; see "Individualism in the Early Italian Renaissance: Burden and Blessing," *Studies in the Renaissance*, XIX (1972), 292–93; "The Florentine Territorial State," *Flor. Studies*, 110–15.

[13] *Lawyers and Statecraft*, 25.

[14] See, e.g., the *Statuti delle arti dei fornai e dei vinattieri di Firenze*, ed. F. Morandini (Florence, 1956). The most recent study of the Florentine guilds is J. Najemy, "The Guilds in Florentine Politics, 1292–1394," Harvard Ph.D. dissertation, 1972.

[15] R. Trexler, "Ritual in Florence: Adolescence and Salvation in the Renaissance," *The Pursuit of Holiness in Late Medieval and Renaissance Religion*, ed. C. Trinkaus and H. Oberman (Leiden, 1974), 205–06; R. Hatfield, "The Compagnia de' Magi," *Journal of the Warburg and Courtauld Institutes*, XXXIII (1970), 143–44.

[16] *Society of Renaissance Florence*, 84–89.

[17] The authoritative work on the Florentine family in the Renaissance is now F. W. Kent, *Family Worlds in Renaissance Florence*. The critical reader will note

owned property and businesses; by common political interests and objectives; above all, by identification with, and loyalty to, a family tradition. The bonds of kinship had changed significantly since the halcyon days of the *consorterie* in the late twelfth and early thirteenth centuries. The infiltration of "new men" into the city, the rise of the *popolo*, the enactment of legislation concerning magnates, the demographic and economic crises of the mid-fourteenth century: these developments had combined to transform, and perhaps to weaken, kinship ties.[18] Florentines in 1400 were rather more reluctant than formerly to participate in vendettas, less willing, perhaps, to risk money on behalf of relatives plagued by economic misfortune[19] or threatened by neighbors or the commune. In 1373, Foligno de' Medici recalled with nostalgia a past time when his family was strong and unified, "and every man feared us."[20] But some scholars have exaggerated the disintegration of the lineage in the fourteenth century, just as they have emphasized too strongly the debility of other corporate bodies. The trend is not a simple declension from strength to weakness, from cohesion to fragmentation, but a more complex pattern of flux and reflux, of breakdown and reconstitution.

A moment in the history of the Strozzi illustrates the problem. In 1387 that large and very potent lineage was severely damaged, and its political authority jeopardized, by the senseless act of a kinsman, Pagnozzino, who killed Piero Lenzi, a member of the Sixteen. Pagnozzino, his brother Nofri, and their sons were all placed under the communal ban; they could be killed with impunity by any of the Lenzi. In

---

how sharply my own views concerning the family have changed, after reading Dr. Kent's work, since I wrote on the subject in *Renaissance Florence*, 97–99, 264–65. Among the distinctive merits of Kent's study are the precision of his definitions, the distinction that he draws between household and lineage, and his sensitive treatment of the relationship between family structure and the larger community. Diane Hughes' article, "Urban Growth and Family Structure in Medieval Genoa," *Past and Present*, no. 66 (Feb. 1975), 3–28, makes some instructive comparisons between family organization in Genoa and Florence. Cf. J. Heers, *Le clan familial au moyen âge* (Paris, 1974).

[18] Kent notes, *Family Worlds*, 11, 297–98, that historians have assumed that the medieval *consorteria* was a monolithic unit, but that the evidence to support this hypothesis is very thin and ambiguous. On this question, see D. Herlihy, "Family Solidarity in Medieval Italian History," *Explorations in Economic History*, VII (1969–1971), 173–84.

[19] Brucker, *Society of Renaissance Florence*, 106–20; G. Morelli, *Ricordi*, ed. V. Branca (Florence, 1956), 237, 242.

[20] Brucker, "The Medici in the Fourteenth Century," *Speculum*, XXXII (1957), 1. Foligno attributed the Medici decline to the plague, but internal discord also played a part; *ibid.*, 17–19.

April 1388 the Lenzi ambushed a party of Strozzi on horseback, wounding one of their servants. By the terms of the law authorizing the vendetta, that was an illegal assault for which the Strozzi immediately claimed damages from the Lenzi. Currado Strozzi reported the incident in a letter to his cousin Leonardo; he was hopeful that the judge would cancel the penalties against the Strozzi, "and we will free ourselves from them." Currado then described the revival of family solidarity among the Strozzi as a result of those events:

> We are seeking for ways and means to satisfy our honor. We will see how this affair develops, and according to what occurs, we will proceed prudently to protect ourselves. We have everything in order. . . . There are twenty of us, and eight servants, and we have sent all of the children away. . . . Everyone has rallied round to help, and Messer P[azzino] and N[ofri] act as though one of their sons was wounded. They denounce G[iovanni Lenzi] in the strongest terms. We will not suffer this indignity. Our lawyers are prepared, and there is plenty of money. I deplore this incident for its effect on the family, but it has been like a tonic for us. I see those who were asleep now aroused, as a result of this incident. I see everyone united and generous with money.[21]

Rare, however, were such occasions when the resources of a lineage, and particularly one so large as the Strozzi, could be fully mobilized. Not since 1343 had the great patrician families fought as blocs in civic disorders.[22] In the late *trecento* and early *quattrocento*, families might still be treated by the commune as units; for example, in 1394, when the Corbizzi and the Pitti were forced to end their vendetta and make peace, or when (1411) the Alberti were expelled from the city.[23] More frequently, the commune made distinctions among kinsmen, by giving *popolano* status, for example, to individual magnates who had merited the commune's benevolence;[24] or by separating delinquents from their more respectable cousins.[25] Excluded from the penalties imposed

---

[21] The provision penalizing the Strozzi in *Prov.*, 76, ff.121r–125r; Currado's letter in *Strozz.*, 3rd ser., 13, no. 1; partly trans. in Brucker, *Society of Renaissance Florence*, 111–15. The reference to 20 Strozzi suggests that only one or two branches of the family were actively involved in this imbroglio.

[22] G. Villani, *Cronica*, ed. F. Dragomanni (Florence, 1844–1845), XII, ch. 16, 17.

[23] *ACP*, 1990, ff.83r–85r, 3 July 1394; *Prov.*, 100, ff.61v–63r. On the peace imposed on the Rucellai and the Barbadori, see *CP*, 43, f.185v, 3 Apr. 1418.

[24] M. Becker, "A Study in Political Failure: the Florentine Magnates (1280–1343)," *Medieval Studies*, XXVII (1965), 267–68, 273.

[25] Petitions to separate branches of families were numerous in the 1380s and 1390s; e.g., *Prov.*, 72, ff.208v–209r (Canigiani); 76, ff.126r–127r (Ricoveri); 78,

on the Strozzi in 1387 were Messer Pazzino and his male descendants, and the heirs of Rosso and Messer Umberto di Geri, "who are called, in the vernacular, the branch of the Strozzi *armati*."[26] In that same year of 1387, three Alberti households—the sons of Messer Niccolò di Jacopo, Francesco di Messer Jacopo, and Marco di Francesco—were exempt from the ban on officeholding that had been imposed on the remainder of that lineage.[27]

But the slackening of kinship bonds did not lead inexorably to that existential situation described by Goldthwaite: the Florentine "left exposed and isolated, unencumbered with the old social obligations and loyalties."[28] Supplementing the family as a focus of loyalty, and a bastion of support, were smaller, more informal coalitions of individuals bound together by ties of kinship and, equally important, of friendship and of neighborhood. The blood connection was a cohesive element in these informal associations, but it was usually limited to close relatives—brothers or first cousins—and not more distant kin.[29] Relations between cousins—between Francesco di Jacopo and Giovanni d'Amerigo del Bene, between Giovanni di Bicci (and later his son Cosimo) and Averardo di Francesco de' Medici—were often the key links in the nuclei "of relatives and friends and neighbors" that formed around these men.[30] Marriage alliances were important means of recruiting others into these groups. The lawyer Rosso d'Andreozzo Orlandi had married a Davanzati girl, and thus became an intimate associate of that branch descended from Chiarino Davanzati. He wrote (September 1396) to his nephew, Piero di

---

ff.94r–95v (Pucci); 84, ff.162r–163v (Nobili); ff.229v–231r (Salterelli); 86, ff.75r–77r (Pecori); 95, f.85r (Velluti); f.117r (Strozzi).

[26] *Prov.*, 76, f.124v.

[27] L. Passerini, *Gli Alberti di Firenze* (Florence, 1869), II, 236.

[28] *Private Wealth*, 261. Cf. M. Becker: "The burgher now stood in greater isolation than ever before"; "An Essay on the Quest for Identity in the Early Renaissance," *Florilegium Historiale: Essays Presented to Wallace K. Ferguson* (Toronto, 1971), 302. For one illustration of a cohesive lineage in the early *quattrocento*, see D. Kent, *Rise of the Medici*, ch. i, ii.

[29] Referring to the descendants of his uncle, Giovanni Morelli wrote: ". . . I' non sono avvisato bene di loro natività e di lor cose. E perche e' non credino ch'i' voglia misurare loro gli anni, non ne voglio domandare; e però faremo fine in quanto a quel lato, non seguendo più di lor innanzi che sia istato fatto"; *Ricordi*, 200. On the distinction between *proximi consorti* and more distant kinsmen, see F. W. Kent, *Family Worlds*, 61–62.

[30] The phrase "de' parenti e degli'amici e de'vicini," in a letter from Tommaso to Forese Sacchetti; *Ashb.*, 1842, vol. I, no. 169. The close bonds between the Del Bene is revealed in their correspondence in the Carte del Bene; examples in Brucker, *Society of Renaissance Florence*, 32–37.

Chiarino Davanzati in Venice, to congratulate him on the marriage of his son Bartolomeo to the daughter of Andrea Peruzzi. "I do not know of a finer marriage connection (*parentado*)," he said, adding that Bartolomeo's father-in-law was the most highly regarded member of that distinguished house, "a liberal, virtuous, and worthy man, whom you will do well to treat as a blood relative."[31] The Davanzati had followed the counsel that Giovanni Morelli gave to his sons: "Take care to arrange marriages with well-regarded citizens, who are not needy . . . and who are not arrogant, but who come from ancient stock, and are respected and good Guelfs. . . ."[32] The godfather-godson connection was another kind of social cement. Cristofano Bagnesi addressed Forese Sacchetti as his *compare*, and his letters reflect a sense of affinity as strong as any blood relationship.[33] Indeed, the mutual obligations in these associations were substitutes for the kinship tie, and were so recognized by those who contracted them. "You may consider me your brother and your particular friend," Giovanni Morelli wrote to Forese Sacchetti (February 1427), "as I have regarded you. . . ."[34] Morelli had formulated the rationale, and the method, for winning friends like Sacchetti in his memorial to his sons:

> If there is someone in your *gonfalone* who can help you and push you ahead, first try to become intimate with him, if possible, by means of a marriage. If that is not practicable, then have dealings with him and his [relatives]; try to serve him, offer him aid, if

[31] ". . . Andrea, padre dela fanciulla, è tenuto et è il da più di chasa Peruzzi et grande cittadino, da bene, libero et bonissimo parente, et da poterne fare chonto, e farete bene e grande senno sapervelo ritenere per parente"; *CRS*, 78 (Badìa), vol. 315, no. 226, 6 Sept. 1396.

[32] *Ricordi*, 264. On marriages as sources of support, see F. W. Kent, *Family Worlds*, 93–99.

[33] "Chiarissimo fratello e honorevole compare chiarissimo"; *CRS*, 78, vol. 324, no. 94. Also *ibid.*, no. 89, 93. A certain Piero, like Bagnesi a close friend of Sacchetti, wrote the latter: "Quanto dite avete più fidansa in Christofano che in persona, e chosì o io, perchè o veduto ciò a fatto e fa in de' nostri fatti; che se fussi istato io, non arei fatto tanto"; *ibid.*, vol. 323, no. 264, 5 Sept. 1412. The relationship between Francesco Datini and Ser Lapo Mazzei was equally close; see my *Renaissance Florence*, 109–13.

[34] *CRS*, 78, vol. 326, no. 39, 4 Feb. 1427. Cf. Donato Velluti's statement about his relations with a former enemy: "e per lui aoperai come fratello. . . . Di che da poi in qua siamo stati fratelli"; *La cronica domestica di Messer Donato Velluti* (Florence, 1914), 20–21. A common sentiment in Florentine correspondence is Piero Baldovinetti's statement to Forese Sacchetti: "Fratello chiarissimo, quando i chasi e bisogni acchorono, e di nicistà a' parenti e agli amici e a quele persone in chui l'uomo a fidanza richorere"; *CRS*, 78, vol. 323, no. 213.

you can do so without too much harm to yourself, when you see that he is in need; give him presents; honor him by inviting him often to dinner.[35]

Morelli cited approvingly the example of his father Paolo, who was exceptionally skilled in the art of making friends among the powerful. Paolo honored those men by entertaining them at banquets, by acting as godfather to their children, by advising them about their private affairs. "And by such wise and provident means, he had so arranged matters that, in his time of great need, he had friends, and not only relatives, who gave him help and support. . . ."[36] Leon Battista Alberti once complained that he had been maltreated by relatives during his youth, and that he had received more assistance from friends than from kinsmen.[37]

The diary of Paolo d'Alessandro Sassetti, written between 1364 and 1400, describes one of these social agglomerates. Paolo was descended from a prominent mercantile family in the quarter of Santa Maria Novella that, by his time, was much reduced in size and political influence. Neither he nor any of his kinfolk qualified for the Signoria, though their social standing, as measured by their marriages, was quite respectable.[38] A schedule of forced loans compiled in 1378 lists five Sassetti households,[39] but Paolo's diary suggests that the bonds uniting his kinsmen were not strong. The plague of 1383 claimed the lives of seven Sassetti;[40] two were buried with none of their relatives present. Pierozzo di Doffo Sassetti died in a neighbor's house in the Via Maggio "with none of us at the funeral, and this we did because we felt ourselves shamed by his desire to die in someone else's house against our will." Letta, the daughter of Federigo di Pollaio Sassetti, died unmourned by her kin because she lived with her paramour, Giovanni Porcellini: "May the devil take her soul, for she has brought shame and dishonor to our family." Rinaldo di Pollaio Sassetti lay moribund in his sister Fiondina's house, but "she did not permit any

[35] *Ricordi*, 253.

[36] *Ibid.*, 150.

[37] Alberti, *The Family in Renaissance Florence*, ed. Renèe Watkins (Columbia, S.C., 1969), 5–6.

[38] On the early history of the Sassetti, see P. Jones, "Florentine Families and Florentine Diaries in the Fourteenth Century," *Papers of the British School at Rome*, XXIV (1956), 184–85; and Martines, *Social World*, 217–18.

[39] *Pres.*, 334, ff.95r–99r, 122r.

[40] Paolo's diary; *Strozz.*, 2nd ser., 4, ff.66v–68v, parts trans. in Brucker, *Society of Renaissance Florence*. Two of the seven deaths were Sassetti wives.

of us to visit him . . . and has treated us as though we were mortal enemies." Only marriages brought together the members of this fragmented family,[41] but the nuptial celebrations did not sustain the feeling of kinship. The significant family unit to which Paolo belonged comprised his household, those of his brothers Niccolò and Bernardo (and the latter's daughter Lena), and the children of Federigo di Pierozzo: Lisabetta, Tommaso, and Bernardo.[42] Although the Sassetti were linked by marriage to other prominent lineages (Strozzi, Peruzzi, Gondi, Covoni), they did not develop intimate ties with them, nor did these connections bolster their political status.[43] Paolo and his kinfolk received more support from, and identified more closely with, their neighbors in the *gonfalone* of the White Lion, and particularly the Anselmi. Gino di Bernardo Anselmi was a prominent politician in the district, whose death in 1390 was noted by Paolo, who expressed the hope that Gino's last testament "would be satisfactory to all of his relatives and friends."[44] Six years earlier, Paolo recorded the details of the marriage between Lisabetta, the daughter of Federigo di Pierozzo Sassetti, and Filippo d'Anselmo Anselmi. "It is a fact," he wrote, "that this marriage was contracted for love of relatives and neighbors"; it was forged to strengthen the affective bonds that held neighborhoods together.[45]

A similar pattern emerges from the diary, written between 1375 and 1427, of Lapo di Giovanni Niccolini, a wealthy merchant and cloth manufacturer in the quarter of Santa Croce.[46] Lapo's circle embraced only his nearest kinfolk, the descendants of his brother Niccolino and his sister Fia, and a select group of relatives by marriage. He apparently had no contact with descendants of his great-grandfather

[41] Descriptions of three Sassetti weddings in Paolo's diary; *Strozz.*, 2nd ser., 4, ff.73r–74r, 111v–112r, 113r–113v.

[42] Excluded were those who had died in 1383, and Piero di Sassetto Sassetti. Manente di Gino Sassetti had some contact with Paolo and his kinfolk; *ibid.*, ff.73r, 99v, 104r, 105r, but the degree of intimacy is not clear.

[43] The Sassetti women had married Verano Peruzzi, Antonio and Lionardo di Simone Gondi, Jacopo di Paolo Covoni, Cambio Arrighi, Bartolomeo Galilei, Giovanni d'Ugo Vecchietti, and Pagnozzino Strozzi; *ibid.*, f.113r.

[44] *Ibid.*, f.105v. On Gino's political career, see my *Florentine Politics and Society*, 33, 69, 334–35, 359.

[45] Paolo's diary; *Strozz.*, 2nd ser., 4, f.73r: "conciò sia chosa che questo parentado si fe' con amore di parentado e di vicinanza. . . ." At a Sassetti wedding, Paolo reported that the procession included "huomini assai, parenti, amici e vicini"; *ibid.*, f.113r.

[46] Edited, with an introduction on the Niccolini, by C. Bec, *Il libro degli affari proprii di casa de Lapo di Giovanni Niccolini de' Sirigatti* (Paris, 1969).

Rucco's brother Lucchese.[47] And though he did recognize the members of another collateral branch, the descendants of Ser Piero Gucci dei Sirigatti, as his blood relations, his ties with those distant cousins were not close.[48] Among those whom he called his "most trusted relatives and friends" were men linked to him by marriage (Rinieri di Bagno Bagnesi, Bese di Guido Magalotti, Messer Zanobi da Mezzola, Giovanni di Bernardo Ardinghelli) and friends from his *gonfalone*: Jacopo di Sandro Covoni, Giovanni di Messer Forese Salviati, Simone Buonarroti, Domenico di Domenico Giugni, Francesco d'Agnolo Cavalcanti, Cristofano del Bugliasse.[49] His wealth and connections with the leading families in Santa Croce gave a powerful stimulus to his political career; by 1400 he had joined the regime's inner circle.[50] With his political eminence buttressing his socio-economic standing, Lapo was able to arrange marriages for his dependents with other families in the ruling elite. When his first wife, Ermellina da Mezzola, died, he married the widow of Rinaldo Gianfigliazzi's son Antonio. His brother Filippo married a Spini and then a Rucellai; his daughters, an Altoviti and an Albizzi; his nieces, a Rucellai, an Ardinghelli, and a Da Filicaia; his nephews, a Bischeri and a Tosinghi.[51] From this large circle of intimates, Lapo selected the godfathers of his children, the executors of the estates of his relatives who had died without leaving wills, and the guardians of their minor children.[52] Such men as the notary Ser Antonio di Niccolò d'Ancisa, whom Lapo described as his "godfather and most intimate and well-disposed friend,"[53] were also selected as *arbitri*, to settle differences among relatives over property and inheritances, and *mallevadori*, who guaranteed that dowries would be delivered or restored, or that loans would be repaid, or that the vendors of real estate possessed a legitimate title to their property. To ask anyone to serve as bondsman, and so risk his own money for a friend or relative, placed a particular strain upon these relationships. Lapo agreed to be a *mal-*

---

[47] "Di quello Luchese e de' suoi figliuoli disciese molta gente e sonno assai a miei dì, ma, perchè non ne anno a ffare alla nostra materia, gli preterischo e ritorno a Ruzza, mio principio e di mio lato"; *ibid.*, 56.

[48] *Ibid.*, 96, 101–02, 116. These relatives lived in Lapo's *gonfalone* but did not achieve any political distinction; *Tratte*, 45, ff.45r–47v.

[49] *Libro degli affari*, 129. Bec states that Lapo's circle numbered about 60 men, perhaps too large an estimate; *ibid.*, 24, 47–48.

[50] See below, ch. v, 268.

[51] *Il libro degli affari*, 71, 88, 92, 94, 98–100, 108, 113, 139.

[52] *Ibid.*, 63, 70, 77, 80–81, 93, 105, 109, 121, 129, 133–34.

[53] "Mio compare e intimo amico e benivolo"; *ibid.*, 130.

levadore for his father-in-law, Messer Zanobi da Mezzola, but only after the latter had promised, "as a trustworthy knight, that I would not be damaged or molested. . . ."[54] He reluctantly agreed to be a guarantor for the debts of a bankrupt nephew, thereby violating Giovanni Morelli's rule against such obligations, "even for relatives or friends, unless you can see with your own eyes that they can repay forty soldi per lire. . . ."[55] Giovanni di Simone Buonaccorsi was that rare phenomenon, a friendless man, who could not find a guarantor for the sale of property to dower his daughters, and so had to petition the commune to approve that transaction.[56]

There is no reference, in Lapo Niccolini's diary, to politics; that important aspect of his career can only be reconstructed from public records. In the voluminous correspondence of the Del Bene family, however, there is some data on the links between these coalitions of *parenti, amici e vicini*, and the political system.[57] The Del Bene were a small family from Santa Maria Novella, making up only three urban households in 1378: Giovanni d'Amerigo, Francesco di Jacopo, and Francesco and Berto di Tano.[58] The key connection linked the two first cousins, Giovanni d'Amerigo and Francesco di Jacopo; neither had close relations with the descendants of Tano. But Giovanni and Francesco were as intimate as brothers, in arranging marriages for each other's children and in protecting the interests of nephews and nieces.[59] The political careers of these men rose and fell with an abruptness unusual even for these years. In the Signoria during the 1370s, they were both proscribed by the Parte Guelfa in 1378. They were active and prominent in the guild regime that followed the Ciompi revolution but then, in 1382, they were exiled by the regime

[54] *Ibid.*, 85–86. See the petition of Piero di Masino dell'Antella: "Propter fideiussionem per eum large et amicabiliter facta pro Antonio ser Martini, vinacterio ad gabellam vini de qua damnificatus est in quantitate florenorum 1500"; *Prov.*, 88, ff.217v, 27–28 Oct. 1399. See also *Prov.*, 92, f.137v.

[55] *Libro degli affari*, 132; Morelli, *Ricordi*, 238, 242: "Se se' richiesto di danari o di malleverie o d'alcuna obbrigazione la quale ti potesse fare danno, guardatene quante dal fuoco. . . . Non t'obbrigare mai per niuno fallito, assai ti sia egli parente o amico; non mai, se tu vedessi coll'occhio ch'egli avesse da rendere quaranta soldi per lira non vi ti affidare mai. . . ."

[56] *Prov.*, 78, ff.177r–179r, May 1389.

[57] On the Del Bene, see H. Hoshino, "Francesco di Iacopo Del Bene cittadino fiorentino del Trecento"; *Istituto giapponese di cultura*, Rome; *Annuario*, IV (1966–1967), 29–119.

[58] *Pres.*, 333, ff.5v, 11v; 334, f.4v.

[59] On their marriage negotiations, see my *Society of Renaissance Florence*, 32–37; and *Acquisti e Doni*, 301, unpaginated, letters of 23 Feb., 14 and 20 March and 25 May 1391.

that came to power in that year.[60] To regain their political status was their primary goal in the 1380s, and one that required a sustained effort by friends and neighbors.

Two men from their quarter, Branca Guidalotti and Bernardo di Giovanni Strozzi were most assiduous in organizing support for the exiles; they may have been connected to the Del Bene by marriage.[61] If so, they displayed more concern for the welfare of their families than did members of other houses (Altoviti, Medici, Cavalcanti, Spini, Guasconi) who had also contracted marriages with the Del Bene.[62] Neighbors—Giovanni Lenzi, Amedeo Adimari, Filippo Bombeni, Nanni di Ricci—sent messages of encouragement and advice to Francesco in Venice, and to his son Ricciardo, a law student at Bologna. Their letters also identify others who were sympathetic to the Del Bene: Bartolino Bartolini, Messer Palmiero Altoviti, Donato Acciaiuoli, Francesco Ardinghelli.[63] Letters on their behalf poured out of Bologna, sent by local notables and law professors to prominent Florentines. Francesco del Bene wrote to his son Borgognone in Padua that "a number of citizens have visited the priors and the Ten [the war magistracy] to speak for me, including Messer Filippo Adimari, Francesco Ardinghelli, Jacopo di Francesco Ventura, Bernardo Strozzi, Meo Bartolini, Leone Acciaiuoli, Bindo Altoviti, and Giovanni Lenzi."[64] In October 1391, a formal petition to cancel the ban against the Del Bene was presented to the Signoria by Leonardo dell'Antella. Another Del Bene partisan, Domenico Lenzi, visited one of the priors, Caccino del Caccia, who promised to support the petition.[65] When an artisan, Francesco di Piero Bartoli, voiced his opposition to the measure, "We sent

---

[60] Stefani, 775, 918.

[61] Branca's letters are in *Acquisti e Doni*, 301, unpaginated, and *Carte del Bene*, 49, no. 132, 133, 137. Examples of Bernardo's letters in *ibid.*, 49, no. 169; 52, unpaginated. For Jacopo's comments on Bernardo Strozzi, *ibid.*, 52, unpaginated, letter to Ricciardo del Bene of 26 May 1391. See also Ricciardo's letter to Jacopo; *Acquisti e Doni*, 301, unpaginated, 13 May 1391. Coluccio Salutati was a good friend of the Del Bene in 1381, but their relations may have cooled after their exile: "E spezialmente abi riguardo a ser Coluccio, che io il truovo tutto nostro e serveci volentieri in ogni nostro caso e di parole e di facto, e sì facti amici si vogliono pur riserbare a bisogni"; Giovanni d'Amerigo to Francesco di Jacopo del Bene, 2 Apr. 1381, *Carte del Bene*, 51, unpaginated.

[62] *Carte dell'Ancisa*, CC, f.811v, KK, ff.263v–264r.

[63] The letters that discuss the rehabilitation efforts are scattered through several files of the *Carte del Bene* (vols. 49, 52, 53) and *Acquisti e Doni*, 301. Only the letters in vol. 49 are numbered; the others can be cited only by date.

[64] Letter of 18 Aug. 1391; *Carte del Bene*, 53. Bernardo Strozzi wrote to Ricciardo, *ibid.*, 52, 19 Aug.: "Asai uomini auno per voi adoperato per modo ch'io mi rendo certo che voi non recevete torto."

[65] *Ibid.*, 53, 21 Oct. 1391.

several of his friends to him [Filippo di Giovanni wrote to Francesco del Bene] and also to the other priors, each one using arguments that seemed appropriate. But they have been criticized for their action, and so are responding quite negatively. Bernardo [Strozzi] went directly to Messer Rinaldo [Gianfigliazzi] and asked him to talk to the priors, and I have heard that he responded favorably. . . ."[66] Eventually, in November, the Del Bene won their struggle for rehabilitation, after the Alberti and the Rinuccini had first been reintegrated into the regime.[67] Those lineages also had their coteries of supporters who had suggested to Bernardo Strozzi that he postpone his campaign to rehabilitate the Del Bene until their friends had been restored to the *reggimento*. "I have been told," Bernardo wrote to Francesco del Bene, "that I have antagonized the Alberti and the Rinuccini by seeking to include you in the group [of the rehabilitated], and they tell me, 'Another time, and soon, your friends will be served.' "[68] Refusing to be intimidated by these pressures, Bernardo wrote to his friend that he would do everything within his power to demonstrate that "you are not inferior in rank to the Alberti and the Rinuccini."[69]

Whether based upon blood or friendship, the ties binding Florentines together in these associations were as important in the political arena as in their private affairs. Behind every petition to the Signoria for an office, a grant of immunity, or a tax reduction was a group of supporters acting on behalf of the appellant. Every officeholder had to find *guarantors* to give surety for his good conduct as prior, or castellan, or keeper of the communal accounts.[70] Men arrested and convicted of non-capital offenses solicited their relatives, and often their friends, to guarantee the payment of their fines so that they could leave prison.[71] The records of the criminal courts thus provide

[66] *Ibid.*   [67] See below, ch. II, 86–87.

[68] *Carte del Bene*, 52, letter of 29 Apr. Cf. Giovanni Lenzi's letter to Jacopo, *ibid.*, letter of 11 May: "Sappi che quivi si mosono parechi cittadini per fare ristituire gl'Alberti, ed altri per fare i Rinuccini." Another letter, undated and unsigned, from that volume contains this remark: "I fatti degli Alberti e Rinuccini erano tirati innanzi pegli amici loro."

[69] *Ibid.*, letter of 18 May: "Non so che seghuirà, ma tanto ti dicho, che giusta mia posa, si farà che voi non siate de'pegore condizione ch'Alberti e Rinuccini. . . ."

[70] Francesco Giovanni listed his *mallevadori* when he was a prior (1436), captain of Pisa (1436) and captain "della Montagna di Pistoia" (1439); *Strozz.*, 2nd ser., 16, ff.12r, 14v, 18r.

[71] Bartolomeo Valori posted bond for Strozza Strozzi; Giovanni di Ciampino da Panzano for Bernardo di Andrea Peruzzi; Tommaso di Neri Ardinghelli for Filippo Soldanieri; *ACP*, 1496, ff.241r–242r; *AP*, 3178, ff.195r–195v, 255r–255v. Bereft of such support was Matteo di Lodovico Covoni, convicted of assaulting

clues to these bonds of blood and friendship. By far the greatest burden that could be placed upon these chains of obligation involved the
posting of bonds for the good behavior of exiles. When Donato Acciaiuoli violated the conditions of his exile in 1397, he betrayed his
relatives and friends—three Acciaiuoli (Michele di Zanobi, Donato
d'Albizzo, and Lodovico d'Adoardo), three Cavalcanti (Giovanni di
Messer Amerigo, Carlo and Otto di Messer Mainardo), Luigi Guicciardini, Nicola di Messer Vieri de' Medici, Niccolò Sinibaldi and
Matteo Malatesta—who had posted 20,000 florins as surety for his
compliance.[72] Citizens who helped relatives and friends accused or
convicted of political crimes were motivated by a strong sense of
obligation, for they were risking not only money, but their reputations
and status.[73]

These coalitions appear to have been as cohesive as were the *consorterie* and factions in Dante's time. The mutual bonds of obligation
between the Niccolini and the Del Bene and their friends were as
strong as those uniting the Donati and the Cerchi, or the Blacks and
the Whites, in 1300.[74] And they may have contributed as much to the
psychic—as well as the physical—security of their members. The differences, however, were substantial. Ties of friendship, particularly
between neighbors, were quite as important as blood in cementing
these coalitions. And, unlike the factions that had proliferated in the
city in Dante's age and before, these associations possessed no ideological dimensions. They were less concerned with Guelfism than with
profit, with promoting the material well-being (*utile*) of their members.[75] Rarely did they use violence or the threat of violence against

---

his cousin Lapa: "et quia dictus Mactheus fideiuxores prestare non potuit, ideo
ipsum pro dicta quantitate recommandatus est in carceribus Stincarum"; *AEOG*,
1060, f.72v, 15 July 1388.

[72] Donato left Barletta, his designated place of exile, for Venice; *ACP*, 2073,
ff.3v–6r; *CP*, 32, f.151r, 23 Oct. 1397. For the names of his *fideiussori* and the
amount of their bonds, *ACP*, 2011, unpaginated, 12 Jan. 1396.

[73] When Luca da Panzano's cousin Matteo was exiled in 1434, Luca pledged
200 fl. (of a total of 500) to guarantee that he would keep the terms of his
confinement; *ASI*, 5th ser., IV (1889), 157. When Buonaccorso and Bartolomeo
Pitti were arrested (1413) as a result of a charge of treason against their brother
Luigi, their friends offered to post bond to obtain their release from prison; *CP*,
42, f.53v, 1 Aug. 1413.

[74] For a different viewpoint, see M. Becker, "Individualism in the Early Italian
Renaissance," *Studies in the Renaissance*, XIX, 273–97.

[75] For the organization, personnel and goals of the Medici "party" in the late
1420s, see D. Kent, *Rise of the Medici*, ch. 1.

their enemies; as Barna Valorini wrote to his father Valorino, "Today vendettas are fought in the palace [of the Signoria] and not with knives."[76]

CORPORATISM AND THE ARISTOCRATIC SPIRIT

The Florentine impulse to seek security through association had persisted throughout the fourteenth century, although the nature of the bonds linking men together had changed. While older corporate bodies had lost some of their cohesiveness and magnetism, new groupings had emerged to attract clienteles. The priorities of allegiance and obligation, so clearly defined and understood at the beginning of the *trecento*, had become confused and blurred by its end. Competition between corporate groups within the commune had also intensified. Central to the commune's function was the premise that its corporate components, representing the interests of particular groups, would reconcile their differences within its ambit and under its guidance. Once defined, the common good (*il ben comune*) was expected to take precedence over the interests of any specific group or constituency. But that principle was challenged with increasing frequency and intensity by factions which identified their own interests with the *ben comune*, and which sought to exclude their rivals from the government. The most pertinacious attack upon the corporate ideal—with its assumptions concerning political equality and the superior claims of the whole community over any single part—was sustained by coalitions of aristocratic families. From their entrenched position in the city's economic and social hierarchy they sought to dominate the commune. They cultivated a distinctive life style and a value system which set them apart from their neighbors of less exalted lineage. They became conscious of belonging to an exclusive social caste: an aristocracy, an elite.

Signs of an aristocratic mentality can be found in Florentine sources long before Dante traced his own ancestry back to Cacciaguida in the twelfth century. But not until the later fourteenth century did the idea of an elite based on blood and social distinction achieve maturity. In the years after the Black Death, members of old and prominent Florentine families began to search for documents that would establish their ancestry, and to construct the genealogies and the records of officeholding (*prioristi*) that would support their claims to social and political distinction. "Today everyone is descended from very

---

[76] *BNF, Magl.*, VIII, 1392, no. 44, undated.

ancient origins," Giovanni Morelli wrote ironically in 1393, "and so I want to record the truth about ours."[77] Nostalgia contributed to this preoccupation with ancestry, particularly in those houses of magnates —Rossi, Tornaquinci, Adimari, Agli, Frescobaldi—whose status and power had declined since the thirteenth century. But the strongest motive in this search for family origins was the more practical objective of establishing membership in the city's aristocracy. Blood—not wealth nor professional status nor personal virtue—was the basic criterion for locating individuals on the ill-defined rungs of Florence's social hierarchy.

Determining membership in an urban aristocracy was not a simple matter in this community without a legally defined nobility, in which the status of magnate was not a privilege but a penalty. In a dialogue (c. 1380) between the eminent canon lawyer, Lapo da Castiglionchio, and his son Bernardo, that question was examined in some detail. The Castiglionchi were a branch of a prominent family in the Valdisieve east of Florence, where they held fiefs with vassals and serfs, and where they "were considered to be the greatest and most noble men of that region." Sometime in the late twelfth century, the Castiglionchi were separated from their kinsmen, the Volognano, who had resisted the commune's efforts to extend its control over the *contado*. The Castiglionchi were "more gentle and modest" than their violent, unruly kinsmen, and more willing to accommodate themselves to the urban world that was encroaching on their district. Eventually, in the 1270s, the Castiglionchi came to live in Florence, but they did not follow the path of so many landed families that migrated into the city in these decades. They never practiced any trade or business except that of the international merchant who trafficked in cloth and wool "as do all of the greatest and worthiest men of the city"; they preferred to live in the country, to hunt and supervise their estates. They did not participate actively in civic affairs, and so did not become as influential

---

[77] *Ricordi*, 81. As early as 1350, the Alberti were searching for family papers to throw light on their origins; L. Passerini, *Gli Alberti di Firenze*, II, 7-9. The Strozzi asked Leonardo Bruni to search for ancestral documents while he was doing research on his Florentine history; *BNF, Fondo principale*, II, v, 10, no. 218, 6 Jan. 1424. That such investigations were not common before the late *trecento* is suggested by a passage in Lapo da Castiglionchio's treatise on his family: "Non ti debbe maravigliare se di più a drieto non truovo memorie, nè scrita, perocchè non è in costume di queste parti di fare di ciò si lunga e continua memoria; e molti cittadini sono che non potrebbero dare a' loro figliuoli informazioni si antica de' loro progenitori"; *Epistola o sia ragionamento di Messer Lapo da Castiglionchio*, ed. L. Mehus (Bologna, 1753), 52. On this issue, see Martines, *Social World*, 57.

in Florence as the Ricasoli who, like the Castiglionchi, were descended from the feudal nobility, but who did play an active role in urban politics.[78]

Though intensely proud of their ancestry, Lapo and his son realized that antiquity alone was not sufficient to maintain their family's status. They had witnessed the decline of many noble houses; they saw signs of decay in their own family. The Castiglionchi's reputation was still high in their rural district of Cuona, but they had lost property, wealth, and legal jurisdiction over the peasants who cultivated their land. To sustain their fortunes, they had to become more involved in urban life. Lapo's grandfather Albertaccio, and a kinsman Ruggiero, were the first Castiglionchi to participate in communal politics; the latter, a lawyer, was a prior in 1289. Albertaccio's son Lapo was twice chosen to the Signoria, in 1319 and 1322; his son described him as "a peaceful man of good reputation, much loved by all, and a man who liked city life."[79] With this generation, the urbanization of the Castiglionchi was complete, and Lapo followed the pattern established by his grandfather. He studied canon law in Bologna and took minor orders, but after the plague of 1348 had decimated his kinsmen, Lapo left the church to marry and raise a family.[80] He practiced law in Florence and lectured in the university; his earnings enabled him to purchase the property in the quarter of Santa Croce that had once belonged to his ancestors, "the better to conserve and enlarge it."[81] Deeply involved in urban politics and in the Parte Guelfa, Lapo became the leader of the aristocratic forces in the commune from the early 1360s until the Ciompi revolution in 1378.[82]

Strongly committed to the principles of hierarchy and elitism, Lapo believed that the commune should be governed by the city's aristocracy, composed of old and worthy families with a long and unblemished record of allegiance to Guelf principles and service to the Guelf republic. Florence's political hierarchy should coincide with her social order, at the apex of which were families like the Castiglionchi, "which had always pursued an honorable existence, had possessed the castle of Castiglionchio with many of its ancient holdings adjacent, which had retained control of the [local] churches . . . which still held its ancient site in Florence . . . and which has kept its citizenship and its relations with noble citizens and its share of the city's

---

[78] *Epistola*, 31–48, 148.

[79] *Ibid.*, 59–60; Stefani, 179, 335, 342.

[80] *Ibid.*, 56: ". . . Veggendo la nostra famiglia quasi mancare di persone, per zelo della nostra famiglia, e per avere famiglia, presi moglie. . . ."

[81] *Ibid.*, 47.   [82] *Ibid.*, 140–42.

highest offices. . . ."[83] Family antiquity, wealth, a respectable profession like the law or international trade, a dignified life style:[84] these were the marks of social distinction, and also the appropriate qualifications for a political career. Lapo relished the deference shown him by a fellow-student at Bologna, whose own family was as old as the Castiglionchi, but had been servile dependents of Lapo's ancestors. Such men never lost the stigma of their origins, even though they (or their forebears) had moved to Florence and prospered, and even gained membership in the Signoria.[85] They might be tolerated in the commune, if their families had always been loyal to the Guelf cause, and if they accepted the leadership of their social superiors.[86] The fastidious Lapo never expressed, in writing, the anger that he must have felt over the participation in the government of artisans and shopkeepers, the practitioners of lowly trades (*vili arti*). But his distaste for such men was certainly as strong as that expressed by Giovanni Guinigi, who wrote in 1413 to his brother Paolo, the lord of Lucca, about his experiences in Siena, "governed by a hundred tyrants—stocking-makers, locksmiths, and other low types (*gentaglia*) —who behave like pigs, so that when one shouts, the rest come running to help him. . . ."[87]

In varying degrees, every well-born Florentine shared these feelings about the guildsmen who could not boast of a distinguished ancestry, nor obtain help from supportive kinsmen. Many of these craftsmen and retailers were "new men" who had recently migrated to Florence from the *contado* and beyond; others had risen from the ranks of the urban poor.[88] A handful were rich or nearly so; the majority enjoyed a modest but not comfortable livelihood. For such men, the guild connection was a prime source of security and status. They habitually supported the commune's authority against all forms of privilege: the church, the Parte Guelfa, the noble clans like the Ubertini and the counts of Poppi. Though considering themselves loyal Guelfs, they

---

[83] *Epistola*, 147, statement by Lapo's son Bernardo.

[84] See Martines, *Social World*, ch. 2.

[85] *Epistola*, 43.

[86] *Epistola*, 116: "Avemo fatta menzione di queste vili e piccole parole per esempio che nullo cittadino, e massimamente popolano, o uomo di piccolo affare, quando ha signoria, non deve. essere troppo ardito, nè persontuoso, ma udire le due e le tre voce in consiglio."

[87] *Carteggio di Paolo Guinigi*, ed. L. Fumi (Lucca, 1925), 316, 2 Feb. 1413.

[88] On the *gente nuova*, see Brucker, *Florentine Politics*, 20–24, 40–46, 53–56, 114–15, 135–38, 161–63; Becker, "An Essay on the 'Novi Cives' and Florentine Politics, 1343–1382," *Medieval Studies*, XXIV (1962), 35–82. For examples of upward mobility, Brucker, *Society of Renaissance Florence*, 17–18.

were suspicious of—and hostile to—the Guelf party that tried to exclude them from communal office. In the priorate and the colleges, and in the legislative councils, they tended to follow the lead of men from prominent families who were, like themselves, committed to corporate values. They demonstrated their hostility to the aristocrats by voting against legislation that served their interests, and by reporting their delicts to the authorities. "Be it known to you, Lord Executor," one anonymous informant reported, "that Nofri di Pagno Strozzi . . . is a potent, arrogant, evil, and violent man, who has already killed and wounded many men and women of the city of Florence. . . ."[89] Aghinolfo de' Bardi was described by his anonymous accuser as the most villainous man in Florence; no one had "a worse reputation or condition, nor . . . has done more harm to his commune or to citizens and residents of the *contado*."[90] Another citizen denounced the entire Bardi clan as "a great and arrogant family" whose members committed acts of violence against their social inferiors every day. They allegedly threatened witnesses called to testify about their misdeeds, and bribed the judge to quash the cases against them.[91] Africhello de' Medici was accused (1377) of exploiting and terrorizing his neighbors in the Mugello, forcing them to surrender their property to him so that he could "live like a nobleman from the possessions of the poor." By such tactics (it was alleged), he had doubled the value of his property, even though "he neither pursues a business career nor any other trade and has never earned a penny honestly."[92]

The artisans, merchants, and notaries of modest social standing— the *mezzana gente* who constituted the bulk of the guild community —were very conscious of the differences, in life style and in outlook, between themselves and those whom they described as "*grandi e possenti*."[93] When Andrea de' Pazzi sought *popolano* status (June 1422), he reminded his fellow-citizens that "since childhood he has been continually involved in mercantile activities and in honest affairs, and

[89] Brucker, *Society of Renaissance Florence*, 125. This accusation was made in 1381; six years later Nofri was placed under the communal ban for his brother's crime; *ibid.*, 111–12; below, 84–85. Nofri's miserable death, by his own hand while inebriated, is described in *Prov.*, 91, ff.26r–27r, 28–29 Apr. 1402.

[90] *Society of Renaissance Florence*, 123.

[91] *AEOG*, 1223, f.4r, 19 Nov. 1394: "Sapiate come questa famiglia di Bardi sono una famiglia grande e arrogante e non churanno a persona e a 'gni omo danno de' le busse tuto dì e minacciono ogn'uomo." Lodovico Giandonati was characterized, in another accusation, as a "homo superbo, altero e arrogante"; *ibid.*, 892, f.88r.

[92] Brucker, *Society of Renaissance Florence*, 120–21.

[93] The phrase is often found in these documents, e.g., against Jacopo di Bindello de'Bardi; *AEOG*, 404, f.99r, 4 Apr. 1363.

he has tried always to imitate the life and the mores of *popolani*. . . ."[94] In his petition to be separated legally from his kinsmen whose behavior he deplored, Andrea Salterelli spelled out in detail his conception of the life style appropriate for a worthy *popolano*: "He has always been and remains a young man of good reputation and of peaceful temperament, who exercises the craft of woolen cloth manufacturer, and who intends to live in peace and quiet, and to have good relations with everyone. . . ."[95] In describing the virtues and vices of their relatives, the lawyer Donato Velluti (d. 1370) and the merchant Giovanni Morelli (d. 1444) defined their conception of the ideal citizen. He should be a competent businessman, capable of enlarging his patrimony without taking excessive risks, and thus able to provide amply for his heirs. Sobriety, honesty, prudence, loyalty, devotion to family: these were the supreme *popolano* virtues, just as infidelity, untrustworthiness, extravagance, and immoderation were, together with *prepotenza*, the gravest flaws in the moral code of the *popolani*. Men who squandered their fortunes, or who failed to maintain the status that they had inherited, were objects of contempt and condescension, rarely of charity and compassion.[96] Giovanni Morelli warned his sons against contracting a marriage with any family that had spawned a traitor, robber, murderer, or bastard: "They should be clean and without blemish, with a reputation as good and loving kinsmen who are not too avaricious, but who are temperate in their hospitality, and are prudent men and worthy citizens."[97]

The Guicciardini did not fully meet these criteria, in the 1390s. When his kinsman appealed for help to obtain his release from prison, Messer Luigi Guicciardini compiled a lengthy catalogue of the "vile and abominable deeds" committed by "the accursed Simone di Machirone Guicciardini."[98] These included a series of assaults on his neighbors, the illegal occupation of a Machiavelli house, the organiza-

[94] *Prov.*, 112, f. 37v. Ridolfo and Guido Cavalcanti described themselves as "mercatores pacifici et quieti et inter artifices et mercatores continue conversati; nunquam . . . alicui nocuerunt vel iniuriam intulerunt et de eorum industria et labore vivere quesiverunt"; *Prov.*, 68, ff.57r–57v, 13–14 June 1379.

[95] *Prov.*, 84, f.229v, Dec. 1395. In July 1406, several Strozzi petitioned the commune for legal separation from their kinsman, Francesco di Giovanni di Messer Niccolò Strozzi, "qui quotidie querit alios offendere indebite et iniuste, et ipsi nollunt quod sub umbra favoris consortium ipse faceret iniuriam alicui"; *Prov.*, 95, f.117r.

[96] See Brucker, *Renaissance Florence*, 104–06. Velluti condemned Piero Pitti and Baldo Frescobaldi for wasting their inheritances; *Cronica*, 100, 137.

[97] *Ricordi*, 208–09.

[98] *Strozz.*, 1st ser., 16, ff.4r–4v, Simone's letter; 5r–5v, Luigi's catalogue, partly trans. in Brucker, *Society of Renaissance Florence*, 127–29.

tion of a jailbreak. Donato Velluti described the career of a kinsman by marriage, Piero di Ciore Pitti, who had fallen so low that he had worked as a laborer in a cloth factory and had married a woman named Bartolomea, "the grand-daughter of Bongianni, the wine seller, who had been the whore of other men and with whom he lived in a miserable state."[99] Another relative, Gherardino di Piero Velluti, was criticized for his addiction to the pleasure-loving, spendthrift ways of the nobility. "He is a good horseman and equerry, and expert at everything save business. . . . He is always dressed and shod well, and he rides with his friends, and keeps horses, dogs and hawks. . . ."[100] These aristocratic extravagances, Donato implied, were not appropriate for the Velluti, who for generations had been committed to the work ethic and to capital accumulation.[101]

No political or social dichotomy is ever so neat in reality as in its defining schema; this Florentine model is no exception. Giovanni Morelli was loyal to his commune, his lineage, and his *gonfalone*; he also embraced aristocratic values that his ancestors—men of worthy but humble stock whose stained hands revealed their trade as dyers—would have deplored. Morelli had a keen sense of his social place, just below the highest ranks of the hierarchy, and separated by a wide gulf from the "new men, the artisans, and those involved in petty affairs."[102] Morelli cautioned his sons against ostentation in dress and deportment, but he also advised them to choose their friends from the aristocracy, and to adopt their habits and life style. They should learn to sing and dance, to hunt, even to joust. They should attend weddings and feasts, and in turn invite their friends to dine and drink, "and so you will possess the social graces, and you will make friends among your peers, and will gain a reputation as a man of culture and gentility."[103] Like others from his social milieu, Morelli was unaware of the contradictions between his ascetic and par-

---

[99] *Cronica*, 137–39.   [100] *Ibid.*, 34–36.

[101] See his comments on his brother Filippo, who returned to Florence from Sicily, "tanto borioso di vestimenti, di cavallo, di famiglia, la qual cosa non si convenia"; *ibid.*, 142–43. Morelli warned his sons against those luxuries: "che si guardi di non vestire di soperchio, nè seta nè panni ricchi, che non tenga fante nè cavallo"; *Ricordi*, 257. Concerning his son Niccolò who died in 1417, Lapo Niccolini wrote: ". . . Non avea niuno proprio e avea dissipato e llogoro del mio molto più non gli toccava in parte . . . ma troppo grande gittatore del suo e dell' altrui, che poco si curava di nulla se non seguire i suoi apetiti e volontà, e a me diede assai fatiche"; *Libro degli affari*, 137.

[102] *Ricordi*, 196.

[103] *Ibid.*, 257, 260–62. On the necessity of entertaining friends, see L. B. Alberti, *Opere volgari*, ed. C. Grayson (Bari, 1960), I, 161.

simonious instincts, derived from mercantile habits and practices, and the aristocratic impulses to entertain lavishly and to spend without restraint.[104] In his diary devoted largely to purchases of real estate and his tax payments, the merchant Francesco Giovanni described the jousts in which he and his brother had participated in the late 1420s. These tournaments had become very popular with upper-class Florentines like the Giovanni brothers, providing them with an opportunity to display their military prowess, but above all, their wealth. Francesco Giovanni described, in lavish detail, the jeweled costumes and trappings worn by himself and his retinue, and furnished "entirely at my expense."[105] In 1430, the vogue for building large and magnificent palaces had scarcely begun, but rich Florentines were discovering other ways to flaunt their wealth and advertise their social eminence.[106]

In seeking outlets for their elitist impulses, Florentine aristocrats were confronted by a suspicious and hostile community of guildsmen, who used legislation and the pressure of public opinion to thwart their social superiors. By the sporadic enforcement of sumptuary legislation, they imposed limits on any public display—in dress, wedding celebrations, or obsequies for the dead—that would publicize the wealth and prestige of a family.[107] Only citizens who died while serving in office were honored at their burial by the display of the communal insignia.[108] Official policy prohibited the burial of citizens in the reconstructed cathedral of Santa Reparata. Vieri de' Medici did receive permission to be buried there next to his ancestors, but his tomb was to be placed in the pavement and "not in the wall or in any prominent place." Relatives of Cardinal Piero Corsini were likewise authorized

[104] On those contradictions, see my *Renaissance Florence*, 103–09, 121–24.

[105] *Strozz.*, 2nd ser., 16, ff.3v–4v. After a hiatus of several years, tournaments were held in Florence in 1368, 1372, and 1377; *Manoscritti*, 222, p. 232; *Diario d'anonimo*, 325. By the 1390s, they had become very common; *Panc.*, 158, ff.169r–170r; *BNF*, *Magl.* VIII, 1392, no. 62. Alberti discusses the pros and cons of participating in tournaments; *Opere*, I, 159–60.

[106] R. Goldthwaite, "The Florentine Palace as Domestic Architecture," *American Historical Review*, LXXVII (1972), 977–1012.

[107] *Statuta populi et communis Florentiae* (Fribourg, 1778–1783), II, 357–84; Brucker, *Society of Renaissance Florence*, 179–83. Violations of sumptuary laws are recorded in *AEOG*, vols. 71, 98, 115, 160, 208 (1346–54), and in *GA*, vols. 28, 60, 61 (1384–85).

[108] Martines, *Social World*, 239–41. Cf. the comment of Niccolò Busini, for the Sixteen, *CP*, 38, f.51v: "Circa licentiam que petitur pro honorando corpus domino Caroli de Cavalcantibus, videlicet, de deferendo signum communis ad sepulturam, quod audiverunt hec esse prohibitum ab ordinamentis et quod non esse honestum contra illa facere, sed si esse permissum, quod libenter concurrerent. . . ."

to bury that prelate in the cathedral, but they could not exhibit the family insignia on the wall, but only "in the enclosure of the tomb."[109] Though the carving of family escutcheons in churches was not formally prohibited by statute, the prejudice against displaying these symbols was so strong that, as late as the 1440s, the Medici were criticized for emblazoning their arms in every church they had rebuilt.[110] By that time, however, the struggle by civic authorities to contain the aristocratic impulse had been largely abandoned.[111]

The widespread acceptance of the axiom that some citizens, by virtue of their birth, were superior to others limited communal efforts to restrain elitism.[112] The republic recognized distinctions among its citizens based upon guild membership, social rank, and knighthood. Lower guildsmen could not hold the office of standard-bearer of justice, nor the most important vicariates and captaincies in the territory. An innkeeper, Cenni di Marco, once suggested that different standards of behavior should be expected of the two groups: "The lower [guildsmen] should act with reverence and humility, and the greater, with benevolence. . . ." Speaking in 1382 for the consuls of the Lana guild, Guido del Palagio enunciated the principle that "everyone in the city should have his portion, according to his quality or rank."[113] In recommending citizens for office or for special consideration by foreign states, the Signoria emphasized their family origins, as well as their personal qualities. Messer Lorenzo de' Ricci was descended from "a well-born and celebrated family of our city"; Messer Antonio Peruzzi came from "one of the most noble and exalted families . . . ."[114] The relatives of a young Florentine convicted of theft, Chiovo

[109] *Lana*, 47, 26 June 1392; 85, ff.70r–70v, 12 Dec. 1389; *Prov.*, 80, ff.15r–16r. The provision authorizing the Corsini tomb was initially rejected in the Council of the Commune, and then approved; *LF*, 43, ff.204r–206v.

[110] E. Gombrich, "The Early Medici as Patrons of Art," in *Italian Renaissance Studies*, ed. E. F. Jacob (London, 1960), 286–87, 291, 299.

[111] In his article, "Further Observations on Masaccio's Trinity," *Art Bulletin*, XLVIII (1966), 382–84, J. Coolidge notes that the building of monumental tombs again came into fashion in Florence in the 1420s, after a long hiatus.

[112] Cf. J. Kirschner, "Ars imitatur naturam: a Consilium of Baldus on Naturalization in Florence," *Viator* (1974), 10: "One must not view political inequality in Florence as a pathology or as a residue of social and political institutions that were dysfunctional. The politics of inequality . . . were in keeping with the hierarchical structures of the tre- and quattrocento. A society conceived and structured hierarchically and a society obsessed with ancestry militated against a true florescence of civic equality in late medieval and Renaissance Florence."

[113] *CP*, 20, ff.117r, 118r, 4 Feb. 1382. On an earlier occasion, Cenni said: "Quod sicut Deus precipit, pro unitate civitatis detur quilibet quod suum est"; *CP*, 16, f.73v, 10 Jan. 1379.

[114] *SCMC*, 27, f.4r; 34, f.33r.

Machiavelli, petitioned for the mitigation of his penalty, arguing that "he should receive some consideration for the many worthy deeds that his Machiavelli ancestors have performed on behalf of the Commune. . . ."[115] After confessing to his involvement in a plot to overthrow the regime in 1396, Messer Donato Acciaiuoli pleaded for mercy: "I am a Guelf and born of Guelf blood." That argument was compelling for the members of the war *balìa*, whose spokesman, Andrea della Stufa, proposed that "on account of his merits and those of his relatives," Donato's life should be spared.[116] In 1407, the Signoria asked Marcello Strozzi to help Cappone Capponi "out of respect and for the honor of his family, the status of which in our city we are certain will be known to you."[117] When Buonaccorso and Bartolomeo Pitti were held as hostages for the return of their brother Luigi, charged with treason, a collegiate spokesman appealed to the Signoria to warn the rector not to maltreat them, "considering the status and the virtues of the prisoners and their ancestors. . . ."[118]

THE CIOMPI REVOLUTION

Ever since the commune had been established in the twelfth century, prominent and well-born Florentines had tried to limit its membership to their kind, while popular elements fought to breach the barriers erected to keep them out of the government. The struggle between these rival groups, with their antithetical value systems and life styles, was particularly intense in the 1250s, when the regime of the *primo popolo* dismantled the towers of the great families, and again in the 1290s, when the guild regime enacted the Ordinances of Justice to restrain the power of the most lawless and violent magnates. Subsequent to the passage of this punitive legislation, periods of equilibrium alternated with periods of crisis, when pressures within the society became too great for the commune to contain them.

One such moment occurred in the 1320s, when the arrogance of the magnates inspired a popular reaction against these prepotent houses. The 1340s witnessed another confrontation between corporate and aristocratic elements. In November 1340 the Bardi headed a group of magnates that sought to expand their authority in the commune and ward off their impending bankruptcy. Two years later, a coalition of magnates and wealthy *popolani* was responsible for the establishment of the dictatorship of Walter of Brienne, the duke of

---

[115] Brucker, *Society of Renaissance Florence*, 178.
[116] *CP*, 32, ff.IV, 2r.   [117] F. W. Kent, *Family Worlds*, 199.
[118] *CP*, 42, f.53v, 1 Aug. 1413.

Athens, who paid for their support by canceling bans against magnates, granting them lucrative offices, and weakening the punitive clauses in the Ordinances of Justice. Not content with these boons, the magnates joined an alliance of *popolano* families—Medici, Altoviti, Ricci, Rucellai, Strozzi—in a revolt against the duke (July 1343), and as a reward they received the privilege of membership in the Signoria. But their triumph was short-lived. Two months later, a popular revolt broke out against this aristocratic regime. The magnates and their supporters were defeated in street battles; their palaces were burned and looted. From these disorders emerged a popular regime from which magnates were excluded and which contained a substantial number of lower guildsmen, artisans, and shopkeepers who were strongly committed to the idea of a corporate polity.[119]

Although the 1343 revolution did mark the momentary ascendancy of popular and collective interests in Florentine politics, it did not signify the permanent victory of these principles. Within five years of this regime's establishment, an aristocratic resurgence occurred in the wake of the Black Death. The number of lower guildsmen and "new men" in communal offices was sharply reduced; their places were taken by members of old and distinguished *popolano* families who now replaced the discredited magnates as the advocates of aristocratic politics. Their objectives were, first, to increase the representation of the great families in the commune, and second, to promote Guelf ideals in domestic and foreign affairs.[120]

The most intense phase of this conflict between guild corporatism and elitism began in the 1360s; it reached its climax with the Ciompi revolution of 1378. Recalling in 1420 a scene from his childhood fifty years before, Gino Capponi described how he and his schoolmates would chant political slogans in the streets: "Long live the hats"— that is, those members of aristocratic families whose headgear symbolized their exalted social status—and "Death to the capes," which meant (he explained) "Death to the guildsmen and to those of lowly condition." The tables were turned fifteen years later, at the height of the Ciompi disorders, when throngs of artisans and laborers were burning the palaces of their aristocratic enemies, shouting "Death to the hats and long live the capes!" Capponi described another gambit employed by his aristocratic friends to demean guildsmen who sat in the councils and the magistracies. They taunted the *lanaiuoli* by shouting, "Go

---

[119] These events summarized by Becker, "The Florentine Magnates: 1280–1343," *Mediaeval Studies*, XXVII (1965), 246–308.

[120] Brucker, *Florentine Politics and Society*; Becker, *Florence in Transition*, I, ch. 5.

back to your cloth-making," and to the druggists, "Go and grind the pepper."[121] In less formal contexts, the gibes were even sharper. A magnate, Ceffo degli Agli, allegedly referred (1381) to the *arteficiali de la merda*, those upstarts (*artifici pidocchiosi*) who had recently come to power; Francesco degli Albizzi spoke derisively of "those louts (*gaglioffi*) who are sitting in the Signoria."[122] Since many artisans had joined the cloth-workers in the Ciompi uprising, aristocrats tended to lump them together into an undifferentiated crowd of "robbers and traitors and murderers and assassins and gluttons and malefactors."[123]

The political struggle between aristocratic and corporate elements in these years centered upon the Parte Guelfa, which was dominated by members of aristocratic houses, of both magnates and *popolani*. The Parte launched a campaign to purge the regime of undesirables; the excuse was their Ghibelline ancestry, and the weapon, proscription (*ammonizione*). Some victims of this political vendetta were indeed "new men" of uncertain origins; others, like Matteo Villani and Francesco del Bene, came from old Guelf stock. The arrogance of these *arciguelfi*, and the arbitrary nature of their tactics, infuriated citizens like the chronicler Marchionne Stefani, who wrote that no one was safe from their vindictiveness, "even if he were more Guelf than Charlemagne."[124] Men like Stefani, from the middle echelons of the guild community, realized the precariousness of their political status, and they organized a campaign against the Parte and against the factionalism that its policies had spawned. In 1366 the Parte's authority to purge suspected Ghibellines was restricted; the two most factious families (the Albizzi and the Ricci) were barred from office for ten years.[125] These measures were adopted and implemented by a civic group organized to defend the commune, and its corporate values, against those who "sought to hold the merchants and artisans of Florence in a state of vassalage. . . ."[126] That coalition included artisans and tradesmen, bankers and *lanaiuoli*, and also men from old and prominent families: Salvestro de' Medici, Sandro da Quarata, Andrea Rondinelli, Filippo Bastari. Around these leaders had formed groups of citizens whose vision of the corporate ideal may have been blurred by their thirst for power and prestige. When it launched an attack on the papacy in 1375, the "civic party" violated the spirit, if

---

[121] "Ricordi di Gino di Neri Capponi," in *Miscellanea di studi offerti a A. Balduino e B. Bianchi* (Padua, 1962), 37.

[122] *AEOG*, 889, f.136r; 892, f.34r.

[123] *Diario d'anonimo*, 394.   [124] Stefani, 766, 788.

[125] Brucker, *Florentine Politics and Society*, 202–21, 244–65.

[126] Velluti, *Cronica*, 248.

not the letter, of legislation that it had adopted in 1372, which prohibited the waging of war or the dispatch of armed troops without the prior approval of a special assembly.[127] To direct and subsidize that war, the leadership delegated unprecedented authority to a *balìa*, and confiscated a large portion of the church's patrimony in Florentine territory.[128] Not since the Guelf regime was established in the thirteenth century had its ideological teguments been so rudely assaulted. To these radical measures, Guelf aristocrats responded in kind, by proscribing nearly one hundred citizens in the early months of 1378. This was the prelude to a plot, organized by the Parte hierarchy, to overthrow the regime during the festivities held on the feast day (24 June) of Florence's patron saint, John the Baptist.[129]

The war party's response to that threat precipitated the Ciompi revolution, when the *popolo minuto* participated, for six weeks, in the government of their city. Posterity's interest in that episode has naturally focused on its socio-economic aspects, for the Ciompi uprising provides a rare glimpse of the political goals and methods of the "underprivileged," whose voices are scarcely ever heard in an age dominated by the rich and the powerful.[130] But the short-lived ascendancy of the cloth-workers did not permanently alter their living standards nor their relations with their masters. More significant, historically, was the impact of these events upon the continuous struggle between corporate and aristocratic forces for control of the government. While Salvestro de' Medici and his allies were pushing through legislation to cripple the Parte, they were also organizing the crowds that burned the palaces of the *arciguelfi*: Lapo da Castiglionchio, Carlo Strozzi, Niccolò Soderini, Piero degli Albizzi. Guildsmen participated in these disorders with poor laborers, but they also acted to keep the violence within limits; the pork butchers repelled a mob attempting to loot the communal treasury.[131] They retained, too, their arms in their shops—and in their minds, the memories of their victory over the *arciguelfi*. When the Signoria responded too slowly to guild demands for reforming the government, they presented a petition to the priors that articulated the corporate ideal in its purest form. Henceforth, all guilds were to participate in the scrutinies for the

[127] Brucker, *Florentine Politics*, 255.

[128] *Ibid.*, 293, 317–19. Forty years later, the powers granted to that *balìa* were remembered by Messer Nello Martini; *CP*, 45, f.165r, 3 Feb. 1424.

[129] Brucker, *Florentine Politics*, 362–63.

[130] For an historiographical survey, see my "Ciompi," *Flor. Studies*, 314–19; and for some documentation of the "voices of the poor," my *Society of Renaissance Florence*, 233–37.

[131] Brucker, *Florentine Politics*, 368.

Signoria and the colleges, and all guildsmen nominated by their districts (*gonfaloni*) were to be voted upon by the electors. Only citizens who actually worked at trades or businesses could hold communal office. The intent of this legislation was to minimize distinctions within the regime: to give the most obscure artisan a greater opportunity to hold office, while excluding the aristocratic rentier who took no active part in trade or industry.[132]

Thus, in those early days of July 1378, the corporate ideal had achieved its greatest triumph since the guild regime's establishment in 1282. But that victory was hollow, since the institutional fabric of corporatism, the commune, had been seriously weakened by the June disorders. The Signoria's authority was further undermined by its capitulation to the guilds, whose members threatened to riot if their petitions were not approved.[133] Contributing to the Signoria's difficulties was the war magistracy, whose members had been among the instigators of the June disorders, and who still exercised control over soldiers hired for the papal war. Instead of placing these troops at the Signoria's disposal, the war *balìa* used them to guard their own houses.[134] Other citizens imported peasants from their country estates to defend their palaces; they placed no trust in the government's ability to keep the peace. As disorders spread through the city, the priors sent urgent appeals for troops stationed in the *contado* to march into Florence to guard the palace of the Signoria. Only eighty lances heeded that call; others may have been detained by the war magistracy. The Signoria's last hope was the civic militia, but only two of the sixteen companies came to their assistance. The final, dramatic moment was described by an eyewitness: outside the palace, a menacing crowd; within, consternation and despair, as the frightened priors and their collegial associates looked to each other in vain for guidance. As the crowd shouted for the priors to leave, or to be killed, they stole away, one by one, leaving the members of the war *balìa* to open the palace doors for the mob.[135]

The regime that ruled Florence for six weeks (22 July–31 August 1378) was not a workers' republic, but a government of an enlarged guild community that included three new corporations of cloth-

[132] *Ibid.*, 376. The law also provided for the Signoria's right to veto any *ammonizione* by the Parte.

[133] *Cronache e memorie dello tumulto dei Ciompi*, 18: "Imperochè li artefici erano tutti alle botteghe delle loro arti armati, e avevano spigati già i gonfaloni dell'arti per rumoreggiare."

[134] These events in Brucker, *Florentine Politics*, 379–86.

[135] *Cronache e memorie*, 31, trans. in Brucker, *Florentine Politics*, 386. See also Morelli, *Ricordi*, 321–22.

workers, some of whom were day laborers, and others, jobbers who operated small shops where they performed some of the steps in the cloth-making process for the *lanaiuoli*.[136] Executive authority was vested in a *balìa* of 130 members recruited from the mass of artisans and shopkeepers who heretofore had enjoyed very little power and status in the commune. The *petit bourgeois* mentality of these lower guildsmen was revealed by the *balìa's* decrees, which were moderate not extreme, and which were patently designed to calm the populace by avoiding radical solutions to the city's problems. Members of the *balìa* demonstrated their commitment to the corporate principle by forming a brotherhood (*consorteria*), and swore an oath that they would "band together, one with the other, in life and in death." They devised an insignia to identify themselves: "a gold lion on a blue field, with the emblem of the *popolo* . . . and a shield of liberty. . . ."[137] Ostensibly, the association was created to defend the regime from attack; to that end, they granted themselves the right to bear arms and to assemble anywhere, day or night.

The cautious policies of the *balìa* may have reassured the "good citizens," but it did not satisfy the *popolo minuto*. In late August, the lower-class districts (San Frediano, Belletri, Camaldoli, San Lorenzo) were seething with unrest. A large crowd of workers assembled in Santa Maria Novella and elected eight of their number to represent them in negotiating with the Signoria. Their political objective, apparently, was the incorporation of that workers' committee into the constitutional system, as a permanent magistracy. Like other collegiate bodies in the commune, they would be consulted by the Signoria, and would vote on all legislative proposals. Though the evidence concerning their organizational plans is ambiguous, and derived from unfriendly sources, they seem to have developed an embryonic bureaucracy, with notaries to record their deliberations and treasurers to collect and disburse funds. Possibly the leaders envisaged their organization as enjoying the privileges similar to those of the Parte Guelfa, and with a particular responsibility for promoting the interests of the poor. Their aspirations, however, were crushed on the last day of August, when the guild community turned on its newest adjunct and in a brief but decisive battle drove the Ciompi out of the piazza della Signoria, and out of the regime.

Florentines reacted to these events in very different ways, according

---

[136] For the material in this paragraph, Brucker, "Ciompi," *Flor. Studies*, 314–56.

[137] *Cronache e memorie*, 79: "E che niuno altro potesse portare questa arme, se non fosse della detta consorteria."

to their places in the social hierarchy. The most detailed formulation of lower-class expectations was recorded by the anonymous "scrutator," who wrote that certain reforms were instituted by the Ciompi regime "to give a part to more people, and so that each would be content, and each would have a share of the offices, and so that all citizens would be united. Thus, poor men would have their due, for they have always borne the expenses [of government] and only the rich have profited."[138] That statement was an idealized version of the corporate ethic: a polity characterized by justice and peace, in which each citizen enjoyed a share of the responsibilities and rewards of government. In a more pragmatic vein, the Ciompi leaders demanded reforms that would improve their living standard: higher wages and guaranteed work, an amnesty for small debtors, a more equitable system of taxation.[139] The changes, which these workers perceived as heralding the end of their exploitation and the creation of a just society, were seen by the propertied classes—from humble artisan to rich merchant—as the destruction of the natural order of things. "If the *minuti* had won," Giovanni Monaldi wrote in his diary, "every worthy citizen would have been driven from his home, replaced by a wool-carder who would have taken everything that he owned, and in Florence and in the *contado*, everyone with any property would have been killed or would have fled."[140] Though the actual losses, in lives and property, from these disorders were quite small, the "good citizens" were persuaded that the *popolo minuto* were about to burn and sack the city, when their evil plans were aborted.[141]

Florentines with a substantial investment in the traditional order were truly frightened by the prospect of social revolution, and also troubled by the sequence of events that had culminated in this nightmare. They did not credit the Ciompi with precipitating the crisis; instead, they saw the workers as the dupes of politicians whose thirst for power or revenge had brought the city to the brink of destruction. Alamanno Acciaiuoli blamed the catastrophe on those responsible for launching the war against "the Holy Church of God." In this interpretation, the Ciompi revolt was divine retribution for the republic's treatment of the papacy and the Florentine clergy. But according to Marchionne Stefani, the villains were the *arciguelfi*, whose indiscriminate proscription of honest citizens had poisoned the civic atmos-

---

[138] *Ibid.*, 76–77, trans. in Brucker, *Society of Renaissance Florence*, 238.
[139] Brucker, "Ciompi," *Flor. Studies*, 339–44, 347–48, 353–54; *Society of Renaissance Florence*, 236–37.
[140] Brucker, "Ciompi," 349, n. 3.   [141] *Ibid.*, 349–50.

phere. Stefani defended the leaders of the war party, as did, too, the anonymous chronicler who praised "the worthy Salvestro di Messer Alamanno de' Medici, that cherished citizen" who had resisted the machinations of the "ravenous wolves" seeking to destroy the regime.[142]

Though differing in their explanations of the Ciompi revolt, these witnesses were all united in their strong commitment to the republic, and to the corporate values that it symbolized. They deplored the factious spirit animating those who could not accept the subordination of private interests to the public welfare, and whose systematic violation of traditional norms had destroyed the precarious balance that had existed between popular and aristocratic elements since mid-century. They were shaken by the spectacle of authority being flouted; of priors scuttling from the palace like criminals; of a wool-carder, Michele di Lando, chosen standard-bearer of justice by the acclamation of the crowd. They yearned for the restoration of orderly government, of the familiar routines and rituals that legitimized the political process. They applauded every sign that the city was again under the Signoria's control, and that its edicts were obeyed.[143] "May God give them [the priors] the will to do what is necessary for the good and peaceful state of the *popolo* and the guilds and the commune," wrote one citizen in his diary on 2 September, "and death to all traitors in the city and *contado* of Florence!"[144]

THE GUILD REGIME OF 1378–1382

The tenure of the Ciompi regime was too brief to show how a polity embracing nearly the whole community might have fared. Its successor survived long enough—three years and five months—to test the viability of a government with a broad social base. That regime was the closest approximation to the corporate ideal that Florence was ever to experience. Its magistracies regularly consulted with the guilds, through their *capitudini*, and advised those representatives to

[142] *Cronache e memorie*, 18; *Diario d'anonimo*, 356, 360. On Stefani's views, see L. Green, *Chronicle into History*, 91–111. Several themes in this paragraph were developed by Dr. Mark Phillips of Carleton University, who wrote a paper on the Ciompi for the seminar of my Berkeley colleague, Randolph Starn.

[143] Acciaiuoli had remarked on the cancellation of the celebrations for the feast of John the Baptist, and the installation of the July priorate without the traditional public ceremonies; *Cronache e memorie*, 17. In October, the Signoria ordered these festivities to be held, and also a celebration of the ratification of the peace treaty with the papacy; *Diario d'anonimo*, 386–87.

[144] *Diario d'anonimo*, 381.

meet often with their constituents.[145] The priors carefully considered every guild petition, and they generally favored the policy, articulated by Tommaso Strozzi, that "the guildsmen should be free to meet, at their volition, in their guild halls and in the palace of the Merchants' Court. . . ."[146]

As leaders of, and spokesmen for, the city's neighborhoods, the *gonfaloni*, the sixteen captains of the militia companies enjoyed a particularly important place in this regime. They were the principal custodians, Donato Barbadori said, of the city's security; in times of turmoil, they were authorized to march to the palace of the Signoria with their armed contingents and their flags.[147] That the guildsmen understood and appreciated their role as the regime's defenders is clear from their response (March 1379) to criticism directed against the Signoria. The linen-maker, Zanobi called Principe, said that "he and the other guildsmen" gave their unqualified support to the priors; Andrea di Mazze, an armorer, and Agostino d'Andrea, shoemaker, placed their corporations "and their persons" at the Signoria's disposal.[148] It was hoped that massive corporate support for the regime would contribute to civic unity, and everyone (in Tommaso di Giovanni da Careggi's words) "would exchange the kiss [of peace] . . . ."[149] That vision was articulated by an unidentified artisan "who came to the rostrum and said that rich and poor should share alike in the offices, so that each would be content . . . and so that each, poor or rich, could say what he wished without fear. . . ."[150]

[145] Guido Fagni, "Quod domini habeant capitudines et cum eis conferrant"; Piero Strada, "quod respondeatur capitudinibus quod sint simul cum veteribus et novis consulibus et aliquibus sapientibus artificibus quelibet ars per se, et ita separatim per scriptura referant sua consilia cras"; Tommaso Strozzi, "quod capitudines habeant suas artifices et consulant super materia"; Ser Martino Ceschi, "domini cum collegiis et cum illis capitudinibus quos volent, ita tamen quod unus sit pro arte ad minus, qui eligant cives bonos, non passionatos, et de omni gradu, qui praticent super unione"; Guccio, a carpenter, "capitudines cum suis artibus consulent super estimo et referant novem et postea dominis"; Niccolò di Giovanni, "quod artifices sint ad artes et cras bona hora respondeant consilia suarum artium"; *CP*, 16, ff.15v, 64v, 69r, 71r; 17, f.69v; 18, f.58r.

[146] *CP*, 18, f.64v. Cf. Uguccione Franceschi, "Quod petitio que datur per artifices procedatur"; Francesco Brunellini, "Domini et collegia provideant circa capitula data per artes"; *CP*, 16, ff.113r–113v.

[147] *CP*, 16, f.126v. Also, Andrea Grandoni, *ibid.*, f.113r; Benedetto Alberti, *CP*, 18, ff.92r, 98v; and the discussion concerning a civic militia, *ibid.*, ff.89r–92r.

[148] *CP*, 16, ff.115v–116r.

[149] "Quod civitas uniatur et omnes se invicem osculentur"; *ibid.*, f.35v, 19 Oct. 1378. For other appeals for unity, see N. Rodolico, *La democrazia fiorentina nel suo tramonto (1378–1382)* (Bologna, 1905), 240–41.

[150] *Cronache e memorie sul tumulto dei Ciompi*, 90.

Yet, when Uguccione de' Ricci told his fellow-citizens in a *pratica* (31 March 1379) that the city had never been so united, or the regime more secure,[151] he was expressing a pious hope that was some distance from reality. This government never enjoyed the full support and approbation of the whole community, nor did it ever include the entire social order within its perimeters. The laborers in the cloth industry, numbering several thousands with their dependents, had been excluded from the commune. And though some citizens—in the early, euphoric days of the regime—had expressed the hope that magnates might be incorporated into the polity,[152] only a few were admitted to *popolano* status, and these were barred from the Signoria and the colleges for twenty years.[153] Guildsmen were no more eager to allow outsiders into their regime than into their corporations, where they would compete with established craftsmen and shopkeepers. Nofri dell'Antella addressed himself to those prejudices when he warned the authorities to guard against pressures by "foreigners and apprentices" to gain control of the city and the guilds.[154] By very substantial majorities, the legislative councils passed a law (August 1379) excluding from communal office anyone whose father had not been born in the city or *contado*.[155] Guildsmen were equally suspicious of those citizens who had been proscribed by the Parte Guelfa as suspected Ghibellines. Anyone branded with this stigma, Stefani reported, was thereafter treated as a pariah.[156] The regime's decision (October 1378) to accept the Asini, a wealthy banking family, as Guelfs aroused the ire of the *popolo*, who remembered (so one chronicler reported) that the family had been so named because their ancestors had carried supplies for the Emperor Henry VII on their donkeys.[157]

The dissolution of the Ciompi guild had alienated the cloth-

---

[151] *CP*, 16, f.118v, 31 March 1379.

[152] Benedetto Alberti, Tommaso da Careggi and Ser Manno Nigi; *ibid.*, ff.35v, 40r, 73v.

[153] Petitions for *popolano* status accepted by the councils; *LF*, 40, ff.312r, 317r, 322r, 328v, 356v; and rejected, *ibid.*, ff.314r, 324r, 333r, 337v, 339r, 356v, 365v, 366v, 370r, 372r.

[154] ". . . Provideant ita quod forenses et discepuli non sint domini civitatis et magistrorum"; *CP*, 16, f.129r, 18 Apr. 1379.

[155] *Prov.*, 68, ff.108r–108v. The votes: 202–73 and 128–43. A revision of that provision was approved three weeks later; *ibid.*, ff.120r–120v, 6–7 Sept. 1379. On this legislation and the opposition to its passage, see Stefani, 818, 820, and J. Kirshner, "Paolo di Castro on Cives *Ex Privilegio*," in *Renaissance Studies in Honor of Hans Baron*, 239–42.

[156] Stefani, 921.

[157] *LF*, 40, ff.312r, 313r, 25–26 Oct. 1378; *Cronache e memorie*, 87: "et per questo furo chiamati 'gli asini nimici di parte guelfa.'"

workers and created a serious threat to the regime's security. Ciompi leaders had fled to avoid capture and execution; from their places of exile in Siena, Pisa, Lucca, and Bologna, they maintained contact with their comrades in Florence. In their incessant plotting to overthrow the regime of the artisans who, they felt, had betrayed them, they formed alliances with Florentine aristocrats who had preceded them into exile. These *arciguelfi* were the regime's most dangerous opponents because they possessed the resources to finance subversion: to hire the agents who recruited supporters in Florence, and troops who could attack the city from outside. Scarcely a month passed without the discovery of a conspiracy, in which laborers and wealthy patricians collaborated, and which claimed its quota of victims who died on the gallows or the scaffold.[158]

The kinsmen and friends of aristocratic exiles who remained in Florence were not imprisoned, but their situation was precarious. Though only a few were deprived of their civic rights,[159] they were all effectively excluded from office, and subject to harassment.[160] Simone Peruzzi's hysterical outburst against his outlawed son Benedetto reflects the tensions under which these citizens lived: "With lies, tricks, and betrayals, he has continually disobeyed and vituperated me, my commune and my family and relatives. As a result of his evil and iniquitous activities, we have suffered many dangers and we have lost honor, status and security. . . ."[161] To escape from this climate of fear, many aristocrats left the city to live in their country villas, only to be recalled by suspicious authorities who wanted to keep them under surveillance.[162] Civic opinion was sharply divided between advocates of repressive policies and those who favored more lenient treatment of these potential subversives. In arguing for tolerance (January 1379), Tommaso Soldani said that he favored harsh punishment for those "who have committed heinous crimes against the state," but for the rest he recommended mercy "to avoid cutting off so many limbs of the body that it dies."[163] Social divisions played a part

---

[158] The judicial records for these years are filled with these cases; for some examples, Brucker, "The Florentine *Popolo Minuto* and its Political Role, 1340–1450," in *Violence and Civil Disorder in Italian Cities, 1200–1500*, ed. L. Martines, 177–80; Rodolico, *Democrazia fiorentina*, 365–405, 475–79; *ACP*, 1197 *bis*, ff.9r–12r, 99v–101r, 130r–132r, 141r–144r; 1198, ff.31r–35r, 47r–49v, 103r–107r.

[159] For the lists of those named magnates, and others deprived of office, Stefani, 843.

[160] Anonymous denunciations against magnates for allegedly conspiring against the regime, or harboring outlaws; in *AEOG*, 820, 821, 830, 832, *passim*.

[161] Brucker, *Society of Renaissance Florence*, 63.

[162] Stefani, 882.   [163] *CP*, 16, f.75r.

in this controversy, since artisans and laborers believed that the judges "did not prosecute the great as they would have liked, but were much harsher in their treatment of the little people."[164]

The regime was thus confronted by hostile and antipathetic groups that either worked actively to subvert it or accepted its rule grudgingly. And within its membership were deep cleavages between socio-economic categories: for example, between the wealthy Francesco Rinuccini and Benedetto Alberti on the one hand, and Giovanni di Feo, a laborer in a dyeing *bottega*, and Banchino di Banco and Cristofano di Andrea, workers in a wool-carding shop, on the other.[165] There were differences, too, between men with previous experience in magistracies and councils, and those artisans and apprentices whose knowledge of communal politics was as limited as their demeanor was awkward and their clothing inappropriate for the palace of the Signoria.[166] Stefani divided the regime into three groups (*brigate*).[167] Forming the largest contingent were the mass of artisans, shopkeepers and apprentices from the lower guilds, and their allies who had been proscribed by the Parte or were suspected of Ghibelline sympathies. The second group (to which Stefani himself belonged) comprised "merchants and guildsmen from old families who wished to live in peace," and who deplored the partisanship displayed by those who had been victims of the Guelf purge. A third party, recruited from those members of the aristocracy who had not been exiled or disgraced, had little influence in the regime. These embittered men could only complain privately about their exclusion from office and hope for some change in their political fortunes.

Though threatened by enemies without and plagued by internal divisions, this regime survived for more than three years. Even some conservatives gave it their lukewarm support; its popular character notwithstanding, it was still a bulwark of legitimacy in a time of chaos.[168] Through ceremonial occasions and a strict adherence to

---

[164] Stefani, 814.

[165] On the wealth of Rinuccini and Alberti, see L. Martines, "Nuovi documenti su Cino Rinuccini," *ASI*, cxix (1961), 80–81. Giovanni di Feo and his comrades were consuls of the dyers' guild in Sept. 1378, and thus played a minor role in the government; Rodolico, *Democrazia fiorentina*, 450.

[166] The disparaging remarks about the Ciompi, "oltre l'essere vili, erano tanto poveri, che con gran difficultà trovavano da vestirsi secondo che appartiene a tali gradi" would apply equally to the new men who first entered the regime after Sept. 1378; *Cronache e memorie*, 41.

[167] Stefani, 814.

[168] The author of the *Diario d'anonimo* represented this viewpoint. He noted approvingly in his diary those official actions that contributed to civic peace: the

familiar rituals, the regime constantly publicized its constitutional and ideological links with the past.[169] By avoiding any sharp departure from traditional forms, the authorities did restore a measure of confidence and keep the administration running quite smoothly. The foreign judges, with their retinues, made their rounds in search of malefactors; their officials seized and imprisoned debtors, and treasury agents harassed tax delinquents.[170] And although hundreds of lower guildsmen enjoyed offices and emoluments that heretofore had been reserved for a small minority,[171] they did not exert a dominant influence in the formulation of public policy. In the *pratiche*, where the critical issues were debated, shoemakers, carpenters and shopkeepers spoke more frequently and candidly than ever before, but their contributions to the deliberations were marginal.[172] Except for a handful of artisans admitted into the leadership, the debates were dominated by patricians—Benedetto Alberti, Tommaso Strozzi, Giorgio Scali, Uguccione de' Ricci, Bettino Covoni, Bernardo Velluti—and by men whose political careers had been launched during the papal war: Giovanni Dini, Paolo Malefici, Donato Ricchi, Tommaso Guidetti. These men possessed the political and administrative expertise that most artisans lacked, and in their comments about the qualifications for particular magistracies or advisory bodies they stressed the im-

---

convocation of the urban militia, the fortification of the walls, the public execution of criminals and conspirators. His yearning for peace was palpable: "Iddio ci mandi pacie in questa città e per tutto il mondo ammè"; *Diario d'anonimo*, 425.

[169] See, e.g., *Diario d'anonimo*, 386–88. For references to the Guelf character of the regime, see *CP*, 16, ff.89v–90r. There were suggestions in the *pratiche* for censoring the slogans that were chanted by crowds in the streets: Francesco del Bene, "quod clamor sit solum 'Vivant populus et artes et pars Guelfa,' " and Francesco Casini for the guild *capitudini*: "et quod clamor sit solum 'Vivant populus et artes' et non aliud"; *CP*, 16, f.59r, 20 Dec. 1378. For the Ciompi regime's concern for legitimacy, see Brucker, "Ciompi," *Flor. Studies*, 333.

[170] For the issuance of orders to arrest delinquent debtors, see *AP*, 2859, 2860, *passim*. For the sequestration for debt of the belongings of cloth-workers, see Brucker, *Society of Renaissance Florence*, 214–15.

[171] Stefani, 813, asserted that the lowliest members of the greater guilds (furriers, shirt-makers, factors, petty retailers) were selected in the scrutinies as representatives of their corporations, while their economic and social superiors were systematically excluded. Large numbers of artisans filled the territorial magistracies; *AEOG*, 856, 870, *passim*; *Camera del Commune, Uscita*, 248, ff.21r–28r. On office-holding in this regime, see Rodolico, *Democrazia fiorentina*, 237–48.

[172] Some of these speakers were identified only by their Christian names and their trade: Lorenzo, potter; Pizzino, coppersmith; Benedetto, shoemaker; Nino, farrier; Niccolò, knife-maker; Buono, doublet-maker, *CP*, 16, f.93v; 18, f.23v; 19, ff.14r, 116v.

portance of choosing "wise, virtuous, ancient and experienced citizens."[173]

Although craftsmen and retailers did not play a major role in the decision-making process, their political influence was not negligible. If they spoke rarely in the *pratiche*, they voted often in the councils to defeat provisions that affected their interests adversely. In addition to rejecting petitions submitted by magnates, they voted against proposals to cancel or mitigate penalties against citizens outlawed for political crimes, to appoint a special police official, to raise gabelle rates.[174] They also exerted pressure upon the leadership to refrain from interfering in economic matters that could be regulated by their own guilds.[175] Marchionne Stefani, a rentier of moderate means, was critical of this guild influence, which resulted (so he alleged) in higher prices for food, "and everyone taking what they can, without any regard for the city's welfare, but each carrying water to his own mill. . . ."[176] In disputes between guilds, the regime limited itself to pious platitudes—for example, Filippo Bastari's admonition that "the fourteen lower guilds should join together so that the city will be pacified . . . and citizens should be chosen to remove all dissension that exists between the guilds, and that might arise in the future."[177] In the past, communal authority had been used in support of the Lana guild's efforts to control workers and jobbers under its jurisdiction, but after the Ciompi revolt the regime adopted a policy of neutrality.[178] Bitter quarrels between *lanaiuoli* and dyers over the price of tinting cloth persisted in these years, and the commune's mediatory efforts were unsuccessful.[179] Stefani's views on this issue are significant, for he had no direct interest in cloth manufacture. He castigated the dyers for their arrogant behavior, for thinking only of their interests and forgetting "that they used to be governed by—and subject to—the *lanaiuoli*, receiving laws from them, and subject to their statutes."[180]

---

[173] Bernardo Velluti, *CP*, 19, f.30v. See also the comments of Donato Ricchi; *CP*, 18, f.117r.

[174] Examples: *LF*, 40, ff.324r, 327v, 331r, 333r, 334r, 339r, 345v, 352r.

[175] No significant legislation was passed concerning the authority of the guilds over their members, or controlling relations between the commune and the guilds. A few guild petitions were approved by the councils, a few rejected: *LF*, 40, ff.308r, 324r, 331r, 353r, 355v, 358v, 370r, 376r; 41, ff.3r, 12r.

[176] Stefani, 877.   [177] *CP*, 16, f.51v, 29 Nov. 1378.

[178] A provision was passed authorizing the Lana guild to reappoint its police official, who disciplined the laborers in the industry, but with the stipulation that he would have no jurisdiction over members of other guilds; i.e., former *sottoposti* like dyers, shirt-makers, shearers; Rodolico, *Democrazia fiorentina*, 457–58.

[179] Rodolico, *I Ciompi* (Florence, 1945), 197–206.

[180] Stefani, 887.

The most remarkable feature of this regime is not the discordances and tensions among its social components, but rather its success in reconciling these diverse interests. Critically important for this process was the cooperation between spokesmen for mercantile and industrial interests, notably Tommaso Strozzi and Benedetto Alberti, and those artisans whom Stefani identified as the leaders of the lesser guilds: Benedetto and Niccolò da Carlone, Simone di Biagio, and Feo di Piero, armorers; Lorenzo di Donato and Salvestro di Giovanni, dyers; Feo Casini and Jacopo di Bartolomeo called Scatizza, cloth-shearers.[181] These men were political brokers. They bargained with each other on behalf of their constituencies, with one eye on their own —and their friends'—interests, and the other on the community's needs.[182] Though their motives for working together were not entirely selfless, they did achieve compromises on two divisive issues, the *monte* and the *estimo*, where the interests of their rich and poor clients appeared to be irreconcilable.

Possibly the most significant reform initiated by the Ciompi regime was the elimination of the funded debt, the *monte*, and the interest-bearing loans, the *prestanze*. The Ciompi correctly judged that wealthy citizens and speculators profited from this fiscal system at the expense of the poor, but they failed to appreciate the *monte*'s importance for the mass of guildsmen with small investments. Responding to the pressures from these creditors, the *balìa* (27 August 1378) decided to restore interest payments on *monte* shares, "to calm the citizenry and satisfy the needs of widows and orphans, so that the commune, as far as possible, would maintain its faith and promises."[183] On this fiscal issue, the interests of the destitute and propertyless workers diverged sharply from those of the poor artisan whose meager patrimony might include forty or fifty florins of *monte* shares.[184] It was for that large constituency, as well as the affluent citizens, that Ser Niccolò Monachi spoke (October 1378) when he warned the authorities against violating the "commune's faith" with respect to the *monte*.[185] That argument was supported by other speakers in the *pratica*, although Tommaso da Careggi and Tommaso Strozzi did express some reservations about the commune's ability to honor those obligations fully. The recurrence of these warnings in the debates

---

[181] "Quelli che più erano capi, e guidavano gli altri . . . e questi si tiravano dietro altri capi, ma pure questi erano il bilico delle 16 arti"; Stefani, 814.

[182] See Brucker, "Ciompi," *Flor. Studies*, 332.

[183] *Ibid.*, 341–44; Rodolico, *Ciompi*, 121–24.

[184] Brucker, *Flor. Studies*, 320, n. 1.

[185] CP, 16, ff.35r–36r; Rodolico, *Democrazia fiorentina*, 272–73.

suggests that proposals for a partial repudiation of the funded debt
were being voiced in the streets if not in the council halls.[186] But no
provision concerning the *monte* gained the approval of the Signoria
until, in November 1380, a fiscal crisis created by the rising costs of
defense forced the regime to act. With a minimum of debate, a provision was drafted to reduce the interest rate on all *monte* shares to
five percent, and to retire those obligations systematically over a
period of several years.[187] The measure, which passed both councils
by substantial majorities, was a victory for fiscal and civic reponsibility. Though many of the estimated 5000 shareholders did suffer
losses, no one was ruined by the law which, had it been fully implemented, would have given a very different shape to the fiscal and
political history of Renaissance Florence.[188]

The controversy over the *estimo* was more acerbic, and much
harder to resolve, than that over the *monte*, to which it was closely
linked. The Ciompi regime had appointed a commission of forty-eight
assessors to draft an *estimo* schedule; this was a direct tax that, unlike
the forced loans, would not earn interest or be repaid.[189] That schedule
was not completed until the summer of 1379, and the first levy imposed
in September.[190] Its publication aroused a storm of criticism over
inequities, and demands for an immediate reform of the assessments.
So concerned were the Sixteen about potential disorders that they
recommended that "whenever any scandal erupts over the *estimo*,
the Eight on Security should bring together the antagonists and induce
them to make peace. . . ."[191] Lower guildsmen and laborers were most
vociferous in their objections to the apportionment of the tax burden,
and most insistent on reform.[192] Wealthy citizens with large assess-

---

[186] Rodolico, *Democrazia fiorentina*, 274–78.

[187] The debate in *CP*, 19, ff.84v–86v is described by Rodolico, *Democrazia
fiorentina*, 277–79, who also summarized the law and printed its text; *ibid.*, 280–81,
458–75. The vote on the provision: 215–62 and 117–57; *LF*, 40, f.381v. For contemporary criticism of the law, see Rodolico, *op. cit.*, 282–83.

[188] Molho, *Florentine Public Finances*, 63–70, summarizes the history of the
monte in the fourteenth century. C. Bayley, *War and Society in Renaissance
Florence* (Toronto, 1961), 65–68, believes that these fiscal reforms contributed
significantly to the regime's downfall, a view I do not share.

[189] Brucker, "Ciompi," *Flor. Studies*, 343.

[190] *Prov.*, 68, f.30r; *CP*, 17, ff.47v–48r; Rodolico, *Democrazia fiorentina*, 297–300.

[191] Benedetto Alberti, spokesman for the Sixteen; *CP*, 17, f.54r, 28 July 1379.

[192] Romolo del Bianco, *ibid.*, ff.62v, 76r. Several artisans, speaking for collegiate
bodies, recommended that the current schedule be valid for only one year, or
eighteen months, and then revised; *ibid.*, f.76v. One artisan, Francesco Martini,
suggested that "ponatur potentibus solvere et non aliis"; *CP*, 16, f.74r. Niccolò

ments wished to have their payments recognized as liens on the treasury, to be repaid in the future.[193] Doubtless they would have preferred to receive interest on their contributions, as had been the custom with *prestanze*, but they prudently refrained from raising that sensitive issue. The first test of strength over this vexing problem occurred in September 1379, when the Signoria and the colleges approved a provision to inscribe all who paid the *estimo* as creditors of the commune. In the Council of the *Popolo*, however, artisan votes killed the measure twice that winter, and again in the spring of 1380.[194] By that autumn, the treasury was so depleted that artisans—a jacket-maker named Nanni and the cloth-shearer Scatizza—agreed with Bernardo Velluti, Benedetto Alberti, and Salvestro de' Medici that *estimo* payers should receive five percent annually on their contributions.[195] Many guildsmen, however, remained steadfast in their opposition, even after the Signoria and the treasury officials had argued that the measure was necessary for the regime's survival.[196] Not until November 1381 was a law finally passed that effectively abolished direct taxation in the city, and restored forced loans and the principle of deficit financing.[197]

This regime's solicitude for the interests of its affluent citizens, and its demonstrated capacity for reconciling the divergent interests of its members, did not save it from disintegration. Its fatal weakness was the alienation of the Florentine aristocracy, which would not tolerate a government in which its power was so restricted. The militants in the Parte Guelfa had been exiled by the Ciompi government; they were later joined by others who refused to live under this guild regime.[198] Their relatives who remained in the city lived in constant fear. Many were accused of participating in conspiracies, others of

---

Martini, carpenter, said that all should pay their *estimo* levies "sine spe rehabendi"; *ibid.*, f.49r.

[193] Thus, Donato Ricchi and Bettino Covoni, *ibid.*, ff.49r–49v. Donato Barbadori proposed that no interest ever be paid on the *estimo*, but that after four years those contributions should be repaid, "secundum statum communis"; *ibid.*, f.49v. Cf. Rodolico, *Democrazia fiorentina*, 300–07.

[194] *LF*, 40, ff.341r, 344v, 361v, 363v.   [195] *CP*, 19, ff.86r–87v.

[196] See the deliberations in Jan. and Feb. 1381; *ibid.*, ff.106r–106v, 113v–117r. One artisan, Salvo di Nuto, said that "interesse non solvatur!" *ibid.*, f.113v.

[197] *LF*, 41, ff.32r–33v. The vote: 187–88 and 119–50.

[198] Buonaccorso Pitti left Florence to join the exiles; he recounted his adventures in his *Cronica*, 44–57. The objectives and methods of these exiles are well described in the captain's judgment against Piero Canigiani and Antonio da Uzzano; *ACP*, 1198, ff.103r–107r, Oct. 1379.

sheltering rebels, and still others of being privy to plots which they did not reveal to the authorities.[199] Fears of counter-revolution reached a climax in December 1379, when several prominent citizens were implicated in a scheme to overthrow the regime with contingents of exiles, fortified by mercenaries, and their sympathizers within the walls.[200] The discovery of that plot infuriated the *popolo*; throngs of armed guildsmen gathered in the square to demand the death penalty for the conspirators, or they would take justice into their own hands.[201] Six aristocrats—including Piero degli Albizzi and Simone di Biagio Strozzi—were executed; twenty more were designated as magnates, and another thirty-nine were declared to be ineligible for communal office for three years.[202]

This conspiracy destroyed any possibility of reconciliation between the regime and its aristocratic opponents. The exiles enlisted the aid of the Angevin prince, Charles of Durazzo, to attack Florence; three of their number murdered Messer Giovanni di Mone, the regime's ambassador to Arezzo.[203] The government's policy toward its opponents hardened noticeably after the December conspiracy. Counselors urged the authorities to punish the ringleaders without mercy, and to confiscate their property.[204] Tommaso Strozzi wanted to penalize the wives and children, by sending them into exile and seizing their dowries. Bernardo Velluti proposed that a civic magistracy be appointed "for the extermination of our enemies, whose figures should be painted in the Parte's palace as a perpetual reminder, and whose

[199] See, e.g., the accusations against Jacopo Cavicciuli, Filippo and Giovanni de' Rossi, Fagina Tornaquinci, Rinaldo and Guido da Castiglionchio, and Gherardo and Francesco Buondelmonti; *AEOG*, 820, ff.130v, 135r, 141v, 154v–155v; 830, f.121r. Another example, *Diario d'anonimo*, 423–24: "Oggi a dì x d'aprile 1381, si trovorono apiccate cierte iscritte in più luogora, per Firenze, e contavano cierti cittadini ciascuno per nome, che dovieno volere guastare lo stato d'ora, ed erano nominati da 45 a 50, e dicieva la scritta, ch'a questi nominati per nome e sopranome si voleva loro far tagliare la testa. . . ." See also Stefani, 892.

[200] The details in Stefani, 829–30, 833–35, and in the sentence against the conspirators; *ACP*, 1198, ff.54v–59v, 63v–66r.

[201] Those threats were also made in a *pratica*: Alessandro Gucci, for the Sixteen: "quod si rectores nollent facere iusticiam, fiat commissio civibus et artificibus qui faciant"; *CP*, 18, f.53v, 19 Dec. 1379.

[202] Stefani, 843. Some 50 exiles, also implicated in the plot, were sentenced to death *in absentia*, and their property confiscated; *ibid.*, 845.

[203] Stefani, 846, 849–51, 860, 870. For the details of conspiracies in 1380 and 1381, *AEOG*, 870, ff.13r–14r, 37r–38v; 900, ff.29r–30v, 36r–36v, 57r–58r; *ACP*, 1313, ff.20r–21v; 1427, ff.11r–12r.

[204] *CP*, 18, ff.50v–53v, 19 Dec. 1379. Typical was the comment of Giovanni di Filippo, shirt-maker: "Quod iusticia fiat pura et mera, que sola est medicina infirmitatis istius civitatis"; *ibid.*, f. 51v.

property should be confiscated. . . ."[205] If relatives of these outlaws tried to recover their possessions by illegal means, Simone di Biagio suggested that they be fined an amount equal to the property's value "and forced to wear yellow shirts in perpetuity. . . ."[206] So pervasive were these fears that some politicians advocated the suspension of the constitutional process, to insure the selection of priors loyal to the regime. Tommaso Strozzi proposed that the incoming Signoria be chosen "by hand"; Bernardo Velluti suggested that lists of eligibles for the supreme executive be compiled by eight "venerable citizens," so that at least six men known for their loyalty would sit in each priorate.[207] A majority of guildsmen, however, rejected these schemes, and the new group of priors was drawn from the pouches in the customary way and (Stefani commented), "by God's grace, without a breath of scandal."[208]

These were the reactions of frightened men, who had lost their faith in the guild community and in constitutional government. Instead of the guilds and the civic militia, they relied upon cliques of their supporters which, in their organization and their tactics, were similar to the factions of the 1370s. Giorgio Scali and Tommaso Strozzi emerged as the leaders of these partisans, displacing the moderates—Benedetto Alberti, Uguccione de' Ricci, Filippo Bastari—whose political influence waned during the regime's last months.[209] So determined were these men to uncover evidence of treasonous activity that, Giovanni Morelli reported, "they had their dogs—that is, their spies—everywhere in Florence, to make arrests and to watch by day and night, so that no one could have a social gathering, nor any conversation, without being denounced to the Eight [on Security]."[210] Their critics

[205] *Ibid.*, ff.95v, 117v. See Paolo Malefici's comments: "Quod filii et coniuncti exbannitorum ponantur in locum ita quod populus sit contentus; et auferantur omnia bona exbannitorum exceptis dotibus et debitis; et quod omnes illi qui sunt contra commune scribantur ad partem pro gebellinis et proditoribus"; *ibid.*, f.96r.

[206] "Puniatur in valore bonorum que peteret; et induatur clamida gialla quam semper portet; et quod filii et descendentes eorum expellantur; et mali homines et suspecti separentur de bursis et habeant devetum X annis"; *ibid.*, f.63r, 5 Jan. 1380.

[207] Velluti: "Quod fiant pallotte officii dominorum et collegiorum ita quod in qualibet pallotta sint ad minus sex confidentes"; Strozzi, "Provideatur de faciendo unam extractionem dominorum et gonfalonerii ad manum"; *ibid.*, ff.50v, 58r.

[208] Stefani, 840. Six of the lower guilds did approve the selection by hand, but the other guilds did not wish to alter the traditional mode of selection.

[209] Giovanni Morelli noted Alberti's retirement; *Ricordi*, 325; it is also apparent from his absence in the *pratiche* after 1380.

[210] *Ricordi*, 325. The author of the *Diario d'anonimo* believed that several citizens executed for conspiracy in 1381 were innocent: "Iddio gli abbi l'anima sua e di tutti coloro che sono morti martiri sanza colpa"; *ibid.*, 431.

charged that they used their power to ruin their enemies; Stefani believed that Tommaso Strozzi was primarily responsible for the death of his rival, Donato Barbadori, executed for treason.[211] That they did pull strings on behalf of friends is proved by the letters sent to Francesco del Bene (when he was vicar of the Valdinievole) by prominent artisans in the regime—Simone di Biagio, Morello di Ciardo, Tommaso Buzaffe—on behalf of one Giovanni di Coluccio, accused of assault in Francesco's court.[212] After their fall from power, their condemnations contain specific information on their illegal activities, though this evidence is naturally suspect.[213] They were accused of meeting secretly with their henchmen to organize armed forays, if these should be necessary, to quash an administrative process against Simone di Biagio and Feo di Piero, and to insure that the officials responsible for internal security would be their friends. These judicial documents also contain details about plans these men allegedly formulated to unseat any Signoria that might oppose them. They were also suspected of planning an uprising as an excuse for massacring their enemies and destroying their palaces.[214]

The regime gradually lost the support of most of its members, who either lapsed into a fear-stricken passivity or became more querulous and intolerant in their behavior. Letters sent to Francesco del Bene in the spring of 1381 accurately reflect this civic mood. The situation was then particularly grave, because the Signoria was filled with unqualified men. "These priors have nearly ruined this city," Giovanni del Bene complained to his cousin; "they have aroused the hostility of

[211] Stefani, 827. For similar charges against Scali and Strozzi, see Brucker, "Ciompi," *Flor. Studies*, 327–28.

[212] These letters, written in April and May 1381, are in *Carte del Bene*, 51, unpaginated. One example: "A miei bisongni io ti richiederei sempre chon tuo honore. Sento che ttu ai presso nella forza tua Giovanni Choluci da Uzano, lo quale è a me charo fratello ed è povero huomo. Se 'l chasso aveniesse che non vi chadesse morte, prieghotti che ttu ti porei abillemente in verso di llui in pero ch'è povero ed è grande mio amicho e quella chortessia che farai allui . . . lla faccia a me proprio. Simone di Biagio chorazaio in Firenze a dì xxii d'aprille."

[213] *ACP*, 1427, ff.35r–36v, 97r–98v.

[214] ". . . Ipse [Tomas] una cum predicto domino Giorgio [Scali] et pluribus aliis in domo dicti domini Tome . . . tractavit . . . et conventiculam et posturam fecit quod si contingeret quod in offitio prioratus esset aliquis confalonerius iustitie et alicui priores pro magiori parte de eorum animo et voluntate de expellando et privando omnes illos qui essent de eorum contraria voluntate de offitiis et beneficiis civitatis Florentine cum fabis et fabas elevando de manibus ipsorum, viz., de Perutiis, de Guasconibus, de Malclevellis, de Medicis, de Ricoveriis, de Straderiis, de Manghonibus, de Billoctis, et quampluribus aliis hominibus dicte civitatis Florentie et predictos de dictis offitiis et beneficiis . . . penitus et omni modo privare"; *ibid.*, f. 97v.

everyone and are in very bad repute. . . ." The artisans were so angry over the Signoria's performance that they threatened to organize another revolution "to cleanse the pouches of the enemies of this regime."[215] Discord within the magistracies was a persistent problem. "The Eight [on Security] are badly divided," Giovanni del Bene noted, and Branca Guidalotti commented that Tommaso Strozzi and Giovanni Dini were harshly criticized by their fellow priors for opposing the majority on an issue of state security.[216] Officeholding was no longer an honor but a burden, Giovanni del Bene wrote to his cousin, after his selection to the Sixteen. He was distressed by the mediocre quality of his colleagues, a majority of whom were ignorant and inexperienced, and he dreaded the prospect of judging those accused of political crimes. "I do not feel any desire to deprive citizens of their rights, and I do not know how to solve this problem. God help me so that if I do badly, only I will suffer; and if I do well, all of us may profit."[217] A few days later, Branca Guidalotti gave his pessimistic evaluation of the political situation: "Francesco, it is my feeling that if God does not provide some remedy, this city will never again experience peace, thanks to those evil men whose false principles have brought us to this extremity."[218]

The remedy was a revolution.

[215] *Acquisti e Doni*, 301, unpaginated, letters of 12 and 26 Apr.
[216] *Ibid.*, letters of 20 March and 3 Apr.
[217] *Ibid.*, letter of 2 May. Cf. *ibid.*, 49, no. 133, 29 Apr.
[218] *Ibid.*, 49, no. 138, 11 May: "Francesco, io credo che se Iddio no' pone rimedio, questa città non arà mai posa: bonta de' rei homini, che per gli loro ma' prencipi l'anno così condotta. Questo dicho perchè se niente sentissi, ne sia avisato; perchè si dichono molte cose di fuori di quello che non è, e chi è di fuori n'a gran pensiero."

CHAPTER II

Domestic Politics, 1382–1400

THE EARLY YEARS OF THE NEW REGIME

THE guild regime fell in January 1382, when one of its leaders, the cloth-shearer Scatizza, informed the Signoria that a prominent citizen and member of the Sixteen, Giovanni Cambi, was plotting to overthrow the government. After investigating these allegations, the priors suspected that Scatizza was himself guilty of defamation, and ordered his imprisonment and interrogation by the captain of the *Popolo*, Messer Obizzo degli Alidosi. Scatizza's friends persuaded the Signoria to release him, but the captain refused to obey that order. Giorgio Scali and Tommaso Strozzi then organized a mob which broke into the captain's palace and rescued Scatizza, whereupon the captain tendered his resignation to the Signoria. With the support of angry guildsmen and contingents of mercenaries who guarded the palace, the priors persuaded the captain to remain in office, authorizing him to prosecute those who had organized Scatizza's escape from custody. Scatizza and Giorgio Scali were seized and executed; Tommaso Strozzi saved his life by fleeing the city. A *balìa* was created to reform the government (20 January); one of its first acts was the dissolution of the guilds of the dyers and shirt-makers that had been established in 1378 by the Ciompi government. These disenfranchised artisans then tried to enlist the support of the lower guildsmen; the butchers marched to the palace of the Signoria to defend their comrades. There they met the cloth manufacturers and bands of aristocrats, who had armed their servants and retainers, and the peasants from their country estates. Had the artisans maintained discipline, so Stefani believed, they might have defeated their enemies and regained control of the city. Instead, they broke ranks to fight individual skirmishes, and were driven from the square by the *lanaiuoli*. That evening, the cloth-manufacturers organized a victory procession in the city; they marched through the streets shouting, "Long live the Parte Guelfa."[1]

This revolution, like that of the Ciompi four years earlier, is well documented in contemporary sources. The most graphic account appears in the despatches of the Sienese ambassadors, who described how tenuous was the new regime's control of the city, and how

---

[1] The details of the 1382 revolution in Stefani, 905; *Diar. anon.*, 433–36; *Panc.*, 158, ff.140v–141r; L. Fumi, ed., *Regesti del R. Archivio di Stato di Lucca*, II (*Carteggio degli Anziani*), (Lucca, 1903), 169–70.

palpable were the fears of the inhabitants.[2] Whenever an alarm sounded or a rumor circulated, citizens seized their arms and ran to the palace of the Signoria. Periodically, the rectors and their retinues would march through the streets seeking to calm the populace, but these parades had little effect. On 7 February, the Sienese diplomat, Giacomo Manni, wrote that "everyone is in suspense, and . . . no one has surrendered his arms; though the shops are now open, there is scarcely any activity. . . ."[3] Manni did report that "very little harm has resulted from so much turmoil and revolution: only fifteen people have been killed, of whom three were executed [by the authorities] and twelve killed in private vendettas."[4] In the palace of the Signoria, the authorities exhorted the citizens to keep the peace. They also deployed units of the civic militia, as well as John Hawkwood's mercenaries, to deter troublemakers.

In addition to describing these disorders in detail, the Sienese diplomats also grasped the significance of the change in regimes. The new rulers of Florence were "the rich *popolani* and the *lanaiuoli*" who were supported by a substantial number of artisans and shopkeepers from the fourteen lower guilds. In the scrutiny for the Signoria held in late January, only the "worthiest and the richest" of the lower guildsmen qualified for the supreme executive. "The good *popolani* are reforming this city," Manni reported, "and while they are not barring any group of citizens by name, they will definitely exclude all of the poor (*minuti*) and the lowliest artisans."[5] Although the lower guilds received one-third of the offices, Manni concluded that "the control of this city rests almost entirely in the hands of the *maggiori*."[6]

The results of this scrutiny confirm the judgment of the Sienese observers and permits a rough analysis of this regime's social com-

[2] *Conc.*, 1803, *passim*. The Lucchese ambassadors also wrote a graphic account of these events; Fumi, *Regesti*, II, 169–77.

[3] *Conc.*, 1803, no. 77. The disruption of normal activity is noticeable in the records of the Merchants' Court for these weeks; no decisions or sentences were promulgated between 16 Jan. and 4 March; *Merc.*, 1183, *passim*.

[4] *Conc.*, 1803, no. 68, 26 Jan. But a week later (7 Feb.), Manni reported that men were being killed daily "per vendette e chi per dispiaceri fatti," no. 77. The Lucchese ambassador reported: "Qui a' molti cittadini da Prato, da Pistoia, da Sangiminiano, da Colle, e d'altri diversi luoghi et tucti sono a casa di loro amici cittadini et ogni uno porta l'arme et ucidensi li homini come pecore: soli quelli che anno nimici. Et la forza è qui la misura della ragione"; Fumi, *Regesti*, II, 177.

[5] *Conc.*, 1803, no. 68, 77.

[6] *Ibid.*, no. 68, 71. The Lucchese ambassador commented: "Li lanaiuoli e 'l popolo grasso insieme con le sette arti si sono riarmati e sono bene da sei milia"; Fumi, *Regesti*, II, 170.

position.[7] An exceptionally large number, 800 of some 5000 candidates, qualified for the Signoria and the colleges.[8] Among those eligibles were textile manufacturers, merchants of all descriptions, artisans, and craftsmen.[9] The scrutators did not discriminate against everyone who held office between 1378 and 1382, although many of the guild regime's leaders were excluded from the priorate. Of the nineteen greater guildsmen from the quarter of Santa Croce who had been priors between September 1378 and February 1382, nine were among the eligibles in this scrutiny, and two others nearly qualified. The most curious result of this election was the limited success of the Guelf aristocracy. Among the *arciguelfi* who failed to qualify were Simone Peruzzi, Bese Magalotti, and Ser Piero di Ser Grifo, while only two Albizzi were among the eligibles.[10] In their voting patterns, the scrutators were pursuing a middle course, excluding partisans of the right and the left, and selecting candidates from the broad middle strata of Florentine society.

The twin themes of pacification and reconciliation occurred again and again in the *pratiche* held during these weeks. "The greater and the lower guilds should be a single body," proclaimed the innkeeper, Cenni di Marco, "and all guildsmen should be preserved in their privileges and rank." Speaking on behalf of the consuls of the Lana guild, the influential Guido del Palagio said that "each citizen should have his rightful share [of offices] according to his quality and rank."[11] Amerigo Cavalcanti made three concrete proposals for restoring order: the deposition of arms, the transfer of mercenaries into the *contado*, and the end of private feuds.[12] The *balìa* that had been created on 20 January by a *parlamento*[13] of the whole guild community did endeavor to pacify the city, by legitimizing the political changes that had been wrought by revolution, and reconciling vengeful exiles with those citizens who had participated in the previous regime. This

[7] *Delizie*, XVI, 125–260; *Tratte*, 396, *passim*.

[8] Compare with earlier scrutinies: Brucker, *Florentine Politics and Society*, 66–67; A. Molho, "Politics and the Ruling Class in Early Renaissance Florence," *Nuova Rivista Storica*, LII (1968), 405.

[9] Among these eligibles were more than 100 "new men" whose families had not previously been represented in the Signoria. Molho, 414–15, n. 41, has calculated that 135 new families obtained this distinction between 1382 and 1389. Only in the 1340s did a higher proportion of new men enter the priorate.

[10] *Delizie*, XVI, 152, 162, 208–38. By contrast, five Medici were qualified for the Signoria.

[11] *CP*, 20, ff.117r–117v, 4 Feb.   [12] *Ibid*.

[13] The deliberations of the *parlamento*, defined as the "innumerabile multitudine hominum dicti populi et civitatis ad parlamentum et ad adunantiam generalem"; *Balìe*, 17, f.5r.

balìa appointed a magistracy of peacemakers (*paciales*) with authority to compel feuding citizens to settle their quarrels or be liable to a fifty-lire fine.[14] It cancelled all condemnations for political offenses between June 1378 and January 1382; it also granted immunity to those involved in the recent disorders.[15] The *balìa* also annulled the legislation, so strongly resented by Florentine aristocrats, that provided for the conferment of magnate status on *popolani* who were found guilty of certain crimes.[16] Although lower guildsmen no longer had parity with the greater guilds in the allocation of offices, they still retained a substantial number of these positions, larger than their share before the Ciompi revolution.[17] The *balìa* also made a conciliatory gesture to the members of the two disbanded corporations by integrating some dyers, tailors and shirt-makers into other guilds.[18] Further evidence of the *balìa*'s reluctance to antagonize its artisan constituency was its acceptance of the legislation enacted by the previous regime. It annulled only one provision that had directly benefited the lower guildsmen: the law of October 1380 that authorized the melting down of silver *quattrini*, to raise the value of those silver coins with respect to the gold florin.[19]

[14] *Balìe*, 17, ff.36v–37r, 5 Feb. This magistracy could not intervene in vendettas arising out of homicide, nor could it force anyone to accept a truce for more than three years.

[15] These decrees, enacted on 21 Jan., are printed in G. Capponi, *Storia della Repubblica di Firenze* (Florence, 1875), I, 610–12. The grant of immunity for those involved in recent disturbances is in *Balìe*, 17, f.20v, 25 Jan.; the cancellation of exile sentences in *ibid.*, f.35r, 4 Feb. Realizing that these exiles would be a disruptive element, the authorities tried to delay their return until the end of February; Fumi, *Regesti*, II, 170, no. 1015; *Panc.*, 158, f.141r; but this decree was violated by the exiles who returned immediately to Florence; *ibid.*, f.141v.

[16] Capponi, *Storia*, I, 609–10; and elaborations of this annulment in *Balìe*, 17, f.25r, 28 Jan. On this legislation, see Brucker, *Florentine Politics and Society*, 129–30, 261–62, 323–24.

[17] They were excluded from the office of standard-bearer of justice, and six major territorial magistracies; Capponi, *Storia*, I, 614. On 22 Jan., the *balìa* decreed that the lower guilds would have four posts in each priorate, but that number was later reduced to three; *Balìe*, 17, f.47r, 17 Feb.

[18] *Balìe*, 17, ff.19v, 22v–23r, 22 and 28 Jan. Dyers and soapmakers were incorporated into the Lana guild; they had two of the ten consul offices. Shirt-makers, silk dyers, weavers, and embroiderers entered the guild of Por San Maria; the tailors were matriculated into the guild of linen manufacturers. The *balìa* did penalize the butchers for their part in the disorders by prohibiting the sale of meat at the city gates or outside the gates; *ibid.*, f.25r. This may have been designed to prevent non-payment of the meat gabelle.

[19] *Ibid.*, ff.26v, 40r. On this law and its implications, see Rodolico, *Democrazia fiorentina*, 265–70. The *balìa* also cancelled the gabelle on oxen in the *contado*; *Balìe*, 17, f.28v.

But the return of the aristocratic exiles who had suffered under the guild regime abruptly changed the political climate. These men bitterly resented their persecution, and they were not appeased by the executions of Giorgio Scali and his henchmen, nor by the ban imposed on twenty leaders of the old regime. The primary targets of these *arciguelfi* were not the artisans and laborers, but those citizens who had been proscribed as suspected Ghibellines prior to the Ciompi revolution. The campaign of harassment began in late January, when the "Ghibellines" hastily moved goods from their houses and sent their wives and children out of the city.[20] Their enemies spread rumors that they had plotted to deliver the city to Bernabò Visconti, the *signore* of Milan.[21] When a "young Guelf" was brought before the *podestà*'s court on a charge of assaulting a member of the once-proscribed Covoni family, his friends accused the judge of being a Ghibelline: "You wish to avenge the Ghibellines with Guelf blood."[22]

In the palace of the Parte Guelfa, the *arciguelfi* formulated their plans to consolidate their position. There they drew up a list of petitions and, on 15 February, presented them to the Signoria and the *balìa*.[23] They demanded, first, that a group of forty-three Guelfs be added to the *balìa*, to give the aristocratic families a greater voice in reforming the regime. Those who had been proscribed as Ghibellines were to be excluded from office. Guelfs who had been exiled were to regain their civil rights and receive compensation for their confiscated property. Another proposal designed to strengthen the aristocratic role in the regime was the conferment of *popolano* status on sixty magnates, who would qualify immediately for the Signoria. A general amnesty was to be proclaimed for all crimes (including homicide) committed since the outbreak of the revolution on 16 January. The list ended with two proposals, quite different in tone and purpose from the others. One clause stipulated that those Ciompi workers who had been exiled in 1378 were to recover their positions and stipends in the civic militia. Finally, all communal debtors were to receive a five-month period of grace to settle their obligations, and the poorest citizens were given the option of paying only one-fourth of their *prestanze* assessments, and still receive credit for their payment in *monte* shares.

[20] *Panc.*, 158, f.141r.

[21] *Ibid*. Giorgio Scali had been accused of the same crime; *ibid.*, f.140v.

[22] *Ibid.*, f.142r. The Signoria sent Salutati to the judge, ordering him to cancel the sentence.

[23] They are summarized in *Panc.*, 158, f.142v; Stefani, 913; *Diar. anon.*, 438. Their form and content invites comparison with the Ciompi petitions in 1378; Brucker, *Flor. Studies*, 347-48, 353-54.

These concessions to the poor by Guelf aristocrats were part of a larger scheme to forge a coalition of social extremes against the guild community. This alliance of opposites was not uncommon in Florence, where personal ties and shared experiences might link together rich and poor, magnate and artisan. The Ciompi radicals who had been expelled from the city in 1378 had joined aristocrats in plotting the overthrow of the guild regime that had deprived them of their political rights.[24] Luca del Melano and the carder Testinella, who in 1378 had fought to establish a regime in which poor laborers were represented, returned to Florence under the aegis of the Guelf exiles, and were reimbursed for their confiscated property by the communal treasury.[25] Stefani believed that the *arciguelfi* and a group of artisans had formed a clique similar in its social composition to that headed by Giorgio Scali and Tommaso Strozzi a few months earlier. A band of some fifty Ciompi, marching behind the Parte's flag, had accompanied the Guelf partisans who presented their petitions to the Signoria. Stefani also reported that certain *arciguelfi*, whose palaces had been burned in 1378, were distributing arms to the poor inhabitants of their neighborhoods, who would presumably follow them in any renewal of civic disorder.[26]

These Guelf leaders, Stefani thought, "wanted to restore things to their previous state, when proscription was practiced, or even worse."[27] Their primary objective was to strengthen the position of the Guelf aristocracy within the regime, at the expense of the guild community and the corporate values which it symbolized. By manipulating the disfranchised *popolo minuto* to achieve their goal, they violated a basic principle of this corporate polity. The guild community objected strenuously to the tenor of these petitions, and also to the manner in which they were presented to the *balìa*, as the demands of a *parlamento*. The *lanaiuoli* were most incensed by these tactics; they now assumed the leadership of the guild community against the Guelf extremists. Using coercive tactics of their own, they "persuaded" the forty-three new members of the *balìa* to resign. They induced the *balìa* to accept some of the Guelf petitions, while annulling or revising others.[28] According to one anonymous source, the rectors were

[24] Brucker, *Flor. Studies*, 355.

[25] On Luca's career, see *ibid.*, 354-55. Payments to Luca and to Testinella in May 1383 are recorded in *APG, rosso*, 56, f.28r. Their condemnation in Sept. 1378 was noted by Stefani, 801.

[26] Stefani, 913, 923.   [27] Stefani, 914.

[28] The measures that were retained are in *Balìe*, 17, ff.47v–53v. These reduced the lower guild representation in the Signoria from four to three, and provided for the restitution of *monte* credits and property formerly belonging to citizens banned between 1378 and 1382.

ordered to apprehend and condemn three *arciguelfi* (Ugolino Gherardini, Moscone Beccanugi, and Fruosino Peruzzi) "because they were
believed to be the leaders of the disturbance on Saturday [15 February]
and they wanted to burn and pillage the city."[29]

The *arciguelfi* did not abandon their campaign, but continued to
press their cause in the palace of the Signoria and in the streets. The
assassination (2 March) of a notary, Ser Giustino, reputed to be in
league with "the Ghibellines and the two disbanded guilds" was probably their work.[30] A week later (9 March), they organized a mob to
burn and pillage the houses of "the Ghibellines," but they were
thwarted when the Signoria assembled a group of armed guildsmen
to keep order. On the following day, Guelf partisans presented another
list of petitions to the authorities, demanding that these be presented
for approval to a *parlamento* of their supporters assembled in the
square. These aristocrats were thus seeking to circumvent the normal
legislative process, by appealing to the mob. Their primary target was
still that group of citizens suspected of disloyalty; those who had been
proscribed as Ghibellines were to be disqualified from all offices, and
twenty-five "enemies of the regime" were to be outlawed. Aristocrats
whose houses had been burned during the Ciompi uprising were to
be reimbursed for their losses, as were those who, between July 1378
and January 1382, had paid fines for political offenses.[31] In this tense
atmosphere, the authorities acted circumspectly but decisively to
restrain the extremists. Some victims were sacrificed to the in-
transigents. These included twenty-five citizens sent into exile, and
six standard-bearers of the companies (including the chronicler
Stefani) who were replaced by "good Guelfs."[32] But several of the
parlamento's decrees were annulled, others revised by a commission
established to review them.[33] While restoring the political privileges
of those who had been proscribed by the Parte, the *balìa* did exclude
them from office for a four-year period.[34] It cancelled the provisions
awarding compensation to the owners of gutted palaces, and those

---

[29] *Panc.*, 158, f.143r; Stefani, 914, 915.   [30] *Panc.*, 158, f.143r.

[31] *Ibid.*, ff.144r–145v; Stefani, 916–21; *Diar. anon.*, 439–40.

[32] The 25 exiles are identified by Stefani, 918; and in *Balìe*, 17, ff.67v–68r.
Several were fined; *Camera del Comune, Entrata*, 205, ff.18r–19v. Stefani's hostility
to the *arciguelfi* was certainly intensified by his exclusion from office. He did not
mention this fact in his history, but the Panciatichi chronicler noted that he
was replaced by Stoldo Altoviti; *Panc.*, 158, f.144v. On the removal of the standard-
bearers of the companies, see *CP*, 20, ff.125v–126r, 11 March.

[33] The most important measure to be annulled was that authorizing the captain
of the *Popolo* to declare 25 citizens as rebels; *Balìe*, 17, f.62v; Stefani, 921.

[34] *Balìe*, 17, f.61r.

who had been fined.[35] Finally, the *balìa* ordered the *podestà* to prosecute four men (including two members of the prominent Beccanugi family) who were implicated in the disorders of 9 March, when two "Ghibelline" palaces had been ransacked.[36]

The memories and experiences of the Ciompi period and its aftermath bound together the members of these political coalitions, the *arciguelfi* and their opponents. Guelf aristocrats who had suffered persecution in those years were determined to receive compensation for their losses, and to punish those who had been prominent in the guild regime. The latter were united by fear and, posing as defenders of a corporate polity, they enlisted the support of guildsmen to resist the demands of the *arciguelfi*. They opposed legislation restoring the confiscated property of exiles.[37] In July and August 1382, the Council of the *Popolo* stubbornly refused to allow the Signoria to elect a commission to administer the confiscated property of the rebels.[38] Eventually, this tenacious resistance to the demands of the Guelf partisans crumbled, and officials began the complicated task of reimbursing former exiles with property seized from the new crop of exiles.[39] The *arciguelfi* also obtained the passage of a law stipulating that in any future revolution the commune was obligated to compensate the priors for any damage to their property.[40] But they were less successful in other phases of their program. They could not persuade the authorities to disqualify more "Ghibellines" from office, nor to send those suspected of disloyalty into exile. They also failed to obtain passage of a law that would have authorized the Signoria to scrutinize any official selected for a post in the dominion, "to determine whether or not he [the official] is competent."[41] Perhaps their most decisive rebuff occurred over the granting of extraordinary powers, which these partisans often favored as a means of gaining political objectives that could not be achieved through regular chan-

[35] For the cancellation of this and other *parlamento* enactments, see *Balìe*, 17, ff.62v–63r, 66v.

[36] This order is not included, however, in the *balìa* decrees.

[37] *LF*, 41, f.45v. Petitions by two exiles, Matteo Arrighi and Alessio Baldovinetti, for the restoration of their property were approved; *Prov.*, 71, ff.73r–74r; 72, ff.51r–51v; that of Bartolomeo di Giotto Peruzzi, was rejected; *LF*, 41, f.45r.

[38] *LF*, 41, ff.55v–61r.

[39] *APG, rosso*, 56, ff.7v–11v, 15r–16v, 21v–22r, 24r–41r.

[40] *Prov.*, 71, ff.175r–175v, 12 Dec. 1382. This measure had previously been rejected; *LF*, 41, ff.55v, 56r.

[41] *LF*, 41, ff.55v–56r. The procedure for designating as magnates those *popolani* guilty of serious crimes was not abolished, as Stefani stated, 912, but its implementation was curtailed; *Balìe*, 17, ff.40v–43r.

nels. In June, the Council of the *Popolo* rejected two provisions: one granting special authority to the Signoria and collegiate groups to provide for the welfare and security of the regime; the other investing the priors with power to impose sentences of exile upon those citizens suspected of disloyalty. In October, the council voted down another proposal to give special powers to a *balìa* "for the consolidation and fortification of the present regime."[42] In December, five separate provisions that enlarged the authority of the Signoria were submitted to the Council of the *Popolo*. All five were rejected on the first vote, although two measures eventually won the grudging approval of the councils.[43]

Conflict was thus largely contained within the constitutional structure in these months, although there were occasional incidents of violence with political overtones.[44] Accused of wounding Marco Tolosini (whose cousin Lapo had been proscribed as a Ghibelline in 1378), Bartolomeo Peruzzi was alleged to have said that "he was not afraid of denunciations made against him, because he had friends in Florence who would protect him, even if he had committed murder."[45] In April 1382, a member of the Giraldi family, accused of Ghibellinism in 1378, killed an artisan, Francesco di Giandonato, in a quarrel over a tax assessment which the latter (with other assessors) had imposed on him.[46] Two months later, a scion of another "Ghibelline" family, Piero Covoni, was condemned for attempting to kill Zanobi di Jacopo, who allegedly had offended him while he was a captain of the Parte Guelfa.[47] A prominent Guelf magnate, Matteo di Messer Luca da Panzano, was the intended victim of an assassination plot organized by two of his neighbors in the Oltrarno parish of San Niccolò.[48] Zanobi Altoviti, rector of a church in Empoli, west of Florence, received this warning from Leonardo Adimari and Luca di Ricco, an armorer who was allegedly a friend of the notorious Simone di Biagio: "If you enter the church of San Donato of Empoli, we will kill you . . . for you are an *arciguelfo*."[49]

Though troublesome, these internal quarrels did not threaten the regime's security as gravely as did the conspiracies organized by dis-

---

[42] *LF*, 41, ff.51v, 54r, 69v-70r.

[43] *Ibid.*, ff.76v-81v. Legislation was passed reorganizing the councils and granting authority to the Signoria to fix terms of exile. A provision conferring *popolano* status on 25 magnates was rejected.

[44] Between 1382 and 1384, nine Strozzi were convicted of assaulting persons who were their social inferiors; Brucker, *Renaissance Florence*, 116.

[45] *AEOG*, 924, f.113v.   [46] Stefani, 925.

[47] Stefani, 930; *AP*, 3084, ff.119r-120r; *ACP*, 1428, ff.65v-67r.

[48] *ACP*, 1128, ff.1r-2r.   [49] *AEOG*, 924, ff.127r-128r.

enfranchised workers and artisans, and by exiles living abroad. In the regime's first months, the authorities uncovered several plots in the districts inhabited by cloth-workers—San Frediano, Camaldoli, San Lorenzo.[50] A more serious conspiracy was organized by exiles in the spring and summer of 1383. The day chosen for the uprising, 21 July, was the fifth anniversary of the Ciompi revolution. The times did indeed seem propitious for a successful revolt. The events of 1378 were still fresh in the minds of the *popolo minuto*, whose miseries had been intensified by a plague epidemic that closed down cloth factories and thus increased unemployment and hunger among the poor.[51] The plague also drove many of the regime's supporters out of the city in search of more healthful surroundings.[52] Participating in this conspiracy were many exiles who had been prominent in the old regime, both patricians (Tommaso Strozzi, the sons of Giorgio Scali, Bernardo Velluti) and artisans (Giuliano, a dyer; Domenico Grazini, a carder; Ciambioccio di Miniato, a cloth-worker).[53] Since these men were scattered all over northern and central Italy—in Padua, Ferrara, Venice, Lucca and Pisa—they developed a courier service to coordinate their plans. Some of the exiles, and their sympathizers, secretly visited Florence to persuade their friends to join the plot and to provide hiding places for other exiles who would arrive just before the uprising.[54] On the evening of the 21st, throngs of conspirators ran through the streets, waving the banners of the disbanded guilds and shouting: "Long live the *popolo* and the guilds! Kill the traitors! Poor people of Florence, arise and escape from your yoke of servitude, for they [the rulers] will starve you to death!"[55] The Sienese ambassador

[50] For details on the seven Ciompi plots uncovered by the authorities in 1382, see *AP*, 3084, ff.19r–20r, 77r–78r, 132r–135r; *ACP*, 1428, ff.47r–48r, 53r–54r; 1496, ff.23r–24r, 114r–115r. See, too, Stefani, 928, 935, 936; *Diar. anon.*, 442, 445–47.

[51] *Datini*, 444, unpaginated, Niccolò and Lodovico di Bono to Francesco Datini, 27 July 1383.

[52] This exodus prompted Coluccio Salutati to write his famous letter criticizing those patricians who fled the city during the plague; *Epistolario di Coluccio Salutati*, ed. A. Novati (Florence, 1891–1911), II, 84–86. See also Stefani, 955, 956.

[53] The names and professions of 100 conspirators are recorded in their sentences; *AP*, 3150, unpaginated, 4 Aug. 1383; *AEOG*, 950, ff.7r–8v, 11r–12r, 15r–18v, 25r–27v, 29r–30v, 33r–36v, 43r–44v, 75r–76r; *ACP*, 1496, ff.159r–161r; *AEOG*, 960, ff.45r–47r.

[54] An agent of a group of exiles living in Siena, Leonardo Benvenuti of Prato, was sent to Florence to rent three houses, where conspirators could assemble; *ACP*, 1496, ff.63r–64r.

[55] *AEOG*, 960, f.46v. One witness wrote: "E poi che novità furono da V anni in quà molti ce n'a auti, ma niuno s'uto prencipio il fatto se no' questo; sanza essersi saputo prima"; *Datini*, 444, unpaginated, 27 July 1383.

reported that the rebels went to the houses of the poor and told them, "Now is the time when we will buy grain for fifteen soldi per *staio* or less, and we will be the rulers."[56] But only a few workers joined the rebels, who were unable to open the city gates to allow their friends outside the walls to come to their aid.[57] From the depleted ranks of the guild community, the Signoria hastily assembled a civic militia to guard their palace. The conspirators then fled to escape capture.

Some plots failed through inept planning or bad luck, but others were thwarted by a newly created branch of the administration, the Eight on Security, established in 1378 after the collapse of the Ciompi regime.[58] In its efforts to control subversion, this magistracy received substantial assistance from two provisions that were enacted, with large majorities, in June 1382.[59] One measure provided for the registration of all convicted conspirators in a special volume, maintained by the Parte Guelfa; they were henceforth prohibited from holding any communal office, even if their sentences were later cancelled. The second law authorized the Signoria to assign life pensions to anyone (including those under communal ban) who revealed a plot to the authorities. Six months after its passage (December 1382), Francesco Marchi and his son Leonardo informed the Signoria of a Ciompi conspiracy; they were rewarded with annual pensions of twenty lire.[60] None of these security measures encountered significant opposition in the councils, but conflict did arise over the severity of penalties for political crimes. Guelf partisans insisted that dissent be punished severely, and that the authorities should exert pressure on neighboring governments to expel Florentine exiles.[61] Resistance to these pressures came from moderates who were influenced by a variety of motives. Some were linked to the rebels by ties of blood and friendship, and may have had some sympathy with their political ideology.[62] Others

[56] *Conc.*, 1809, no. 99, 23 July 1383.

[57] Stefani, 954, reported that the rebels could have accomplished their objective if the uprisings in the three working class quarters (Belletri and S. Ambrogio, S. Frediano and S. Piero Gattolino) had been better coordinated. On this conspiracy, see also *Panc.*, 158, f.147r.

[58] On this magistracy, see G. Antonelli, "La magistratura degli Otto di Guardia a Firenze," *ASI*, cxii (1954), 3–23, and the comments in Martines, *Lawyers and Statecraft*, 124–25, 135–36, 431–33.

[59] *Prov.*, 71, ff.57v–58v.   [60] *Ibid.*, ff.172r–172v.

[61] See the letter to the Sienese commune, requesting that Florentine exiles be expelled from Sienese territory; *Conc.*, 1809, no. 28, 7 May 1383.

[62] Advocates and sympathizers of those under communal ban voted against a provision of Dec. 1382 which increased the hardships of certain outlaws, by requiring them to stay more than 100 miles from Florence; *Prov.*, 71, ff.181r–181v. This measure passed by votes of 189–76 and 121–48 after being twice rejected; *LF*, 41, ff.76v, 78r.

may have believed that leniency would promote reconciliation with the dissidents. In November 1382, the partisans of these opposing viewpoints clashed over the reappointment of the captain of the *Popolo*, Messer Cante de' Gabrielli, for a six-month term. Gabrielli had been very active in ferreting out subversion and prosecuting rebels; his methods had not gained the universal approbation of the citizenry. First proposed in late October, Gabrielli's appointment was blocked in the councils for a month before it was finally approved in late November by small majorities.[63]

While appeals for restraint and magnanimity continued to be heard in the debates on internal security, civic opinion hardened against those who fomented unrest. In December 1382, after the seventh conspiracy of that year had been discovered by the authorities, one exasperated citizen, Agnolo Bandini, pleaded for an end to disorder, "so that merchants and artisans and others who wish to live by the sweat of their brows may be secure."[64] In the *pratiche*, counselors demanded that the populace be disarmed[65] and that guild autonomy be limited. When a delegation of guildsmen assembled in September 1382 to present a list of grievances to the Signoria, the colleges were very critical of that practice, so reminiscent of the Ciompi period and its aftermath. "The guilds should not be allowed to assemble for the purpose of presenting their views to the Signoria," the Sixteen insisted. Though somewhat more conciliatory, the Twelve did not welcome this manifestation of the corporate spirit: "No guild should be prevented from addressing [the Signoria], although they doubt that any good can come from it; but reply to them in a friendly manner if they speak properly, and change the tone of the response according to their statement."[66] In this increasingly repressive climate, sympathy for the poor workers also subsided. The Ciompi who participated in the conspiracy of July 1383 were to be punished "without mercy"; their comrades who had been employed in the civic militia were to be dismissed. "See to it that the Ciompi receive no salaries from the commune," Giovanni Rucellai counselled the Signoria on behalf of the Twelve.[67]

The aristocrats, merchants, and artisans who made up this regime had reached a consensus over the problem of subversion and its con-

---

[63] The votes were 207–87 and 115–52; *LF*, 41, ff.74r, 75v. For the debate on this provision, see *CP*, 21, ff.98r–98v, 101r; *LF*, 41, ff.72r–73r, 75r.

[64] *CP*, 21, f.117r.

[65] *CP*, 20, ff.180r–180v.   [66] *CP*, 21, f.76v. Cf. Stefani, 935.

[67] *CP*, 22, ff.75r–76r, 87v. Since the Ciompi revolution, the commune had regularly recruited laborers into the militia; Brucker, *Flor. Studies*, 334; *CP*, 21, ff.26r, 67v.

trol. But they could not agree on another divisive issue: the size and composition of the officeholding class, and the criteria to be employed in determining eligibility for office. Although some decisions had been made in January 1382, when the guilds of dyers and shearers were disbanded and their members disenfranchised, the question of eligibility had not been settled definitively by the *balìa*. The problem was complicated by the persistent usage of those anachronistic terms, Guelf and Ghibelline, in discussing the problem. Yet, though the terminology was archaic, the issue was real. When Simone Peruzzi and Michele Castellani emphasized the need to create a Guelf electorate cleansed of its foreign, potentially subversive elements, they were arguing for an elitist regime dominated by those aristocratic families that had monopolized Florentine politics before the Black Death. When other citizens demanded the abrogation of sentences against true Guelfs who had been proscribed unjustly, they were promoting the idea of a large and socially heterogeneous electorate, in which membership might be determined by factors other than family antiquity and reputation. The main focus of the aristocratic campaign was the resuscitation of the Parte Guelfa, and the revival of its influence in the regime. By posing as the guardians of Florence's ancient traditions, the Guelf aristocrats commanded broad sympathy and support. Also enhancing their position was the widely held belief that the root of Florence's recent tribulations was the fateful decision taken by the "Ghibellines" in 1375 to attack the papacy, and thus to violate the most sacred principle of the Guelf credo.[68] Only by oblique and covert means, and never openly in public debates, could the machinations of the Parte's leadership be resisted by those who favored a guild regime with a broad social base. It was necessary to publicize one's commitment to Guelfism, even while resisting the efforts of the Parte and its leaders to restrict the electorate.

In the autumn of 1382, the Parte made its first serious effort to regain some of its authority in communal politics. The captains appointed a commission of forty-eight Guelfs to consider the internal problems confronting the state; then they urged the Signoria to discuss those issues with a delegation of Parte chieftains.[69] The next step was the enactment of a provision temporarily suspending (for the month of October) the legal prohibitions against the public discussion of such delicate issues as the Parte Guelfa and the proscription of Ghibellines and others suspected of disloyalty to Guelfism.[70] But resistance

---

[68] Cf. the views of Alamanno Acciaiuoli, above, ch. 1, 45.

[69] Stefani, 937.

[70] *Prov.*, 71, ff.120v–121r. This provision was first rejected in the Council of the Commune before it was finally passed; *LF*, 41, ff.62v, 63r–63v, 25–27 Sept. 1382.

in the councils was building up to these schemes; they were decisively rejected in the Council of the *Popolo*.[71] The Parte sought to obtain communal sanction for a register of Guelfs and Ghibellines, to be compiled and maintained by the Guelf society.[72] Had this proposal been enacted and enforced, it would have given the Parte effective control over the electorate. The Parte captains continued to agitate for a greater voice in the selection of qualified citizens for office, but they could not persuade the Signoria to submit their reform proposals to the councils.[73] Nor were they successful, two months later, in their attempt to enlarge their political constituency, through the designation of twenty-five magnates as *popolani*.[74] In January 1383, counselors debated another cluster of reform proposals, including the compilation of a Guelf register and the elimination of certain disabilities pertaining to the status of magnates. Though these provisions won the support of such leading statesmen as Benedetto Alberti, Simone Peruzzi, and Stoldo Altoviti, they failed to gain a two-thirds majority in the councils.[75]

The Parte Guelfa launched its final campaign to reform the regime in the autumn of 1383. Hoping to gain some advantage from the conservative mood in the city after the July rebellion, Parte leaders pressed for the enactment of their program. They sharply criticized those who still favored a policy of reconciliation; Luigi Canigiani announced that he was adamantly opposed to any plan "to unite the exiles and the *ammoniti* with the Guelfs and those within [the regime]."[76] On the agenda of Guelf reform were several proposals, including the earlier plan of registering Guelfs and Ghibellines, the holding of a new scrutiny, and the utilization of *accoppiatori* to screen nominees for office and to disqualify those whose loyalty was suspect.[77]

---

[71] *LF*, 41, ff.69v–70r, 9 Oct. 1382. The short title described the measure: "Disponentem baliam concessam dominis prioribus et eorum collegiis et capitaneis partis guelforum . . . et certis aliis civibus florentinis in providendo et ordinando circa solidationem et confirmationem presentis pacifice status civitatis Florentie et partis guelforum prout eis placuerit."

[72] *CP*, 21, f.82v, statement of Filippo Bastari. For other discussions concerning the Parte and its reform plans, see *ibid.*, ff.80v–83v, 86v–87v.

[73] See the views of the colleges, *ibid.*, ff.91r–91v, 100v, 10 and 13 Oct. and 3 Nov. 1382.

[74] *LF*, 41, ff.77r, 78r, 80r. Only three magnates succeeded in obtaining *popolano* status between 1382 and 1392; *Balìe*, 17, ff.217r–218v. Dozens of anonymous denunciations were made against individual magnates, for crimes against *popolani*. See, e.g., *AEOG*, 924, ff.92v, 117v–118r, 122v–123r; 941, ff.4v–5r, 9r–10r, 20r, 22v–23r.

[75] *CP*, 21, ff.126r–126v, 132r–132v.

[76] *CP*, 22, f.99v, 3 Oct. 1383.

[77] *Ibid.*, ff.99v–100v, 115r–116v, 117r–118r.

From mid-September to mid-November, the colleges and the *pratiche* discussed these proposals. Two provisions emerged from these deliberations: one to hold a new scrutiny of offices in the city and *contado*, the other to establish registers of Guelfs and Ghibellines. On 21 November, the Council of the *Popolo* rejected both provisions, to the annoyance of the Guelf leadership.[78] Finally, on 30 December, Guccio Bartolini conceded defeat; the provisions should be abandoned, he advised, "since they are not pleasing to the *popolo*." He concluded his speech with the pious hope that "all should live together fraternally, in justice and in reverence to the Signoria."[79]

Thus, by the second anniversary of the new regime, there existed a precarious balance between the *arciguelfi* and the moderates. The Guelfs had been thwarted in their efforts to make the regime more exclusive; they had failed, too, in their campaign to restore the Parte's former influence and prestige. Though a minority, they were well represented in the leadership, and their ideological weapon, Guelfism, still retained some potency.[80] Those citizens identified as Ghibellines or pseudo-Guelfs bore the political disabilities of that stigma, even though the Parte was not allowed to add new names to the proscribed list. The aristocratic families had registered some tangible if marginal gains in the *contado* rectorships and vicariates and in the legislative councils, where artisan representation declined significantly.[81] Those returning from exile had recovered their confiscated property, including their *monte* shares and the accumulated interest on those credits.[82] Under their incessant prodding, the commune was grudgingly returning ecclesiastical property (which had been confiscated and sold during the papal war) to the former owners.[83] Still, the Guelf con-

---

[78] *LF*, 41, ff.120v, 121r. For discussion of the merits of these provisions, see *ibid.*, ff.121r–124r; *CP*, 22, ff.117v–118r.

[79] *CP*, 22, f.123v. See the comments of Messer Francesco Bruni, *ibid.*: "Et alia colloquia habita de unitate guelforum et de favendo sibi invicem et quod fiat iusticia et minuantur expense et tollendo oblocutiones civium et detractores etiam procedant."

[80] On the Guelf issue in foreign policy, see below, ch. III.

[81] A *balìa* decree of 22 Jan. 1382 reserved six major rectorships for citizens of the seven greater guilds. Lower guildsmen were still selected (though in diminishing numbers) for the lesser posts in the *contado* and district; see *Tratte*, 65, ff.1v–5v, 10r–42v. For the legislation reducing the number of lower guildsmen in the legislative councils, see *Balìe*, 17, f.16v; *Prov.*, 71, ff.185r–185v.

[82] See the payments recorded (Apr. 1383–July 1384) in the books of the "officials of the towers," who handled the property confiscated from rebels and also the repayments to former exiles; *APG, rosso*, 56, ff.7v–52r; 57, ff.53r–70v.

[83] *Prov.*, 71, ff.55v–56r, 19–20 June 1382.

servatives could not alter the political balance in their favor; guildsmen committed to a corporate polity resisted every aristocratic attempt to restrict the size of the electorate or to revise the qualifications
for office. In May 1385, the councils approved liberal rules for the new
scrutiny to be held for the Signoria and the colleges. "For the peace,
unity, and contentment of the entire citizenry," an anonymous witness
reported, "it was decreed that every citizen, of whatever rank or condition, could be nominated for office without being disqualified as a
Ghibelline or an *ammonito*. This was the desire of the good Guelf
citizens, on account of their benevolence and tolerance, and not because they [the Ghibellines] merited this privilege. . . ."[84]

THE DEFEAT OF THE ALBERTI

After five years of political turbulence, of revolution and the threat
of revolution, the mid-1380s were relatively tranquil. No conspiracies
of any magnitude came to light either in the city or among the exile communities abroad.[85] The regime was more preoccupied with
foreign policy—the acquisition of Arezzo, relations with Siena and the
papacy—than with domestic affairs. The protracted struggle in 1385
over the holding of a scrutiny for the Signoria and the colleges[86] was a
sign that the basic disagreements over the regime's composition
had not disappeared. Nor had the feuding between "Guelfs and
Ghibellines" subsided. In October 1384 vandals defaced the Parte's
coat of arms; the captains hired a painter to restore it "in defiance of

[84] Minerbetti, *anno* 1385, ch. 15. Another chronicler (*Panc.*, 158, f.150r) wrote:
"Il regimento tornava ne' buoni cittadini guelfi più che non era lo squitino di
prima." The provision authorizing a new scrutiny was passed on 13–14 May
1385; *Prov.*, 74, ff.51r–52r. First presented to the Council of the *Popolo* on 24
Jan., it was rejected seven times before it finally passed; *LF*, 42, ff.36r, 37r–38v,
41v–42r, 44r, 48r–50v. The vote was 152–69 and 133–65. The provision made no
mention of Ghibellines and *ammoniti*, but merely states that *consueta forma*
was to be observed. On this scrutiny, see *CP*, 24, ff.21v, 56v, 63v–65r.

[85] There are a few references to abortive conspiracies; *CP*, 23, ff.40v–41v, 68r;
AP, 3178, ff.69r–70r; 3204, ff.92r–93r; *Conc.*, 1815, no. 47, but these did not
materialize.

[86] In that same year, a dispute arose over offices in the Aretine *contado*, recently incorporated into the Florentine dominion. Dissatisfied with their share
of these offices, lower guildsmen voted against a provision to hold a scrutiny
for these posts; *LF*, 42, ff.60v–70r, 8 Aug.–28 Sept. 1385. The measure finally
passed after four rejections; *Prov.*, 74, ff.140r–141r. Two vicariates were reserved
for the greater guilds. Perhaps to win artisan support for this provision, a clause
was added which guaranteed the lower guilds one-third of the *podestà* and
castellan posts in the Aretine *contado*.

the Ghibellines and those who committed that outrage."[87] More specifically partisan were the quarrels that swirled around Charles of
Durazzo, king of Naples, who had a large following among the Guelf
extremists, including many former exiles who had joined his army in
1380. Their commitment to this Angevin ruler was so intense that they
even sought to justify his despoliation of Florentine merchants in
the Regno, arguing that his great need excused that arbitrary action.[88]
When the news of Charles' coronation as king of Hungary reached
Florence in February 1386, the Signoria ordered an official celebration: parades, bonfires, and a proclamation to the citizenry. Perhaps
hoping to allay suspicions that they were not good Guelfs, the members of the Alberti family organized their own parade in honor of the
Angevin monarch.[89]

The most puzzling aspect of this Angevin issue in Florentine politics
was the intensity of the passions aroused by Charles, which were so
disproportionate to his stature and his role in Italian politics. How
does one explain the enthusiastic throngs of young men who ran
through the streets shouting his name, and threatening those skeptics
who did not share their love for this foreigner who (as Stefani sourly
noted) had brought nothing but trouble to Florence?[90] Some Guelf
partisans refused to believe the report (20 February 1386) that
Charles was dead. Stefani described these bizarre reactions:

> For nearly two months, some said that he was not dead and [others
> that] he was dead, and they even had letters brought with their own
> messengers which purported to come from there [Hungary] saying
> that he was alive, and the others had letters which said that he was
> dead. . . . And a group of fanatics threatened anyone who said that
> he was dead. . . . Truly, if he had been the legitimate ruler of
> Florence, and who had done much to exalt the city, there would
> not have been such discussion, or so much exaggeration.[91]

The irrationality of that behavior might be explained in psychohis-
torical terms, as a reaction by guilt-ridden Guelfs to their city's assault
on their traditional lord, Pope Gregory XI, and their choice of Charles

---

[87] *Diar. anon.*, 454. See also *ibid.*, 466. Three men were convicted of burning
a house belonging to the Parte; *AP*, 3239, unpaginated, 27 March 1386.

[88] Stefani, 992.

[89] Stefani, 995; Minerbetti, *anno* 1385, ch. 8; *Diar. anon.*, 464.

[90] Stefani, 995: "Sichè a buona ragione si può dire, da lui non avere auto altro,
che male. . . ."

[91] *Ibid.* On the news of his death and the uncertainty, see also *Diar. anon.*,
464–65.

as his replacement.[92] The pragmatic Stefani, however, believed that the *arciguelfi* were exploiting Charles' image to embarrass their enemies. "They realized that they could not be *signori* and expel those whom they wished, and so they seized upon his name and repeated it frenetically, claiming that whoever did not support the exaltation of King Charles and the enlargement of his authority was not a true friend of the Florentine regime."[93] In Stefani's analysis, the most fervent supporters of the Angevin were those "who had joined him [in 1380] to attack Florence so that they might return to their homes, and to tell the truth, many [of the exiles] had been unjustly expelled." Yet among their opponents were "men who had been offended, outraged, and proscribed," and who sought to recover their political rights and their honor. There was guilt on both sides, Stefani concluded, and he could see no resolution to the conflict.[94]

Stefani's political career had been blighted by this quarrel, and in 1386 he expressed his frustrations in a different, and more dangerous, context. He was convicted by the *podestà* of making a public statement that threatened the regime's security:

> We cannot continue in this state of discord and internal strife. We cannot live in this city. . . . There are between fifty and sixty of us, prominent Florentine citizens, who are neither Ghibelline nor *ammoniti*, and we are determined that we will no longer submit to these outrages. We will take measures so that one of two things will follow. Either we will have the offices and the honors that the other Florentine Guelfs possess, or we will all die.[95]

For voicing these seditious views Stefani was fined 500 florins and permanently excluded from communal office. His statement hints at clandestine meetings of disgruntled citizens, and even of conspiracy. If such sentiments were as common as the chronicler suggests, then the events of May 1387 become more explicable, even though the origins of that political crisis remain obscure.

[92] Gregory's successor, Urban VI, was not a suitable father figure; he was very hostile to the republic. See the comments by Alberto Albizzi and Guccio Nobili; CP, 25, f.179r; 26, f.19r.

[93] Stefani, 961, 974, 990, also notes earlier examples of quarreling between Guelf extremists and their opponents over Charles of Durazzo.

[94] Stefani, 995.

[95] ACP, 1635, ff.55r–56v, 13 June 1386. Stefani had been removed from one of the colleges in Feb. 1382; see above, 66. He also failed to qualify for the Signoria in the 1382 scrutiny; *Delizie*, XVI, 177.

The trouble began (so the official version read)[96] when Benedetto Alberti's son-in-law, Filippo Magalotti, was chosen standard-bearer of justice.[97] When it became known that Magalotti was too young to hold that prestigious office, "several of our citizens [i.e., the Alberti], motivated by ambition, sought to violate the laws by insisting upon his selection." Angered by this blatant disregard of legality, the report continued, the citizens demanded that the statutes be obeyed, that Magalotti be disqualified, and that those who had promoted his election be punished. It is clear that the Magalotti issue was the catalyst that aroused the citizenry, and led to the creation of a *balìa* empowered to restore civic peace.[98] The question of Magalotti's qualifications may have arisen unexpectedly and then expanded into a major crisis, or it may have been planned by Guelf partisans to give them an opportunity to reform the regime. In support of the second hypothesis is a letter written on 4 May by Lorenzo Buoninsegna, a member of the *balìa*, to Francesco Datini, stating that certain *popolano* families had decided "several months ago to accomplish these things" which the *balìa* had on its agenda.[99] If the *arciguelfi* did provoke a confrontation deliberately, the intemperate actions of Benedetto Alberti furthered their scheme. Seeking to retain his son-in-law Magalotti in the Signoria, he cajoled officials and other citizens, thus arousing their suspicions "that he wished to be *signore* of Florence."[100] The fears stimulated by Alberti's tactics undoubtedly strengthened the hand of his enemies and facilitated the passage of the law creating a *balìa*.

The five letters written by Buoninsegna between 4 and 24 May provide an inside view of the *balìa*'s deliberations and the factions contending for supremacy.[101] A merchant and a political moderate,

---

[96] This account was sent to neighboring states; SCMC, 20, ff.249r–249v, 13 May. See a similar letter to Giangaleazzo Visconti, *ibid.*, ff.253r–253v, 29 May.

[97] The official notice of this controversy is a statement of 29 April by the Sixteen: "Quod videatur si dominus Filippus potest esse vexillifer iusticie nec ne de iure. Et si leges non patiuntur, non sit et fiat cito. Et prius non fiat aliud"; CP, 26, f.30r. The chronicler, Ser Naddo di Ser Nepo, stated that Filippo Magalotti's kinsman Bese was the informant who alerted the authorities to Filippo's ineligibility; *Delizie*, XVIII, 92.

[98] The *balìa* was approved by the councils by narrow margins, on 3 and 4 May; *Prov.*, 76, ff.35r–37r. The votes: 184–79 and 145–64. For the discussion on the *balìa* and its authority, see CP, 26, ff.31r–33v. Several counselors opposed the creation of a *balìa*.

[99] *Datini*, 326, unpaginated, 4 May 1387. The other letters by Buoninsegna are in this *filza*.

[100] *Panc.*, 158, f.151v.

[101] The *balìa*'s authority terminated on 7 May. Thereafter, political battles were waged within the regular executive offices and the councils.

Buoninsegna was an Alberti supporter, one of the "good citizens" who resisted the pressures of the Guelf extremists. He expressed his strong distaste for the *balìa*'s activities: "I would rather be ill with a fever than be in office now. . . . It depresses me so much to see our government change every day, that I would rather be a hermit."[102] Some of his annoyance stemmed from economic considerations—"It troubles me that every third day we take up arms; this will ruin trade and industry"[103]—and some from his sympathies for the Alberti, and perhaps for the political values they represented. He realized immediately that the Alberti were the primary targets of this reform movement: "There is considerable sentiment against allowing Messer Benedetto to be a standard-bearer [of the companies, one of the Sixteen]," he wrote on 4 May. "And this is a result of spite and envy, an evil thing that can be likened to those honest men who were expelled from Rome on account of their virtue and good works." Every day the campaign against the Alberti gained momentum. On 4 May, the *balìa* banned Benedetto and Cipriano Alberti from all communal offices. "Don't repeat this," Buoninsegna wrote to Datini, "but there were many in that faction who favored even harsher measures, but the good citizens prevented them from doing worse."[104] But with each partisan triumph, the pressures and rancors increased, and on 6 May, the *balìa* ordered Benedetto and Cipriano into exile for two years and, with a few exceptions, barred the whole family from office for five years.[105] Although this vendetta against the Alberti was partly motivated by personal malice, it did possess a broader political significance, as later actions of the *balìa* reveal. The Alberti were the acknowledged leaders of a loose coalition of political moderates, the "liberals" of *trecento* Florence. Their political disgrace was a prelude to an attack on the guild community by those who favored a more aristocratic regime purged of its popular elements. Having disposed of the Alberti, they moved next against the *ammoniti* whom they had tried to exclude from office in 1382. The Scali, Corbizzi, and Mannelli families were barred from holding office for five years, as were some fifteen others whom the Parte Guelfa had proscribed a decade

---

[102] Letters of 6 and 7 May.

[103] Letter of 6 May; on 13 May he wrote: "Ma danno fan ala merchatantia queste novità, a faracisi meno non suole a riscoterasi asai pegio."

[104] Letter of 6 May. This reference to political support in the *balìa* for the Alberti casts some doubt upon Molho's contention that Benedetto was "a man strongly disliked by the vast majority of the *maggiori*"; "Politics and the Ruling Class in Early Renaissance Florence," *Nuova Rivista Storica*, LII, 418.

[105] Letter of 7 May. The decrees of the *balìa* of 4 and 6 May are printed in Passerini, *Alberti*, II, 232–40.

earlier. Eight men, including Francesco and Giovanni del Bene, were exiled for five years.[106]

The ironic feature of this political struggle was the demand for innovation by Guelf partisans, who viewed themselves as the guardians of tradition and orthodoxy. "The good and wise citizens who said that such things had never been done before"[107] denounced the proposals to change the electoral system. Niccolò Tecchini wrote to Francesco Datini (20 May) that "so many innovations are being proposed, new matters and fashions, that I don't understand them; some who discuss these things are motivated by ambition, others by malice and others by a passion for novelty, so that in brief, there are more opinions than men. . . ."[108] This campaign to reform the system had already begun on 4 May, when Lorenzo Buoninsegna reported widespread dissatisfaction with the traditional method of sortition, by which the personnel for the executive offices were drawn by lot from pouches of qualified candidates.[109] Many felt that sortition left too much to chance; they favored some device for manipulating the electoral process to insure the selection of citizens loyal to the regime and to Guelf principles. Aristocrats had long felt that the list of eligibles in the 1382 scrutiny contained too many names from the lower echelons of the guild community: artisans, shopkeepers, professional men, petty entrepreneurs. Of the fifty-four members of the Signoria selected between May 1386 and April 1387, only nine were from old and prominent families.[110] Since these guildsmen could not be excluded from office by proscription, the Guelf aristocrats invented two new devices for regulating the electoral process: the grant of discretionary authority to electoral officials, the *accoppiatori*, and the concept of election *a mano*, by hand instead of by lot. Both were to play important roles in the constitutional history of the republic.[111]

[106] Most of these individuals had been proscribed in 1377 and 1378, during the Guelf purges of those years; see Stefani, 770, 775, 788; Brucker, *Florentine Politics*, 340–50. When their names were drawn from the *borse*, they were torn up. See *Tratte*, 194, unpaginated, for the extraction to the Signoria, and the disqualifications, after 1 May 1387.

[107] Minerbetti, *anno* 1387, ch. 10.   [108] *Datini*, 326, unpaginated, 20 May.

[109] *Ibid.*, letter of 4 May. The Signoria of March–April 1387 was criticized as incompetent, and the reform proposals were aimed at preventing the selection of a similar priorate, "aciò non avengha come a'prioraticho passò ora, che furono uomini sì pocho pratichi ch'ano meso questa tera in puntegli."

[110] Ser Naddo di Ser Nepo, *Delizie*, xviii, 89–92. The Signoria of March–April 1387 had no patrician members; that of May–June 1386 included three butchers, a goldsmith, a money-changer, a *lanaiuolo*, and only two patricians.

[111] N. Rubinstein, *The Government of Florence under the Medici (1434–1494)*, (Oxford, 1966), 4–7, 45–46. One proposal for reforming electoral procedures,

After the *balìa*'s authority expired on 7 May, the Signoria and the colleges continued to debate the issue of electoral reform.[112] On 22 and 23 May, the councils approved a provision annulling earlier legislation that prohibited any change in the distribution of offices between the seven major guilds and the fourteen lower guilds.[113] With this legal barrier removed, the councils then enacted a provision that substantially reduced the representation of the lower guilds in communal offices.[114] In the Signoria, for example, their number declined from three to two; their share of the colleges was fixed at one-fourth.[115] This provision also established the machinery for identifying foreigners who were enrolled in the lower guilds and who were thus disqualified from communal office.[116] Proponents of this restrictive legislation hoped to limit the officeholding group to those native Guelfs whose ancestry would presumably guarantee their loyalty to the regime.

This reform was a substantial victory for those Guelf partisans who since 1382 had tried to limit the size of the officeholding group. The sources do not identify the ringleaders of this movement;[117] Lorenzo Buoninsegna said only that "certain families" were the instigators of

---

noted by Buoninsegna (letter of 4 May), was to rearrange the personnel of the various priorates into satisfactory groupings: "Ma quelo più disiderano queste famiglie si è fare l'uficio de' singniori, metegli tuti a nove in una palotola di ciera per fare chatuno priorato agualgliato." This technique had been utilized in the 1370s for the captaincies of the Parte Guelfa; *Diar. anon.*, 361–62, and also proposed in 1379; above, ch. 1, 57. The idea of giving electoral officials authority to designate certain citizens as most worthy and qualified for office appears in the plan for a special *borsellino*, described by Minerbetti, *anno* 1387, ch. 10.

[112] *CP*, 26, ff.34r–40r.

[113] *Prov.*, 76, ff.48v–49v; the votes were 126–60 and 134–63. The law establishing the *balìa* had stipulated that it could not tamper with the distribution of offices; *ibid.*, f.35v. Speakers in a *pratica* session of 2 May had insisted upon that limitation; *CP*, 26, ff.32r–33v.

[114] *Prov.*, 76, ff.51v–55v, 23 and 24 May; the votes were 181–52 and 142–50.

[115] The lower guilds were given one-fourth of the offices in the dominion, but they were excluded from eight important offices (in addition to the six for which they had been disqualified in 1382); *ibid.*, ff.52v–53r.

[116] The guild consuls were required to present lists of foreigners in their guilds to the chancellor, Coluccio Salutati. Those so designated could appeal to the Signoria to declare them eligible for office. For a summary of this statute, see Buoninsegna's letter, *Datini*, 326, 24 May.

[117] Bardo Mancini, who replaced Filippo Magalotti in the Signoria, was a leader of the Guelfs; Naddo di Ser Nepo, *Delizie*, XVIII, 96. The Panciatichi chronicler mentioned the Albizzi, Peruzzi and Medici families as being very active in this campaign; *Panc.*, 158, f.152r.

the electoral reforms and the vendetta against the Alberti.[118] Moderates like Filippo Bastari and Alberti sympathizers like Buoninsegna accepted and perhaps even voted for these reforms, hoping that their enactment would bring peace, and fearing that resistance and obstruction would increase tensions.[119] But these tactics did arouse resentment, expressed privately in letters and chronicles but also voiced publicly, and strongly enough to provoke a demand from Andrea di Francesco degli Albizzi that "measures be taken against those dissidents who criticize the Signoria so that others will be terrorized [into silence]."[120] An anonymous chronicler described one rumor circulating in the city, "that the Guelfs wished to destroy the lower guilds, that is, to reduce the number of guilds from twenty-one to fourteen." This witness also reported that a poster had been displayed in the *Mercato Vecchio* announcing that "the artisans have been tricked by the rich who were intent upon their downfall, and that the butchers would be ruined because they had permitted the expulsion of the good merchants," presumably the Alberti.[121]

Such manifestations were gestures of resentment by guildsmen who realized that the political balance had shifted in favor of the aristocratic houses. Still, the political strength of the artisans and petty merchants had not been destroyed by the 1387 reforms. The issue that most sharply revealed the vitality of the guilds' opposition to the aristocratic leadership was the establishment of a *balìa* to con-

[118] "Ma quelo più disiderano queste famiglie. . . . Ancora vogliono queste famiglie," letter of 4 May; "Seguì poi deto dì non parve a queste famiglie bastare," letter of 7 May.

[119] Buoninsegna reiterates this theme in his letters. "Idio ci dia ci posiamo riposare in pacie," letter of 6 May; "Qui sono le cose chetate asai bene, e con la grazia di Dio pure ci riposeremo," 13 May; "Isperasi le cose rimarano bene e d'acordo per modo ci riposeremo e così piacia a Dio che sia," 24 May.

[120] *CP*, 26, f.38r, 20 May. Three days earlier, the lower guildsmen in the Council of the *Popolo* had fiercely opposed a provision (one of three submitted to the councils) authorizing the appointment of a *capitano di balìa* with very extensive police powers; *Panc.*, 158, f.152v: "Le chapitudini e 'l popolo non voleano che lle si vincesno, perchè diceano i ghuelfi volere fare questo chapitano per fare ismozichare chi e' voranno; e dopo molte tirate e minaccie, si fè savi richiesti e molte cose si disse sopra le dette petitioni e questo dì feciono i ghuelfi venire in Firenze molta fanteria per ghuardia di loro e perchè si vincesero quelle petizioni. . . . Fune gran favelio pero chè gli artefici non voleano che se ne vincesse niuna. E guelfi che anno lo stato in mano le vogliono vincere tutte o per forza o per amore a lor dispetto. . . . L'arte minute sono malchontente che queste pitizioni si vinchano perchè temono di loro stato." The provision authorizing the captain's appointment did not pass; *LF*, 41, ff.2r–3v.

[121] *Panc.*, 158, f.153r.

trol the republic's military and diplomatic activities. When the Signoria first raised this issue in August 1387, every collegiate group favored its implementation, but the measure failed to pass the first legislative hurdle, the Council of the *Popolo*.[122] Three months later, the *balìa* provision was again defeated in that council, even though the colleges enthusiastically supported its enactment.[123] As in the past, when an important piece of legislation encountered strong resistance, some counselors urged the Signoria to coerce the dissidents into approving the provision.[124] On this occasion, however, the priors preferred to wait until the seating of a new council, which might be more amenable to their desires. This strategy was successful. On 13 January 1388, a provision establishing a *balìa* for nine months was approved by narrow margins in both councils.[125] Since tradition and prudence dictated that only favorable opinions be expressed publicly on issues favored by the Signoria, the sources provide no clues to the motives of those who voted persistently against this magistracy. Among the rank and file of guildsmen who were members of the councils (but not of the executive offices), there persisted a vague prejudice against these extraordinary magistracies, and this negative bias was certainly reinforced by the activities of the 1387 *balìa*. Some viewed that magistracy as a tool of the aristocratic elements in the regime. To disarm these critics, the Signoria submitted the membership of the *balìa* (which included two artisans) to the councils for approval and sponsored a law barring these officials from serving again in that office for three years.[126] These marginal concessions to guild sentiment did not placate the opposition, and in September 1388 the proposal to appoint another *balìa* was

[122] The records of the *Libri Fabarum* do not indicate whether the provision was submitted to the Council of the *Popolo*, although it was discussed and approved by the colleges; *LF*, 43, ff.11r–11v, 17 and 19 Aug. In a discussion on 22 Aug., several advisory groups favored the "resubmission" of the controversial measure; *CP*, 26, ff.92r–92v.

[123] *LF*, 43, ff.21r–26r, 20 Nov.–4 Dec. 1387.

[124] See the statements of Niccolò Giugni, "Quod obtineatur omni modo et recordatus est parlamentum," and Filippo Pandolfini, "Quod provideatur quod provisio sit obtentus ante discessum; et quod omnibus modis teneatur, etiam recolligendo [fabas] per manum vel alio modo quod obtineatur," *ibid.*, f.22v. See also *Panc.*, 158, ff.154r–154v.

[125] *Prov.*, 76, ff.185r–189v. The vote in the council of 131 was 91–26; in the other councils, 160–76 and 133–49. See Minerbetti, *anno* 1387, ch. 40. One witness claimed that the *balìa*'s authority was so great "che a loro parrà poter impegniare la città e vendere gli uomini se bisogna fusse," *Panc.*, 158, f.154v.

[126] The names of the *balìa* members were included in the provision; on the legislation imposing a three-year ban on *balìa* personnel, see *LF*, 43, f.30v.

passed after seven rejections and a struggle of three weeks' duration with a refractory Council of the *Popolo*.[127]

In describing the bitter fight over the *balìa*'s renewal, one observer stated that opponents did not reject a *balìa* in principle, but were against those who had been selected for this magistracy.[128] While this analysis perhaps underestimates the political dimension of this controversy, it does give appropriate weight to the personal factor. Private quarrels and family feuds were exceptionally common in the months following the 1387 crisis. The prosecution of Giovenco Bastari, accused of malfeasance while serving as vicar of San Miniato del Tedesco, may have been instigated by an aristocratic Guelf partisan seeking to discredit the Bastari, whose political orientation was liberal.[129] The quarrel between the Pitti and the Corbizzi had political as well as personal dimensions: the Pitti had been bitter opponents of the guild regime, supported by the Corbizzi, which had been overthrown in January 1382. This feud had so endangered civic peace that the authorities intervened directly to impose a truce upon these families, and provided for heavy criminal penalties against anyone who violated the settlement.[130]

Two other incidents, which acutely embarrassed the regime and particularly its aristocratic contingent, involved an important patrician family, the Strozzi, and a statesman of the highest rank, Buonaccorso di Lapo Giovanni. In a quarrel over a gambling debt (October 1387), Pagnozzino Strozzi assaulted and killed a *lanaiuolo*, Piero Lenzi.[131] This crime assumed political significance since Piero was then a member of the Sixteen. Responding to the popular clamor for revenge, the Signoria, the colleges, and the councils approved a harsh and vindictive provision against the assassin. Pagnozzino and his

---

[127] *Ibid.*, ff.66v–72v. The *balìa* was first proposed on 27 Sept. and finally passed (157–77 and 108–49) on 13 Oct.; *Prov.*, 77, ff.156r–157v.

[128] "Tutti i cittadini di Firenze sapeano ch'era di bisogno dare balìa a cittadini per riparare alle operazioni che faceva il Conte di Vertù . . . ma non piacea loro tutti quelli cittadini nominati; ma arebbono voluto fare altri cittadini"; Minerbetti, *anno* 1388, ch. 20.

[129] The Bastari case is discussed fully by Martines, *Lawyers and Statecraft*, 147–54.

[130] Buonaccorso Pitti furnishes some details on this feud in his diary; *Cronica*, 49–52. A provision imposing a truce was defeated in the Council of the *Popolo* in Oct. 1388; *LF*, 43, f.69r; but the authorities persisted and in Jan. 1389 they formulated a settlement which the Corbizzi were accused of violating; *CP*, 27, ff.70v, 77v, 78r. A decree of the captain of the *Popolo* of July 1395 proclaimed a truce and provided for the punishment of violators; *ACP*, 1990, ff.83r–85r.

[131] The incident is described in *Diar. anon.*, 473, and in the chronicle of Ser Naddo, *Delizie*, XVIII, 96–97.

brother Nofri were placed under the communal ban; their property was to be destroyed, and their kin were declared ineligible for the Signoria and the colleges unless within three years they had either killed Pagnozzino and Nofri, or delivered them to the communal authorities.[132] With an adult male contingent of seventy, the Strozzi were the largest (and potentially the most dangerous) lineage in Florence, and so aroused the greatest fears in a populace traditionally fearful of aristocratic prepotence. They also had influential friends who attached clauses to the provision that limited the responsibility and the penalties to be borne by members of that family.[133] Equally damaging to the aristocratic cause was the treasonous behavior of Buonaccorso di Lapo Giovanni. While on a diplomatic mission to Milan in the autumn of 1388, he allegedly revealed certain state secrets to Giangaleazzo Visconti, in return for a payment of 1000 florins. Neither his judicial condemnation, nor the other sources which described this incident, explain how news of this betrayal became known in Florence.[134] Buonaccorso had obviously made enemies during his long political career, but like the Strozzi, he also had friends who could save him, not from disgrace, but from the executioner's sword. In exchange for a three-day grant of immunity from seizure and prosecution, he revealed the details of his transactions, and then fled from the city.[135]

While these incidents were embarrassing to the regime and potentially harmful to its security, they were isolated occurrences in a period when the focus of the republic's concern was shifting from

[132] *Prov.*, 76, ff.121r–128r. The vote: 141–63 and 111–49; *LF*, 43, ff.14v–17r.

[133] Friends of the Strozzi modified the punitive provisions of the law in the Council of the Commune. For almost two weeks, from 7 to 19 Oct., that council refused to approve the original provision, until the qualifying clauses were added; *LF*, 43, ff.14v–17r; *CP*, 26, ff.116r–117r. For another aspect of this affair, see above, 19–20.

[134] Buonaccorso was sent on two missions to Giangaleazzo, in June and again in Aug. 1388; *DBCMLC*, I, 103–05, 112, 129. His companion on the second mission was Rinaldo Gianfigliazzi. Buonaccorso's treason is mentioned in *Diar. anon.*, 480; the chronicle of Ser Naddo, *Delizie*, XVIII, 103–14; and Minerbetti, *anno* 1388, ch. 21. He was apparently in economic difficulties and was being pressed by his creditors; *Lana*, 81, f.98r; *Merc.*, 1199, unpaginated, 6 Aug. 1389. Perhaps hoping to minimize his guilt, Giangaleazzo wrote to the Signoria, stating that Buonaccorso had simply asked him for a loan which he had granted; *SCMC*, 21, ff.70v–71r. In addition to divulging state secrets, Buonaccorso was also convicted of extortion and simony while in the Signoria; *AEOG*, 1074, ff.39v–40r.

[135] For the debate on granting Buonaccorso temporary immunity from prosecution, *CP*, 27, ff.43r–43v. Buonaccorso confessed that he had received money from Giangaleazzo, so the Signoria claimed in a letter to the Milanese *signore; SCMC*, 21, f.70v.

internal to foreign affairs. The regime was increasingly preoccupied with the threat posed by Giangaleazzo Visconti, who had consolidated his power in Lombardy and was also establishing bases on Florence's southern and western flanks, in Siena and Pisa. After two years of diplomatic maneuvering, war broke out between Florence and Milan in April 1390 and continued for nearly two years, before it terminated in a peace treaty signed in February 1392. Internal discord did not subside during the war, but it was strongly influenced by military events and by the burdens that the war imposed on the citizenry.[136]

The rehabilitation of the victims of the 1387 purge was the most controversial issue in domestic politics during the first Milanese war. Behind the campaign to restore the political rights of the Alberti, Rinuccini, Del Bene, and other exiles were two different motivations, one personal and the other political. Each of the disgraced families had a circle of friends who were constantly seeking to reintegrate them into the regime, and support also came from men who shared their political outlook and who favored an open and broadly representative regime. The need to foster civic unity in wartime may have gained some votes for the reintegration of the exiles.[137] But these arguments had little effect upon those citizens—motivated by personal animus, political calculation, or ideological conviction—who strongly resisted the efforts to undo the work of the 1387 *balìa*. The campaign to cancel the bans was first launched in the spring of 1391, but it failed because the friends of the *fuorusciti* did not coordinate their efforts.[138] In October of that year, a Signoria sympathetic to the exiles approved provisions rehabilitating the Alberti and the Rinuccini; they were accepted by the councils by substantial margins.[139] A month later, however, the Council of the Commune rejected legislation that would have restored the political rights of the Del Bene and other exiles:

[136] The impact of the war on Florentine politics is discussed in ch. III.

[137] This motive also lay behind the campaign to cancel or mitigate the penalties against outlaws whose crimes were not political; see *CP*, 28, ff.99r, 162v, 168r–169v, 179v, 180v, 185r–186r. This culminated in a decree (17 Sept. 1391) authorizing the cancellation of bans against those who enrolled in the Florentine army commanded by John Hawkwood "e farsi iscrivere e pigliare il soldo e valentemente provare contra nimici"; *Panc.*, 158, f.162v. Rebels and political criminals did not qualify for this amnesty. For the identification of certain *banniti*, including murderers, whose sentences were cancelled, see *Prov.*, 80, ff.78v–80r, 239r–243r, 245r–249r.

[138] Letters of Bernardo Strozzi, Amedeo Adimari, Giovanni Lenzi, and Ricciardo del Bene to Jacopo di Francesco del Bene; *Carte del Bene*, 52, unpaginated, 29 and 30 Apr., and 11 and 13 May.

[139] *Prov.*, 80, ff.141r, 151r. See too *CP*, 28, ff.171r–175r.

Scali, Corbizzi, Covoni, Petriboni, Bonsi.[140] Only after an extraordinary effort by Del Bene supporters were Giovanni and Francesco authorized to return home;[141] the others were not rehabilitated, despite the appeals of collegiate groups.[142] The Panciatichi chronicler described these provisions as "just and holy" and reported that their rejection by the Council of the Commune "was deplored by men of every condition, and most strongly by the artisans. . . ."[143]

This controversy reflected the precarious balance of power in the tenth year of the regime's existence. The *arciguelfi* had been forced to accept the rehabilitation of the Alberti, Rinuccini, and Del Bene but, by thwarting the efforts to restore all the victims of the 1387 purge, they had preserved the concept of proscription.[144] The Guelf partisans were more influential than their modest numbers might suggest. Drawn primarily from the aristocratic families, they were well represented in the regime's inner circle, and in the prestigious magistracies filled by election instead of sortition. They were also better organized than their opponents. Except for their allegiance to a corporate policy, no strong ties of interest united such heterogeneous elements as cobblers and stonemasons from the lower guilds, parvenu merchants like the Lenzi and the Vespucci, and the wealthy and socially prominent Alberti and Covoni families. While these groups might occasionally coalesce to oppose an aristocratic stratagem, they were not capable of taking the initiative, or of formulating and implementing a consistent policy.

The records of the 1391 scrutiny for the Signoria and the colleges corroborate this impression of political equilibrium. This election did reverse a trend, by reducing the number of eligible candidates for the republic's highest offices. A total of 677 citizens qualified for the Signoria in 1391, compared to some 850 in 1382.[145] The most significant

---

[140] *LF*, 43, ff.225v–227r, 9–15 Nov.   [141] *Prov.*, 80, ff.167v–170r; above, 28.

[142] *CP*, 28, f.186v; 29, ff.21v, 23v, 25r–26v, 27v, 32r; *LF*, 43, ff.226r, 228r–229v; 44, ff.2r, 24v.

[143] ". . . Per gli uomini che vogliono bene vivere et cittadineschamente"; *Panc.*, 158, f.164v.

[144] An oblique reference in Bernardo Strozzi's letter to Jacopo del Bene suggests that Rinaldo Gianfigliazzi and Maso degli Albizzi led the resistance to rehabilitation: "Tu sai che tra costoro ci era il vechio cavaliere e 'l giovane, e mai a nulla si vollono accordare in beneficio dell'amico nostro"; *Carte del Bene*, 52, unpaginated, letter of 29 Apr.

[145] These figures are higher than those cited by A. Molho, "The Florentine Oligarchy and the Balìe of the late Trecento," *Speculum*, XLIII (1968), 27, since they include estimates for the two *gonfaloni* from S. Spirito (Scala and Nichi) whose records are missing in the 1382 scrutiny.

decline, over fifty percent, occurred in the fourteen lower guilds, while the number of eligibles in the seven greater guilds fell by only twelve percent.[146] The representation of the old Guelf families did not change significantly between 1382 and 1391. In the quarter of Santa Croce, for example, thirty-three members of the ten leading aristocratic families were nominated in the 1382 scrutiny, compared to twenty-five in 1391.[147] The pattern was reversed in the quarter of Santa Maria Novella, where the number increased from thirty-five to forty-four. New families continued to qualify for the Signoria in substantial numbers, although the trend was downward after 1391.[148] An examination of the electoral data from one district, the *gonfalone* of White Lion (*Leon Alba*) in the quarter of Santa Maria Novella, illustrates this pattern.[149] White Lion was one of the smallest of the sixteen districts in the city, with a high proportion of aristocratic households: Strozzi, Baldesi, Vecchietti, Malegonelle, Mangioni. In the 1382 scrutiny, the "new men" had a slight numerical advantage (14–12) over the aristocratic bloc, but a decade later, the old families qualified twenty-five of their number, while the representation of the *gente nuova* declined to eleven. Of the fourteen "new men" who qualified in 1382, only three were among the eligibles chosen in

[146] These ratios, the number of eligibles and the number of nominees, are based on figures in D. Kent, "The Florentine *Reggimento* in the Fifteenth Century," *Renaissance Quarterly*, xxviii (1975), 633.

Quarter	1382		1391	
	maggiori	*minori*	*maggiori*	*minori*
S. Spirito				
(two *gonfaloni*)	68–555	39–217	144–1309	39–384
S. Croce	154–946	70–281	120–928	32–308
S. Maria Novella	120–799	53–367	132–934	32–387
S. Giovanni	145–1068	103–535	139–1413	39–647
TOTAL	487–3368	265–1400	535–4584	142–1726

[147] Two criteria were used to select the ten leading families in each quarter: the number of family members scrutinized, and the number of eligibles selected. For S. Croce, where the Peruzzi and the Alberti were preeminent, the ratios were 33–104 (1382) and 25–120 (1391). In both scrutinies, the ten leading families gained slightly more than 20% of the total number of eligibles from the greater guilds: 33 of 154 and 25 of 115. Among the most prominent families in the quarter of S. Maria Novella were the Strozzi (5–68 in 1382 and 7–60 in 1391), Altoviti, Spini, and Rucellai. The ten-family statistics for that quarter were 35–171 (1382) and 44–172 (1391).

[148] A. Molho has calculated the number of new families (including artisans) in the Signoria for the years 1382–1389 at 135; for the 1390s, the number declined to 114; *Nuova Rivista Storica*, LII, 414–15.

[149] *Delizie*, XVI, 200–08; *Tratte*, 397, ff.121r–132r.

1391,[150] but that remnant was supplemented by eight new guildsmen, including four *lanaiuoli* and two money-changers. The lower guild representation of White Lion was cut in half, from fourteen to seven. Of that decimated artisan contingent, four had qualified a decade before, and two others were kinsmen of 1382 nominees. Within the lower guilds there now emerged an elite of officeholders, with the sons and grandsons of favored artisans inheriting their fathers' places in the roster of those qualifying for the supreme executive.

The scrutiny of 1391 also provides some information on the political fortunes of those citizens proscribed by the 1387 *balìa*. To be designated a potential subversive did not automatically ruin one's political career, even though some families (the Covoni and the Corbizzi) and some individuals (Valorino Curiani and Ruggiero Carucci) were permanently barred from public life.[151] But the sons of Francesco Rinuccini failed by very narrow margins to qualify for the Signoria, even though they had been excluded from the regime in 1387.[152] Even more remarkable was the popularity of the Alberti among the scrutators; five members of that family qualified for the priorate, compared to only one Peruzzi.[153] The strong showing of the Alberti may have encouraged their political ambitions, but it may also have intensified the fears of their aristocratic opponents, and thus hastened the day of reckoning for this potent and wealthy lineage. Maso degli Albizzi failed to qualify in this scrutiny; his rejection was a stain on his honor and a blow to his family's prestige.[154] It is quite likely that he was penalized for his role in the persecution of the Alberti. Bardo Mancini, whose part in that vendetta is better documented than Maso's, also did not qualify in this scrutiny, receiving only 85 of 150 votes compared to 144 of 170 ballots in the 1382 scrutiny.[155]

---

[150] Of the 11 who did not qualify again in 1391, several had died; only three were renominated and failed to receive a two-thirds majority. At least four of these "new men" had been named eligible for the Signoria in the scrutinies of 1363 and 1367.

[151] The three Covoni nominated in 1391 (compared with fifteen in 1382) received very few votes. None of the Corbizzi were nominated for the scrutiny. In 1382, Francesco and Jacopo del Bene had received 98 and 89 votes respectively, just failing to qualify; *Delizie*, XVI, 178; in 1391, they were not nominated. The Bastari also failed to qualify any member in the 1391 scrutiny.

[152] *Tratte*, 397, f.64v.

[153] *Ibid.*, ff.74r–84r.

[154] *Ibid.*, f.160r. Maso barely failed to obtain a two-thirds majority: 96 of 147.

[155] *Ibid.*, f.78r; *Delizie*, XVI, 152. Filippo Magalotti, the man whom Mancini replaced as standard-bearer of justice in 1387, obtained 117 votes, sufficient to qualify, in the 1391 scrutiny.

THE CRISIS OF 1393

The political scene was remarkably quiet in the months preceding the convulsions of October and November 1393, which brought Florence to the brink of civil war. The regime had concluded a peace settlement with Giangaleazzo Visconti early in 1392, thus reducing some of the tensions created by the war and its fiscal burdens. Only once (April 1393) did a manifestation of discontent appear serious enough to warrant discussion by the colleges.[156] In August 1392, the head of the Alberti, Cipriano, recovered his political rights, and his voice was once again heard in the *pratiche*.[157] One domestic issue that continued to trouble the regime was amnesty for political crimes; several provisions designed to facilitate the rehabilitation of outlaws were rejected in the councils.[158] But the controversy over this issue was neither lengthy nor bitter; the friends and relatives of those exiles who remained under the communal ban were too few and impotent to gain much sympathy for their cause. And, after their flurry of conspiratorial activity in 1390 and 1391, the exiles had apparently abandoned their efforts to overthrow the regime by force.

It is this background of relative tranquility that makes the events of 1393 so difficult to comprehend. As in 1387, the crisis erupted without any warning. On 9 October, the authorities announced that a conspiracy had been discovered, involving exiles living abroad and also some persons in the city. A farrier named Paolo di Bartolo and a dyer, Andrea Franceschini, were seized and interrogated by the *podestà*; they revealed the details of the plot, as well as the names of their alleged accomplices. They implicated two of the Alberti, Cipriano and Alberto, and also an exile group in Bologna headed by Gino di Messer Giorgio Scali. The *signore* of Faenza, Astorre Manfredi, and the counts Guidi of the Casentino were also accused of participating in the conspiracy. An assault on the city by the exiles and a mercenary band was scheduled to coincide with an uprising of workers and artisans hostile to the regime.[159] In addition to the confessions of the two conspirators, the sources also mention the discovery of letters ex-

---

[156] CP, 30, ff.22r, 23r, 24 Apr. 1393. The colleges and the Eight on Security were the targets of this attack.

[157] *Prov.*, 81, ff.164v–165r, 171r–172r; CP, 30, ff.11r, 12r, 19v.

[158] LF, 44, ff.2r–12r (26 Jan.–22 March 1392); 24v (21 June 1392); CP, 29, ff.21v, 27v, 8 and 22 Jan. 1392.

[159] The most detailed account of the plot is in *Panc.*, 158, f.172v, and Minerbetti, *anno* 1393, ch. 21. There are references to the conspiracy in CP, 30, ff.75r–77r, 14 Oct., and in the deliberations of the *balìa*, printed in Passerini, *Alberti*, II, 249–51.

changed between the Alberti and Gino Scali, which described the conspirators' plans and objectives.[160] But letters can be forged, and false confessions extracted by torture. If the Alberti were guilty, it is surprising (as one of their kinsmen noted) that they did not flee when Paolo di Bartolo was seized.[161] Another perplexing aspect of the case was the *podesta*'s refusal to obey the *balìa*'s order to interrogate Cipriano and Alberto Alberti, for which he was relieved of his office.[162] In the *pratiche*, counselors urged the authorities to discover the truth about the conspiracy, but many were not convinced of the Alberti's guilt. Some proposed that the case be turned over to the criminal courts, while others preferred to keep this explosive case in the hands of the executive.[163] Following a disturbance on 18 October, the Signoria convened a *parlamento* which granted authority to a special *balìa* to resolve the crisis.[164] This magistracy assumed responsibility for penalizing those who were judged guilty of conspiracy. Five Alberti— Cipriano and his son Giovanni, Alberto and Nerozzo di Bernardo, and Piero di Bartolomeo—were sent into exile; other members of the family were excluded from office in perpetuity.[165] Considering the gravity of the alleged offense, these penalties were quite mild. But the

---

[160] ". . . Avendo trovate molte lettere che parlavano di ciò . . . . A dì xiii si fe' gran consiglio di richiesti e piuvichosi [publicosi] lettere trovate per questo trattato e tutto l'ordine dato dovere tenere, e chome mercholedi notte a dì xv dovevano que' dentro cholla gente che menavano di messer Giorgio di Romagna"; *Panc.*, 158, f.172v. The *balìa* records (Passerini, *Alberti*, ii, 251–52) mention the letters exchanged between the Alberti and Gino Scali, but do not divulge their contents.

[161] Messer Antonio Alberti: "Quod diligenter inquiratur de suis consortibus et reperta veritate, clare puniatur. Et in hoc consideretur conditio accusatorum et illorum qui accusant. Et non est verisimile quod Astorgius vel comites Casentini attenderent ad hoc et habeatur respectus quod dominus Ciprianus et Albertus sciverunt capturam Pauli"; *CP*, 30, f.75r.

[162] *Balìa* decree of 23 Oct., Passerini, *Alberti*, ii, 249–50. The Panciatichi chronicler, *Panc.*, 158, f.174v, added these interesting details: ". . . Il podestà volea che si gli dessono que' prigioni[eri] a farne giustizia, e che volea la balìa che avea messer Francescho da Cantiano [de' Gabrielli, captain of the *Popolo*] sei mesi, e dopo sei mesi esere rafirmo per altri sei mesi. I signiori, udendo questo . . . dissono a cholegi e a quegli della balìa ciò che il podestà voleva. Di che tutti a una boce gridarono: 'Cassisi! Cassisi!'"

[163] *CP*, 30, f.79v, 23 Oct.

[164] *Panc.*, 158, ff.172v–173r. The official convocation of the *parlamento* and the establishment of the *balìa* are in Capponi, *Storia della Repubblica di Firenze*, i, 625–27.

[165] Cipriano and Alberto were also fined 1000 and 2000 fl. respectively. The sons of Messer Niccolò Alberti were exempt from the officeholding prohibition. Paolo di Bernardo was exiled to Sardinia and Andrea Franceschini imprisoned for life; Passerini, *Alberti*, ii, 253–63.

balìa insisted that it was imperative to act rapidly, and with clemency, to calm the populace.[166]

Neither the culpability of the Alberti, nor their victimization by the Albizzi, can be proved by the surviving evidence.[167] In concert with their political allies, the Albizzi took advantage of the crisis to reform the regime. Dominated by citizens from old families,[168] the *balìa* was the instrument for redressing the political balance in favor of the Guelf aristocracy. After nullifying the results of the 1385 scrutiny, as well as the scrutinies for territorial magistracies, it authorized new elections for those offices.[169] In a significant departure from constitutional practice, the *balìa* stipulated that citizens who obtained majorities in the 1393 scrutiny would also be included in the pouches of the previous elections, in 1382 and 1391.[170] The names of citizens who had qualified for the supreme executive, and who were judged to be particularly loyal and trustworthy, were to be placed in special pouches (*borsellini*), by officials (*accoppiatori*) entrusted with this delicate task.[171] For every priorate, three names were to be drawn from these *borsellini*, thus guaranteeing that every Signoria would include some citizens whose

[166] "Magis cedunt ad pacem civitatis et ad quietem, quam aliter procedere; et quod via infrascripta est magis benigna et misericordie proxima, quam rigidius procedere"; *ibid.*, II, 252.

[167] Molho is persuaded that the Alberti were guilty of treasonous activities; *Nuova Rivista Storica*, LII, 418, n. 53. For the view that Maso degli Albizzi trapped the innocent Alberti, see the passage in the Ridolfi *priorista, Manoscritti*, 225, f.122v, printed in the chronicle of Naddo di Ser Nepo, *Delizie*, XVIII, 140–41, and below, ch. v, n. 143. Only circumstantial evidence can be cited to support the hypothesis of an Albizzi plot. Maso was a member of the Signoria in Sept.–Oct. 1393, and three of the Eight on Security who discovered the evidence against the Alberti (Luigi Canigiani, Piero Serragli, and Simone Bordoni) were members of families with strong Guelf sympathies. Was it coincidence that Serragli and Bordoni were chosen by hand to the succeeding priorate?

[168] The *balìa* included 60 *ex officio* members and 79 coopted members. The latter group was strongly aristocratic; it included only seven lower guildsmen; *Balìe*, 17, ff.90v–91v.

[169] Capponi, *Storia*, I, 634–38. The scrutinies of the Parte Guelfa were also nullified, *ibid.*, 633.

[170] "Quod omnes et singuli illi qui obtinebunt in isto novo scrutinio, possint et debeant imbursari in quocumque ex dictis duobus scrutiniis remanentibus"; Capponi, *Storia*, I, 636. This particularly benefited the younger members of patrician families who, as juveniles, had not been successful in earlier scrutinies. The *balìa* records do not corroborate the statement of the Panciatichi chronicler, "chi non rimanesse in questo novo [1393] non s'intendea essere negli altri [1382 and 1391]"; *Panc.*, 158, f.174v.

[171] Capponi, *Storia*, I, 636. Since those elected as standard-bearers of justice were also picked by election officials (*accoppiatori*), this guaranteed a bloc of four men in each priorate who had been certified as loyal to the regime.

devotion to the regime was certain. By such methods, the aristocratic forces hoped to strengthen their position in the regime, and to weaken the corporate element, without dismantling the traditional procedures for filling communal offices.[172] The *balìa* introduced still another innovation which, though temporary, established an important precedent. The Signoria of November and December was to be selected by hand (*a mano*), to insure that these reforms would not be cancelled by disgruntled citizens who might have been drawn for the priorate.[173] In yet another bold departure from tradition, the *balìa* enacted several decrees in favor of the magnates. It conferred *popolano* status upon certain members of the Ricasoli, Adimari, and Rossi families. Finally, it suspended—for a five-year period—the requirement that magnates had to provide surety for their good behavior, and also the procedure whereby the authorities were required to investigate every anonymous denunciation which accused them of certain crimes against *popolani*.[174]

Although the *balìa* did not tamper with the quotas of offices assigned to the lower guilds, many artisans feared that aristocratic pressures would eventually undermine their position in the regime. In the church of Santa Maria Maggiore, a butcher, Salvi di Guglielmo, was alleged to have made this statement to his acquaintance, a furrier named Bonaguida di Stagio: "Let us find a way to abrogate those decrees made by the *parlamento*. . . . It is necessary to overthrow the present regime, and that can be done by starting a riot, and then we will become strong [by allying ourselves] with the guildsmen of this city. To achieve this end, we will begin to cry: 'Long live the guilds! Long live the *popolo* and the guilds!' And the guildesmen will all come together and we will fight against the rulers of this regime. . . ."[175] According to Salvi's condemnation, he assembled a mob in the quarter of San Giovanni, and marched to the square adjacent to the Signoria's palace, where he was joined by other contingents of armed guildsmen. These rebellious artisans would have overthrown the regime (so the sentence read) if they had not encountered "true, catholic, and faithful Guelf citizens who were supporters of this regime" and who, with divine favor, defeated the artisans and drove them from the square.[176] Unlike earlier disorders in which disenfranchised cloth-workers and

---

[172] The *balìa* substantially increased the authority of the electoral officials, the *accoppiatori*, who were empowered to transfer names (*cedule*) of citizens from one pouch to another. For example, they could promote those whom they favored from the ordinary *borse* to *borsellini* and to the standard-bearer's *borse*; and they could also demote those whom they considered unworthy; Capponi, *Storia*, I, 636.

[173] *Ibid.*, I, 637-38.   [174] *Balìe*, 17, ff.113r-113v, 123v-124r.

[175] *ACP*, 1988, ff.9r-10r, 27 Nov. 1393.

[176] For an account of this revolt, see above, ch. I, 17.

laborers were represented, this revolt was organized by artisans and shopkeepers, the lower echelons of the guild community. Among those identified as active participants were three butchers, four old-clothes dealers, a goldsmith, a druggist, a purse-maker, a wineseller, an inn-keeper, a brick-maker and only three textile workers: a dyer, a weaver, and a washer.[177]

The regime that survived this abortive revolt was more distinctly aristocratic than that of 1382 had been. Its political style was also tougher and more ruthless; its leaders were more intensively preoccupied with their regime's security. Reflecting these changes of mood and perspective was the *balìa*'s decision to create a militia of 2000 citizens, to be chosen by the Eight on Security on the basis of loyalty to the regime and to Guelf principles.[178] The old militia, recruited from the sixteen *gonfaloni*, had not been a reliable force in the recent disorders; some of its members had joined the insurgent guildsmen.[179] These armed citizens were to wear white shirts on which were displayed the symbols of the *popolo* and the Parte Guelfa.[180] In one of its last decrees before its dissolution on 31 October, the *balìa* authorized the recruitment of 400 Genoese crossbowmen to be stationed in the square adjacent to the Signoria's palace for a one-year period.[181] The regime came to rely more heavily for its security on these mercenaries than on its own militia, or the retinues of the *podestà* and the captain.[182] Constitutionally, the *balìa*'s most significant action was its decree (20 October) providing that future elections of the war magistracy would be made by a select commission of eighty-one citizens, instead of the councils of the *Popolo* and the Commune. By thus restricting the power of these legislative assemblies, this decree weakened the voice of the guild community, which was well represented in these councils, and further enhanced the authority of the Guelf aristocracy in the conduct of foreign affairs.[183]

The presence of a large mercenary force in the city inhibited manifestations of opposition to the regime, but it could not stifle dissent. In December 1393, the captain sent six men into exile who

[177] *ACP*, 1988, ff.5r–11r; *Panc.*, 158, ff.174v–175r.

[178] *Balìe*, 17, f.125r, 29 Oct.

[179] Some members of that militia had joined the insurgent guildsmen on 24 Oct.; *ACP*, 1988, ff.9r–9v.

[180] Morelli, *Ricordi*, 335. Morelli suggested that this Guelf militia did not become a permanent part of the regime's system of defense.

[181] *Balìe*, 17, f.126r.

[182] For payments to these mercenaries from Dec. 1393 through March 1395, see *Camera, Uscita*, 301, 302, *passim*.

[183] Capponi, *Storia*, I, 631–32. See Molho, *Speculum*, XLIII, 31–32.

were charged with fomenting unrest. The sentence against Maestro
Leonardo di Maestro Dino stated that "he has incessantly sought to
sow discord and controversy among the peaceful citizens of good will,
by means of diabolical arguments and reasoning. . . ."[184] So vaguely
worded were the charges against these men that the strength of this
opposition cannot be determined. Like two other exiles, Valorino
Valorini and Andrea Adimari, Leonardo belonged to that group
stigmatized as Ghibelline, and thus ineligible for office.[185] Lacking the
support that the Alberti and the Del Bene could muster, they could
express their views only in private meetings with other dissidents,
or by circulating defamatory broadsides against the regime and its
leadership.[186] Within that inner circle, peace and harmony did not
prevail either. The Alberti still had friends and supporters in the city;
and others, though indifferent to the fate of that powerful family, were
disturbed by the methods employed to discredit them. The cases of
Filippo Bastari and Donato Acciaiuoli attest to the existence of this
discontent, and the leadership's response to these challenges to its
authority.

Filippo Bastari had been a prominent figure in Florentine politics
since 1343 when he had first qualified for the Signoria. A moderate
who had always remained aloof from factions, he had alienated the
Albizzi in the 1370s,[187] and his position became increasingly vulnerable after 1387. One of his kinsmen was convicted of malfeasance in
1388, and for the first time in forty years neither he nor any member
of his family qualified for the Signoria in the 1391 scrutiny.[188] Perhaps
motivated by the fear that his family would suffer Alberti's fate, Filippo
indiscreetly engaged in a conversation with Rinaldo Gianfigliazzi, in
April 1394. The subject of their discussion, he told the Signoria later,
was a marriage that Rinaldo had arranged with the daughter of
Jacopo Alberti and from which, at the insistence of the Albizzi, he had
then withdrawn.[189] Filippo said that he had offered to petition the
incoming Signoria to approve that marriage, and that Rinaldo had

---

[184] These sentences of exile are in *ACP*, 1988, ff.11r–11v, 23r–24r, 44r–44v,
74r–75v.

[185] Maestro Leonardo's brothers, Lorenzo and Martino, had been *ammoniti* in
1378; Stefani, 770. Valorini and Adimari had been banned from office by the
1387 *balìa; Delizie*, XVIII, 95.

[186] *Prov.*, 83, ff.206r–207r.

[187] Brucker, *Florentine Politics and Society*, 251–56.

[188] Save for one lapse in 1357, Bastari had been nominated in every scrutiny
(for which records are extant) since 1343. He failed to qualify in 1391; *Tratte*,
397, f.85r.

[189] On this marriage, see below, ch. v, 276.

consented to the scheme. But in the latter's version of the conversation, the subject was not marriage but politics.[190] On two occasions, he reported, Filippo had reprimanded him for submitting to the Albizzi veto of his marriage.[191] In their most recent conversation, Filippo asked him whether he had accepted an ambassadorial mission to Pavia; Rinaldo replied that he did not wish to go. Filippo then said: "I don't want you to go, nor Guido [del Palagio] either, because the good citizens who support you have faith in you. It is my opinion that some forty or fifty honest citizens should appeal to the new Signoria to resist the tyranny and audacity of others. And I have discussed this with Riccardo Alberti." Rinaldo responded: "Filippo, this is not very sensible, for if fifty support this action, soon there will be one hundred opposing it."[192] Presented with these divergent accounts, the colleges declined to judge the issue, but advised the Signoria to turn the matter over to the Eight on Security and the captain.[193] On the following day (15 April), they accepted Rinaldo's version of the incident, but urged the rector to be lenient in punishing Filippo Bastari.[194] The latter simplified the task of his interrogators by confessing to the veracity of Rinaldo's account; he was fined 1000 florins and sentenced to perpetual exile in the Dalmatian city of Ragusa.[195]

Although similar in many respects to the Bastari case, the Acciaiuoli affair was more significant politically and its ramifications were far greater. Early in January 1396, Agnolo Ricoveri informed the authorities that Donato intended to present an important petition to the

[190] The two men made their statements to the Signoria and the colleges on 14 April 1394; CP, 30, f.112r.

[191] Ibid.: "Dominus Raynaldus dixit quod cum esset in camera regulatorum, Filippus dixit sibi in aurem: 'Qui negligit famam suam est homicida sui.' Et quod ipse respondit quod quia negligebat famam suam faciens contra guelfos, ideo se correxit. Et quod alia vice in platea dixit sibi: 'Vos consuevistis esse animosus et indignans. . . .'"

[192] Ibid. The version in Panc., 158, f.177v, is similar to Gianfigliazzi's account. Filippo allegedly told Messer Rinaldo: "Noi siamo una brigata di cittadini che ne siamo molto lieti che voi non vi andiate pero chè noi intendiamo, entrati i priori nuovi, d'andarcene in palagio e di volere che queste cose che anno fatto questi tiranni si rivanghino. . . ."

[193] CP, 30, f.114v.

[194] Francesco di Bicci de' Medici for the Twelve: "Quod super verbis dictis per dominum Raynaldum, capitaneus se fundet in processu Filippi"; ibid., f.115v.

[195] ACP, 1988, ff.162r–163v, 18 April 1394. This confession is not conclusive proof of Bastari's guilt; it may have been extracted by threats of torture. But there is no evidence that Bastari, or any of his kin, ever denied his injudicious overture to Gianfigliazzi.

Signoria. All sentences of exile and bans against rebels were to be cancelled; all previous scrutinies were to be destroyed and new elections held for every communal office. One chronicler reported that Donato and his associates had decided that, if the petition were not accepted, they would call for an uprising of the citizenry and assassinate Maso degli Albizzi and Rinaldo Gianfigliazzi.[196] Ricoveri had been privy to this conspiracy, and had served as liaison between Acciaiuoli and members of the Alberti and Medici families.[197] So confident was Donato of his impregnable position that he went voluntarily to the palace to answer the charges against him. When news of the affair circulated through the city, a crowd assembled in the square before the palace, demanding Acciaiuoli's execution.[198] For two days his fate was debated among the priors, the colleges, and a select commission of citizens appointed to investigate the case. Many favored his execution as a penalty appropriate to his crime, and to placate the angry populace. But others, without denying Acciaiuoli's guilt, appealed for leniency, on the grounds that his execution would alienate his influential family, which had a long tradition of service to the Guelf cause, as well as important connections in the Roman curia and the kingdom of Naples.[199] Two of Donato's intimates, Michele Acciaiuoli and Biliotto Biliotti, informed him of the sentiment against him, and urged him to confess to the charges in order to avoid the death penalty. From Donato's own account, we learn of his anguished decision to make a confession which, so he later insisted, was false.[200]

[196] The plans for revolution are described in *Panc.*, 158, ff.181r–181v, but not in Minerbetti. These are the two main chronicle sources, but some additional details may be gleaned from *Manoscritti*, 225, f.129v.

[197] This is suggested by a judicial sentence absolving Ricoveri and Ser Guido of Empoli; *ACP*, 2012, ff.71r–72v, and mentioned by the Panciatichi chronicler, ff.181v–182r: "E tutte queste cose a rivelato Agniolo di Nicholò Ricoveri, perchè trattava ogni cosa cho' Messer Donato e andava avisando ogni loro amicho il dì e lla notte, perchè avea il bulettino che era il padre gonfaloniere di giustizia."

[198] *Panc.*, 158, f.181v.

[199] None of this debate is recorded in the *Consulte e Pratiche*, but reported only in the chronicles. The collegiate reaction to Acciaiuoli's confession is in *CP*, 30, ff.2r–2v.

[200] Donato's detailed account of these events is contained in two exculpatory letters which he sent to the Signoria from Barletta. One, dated 30 May 1396, is in *BNF*, Palatino, 545, ff.24v–30r, and in *Panc.*, 158, ff.183r–185r; the second, dated 10 Nov. 1396, is printed in *I sermoni evangelici, le lettere ed altri scritti inediti e rari di Franco Sacchetti*, ed. O. Gigli (Florence, 1857), 188–98. A. Molho has discovered another letter in a private archive, the *Archivio Ricasoli-Firidolfi*, sent by Acciaiuoli to Fra Domenico of Certosa: "Iddio, e la verità del mondo, vede quanto oscuro pecchato contra Iddio e contro alla giustizia e libertà del popolo, contro a me è suto chomesso, e con disonesto modo, abominoso a ricordarlo, e

Brought before the Signoria and the colleges, whose members had previously refused to hear his testimony, he acknowledged his guilt and pleaded for mercy.[201] His life was spared and he was exiled to Barletta on the Adriatic coast for twenty years. Two of his sons were to remain in prison until he had sent proof of his arrival in Barletta; his friends were also required to post bond of 20,000 florins that he would abide by the terms of his exile.[202] Two weeks later, eight others (including three Medici) were sent into exile for their alleged participation in Donato's conspiracy.[203]

Acciaiuoli's involuntary confession cannot be used to demonstrate his guilt,[204] but independent evidence does suggest that he was deeply involved in a campaign to rehabilitate the Alberti.[205] His abrasive personality is the key to his political role and to his ultimate downfall. He assaulted a baker, Lorenzo d'Andrea, when they were both members of the war *balìa*.[206] He had many enemies in Florence and Pistoia; their attacks upon Acciaiuoli were so sharp that the Signoria discussed the issue with the colleges in November 1395.[207] A man with his talent for making enemies might well become suspicious of his peers, and ready to believe that his influence was declining. In the months before his disgrace, he spoke out boldly against policies advocated by the regime's leadership. He favored peace with Milan

---

non della volontà del comune, nè dalli ordini del popolo, ma dalla volontà d'alcuni"; "The Florentine Oligarchy of the Late Trecento, 1393–1402." Western Reserve University Ph.D. thesis, 1965, 96.

[201] This statement is briefly summarized in *CP*, 32, f.iv, 11 Jan. 1396.

[202] *ACP*, 2012, ff.39r–41r, 12 Jan. That bond was later forfeited when Donato violated the terms of his exile; above, ch. 1, 29.

[203] *ACP*, 2012, ff.54r–57r, 21 Jan. 1396. The Medici were: Antonio di Bartolomeo, Alamanno di Messer Salvestro, and Antonio di Giovanni di Cambio.

[204] In his letter to Fra Domenico (above, n.200), Acciaiuoli mentioned some hidden documents which were not to fall into the hands of his enemies. Molho, "Florentine Oligarchy," *Speculum*, xliii, 32, suggests that those papers contained evidence incriminating him.

[205] Only one chronicler suggested that Donato might have been innocent: "Si disse che cercava cose nuove de' fatti del reggimento; e chi disse che fu per invidia"; *Ricordi storici di Filippo di Cino Rinuccini dal 1282 al 1460*, ed. G. Aiazzi (Florence, 1840), xlii.

[206] "Fu questa cosa cacciata gagliardamente da Lorenzo fornaio, uno de' Signori . . . perchè M. Donato, quando erono già insieme de' Dieci di guerra passati, gli haveva dato uno schiaffo. Era, come si è detto, M. Donato non solo grandissimo cittadino, ma havendo il fratello cardinale, era tanto più invidiato et chiamato da i suoi inimici Doge et Signore per calumniarlo"; *Manoscritti*, 225, f.129v.

[207] *CP*, 31, f.123r, 8 Nov. 1395. Molho, *Speculum*, xliii, 5, notes that Leonardo Bruni commented on Acciaiuoli's habit of criticizing his fellow citizens.

and a reduction of military expenditures; he also urged that the authority granted to the captain be limited, since it was too broad.[208] By his vocal support for these policies, Acciaiuoli may have been seeking to curry favor with the *popolo*. His posture suggests a willingness to provoke a confrontation with the Albizzi; he certainly furnished them with a powerful motive for seeking his downfall.[209] Schiatta di Ambrogio and Riccardo Alberti both admitted that they had discussed the scheme to rehabilitate the Alberti with Ricoveri.[210] Acciaiuoli's plan to submit a petition was not a violation of the law, but his enemies were convinced that he intended to achieve his objective through violence.[211] If he was planning a revolutionary coup, he had done little to prepare for its implementation.[212] His actions prior to and during the crisis were characteristically amateurish, the distinguishing quality of most Florentine conspiracies.

By expelling one of the city's most influential statesmen, a man with important connections abroad,[213] the regime had increased the size and potency of its opposition. On the other hand, it enjoyed more fervent support from Donato's enemies, and from those who longed for domestic peace and security, and who reacted violently against those who disturbed the status quo.[214] The regime's decision to spare Ac-

[208] For Acciaiuoli's disagreement with other leaders of the *reggimento*, see *CP*, 31, ff.69r, 102v, 111v, 130v, and especially f.66v, 16 March 1395: "Quod via data per Decem est periculosa et scandalosa." See below, ch. III, 154–55.

[209] Describing the Acciaiuoli incident in a letter to Bologna, the Signoria wrote: "Verum sicuti per alias nostras litteras fraternitati vestri duximus intimandum electa est pestilens illud virus quod totam civitatem nostram sub nomine securitatis et pacis et minuendarum expensarum obtentuque voces populares in omni re publica semper fuerunt semperque vulgus insipiens solite sunt decipere corrumpebat. Que pestis intestinumque malum adeo se late diffuderat, quod omnium deliberationum summa iam in unius reducta voluntatem pendereque ab unius arbitrio videbatur"; *SCMC*, 24, f.177v, 14 Jan. 1396. This statement lends some credibility to the hypothesis that Acciaiuoli was convicted with false testimony, by his enemies who feared his popularity.

[210] *ACP*, 2012, ff.59r–60r, 66r–67r.

[211] The 1393 *balìa* stipulated that the petition had to be approved unanimously by the priors and the colleges; Passerini, *Alberti*, II, 261–62. This would not have occurred without some form of coercion.

[212] Acciaiuoli's testimony, *BNF, Palatino*, 545, f.16r: "Fu domandato d'alchuni se io avevo raghunata di fanti in chasa. Rispuosi di no; e che sapevano bene dove n'avevo, e mandaro[no] a cherchare e trovarono ch'io dicevo il vero."

[213] Donato's kin included a cardinal in the Roman curia and officials in the Regno; see the regime's response to their criticism of his exile; *SCMC*, 24, f.185r; *CP*, 32, ff.54r–54v.

[214] Donato was aware of the intense hostility which he had aroused: "Di fuori si chiedeva charne, e anchora per alchuni di quegli dentro"; *Palatino*, 545, f.27v.

ciaiuoli's life was a manifestation of its established policy to avoid bloodshed and thus minimize the hostility which inevitably accompanied a political purge. Exiles were potentially dangerous, but they did not stir up the deep and lasting hatreds born of a political execution.[215]

Filippo Bastari and Donato Acciaiuoli were the most notable political figures accused of sowing discord in the city. Their banishment should have promoted unity and harmony,[216] but the evidence points to a different conclusion. The guild community had not been cowed into supine acceptance of the policies formulated by the leadership. The Council of the *Popolo*, for example, refused to grant an extension to the broad police powers exercised by the captain, and it also voted down provisions for levying new forced loans.[217] The magistracies were the targets of defamatory letters and criticism in the streets.[218] Bolstered by new recruits, the exile groups in Bologna, Faenza, and Venice pursued their revolutionary goals. In the summer of 1397, a group led by Bastardino de' Medici, and including members of the Adimari and Ricci families, made plans for a rebellion in Florence.[219] They secretly entered the city and hid in a house belonging to a sympathizer. They had two principal objectives: the assassination of Maso degli Albizzi and Rinaldo Gianfigliazzi, and the incitement of workers and dissident guildsmen to revolution. But the rebels were foiled in their attempt to kill the regime's leaders. "They ran through the streets for two hours urging the *popolo* to seize arms," the Lucchese

[215] By extending mercy to the culpable, and limiting the scope of the investigation of the "conspiracy," the authorities hoped to reduce tensions by limiting the number of those implicated; *LF*, 45, f.8r, and the opinions of Filippo Strozzi and Filippo Corsini; *CP*, 32, ff.4r, 5r. Every condemnation for a political offense created enemies for the regime.

[216] This was the Signoria's contention: "Preter quod illius talis expulsio, divisio sit aliqua civitatis, sed talis unio tantaque redintegratio quod totus noster populus . . . factus est corpus unum et animam unam postquam illius contagiosi membri, quod omnia corrumpebant, exetio facta fuit"; *SCMC*, 24, f.177v.

[217] For opposition to the appointment of a *capitano di balìa*, see *CP*, 32, ff.21r–21v, 23r–23v, 69v, 76r; *LF*, 45, ff.32r, 40r, 43r–44r, 47r–50r. This official was the commander of the Genoese mercenary force, and its retention may have depended on his appointment.

[218] *CP*, 32, ff.39v, 40v, 100v. Intense public criticism must have prompted the sharp reaction of Alessandro Alessandri: "Quod domini eligant octo cives bonos et discretos, amatores boni publici qui provideant de pecunia; et id quod faciant sit ratum, et qui contradixerit, puniatur, abscindendo linguas eorum qui obloquerentur"; *ibid.*, f.104v, 17 March 1397.

[219] This plot is described in the sentences against the conspirators; *ACP*, 2056, ff.65r–71r, 76r–80r, 92r–94r, 97v–99r; *AEOG*, 1321, ff.19v–21r, 25r–27r. The year before, Bastardino had been sentenced to death for murder; *ACP*, 2044, ff.38r–40r.

ambassador reported, "but no one moved to join them."[220] After taking refuge in the cathedral, the conspirators were seized and executed.

Commenting upon the failure of Bastardino's conspiracy, the Lucchese ambassador wrote: "All is now quiet and peaceful, by God's grace, and those who govern the city are united with all of the others. . . . And if any shadow [of discord] still lingers, this episode will dispel it and motivate everyone more strongly toward virtue. . . ."[221] To his friend Piero Davanzati in Venice, Rosso Orlandi wrote: "One sees clearly that this regime is much more secure, and the citizens neither so discontented or faction-ridden, as many have foolishly believed."[222] While this image of harmony should not be overdrawn, the regime was more stable, and more unified, than at any time since 1382. Its durability, its demonstrated capacity for survival, was an important source of strength. Among the workers and artisans who failed to respond to Bastardino's appeal were hundreds—perhaps thousands—who sympathized with the rebels, but who had seen too many comrades being escorted to the gallows by officials of the *podestà* and the captain. Rid of its dissident (or potentially dangerous) elements, the regime's leaders were generally in agreement on basic issues: internal security, officeholding, the fisc, foreign policy. Promoting this cohesiveness was that perennial threat to Florentine security: Giangaleazzo Visconti, lord of Milan. For this republican community, war was both a divisive and a unifying force.[223] The regime was, however, able to use the Visconti threat to its own advantage: to arouse patriotic sentiment, to mobilize civic support for its policies and for the sacrifices, in wealth if not in blood, that war exacted.

[220] Report of Ser Guido da Pietrasanta, in Fumi, *Regesti*, ii, no. 1804; also printed in Molho, *Nuova Rivista Storica*, lii, 419.

[221] Fumi, *Regesti*, ii, no. 1804.

[222] CRS, 78 (*Badìa*), 315, no. 228, 4 Aug. 1397.

[223] For general considerations of this problem, see C. Bayley, *War and Society in Renaissance Florence*, ch. 2; and Brucker, *Renaissance Florence*, 160–71.

CHAPTER III

Foreign Affairs: 1382–1402

FLORENTINE IMPERIALISM, 1382–1388

THE primary objective of Florentine diplomacy in the early 1380s was survival. Weakened by internal struggles for power, the regime could not muster the will and the resources to play an influential role in Italian politics. The peninsula was in an unusually chaotic state in these years, for which the republic bore a heavy responsibility. Her campaign against the papacy's territorial state in central Italy (1375–1378) had destroyed the old Guelf entente that had given some measure of stability to Italian politics, and had also wrecked the military and administrative structure in the Papal States so painstakingly constructed by the Avignonese popes.[1] The rebellions fomented by Florence in papal territory brought Pope Gregory XI back to Rome in 1377, a development that set the stage for the outbreak of the Great Schism a year later. Florence's alienation from her traditional Guelf allies was nearly total in these years.[2] Urban VI was suspicious of Florentine motives and angered by the republic's failure to pay the indemnity stipulated in the 1378 peace settlement. With his temporal possessions and his revenues drastically reduced, and one-half of Catholic Europe rejecting his authority, the Roman pope would have been a weak and ineffectual ally in any event. The major Guelf powers beyond the Alps, France and Hungary, were locked in a bitter rivalry over the possession of the kingdom of Naples. The contenders for that prize, Louis of Anjou (uncle of the French monarch, Charles VI) and Charles of Durazzo (the son of King Louis of Hungary) both demanded aid from Florence; neither was in a position to provide support for the republic. The Great Schism completed the demolition of the Guelf alliance: the Hungarian branch of the

---

[1] P. Partner, *The Lands of Saint Peter* (Berkeley and Los Angeles, 1972), 362–64. Cf. P. J. Jones, *The Malatesta of Rimini and the Papal State* (Cambridge, 1973), 91–99.

[2] Florentines continued to profess their allegiance to Guelf principles, e.g., Benedetto Alberti's statement, "procurent ostendere eidem [regi Ungarie] quomodo comune est devotum sue maiestatis et regitur per guelfos"; and Alessandro dell'Antella, "mittatur ambasciata ad regem pro pace inter eos et dicant de malis operibus illorum qui destruxerunt civitatem et devotionem populi et regiminis, et quomodo sunt vere guelfi et ostendendo quod singulari Dei gratia, pars Guelfa reassumpsit in civitate Florentie maximas vires et Gebellina est extincta quod non fuit tempore aliquorum suorum progenitorum"; *CP*, 16, f.90r.

Angevin house favored the Roman pope, Urban VI, as did Florence; France was the major ally of his rival in Avignon, Clement VII.

The conflict over Naples was the greatest source of anxiety for the republic in these years, and it revealed most acutely her vulnerability. With the blessing of Urban VI, Charles of Durazzo had occupied the kingdom in the autumn of 1381, and then defended his conquest against Louis of Anjou's army, which invaded Italy in the summer of 1382. Each of these princes sent embassies to Florence requesting an alliance and demanding military assistance against his enemy. Charles of Durazzo was favored by most Florentines and particularly the *arciguelfi*,[3] but officially the government did not dare to take sides in this quarrel. Simone Peruzzi formulated the argument for neutrality in June 1382: "Reply to the ambassador of King Charles so that he will not break off relations completely, and also so that the duke of Anjou will not be provoked to anger. The ambassadors should be told that both [princes] have been benefactors of the commune, which deplores the division that has arisen between them."[4] To walk the tightrope of neutrality was difficult, and the regime sometimes faltered in its efforts to avoid any sign of partisanship.[5] Louis of Anjou was the most immediate threat to Florentine security, and he presented the commune with the most troubling decisions. The regime did provide limited financial and military aid to Anjou's enemy, Pope Urban VI,[6] and her spokesmen reacted angrily to criticisms of the Roman pope voiced by the duke's ambassadors. "Refute the calumnious statements against the pope and the king [Charles of Durazzo]," Simone Peruzzi counseled the Signoria, "and tell them that this is a free city and that for our liberty we will do everything, and this should be stated forcefully and without any display of fear."[7] When Anjou's army approached Rome in August 1382, one counselor urged the government to send more aid to Urban VI, "for if he falls, our city will perish." But the republic was unwilling to declare its support for the pope's ally,

[3] Some Guelf partisans had joined Charles' army in 1380; see above, 56. For indications of support for Charles, see the statements of Biagio Guasconi and Guido del Palagio; *CP*, 21, ff.20v, 31r.

[4] *CP*, 21, f.19v. Cf. the opinions of Giovanni di Ser Dati and Alessandro de' Bardi; *ibid.*, ff.61v–62r.

[5] Fearing leaks, Francesco Bruni and Simone Peruzzi objected to voting on the proposal to ally with Charles; *ibid.*, ff.14r–14v.

[6] On differing opinions about releasing John Hawkwood to fight for Urban VI against Anjou, see *ibid.*, ff.61v–62v, 67v–68r, 71r–72r, 14–23 Aug. 1382. Later the commune justified its decision to release Hawkwood; *CP*, 22, f.17r, statement of Donato Acciaiuoli.

[7] *CP*, 22, f.17r, 14 Feb. 1383.

Charles of Durazzo. When an episcopal official published Urban's condemnation of Anjou, several citizens angrily denounced this action and demanded that the offending cleric be imprisoned for his temerity.[8] So great was the anxiety over this blunder that the regime was willing to risk papal anger over the maltreatment of a priest, rather than alienate the duke of Anjou and the French crown, and so endanger Florentine merchants trading in France.

Out of this Neapolitan imbroglio emerged an opportunity and a decision that dramatically changed the course of Florentine foreign policy. The turning point was the acquisition of Arezzo in November 1384. Earlier that year, a French army under the command of Enguerrand de Coucy crossed the Alps and moved southward to bring help to the beleaguered duke of Anjou, whose campaign to conquer the Regno was faltering. This invading force moved slowly through Tuscany, arousing great anxiety in Florence; it occupied Arezzo at the end of September.[9] When news reached Coucy of Anjou's death and the disintegration of his army in the Regno, he sold Arezzo to Florence for 40,000 florins. This acquisition had several momentous consequences for the republic. It substantially enlarged Florence's territory, her subject population, and her resources (and also her burdens and responsibilities), and it brought the city into more direct contact, and also into potential conflict, with her neighbors in southern and eastern Tuscany. But the most direct consequence was the dramatic change in the civic mood, from anxiety and defensiveness to buoyancy and even arrogance.

The decision to acquire Arezzo was not an impulsive gesture; it had a history. Since June 1382,[10] the issue had been raised by successive priorates and had been frequently discussed in the *pratiche*. While some citizens favored the scheme, others warned that it was too dangerous and expensive. Gino Anselmi commented (December 1382) that "the Arezzo enterprise is fraught with peril, but if the town can be obtained without any restrictions, then we should seize it."[11] A year later, in the spring of 1384, civic opinion had shifted decisively in favor of acquisition, at the lowest possible cost. The plan was supported by Guelf aristocrats (Simone Bordoni, Buonaccorso di Lapo Giovanni, Filippo Corsini) and also by citizens affiliated with the Alberti (Benedetto Alberti, Giovanni de' Ricci, Filippo Bastari, Tom-

---

[8] *CP*, 21, ff.96r–97r, 20 Oct. 1382.

[9] On the commune's reaction to Coucy's campaign, see *CP*, 23 ff.65r–67r, 76v–77r, 84v–90r, 93v, 95v, 102v–113v, 128r–131v, 134v.

[10] *CP*, 21, f.3r, 9 June 1382.   [11] *CP*, 22, f.7r, 30 Dec. 1382.

maso Guidetti).[12] Still, there was opposition, though it was not voiced publicly. Two measures were submitted to the councils in the summer and autumn of 1384, providing for the election of commissioners to negotiate with the French for Arezzo's purchase. These provisions passed the councils by very narrow margins, with negative votes of 153 and 122 cast by the dissenting minority.[13]

The shift in Florentine attitudes from tremulous anxiety to ebullient confidence is reflected in the *pratiche* convened in the autumn of 1384, after Coucy's army had occupied Arezzo. There was no trace of obsequiousness or the desire to placate French sensibilities that had characterized the debates in 1382, when the duke of Anjou's army moved south through Tuscany toward Naples. Typical of the reaction to Coucy's incursion was Filippo Bastari's statement: "The commune should fortify itself with troops . . . without sparing any expense . . . and prevent the French army from attacking us. . . . By every means possible, give aid to Arezzo [against Coucy], having no consideration for anything." Paolo di Ser Guido concurred: "All of the commune's strength should be sent to the frontiers . . . and Arezzo should be beseiged so that we have the city."[14] Not since the early months of the war against Pope Gregory XI in 1375 had such bellicose sentiments been expressed in the *pratiche*.

The implications of Florence's occupation of Arezzo were not lost upon her neighbors, particularly Siena. The most powerful state in Tuscany now replaced a weak Aretine regime on Siena's eastern frontier. The Sienese were very frightened by this move, the Lucchese ambassador in Siena reported to his government.[15] That anxiety was legitimate. Boundaries between the Sienese and Aretine territories had long been the subject of controversy, and noble clans in this border region were a perpetual source of turmoil. The Sienese regime was particularly vulnerable, since it had exiled members of prominent noble families who sought Florentine aid to recover their status. Diplomatic relations between the two republics had been cool though correct since 1382, but they deteriorated rapidly in the winter of 1384–1385. Sienese ambassadors received a chilly reception in Flor-

---

[12] See the discussions on Arezzo in *CP*, 23 ff.4r–5r, 8v–9r, 13v, and in particular, the debate on 10 May 1384, *ibid.*, ff.45r–46r. Two lower guildsmen (Niccolò di Chiaro, blacksmith, and Lapacino Tosi, linen-maker) supported Arezzo's acquisition, *ibid.*, ff.45r–45v.

[13] *LF*, 42, ff.10r–10v, 10 June 1384; 22r–22v, 17 Sept. 1384.

[14] *CP*, 23, ff.127v, 129r, 30 Sept. 1384.

[15] Fumi, *Regesti*, II, part 2, 234–35, 18 Nov. See also the Florentine letter of 4 Nov., *Conc.*, 1814, no. 90.

ence, and their petition for an alliance was rebuffed by the Signoria.[16] Siena complained about the depredations of Florentine troops in her territory; the Arno republic charged that the Sienese had imprisoned her citizens without cause.[17] Sienese diplomats heard rumors that Florentine agents were assembling troops in the Chianti for an invasion, that their spies were inspecting the walls of Siena for weak spots, and that a plot against their regime was being organized under Florentine auspices.[18]

That these reports had some factual basis is clear from the *pratiche*, which reflected the new spirit animating Florentine diplomacy as well as the city's political divisions. Most aggressively hostile to the Sienese were Guelf aristocrats like Rinaldo Gianfigliazzi, who called for the use of force to rescue Florentine citizens in Sienese captivity and "the extermination of the commune's enemies."[19] The social bias of these aristocrats against the artisans in the Sienese regime was most clearly articulated by Francesco Bruni, the humanist-diplomat who had spent several years in the papal chancery. Bruni argued that "it is both necessary and desirable to restore the Sienese government into the hands of worthy men, lest the idiots (*fatui*) who now rule bring the whole country to ruin."[20] These sentiments frightened men of a more cautious temperament, who warned of the dangers inherent in this posture. "We should not wage war either openly or secretly," Cipriano Alberti said, "for it is immoral, dangerous, and expensive. Instead, we should recall our troops, send an embassy [to Siena], and work for a good government in that city without force of arms."[21] The armorer Salvo di Nuto, who may have been expressing the feelings of most Florentine craftsmen and shopkeepers, was sharply critical of this imperialist policy. "Do not embark upon any new military enterprise," he urged, "and do nothing that will be against God; but act so that the city of Siena will not be destroyed, and so that their citizens are restored to harmony."[22] By introducing a moral theme into this dis-

[16] Reports of the Sienese ambassadors, *Conc.*, 1815, no. 12, 27, 37, 41, 47, 64, 65, 67.

[17] *CP*, 24, ff.9v–10r, 18 Dec.　　　　[18] *Conc.*, 1815, no. 37, 41, 67.

[19] *CP*, 24, f.9v. See also the arguments of Buonaccorso di Lapo Giovanni, Alessio Baldovinetti, Vieri Cavicciuli, Rinieri Peruzzi; *ibid.*, ff.12r–12v.

[20] *Ibid.*, f.14v, 27 Dec.

[21] *Ibid.* Similar views were expressed by Giovanni de' Ricci, Tommaso Guidetti, and Ridolfo di Jacopo; *ibid.*, ff.9v, 12r, 15r–15v.

[22] *CP*, 24, f.33v, 23 Feb. 1385. This controversy is one example of an internal disagreement over foreign policy, which Peter Herde minimizes in his analysis of Florentine diplomacy in these years; "Politische Verhaltensweisen der Florentiner Oligarchie 1382–1402," in *Geschichte und Verfassungsgefüge: Frankfurter Festgabe für Walter Schlesinger*, 173, 185.

cussion, Salvo was suggesting that an attack on Siena would violate divine law, since (and this is implicit) the Sienese regime was not a serious threat to Florentine security. That argument was less persuasive than were those based on expense and danger, and particularly the negative reaction of other Tuscan city-states to aggression.[23] The conversion of the moderate Filippo Bastari to a strategy of subversion may have reflected a general shift in Florentine attitudes. Speaking about the Sienese issue in late December, Filippo counseled restraint. Two weeks later, he conceded that the Sienese were truly enemies of the Florentine republic, and while still opposing the use of force, he recommended that the war magistracy establish contact with Sienese exiles to subvert that regime.[24] Benedetto Alberti made a similar proposal in February 1385;[25] two months later, the government of the Nine was overthrown and replaced by an aristocratic regime more friendly to its northern neighbor.

This event was an occasion for celebration in Florence.[26] With a friendly regime in Siena, Florentine exiles would be deprived of a base for plotting conspiracies, and an alliance between the two republics would bring a greater measure of stability to Tuscany. When the Sienese ambassador, Ser Giacomo Manni, arrived in Florence to discuss these issues, he reported, "I cannot walk through the streets without being accosted by citizens who display such pleasure, and show me such honor, that it would not be appropriate for me to describe their sentiments."[27] The Sienese government had commissioned Manni to negotiate an alliance and to settle border disputes arising from Florence's annexation of the Aretine *contado*, and particularly the village of Lucignano some twenty-five miles east of Siena.

Although the Lucignano episode hardly qualifies as a major event in Tuscan history, it does illustrate the new style of Florentine diplomacy. From Giacomo Manni's correspondence, we are unusually well informed about the negotiations over Lucignano, and particularly

[23] The statement of Alessandro Alessandri: "quod Senensibus non fiat guerra . . . ne vicini per invidiam ad aliquid moveantur"; CP, 24, f.22v.

[24] Bastari's opinions are in *ibid.*, ff.15r, 22r.

[25] *Ibid.*, f.33r, 23 Feb. Filippo Bastari later admitted that he had participated in secret negotiations with Sienese exiles; *ibid.*, f.74v, 17 June 1385.

[26] See the comments of the Panciatichi chronicler; *Panc.*, 158, f.149v: "Venerdì a dì xvii di marzo [1385] vene in Firenze la novella . . . chome i gentili uomini e 'l popolo grasso di Siena aveano corsso la città e chaciate a ttera il popolo minuto. Feciene gran festa in Firenze e lla sera molto falò per la città en sul palagio di signiori e vestironsi molte brighate d'armigiatori tuti giovani ghuelfi vestiti a drappi di molti cholori armegiando per la città. . . ."

[27] *Conc.*, 1816, no. 27, 9 May 1385.

the secret parleys between him and Florentine citizens who were friendly to Sienese interests, and who worked assiduously to achieve a settlement.[28] These men favored the aristocratic regime in Siena that had been purged of its artisan elements. Manni reported that they were willing to give Lucignano to Siena, to strengthen that regime and the "good citizens" of Siena, and to promote cordial relations between the two republics. "Truly, my lords," he wrote, "the more I discuss and negotiate with your friends here and with others, the more I am aware of the benevolent disposition of all the good citizens of this community. . . ."[29] In exchange for a minor territorial concession, Florence would gain a staunch ally in Tuscany. The opposition to this conciliatory policy came from the *popolo*, whose latent xenophobic feelings had been aroused against the Sienese, and who may have felt some sympathy for the fallen artisan regime in Siena, similar in its social composition to the guild republic that had governed Florence between 1378 and 1382. Manni and his Florentine confidants hoped that the territorial disputes could be settled quickly and quietly, so that they did not become controversial. But Sienese anxieties delayed a settlement until popular opposition reached such proportions that concessions were no longer feasible. Manni's despatches trace the progressive hardening of the regime's posture on Lucignano. In a sanguine report of 14 May, he stated that most Florentines were favorably disposed to the Sienese regime "although there are some who, for whatever reason, are not so friendly toward you." A week later, he wrote in a more sober vein: "Our friends here secretly comfort us and give us hope, even though the populace grumbles. . . ."[30] Some resentment against the Sienese government was fomented by exiles who established contacts with artisans and cloth-workers in Florence. They spread rumors, Manni wrote, "that Lucignano is fertile and has an abundance of grain which would feed half of the Florentine poor."[31] Lucignano had become a divisive issue[32] that could no longer be settled by secret diplomacy. In late June, reports circulated that the town was to be surrendered to Siena, but so violent was the popular

[28] Manni identified two prominent Florentines, Filippo Corsini and Buonaccorso di Lapo Giovanni, who were sympathetic to Sienese interests; *ibid.*, 1816, no. 47. The Salviati and the Castellani also had close ties with the Sienese aristocracy.

[29] *Ibid.*, 1816, no. 28, 10 May.

[30] *Ibid.*, 1816, no. 35; 1819, no. 24, 14 and 20 May. Also, 1816, no. 40, 30 May.

[31] *Ibid.*, 1819, no. 24. For the identity of some Sienese artisan exiles, see *ibid.*, 1817, no. 30, 15 July.

[32] "Fra la cittadinanza se ne parla assai, ma la buona gente vorrebe di largo affare le cose dovuti; altri più comuni ne parlano per altro modo, chi per loro divisioni, che ci è assai, chi per altri rispetti"; *ibid.*, 1817, no. 12, 7 July. See also *ibid.*, no. 29.

outcry that an apprehensive Signoria abandoned the plan. On 2 July Manni wrote that "the mob and the populace of Florence say that Lucignano belongs to Arezzo [and so to Florence], and it is extremely difficult to drive that idea from their minds; furthermore, there are certain ones here who maliciously seek to sow discord between the two communes. . . ."[33]

Manni's analysis of the Lucignano dispute was remarkably astute. Most Florentine aristocrats were well disposed toward his government and were eager to reach a settlement. Manni may have exaggerated the benevolence of those citizens who met with him privately, and who sought to persuade the Sienese to give the Signoria authority to settle the issue. If he was deluded about their motives, which may have been more selfish than he assumed, he did not misinterpret the hostile feelings of the populace and the strength of that sentiment in preventing a compromise. Manni was highly critical of those Florentines who opposed the transfer of Lucignano to Siena,[34] but they could base their arguments upon law. "It is generally believed," asserted Filippo Bastari, "that Lucignano belonged to Arezzo . . . and what is Caesar's should be given to Caesar and what is God's, to God. If by law or by valid reasons Lucignano belongs to us, then let us accept it without arousing anger among the Sienese."[35] The Lucignano issue had raised some basic issues in the formulation of foreign policy.[36] It might be argued that statesmen who favored accommodation with Siena were taking a realistic, long-range view of Florence's interests, and that those opposing a settlement were selfish and short-sighted. In this dispute, partisan politics and xenophobia were stronger than the forces of moderation and compromise. Stubbornly refusing to surrender Lucignano, the Signoria forced Siena to submit the case to arbitration. Whether awed by Florentine power or persuaded by the legitimacy of her claims, the commune of Bologna gave Lucignano to Florence. The sum of 18,000 florins awarded to the Sienese was little consolation to that embittered community, whose citizens were convinced that they had been robbed of their legitimate possession.[37]

---

[33] *Ibid.*, 1817, no. 3.

[34] "Certi che per malitiosa industria studiano di mettere disdegno e rancore tra l'uno comune e l'altro"; *ibid.*, no. 3, 2 July; "tanti altri che sotto pretesto d'aquistare le ragione di loro comune e chi per altri rispetti volgliono tutte queste terre, pero chè dicono sono d'Arezzo"; *ibid.*, no. 29, 7 July.

[35] *CP*, 24, f.69r.

[36] I have discussed some of the implications of the Lucignano crisis in my *Renaissance Florence*, 165–66.

[37] For Sienese criticism of Florentine pressures on the Bolognese government, see *Conc.*, 1819, no. 95, 25 Oct. 1386. On this settlement, see Martines, *Lawyers and Statecraft*, 349–50.

Giacomo Manni's mission was not typical of Florentine diplomacy; his relations with his hosts were exceptionally intimate, and the popular reaction to his embassy was far stronger than was customary. Nevertheless, his correspondence is a revealing source for the style of diplomacy practiced by this regime. The official aspects of his mission involved periodic meetings with the Signoria and with the seven citizens (uditori) delegated by the priors to negotiate with the Sienese ambassadors.[38] This procedure allowed the Signoria to delegate some responsibility to specialists while preserving its freedom to modify or reject their recommendations. The natural inclination of these officials was to settle controversial issues in secret, to minimize public involvement and debate.[39] But Florence's relations with Siena had become a matter of acute civic concern. Although the intensity of popular feeling over Lucignano was exceptional if not unique, the episode does suggest that such issues could generate intense excitement in the "multitude,"[40] and that public opinion was always a factor in Florentine diplomacy. Manni's conversations with private citizens were quite as important as his official functions; he was both the purveyor and the recipient of propaganda, and a sharp observer of the Florentine political scene. Although he did not reveal everything that he learned in his despatches,[41] he was obviously well informed about the partisan divisions created by the Lucignano issue. His Florentine sources leaked information about secret deliberations and, in all likelihood, about the identity and the strategy of those who opposed Siena's claims to Lucignano.[42] Such intimacy between foreign diplomats and private citizens was doubtless as rare as it was illegal.[43] But this experience does throw light upon the role of partisanship in diplomacy, and the inclination of some Florentines to engage in unconstitutional practices to further their political objectives.

[38] These official visits, including one meal with the priors, are described by Manni; Conc., 1816, no. 26-28, 31, 37, 40; 1819, no. 24.

[39] However, the Signoria did grant Manni the rare privilege of addressing an assembly of 400 citizens; ibid., 1816, no. 66, 23 June.

[40] The word is Manni's and he used it in a pejorative sense; ibid., no. 28, 40; 1817, no. 29. Citizens who supported Sienese interests were "buoni e cari cittadini e nostri amici e bene intendenti"; ibid., no. 28.

[41] "Di qui e di costà sono di quelli che non amano vostro buono stato nè amano e buoni gentiluomini e' popolari dela vostra città, che intizzano e mettono dele lengna nel fuoco e non è licito ongni cosa scrivere"; Conc., 1817, no. 29. See also ibid., no. 53, 28 July.

[42] Ibid., 1816, no. 66, 68; 1817, no. 30.

[43] For discussions about punishment to be meted out to those who revealed communal secrets, see below, ch. VI, 345-46, 357-58.

One aspect of the Lucignano affair that is not well described in Manni's reports is the motivation of those Florentines who assured him of their devotion to Sienese interests. Were these men sincere in their protestations of friendship and their willingness to surrender Lucignano, or were they engaged in an elaborate game to dupe the Sienese? No speaker in a *pratica* was willing to recommend territorial concessions to Siena, although several did urge the Signoria to avoid scandal and to have some regard for Sienese sensibilities.[44] Though Manni described the attitudes of his Florentine friends in the most favorable light, he did reveal, perhaps unconsciously, their condescending attitude toward their weaker neighbor. In their comments to Manni, Florentines assumed that the Sienese would recognize the superior weight of their judgments, and their obvious commitment to equity and justice. In an early report (13 May), when he was still optimistic about his mission, Manni wrote: "I perceive the benevolent attitude of these citizens. . . . They are very open with me in private conversation, and they are less interested in gaining possession of those lands than in receiving from you full authorization [to arbitrate], so that the citizenry will be satisfied."[45] When the Sienese were unwilling to trust so fully in their neighbors' sense of justice, the Florentine mood changed from benevolence to exasperation. The inconclusiveness of the negotiations was particularly galling; Manni's friends told him repeatedly that the uncertainty over Lucignano could not continue indefinitely but that a resolution of the problem was essential.[46] Similar in tone were the statements by counselors who urged the Signoria to show the Sienese the error of their ways, and to induce them to be sensible and rational.[47] This paternalistic attitude was typical of Florence's diplomatic posture toward the city-states on her frontiers; it was not appreciated by her resentful neighbors.

The revival of imperialistic impulses in Florence naturally aroused the anxieties of other communities besides Siena. While the main thrust of Florentine expansion was toward the south and east,[48] the republic was also acquiring territory in the Apennine region adjacent to Bolognese territory. Her preoccupation with Lucignano did not im-

---

[44] See the statements of Ugo Vecchietti, Lotto Castellani, and Filippo Corsini; *CP*, 24, ff.75r, 83r, 83v.

[45] *Conc.*, 1816, no. 31.

[46] *Ibid.*, 1817, no. 3 and 29, 2 and 7 July.

[47] The statements of Simone Capponi, Gino Anselmi and Matteo Arrighi; *CP*, 24, ff.82r–82v.

[48] The Sienese were concerned about rumors that Florence was secretly planning to annex Cortona; *Conc.*, 1817, no. 66 and 70, Sept. 1385.

pede her attempts to obtain, by force or negotiation, four castles on
the Bologna frontier in the spring of 1385. Civic opinion was generally
favorable to these acquisitions, although some speakers were concerned about Bologna's reaction.[49] In September, a Bolognese embassy
came to Florence to complain about the republic's diplomatic and military incursions into their territory. Responding to these complaints,
citizens advised the Signoria to reassure the Bolognese of their good
intentions, and more generally, "to restore amity between ourselves
and our neighbors."[50] But such protestations of good will did not
assuage Bolognese fears, and relations between the two republics remained tense.[51] In the autumn of 1386, a dispute over the possession
of an Apennine castle threatened to erupt into a major diplomatic
crisis.[52] Florence was no more successful in establishing good relations
with her northern neighbor and erstwhile ally, Bologna, than with
Siena on her southern frontier.

Though the republic gained Arezzo and the Apennine castles without using force, her power was certainly a factor in these acquisitions.
Florence's only significant military enterprise in these years involved
no territorial ambition, although it was related to her heightened interest in Umbrian politics as a consequence of Arezzo's annexation.
The lord of Urbino, Count Guido of Montefeltro, had attacked a
Florentine client, Francesco Gabrielli of Gubbio, imprisoned him, and
confiscated his estates. The count then insulted a Florentine ambassador sent to remonstrate with him; this prompted the Sixteen to call
for punitive measures to wipe out the stain on Florence's honor: "The
commune cannot submit to this outrage; it must have vengeance!"[53]
Opinion in the *pratiche* was unanimous in support of military action
against Count Guido.[54] However, a provision to create a war *balìa* was

[49] These castles were Gaevia, Anghiari, Valliala, and Castiglione; *CP*, 24, ff.53r–
53v, 60v–61v. Only Maso degli Albizzi expressed his opposition to this enterprise,
arguing that it would antagonize the Bolognese; *ibid.*, f.60v.

[50] Statement of Franco Sacchetti; *ibid.*, f.106r, 5 Sept. 1385. For the discussion,
see *ibid.*, ff.105r–106r.

[51] For references to Bologna in the spring of 1386, see *CP*, 25, ff.71r–73v, 76r–76v.

[52] This was reported by Giacomo Manni from Florence; *Conc.*, 1819, no. 80 and
87, 10 and 15 Oct. 1386. In the debate on this issue, Alessandro Alessandri adopted
a bellicose posture and Filippo Bastari a moderate position. Bastari argued "quod
bellum fugiatur et nullo modo precipitetur in impresam"; *CP*, 25, f.124v. Alessandri
had also been uncompromising in the Lucignano affair; "et omnino Lucignanum
habeatur"; *CP*, 24, f.82v.

[53] Statement of Francesco di Angelo; *CP*, 25, f.20v, 30 Dec. 1385. For earlier
discussions, see *ibid.*, ff.9v–11r, 14v–15r.

[54] "Eligantur decem cives . . . qui vigilent circa destructionem comitis Urbini.
. . . Omnia fiant in destructionem comitis Antonii. . . . Impresa fiat magnifice";
CP, 25, f.34r, 3 Feb. 1386. See also *ibid.*, ff.34v–35r.

first defeated in the Council of the *Popolo* before it finally passed by narrow margins;[55] some citizens were apparently unwilling to spend money on a campaign to defend Florentine honor. This inflammatory rhetoric notwithstanding, the war waged against the Montefeltri was a limited effort; the republic did not wish to intensify fears aroused by her aggressive posture in central Italy.[56] The Signoria was sufficiently concerned about the diplomatic reactions to send ambassadors to Bologna and to the new lord of Milan, Giangaleazzo Visconti, justifying the campaign against the Montefeltri and disclaiming any territorial ambition. The realization that her image as a peace-loving republic had been tarnished probably contributed to her decision to negotiate an early settlement with Count Guido in June 1386.[57]

Urbino and Gubbio were towns in the Papal States. Florence's campaign in this part of Umbria was her first direct intervention in papal territory since the 1370s, and a sign of Pope Urban VI's weakness. The republic did not feel any compulsion to obtain papal approval for her campaign against the Montefeltri;[58] her statesmen realized that Florence had no rivals to challenge her dominant position in central Italy. In the absence of a strong papal government, the Urbino campaign could be interpreted as a manifestation of Florence's custodial function in the northern parts of the papal dominion. Florentines enjoyed this role of peacemaker and policeman; it bolstered their egos and their feelings of moral superiority. Successive priorates wrote to the Perugian commune, urging the citizens of that strife-torn republic to settle their differences and live in peace.[59] In March 1386, the citizens of Todi asked the republic to accept the lordship of their city, some fifty miles south of Perugia. Prudence dictated a negative response to this offer, and to a similar opportunity to acquire the lordship of Corneto.[60] But Florence's hegemony was challenged in that same year by Pope Urban VI, who was determined to regain control of the Papal States, and to stabilize it by establishing his court in Perugia.

[55] *LF*, 42, ff.82v–83v, 6–8 Feb. 1386. The votes: 167–76 and 128–60.

[56] In the minority were Filippo Corsini and Simone Peruzzi who favored a full-scale assault; others (Filippo Bastari, Simone Capponi, Forese Salviati, Giovanni de' Ricci) wanted a more limited campaign; *CP*, 25, ff.72v–74r, 25 May 1386.

[57] Florence's terms for peace are stated in *DBCMLC*, 1, p. 34, 8 June 1386.

[58] Florence described her war against the Montefeltri in a letter to Urban VI; *SCMC*, 20, ff.162r–162v, 10 March 1386.

[59] For examples, see *SCMC*, 20, ff.17r–17v (19 Aug. 1384); 258r–259r (2 July 1387).

[60] *CP*, 25, ff.42v–43v, 50r, 5 and 17 March 1386. Buonaccorso di Lapo Giovanni cited the reasons for refusing this offer; Todi was in papal territory and its acquisition would anger Perugia; *ibid.*, f.42v.

Prior to Urban's decision to move north, Florence's relations with him had been civil if not warm. Citing heavy defense expenditures, she had consistently refused Urban's request for payment of the indemnity stipulated in the 1378 peace treaty.[61] While hoping that Urban would use his influence in support of the Florentine candidate for the Neapolitan throne, the young prince Ladislaus,[62] the republic was not eager to enter into an alliance with the pope.[63] Florence wanted a compliant and distant pontiff, who would give his moral support to her diplomatic objectives, but who would make no demands for help. Urban's weakness was a factor in shaping Florentine policy; a pope without troops or money to defend himself or help his friends had little bargaining power in Italian politics.[64] This indifference to papal sensibilities may also have been animated by vestiges of anticlerical and anticurial sentiment surviving from the papal war, and by the confidence inspired by recent diplomatic successes. A *pratica* in June 1386, upon the conclusion of the Urbino campaign, reflected this mood.[65] The papal legate in Romagna and Umbria was the archbishop of Ravenna, who hoped to obtain Florentine support for the reestablishment of the church's rule in those regions. As an inducement to the republic, he offered to sell Florence the town of Castrocaro on the Forlì road. Speaking for the *pratica*, Giovanni Biliotti urged the Signoria to acquire Castrocaro, which would increase the republic's food reserves and contribute to her security.[66] But the counselors adamantly opposed the establishment of direct papal control over Gubbio or any other town in that region. The republic wanted no revival of the papacy's temporal power to challenge her dominant position in central Italy.

When, in the spring of 1386, Urban established his court in the nearby city of Lucca, Florence sent an embassy there to ask the pontiff not to interfere in the papal dominions, and specifically in the internal

---

[61] See, for example, the discussions in *CP*, 24, ff.119v–123r, 7 Oct. 1385.

[62] The Neapolitan kingdom became a critical issue after the assassination in Hungary of King Charles of Durazzo, whose heir was his infant son Ladislaus. Florence consistently supported Ladislaus' claim to the throne; *CP*, 25, ff.38r–39v, 46v–48v, 63r–64r, 21–22 Feb., 13 March and 28 Apr. 1386.

[63] For the negative reaction to the papal request for an alliance, see *ibid.*, ff.42v–43v, 13 March 1386.

[64] Andrea degli Albizzi opposed a papal alliance, "quia papa est sine pecunia et [nobis] opporteret res expendere"; *ibid.*, f.194r.

[65] *Ibid.*, ff.81r–83r, 18 June 1386.

[66] *Ibid.*, f.83r. Urban VI later refused to sell Castrocaro, which angered some Florentines; *ibid.*, ff.111r–113r, 7–15 Sept. 1386.

affairs of Bologna and Perugia.[67] This embassy had little effect upon Urban, who announced his plan to establish his court in Perugia. This plan was anathema to the republic, whose statesmen correctly perceived that the pope's intervention could only lead to greater disorder, since he did not possess the resources to bring peace to that region. When Urban ignored the appeals of Florentine diplomats to abandon his project and return to Rome, the Signoria sent letters and ambassadors to Perugia, urging that community to withdraw its offer to receive the pope. The arguments were identical to those advanced by Florentine propagandists during the papal war: liberty versus servitude.[68] There were strong indications, too, of a readiness to support those rhetorical appeals with force. When Bologna was threatened (February 1387) by Urban's machinations, several counselors recommended that troops be sent to that city, "whose defense is our own."[69] The most striking feature of these debates was the intense hostility that Urban's policy provoked; he was subjected to sharper criticisms than his predecessor, Gregory XI, had ever received in the 1370s. Alberto degli Albizzi expressed the view that "the pope is the greatest enemy of this community and of the Guelfs of this city; we should do everything possible to expel him from Tuscany."[70] That a member of a notoriously philopapal family should speak so bluntly is an indication of the degree to which Florentine Guelfs had been disillusioned by the titular leader of their cause. The prospect of a reconciliation with Urban temporarily moderated that language, and prompted the articulation of traditional sentiments of filial obedience.[71] But such moments were brief; they were invariably followed by angry criticism of papal duplicity. In a *pratica* held on 24 May 1387,[72] Filippo Corsini, Biagio Guasconi, and Gherardo Buondelmonti conceded that Urban was indeed their enemy, and that Florence must

---

[67] Minerbetti, *anno* 1386, ch. 25. On this general aspect of Florentine policy, see Partner, *Flor. Studies*, 325.

[68] *SCMC*, 20, ff.258r–259r, 2 July 1387, printed in G. degli Azzi Vitelleschi, *Le relazioni tra la Repubblica di Firenze e l'Umbria nel secolo XIV* (Perugia, 1904), I, 680. For discussions of the appropriate appeals to Perugia, see *CP*, 25, ff.189v–191v.

[69] *CP*, 25, ff.178r–178v, 10 Feb. 1387.

[70] *Ibid.*, f.179r, quoted in Herde, "Politische Verhaltensweisen," 188. Herde argues that in the Florentine view Urban VI was as great a threat to the city's liberty as were Giangaleazzo and Ladislaus in later years; *ibid.*, 186, 188.

[71] Examples are instructions to a Florentine embassy, 22 Nov. 1386; Degli Azzi Vitelleschi, *Relazioni*, I, 685; *CP*, 25, ff.143v, 155r–155v, 165r–165v; 26, ff.19r–20v.

[72] *CP*, 26, ff.42r–43r.

defend herself against him. Maffeo di Ser Francesco de' Libri, a man of strong antipapal sentiments, proposed that the republic make a public appeal for a church council to end the schism. Embassies financed by the papal tithe should be sent abroad to promote support for the conciliar idea, and a banner made "with these words, 'Faith and Council,' embroidered in gold letters on a blue background."[73]

Had it been implemented, Maffeo de' Libri's plan would have terminated Florence's allegiance to Urban VI. But the theological and diplomatic implications of this vision were too radical for Maffeo's fellow citizens.[74] The general dissatisfaction with Urban and his policies was so strong that the republic opened diplomatic contacts with the Avignonese pope, Clement VII. In the summer of 1386, Florentine ambassadors, who had been sent to the French court to negotiate a settlement of the Neapolitan question, stopped at Avignon to visit Clement, who received them warmly.[75] A year later, he sent an embassy to Florence with a very attractive offer, described by the Minerbetti chronicler in these terms:

> Pope Clement and his predecessors had not previously recognized the magnificence, the power and the good will of Florence, but they were aware of it now; accordingly, Pope Clement was prepared to do whatever was appropriate to promote the honor, greatness, security and welfare of the Florentine commune. He would gladly grant whatever they asked of him and furthermore, he would always seek to aggrandize and enlarge their dominion and extend their boundaries. . . . He had a great desire to make the Commune of Florence his vicar over those lands in Italy which belonged to Holy Church, because he knew that Florence would hold and govern them in such a way as to earn the praise of their subjects.[76]

[73] *Ibid.*, f.42r: "Quod procuretur sublatio scismatis et fiat vexillum in quo sint littere auree in campo azurro que dicant 'fides et concilium'; et cum bona clericorum, videlicet, decimis et aliis responsionibus, mittantur oratores ad providendum de concilio." Two months later, Maffeo again spoke on this issue: "Quod papa est vir capitosus et inimicus nostri communis . . . et omnes redditus, qui vadunt ad papam, arrestentur donec aliud declaretur. Et teneatur pratica cum papa de Avinione"; *ibid.*, f.64v, 17 July 1387, quoted in Herde, "Politische Verhaltensweisen," 191, n.184.

[74] I cannot agree with Herde's argument, 192, that the issue of obedience had only political (and not religious) implications for the Florentines. How important were the theological and spiritual dimensions of this problem is seen most clearly in the debates over the council in 1407–09; below, ch. v, 295–98.

[75] N. Valois, *La France et le Grande Schisme d'Occident* (Paris, 1896–1902), II, 132–33. I have found no record of this embassy in the Florentine archives.

[76] Minerbetti, *anno* 1387, ch. 33. See Herde, 192–93.

Florentines responded very cautiously to these blandishments. The republic could not assume sole responsibility for determining who was the legitimate pope, so argued the Sixteen; they advised the Signoria to employ legal and theological experts to draft a reply justifying Florence's current policy. They also opposed formal discussions of the embassy's proposals, alleging that this would only exacerbate civic discord.[77] A leading advocate of the Clementine cause, Filippo Corsini, failed to persuade the Signoria to permit the ambassadors to address a civic assembly.[78] After several weeks of delay, the Signoria (January 1388) finally responded to the embassy. Although expressing their gratitude to Clement for his benevolent attitude, they rejected his appeal, stating that they would not switch their allegiance from Urban until it had been determined who was the legitimate head of the church.[79]

The chroniclers reported that the citizenry was divided between Urbanist and Clementine factions, but they do not identify the partisans nor do they discuss their motives. The issue was so troublesome to the Florentines because it touched upon issues of personal salvation and communal honor as well as the mundane problems of political advantage and expediency. The internal divisions did not follow the traditional cleavage between philopapal patricians and populist anticlericals.[80] Alignments were as mixed and confused, politically and socially, as were the motives for keeping or breaking faith with the Roman pope. The Albizzi and the Corsini, who were strong supporters of Pope Gregory in the 1370s, had been committed to Clement VII ever since Cardinal Piero Corsini defected to Avignon in 1380. For the cardinal's brother and nephew, Filippo Corsini and Maso degli Albizzi, the blood tie was probably the decisive factor in their allegiance to Clement,[81] but their associates Biagio Guasconi and Alessandro Alessandri apparently supported their cause for political reasons.[82] The Clement faction was not exclusively aristocratic;

---

[77] CP, 26, ff.150r, 155r, 17 and 27 Dec. 1397.

[78] Panc., 158, ff.154v–155r.

[79] Minerbetti, anno 1387, ch. 33.

[80] See my Florentine Politics and Society, ch. 7.

[81] Filippo Corsini's support for Clement is noted in Panc., 158, f.154v. A letter that Corsini allegedly wrote to Clement VII came into the hands of Urban VI, who complained to the republic. The war balìa insisted that the letter was a forgery, and that Corsini had always recognized Urban as the legitimate pope; DBCMLC, 1, p. 44, 17 July 1387.

[82] For strong statements by these men against Urban, see CP, 26, ff.64r, 68v, 194v. Giovanni de' Ricci and Filippo Pandolfini voiced similar views; ibid., ff.66v–67r.

one of its most articulate spokesmen was Maffeo de' Libri,[83] member of an affluent parvenu family who may have absorbed some of the anticlerical sentiments that had existed in his quarter of Santa Croce a decade earlier. Among those citizens with strong Urbanist leanings were the patrician Giovanni Biliotti, and Bartolomeo Bonaiuti, a representative of that middling class of merchants and professional men to which Maffeo de' Libri belonged.[84] Support for Urban, and for the commune's allegiance to Rome, was probably stronger in the lower orders of society than in aristocratic families. Despite their resentment of Urban's interference in Tuscan affairs, most Florentines continued to regard him as the legitimate head of the church. They could not place any credence in Clement's promise of a vicariate,[85] nor could they see that a shift in allegiance would promote the settlement of the Schism or the peace of Italy. But moral and psychological considerations were as important as these practical ones. Even though it had been made by a regime that had been overthrown, the Florentine pledge of loyalty to Urban was a binding obligation for most citizens. Finally, a decision to support Clement would have been a daring diplomatic gamble, with unforeseeable consequences for the republic, for Italy, and for Catholic Europe.[86] In 1386, Florentines had not yet achieved that degree of psychological security that, twenty years later, would inspire them to seize the initiative to end the Schism.[87]

Urban's arrival in Tuscany terminated Florence's brief moment of hegemony, when her prestige and influence in central Italy were unchallenged. The querulous tone of the debates on relations with the pope was an indication that Florentine statesmen recognized and resented that fact. Urban's presence encouraged the republic's enemies to assert their independence and to reject her leadership. Though not

[83] For information on Maffeo's wealth, see *Pres.*, 333, f.30v; 367, f.22v. He was nominated for the Signoria in the 1382 scrutiny; *Delizie*, XVI, 152, but died sometime before November 1390, when he was selected for that office; *Tratte*, 194, at date.

[84] Biliotti's statement is in *CP*, 26, f.64v: "Quod papa Urbanus est papa et in rebus ecclesiasticis nulla novitas fiat." See also the statements of Bonaiuti, *ibid.*, ff.15v, 59r; and of Arrigo Macinghi: "Quod de scismata nichil fiat quia ipse certus Urbanum esse papam"; *ibid.*, f.163r.

[85] To potential supporters, Clement made generous grants of territory over which he had no control. Earlier he had offered the vicariate of the Papal States to Louis I of Anjou and to the duke of Orleans; Valois, *La France et le Grande Schisme*, I, 167; II, 139.

[86] Donato Acciaiuoli's reaction to a Florentine initiative on the Schism was probably typical: "Quod de scismata non tractetur principaliter; sed si aliquis princeps incipiat, sequatur"; *CP*, 26, f.43v, 24 May 1387.

[87] See below, 295–98.

strong enough to challenge Florence directly, the pope could harass her allies: the *condottiere* Rinaldo Orsini, Count Guido of Montefeltro (now a Florentine client), and the communes of Gubbio and Città di Castello.[88] In response to these provocations, Florentine statesmen could only indulge in angry recriminations. The frustrated republic could not take offensive action against the pope; internal opposition was too strong, the painful memories of 1375–1378 still too fresh.[89] The temper of Florentine diplomacy in 1387 had become distinctly bleaker, like that of the regime's early years. For this changing mood, Urban was only partly responsible. Florentines were also reacting to the wave of troubles engulfing the whole peninsula, the Neapolitan kingdom and Lombardy as well as the central regions. "Because of the disorders which are spreading everywhere today," observed Niccolò Baldovinetti in February 1387, "the commune should take sensible and speedy measures."[90] A major conflict had broken out in eastern Lombardy, where Giangaleazzo Visconti was expanding his territory at the expense of the lords of Verona and Padua. Tuscany and Emilia were witnessing a revival of armed companies: one commanded by Giovanni d'Azzo degli Ubaldini (reputed to be in Giangaleazzo's pay) in the Bolognese *contado*, and three others led by Bernardo della Sala, Averardo della Campana, and Guido d'Asciano on Florence's southern and western frontiers.[91] The depredations of these bands were vivid reminders of the shaky foundations of Florentine hegemony in Tuscany, and of her vulnerability.

Whenever the republic's security was seriously threatened the authorities hired mercenaries, formed alliances, and created a war magistracy. These were the regime's paramount concerns in the winter and spring of 1387–1388, but the leadership encountered exceptional difficulty in implementing them. Provisions to recruit 500 lances and 1000 infantry, and to appoint John Hawkwood as war captain passed the councils by very narrow margins,[92] and the Signoria's plan to establish a war *balìa* was repeatedly rejected. Initially submitted in November 1387, the provision authorizing a *balìa* was not approved by the councils until the following January, and only then after sustained pressure

[88] Minerbetti, *anno* 1387, ch. 43.

[89] The general reluctance to become involved in a military attack on the pope was expressed in a discussion of 21 Oct. 1387; CP, 26, ff.117v–119r. Proposals to suspend payment of all taxes and subsidies owed by the Florentine clergy did win support; CP, 26, ff.163r, 194v, 201r–202v; 15 Jan., 6 and 21 May 1388.

[90] CP, 25, f.177r. In that month, the councils approved the election of a war *balìa*; Prov., 75, ff.222v–226v.

[91] Minerbetti, *anno* 1387, ch. 35, 36.

[92] LF, 43, ff.24v, 25v–26v; Prov., 76, ff.152v–153v, 158r–159v.

that verged on illegal coercion.[93] On the diplomatic front, the government was even less successful in contracting alliances. Counselors repeatedly urged the Signoria to join leagues with other city-states and even with *signori*. In November 1387 Andrea Minerbetti favored a league that would include every major Italian power: the republics of Genoa and Venice, the lords of Milan, Padua, and Verona.[94] However, federations of such broad scope, embracing so many states, had not been very effective in the past; of greater value were the leagues of Tuscan city-states, and particularly the pacts of mutual assistance with Siena, Pisa, and Bologna. But these cities had felt the heaviest pressure from Florence's expansionist thrust in the 1380s, and their enthusiasm for collective action was not great. That relations with her neighbors were in need of repair had long been apparent to the leadership but, except for the occasional embassy bringing messages of fraternity and solicitude, nothing concrete was done to improve her image in Tuscany.[95] Even the republic's most loyal ally, Pietro Gambacorta, the lord of Pisa, could not control a surge of anti-Florentine sentiment in his city.[96] Most crucial, however, was the attitude of the Sienese, whose feelings were still bruised from the Lucignano affair. But the crisis over Montepulciano, which erupted in the summer of 1388, was far more dangerous to Florentine security than the Lucignano episode. Though acutely aware of the need to preserve her friendship with Siena,[97] the republic pursued a policy so rigid and

---

[93] *LF*, 43, ff.21r–26r, 30v–31r. The Panciatichi chronicler described the pressures on the councilors: "Istettono i cholegi in palagio infino alle due ore di notte sanza mangiare o bere insieme chol XLVIII; e nel fine la petizione si vinse fra le minacce e vilanie. Anne grande favelio per la città perchè pare loro vivere quasi a ttirani, per li modi che tiene messer Luigi Guicciardini ghonfaloniere di giustizia"; *Panc.*, 158, f.154v. The authority of the war commission, finally approved in Jan. 1388, was so extensive that "a loro parrà potere inpegniare la città e vendere gli uomini"; *ibid*. The magistracy announced its election "con grandissima balìa"; *DBCMLC*, 1, pp. 46–47.

[94] *CP*, 26, f.137r. See also the statements of Alessandro Alessandri and Gherardo Buondelmonti; *ibid.*, ff.167r, 198v. In Jan. 1388, the war *balìa* announced that it was sending envoys to Ferrara, Padua, Genoa and Venice to promote an alliance; *DBCMLC*, 1, pp. 46–47.

[95] Examples of these contacts are letters to Bologna and Perugia, 2 July and 7 Sept. 1386; *SCMC*, 20 ff.162v–163r, 258r–259r, and an embassy to Siena in Nov. 1386; *Conc.*, 1820, no. 6.

[96] Pisans believed that the companies ravaging their *contado* were in Florentine service; Minerbetti, *anno* 1387, ch. 36. Florence sent an embassy to Pisa in June 1388 to deplore the "disoneste parlanze che si fanno contro alla nostra comunità"; *DBCMLC*, 1, pp. 99, 106–07.

[97] *CP*, 25, ff.133r, 135r; 26, ff.122v–124v, 167v.

insensitive that it impelled the Sienese to surrender their liberty to gain revenge upon Florence.

Initially, the republic had no territorial interest in Montepulciano, a hill town twenty-five miles southwest of Arezzo. To promote the security of this region, the government supported Siena's claim to control the town and its *contado*. Niccolò Malavolti, the ambassador sent by Siena to Florence in June 1388, had conversations with those "friends of Siena" who had encouraged Giacomo Manni two years earlier. They urged the Sienese to act decisively to settle the Montepulciano question, fearing that its prolongation would increase the danger of revolution.[98] Yet, while generally supporting Sienese interests in Montepulciano, Florentine authorities could not resist the temptation to intervene there. The Signoria sent an embassy to Montepulciano, ostensibly to persuade the town to submit to Siena. As a consequence of this diplomatic venture, the Poliziani became more determined to resist the Sienese, who in turn were increasingly suspicious of Florentine motives.[99] Malavolti obviously suspected the republic of duplicity, and his letters are filled with bitter comments about Florentine arrogance. In this as in the Lucignano imbroglio, Florentines were quite insensitive to Sienese fears.[100] Believing firmly in their right to intervene in this area to promote order, they could not understand why their motives might be questioned by others. As late as October 1387, a majority of counselors appeared to favor a settlement that would satisfy the Sienese by giving them control of Montepulciano.[101] Then opinion shifted toward a policy of freedom for the Poliziani. In February 1388, Rinaldo Gianfigliazzi announced his conversion to that position: "We should conserve the devotion of the Poliziani to our commune and keep them from being oppressed by the Sienese."[102] Florence had proposed a settlement by which Montepul-

---

[98] *Conc.*, 1821, no. 18, 24, 29; 26 June, 8 and 10 July 1388. For instructions to the Florentine embassy to Siena, justifying her interference in Montepulciano, see *DBCMLC*, 1, p. 108, 18 June 1388.

[99] The Sienese complained that Florentine subjects were being recruited to fight in Montepulciano territory; *Conc.*, 1821, no. 54, 8 Aug. The Sienese ambassador reported on the Florentine embassy to Montepulciano; *ibid.*, no. 58, 59 and 61; 12–14 Aug. See also *CP*, 26, f.88r.

[100] "Tanto è la loro superbia, la quale pregho Iddio che l'attuti, per modo che rimangano a pari de' loro vicini"; *Conc.*, 1821, no. 57, 10 Aug. See also *ibid.*, no. 63, 17 Aug.

[101] *CP*, 26, ff.122v–124v, 28 Oct. Stoldo Altoviti's comment: "Detur sententia quod commune Montepulciani sit perpetuo cum Senensibus, ne ad guerram veniantur."

[102] *CP*, 26, f.167r, 5 Feb. 1388.

ciano would be placed under Sienese control for a fifty-year period.[103] But the Poliziani rejected this plan, and in May 1388 they organized a demonstration in which Florentine banners were paraded through the streets amidst shouts of "Long live Florence!"[104] Though the Signoria denied any complicity in this affair, the infuriated Sienese were convinced of Florentine treachery, and her determination to annex Montepulciano.[105] For several months thereafter, the problem of Montepulciano was discussed by representatives of both republics, but the breach had widened irreparably. The Lucchese ambassador in Siena described the bitter feelings of the citizenry, "who can recognize the trot of the wolf. . . ." He warned his government to be alert for Florentine treachery: "Everywhere they probe with their heads and their vulpine tails. . . . I beg you to guard your fortresses, because the accursed Judas, full of evil and simony, never sleeps!"[106]

The most significant theme in Florentine diplomacy in the 1380s was the republic's campaign to achieve hegemony, not only in Tuscany, but throughout central Italy, including a substantial part of the Papal States. As Florentine territory expanded, so did her confidence. Her sphere of influence extended as far south as the lands of Rinaldo Orsini and the prefect of Vico near Rome, east to Gubbio and Urbino, and north into the Apennines from La Spezia to Bologna. "You can see that their power is so great in the region that they have no rivals and no superiors," observed an acquaintance of the Sienese diplomat, Niccolò Malavolti.[107] For the Florentines themselves, expansion signified greater security, a more ample food supply, and control of trade routes; for others (so she insisted in the letters drafted by Coluccio Salutati), her authority contributed to peace and order. Yet, though she might have desired more stable conditions in central Italy, she was not strong enough to enforce a general peace. Indeed, her policy of subsidizing clients like Rinaldo Orsini and the Gabrielli of Gubbio contributed to the anarchic conditions that prevailed in large parts of the Papal States and in Tuscan lands adjacent to papal territory. In these

---

[103] Florentine Signoria to Siena; *SCMC*, 21, ff.20r–20v, 31 March 1388.

[104] See the account of this demonstration in Minerbetti, *anno* 1388, ch. 9; and also in *SCMC*, 21, ff.28r, 44v, 29 May and 11 Aug.

[105] For the Sienese reaction, see Fumi, *Regesti*, II, part 2, 256–60. Florence sent a contingent of lances to Montepulciano to protect the town from the Sienese; Minerbetti, *anno* 1388, ch. 9. Florence was less than candid with the Sienese about her policy. While insisting, in a letter to Siena, that she was seeking to persuade the Poliziani to accept Sienese rule, she was concurrently urging them "mantenere loro stato e loro libertà bene e francamente"; *DBCMLC*, 1, pp. 107, 123, 18 June and 31 July 1388.

[106] Fumi, *Regesti*, II, part 2, 260.   [107] *Conc.*, 1821, no. 59, 13 Aug. 1387.

regions on her frontier the republic sought recognition as the superior power: the arbiter of disputes, the protector of friends, the employer of mercenaries.[108] Her greed for territory and her arrogance alienated many former friends and allies in Tuscany, but her power was unchallenged and her tactics appeared to be successful. "The pope has no strength, and the emperor is too weak to intervene," Niccolò Malavolti's confidant concluded, "and the count of Virtù is colder than marble, so that one cannot expect anything from him." Giangaleazzo was to prove him wrong.

This aggressive foreign policy never gained the complete approval of the Florentine citizenry. A minority stubbornly opposed territorial expansion and voted against the measures designed to implement it. Their spokesmen in the *pratiche* cited the dangers of arousing local animosities, and the expenses incurred if war broke out. Montepulciano was a case in point; so was the republic's policy in the Papal States in the winter and spring of 1387–1388 when her relations with Urban VI were strained. In April 1388, Alessandro Alessandri urged the Signoria to move forcefully against the pope "so that Perugia will not be ruled by a *signore*."[109] This proposal was too extreme for most of Alessandri's colleagues. One speaker noted that the Perugini had invited Urban to reside there; others recommended that aid be sent to that city only if it were requested. Simone Bordoni was more fundamentally opposed to Alessandri's suggestion: "Without engaging in any military action, we should use words to persuade the Perugini to preserve their liberty; and we should never participate in an unjust war. . . ."[110] Summarizing the opinions of a subsequent *pratica*, Biagio Guasconi counseled the Signoria to avoid any hostile action, either open or secret, against the pope.[111] Simone Bordoni reiterated this viewpoint a month later, in a discussion of the Montepulciano crisis: "War is extremely perilous, and since it appears that the citizens are opposed, we should not launch [a campaign against Siena] unless civic opinion strongly favors it."[112]

The debate over expansion was the most important, but not the only, issue to stimulate controversy within the *reggimento*. The Florentine

[108] P. Partner, *Flor. Studies*, 385–86.

[109] *CP*, 26, f.184v, 3 April. Several months earlier, Alessandri had advocated a Florentine alliance with the lords of the Marches in papal territory, an enterprise which would have extended her zone of influence some 150 miles southeast of Florence; *ibid.*, f.117v, 21 Oct. 1387.

[110] *Ibid.*, ff.184v–185r. [111] *Ibid.*, f.187r, 6 April.

[112] "Impresa est maximi periculi, et attento quod cives non videntur contentari de impresa, nullo modo imprendatur nisi forte alias concorditer consulatur"; *ibid.*, f.208r, 27 May.

electorate was confronted with a series of complex diplomatic issues in these years, from the delicate matter of the Schism to the question of intervention in Sienese internal politics. Opinions were solicited from a broad spectrum of the community: from artisans and merchants, physicians and notaries, as well as prominent statesmen like Filippo Corsini and Biagio Guasconi who devoted much of their time to politics. And since the inner core of leadership had not yet crystallized around Maso degli Albizzi and his associates, the debates were not monopolized, as they were later, by a select group of experts who spoke in every *pratica*. While a trend was developing toward a smaller, more exclusive cadre of consultants, these deliberations still brought together citizens of diverse viewpoints. Among the fifteen men, predominantly aristocrats, who spoke in a *pratica* on 25 November 1388 were the silk merchant Simone Vespucci, the physician Maestro Tommasino di Maestro Simone, the notary Ser Niccolò Pierozzi, and the artisan Domenico Bartolini.[113]

The *pratiche* demonstrate that foreign policy was controversial in these years, but the alignments are not clearly defined. The reports of Sienese diplomats contain hints of a popular position that conflicted with the views of the leadership. This division, however, was not permanent but sporadic, emerging into public view only when the feelings of the *popolo* were engaged by a particular issue. Popular opinion disapproved of the regime's decision (1385) to subvert the artisan regime in Siena and replace it with a government dominated by aristocrats.[114] The *popolo* gained its revenge when it thwarted efforts of the leadership to negotiate a settlement with the Sienese government. The divisions within the inner circle of the *reggimento* were more significant than these intermittent conflicts between regime and populace. Some of these partisan quarrels were tinged with ideology; others had pragmatic origins. The controversy over King Charles of Durazzo in 1385 and 1386 rekindled the feuds of 1378–1382 between *arciguelfi* and those whom they denounced as Ghibellines.[115] Some disagreements over territorial expansion pitted Guelf imperialists against citizens who had belonged to the Alberti party and who advocated a low profile in foreign affairs.[116] In one of his despatches (August

[113] *CP*, 27, ff.56r–57r. For the identity of these men, see *Delizie*, XVI, 145, 151, 183, 243.

[114] Giacomo Manni commented on the hostility of the populace against Siena which he encountered on his first embassy to Florence in May 1385; *Conc.*, 1816, no. 27.

[115] See above, ch. II, 76–77.

[116] Among the former were Alessandro Alessandri, Simone Peruzzi, and Rinaldo Gianfigliazzi; among the latter, Filippo Bastari, Tommaso Guidetti, Benedetto

1387), the Sienese ambassador Niccolò Malavolti attempted to describe the range of opinion that he had encountered in his conversations with Florentines of every social rank.[117] One group was friendly to Siena; a second sought partisan advantage by straining relations between the two communities; a third category was composed of patriots who complained of Sienese affronts to Florentine honor. Malavolti's model—realists, partisans, and xenophobes—is too neat, but he did identify some of the categories that formed the Florentine political community.

THE FIRST VISCONTI WAR

The events culminating in the outbreak of hostilities between Florence and Giangaleazzo Visconti are reported in exceptionally full detail in the sources.[118] The story is complex: the participants were numerous, and their interests and objectives were neither clearly defined nor always pursued rationally. When the Visconti challenge to Florence's preeminence in central Italy first became apparent in 1388, the republic was diplomatically, if not militarily, vulnerable. Her aggressive foreign policy had so alienated her neighbors in central Italy that she was virtually without allies.[119] The widening of her sphere of influence had greatly enlarged the area of her responsibility and her network of *raccomandati*, who could now demand her support if they were threatened by a neighbor who in turn might be a client of Giangaleazzo.[120] A congenital inability to define clearly her needs and priorities also contributed to her difficulties; to decide, for example, the importance for her security of the Romagna alliances,[121] or

---

Alberti, Simone Capponi, and most of the lower guildsmen who expressed their views on these issues.

[117] "Et in efetto parlato e chon grandi e chon mezani e chon piccioli, io ci trovo tre gienerazioni di giente d'ogni ragione"; *Conc.*, 1821, no. 59, 13 Aug. 1387.

[118] The most detailed and objective account is D. Bueno de Mesquita, *Giangaleazzo Visconti, Duke of Milan (1352-1402)* (Cambridge, 1941), ch. 8 and 9. Mesquita has explored Florentine and Sienese archival sources, as well as Milanese records, and has also utilized the important articles, with their published documents, by G. Collino and A. Mancarella cited in his bibliography, 380-81, 384. See also the more recent interpretation of these events by Hans Baron, *Crisis*, 2nd ed., 14-40, *Storia di Milano*, v (Milan, 1955), 520-67; and P. Herde, "Politische Verhaltensweisen," 195-249.

[119] Mesquita, *Giangaleazzo*, 91-92.

[120] An example was Count Guido of Montfeltro, lord of Urbino, who had been a client of Giangaleazzo as early as 1384 and who was also, after 1386, a *raccomandato* of Florence; Mesquita, 30, 88, 94.

[121] Mesquita, *Giangaleazzo*, 88-89, 93.

whether Siena's friendship was worth sacrificing for the possession of Montepulciano. Giangaleazzo's policy toward Florence and Tuscany was equally ambiguous. Uncertain of the other's motives and of their own interests, each power vacillated and temporized, exchanged cordial messages while indulging in private complaints and recriminations, until finally both were trapped into war by their fears and commitments.

Florence had not been at war with Milan since 1370. For twenty years the two states had lived together in amity and had occasionally cooperated to achieve common objectives.[122] Florentines of this generation were not haunted, as their fathers had been, by the specter of the Visconti as the ancient Ghibelline foe of Tuscan Guelfs. The republic's relations with Giangaleazzo Visconti were particularly cordial. The Signoria sent an embassy to congratulate the prince on the capture and imprisonment of his uncle Bernabò in May 1385, which gave him possession of Milan. Civic opinion generally favored the despatch of a military contingent to support Giangaleazzo's efforts to gain control over his Lombard state.[123] By large majorities, the legislative councils passed two provisions authorizing and then ratifying a five-year pact of friendship with the Count of Virtù, as he was known to his contemporaries.[124] There may have been some instinctive distrust of this Visconti prince in Florentine minds, but it was not expressed publicly.[125] Indeed, Florentine diplomats regarded Giangaleazzo as a stabilizing force in Italian politics, a ruler who was preoccupied with consolidating his authority in his dominion and who displayed no thirst for territorial aggrandizement. Not until the spring of 1388 do the first notes of disquiet appear in the sources.[126]

---

[122] See Brucker, *Florentine Politics and Society*, 141–42, 239–40, 294–95, 353, 355.

[123] The first reaction of the colleges to the *coup* (12 May) was reserved; *CP*, 24, ff.63v–64r; but opinion then became more positive; *ibid.*, ff.66r–67r, 23 May. On 10 May, Giacomo Manni reported from Florence that there was rejoicing in the city "perchè l'opera sia optima novella per tutta Ytalia e maxime per questa città e tutta Toscana"; *Conc.*, 1816, no. 28.

[124] *Prov.*, 74, ff.82r–82v, 138r–138v; 5–6 July, 23–24 Sept. 1385. While 78 councilors opposed the enabling provision, only 16 voted against ratification of the pact. On this league, see Mesquita, *Giangaleazzo*, 85.

[125] Mesquita, 34, quotes a statement of the chronicler Giovanni Morelli that wise men in Florence were skeptical of Giangaleazzo, but there is no trace of this sentiment in the official records.

[126] See the discussions concerning a Milanese alliance; *CP*, 25, ff.85v–86r, 172v–173v; *LF*, 42, f.96v. Authority was granted to the Signoria and the colleges to negotiate a defensive alliance; *Prov.*, 75, ff.81r–82r (17–18 July 1386). For an example of the Florentine posture toward Giangaleazzo, see *DBCMLC*, 1, pp. 25–27, 28 March 1386. Herde cites a statement by Biagio Gusconi in Oct. 1387,

Two developments in that year kindled the republic's suspicions of Giangaleazzo: his campaign against the *signori* of Verona and Padua and the annexation of their territories in eastern Lombardy, and his negotiations with Siena for an alliance that would involve him directly in Tuscan politics. Florentines were uncertain about his objectives, but many would have agreed with Donato Acciaiuoli's evaluation of him as "a *signore* with an appetite for conquest."[127] Yet, though convinced of his hostility and aware of his reputation for deception, they could not agree upon the appropriate response to his maneuvers.[128] Opinions in the *pratiche* during the summer and autumn of 1388 fluctuated sharply from provocative and hostile to temperate and conciliatory. Not since 1382 had Florentine statesmen been so unsure of themselves, nor the regime's policy so ambivalent. A mood of vulnerability pervaded the meetings convened by successive priorates to give them advice in these anxious months. They were told to hire troops and strengthen defensive positions, to levy forced loans to pay for military expenditure, to strengthen ties with allies and search for new sources of diplomatic support. While a few counselors favored the ambitious proposals of Filippo Corsini for an alliance with the duke of Savoy and the recruitment of troops in French territory,[129] the majority believed that the commune's salvation lay in her own resources and in the help that she might commandeer from her neighbors. The possibility of Siena's defection weighed most heavily upon Florentine spirits, for both material and psychological reasons. It would deprive her of military aid, and it would destroy the illusion that Florence could rely upon the support of all Tuscan republics in a struggle with the Milanese ruler.

Florentines reacted with shock and dismay to the initial reports of Siena's overtures to Giangaleazzo. Counselors urged the Signoria to exert pressure upon the Sienese to terminate their negotiations with the lord of Milan, and to join Florence and the other free republics of central Italy in a federation to defend their liberties.[130] But none were

---

as reflecting the first hint of anxiety concerning the lord of Milan; "Politische Verhaltensweisen," 196, n.217.

[127] *CP*, 26, f.211r.

[128] See the statements of Lotto Castellani and Forese Salviati; *ibid.*, ff.224v, 229v. Herde stresses Florentine anxiety over Urban VI in these months; 202–08.

[129] *CP*, 26, f.229v.

[130] See the statement of Filippo Corsini; *CP*, 26, f.220r, 1 July; printed in G. Collino, "La preparazione della guerra veneto-viscontea contro i Carraresi nelle relazioni fiorentino-bolognesi col conte di Virtù"; *Archivio storico lombardo*, XXXIV (1907), 287.

willing to placate the Sienese by recognizing the legitimacy of their grievances, though some did suggest that the disputed issues be submitted to arbitration.[131] If diplomacy failed, then other measures would be necessary, but there was no agreement on the appropriate response. Citizens favoring a policy of restraint proposed that castles on the Sienese frontier be fortified, but Guccio de' Nobili called for war: "Send an army against the Sienese and destroy that regime."[132] In the *pratica* of 4 July, such belligerent statements were common; the republic appeared to be on the verge of launching an invasion of Sienese territory.[133] But this aggressive mood evaporated as diplomatic negotiations continued. By the end of July, the proponents of a diplomatic solution of the Sienese crisis had triumphed over the militants.[134] However, the prospects for a settlement were no greater than before; the territorial disputes over Lucignano and Montepulciano were now overshadowed by the more fundamental issue of Sienese sovereignty.[135]

A limited war against Siena might be rationalized on strategic grounds; it could be won, and Siena's independence was essential for Florence's security. But neither of these arguments could be used to justify a military confrontation with Milan. In this initial stage of their long struggle with Giangaleazzo, Florentines were already experiencing the frustrations of contending with a shrewd opponent who could exploit their weaknesses without revealing his own. While a few angry citizens called for war, majority opinion favored a more cautious posture. Conceding that Giangaleazzo could not be trusted, Filippo Corsini nevertheless opposed an open declaration of war, preferring instead to resist him secretly. Gucciozzo de' Ricci believed that the republic would eventually have to fight, but he questioned the advisability of an immediate confrontation. Guccio de' Nobili spoke for that minority which favored decisive action. The Signoria should demand that Giangaleazzo cease his attack upon Florence's old friend, the lord of Padua and, failing in that tactic, should then order John Hawkwood to invade Milanese territory.[136] But war with Milan

---

[131] Niccolò Gherardini Giani and Giorgio Gucci; CP, 26, ff.220v, 221v.

[132] *Ibid.*, f.229v.

[133] Also favoring a militant policy were Donato Acciaiuoli, Gino Anselmi, Alessandro Alessandri, and Luigi da Quarata; *ibid.*, ff.229r-231r.

[134] The subsidence of war sentiment is apparent from the deliberations; *ibid.*, ff.232r-233r; CP, 27, ff.5r-5v, 6v-7r, 7v-8r, 9r-14r, 16v-17v.

[135] The Sienese were to promise that they would never submit to any lord: "Et promissio de non summittendo se alicui domino, non solum fiat pro V annis, sed pro imperpetuum"; CP, 27, f.16v.

[136] For the views of Corsini, Ricci and Nobili, see CP, 27, ff.9r, 10r-10v.

was a perilous enterprise for a state with only one dependable ally, the commune of Bologna. Without any legal basis for intervening in the war between Milan and Padua, Florence could only appeal to Giangaleazzo to desist, and threaten to denounce him "to all of the rulers of the world,"[137] if he ignored their appeal. But Giangaleazzo had already obtained approval for his campaign from the only power that could effectively resist him, the republic of Venice.[138] Isolated diplomatically and lacking the military strength to thwart him, the republic could only complain about his aggression.

After the threat of war subsided, the republic failed to take any concrete action to improve her diplomatic and military situation. The extent of the regime's paralysis was demonstrated in October by a bitter controversy over the election of a new war magistracy. The provision authorizing the balìa encountered strong opposition in one executive council and in the Council of the Popolo before it finally won approval.[139] Members of the pratica convened by an embarrassed Signoria to discuss the question counseled against employing illegal tactics to gain the necessary votes, and implied that the measure's opponents were ignorant men who should not be taken seriously.[140] The issue was not the need for a balìa, but rather the qualifications of the citizens who had been selected as members.[141] But the quarrel was a manifestation of the persistent divisions over foreign policy that have left other traces in the sources. In November, a debate over Montepulciano revealed two clearly defined positions, one favoring an accommodation with Siena and the abandonment of the Poliziani, while the other advocated the occupation of Montepulciano by Florentine troops, and even argued that the republic had legitimate claims to the territory.[142] Opinions had hardened and, as in the Lucignano episode three years before, the prejudices of the populace were being exploited by the imperialists. Simone Bordoni called for a popular refer-

---

[137] "Commune de hoc condolebit cum omnibus principibus mundi"; ibid., f.31v. Filippo Bastari, ibid., f.32r, defined the Florentine interest in Padua: "Dicatur comiti quod non miretur si commune se interponit pro pace domini Paduani quia commune dedit sibi statum."

[138] Mesquita, Giangaleazzo, 107, 117.

[139] Prov., 77, ff.156v–157v. The vote: 156–77 and 108–49. Donato Acciaiuoli and Lotto Castellani were the most prominent members of that commission.

[140] CP, 27, ff.38r–39v, 11 Oct. 1388. Several speakers referred to ille oblocuturus who had criticized the provision, but they did not wish to punish him.

[141] Minerbetti, anno 1388, ch. 20.

[142] CP, 27, ff.44v–46r. Gagliardo Bonciani, Lodovico di Banco di Ser Bartolo, Cristofano Spini, Andrea Minerbetti, and Simone Capponi favored accommodation with Siena; those desiring to acquire Montepulciano included Donato di Jacopo Strada, Giovanni de' Ricci, Luigi Canigiani, and Simone Bordoni.

endum on Montepulciano, "and if the *popolo* with their votes decide that the castle [Montepulciano] should be annexed, then let it be done."[143]

But these disagreements were tangential to the more fundamental controversy over the appropriate response to Giangaleazzo's challenge. "We are in grave danger from the count's power, but there is a greater peril in going to war"; thus Filippo Corsini defined the republic's dilemma.[144] While some of Corsini's colleagues in that *pratica*—Alessandro Arrigucci, Filippo Bastari, Franco Sacchetti—hoped that a cogent presentation of the commune's benevolent attitude would placate Giangaleazzo, others were less sanguine about the prospects for peace. Luigi Guicciardini was most eager for a confrontation; he recommended a break in diplomatic contacts and the launching of a military offensive.[145] But Biagio Guasconi stressed the danger of declaring war "without just cause, for it would displease God and men, and also our citizens."[146] In November the most immediate problem was the fate of Padua: should Florence send John Hawkwood into Lombardy to help the beleaguered Francesco da Carrara? Rinaldo Gianfigliazzi favored that scheme, although he hoped that Florence would be supported by Bologna and her Tuscan allies. Arguing most eloquently for war was the notary Ser Biagio Bernabucci: "A gangrenous wound must be cut away lest the healthy part be infected; whoever wants to be powerful should join the strong, and tyrants who are feared by everyone are not as powerful as they appear."[147] But this was a minority view resisted by cautious men like Franco Sacchetti, who opposed the despatch of any assistance to the Carrara, claiming that it would antagonize Giangaleazzo, the lord of Ferrara, and the Venetian republic. Biagio Guasconi was fearful that intervention would endanger the merchants trading in Lombardy and Venice; Pazzino Strozzi and Giovanni Baroncelli felt that Florence was too weak to furnish effective aid to Francesco da Carrara.[148] After Padua had fallen to his army, Giangaleazzo sent another embassy to

---

[143] *Ibid.*, f.45r. Bordoni was calling not for an assembly of the whole citizenry in the piazza (*parlamentum*) which made decisions by acclamation and not by votes, but rather for a very large assembly of citizens in the palace, "et deliberatio fiat ad fabas."

[144] *CP*, 27, f.31r, 17 Sept., in Collino, *Arch. stor. lombardo*, xxxiv, 57.

[145] *CP*, 27, f.32v.   [146] *Ibid.*, f.47r, 21 Nov.

[147] *CP*, 27, f.50r, 23 Nov., in Collino, 340.

[148] These statements are in *CP*, 27, ff.51v, 53r, 53v. Speaking in favor of aid to Padua were Rinaldo Gianfigliazzi, Ugo Vecchietti, and Benedetto Peruzzi, who called for the revival of a Guelf federation "cum antiquis amicis dominis et regalibus"; *ibid.*, f.53v.

Florence (December 1388) to renew his invitation for a non-aggression pact.[149] Filippo Corsini presented the most pessimistic analysis of Florence's situation: "Peace is dangerous, for he [Giangaleazzo] has a standing army of 2000 lances and the keys to Germany. If he can gain a brief respite and make an agreement with France, we are lost."[150] Either Corsini's forebodings were not shared by his colleagues, or they suppressed their fears. Rejecting war in favor of negotiation, they urged the Signoria to consider again the proposal for a league, to include as many states as possible, so that "all Italians will form a single body."[151]

After six months of inconclusive debate, the republic decided in the spring of 1389 to seek a peaceful settlement with Giangaleazzo and a reconciliation with Siena. Some Florentines, perhaps the majority, genuinely believed that an accommodation could be achieved; others, more skeptical and suspicious, nevertheless supported diplomatic exchanges with Giangaleazzo, to gain time for the conflict that (they thought) was imminent. The most striking manifestation of this conciliatory mood was a speech by Alessandro Alessandri, who proposed (March 1389) that a provision be enacted declaring that the commune would not annex any territory for a period of forty or fifty years.[152] This remarkable statement by an ardent imperialist was a tacit admission that Florence's territorial ambitions were largely responsible for her present difficulties. The government was urged to placate the Sienese by exerting pressure upon the Poliziani to accept the overlordship of the Sienese republic.[153] In response to Giangaleazzo's invitation, the war *balìa* sent two ambassadors, Luigi Guicciardini and Giovanni de' Ricci, to Pavia to discuss a formal alliance. Florence's price for a federation was Giangaleazzo's written promise that he would not intervene in Tuscany and Romagna, and on this issue negotiations foundered.[154] On 4 March, opinions voiced in a *pratica* were uniformly conciliatory, and also optimistic about the prospects

[149] For the proposal of Bevilacqua, the Visconti ambassador, see Collino, 374–75. The discussion on this proposal is in *CP*, 27, ff.60r–66r; and partially published in Collino, 376–80.

[150] *CP*, 27, f.60r.

[151] The statement of Andrea Benini, *ibid.*, f.65r. Similar arguments were made by Giovanni de' Ricci, Alessandro Arrigucci, Gino Anselmi, and Guido del Palagio; *ibid.*, ff.60v, 61r, 64v, 65r.

[152] *CP*, 27, f.83v.

[153] See the opinions of Biagio Guasconi and Filippo Corsini, *ibid.*, f.101r, 26 March. In return for Montepulciano, Siena would be required to join a league with Florence.

[154] Mesquita, *Giangaleazzo*, 100–02.

for a settlement.[155] Then news arrived of a provisional agreement, already publicized by Giangaleazzo, that did not include his pledge to abstain from intervention in Tuscan affairs. The Florentine reaction was predictably angry. Two new ambassadors were sent to Pavia to replace Ricci and Guicciardini, and to reject the settlement.[156] For those who had long believed in the inevitability of war, the moment seemed propitious for a formal break in relations as a prelude to open hostilities. Filippo Corsini and Alessandro Alessandri urged the Signoria to publicize the evidence of Giangaleazzo's duplicity, to prepare the citizenry for war.[157] But they were not able to persuade the majority that conflict was inevitable, and negotiations continued in an atmosphere of rising tension.

Florentines who were involved in these deliberations were very conscious of their two audiences, one domestic and the other foreign. The decision to prolong negotiations with Giangaleazzo was strongly influenced by the need to persuade those two constituencies of the republic's good faith and her sincere desire for peace. With increasing frequency, counselors called upon the Signoria to publicize the details of Giangaleazzo's proposals for a settlement, to assemble large numbers of citizens to learn the truth about his deceptions. The populace had to be persuaded that the government's position was just so that it would make the necessary sacrifices for defense, and would unite behind its leaders in the event of war.[158] The importance of Italian opinion was also generally recognized in Florence (as in Pavia), though the weight of that opinion was assessed differently. Those who favored a diplomatic settlement with Giangaleazzo even with unsatisfactory terms placed the greatest value upon preserving the friendship of Florence's neighbors, particularly the Pisans and the Sienese. If the republic joined a league with Giangaleazzo, they argued, she would ingratiate herself with her neighbors who were so desirous of peace, and she would place herself in a strong position, legally and morally, if he should violate the pact. If he broke the agreement, "then we would have the support of God and of our neighbors, and before all of the rulers of the world, our cause would be just."[159] These argu-

---

[155] CP, 27, ff.83v–86r.   [156] Mesquita, 102–03.

[157] The statements of Alessandri, Corsini and Simone Bordoni; CP, 27, ff.94v–96r. Arguing most strongly for further negotiations was Filippo Bastari, ibid., f.95v.

[158] See the statements of Alessandro Alessandri, Simone Bordoni, Andrea Vettori and Francesco Ardinghelli; CP, 27, ff.94v–95r (23 March); and Niccolò Gherardini Giani, f.136r (9 July).

[159] This statement is contained in an undated memorandum (July or August 1389) which listed twelve arguments for, and thirteen against, a league with Giangaleazzo, ibid., ff.1r–4r. Though roughly formulated, this represents the beginnings of an analytical approach to decision-making.

ments were advanced by proponents of negotiations in an important *pratica* held on 3 July,[160] but they were rebutted by a minority that vehemently opposed further communication with him. Alessandro Alessandri argued in favor of a law that would condemn to death anyone advocating a league with Giangaleazzo; Andrea Minerbetti spoke of the superior wisdom of ancestors "who never wished to have anything to do with the Visconti." The perils of a settlement far outweighed any benefits that might accrue to Florence. Filippo Corsini stated the case succinctly: "The count enters this league to deceive us, and from it he will emerge as the greatest power in Italy; his enemies and those who are under his domination will lose hope."[161] Corsini was already looking to the future when Florence would be searching for allies among Giangaleazzo's frightened neighbors and his subjects, in their efforts to thwart his imperialist designs.

In the *pratica* of 3 July an eminent statesman, Guido del Palagio, announced his support for a league with Giangaleazzo, stipulating that it should be limited to three years. If he observed the agreement, Guido concluded, then all would be well; if not, "then God, justice, our citizens and neighbors will be united against him."[162] This counsel was accepted by the Signoria and the war *balìa*, although the agreement was not formally concluded and signed until three months later (9 October).[163] Though Guido's great prestige may have contributed to the adoption of his scheme, he was articulating the sentiments of many citizens who still hoped for a peaceful solution to the crisis.[164] For those who opposed the league, Guido's plan had one virtue: it would gain time for the republic to prepare for hostilities. While Florentine diplomats in Pisa were bargaining with their counterparts from Pavia, Siena, Perugia, and Lucca, other emissaries were sent by the war magistracy to Venice and Bavaria in search of support against Giangaleazzo.[165]

The key to the crisis was Siena. As long as that republic remained

---

[160] See the arguments of Alessandro Arrigucci, Filippo Bastari and Forese Salviati, *ibid.*, ff.133r–133v.

[161] *Ibid.*, ff.127v, 133r, 133v.

[162] "Pro unione vicinorum, fiat liga cum comite, limitando capitula; et fiat pro III annis ad plus; et si acquiretur tempus, et si observat ligam, bene erit; alia autem Deus iusticia et totus populus erit unitus contra eum et vicini"; *CP*, 27, f.133v.

[163] Mesquita, *Giangaleazzo*, 109–10. Guido del Palagio was one of three ambassadors sent to Pisa to negotiate an agreement; P. Silva, "Il governo di Pietro Gambacorta in Pisa," *Annali della R. scuola normale superiore di Pisa*, XXIII (1912), 327.

[164] An example of mercantile opinion was Domenico di Cambio's letter to Francesco Datini, 26 August: "Qui s'avisa che noi areno pacie, e chosì piacia a Dio che sia"; *Datini*, 1092, unpaginated.

[165] Mesquita, *Giangaleazzo*, 107.

hostile, she represented the greatest threat to Florentine security, as the instrument of Giangaleazzo's penetration into Tuscany. After their first overture to the count in June 1388, the Sienese apparently remained steadfast in their determination to surrender their liberty to him, though their precise intentions are not stated in the documents. Giangaleazzo seems to have been the more cautious partner, unwilling to commit himself to accepting the lordship of their republic.[166] Still hoping for a reconciliation with Siena, in May the Florentine government had agreed to withdraw its troops from Montepulciano,[167] but a delay in implementing that commitment intensified Sienese suspicions that these promises were worthless. The Florentines, on the other hand, complained that Siena had broken her agreement to form an alliance. The ambassador reported that some of the "good citizens" still spoke favorably of Siena, but most were persuaded that the Sienese had no intention of entering a league with Florence.[168] To make matters worse, the troops of John Hawkwood, who was in Florentine service, were pillaging farms and villages in the Sienese *contado*. In response to their appeal for help, Giangaleazzo sent a contingent of 200 lances to Siena to protect the city.[169]

When reports of Visconti troops in Siena reached Florence, they stimulated another surge of war fever. The council halls resounded with demands for offensive action against Giangaleazzo which, for the moment, were successfully resisted by men of more cautious temperament.[170] The efforts of the diplomats at Pisa nearly foundered as a consequence of the Sienese developments.[171] So convinced were some citizens of Siena's capitulation to the Visconti that in a *pratica* held on 3 September, they urged the Signoria to occupy Montepulciano.[172] Among the counselors who supported this action were two artisans, the farrier Nino di Andrea and the blacksmith Niccolò di Chiaro. Simone Bordoni conceded that this would be tantamount to a declaration of war, and he called for an invasion of Sienese territory. Two

---

[166] *Ibid.*, 108–09, 341–42.

[167] *Conc.*, 1825, no. 63. Though Minerbetti, *anno* 1389, ch. 3, stated that the troops were withdrawn, he may have been mistaken.

[168] *Conc.*, 1825, no. 63 and 65.

[169] Minerbetti, *anno* 1389, ch. 9; Mesquita, *Giangaleazzo*, 106. For Sienese fears of a Florentine invasion, see the letter of the Sienese ambassador in Pisa, 22 August; *Conc.*, 1826, no. 17.

[170] Among those advocating war were Alessandro Alessandri, Guccio de' Nobili, and Rinieri Peruzzi; *CP*, 27, ff.143v–144v, 23 July.

[171] In a session of 30 August, Alessandro Alessandri and Matteo Tinghi argued for breaking off negotiations in Pisa; *ibid.*, ff.158v–159v.

[172] *Ibid.*, ff.163v–164r.

lawyers, Giovanni de' Ricci and Tommaso Marchi argued that the annexation of Montepulciano would induce the Sienese to opt for peace. Had the Florentines known of the agreement, signed on 22 September, by which Giangaleazzo accepted the lordship of Siena,[173] they would surely have declared war. But this secret was well kept, though rumors of the pact were circulating in Florence in November.[174]

Six months elapsed after the signing of the peace agreement at Pisa before hostilities began in April 1390.[175] The delay was partly tactical, as each side maneuvered to gain allies and to build up reserves of money and troops.[176] Initially, Florence may have enjoyed a military advantage over Giangaleazzo. The republic had the services of John Hawkwood, the most competent and trustworthy captain in the peninsula, and she had not been involved in a major war since 1378. Giangaleazzo, on the other hand, had been fighting in eastern Lombardy since 1387, and his subjects were hard pressed to support his military enterprises. But in the realm of diplomacy, the republic was less successful than her Lombard rival. In addition to Siena's allegiance, Giangaleazzo had strong support in Lucca and Perugia, and also in Pisa, where the authority of Florence's staunch ally, Pietro Gambacorta, was declining perceptibly. "We can place little faith in the unity of our neighbors," Tommaso Marchi observed, "for they are so committed to the count that they neither can nor will assist us."[177] The republic's diplomatic forays outside of Tuscany were equally fruitless. Venice and Genoa remained neutral, and the newly elected Roman pope, Boniface IX, was too weak and distracted by local problems to offer more than mediation.[178] Negotiations for an alliance with Stephen of Bavaria dragged on inconclusively,[179] while Florence's ef-

---

[173] Mesquita, *Giangaleazzo*, 109.

[174] The statement of Filippo Bastari: "Comune se certificet de intentione comitis Virtutum et de conventionibus et liga quam dicitur habere cum comuni Senarum"; *CP*, 28, f.3v, 10 Nov.

[175] The diplomatic events of this period are well described by Mesquita, *Giangaleazzo*, 110–20; see also Herde, "Politische Verhaltensweisen," 208–10.

[176] See the discussions concerning military preparations; *CP*, 28, ff.33r–34r, 41v–42v, 18 Jan. and 25 Feb. 1390.

[177] *Ibid.*, f.19v, 9 Dec. 1389, quoted in Herde, 210, n.306.

[178] The fundamental work on Boniface's pontificate is now A. Esch, *Bonifaz IX. und die Kirchenstaat* (Tübingen, 1969); see ch. 2.

[179] The alliance was signed in April 1390; Mesquita, 119. Stephen received 78,915 fl. but gave no military assistance to his ally; *ASF, Camera, Uscita,* 295, part 1, payments of 2 May, 8 July, 10 Sept. and 13 Oct. On Florentine negotiations with the German emperor Wenceslaus, see Herde, "Politische Verhaltensweisen," 213–14.

forts to enlist the aid of the French crown were effectively thwarted by Milanese agents at the Valois court. Florence's only dependable ally was Bologna, whose communal regime had recently uncovered a plot linked to Giangaleazzo, and whose citizens felt as threatened by Visconti power as did the Florentines.

The military and diplomatic aspects of the war (April 1390–January 1392) can be summarized as a struggle in which both protagonists failed to gain a decisive advantage.[180] Giangaleazzo's forces moved first, launching an attack against Bologna, but they were not able to subdue that key city. The count had to deploy his forces in eastern Lombardy, where an invading army led by the exiled Carrara had reconquered Padua and temporarily occupied Verona. The balance then swung in Florence's favor and in the spring of 1391 she and her allies planned a double assault upon Milan by John Hawkwood, attacking from the southeast, and by a French army under Count Jean of Armagnac, moving toward Milan from the west. Had these two armies been able to synchronize their movements, they might have achieved a decisive victory. But Hawkwood was forced to retreat from Milan's environs, and Armagnac's army suffered a crushing defeat near Alessandria (July 1391).[181] For a brief moment, the initiative passed again to Giangaleazzo, when his army moved south into Tuscany to test Florence's defenses. So grave was this threat to the city's security that some counselors suggested that citizens and *contadini* be encouraged to join Hawkwood's army to fight against the Visconti forces.[182] Hawkwood's mercenaries repelled the invasion, and the combatants limited their military activities to raids on farms, villas, and grain convoys. The military stalemate ended with the conclusion of a peace treaty, signed in Genoa in January 1392, which provided for the restoration of the old boundaries and arrangements.

No war fought by the Florentine republic ever enjoyed the universal approbation of the citizenry, and this first confrontation with Giangaleazzo was no exception. In its initial stages, it appeared to have the support of the majority of the guild community, if not of the whole populace. But as the conflict continued with dwindling prospects of a

[180] For the military and diplomatic developments, see Mesquita, ch. 10; Herde, 210–15.

[181] Armagnac received a subsidy of 120,000 fl.; *Camera, Uscita*, 298, part 2, f.88v; 297, f.183v.

[182] *CP*, 28, ff.168v–169v, 21–22 Sept. 1391. Speaking for the Sixteen, Lapo Niccolini said: "De mittendis civibus ad campum, quia res est insolita, praticetur per dominos, collegia et Decem, offerentes se ad omnia; non recusando laborem aut onus"; *ibid.*, f.169v.

decisive military victory, opposition to the war intensified. Scarcely a month passed without some reference in the *pratiche* to criticism directed at the authorities and their conduct of the war. The identity of these "slanderers" was rarely disclosed, and only occasionally do the sources refer to the targets of discontent: the ten war commissioners, the officials in charge of raising revenue, and the magistrates who supervised the grain supply. In February 1391, Rinaldo Gianfigliazzi urged the Signoria to prohibit all public criticism of the government.[183] Six months later, the councils approved the appointment of a "captain of the guard" who received the authority, in the words of one chronicler, "to send to the gallows or the block anyone . . . who criticized the regime."[184]

The *pratiche* are a useful but not infallible guide to civic opinion in wartime, when the pressures for supporting the government were most intense, and when public expression of dissenting views could lead to penalties and reprisals. The leaders of the war party are easily identified. Alessandro Alessandri, Filippo Corsini, and Rinaldo Gianfigliazzi had consistently favored an expansionist foreign policy and had expressed the greatest concern over Giangaleazzo's motives and tactics. These men agreed with Stoldo Altoviti's contention that "the count is seeking by every means to make himself king [of Italy] and to subjugate our state."[185] They believed, too, that the only feasible defense against him was a spirited counteroffensive culminating in a total military victory. Alessandro Alessandri's prescription was simple and dramatic: "Appoint good, loyal, and valiant citizens with responsibility for internal security who dare to act and to exercise authority where it is needed . . . and choose men for the war commission who are dynamic and who will search out the enemy. And call an assembly to inspire the citizens to defend themselves."[186] While the war faction was dominated by members of aristocratic Guelf families (Albizzi, Guasconi, Castellani, Peruzzi), it also included citizens from obscure families and backgrounds: Ser Biagio Bernabucci, Cristofano di

[183] For specific references to magistracies that were criticized, see *CP*, 28, ff.56r, 77r, 117r, 187v; 29, f.19v.

[184] *Panc.*, 158, f.162r. The chronicler added: "Et questo feciono fare gli arcighuelfi per chè altri non parlasse contro a loro." This measure was first proposed in February but it did not pass; one speaker argued that it would terrorize the populace; *CP*, 28, f.123v.

[185] *ASF, Acquisti e Doni*, 140, part 7, no. 63, letter to Donato Acciaiuoli, 25 Aug. 1389.

[186] *CP*, 28, f.31v, 18 Jan. 1390. For similar views, see Herde, "Politische Verhaltensweisen," 210–13.

Giorgio, the blacksmith Niccolò di Chiaro, Nofri Brie. These men advocated an invasion of Lombardy, and urged citizens to make greater sacrifices for the war effort.[187]

The political strength of this group derived less from numbers than from its cohesiveness and the intensity of its convictions. Opposition to the war was less openly expressed, because it was (or could appear to be) unpatriotic, and because it was so unfocused and inchoate. There was little enthusiasm for the war among artisans and workers, who did not experience the anxieties that Giangaleazzo aroused in the patriciate and who suffered most from the food shortages, rising prices and unemployment that accompanied every major conflict.[188] For merchants who felt more strongly about profits than about politics, the war was, at best, an unfortunate if inevitable burden and, at worst, a calamity that ruined trade.[189] A letter written in August 1391 by Ambrogio di Meo, an employee of Francesco Datini, clearly expressed the mercantile viewpoint. "The citizens of this republic are in poor condition; they can no longer bear the tax burdens and they have not imported any grain for six months. If the count were to launch an attack from either Siena or Bologna, there would be a serious famine."[190] Ambrogio did not shed any tears for his city; instead, he suggested to his friends that grain shipped to Florence would yield a handsome profit. There are no echoes of this callous viewpoint within the regime itself, where advocates of peace based their arguments upon the deleterious effects of war upon the city and its government.[191] In July 1391 Franco Sacchetti wrote to Donato Acciaiuoli, the standard-bearer of justice, urging him to use his influence to end hostilities. Sacchetti's letter is a florid piece of rhetoric, studded with references to classical authors who lauded peace. Nothing is more inimical to liberty, he wrote, than war with its heavy expenditures. On two previous occasions, Florence had nearly lost her freedom as a result

[187] *CP*, 28, ff.86r, 114r; 29, f.10v.

[188] For references to the popular clamor for peace, see *CP*, 28, ff.120r, 159r, statements of Ser Ristoro di Ser Jacopo and Filippo Bastari. Grain prices were abnormally high during the war years, from 1389 through 1391; R. Goldthwaite, "I prezzi del grano a Firenze"; *Quaderni storici*, x (1975), 33.

[189] For mercantile sentiment favoring peace, see the letters of Giovanni di Ser Nigi to Luca del Sera, 16 Oct. 1389; *Datini*, 1112, unpaginated; and of Domenico di Cambio, 8 Jan. 1392; Piattoli, *Archivio storico pratese*, VIII (1928), 143.

[190] The contents of Ambrogio's letter are in a letter written by Domenico di Cambio to Datini; Piattoli, *op. cit.*, 140–41.

[191] Thus, Filippo Bastari: "Per omnem modum procuretur pax quia ipsa est conservatio libertatis"; *CP*, 28, f.54r, 7 April 1390, quoted in Herde, "Politische Ver haltensweisen," 210, n. 307.

of military adventures. "May we avoid a third disaster with God's help."[192]

For the regime's opponents, the war was an opportunity to embarrass and discredit the government, and even to work for its downfall. Among those Florentines who had been forced out of politics since 1382 and who nursed their resentment in secret were some who subscribed to the views of Messer Ventura Monachi: "The count of Virtù has won the support of everyone, and now that he controls Verona, Padua, Siena, and Perugia, you will see what he will do."[193] Monachi saw Giangaleazzo as the invincible conqueror; others saw him as a Ghibelline hero, the heir of Henry VII, who would crush the Guelfs then ruling Florence. When rumors of a peace agreement were circulating in Florence (January 1392), Domenico di Cambio wrote Francesco Datini that the Guelfs were all delighted with the news, but then added: "This is not true of Stoldo [di Lorenzo, Datini's partner], who still is a Ghibelline at heart, and I don't know whether he is happy or sad."[194]

The colony of Florentine exiles in Pisa did not wait for hostilities to begin before intensifying their conspiratorial activities. The news from Florence had persuaded them that the workers were ready to revolt, "since food is so scarce that no one can live, and three-quarters of the *popolo* would support a change of regime."[195] After assembling secretly at night, they planned to occupy the palace of the Signoria, and then capture the leaders of the regime—Albizzi, Peruzzi, Ricci, Medici—in their homes and expel them from the city. The details of this plot, and the identity of the ringleaders, were revealed to the authorities "by certain zealous and dedicated supporters of the regime"; three men were hanged for their participation in the conspiracy.[196] Undaunted by betrayal and failure, the exiles laid plans for another

[192] *I sermoni evangelici*, ed. Gigli, 184–86. The references were to the dictatorship of the duke of Athens in 1342–43 and the Ciompi revolution of 1378.

[193] Monachi was fined 350 l. for his indiscreet remarks; *AP*, 3351, unpaginated, 2 July 1390. He was the son of a former chancellor, Ser Niccolò Monachi, who had been deprived of his office in 1374 and replaced by Coluccio Salutati.

[194] Piattoli, 143. Domenico made a similar comment a month later, when he informed Datini that the peace treaty had been signed; *Arch. stor. pratese*, IX (1930), p. 89 n.2: "Pensate a fare festa e alegreza chon chotesti vostri vicini originali guelfi; non è pero Istoldo di quelli."

[195] *ACP*, 1828, f.12v, condemnation of Domenico di Bartolo, 14 April 1390. Domenico was later absolved of the charge; *Prov.*, 79, ff.63v–64r.

[196] *AP*, 3351, ff.20v–21r, condemnation of Apollonio Mancini, 23 March 1390. Other sentences for participation in this plot are in *ibid.*, ff.24r–26r. Among those involved in the conspiracy were Michele di Lando and Morello Ciardi, veteran leaders of the Ciompi.

uprising in the autumn of 1390, hoping to capitalize on the discontent of a war-weary populace. To stimulate revolutionary sentiment among the Florentine poor, the exiles claimed that they could assemble a force of 300 men, who would march on the city and join the revolt. But like its predecessors, this plot collapsed when a messenger for the rebels was seized and interrogated by agents of the captain of the *Popolo*.[197] The most serious threat from the exile community developed a year later, in the summer of 1391. Giangaleazzo had sent an emissary, Inghirammo de' Bracci, to see leaders of the Florentine exiles in Pisa, and to enlist their aid for his invasion of Tuscany. The exiles renewed their contacts with friends and sympathizers in Florence, to organize a revolt that would coincide with an assault on the city's defenses by Giangaleazzo's troops.[198] The leaders of this conspiracy had ambitious plans for uniting the scattered groups of Florentine exiles—in Pisa, Lucca, Siena, Venice and Genoa—to support their enterprise. Contacts between them were established and maintained by Giangaleazzo's agents: Inghirammo de' Bracci in Pisa, Cavallino Cavalli in Venice, Ruggero Cane in Genoa. One Florentine exile in Venice allegedly predicted that Giangaleazzo would soon be lord of the city. But nothing came of these grandiose plans except the execution of one rebel and capital sentences against three others *in absentia*.[199]

Though the efforts of Giangaleazzo's men to foment an uprising in Florence were unsuccessful, they did constitute a formidable agency of subversion. From their bases of operation along Florence's frontiers (Pisa, Siena, Lucca, Parma), they blanketed northern and central Italy with a network of spies who collected information and probed for vulnerable spots in Florentine defenses. The remarkable success of their campaign is attested by the large number of condemnations in the judicial records. Among Florentine citizens and subjects whom they recruited to serve in the Visconti armies were the Ciompi exile Antonio di Paolo of Castro San Giovanni and the outlaw Piero di Andrea, who ravaged Florentine territory on the Sienese frontier.[200]

[197] *ACP*, 1843, ff.17v–18v, 20 Sept. 1390.

[198] *AP*, 3389, ff.47r–48r, 15 Nov. 1391, condemnation of Marco di Piero.

[199] The details of these contacts are found in the record of acquittals of Donnino Machiavelli; *AP*, 3389, f.34v; and a group of Florentine exiles in Venice, *ibid.*, ff.116v–117v. Though the individuals charged with treason in these processes were found innocent, the details of the Visconti campaign of subversion are plausible.

[200] Captured by Florentine authorities in 1391, Antonio di Paolo claimed immunity from prosecution as a cleric. The Florentine government asked Pope Boniface IX to defrock him, so that he could be executed; *SCMC*, 22, ff.171r–171v. The

They hired Andrea di Giovanni Angeli to persuade Florentine mercenaries to desert and fight for Giangaleazzo.[201] They also recruited spies in Florentine service, for example, Niccolò di Bartolomeo, who sent information concerning troop deployment to officers in the enemy camp. One of their couriers, Antonio di Piero of Sirano near Como, carried messages between Milan and Siena; he was instructed to travel through Florentine territory and "to collect information about the condition of the Florentines and to deliver it to the authorities in Siena."[202] Antonio was detained by Florentine officials near the *contado* village of Staggia; they found the incriminating correspondence from the Visconti chancery hidden inside a loaf of bread.

Visconti subversion was on a scale unprecedented in Florentine experience; it enhanced Giangaleazzo's reputation as a wily and formidable antagonist who used every available weapon to achieve his objectives. The most disturbing feature of this campaign, from the Florentine viewpoint, was the success of Visconti agents in buying the services of prominent citizens like Buonaccorso di Lapo Giovanni, an ardent Guelf partisan who in the autumn of 1388 sold state secrets to Giangaleazzo for 1000 florins. Three years later (July 1391) four others were convicted of betraying the republic. Two of these malefactors, Filippo di Riccardo Figliopetri and Betto di Messer Pino de' Rossi, were magnates whose families had long been excluded from the *reggimento*. Michele and Paolo da Castiglionchio, sons of the distinguished canon lawyer, Messer Lapo, were allegedly recruited as spies by two of Giangaleazzo's men, Milano Jacomelli and Cavallino Cavalli. From Florence, Paolo sent letters to his brother in Genoa (who gave them to Jacomelli), describing the military and diplomatic maneuvers of the Florentine government, and also the low morale of the citizens who were complaining about the heavy tax burden.[203] If men of such illustrious Guelf ancestry could be seduced by the count's agents, then no Florentine was above suspicion.

---

career of Piero di Andrea ended on the scaffold; *AP*, 3394, unpaginated, 1 Feb. 1392.

[201] Andrea was a native of Borgo San Sepolcro; he was executed for his subversive activities; *ACP*, 1877, ff.6r–7r, 1 April 1391.

[202] *ACP*, 1916, ff.3r–4v, 21 Jan. 1392; 1847, f.61r, 14 Dec. 1390.

[203] The accusations are in *ACP*, 1896, ff.2r–3v, 10r–11r (Sept. 1391); the condemnations have not survived. Michele's condemnation was cancelled in April 1414; *Prov.*, 103, ff.9v–10v. Michele was also accused by Vieri de' Medici of seizing one of his employees in Venice and forcing him to write drafts on Vieri's banking agencies in Genoa and Rome for 17,000 fl.; *ibid.*, 1874, ff.97r–98r, 24 July 1391. On this case, see *Panc.*, 158, f.162r.

The most fruitful area for Visconti subversion was Florence's *contado* and district, where loyalty to the republic was weakest and the burdens of her rule most resented. To obtain more revenue to pay for the war, the government had tightened the fiscal screws on its dependent communities. Even the loyal citizens of Prato were so aroused by the escalating levies that hundreds assembled in the piazza della Signoria to voice their complaints.[204] The themes of misery and high taxes struck responsive chords throughout the territory. "You see, Battista, to what misery and shame our city has been reduced," a native of San Miniato said to his neighbor, "and every day people are forced to leave on account of the taxes." To a poor priest of the same town, one of Giangaleazzo's agents said, "Barna, you are a poor man and the taxes of the Florentine commune that you are forced to pay are too heavy and they are destroying you." The prospects of wealth and higher status were strong incentives to join the plots then being fomented throughout Florentine territory by Giangaleazzo's men, one of whom made this proposition to the priest Barna: "You see that the Count of Virtù is a great lord and a man who generously rewards those who serve him, and that his affairs are prospering. He desires to have a fortress in this territory and I want you to arrange to surrender [the castle of] Agliati to him, and I will give you 200 florins."[205] For others who joined in this dangerous activity, the motives were more political than economic. Another resident of San Miniato, Bernardo di Rosso de' Guichi, addressed a friend in Florence with these words: "Do you see those *contadini* who are in the loggia of the Signoria? They are from Barga, and it is said that a conspiracy has just been discovered there. And we of San Miniato are so abject and vile that we do not have the courage to do anything, even if we were to be in a worse condition than we are now." These men planned to organize a revolt with support from Visconti troops stationed in Siena. "We will seize San Miniato and escape from the subjection of the Florentine commune . . . and we will rule this city according to our desires, and we will wash our hands and feet in the blood of our enemies."[206] Like so many other conspiracies, this plot failed and its ringleaders died on the scaffold. Their deaths may have been a deterrent to other malcontents, but

---

[204] *GA*, 70, part 1, f.97r, 5 May 1391. "Multitudo dicte terre Prate . . . in numero ultra VIᶜ . . . venerunt ad civitatem Florentie et iverunt ad plateam dominorum priorum . . . et inceperunt omnes fortiter exclamare quod divites et potentes terre Prati imposuerunt eis intolerabiles prestantias et gravedines. . . ." On the territory's economy in these years, see Molho, *Florentine Public Finances*, 23–45.

[205] *GA*, part 1, ff.145r–149r, 12 June 1391.

[206] *AP*, 3389, ff.119r–121r, 17 Oct. 1391. For other condemnations of participants in this conspiracy, see *ibid.*, 3351, ff.4r–7r, 12 Feb. 1390.

the conditions that drove them to rebellion did not improve. Florence's subject population remained susceptible to the blandishments of Visconti agents.[207]

Complaints about taxes, which fueled so much of the discontent in the countryside, were also heard in Florentine streets. The war cost the republic nearly two million florins; forced loans in excess of one million were levied to subsidize the mercenaries fighting under Florentine banners.[208] The magnitude of this expenditure was unprecedented in the city's history. In addition to making the usual demands for equity in forced-loan assessments and elimination of unnecessary outlays, counselors proposed a series of radical measures to alleviate the fiscal crisis. Gherardo Buondelmonti favored a moratorium on all communal expenses, except for the magistracies responsible for military operations; Franco Sacchetti suggested that citizens serve without salary in administrative posts.[209] The Sixteen claimed that arrears in *prestanza* payments would be paid quickly if the houses of delinquents were torn down; the Twelve suggested a milder remedy, that debtors be designated as magnates.[210] Others argued that forced loans would be paid more willingly if the interest rate of five percent were increased to eight or even ten percent. In May and October 1391, the Signoria and the colleges approved legislation for increasing the rate, but it was voted down by the councils.[211] The heavy deficits were partly met by subsidies from rich Florentines who lent large sums to the treasury over and above their regular assessments. This idea was first suggested in May 1390 by Rinieri Peruzzi, who "announced his readiness to join with 200 or 300 citizens" to contribute toward the costs of the war. Stoldo Altoviti approved this proposal and stated that he would give

[207] The judicial records of these years are filled with details of conspiracies involving residents of the *contado* and district; e.g., *ACP*, 1847, ff.45r–46r (Colle); *AP*, 3389, ff.122v–123v (S. Gimignano).

[208] For the years 1390–92, expenses for mercenaries were 2,158,000 fl.; forced loans totaled 1,473,000 fl.; Molho, *Florentine Public Finances*, 10. Even though hostilities ended early in 1392, the expenditures for troops remained high (701,000 fl.), since contracts with *condottieri* had been signed before the peace, and had to be honored.

[209] *CP*, 28, ff.44v, 142v.

[210] *Ibid.*, ff.99v, 131v, and Casino di Niccolò's statement: "Qui non vult facere defensionem, expellatur et auferantur bona sua"; *ibid.*, f.70r. Other counselors suggested that the names of delinquents be read aloud to the colleges, and that no immunities (*bollettini*) be issued to those who failed to pay their assessments; *ibid.*, ff.94r, 123r. Officials were appointed to sell the property of delinquents; *Prov.*, 80, ff.138r–139r; *Camera, Uscita*, 297, 30 Dec. 1391.

[211] For these proposals, see *CP*, 28, ff.44v, 145r, 163v–164r, 172r–172v; and for their rejection, *LF*, 43, ff.207r, 222r.

an amount equal to the largest loan made by another citizen. Bartolomeo Valori suggested that the priors might set an example for others by making the initial contributions, and another counselor recommended that the commission established to collect these subsidies be composed of wealthy citizens who were most able to lend money.[212] According to one anonymous source, these contributions totaled 834,000 lire for the year 1391. The largest sum (40,000 l.) was advanced by the banking firm of Gucciozzo de' Ricci; other substantial amounts came from Donato Acciaiuoli (14,000 l.), Maso Alessandri (20,000 l.), Filippo Corsini (9000 l.), Giovanni Castellani (15,000 l.) and Rinaldo Gianfigliazzi (9000 l.). By such extraordinary outlays of capital, these citizens were making a very strong statement of allegiance to their regime.[213]

THE BELEAGUERED REPUBLIC, 1392–1398

The first Milanese war of 1390–1392 was militarily and diplomatically inconclusive, but it did mark the beginning, for Florence and for the rest of Italy, of an age dominated by war and the threat of war, that continued with only brief interludes until the peace of Lodi in 1454. During the twenty-two months of this first conflict with Giangaleazzo, the republic was confronted by a host of war-related problems that would recur again and again in later years. How could these expensive conflicts be financed? How could public opinion be mobilized to support war, and how should civic dissent be handled? By what means could the government control disaffection and rebellion in the towns and villages of the dominion? What diplomatic moves would gain support among neighboring states? Could the political and military resources of France and Germany be utilized effectively against the Visconti? How serious was the threat of a blockade to Florence's mercantile activity and her food supply? Finally, how could the machinery of government be adapted to the requirements and pressures of large-scale warfare? By what methods were the crucial decisions of war and peace, of finance and diplomacy, to be made in this republican polity?

[212] CP, 28, ff.69v–70v, 24 May 1390; 126r, 15 Feb. 1391.

[213] BNF, Magl., xxv, 413, pp. 198–201. A total of eighty-three names are included in this list which has this heading: "cittadini che l'anno 1391 prestarono alla Repubblica lire 834,060 per la guerra contro il Conte di Virtù, gratis quantunque gli fusse assignati cinque per cento, cavata questa nota dal dicto priorista." For another copy of this list, in BNF, Fondo principale, II, II, 196, pp. 104–107, see Molho, Florentine Public Finances, 164.

Historians who have studied Florentine politics after the 1392 peace settlement have noted the vacillating character of the republic's foreign policy, and the apparent inability of her leaders to develop and implement a coherent program for resisting Giangaleazzo Visconti. This faltering posture was partly due to basic disagreements within the *reggimento* over foreign policy, and specifically, over the magnitude of the Milanese threat to Florentine security.[214] The "patriots" who had been most adamant in their opposition to the despot, and most eager to fight, suffered a loss of prestige when the war went badly in the late months of 1391, and when only a stalemate could be salvaged from the wreckage of Florentine aspirations. Chastened by their failure to defeat Giangaleazzo decisively, the leadership acted with great circumspection, aware of the strong pacifist sentiment, and resistance to taxes, among the *popolo*.[215] Coinciding, and interacting, with this paralysis of will and purpose was the leadership's failure to consider problems analytically, as related parts of a coherent structure of goals and priorities. Each issue was examined on an *ad hoc* basis, without any clear reference to its implications or to any larger context.

The debates over the fisc illustrate the problem. The heavy military expenditures had revealed serious flaws in the fiscal system and the need to overhaul it in the event of future wars with the Visconti. But instead of demanding a thoroughgoing reform of the fisc, citizens were insisting that the commune abandon its reliance upon forced loans and "live on its own."[216] In the context of peninsular politics in the 1390s,

[214] Neither Molho, "Florentine Oligarchy," *Speculum*, XLIII, 28–36, nor Baron, *Crisis*, 2nd ed., 28–46, mentions internal discord as a factor in Florentine foreign policy in the 1390s, although Molho does note the popular resistance to military expenditures. Molho attributes the indecisiveness of Florentine policy to an inability to translate their "implacable hostility toward the Visconti" into an effective program of deterrence; 36. For Baron, the failure was rather one of commitment and vision; the first Milanese war "had not revealed any new energies in the Florentine citizenry that promised lasting resistance to the aims of the Visconti"; *Crisis*, 29. Herde sees more coherence in Florence's "sober and pragmatic policy" than do most historians; "Politische Verhaltensweisen," 217, n.362; see also *ibid.*, 173, 187–88, 194.

[215] Concrete evidence of the public attitude toward the war is found in a letter from Domenico di Cambio to Francesco Datini: "Io mi credo che ongn'uomo sia sì stracho di questa guerra, che volentieri si riposerà, e chosì piacia a Dio che sia"; *Datini*, 1092, unpaginated, 25 Jan. 1392.

[216] See the statement of Niccolò da Uzzano, spokesman for his quarter of S. Spirito: ". . . Provideatur ita quod commune sit ordinatum; et quod prestantie non imponantur post hac; sed commune vivat de suis redditibus"; *CP*, 29, f.85v, 10 June 1392. For other statements opposing *prestanze* levies, see *ibid.*, ff.86r, 151r, 154r, 157r.

such statements were quite unrealistic, but they had strong support from the guild community. So provisions were formulated by the Signoria and the colleges, and approved by the councils, for raising the gabelles on foodstuffs and the *estimo* rate in the *contado*, where economic conditions were already so depressed that thousands had fled from Florentine territory to escape taxes.[217] There was even some sentiment in favor of imposing a gabelle on merchandise, but this scheme was strongly resisted by spokesmen for commercial interests.[218] Other traditional methods of increasing revenues, within the existing fiscal structure, were the coercion of tax delinquents and the search for illegal possessors and exploiters of communal property. In October 1391 a magistracy was established to sell the holdings of citizens who had not paid their *prestanze*. Its success in recovering tax debts was doubtless greater than was the proposal to shame delinquents into paying their obligations by reading their names at council meetings.[219]

Even if the regime's leadership had understood the nature of the fiscal crisis and had proposed significant reforms, these reforms would have encountered opposition in the legislative councils whose guild members were suspicious of every fiscal measure submitted for their approval, and stubbornly resisted any effort to change fiscal policy.[220] Councilors were not afraid to vote against *prestanze* levies even in wartime, despite the pleas of a desperate leadership that the money was needed to save the republic from disaster.[221] In August 1390 a provision was enacted that established a commission of thirty-two citizens to allocate forced loans more equitably; that new distribution had scarcely been implemented when an angry citizenry forced the

---

[217] The *estimo* rate was raised from 15 s. to 20 s.; *Prov.*, 81, ff.159v–161v, 24 July 1392. For descriptions of the plight of the districts adjacent to the Sienese frontier, see *ibid.*, 82, ff.102v–109r. The commune of Volterra, *ibid.*, f.103r, claimed that "tam occasione dicte guerre et ob maxima damna recepta . . . quam etiam ex multis gravedinibus quas . . . habent suportare, ulterius respirare non potest, set ultra quingentos homines de comitatu ipsius communis propter necessitatem et non habentes unde vivere possent se ab ipso comitatu absentaverunt et super territorio pisano cum earum familiis pro maiori parte mendicando se contulerunt."

[218] Speaking in favor of this gabelle was the lawyer Filippo Corsini, Vieri Cavicciuli and Arrigo Mucini; *CP*, 29, ff.75v, 91v; *LF*, 44, f.19r; but it was strongly opposed by Alessandro Alessandri and Soldo Soldani, *ibid.*

[219] *Prov.*, 80, f.138r. In a case involving one of the Acciaiuoli, the officials sold his property to a relative for a low figure, which covered the tax debt, and the relative then resold it back to its original owner. For demands that the names of tax delinquents be publicized, see *CP*, 29, f.157r.

[220] Molho, "Florentine Oligarchy," *Speculum*, XLIII, 46.

[221] See the deliberations and the votes on a series of fiscal provisions, 17 March–2 April 1391; *LF*, 43, ff.196r–203r.

Signoria to return to the legislature with proposals for adjusting the assessments.[222] An extreme example of civic resistance to the fiscal system was the sustained opposition to the appointment of a special magistracy (*ragionerii straordinarii*) to search for communal property in the possession of individuals. Legislation to appoint these officials was frequently voted down in the councils by citizens who complained loudly of these abuses.[223] To execute their mandate, the *ragionerii* had to inspect records and interrogate individuals; this invasion of privacy apparently aroused widespread resentment, even though it was designed to promote civic welfare. After one official, Barduccio Cherichini, had been maltreated by an irate citizen, the government enacted a law providing penalties for anyone who killed these agents.[224]

The one significant fiscal innovation in these years was a product of the constitutional crisis of 1393, when the *balìa* created a permanent council of eighty-one citizens with authority to levy forced loans without the approval of the councils. This measure substantially increased the executive's authority in fiscal matters, while sharply reducing the legislative control over the communal purse.[225] Those members of the *balìa* who voted for this change were obviously recalling the frustrations of the war years, when measures to levy *prestanze* were so frequently defeated by the councils. If this Council of Eighty-one was more responsive to the regime's fiscal needs, then its ability to subsidize future wars was greatly enhanced. But though it was authorized to impose forced loans without interest, and even to levy direct taxes

---

[222] *Prov.*, 79, ff.166v–167v (18–19 Aug. 1390), and 372v–375v (19–20 March 1391). The preamble of the latter read: "Auditis querelis multorum civium . . . super nova distributione prestantiarum . . . dicentium se in illa nimis fore gravatos et petentium super his cum iustitia provideri." That measure passed with great difficulty.

[223] *Prov.*, 79, ff.93r–95r (1–2 June 1390); 80, ff.283v–285r (12–13 March 1392); both passed by slim margins. A measure enlarging the authority of the *ragionerii* was rejected in the Council of the *Popolo*; *LF*, 44, f.24v, before it later passed; *ibid.*, f.27r; *Prov.*, 81, ff.110r–114v, 27–28 June 1392. In the summer of 1393 and the spring of 1394, a provision to reactivate the *ragionerii* was defeated seven times; *LF*, 44, ff.90r, 92v, 95r, 115r, 124v, 127r, 129r. For later resistance in the councils to this magistracy, see Molho, "Florentine Oligarchy," 47.

[224] The incident occurred in Nov. 1392; *CP*, 29, ff.146v–148v; but the law was not passed until Jan. 1393, after several rejections; *Prov.*, 81, ff.289r–291r. Some concern was expressed that these officials were so intimidated by threats that they were not searching diligently for alienated property and money owed to the commune; *CP*, 29, ff.149v, 150r, 154r.

[225] Molho, "Florentine Oligarchy," *Speculum*, XLIII, 40–41, was the first scholar to call attention to the importance of this enactment and to describe its implementation. The councils still had to approve any measure for redistributing the *prestanze* levies; *ibid.*, 43–46.

upon urban residents without repayment, it did not adopt these radical measures that, in the past, had often been discussed but never introduced.[226] So great a departure from tradition would have aroused widespread concern that the republic might violate its obligation to its creditors; no theme was more frequently reiterated in public debates on the fisc than the necessity to guarantee "the faith of the commune."[227] The foundations of communal finance thus remained the interest-bearing *prestanze*, while the servicing of the public debt became an increasingly heavy charge.[228] A provision enacted in July 1392 recognized the danger of these spiraling costs. For a period of three years, one-third of the interest on *monte* shares was to be withheld from creditors, and the money used to repurchase those credits at the market price. But this modest attempt to reduce the size of the public debt was ineffectual; even during the peace years 1392–1396, the regime had to levy new *prestanze* to balance its budget.[229]

Though the fiscal crisis subsided once the mercenaries were off the communal payroll, the memories of wartime did restrain the militant impulses of Florentine statesmen in the months following the peace settlement. The evidence of widespread disaffection in city and countryside could not have encouraged them to believe that the regime would have survived a prolonged siege, particularly if Visconti troops had been able to cut off food supplies. The costly efforts to recruit German and French aid had failed completely; only good fortune and the loyalty of John Hawkwood had enabled the republic to resist the Visconti assault. Florence did achieve an important diplomatic victory with the conclusion (April 1392) of the treaty of Bologna, a pact of mutual defense uniting Florence, Bologna, and the lord of Padua with Giangaleazzo's former allies, the *signori* of Mantua and Ferrara. That league was obviously designed to resist Giangaleazzo, and it gained more strength from the covert support of the Venetian republic. But the advantages accruing to Florence from this Lombard federation were partly nullified by the survival of Visconti influence in Siena and Perugia. Giangaleazzo maintained a military garrison in Siena, and from that base on Florence's southern flank his agents established links

[226] Brucker, *Flor. Studies*, 341–44; Molho, *Florentine Public Finances*, 64–67. One statement (Dec. 1392) by Andrea Minerbetti, spokesman for the Sixteen, suggests that a direct tax on urban households may have been discussed: "Quod illi octo cives provideant per alium modum quam per prestantiam vel per ignem vel per fumatorium vel alium quemcumque modum"; *CP*, 29, f.157r.

[227] *CP*, 29, ff.76v, 152v, 154r; *LF*, 44, ff.19r–19v.

[228] Molho, *Florentine Public Finances*, 69–72.

[229] *Prov.*, 81, ff.151r–158v. For later suspensions of interest payments, see Molho, *Speculum*, XLIII, 42, n.52.

with Tuscan nobles and communities hostile to Florence. The opportunities for intrigue were enhanced by the presence of large bands of unemployed mercenaries who ranged over this troubled region, a potential threat to the security of both Florence and Siena. The Visconti position in Tuscany became even stronger in October 1392 when Jacopo d'Appiano, who had secretly supported Giangaleazzo during the war, seized control of Pisa from Florence's longtime friend and ally, Pietro Gambacorta.[230]

The Florentine reaction to the Pisan crisis was remarkably mild, considering the potential threat to her security that Jacopo d'Appiano's coup signified. A few alarmed citizens called for a mobilization of troops on the Pisan frontier, but the dominant mood was expressed by Uguccione de' Ricci: "Let us avoid war by every means possible . . . and maintain friendship with the Pisans."[231] Counselors advocated similar restraint in relations with Giangaleazzo. Filippo Corsini argued that the republic's policy should focus upon persuading her neighbors, and especially the count of Virtù, that she desired to avoid war.[232] She urged her Lombard allies to avoid any provocative act that might endanger peace. When Francesco da Carrara, lord of Padua, sought Florence's support to avoid paying his debt to Giangaleazzo, Alessandro Arrigucci advised the Signoria to inform him "that he should pay the Count of Virtù and . . . that we want peace not war, and that if he begins war, he will have to finish it alone."[233] When the ruler of Mantua, Francesco Gonzaga, became embroiled with Giangaleazzo over the building of fortifications on the Mincio river, Donato Acciaiuoli proposed that an embassy be sent to ask the count to abandon the project, but also to urge Gonzaga to refrain from antagonizing the lord of Milan.[234] In relations with her neighbors to the south and east, the republic's policy was likewise conciliatory. Florentine statesmen resisted the urge to meddle in the local politics of Romagna and Umbria. When civil turmoil erupted in Perugia in the spring of 1393, counselors advised the Signoria to send an embassy there to pacify the factions, but not to involve the republic in any military campaign.

[230] There is a good account of these developments in Mesquita, *Giangaleazzo*, ch. 11, who argues that Giangaleazzo was planning another attack on Florence. See too Herde, "Politische Verhaltensweisen," 218-19.

[231] *CP*, 29, f.151r, 29 Nov. 1392. Similar views were expressed by Andrea della Stufa and Matteo Arrighi; Maso degli Albizzi advocated a more aggressive policy; *ibid.*, ff.151v, 158v. See also Herde, 219, n.371.

[232] *CP*, 30, f.3v, 15 Feb. 1393. For similar opinions, see *ibid.*, ff.19v, 20v.

[233] *Ibid.*, f.134v, 22 June 1394; also *ibid.*, ff.131r, 135r.

[234] *Ibid.*, f.39r, 26 June 1393, quoted in Herde, 221, n.387. More belligerent was the counsel of Alessandro Alessandri: "Quod viriliter dicatur [ei] intentio communis et non timide nec remisse"; *ibid.*, f.40r.

Quarrels in the Romagna between Bologna and Imola, and between the lords of Ferrara and Faenza, disturbed the peace on Florence's eastern frontier, but no citizen advocated intervention in these disputes.[235]

This unheroic posture, so different from the aggressive diplomacy of the previous decade, was approved by the *popolo*.[236] But to those citizens—Alessandro Alessandri and Filippo Corsini, for example—who had been most vocal in advocating war with Giangaleazzo this policy must have seemed like appeasement. Still, there was no discernible pressure to change the course of peaceful co-existence, even after the expulsion of the Alberti and their sympathizers from the *reggimento* in the autumn of 1393. During the next year, the republic still relied heavily upon diplomatic cajolery to keep intact the league of Bologna, and thus to maintain the precarious balance of power in northern and central Italy. In instructions sent to the republic's ambassadors at the court of Ferrara in July 1394, the Signoria articulated the principles of Florentine policy: "It is much better to spend the time in embassies, than to break off negotiations and embark on a war, which would involve more expense every day than these embassies cost in a year."[237] By the early months of 1395, however, the mood within the *reggimento* had become more belligerent, and after a four-year truce, advocates of war and pacifists were again confronting each other in the palace of the Signoria.

Giangaleazzo's persistent efforts to find allies on both sides of the Alps to enable him to subvert the Bologna league certainly contributed to the intensification of Florentine fears about his motives.[238] Still, the

---

[235] *CP*, 30, ff.10v, 12r, statements of Vieri Cavicciuli and Pazzino Strozzi. As Molho notes, "Florentine Oligarchy," *Speculum*, XLIII, 36, n.32, Florence was always eager to serve as mediator in disputes involving allies and neighbors, but her posture was distinctly less assertive and overbearing in these years, compared to the 1380s; see above, ch. III, 105–12, 120–22.

[236] The civic mood was neatly captured in an anonymous letter, undated but probably written in 1393, sent to Jacopo del Bene in Padua: "Di pacie o di guerra tra noi e 'l Conte pocho si ragiona, bene ch'ogniuno ista in su' suoi, e sì di giente in punto e sì d'ogni altra cosa, come vedi; e quanto per ora non mi pare si speri guerra. E sia cierto, se l'uno non ingrasa più che l'altro, guera no' fia; e in ultimo, come le munete [monete?] prospereranno più a l'uno c'a l'altro, così puoi ragionare la guera"; *Carte del Bene*, 49, no. 57.

[237] Mesquita, *Giangaleazzo*, 167. For similar views in the *pratiche*, see Herde, "Politische Verhaltensweisen," 221–22.

[238] Mesquita, ch. 12, summarizes Visconti diplomacy in these years. Baron, *Crisis*, 2nd ed., 30–31, argues that Florence's diplomatic position was progressively weakening in these years, and Giangaleazzo was growing stronger. That is not the impression given by Mesquita or by Cognasso in *Storia di Milano*, VI, 3–27.

resurgence of bellicosity was due more to internal than to external developments and specifically, to the greater influence in the *reggimento* of the war faction led by Maso degli Albizzi and Rinaldo Gianfigliazzi. A debate over the creation of the war *balìa* signaled this group's initial effort to reorient Florentine foreign policy. The occasion was a minor crisis in Ferrara, where a rebel band was seeking to wrest control of that state from its legitimate ruler, the nine-year-old Niccolò d'Este. Although there is no evidence that Giangaleazzo gave any concrete assistance to the rebels, Rinaldo Gianfigliazzi and Alessandro Alessandri called for the establishment of a *balìa* to counteract "the deceptions of the Count of Virtù." The members of that magistracy should be "distinguished, wise, virtuous, virile, and Guelf," counseled Niccolò Gherardini Giani, and he added that "every citizen should be ready to pay for the defense of liberty."[239] While some favored a delay and further consultation before creating a *balìa*, which would be viewed by Giangaleazzo as a provocative act, the sentiment in the *pratica* was strongly in favor of a war magistracy. Luigi Canigiani even argued for the periodic renewal of the *balìa* "as long as the count lives." To ensure that the office would be staffed by citizens with zeal and determination, the Sixteen proposed that the election be made by the Signoria "and not placed in the hands of fortune, as had formerly been done."[240] The Panciatichi chronicler wrote that many citizens opposed the *balìa* "for fear that it would lead to war" but their resistance was futile. On 2 February, the Council of Eighty-one elected a war magistracy for one year with very broad authority to direct foreign policy.[241]

The *balìa* acted quickly to justify its appointment by sending a contingent of lances to Ferrara, and other troops to Florence's allies in Lucca and Faenza. For the first time since 1392, the republic was relying upon arms to reinforce its diplomatic position. In a letter to his brother Piero in Venice, Marco Davanzati justified these measures

---

[239] *CP*, 31, ff.57r–58r. Others who argued strongly for the *balìa* were Francesco Ardinghelli, Niccolò Guasconi, and Agnolo Ricoveri; *ibid.*, ff.54r, 57r. The only lower guildsman to participate in the debate, the innkeeper Cenni di Marco, also favored the *balìa*; Arrigo Mucini and Pazzino Strozzi wished to delay its appointment; *ibid.*, ff.57v–58r.

[240] *CP*, 31, f.61r. Canigiani spoke in a *pratica* in which 46 citizens expressed their views; *ibid.*, ff.59v–60v, 30 Jan.

[241] *Panc.*, 158, f.179r. The creation of a *balìa* no longer required the approval of the legislative councils, but only of the Council of Eighty-one; Molho, "Florentine Oligarchy," *Speculum*, XLIII, 32. The Signoria wrote to Giangaleazzo to assure him that the *balìa*'s appointment was designed to promote peace; *SCMC*, 24, ff.107r–107v, 4 Feb. 1395.

as necessary for the republic's security. Giangaleazzo was responsible, Davanzati argued, for the seizure of a Florentine castle in the Aretine *contado*, and also for encouraging Jacopo d'Appiano, the lord of Pisa, to attack Lucca. Furthermore, he had gained support among the petty *signori* of Romagna and was ready to enter an alliance with the republic of Genoa.[242] None of these suspicions about Visconti projects can be verified by the surviving evidence, but they were used by the war party to gain support for their policy of military preparedness.[243] Illustrating the expanding scope of their diplomatic interests, and the growing boldness of their vision, was the debate over a proposal to contract an alliance with Genoa. That city was so divided by factional discord that its independence was gravely jeopardized. Those Florentines who saw Giangaleazzo's fine hand behind every Italian crisis speculated that he would gain control of Genoa. Donato Acciaiuoli strongly favored the Genoese alliance, "considering the dangers that we will face if the [Tyrrhenian] sea were to become unsafe for us."[244] Acciaiuoli's arguments persuaded many citizens who believed that if Florence did not help the Genoese, the city would inevitably fall to the Visconti. Others, however, contended that the Genoese regime was so fragile that Florence could not save it from collapse, and that her intervention would alienate the French king. Leading this opposition to the Genoese alliance were Filippo Corsini, Ridolfo Peruzzi, and Maso degli Albizzi, who were strongly committed to a pro-French policy and who in the following year succeeded in forging an alliance with King Charles VI.[245]

The dramatic shift in the Florentine attitude toward Giangaleazzo in the early months of 1395 is reminiscent of the fluctuations in civic opinion prior to the outbreak of hostilities in 1390. Between 1392 and 1394, no overt criticism of Giangaleazzo was ever voiced in the *pratiche*, nor recorded in diplomatic correspondence. In the spring of 1395, however, the council halls reverberated with denunciations of the perfidious tyrant. "We can never trust him an inch, and so we must chart a different course, since his promises are worthless," was the

[242] *CRS*, 78 (*Badia*), 315, unpaginated, 30 Jan. 1395.

[243] Mesquita, *Giangaleazzo*, 164-65, notes that Giangaleazzo arranged for the return to Florentine control of the captured castle of Gargonza. For escalating demands for money to subsidize military projects, see *CP*, 31, ff.64r–64v, 65v–66r.

[244] *CP*, 31, f.69r, 2 Apr. 1395.

[245] *Ibid.*, ff.69v–70r, 74v. Maso degli Albizzi's argument is instructive: "In liga Janue consideretur quod contra regem Francie non fiat, et quod guelfi Janue non destruantur et considerentur expensa. . . ." The discussion over the Genoese alliance continued into June; *ibid.*, ff.75v–76r, 79v–83v. See Herde, "Politische Verhaltensweisen," 222–23.

judgment of Gherardo Montebuoni. Alessandro Arrigucci claimed that Giangaleazzo was intent upon sowing discord between Florence and her allies, and he warned that Lucca in particular could fall into the Visconti orbit. Giovanni Biliotti touched upon the same theme; the count had first attempted to subvert Ferrara, then Lucca, and now he was trying to insert himself into Genoa. Rinaldo Gianfigliazzi referred to a statement of King Solomon in the Book of Kings, "who said that you should never trust an enemy with whom you have been reconciled, and so with respect to the Count of Virtù, you should never ask anything from an enemy and you will never be deceived." To illustrate his argument, Rinaldo recalled his conversation with Giangaleazzo when he had been an ambassador at the Visconti court. "The count told him that in order not to lose what he had gained, he would have to be lord of all Italy, and that from his revenues he wished to marry his daughters honorably and to spend grandly and to expand, and that never would there be peace until he was lord of all Lombardy."[246]

Within weeks of this public declaration by the *reggimento*'s leadership that a renewal of the struggle with Giangaleazzo was imminent, an issue arose to test the political strength of the war party. Earlier in the year, Florence had concluded an agreement with Pope Boniface IX to take possession of the papal town of Castrocaro near Forlì as surety for a loan that the republic had made to the impecunious pontiff. When Florentine troops moved to occupy the city, they encountered stiff resistance from the local *signori*, and also the Bolognese, who raised the specter of Florence's imperialist designs in the Romagna.[247] The same fears had been articulated a decade before, but Florence could ignore them since she did not then need Bologna's help against the Visconti. Despite the strong possibility that her possession of Castrocaro would so alienate Bologna that the anti-Visconti league would crumble, a group of imperialists led by Alessandro Alessandri demanded that the republic stand firm in its determination to hold the town. The territory was needed for its grain, they argued,

---

[246] The speeches were delivered in a *pratica* of 18 June 1395; *CP*, 31, ff.82r–82v. Gianfigliazzi's statement is printed in Herde, 224, n.406. One may doubt whether Giangaleazzo would have been so indiscreet in describing his goals to a Florentine diplomat; see Mesquita, *Giangaleazzo*, 160.

[247] Esch, *Bonifaz IX*, 139–41; Mesquita, 193–94; *DBRA*, 1, ff.2v–3r, which contains the Bolognese view of the enterprise: ". . . 'l comune di Firenze volea Castrocaro per avere Furlì e Ravenna e il porto in mare e poi anche altro e volea fare in Romagna come in Toschana d'occupare i vicini e che questo non si poterrebbe etiandio se dovessono mettere mano alla spada e che ci piacesse levarci da Castrocaro." For earlier negotiations (June 1394) for Castrocaro's acquisition, see *SCMLC*, 1, ff.19v–22r.

but they also stressed the importance of the republic's honor, which would be tarnished if she were forced to abandon her position.[248] The opponents of this intransigent posture moved slowly to defuse the situation, and then to consider the problem rationally. They suggested, first, that the issue be discussed in a large assembly, "since it concerns the whole *popolo*." The crucial issues were fiscal and military, Giovanni de' Ricci insisted: "If it is possible to settle the Castrocaro affair without too much expense or danger, then do so; otherwise, it would be better to withdraw. . . ." Donato Acciaiuoli spoke more bluntly: "Considering the dangers involved, and the fact that the commune does not have sufficient force, do not lay siege [to Castrocaro] since the castle is impregnable; and this campaign has angered the Bolognese and all of the lords of the Romagna. . . ."[249] In a final *pratica* (23 August 1395) on the Castrocaro crisis, all the speakers counseled the Signoria to avoid further military action and to settle the dispute through negotiation. Only Filippo Corsini announced his support for war if the settlement did not redound to the commune's honor.[250]

The dispute over Castrocaro was a revival of a longstanding disagreement between those citizens who believed that offense was the best defense, so were committed to an aggressive posture in foreign affairs, and those who preferred a low profile in diplomacy and habitually sought to temporize rather than seek a confrontation. These differences were not so rigid that their adherents formed parties or factions; a more appropriate description would be alignments. The most significant political result of the Castrocaro debate was the emergence of Donato Acciaiuoli as the leader of, and spokesman for, those citizens who favored restraint and retrenchment in foreign affairs, and a sharp reduction in military expenditures. In two important speeches delivered in September and October 1395,[251] Acciaiuoli proposed that most of the mercenaries hired by the war *balìa* be released, and that only 400 lances be retained. He further recommended that all the stipends to foreign pensioners (*provisionati*) be cancelled, "and everywhere cut all expenses that can be eliminated." Acciaiuoli favored an intensive diplomatic effort "to

[248] See the discussions in the *pratiche* of 2 and 5 August; *CP*, 31, ff.98r–100r. Tommaso Marchi, Cristofano Spini, and Benedetto Peruzzi supported Alessandri.

[249] *Ibid.*, ff.101v, 102v, 11 Aug. Benino Gucci, Niccolò Guasconi, and Alessandro Arrigucci agreed with Ricci and Acciaiuoli. Opposing them were Filippo Corsini, Simone Capponi, Cristofano Spini, and Benedetto Peruzzi.

[250] *Ibid.*, ff.106v–107r. Cf. Esch, *Bonifaz IV*, 145–47.

[251] *CP*, 31, ff.111v, 115v, 17 Sept. and 11 Oct. 1395. Acciaiuoli's speech of 11 Oct. revealed an exceptional talent for analysis.

restore the league" that had been weakened by the Castrocaro affair. Implicit in his program was the assumption that Giangaleazzo was not an immediate threat to Florentine security, that he could be restrained within the existing system of diplomatic alignments, and at a moderate cost. This program was directly opposed to the policy of those leaders of the *reggimento* who had agitated for a war *balìa* in January, and who had denounced Giangaleazzo in June. For those statesmen—Maso degli Albizzi, Rinaldo Gianfigliazzi, Alessandro Alessandri—the disarmament program encouraged Visconti aggression, and Acciaiuoli's bold articulation of that program challenged their leadership of the *reggimento*.[252] There is no evidence that these men were responsible for the campaign to vilify Donato, which came to the attention of the Signoria in early November.[253] But his advocacy of fiscal and military retrenchment had made him unpopular with the war party and contributed to his political disgrace in January 1396.

Acciaiuoli's exile eliminated the most influential voice resisting the efforts of those eager to renew hostilities. Though Giangaleazzo had not succeeded in shifting the political balance in his favor,[254] Maso degli Albizzi and his associates chose that moment to seize the diplomatic initiative and provoke a confrontation with "the tyrant." The chosen instrument was King Charles VI of France, and the beginning of their campaign can be traced to the spring of 1395, when Maso and Filippo Corsini opposed a league with Genoa, which Donato Acciaiuoli favored, arguing that it would antagonize the French monarch, who had his own eyes on that Ligurian prize.[255] Though concerned about the possibility that the faction-torn city would fall into Visconti hands if it did not receive help, they were even more fearful

---

[252] Acciaiuoli reiterated his opposition to increasing military expenditures in later speeches; *ibid.*, ff.118r, 126r.

[253] *Ibid.*, f.123r, 8 Nov. Scolaio Spini for the Sixteen: "Quod habeantur illi qui oblocuti sunt contra dominum Donatum, tam in civitate Florentie quam Pistorie, et . . . mittantur ad unum rectorem et reperiatur fundamentum, et quicumque erravit, puniatur." Speaking for the war *balìa*, Guido del Palagio said: "Quod de illis verbis faciunt parvam existimationem; tamen ne res crescat, potius extinguantur quam propagentur. Et dominus Donatus hortetur. Et quod domini . . . moneant illos qui oblocuti sunt in forma quod similia non fiant imposterum. Et quod omne scandalum inter guelfos tollatur. . . ."

[254] Giangaleazzo's most spectacular failure was in France (Mesquita, 155-60), but his efforts to woo Boniface IX and King Ladislaus of Naples yielded no positive results, since neither prince was strong enough in his own territory to give effective assistance to Giangaleazzo; *ibid.*, 189-95. Giangaleazzo continued his efforts to divide Florence's allies in the league of Bologna, but with little success. He had recently purchased the ducal title from the emperor-elect Wenceslaus.

[255] *CP*, 31, ff.69v, 74v, 75v, 79v, 112v, 117v.

of angering Charles, who apparently had received a Florentine promise to stay out of Genoese affairs.[256] In a *pratica* held on 19 January 1396, Maso degli Albizzi, Alessandro Alessandri and Filippo Corsini all opposed the Genoese alliance.[257] A few weeks later the war magistracy sent a secret agent to Avignon, who was instructed to meet with Cardinal Piero Corsini, Filippo's brother and the uncle of Maso degli Albizzi.[258] The agent was to ask the cardinal to inform the French monarch that Florence had steadfastly refused to enter an alliance with the Genoese doge out of respect for him. Cardinal Corsini communicated regularly with Maso, and worked hard to improve relations between his native city and the French court.[259] The agent of the war commission, Ser Piero di Ser Piero of San Miniato, received a second, and more important, assignment: to persuade the count of Armagnac (whose father had been killed in the ill-fated invasion of 1391) to recruit another army to cross the Alps and attack Giangaleazzo. Simultaneously with this diplomatic initiative in France, other efforts were being made to recruit mercenaries in the Romagna, and as far away as Hungary. In May 1396 the Ten sent Maso degli Albizzi to the French court with specific proposals for an alliance, and for Florence's subsidy of a French army to invade Lombardy.[260]

There is no evidence that the French alliance, and the fiscal obligation that it entailed, were ever discussed in consultative assemblies during the winter and spring of 1396.[261] The legislative councils were given no opportunity to express an opinion, even upon renewal of the war *balìa*, whose original term had expired in February 1396.[262]

[256] *Ibid.*, f.79v, Filippo Corsini: "Consideranda est promissa facta regis Francie," and the statement of Rinaldo Gianfigliazzi, *ibid.*, f.115v. But see the Signoria's statement to Boniface IX concerning its solicitude for Genoa's liberty; *SCMLC*, 1, f.89r.

[257] *CP*, 32, ff.8v–9r. Only Rinaldo Gianfigliazzi gave qualified support to the alliance, "non faciendo contra regem Francie."

[258] *DBCMLC*, 2, ff.3r–3v, 6 March 1396.

[259] See Cardinal Corsini's letters (undated but written between 1391 and 1396) to Maso; *BNF, Fondo principale*, II, III, 434, no. 4–16.

[260] *DBCMLC*, 2, ff.6r–16r, 17r (embassy to Hungary), 19r–21r (instructions to Maso degli Albizzi), 35r (instructions to Buonaccorso Pitti in France). On the diplomatic background, see Herde, "Politische Verhaltensweisen," 225–26.

[261] In March there was a debate concerning financial needs, and proposals for a forced loan of 50,000 fl., but this was not related to the French negotiations; *CP*, 32, f.29r. A month later, Filippo Pandolfini proposed that money be raised by a gabelle on commerce instead of forced loans; Giovanni Biliotti wanted the commune to live on its regular revenue; *ibid.*, f.33r.

[262] The decision for renewal was made by the Council of Eighty-one, and the membership of the magistracy is not known.

Through its predominant influence in the war magistracy and in the Council of Eighty-one, the war party had led the republic into another conflict with Giangaleazzo without receiving a clear mandate from the electorate. Not until 8 June, when Maso degli Albizzi was already at the French court, was there a reference to the alliance in any debate. Speaking for a collegiate group, Filippo Adimari spoke in favor of the French alliance, and suggested that the negotiations be entrusted to the war *balìa*.[263] But the issue quickly disappeared from the agenda, and there is no reference in the protocols to Buonaccorso Pitti's mission to France "with a mandate authorizing Messer Maso and myself to conclude an alliance with the French king."[264] The terms were settled in September. They stipulated that a French army of 12,000 horse would invade Lombardy and that Florence and her allies would furnish some 4000 cavalry for the assault.[265] With the conclusion of this alliance, war became inevitable.[266]

Opposition to the Albizzi party and its war policy was not voiced publicly in the councils, and the only concrete evidence of dissent appears in the trial of Ardingo di Gucciozzo de' Ricci,[267] a merchant from a prominent family that had been in political disfavor for several years. Ardingo was convicted of supplying a business associate in Pisa, Giovanni Grassolino, with information about Florentine troop movements and diplomatic activities. His accomplice was a certain Matteo di Guccio, who brought messages to Pisa that a Florentine force of 3000 horse was being sent to Mantua "to make war on the duke of Milan . . . and force him to withdraw his troops in Pisa." Matteo also informed his Pisan contacts that most Florentines did not want war because they neither desired, nor were able, to pay the costs, and that they were being forced into the conflict against their will. He added that if hostilities did break out, the Pisans should stand firm because there would be a revolution in Florence. He calculated that only four or five members of the war magistracy favored the attack on Giangaleazzo; they were supported by four or five other citizens who

---

[263] *CP*, 32, f.46r.   [264] Pitti, *Cronica*, 96.

[265] The details are in the treaty draft that Pitti took to Paris; *DBCMLC*, 2, ff.40r–40v; for Pitti's instructions, see *ibid.*, ff.35r–36r. On the alliance, see Minerbetti, *anno* 1396, ch. 7. For an official version of the negotiations and the treaty, as related to Boniface IX, see *SCMLC*, 1, ff.89r–89v, 16 July 1397. The Signoria denied that Florence was promoting a French invasion of Italy.

[266] This is also Mesquita's judgment, 205; see also Herde, 226–27. For a different view, cf. Molho, "Florentine Oligarchy," *Speculum*, XLIII, 36.

[267] *ACP*, 2044, ff.19r–22r, 26 Aug. 1396. The case was discussed by the colleges; *CP*, 32, ff.34v–35v, who recommended leniency for Ardingo: "Rogetur [capitaneus] quod habet recommendationem honoris illius familie de Riccis."

profited from the war. From his merchant's point of view, Ardingo realized that Florence was vulnerable to a Pisan blockade. "If they were to seize Florentine merchandise, there would be a great scandal. Those whose goods were confiscated would go to the Merchants' Court and make them go to the palace of the Signoria to appeal [to the priors] not to declare war, and a great turmoil would ensue." The details of these communications came, not from Ardingho, who fled to escape arrest, but from the hapless Matteo di Guccio, who was captured while enroute to Pisa and who was executed after he confessed. For suppressing evidence of Ardingho's crimes, his father Gucciozzo was barred from holding any communal office for four years.

Ardingo de' Ricci's trial suggests that opposition to a renewal of warfare was stronger and more widespread, especially in mercantile circles, than the records of the *pratica* deliberations and the diplomatic contacts with France would indicate. During the hostilities between Pisa and Lucca in the summer of 1396, Florence furnished troops for Lucca's defense. However, the tenor of *pratica* deliberations was not hostile toward Pisa but very conciliatory.[268] Counselors urged the Signoria to restrain the Lucchese and to send ambassadors to Pisa to seek a settlement with Jacopo d'Appiano. Guido del Palagio, Pazzino Strozzi, and Giovanni Biliotti were most ardent in their desire for peace, but even men like Cristofano Spini and Filippo Corsini spoke very circumspectly. The most belligerent statement was made by an artisan, the blacksmith Niccolò di Chiaro, who argued that an attack on Pisa would bring peace and a restoration of trade.[269] But opinion in the palace (if not in the city at large) became more aggressive when news of the French alliance arrived in Florence on 30 October. The letter from Paris announcing the pact was read to a civic assembly in the piazza della Signoria, and bonfires were lit to celebrate the event. In appealing to King Charles to send help promptly, the Signoria wrote that "after God, all our faith now resides in the Kingdom [of France]!"[270] Lotto Castellani proposed that the republic maintain a permanent embassy at the French court, and Bernardo Marsili wanted the king to send an army into Italy "so that the count will have to think about his own defense and will not be able to offend us."[271] Their spirits raised by the prospect of a French invasion, counselors advised the Signoria to break off peace negotiations with Giangaleazzo and to

[268] The *pratica* discussions on Pisa were held on 21, 28 and 30 July, 4 Aug., and 11 Sept.; CP, 32, ff.55r–59v, 63r–64r, 71r–72r. For details of a Florentine embassy to Pisa in October, see DBRA, 1, ff.31v–32r.

[269] CP, 32, ff.55v, 57r, 64r.

[270] DBCMLC, 2, f.57v.

[271] CP, 32, ff.81v, 86r, 18 Dec. 1396 and 10 Jan. 1397.

ignore the complaints of Pope Boniface IX and the Venetians concerning the French alliance. Though seemingly confident that this league would guarantee their victory, they were reluctant to strike at their enemy but instead preferred to remain on the defensive. Only after Giangaleazzo had begun operations against Mantua in March 1397 did Alessandro Alessandri and Benedetto Peruzzi call for an invasion of Lombardy.[272]

One reason for this reluctance to begin hostilities was Florence's apprehension over the reaction of Italian states to the French alliance. Neither the Signoria nor the war magistracy had informed Florence's partners in the league of the negotiations with the Valois monarch; instead they harped on Giangaleazzo's violations of the peace treaty. Envoys sent to Bologna and Ferrara in November 1396 to announce the league with Charles VI were not authorized to mention the military clauses concerning the French invasion force.[273] By not revealing those plans, Florentine statesmen apparently hoped to avoid any charge that they had provoked a renewal of hostilities, which, they insisted, was entirely the duke's responsibility. Florence's Lombard allies might well have resented their involvement in a war that their Tuscan partner had precipitated, and that was being fought on their territory.[274] To placate an irate Pope Boniface, who accused the republic of inviting the French into Italy, the war magistracy insisted that the initiative for the alliance came from France, and the republic had no choice but to accede to the king's request.[275] Even after fighting had begun in March 1397, the war magistracy failed to mention to their allies the projected French invasion. As late as July of that year, Florentine ambassadors at the papal court were instructed to deny that the republic had requested French military aid in her struggle with Giangaleazzo.[276]

[272] *Ibid.*, ff.94v–95r, 97v–98v, 102r–106r. Typical was the counsel of Guido del Palagio, *ibid.*, f.104v, 17 March: "Quilibet veniat ad subveniendum communem. Et quod fiat offensio hostium et guerra fiat in partibus Lombardie." See, too, Herde, "Politische Verhaltensweisen," 227, n.421.

[273] The first notice of the French negotiations in correspondence with the allies was on 9 Nov. 1396; *DBCMLC*, 2, ff.59v–60r.

[274] The Signoria instructed the ambassador sent to Bologna and Ferrara to reject any proposal by the allies to negotiate with Giangaleazzo; *SCMLC*, 1, f.77r, 28 March 1397.

[275] *DBCMLC*, 2, ff.70r–71r, 9 Dec. 1396; *SCMLC*, 1, ff.89r–92v, 15 July 1397. This account is contradicted by the instructions given to Maso degli Albizzi in May 1396; *DBCMLC*, 2, ff.19r–21r.

[276] *SCMLC*, 1, ff.74v–77r, 86r–87r. However, the war *balìa* instructed Buonaccorso Pitti to inform Charles VI (12 Jan. 1397) that the allies had ratified the French alliance and were "disiderosi dell'avenimento delle sue forze di gente alle parti di Lombardia"; *DBCMLC*, 2, f.80v.

Four years of intensive diplomacy in Italy had not changed the power balance significantly, and both Giangaleazzo and Florence searched abroad for an ally to break the stalemate. With the signing of the French alliance, Florence had won that contest, but her diplomats now had to convert treaty obligations into French troops crossing the Alps into Lombardy. The military forces and financial resources of the combatants were nearly equal, and the fighting in the early months of 1397 was sporadic and inconclusive. So the outcome of the war would be decided in Paris. There the Florentine ambassadors struggled against heavy odds to obtain military support from the king and his advisers.[277] Their arrival in Paris (February 1397) had coincided with the news of the disaster at Nicopolis, where a French crusading army had been crushed by the Turks. For several months, Pitti reported in his diary, "no one in Paris had a mind for anything except the funerals of the royal princes and gentlemen killed in Turkey and for the malady and madness of the king who had had to be locked up."[278] After Charles VI had recovered sufficiently to receive the ambassadors and to realize the nature of his obligation, he appointed the count of Armagnac to command the Italian expedition. The count promised the Florentine ambassadors that he would lead an army of 10,000 cavalry into Italy in the spring of 1398, and that "he would pitch camp as close as possible to the Duke of Milan's forces." With that welcome news, Vanni Castellani left Paris for Florence to inform the Signoria and the war magistracy that help was finally on the way.[279]

The news from France bolstered the depressed spirits of Florentine statesmen and aroused some enthusiasm in the populace. The Lucchese ambassador reported on 25 September that citizens were now willing to pay their *prestanze* and were loudly boasting that the tyrant would be destroyed by the French army. Maso degli Albizzi, the ambassador added, "is jumping with joy," since he had been instrumental in concluding the alliance and had been humiliated by King Charles' failure to fulfill his treaty obligations.[280] But reports of

[277] The war *balìa* (12 Jan. 1397) instructed Pitti to expedite the coming of the French army; *DBCMLC*, 2, ff.80v–82r.

[278] Pitti, *Cronica*, 101. The Lucchese ambassador reported from Florence in the spring of 1397 that the news from France was not promising; Fumi, *Regesti*, II, part 2, 349, no. 1690. The Signoria (30 March 1397) sent a mission to the French governor of Genoa, urging him to encourage French nobles to join the invading force; *SCMLC*, I, ff.78r–79r.

[279] Pitti, *Cronica*, 102–05. The count of Armagnac had first been contacted by a Florentine agent two years earlier, in June 1396; *DBCMLC*, I, ff.20v–21r.

[280] Fumi, *Regesti*, II, part 2, 401. Copies of the letters from France are published in *ibid.*, 402–03.

delays in the French invasion filtered across the Alps into Tuscany, changing the mood in Florence from euphoria to despair. Decribing the low morale of the citizenry in late November, the Lucchese ambassador reported that those favoring a peace settlement with Giangaleazzo were convinced that the leaders of the *reggimento* had manipulated the news from France to create a false impression that aid from that quarter was imminent. By these tactics, they hoped to dampen the peace sentiment among the *popolo*, who were becoming very restive over the prolongation of hostilities.[281] The ambassador described his conversation with a prominent political figure, Lotto Castellani, who voiced his deep suspicion of Giangaleazzo, and his fear that a peace settlement in Lombardy would give the duke an opportunity to throw all his resources against Florence in Tuscany. But that argument did not persuade the *popolo*, "all of whom believe that Messer Lotto and his associates, that is to say, the leaders of the *reggimento*, only make those statements to nourish and continue the war."[282]

A prime source of discontent was taxation. The Lucchese ambassador noted that Florentines could talk of little else, "and it appears to them that they are throwing their money, not into a well, but into a very deep chasm, without any results."[283] They grumbled loudly and openly about their assessments and the inequities of the distribution, but when a Signoria proposed reforms, those who sat in the legislative councils cast their white beans against these measures. In an eighteen-month period between October 1397 and March 1399, the Council of the *Popolo* rejected a total of twenty-eight provisions pertaining to the redistribution of *prestanze* assessments.[284] By these constant rebuffs to the executive, the guild electorate was expressing its opposition to the regime's fiscal system and, more generally, to its foreign policy. More effective gestures of protest were made by those citizens who, in increasing numbers, failed to pay their assessments, or paid only a portion of their obligations.[285] This alarming trend substantially reduced

---

[281] *Ibid.*, 416: "E questo è lo scomento di questo popolo e parlassine sì largo che nullo nullo se ne guarda." Also pessimistic was the report from Francesco Datini to his office in Valencia, 17 Nov. 1397: "E poi di Francia viene più parole che gente d'arme"; *Datini*, 984, unpaginated.

[282] Fumi, *Regesti*, II, part 2, 426–27, 2 Jan. 1397.

[283] *Ibid.*, II, part 2, 410.

[284] Molho, "Florentine Oligarchy," *Speculum*, XLIII, 43–45.

[285] Molho, *Florentine Public Finances*, 68, has shown that there was a sharp increase during the 1390s in the number of those who paid no *prestanze*, and who paid only a part *ad perdendum*. Money was in short supply "per questa maladetta guerra"; Francesco Datini to his office in Majorca, 18 May 1397; *Datini*, 1062, unpaginated.

the amount that a *prestanza* would yield, and it forced the government to search for alternative sources of income. To make up an annual deficit of some 200,000 florins,[286] counselors in the *pratiche* recommended measures that were invariably proposed, and often implemented, in wartime. Tax delinquents should be coerced or shamed into paying their levies; the clergy should make their contribution to Florentine liberty from which they derived as many benefits as laymen did; the money set aside to reduce the public debt should instead be diverted to pay mercenaries.[287] These were conventional remedies. More radical were the proposals of Niccolò Guasconi that two forced loans, which would not be repaid, be levied annually, and that the right to hold major offices be limited to those affluent citizens with a *prestanza* assessment above five florins.[288] This proposal reflected the growing strength of elitist ideas within the *reggimento*, and it hinted at a solution to the republic's fiscal problems that had been initiated in 1391. In addition to their forced loans, the wealthiest citizens were solicited for additional contributions whenever a money shortage hampered the war effort. These loans were the particular responsibility of the special commissions of "very astute citizens" who were charged with finding revenue "by means both ordinary and extraordinary, so that our troops will be ready to fight."[289]

Against this background of popular discontent over war and taxes, an unpromising military situation in Lombardy, and growing skepticism about the invasion, the regime reluctantly agreed to participate in peace discussions in the early months of 1398. An embassy was sent to Venice to discuss terms with Florence's allies and with Venetian diplomats who were trying to end the hostilities. Counselors in the *pratiche* displayed little enthusiasm for these negotiations, although they did recognize the difficulties in pursuing a war with an empty treasury, lukewarm allies, and an exhausted citizenry.[290] "Truly, if we do not have peace," Francesco Datini wrote to his partners in Majorca, "the merchants and the guildsmen will be ruined by the taxes. Note that we have to pay four or five forced loans each month. . . . May it please God to give us peace quickly so that these levies will cease.

---

[286] I base this figure on Molho's calculations, *Florentine Public Finances*, 61–62, for the year 1402, when income and expenditure was roughly comparable to that of the year 1397, and when the treasury had a deficit of 200,000 fl.

[287] *CP*, 32, f.86r; 33, ff.25r–26v.   [288] *Ibid.*, 32, ff.74r, 137r.

[289] *Ibid.*, ff.158v, 159r, statements of Rinaldo Gianfigliazzi and Giuliano Nerini.

[290] The Florentines felt that the Bolognese had not contributed their share to the Mantua campaign; Mesquita, 229–30. Conversely, some of the allies complained that Florence had been responsible for the outbreak of hostilities by signing the French treaty, and by attacking her neighbors; *SCMC*, 1, f.87r, 30 June 1397.

. . ."[291] Maso degli Albizzi and Matteo Tinghi vainly resisted these peace pressures; the latter offered to contribute 1300 florins from his private fortune to subsidize the war.[292] These men were so obsessed with winning a decisive military victory that they sent an embassy (March 1398) to offer 150,000 florins to Duke Leopold IV of Austria if he would attack Giangaleazzo.[293] Maso continued to hope that the French invasion would materialize, and he wanted to avoid a truce until the military balance had shifted in Florence's favor. Buonaccorso Pitti arrived from France in late March with the news that the count of Armagnac was collecting his army in Avignon, and that he wanted a subsidy of 25,000 florins to be sent to him at Asti. The war magistracy first agreed to this demand, but when Armagnac later requested that the money be paid to him in Avignon, the officials concluded that this meant further delay and instead decided to sign a truce with Giangaleazzo.[294] In a *pratica* on 23 April, the Signoria tested civic sentiment.[295] Alessandro Arrigucci wanted no part of peace negotiations: "Let us hire the duke [*sic*] of Armagnac and then await victory!" But his colleagues had no stomach for more fighting, and no confidence in the French. Maso degli Albizzi finally realized that the French invasion was a chimera, and he recommended a truce, stipulating only that its terms should not violate the treaty with Charles VI, and that some attention be paid to Florence's honor. Francesco Federighi counseled the Signoria to sign the truce without delay, and to invite Armagnac only if the negotiations collapsed. That policy, approved by a majority of the counselors, was accepted by the Signoria, and, three weeks later, the truce terms were published in Pavia.[296]

[291] *Datini*, 1062, unpaginated, 13 Feb. 1398. On the depressed condition of the woolen cloth industry in these months, see *ASF, Lana*, 48, ff.12r–12v.

[292] *CP*, 33, f.8r, 16 Feb. 1398. For more pacifist views, see the statements of Giovanni Biliotti, Simone Capponi and Cristofano Spini, and also that of Giovanni di Bicci de' Medici: "Quod . . . non obstante scripta de Francia, pax fiat"; *CP*, 32, f.177v, 6 Feb. For earlier statements favoring peace, see Herde, "Politische Verhaltensweisen," 231.

[293] *SCMC*, 1, ff.105v–107r. The invading army was to comprise 2000 lances and 2000 infantry. The duke would receive 50,000 fl. upon arrival in Italy, and an additional 100,000 fl. after three months.

[294] Pitti, *Cronica*, 106–09. Pitti thought that this decision was a mistake. On the negotiations between Armagnac and the Florentine ambassador, Berto Castellani, in the spring of 1398, see *DBRA*, 1, ff.58v–61v.

[295] *CP*, 33, ff.31r–32v. This was a large *pratica* with 34 recorded speeches.

[296] Mesquita, *Giangaleazzo*, 222–23; Herde, "Politische Verhaltensweisen," 232–34. The Florentine government was not pleased with Venice's conduct of the negotiations; *SCMLC*, 1, ff.175v–178v, 180v–181r. Cf. Datini's letter to his Majorca branch; *Datini*, 1063, unpaginated, 8 June 1398.

For Maso degli Albizzi and his associates, this war was an un-
mitigated disaster. It had cost a million florins,[297] and had gained the
republic nothing but resentment and opprobrium. The hopes of the
Albizzi party had been pinned on the French, and the failure of that
enterprise had doomed the plan to crush Giangaleazzo between two
invading armies. Florence's allies blamed her for initiating hostilities
and for pursuing the struggle in Lombardy to avoid the ravages of war
in her own territory. Though Venice played a more active diplomatic
role than heretofore, she was not really concerned with Florentine
security, but only with restraining Giangaleazzo's power in eastern
Lombardy. In Tuscany, Florence's only success was her contribution
to Lucca's defense, which won her no gratitude from the Lucchese.
The republic's sole opportunity to gain an advantage over Giangaleazzo in Tuscany occurred late in 1397 when the lord of Pisa,
Jacopo d'Appiano, expelled the Visconti garrison from that city.[298] The
Signoria sent an embassy to Jacopo, who seemed willing to negotiate
a peace settlement that would again permit Florentine merchants to
use the Pisan port. But he was not prepared to grant the same privileges that Florentines had enjoyed under Pietro Gambacorta, and on
this issue the negotiations foundered. Initially, Florentine opinion was
rigidly opposed to Pisan demands for a revision of the commerical
treaty, but in later discussions some speakers favored a more conciliatory posture, recommending that the dispute be submitted to the Lucchese government for arbitration.[299] But this gesture was too little
and too late, and Jacopo d'Appiano quickly repaired his relations with
Giangaleazzo. Once again, Florentine obstinacy, and her failure to
react quickly to events, had ruined any prospects for gaining a diplomatic advantage through a small concession.[300]

Although the regime achieved none of its military and diplomatic
objectives, it did exhibit a remarkable stability, and an ability to

[297] Based on Molho's calculations, *Florentine Public Finances*, 10.

[298] *Ibid.*, 218–19. See the description of these events; *SCMLC*, 1, ff.172r–172v,
11 Jan. 1398.

[299] *CP*, 32, ff.173r, 174v, 177r, and two important *pratiche* on 6 and 8 Feb. 1398,
ibid., ff.177v–178r; and *CP*, 33, ff.3v–4v.

[300] The Signoria first sent ambassadors to Lucca (10 Jan. 1398) to discuss the
Pisan situation, and told them to use their judgment about visiting Pisa. They
were not given specific instructions for negotiating with Jacopo d'Appiano;
SCMLC, 1, ff.104v–105r. A report from a Datini source suggested that the ambassadors were duped by Jacopo; *Datini*, 769, unpaginated, 3 March 1398; letter
from Andrea e Antonio & C.¹ in Florence to Francesco di Marco e Andrea di
Bonanno & C.¹ in Genoa. See too the letter from Calcidonio e Niccolaio degli
Alberti & C.¹ in Florence to the Datini office in Barcelona, 24 Feb. 1398; *Datini*,
861, unpaginated.

govern effectively, during the fourteen months of an unpopular war. Through its control of the executive, and specifically its authority to create *balìe* and impose *prestanze*, the leadership could prosecute a war, at least for a limited period, without a mandate from the legislative councils. Scarcely any trace of dissent appears in the debates; only the pertinacious resistance of some councilors in voting against tax and security measures testified to the existence of a covert opposition to the leadership.[301] But neither the ravaging of enemy troops in Florence's *contado*, nor the call for an uprising (July 1397) by Antonio de' Medici and his followers, ignited any popular rebellion in the city. In the judgment of the Lucchese ambassador, that bizarre plot had strengthened the regime, since it revealed the indifference of the *popolo* to such appeals.[302] The authorities were much less concerned about domestic unrest than they had been during the first conflict with Giangaleazzo,[303] and the number of conspiracies in the territory also declined significantly, by comparison with 1390–1392. The only serious revolt occurred in San Miniato in February 1397, when Benedetto Mangiadori led a group of sixteen horsemen into the town, assassinated the Florentine vicar, and with shouts of "Long live liberty" tried to ignite an uprising. But no one joined them and they had to flee to avoid capture.[304] Neither Giangaleazzo nor his Pisan confederate, Jacopo d'Appiano, made a real effort to exploit discontent in Florentine territory,[305] whose inhabitants may have had the opportunity to compare their situation with that of their neighbors in Pisa and Siena, who lived under a different type of regime.

The Final Confrontation, 1398–1402

After the failure of the Florentine scheme to crush Giangaleazzo with French arms, the duke gained the diplomatic initiative in Italy. The truce of Pavia provided for the restoration of the *status quo* in Lombardy. An unstated codicil was Venetian acquiescence in Gian-

---

[301] In addition to opposing fiscal measures, the Council of the *Popolo* repeatedly rejected a measure giving broad police authority to a *capitano di balìa*; LF, 45, ff.32r, 40r, 43r–50r; CP, 32, ff.48v, 69v, 76r. The measure was finally approved by narrow margins in August 1397, after an abortive revolt; Prov., 86, ff.103r–105r.

[302] Fumi, *Regesti*, II, part 2, 389–90, no. 1803.

[303] For the only reference to *oblocutores*, see the comments of Alessandro Alessandri and Bartolomeo Valori; CP, 32, ff.104v, 105v, 17 March 1397.

[304] Fumi, *Regesti*, II, part 2, 335, no. 1626; AP, 3603, unpaginated, 14 April 1397.

[305] Jacopo d'Appiano was implicated in a plot to organize a revolt in Pescia near Pistoia; CP, 32, ff.77v–80r, 8–10 Nov. 1396; and the conviction of four conspirators; GA, 71, part 1, ff.118r–121r, 12 Aug. 1396.

galeazzo's efforts to establish his dominion over Tuscany (including Florence) in exchange for the stabilization of eastern Lombardy. The main bulwark against Visconti expansion, the league of Bologna, did not survive the war. The marquis of Mantua switched his allegiance to Giangaleazzo, and the young lord of Ferrara, while still nominally an adherent of the league, in effect declared his neutrality. The situation in Bologna deteriorated as Visconti intrigues stimulated the factional quarrels that had always been a threat to that city's stability and to the Florentine alliance. Giangaleazzo also scored points against Florence in the Romagna, winning the formal allegiance of the Ordelaffi *signori* of Forlì and the Malatesta of Rimini, and even the friendship of a longtime Florentine ally, Astorre Manfredi of Faenza. Even more damaging was the defection of several nobles in the Apennines, who rebelled against Florentine rule and declared their allegiance to Giangaleazzo.[306] These scions of old Ghibelline families, led by Count Roberto of Poppi, were persuaded (so a Florentine witness reported) that the republic would inevitably surrender to Giangaleazzo, and they were preparing early for that contingency.[307] Florence's decision against using force to crush this rebellion may have been dictated by strategic considerations, but it was a serious blow to civic morale and a stimulus to other subjects who chafed under the Florentine yoke.

A greater threat to Florentine security was the duke's brilliant success in solidifying his authority in central Italy, first in Pisa (February 1399), then in Siena (August 1399), and finally in Perugia (July 1400), by formally accepting the overlordship of these cities.[308] Prior to the consummation of these diplomatic coups, Florence had established contacts with the governments of Pisa and Siena, in an effort to improve relations, and specifically to sign a commerical agreement that would give her a Mediterranean port. But her tactics in negotiating with her neighbors had not changed since the 1380s. Refusing to make any concessions on toll rates to the Pisans, she sought to force them to grant her merchants the same privileges they had enjoyed under Pietro Gambacorta, by negotiating simultaneously with Siena

---

[306] These developments are well summarized in Mesquita, *Giangaleazzo*, 239–45. As early as March 1398, Carlo Malatesta had warned Florence of the subversive activities of the duke's agents and Florentine exiles in the Apennine region, "e che in Firenze era bene che darebbe loro favore, e che degli usciti mettevano danari in questi fatti e anchora de' cittadini dentro vi concordano"; DBRA, 1, f.54v.

[307] Morelli, *Ricordi*, 366–67.

[308] Summarized in Mesquita, 246–54. On Florentine policy toward these cities, see now Herde, "Politische Verhaltensweisen," 234–41.

for the use of the port of Talamone. A further complication to these discussions was Florence's insistence that the Pisans (and the Sienese) should abandon their connection with Giangaleazzo.[309] Since they were demanding so much and offering so little, the Florentines should not have been surprised by the failure of these negotiations. But the tone of the deliberations on this issue revealed a curious failure to appreciate realities and, specifically, to grasp the vital importance of gaining a secure outlet to the sea. On 11 October 1398, the Signoria convened a large *pratica*, in which Simone Bordoni and Tommaso Marchi favored an agreement with the Sienese, "since without any doubt this will restore our old friendship." Maso degli Albizzi and Jacopo Guasconi supported that policy, the latter arguing that the Pisans would never become true friends of Florence. But Giovanni Biliotti insisted that Pisa offered more advantages for commerce.[310] This disagreement over the relative advantages of Pisa and Siena as commercial outlets was not resolved, and it may have impeded a settlement with either city.[311] The situation in Pisa became more critical in the winter of 1398–1399 when Jacopo d'Appiano's uncertain control of that city increased the possibility of direct Visconti rule. In Florence, there was no sense of crisis until it was too late to act. On 16 December, Guccio Nobili suggested that the Signoria offer to send 100 lances to defend the city "if the Pisans will enter this alliance voluntarily and sincerely," and if they agreed to restore the old trading privileges to Florentine merchants. In Vanni Castellani's opinion, the Pisans should be persuaded to accept "reasonable and appropriate terms," and no commercial pact should be approved unless they agreed to a formal alliance.[312] By mid-January, some counselors were expressing greater concern, but the mood was predominantly passive and even fatalistic. Giovanni de' Ricci saw no workable alternative to "waiting for time to pass and living peacefully with the Pisans and our other neighbors," and Simone Bordoni remarked petulantly that "if they wish to give themselves to the duke, let them do so."[313] No one favored military

---

[309] See the statements of Simone Capponi and Benedetto Peruzzi, *CP*, 33, f.100r. Concerning these negotiations, see Datini's letters to his partners in Majorca; *Datini*, 1063, unpaginated, 20 July and 25 Dec. 1398; and *SCMLC*, 1, ff.120r, 124r–126r, 128r.

[310] *CP*, 33, ff.84r–85v.

[311] *Ibid.*, ff.100r–100v, 14 Nov.

[312] *Ibid.*, f.106r. The rigidity of the Florentine position is documented by the instructions to her ambassadors; *SCMLC*, 1, ff.157r–159v.

[313] *CP*, 33, f.116v, 12 Jan. 1399. As late as 8 Jan., Florentine envoys were still insisting on a Pisan surety of 100,000 fl. as a condition for a commercial pact; *SCMLC*, 1, f.133r.

intervention in Pisa to keep the city out of Visconti hands and to secure Florence's vital link with the sea.

The republic's failure to react more forcefully to the Pisan crisis may have reflected some uncertainty about the gravity of the issue, but, more generally, it was a consequence of the disastrous foreign policy that had been pursued in 1396 and 1397.[314] Sensing the city's disillusionment with a war that had been expensive and inconclusive, the leadership was wary of any situation that might involve fighting or heavy expenses. Giovanni Biliotti proposed a sharp reduction in the military budget (July 1398), reiterating that "the commune should live on its own"; Maso degli Albizzi concurred with Biliotti's argument "that the commune should avoid the troubles of war."[315] During the Pisan negotiations six months later, Maso's attitude was very cautious: "If the Pisan league violates the truce [with Giangaleazzo], then do not sign it, and commit ourselves only to expenditures that are modest and tolerable." Speaking for the war magistracy, Niccolò da Uzzano was willing to spend 30,000 florins annually, but others felt that no money, and only a limited number of troops, should be invested in the Pisan alliance.[316] However, when the Pisan negotiations were foundering, some counselors became apprehensive of public criticism and urged the Signoria "to justify to our *popolo* and to the Pisans the commune's role in the negotiations over the port, to demonstrate that we did everything possible. . . ."[317] Mercantile correspondence in the Datini archives contains no specific criticisms of Florentine diplomacy, but it does reveal the anxieties stimulated by the news that Giangaleazzo had purchased Pisa from Jacopo d'Appiano for 200,000 florins. "We would gladly have offered 600,000 florins if he wished to sell it to us," Francesco Datini commented. Neither Pisa nor the Lucchese port of Mutrone was now a feasible outlet for Florentine mer-

---

[314] The similarity with the Florentine mood in 1392 is striking; see above, 145. Months later (July 1399), the Signoria sought to place the main responsibility for Pisa's subjection on the Venetians: "se loro ambasciadori fussono venuti a Pisa, innanzi le cose avessono preso quella forma, ogni cosa sarebbe intorbidita et non serebbe quella città in servitù"; *SCMLC*, 3, f.4r.

[315] *CP*, 33, ff.57r–57v. Guido del Palagio proposed an army of 500 lances and 1000 infantry. In July 1398 the Signoria wrote to Florentine ambassadors in Venice "per levarci le genti da dosso e contentare e' nostri caporali ci è convenuto e conviene pagare tanta somma di denari che serebbe uno stupore a dirlo"; Mesquita, 363.

[316] *CP*, 33, ff. 104r, 106v. Maso degli Albizzi's comment: "Et si expensa essent tam magna que displiceret populo, non fiat." See Herde, "Politische Verhaltensweisen," 237–38.

[317] Filippo Magalotti, *CP*, 33, f.109v. See also his statement, "quod cum civibus se large aperiant," and that of Cristofano Spini, *ibid.*, f.111r, 3 Jan. 1399.

chandise. "This is very bad news for us," Giovanni Orlandini wrote to the Datini branch in Barcelona; "the tyrant has established a foothold in Tuscany and will soon do the same in Siena, so that the fire is at the door. Never before have we had so powerful a *signore* for a neighbor. . . ."[318]

Very similar was the Florentine reaction to events in Perugia, which culminated in that community's recognition of Giangaleazzo as its ruler. Since the political situation in Umbria was more complex, and the solutions to the crisis more varied, Florentine policy was even more ambivalent than it had been toward Pisa. Though encouraging the Perugini to defend their liberty, the Florentines would have been quite content if Boniface IX established himself as temporal ruler of that city, particularly if the pope could be induced to enter an alliance with the republic.[319] In letters composed by Salutati in his most florid rhetorical style, the Signoria recalled the ancient friendship between the two cities, and those past occasions when they had fought together to defend their freedom.[320] But the Florentines offered very little concrete help to reinforce their appeals, though some citizens were now insisting that Perugia's independence was crucial to the republic's security.[321] They delivered a series of patriotic orations designed to arouse a war-weary citizenry from its lethargy. "Let us defend our liberty with spirit and determination," cried Matteo di Jacopo Arrighi, "and by every possible means prevent the tyrant's power from growing." But these appeals did not persuade those who worried about the danger of renewed hostilities, and of heavier fiscal burdens. Niccolò Guasconi and Leonardo Beccanugi opposed the reappointment of the war magistracy on the grounds that it would signal the republic's intention to renew the war.[322] At year's end, these problems were still the focus of inconclusive debate. Vieri Cavicciuli

[318] *Datini*, 1063, unpaginated, letters of Datini to Majorca, 15 Feb. and 15 March 1399.

[319] The authoritative study on Perugia's submission to Giangaleazzo is now H. Goldbrunner, "Die Übergabe Perugias an Giangaleazzo Visconti (1400)," *Quellen und Forschungen aus Italienischen Archiven und Bibliotheken*, XLII–XLIII (1964), 285–369. See also Esch, *Bonifaz IX.*, 280–90, 298–301, 311–31.

[320] For examples see Goldbrunner, 359–62; Herde, "Politische Verhaltensweisen," 235; *SCMLC*, I, ff.122r, 129v–131r, 135v–137r, 140v–141r.

[321] Statement of Francesco Fioravanti, *CP*, 33, f.140v, 11 Apr. 1399. Florence did loan Perugia 10,000 fl. to pay her debt to Boniface; *SRRO*, I, f.31r, but did not provide any military assistance to the beleaguered commune. Just before Perugia's decision to submit to Visconti rule, Florence offered to pay for 100–150 lances to defend the city; Degli Azzi Vitelleschi, *Relazioni*, I, no. 925.

[322] *CP*, 33, f.134r, 16 Feb. 1399. See the statements of Maso degli Albizzi and Giovannozzo Biliotti; *ibid.*, ff.122v, 134r.

warned against military adventures, and Jacopo Guasconi urged the government to pursue a peaceful course. In a debate held at the height of the Perugia crisis (29 January 1400), the counselors could not agree on the need for a war magistracy, although a majority favored its appointment. While Vieri Cavicciuli and Filippo Magalotti continued to argue for caution and restraint, Gino Capponi and Rinaldo Gianfigliazzi called for stronger resistance to Giangaleazzo, even though this would involve risks and expense.[323]

Those leaders of the *reggimento* who, like Maso degli Albizzi,[324] resisted the pressures of their more warlike colleagues were guided by their sense of the civic mood.[325] Critics of the leadership did not articulate their grievances in public debates, but they did vote consistently against legislation formulated and promoted by the executive: to hold a new scrutiny for the Signoria, to reappoint the magistracy on internal security,[326] to reform the distribution of forced loans, to elect *ragionerii straordinari*. Civic morale was not improved by a visitation of the plague in the summer of 1399, which forced thousands to flee the city and brought business to a standstill, nor by a severe grain shortage in the winter and spring of 1400.[327] Some citizens grumbled about official malfeasance; others suspected their neighbors of unpatriotic behavior. From Spalato in Dalmatia, Bernardo Davanzati wrote to his son Piero in Venice that a Florentine merchant, Baldassare Ubriachi, was an agent of the Visconti, and had been sent to Paris on a diplomatic mission for the duke.[328] Accused by an in-

---

[323] *CP*, 34, ff.70v–73v.

[324] Maso's views on foreign policy in these months were consistently cautious; *CP*, 33, ff.104r, 106v, 107r, 134v; 34, ff.12v, 61v.

[325] Counselors displayed a greater solicitude for public opinion in these months than was customary; for example, in the selection of a war captain: "Sit Bernardone qui placet populo. . . . Sit Bernardone quia populus contentatur ante omnes alios"; *CP*, 34, ff.33v–34r.

[326] The provision authorizing a scrutiny was finally approved, after two rejections; *Prov.*, 87, ff.350r–351r; see the debate, *CP*, 33, f.101v. The provision authorizing the re-election of the Eight on Security was first rejected, then approved; *LF*, 46, ff.67r, 70r. For resistance to fiscal reforms, see Molho, "Florentine Oligarchy," *op. cit.*, 45; and for opposition to the appointment of the *ragionerii straordinarii*; *LF*, 46, ff.61r, 62r, 65r, 67r, 72r–74r.

[327] There are numerous references to plague in the Datini archives: *Datini*, 719, letter of G. Cirioni to Datini, 29 Sept. 1400; 864, Datini to Barcelona, 1 and 27 Sept. 1399; 985, Datini to Valencia, 17 and 30 Oct. 1400; 1064, Datini to Majorca, 22 Nov. 1399; 1065, Datini to Majorca, 12 Aug. 1400. On the grain shortage, *CP*, 34, ff.55r–56v, 99r.

[328] *CRS*, 78 (*Badìa*), vol. 315, no. 231, 232. On Ubriachi, see I. Origo, *The Merchant of Prato* (London, 1957), 98. Ubriachi was a famous ivory craftsman who had worked for Giangaleazzo in the Certosa near Pavia. See J. von Schlosser, "Die

former of making derogatory remarks about the commune, Francesco Datini had to send an exculpatory letter to the Eight on Security, admitting his guilt and begging their indulgence.[329] Giovanni Alderotti was convicted of making treasonable statements while complaining about his *prestanze*. "I would prefer that we accept the lordship of the duke of Milan," he allegedly said, "and even the rule of the devil himself so that we could escape from the subjugation of our arrogant rulers." Alderotti claimed to be speaking for a majority of Florentines "who share my opinions that we cannot continue in this manner."[330]

It is impossible to know how many citizens shared Alderotti's sentiments. A majority would probably have agreed with his critical appraisal of the government, though certainly not with his statement about preferring Giangaleazzo's rule. The most concrete evidence of patrician alienation is found in the documents pertaining to a conspiracy organized by Florentine exiles in the summer and autumn of 1400, and discovered in November before it could be implemented.[331] Though most of the plotters were members of the exile communities in Bologna, Faenza, and Venice (and thus receptive to any plan that might restore their status), others were recruited from citizens who had come to Bologna that summer to escape the pestilence, and who had been persuaded to join the conspiracy.[332] They belonged to some of Florence's most prominent families: Altoviti, Strozzi, Adimari, Quaratesi, Del Bene. One of the conspirators, Francesco Davizzi, wrote a detailed confession implicating those who had been privy to the enterprise, and listing others who were considered to be sympathetic to the rebels' objectives. Among those whom the ringleaders had judged to be qualified for high office in the new regime were Jacopo

Werkstatt der Embriachi in Venedig"; *Jahrbuch der kunsthistorischen Sammlungen des allerhöchsten Kaiserhofs*, XXII (1899), 220–82. I am indebted to Professor Richard Trexler for this information. In 1408 Bartolomeo Valori stated that Giangaleazzo obtained most of the financing for his wars from Florentine bankers; *CP*, 39, f.45v. That contention is surely exaggerated.

[329] *Lettere di un notaro a un mercante del secolo XIV*, ed. C. Guasti (Florence, 1880), I, 282, 288–89; II, 188. See, too, the letter from Datini to Majorca, 14 Feb. 1400, complaining about poor business conditions resulting from the plague and the insecurity of trade routes; *Datini*, 1064, unpaginated.

[330] *AP*, 3762, ff.37r–37v, 16 Oct. 1400. Alderotti was the son of a once prominent citizen who had been excluded from office in 1387 and restored in 1391.

[331] The condemnations are in *AP*, 3763, ff.9r–11r, 15r–17r, 23r–38v, 51r–58v. The Signoria described the conspiracy in a letter to Bologna; *SCMC*, 25, ff.18v–19r, 14 Nov. 1400. On this conspiracy, and civic reaction to it, see Herde, "Politische Verhaltensweisen," 228–30.

[332] G. Morelli, *Ricordi*, 369–70.

Ardinghelli, Francesco and Alessio Baldovinetti, Veri Rondinelli, Giovanni Altoviti, Tommaso Soderini, Barduccio Cherichini, and the humanist scholar Niccolò Niccoli.[333] Writing to Francesco Datini in Bologna, Giovanni Cirioni reported these events and noted that 102 individuals had thus far been identified as conspirators. He added that Francesco Davizzi had implicated an even larger number, whose names (so it was rumored) were in the possession of a Franciscan friar from Bologna.[334] The decision not to interrogate the suspects on Davizzi's list was made by the priors, who ordered the *podestà* to limit his investigation.[335] When one of the conspirators, Sanminiato de' Ricci, was being led to the place of execution, a crowd assembled in front of the church of Santa Croce. Fearing that sympathizers might rescue Ricci from the *podestà*'s retinue, the Signoria ordered his execution next to the church, instead of at the customary site outside the city walls.[336]

One of the leaders of this conspiracy, Paolo Giraldi, had close ties with the rebellious nobles in the Apennines and the Casentino. He confessed that his group had communicated with Giangaleazzo's agents for assistance in their enterprise, promising in return to accept the duke's rule over their lands.[337] The extent of Giangaleazzo's involvement in this affair is not clear,[338] but his agents were actively encouraging rebellions throughout Florentine territory, on a scale comparable to that of the early 1390s. The Signoria complained to Venice (April 1400) that the duke was continually promoting rebellions in Tuscany, "and that he has invested so much energy and so many resources that . . . we have discovered plots in San Miniato, in

---

[333] Davizzi's confession, and those of Michele Benini and Sanminiato de' Ricci, are in L. Passerini, *Gli Alberti del Giudice di Firenze*, II, 266–79. On the vicissitudes of Niccoli's political career, see Martines, *Social World*, 161–63; Baron, *Crisis*, 2nd ed., 326–28.

[334] *Datini*, 78, unpaginated, letters of 18 and 20 Nov. 1400. The Signoria asked the Bolognese government to obtain a copy from the Franciscan, Fra Jacopo; *SCMC*, 25, ff.21v–22r.

[335] *CP*, 34, f.134r, statement of Rinaldo Gianfigliazzi.

[336] *Panc.*, 158, ff.197r–197v; *Datini*, 78, unpaginated, letter of 19 Nov. 1400, Cirioni to Datini.

[337] *AP*, 3763, ff.9v–10r. Testifying to the success of Visconti proselytization among the Apennine nobility was a statement by one of the Ubaldini: "Io veggio tucti i gentili huomini dintorno acostarsi col duca di Melano, e se io m'indugio ad acostarmi col detto duca di Melano, forse a tale ora vorrò ch'io non potrò, però chè come sai, Bartolomeo da Pietramala è mio nimico, e se io non mi concio a buon'o ra, elli mi potrebbe notare"; *GA*, 97, unpaginated, process against Ser Lodovico di Ser Paolo of Città di Castello, 7 Feb. 1402.

[338] Chronicle sources reported links between Giangaleazzo and the Bologna rebels; *ASF, Manoscritti*, 225, f.134v; *Panc.*, 158, f.197r; but the confessions did not mention these contacts.

Arezzo, in Montepulciano, in Volterra, and in Pietrabuona. . . ."[339] A Sienese nobleman, Niccolò Salimbeni, and Giangaleazzo's lieutenant in Pisa, was implicated in a plot to introduce Visconti troops into Montepulciano (October 1399). Siena was also the base for a group of exiles from San Miniato, led by Benedetto Mangiadori, who had been outlawed for rebellion.[340] Along Florence's northwestern frontier, in the hill region above Pistoia, the danger of subversion promoted by Visconti gold and arms was particularly acute. In the winter of 1401, a prominent Pistoia family, the Cancellieri, tried to seize control of that city and, when they failed, occupied Sambuca, a frontier village on the Pistoia-Bologna road.[341] Though Pistoia remained under Florentine rule, Riccardo Cancellieri successfully repelled all attempts to dislodge him from Sambuca, which he defended with the aid of Visconti arms.

In considering the appropriate response to these challenges, Florentine authorities, and the citizens who advised them, wavered between restraint and ruthlessness. Initially, civic opinion favored clemency for those involved in the 1400 conspiracy, and punishment by exile instead of execution. "Let justice be done with moderation and with a full revelation of the affair," Maso degli Albizzi counseled the Signoria.[342] Five citizens were executed and twelve others (including two Scali, three Ricci, two Medici, and three Alberti) were declared outlaws, with rewards of 2000–3000 florins for anyone who killed them.[343] A month later, Antonio Alberti was accused of being privy to the conspiracy and failing to report it to the Signoria. In the judgment of several counselors, he deserved to die a thousand deaths, but they recommended clemency, "since hatreds are nourished by the shedding of blood."[344] Released from custody, Antonio was fined 3000 florins and sent into exile. After this gesture of clemency, the mood within the *reggimento* hardened. Speaking in a *pratica* on 20 May 1401, Niccolò

---

[339] Mesquita, *Giangaleazzo*, 368. For other complaints about Visconti-inspired plots in Montelupo, allegedly organized by Giangaleazzo's lieutenant in Siena, the bishop of Novara, and in Montepulciano and Volterra; see *SCMLC*, 3, ff.12r–12v, 16 Nov. 1399.

[340] *GA*, 97, ff.80r–81r; *AP*, 3712, unpaginated, condemnation of Domenico di Francesco of Chiusi.

[341] *AP*, 3821, ff.66r–70v; *CP*, 35, ff.15r, 17v.

[342] *CP*, 34, f.132r, 13 Nov. 1400.

[343] Passerini, *Alberti*, II, 281–89. That *balìa* decree stipulated that if a Florentine outlaw killed any of the rebels, his ban would be cancelled.

[344] *CP*, 34, ff.145r–148r; see Herde, "Politischen Verhaltensweisen," 230. Alberti was one of the Sixteen, and contrary to opinions expressed in the *pratica*, his guilt was not proven; Morelli, *Ricordi*, 371.

Guasconi urged the authorities to "use iron and poison against those seeking to destroy the city." Lotto Castellani approved this counsel, adding that the campaign against the rebels should be conducted "according to the laws and by every other means."[345] Some Florentine politicians may have employed "other means" to harm their enemies. In August 1398, Astorre Manfredi, lord of Faenza, informed a Florentine ambassador of the confession made to his officials by one Nardo di Benedetto, that he had been hired by Maso degli Albizzi, Rinaldo Gianfigliazzi and Cionaccio Baroncelli to assassinate certain Florentine exiles, specifically Donato Acciaiuoli, Salvestro de' Ricci, and Riccardo Alberti.[346] The Signoria indignantly denied that charge, insisting that Nardo confessed to his crime because he had been tortured. The judge who had interrogated Nardo and sentenced him to death was a Florentine, Jacopo Covoni, who was himself exiled to Naples for fifteen years for his complicity in what the republic called a miscarriage of justice.[347]

Florentine policy toward the rebels (or potential rebels) in the Pistoia area was no more consistent than the treatment of her exiles, although in this sphere, too, leniency gave way to rigor. The news of the Pistoia revolt and the seizure of Sambuca had stunned the citizenry, some of whom demanded the extirpation of the Cancellieri, while others were in favor of negotiating a pact with the rebels. The colleges were so incensed that they demanded the imprisonment of all the Cancellieri, even their wives and sisters. The Signoria finally decided to take over direct control of Pistoia and by a show of force in that city, coerced the local authorities into approving the enabling legislation.[348] The Signoria then ordered the Florentine magistrates in Pistoia to select eight members of the Cancellieri and eight from the rival Panciatichi family; these men were to live in Florence for a fifteen-year period as hostages for the good behavior of their families and the peace of their community.[349]

These manifestations of dissent and alienation in city, *contado*, and district adversely affected the republic's capacity to resist the Visconti

---

[345] *CP*, 34, f.185r.

[346] *SRRO*, 1, f.21r, 30 Aug. 1398. Others named in the confession as parties to this affair were Cionaccio Baroncelli, Domenico Giugni, and Marcello Strozzi. The price was 800 fl., and Nardo and his companions allegedly promised a Florentine pension and the license to bear arms to the assassin. For a similar accusation, see *SCMLC*, 1, ff.103r, 104r.

[347] *ACP*, 2107, unpaginated, 5 Dec. 1399. The Covoni were victims of a purge by the *arciguelfi* in the 1380s; see above, 86–87.

[348] *CP*, 35, ff.15r, 17v, 19r–21v, 27v; *Panc.*, 158, f. 199r.

[349] *SCMLC*, 3, f.38v, 19 Nov. 1401.

in two ways: first, by distracting the leadership's attention from the critical problems of defense, and second by disseminating a sense of Florentine weakness and vulnerability throughout the peninsula, among enemies and friends. From their sanctuaries in Pisa, Bologna, Faenza, and Venice, Florentine exiles spread tales of popular dissatisfaction with the tax burden, the stagnation of trade, and the arrogant rule of the "tyrants" who were destroying their city. The republic's inability to stamp out the rebellions in the northern and eastern parts of the territory, and to recover Sambuca from the Cancellieri was particularly damaging to her reputation. The statement by a member of the Ubaldini clan in 1401 reflected the sentiment in the Apennines that Florence's fate was sealed, and that prudence dictated an accommodation with the conqueror. "I see that all of the nobles in the region are allying themselves with the duke of Milan," he told a Visconti agent, "and if I delay in my own settlement with him, it may be too late. . . ."[350] The tone of Florence's diplomatic communications with her allies, and with potential allies, betrayed her insecurity and her bafflement over her inability to suppress these revolts. To Venice, the titular head of the league that had been formed to resist Visconti aggression, the republic appealed for support against the viper, whose goal was the subjugation of Italy. Likewise, to Pope Boniface IX and his protégé, young King Ladislaus of Naples, Florentine diplomats spelled out the record of Giangaleazzo's aggression, his appropriation of ecclesiastical territory, his threat to their own security.[351] None of these arguments moved the Venetians or the pope, the former perceiving no connection between Florence's independence and their own, the latter being too weak to risk a confrontation with Giangaleazzo in support of a regime that was so vulnerable.

In their deliberations during the spring and summer of 1401, Florentines were nervous, vacillating, uncertain—seemingly unable or unwilling to agree upon policy, or to execute it forcefully. The priors and the war magistracy were engaged in feverish diplomatic activity—missions to Rome and Naples, to Venice, to Genoa—but none of these overtures bore fruit. Opinions on fiscal problems were either litanies about correcting inequities and forcing everyone to pay his obligations, or radical proposals for increasing revenues by imposing a

[350] *GA*, 97, unpaginated, process of 7 Feb. 1402 against Ser Lodovico di Ser Paolo.

[351] The Signoria's instructions to Florentine ambassadors in Venice and Rome are filled with warnings against Giangaleazzo's machinations, and exasperation because the Venetians and the pope did not appreciate the threat to their states; *SCMLC*, 2, ff.30v–32r, 45v–48r; 3, ff.1r–1v, 3v–4v, 11v–12r, 21r–21v, 28r–29v.

gabelle on all commercial transactions, by levying a tithe on property, and by sharply reducing the *prestanze*.[352] When a Visconti army threatened Bologna in the early months of 1401, counselors urged the war *balìa* to send troops and money to defend the city, so crucial for Florentine security. However, after the immediate threat to the city had passed, a Bolognese request for more help encountered strong opposition in the *pratiche*, despite arguments that a rejection might alienate their allies.[353] In September, counselors were deliberating whether to negotiate with the lord of Bologna, Giovanni Bentivoglio, for an alliance; Lotto Castellani warned the Signoria to be alert "lest the Bolognese deceive us or involve us in expenses that we cannot support."[354] A month later, the term of the Ten on War expired, and when the proposal to renew that magistracy was submitted to the Council of Eighty-one, it was rejected. The irresponsibility of that decision prompted a loud outcry in the *pratica*, and the vote was quickly reversed.[355]

The decision of the leadership to gamble, once again, on foreign intervention stands out in stark contrast against this background of uncertainty over strategy and quibbling over small expenditures. The new Galahad was the German prince, Rupert of Bavaria, chosen by the electors to replace the deposed Wenceslaus as head of the Holy Roman Empire. Ambassadors for the emperor-elect visited Florence in January 1401, announcing Rupert's decision to travel to Rome to receive the imperial crown from Pope Boniface IX. Although this overture was discussed briefly in *pratiche* held that month, there was no full-scale debate on the proposal to hire Rupert and his Germans.[356] The significant details of these negotiations are found in Buonaccorso

[352] Favoring the tax on merchandise (6 d. per l.) were Leonardo dell'Antella and Arrigo Mucini; *CP*, 34, ff.46v, 78r, 129r; Simone da Quarata proposed "quod habeantur IIII^M homines de civitate et comitatus et imponant eis decimum de eo quod habent et solvatur in VI annis"; *ibid.*, f.65r. Maso degli Albizzi was one of several who recommended "quod commune vivat de suo sine prestantiis siquis modus est in toto vel in magna parte"; *ibid.*, f.19v. Francesco Datini wrote an acquaintance (28 Apr. 1401) that he planned to stay in Bologna unless his *prestanza* assessment was lowered; F. Melis, *Aspetti della vita economica medievale* (Siena, 1962), I, 57.

[353] *CP*, 34, ff.167v, 168r, 172v; 35, f.6v.

[354] *Ibid.*, ff.26r–28v.   [355] *Ibid.*, ff.40v–41v.

[356] There is a reference to the German embassy in *CP*, 34, ff.153v–154r, 31 Jan., but the negotiations with Rupert are not mentioned again until late April; *ibid.*, ff.177r–177v, when Pitti was already in Germany. On 4 April, the Signoria instructed its ambassador at the papal court to inform Boniface IX of Rupert's plans, and asked the pope to urge the emperor-elect to come to Italy; *SCMLC*, 2, ff.45v–48r.

Pitti's report to the Signoria on his embassy to Rupert, and in his private diary. Pitti left Florence on 15 March, with instructions to offer Rupert a subsidy of 100,000 florins if he came to Italy that summer with his army. But Rupert was cautious and diffident; he told Pitti that he had no money, that he preferred to postpone his journey until the following year, and that he would need 500,000 florins to organize an effective invasion of Lombardy that summer.[357] In Florence, those citizens who saw Rupert as the Florentine savior were urging Pitti to persuade the emperor-elect to move quickly while, on the domestic front, they sought to create enthusiasm for the German enterprise. According to Giovanni Morelli, the propaganda campaign was intense, and replete with falsehoods and fantasies; with uncharacteristic irony, he noted that in the debates, "Aesop was the authority most often cited." Andrea Vettori was sent to Germany to join Pitti, and "they described so many miraculous things that the paladins of Charlemagne were children compared to these [Germans]."[358] A regime that had been reluctant to invest more than 12,000 florins in Perugian independence, or the cost of 100 lances to keep Giovanni Bentivoglio's friendship, now authorized Giovanni di Bicci de' Medici to pay Rupert 200,-000 florins, upon his arrival in Italy.[359] But the war magistracy sought to limit the risk by refusing to give him any money until his troops had crossed the Alps. The result, inevitably, was a delay in the assembly of the German army at Trent and, more seriously, a much smaller force (only 4000 cavalry) than the Florentines had expected. While journeying to Venice to get more money for the impecunious Rupert, Pitti learned that he had ventured south toward Brescia and there had been defeated in a skirmish with a superior Visconti force (24 October 1401). Rupert then retreated with his army to Trent.[360]

Those citizens who, like Giovanni Morelli, had reservations about the German invasion[361] did not voice their doubts on the rare occasions

---

[357] *Cronica*, 116–25. Giovanni Morelli also describes these negotiations; *Ricordi*, 383–85, and an earlier embassy to Rupert by Andrea Salvini, *ibid.*, 381–83. On Florentine relations with the Bavarian, see Herde, "Politische Verhaltensweisen," 199–202.

[358] Morelli, *Ricordi*, 381, 383–85.

[359] Morelli stated that only 140,000 fl. was authorized to be disbursed by Giovanni de' Medici; *ibid.*, 385–86. The figure mentioned in the *pratiche* was 200,000 fl.; *CP*, 34, ff.177r–177v. Minerbetti, *anno* 1401, ch. 8, stated that Florence had promised to give Rupert 200,000 fl., by October, if he had come to Italy, and to lend him an additional 200,000 fl. for six months, "perchè meglio potesse fornire quello, che promettea di fare."

[360] *Cronica*, 126–35.

[361] Francesco Datini's associate, Domenico di Cambio, was also skeptical of the German enterprise: "Qui no' si fa nulla di merchatantia, ma pònciesi danari assai

when the subject was debated in the *pratiche*. No criticism of this, or any other aspect of Florence's military or diplomatic strategy, was recorded in the protocols. The tone of public debate was epitomized by a statement (14 October 1401) of Alessio Baldovinetti on behalf of both colleges: "The Ten should do everything they deem necessary against the tyrant in Tuscany, and for the exaltation of the commune and the liberation of the homeland." Baldovinetti went even further to encourage the war magistracy by announcing collegiate support for every decision they might make, even if fortune were to negate their efforts.[362] Despite this expression of confidence, the leaders of the *reggimento* were naturally concerned about the German invasion, which they had touted with such enthusiasm. The news of Rupert's defeat outside Brescia did not provoke criticism, but instead a strong appeal for continuing aid to the emperor-elect.[363] So many reputations were involved in promoting Rupert's journey that no one was willing to call it a fiasco. Instead the leadership sent an illustrious embassy—Maso degli Albizzi, Rinaldo Gianfigliazzi, Filippo Corsini, Tommaso Sacchetti—to persuade Rupert to remain in Italy, and thus to keep alive the possibility of another German attack on Giangaleazzo in the following year. But the issue of faith and credibility now intruded into the negotiations. The Florentines argued that Rupert had not kept his promise to lead a powerful army into Italy; the emperor-elect accused them of failing to give him the money they had promised. Responding to Venetian pressure and their own hopes for a favorable outcome, the ambassadors doled out small amounts to induce him to remain through the winter in Padua, where the pitiful remnants of his invasion army were quartered.[364] In March 1402 Rupert sent two ambassadors to petition the Signoria for more aid. A few diehards like Matteo Tinghi and Giovanni Orlandini still urged an accomodation and further subsidies, but the majority supported the judgment of Gino Capponi and Tommaso Sacchetti that money given to him was money

---

per la venuta dello inperadore che viene a Roma a choronarsi, poi dicie che vuole andare chontro al chonte per disfallo, chome ch'i'ò paghura che no'ci dia brigha assai. Tòchane a paghare alla nostra chompangnia XV prestanze tutte insieme: tòchane alla nostra chompangnia fior. ML d'oro"; *Datini*, 866, unpaginated, 20 Aug. 1401.

[362] *CP*, 35, f.38v.

[363] *Ibid.*, ff.43r–43v, 3 Nov. The speakers included Rinaldo Gianfigliazzi, Niccolò Guasconi, Francesco Ardinghelli, Matteo Tinghi and Lotto Castellani.

[364] Pitti, *Cronica*, 131–33; Minerbetti, *anno* 1401, ch. 12; Herde, "Politische Verhaltensweisen," 202.

thrown away. On 23 April the Signoria learned that Rupert had left Padua and was returning to Germany.[365]

The negotiations with Rupert of Bavaria had been unduly prolonged by Florentine officials because they saw no help available from any other quarter. At one point in the discussion concerning the emperor-elect, Lorenzo Ridolfi expressed the pious hope that the Venetians and the pope could be induced to contribute something to Rupert's expenses, but few of his colleagues wasted much thought on such unrealistic expectations.[366] As they perceived their predicament more clearly, in the spring and early summer of 1402, they discussed their problems and options more intelligently and realistically, without panic or despair. The discussions became more sharply focused on specific issues and concrete remedies. In late March, the colleges proposed that the war magistracy establish a goal of 1200–1250 lances as a reasonable estimate of defense needs. A week later, a spokesman for the Twelve urged the war *balìa* to keep open one trade route for merchants, through either Lucca or Romagna.[367] The critical point in Florence's defensive system was Bologna, where Giovanni Bentivoglio maintained a precarious hold on his city, threatened by a Visconti army. The Ten had sent a large contingent of 5000 cavalry to support Bentivoglio, although several counselors questioned the stability of his regime and expressed the hope that the city might be restored to papal rule.[368] As for the military tactics to be followed in the Bologna area, the Twelve believed that the Florentine army should remain on the defensive and not provoke a battle with the Visconti army. Speaking for the war magistracy, Rinaldo Gianfigliazzi deplored this discussion of strategy; it was better to say nothing, he argued, than to advocate a defensive posture, "since the enemy will know that he can assault us with impunity for he will not be attacked."[369] No evidence survives concerning any instructions that the war magistracy may have sent

---

[365] *CP*, 35, f.11r. The debates on support for Rupert are in *ibid.*, ff.98r–99r, 102r–105r, 107v–108r.

[366] *CP*, 35, f.98v. On Florentine diplomatic approaches to Boniface and Venice, see Herde, "Politische Verhaltensweisen," 239–40, 243; Esch, *Bonifaz IX*, 354–60.

[367] *CP*, 35, ff.108v, 109v. Pisa had been closed to Florentine traffic since the previous summer; *Datini*, 866, unpaginated, 20 Aug. 1401; but the Lucchese port of Mutrone was still open during that autumn; *ibid.*, 977, 24 Sept. 1401. The Signoria sent ambassadors to Lucca and Rimini, to obtain the permission of their *signori* for the use of their ports; *SCMLC*, 2, ff.48v–49r.

[368] Morelli, *Ricordi*, 389; *CP*, 35, ff.111v, 118v. On relations with Bologna, see Herde, 241–44.

[369] *CP*, 35, ff.117v–118r, 122v.

their colleagues, Niccolò da Uzzano and Bardo Rittafè, who were with the Florentine army in the field. Nor do the chroniclers agree on fixing responsibility for the tactical decisions that led to the defeat of that force at Casalecchio on 26 June. In the turmoil that followed that battle, the Bolognese rebelled against Giovanni Bentivoglio, and shortly thereafter, the city was occupied by Visconti soldiers.[370]

Much has been written about the historical significance of Bologna's occupation, of Florence's grave condition, and of the Florentine appreciation of, and reaction to, her peril.[371] The news of the defeat at Casalecchio was a shock to the *reggimento*, whose leaders discussed the crisis in a *pratica* held on 27 June, the day after the battle. The basic theme was the need to sustain civic morale in the face of adversity, and to resist the enemy with courage and audacity.[372] The oratory was a degree more florid than was normal, and the appeals for unity and sacrifice more eloquent. But neither the message nor the tone was unique to this occasion. Merchants complained incessantly about heavy taxes and the stagnation of trade, but these laments were not exceptional in their frequency or intensity.[373] Having expressed their

[370] Morelli, *Ricordi*, 390–95, blamed the defeat on Bentivoglio's recklessness; but Minerbetti, *anno* 1402, ch. 7, charged the Florentine captain, Bernardone da Serra, with selecting a weak position for a campsite.

[371] Baron, *Crisis*, 1st ed., I, ch. 2; II, 379–90.

[372] Selections from this *pratica* have been edited by C. Guasti, *Commissioni di Rinaldo degli Albizzi* (Florence, 1867–1873), I, 11, and quoted by Baron, *Crisis*, 2nd ed., 43. Four speeches, not published by Guasti, by Alessio Baldovinetti, Tommaso Marchi, Bartolomeo Popoleschi, and Matteo Tinghi, repeat the arguments of Maso degli Albizzi, Filippo Corsini, and others. Matteo Tinghi's statement, *CP*, 35, f.127v, is particularly forceful: "Quod animose et fortiter erigatur et opponatur fortuna, et omnes uniantur; et provideatur de pecunia et commune se gentibus fortificet."

[373] See the Datini letters of 15 Jan. and 5 Aug. 1402; *Datini*, 987, 1066, unpaginated. In August Datini wrote: "Qua no' si fa nula di merchatantie; atèndesi a paghare danari in Chomune pe' questa maladeta ghuera ch'abiamo chol ducha, che ma' fune la più ischura ghuera, che ci à seratto per modo no' si può mandare nula fori del nostro chontado, ch'ogni chosa è suo. Dio ci dia ghrazzia no'ci posiamo difendere da lui, chè paghura n'abiamo." In April, a Bolognese correspondent of Datini, Niccolò Migliorati, had suggested that he transfer his business operations to Venice: "E convienvi prender partito presto, perchè mi par vada la cosa e'l giuoco di male in pegio, sanza speranza a voi d'alcun ristoro costì, o volete di traffichi o volete d'ufitii o d'altro, per le invidie e superbie et avaritie vi sono"; *ibid.*, 1097, unpaginated, 20 April 1402. The only specific reference to internal opposition to the regime is contained in a criminal process against Niccolò di Messer Bettino Covoni, convicted in Aug. 1402 of uttering "verba scandalosa et viciosa contra pacificum statum Florentie." In a conversation with Matteo Asini, Covoni allegedly said that "si parla per città di rimettere dentro di quegli che sono di fuori," and "tu vedi le sospictioni che ci sono"; *Prov.*, 92, ff.285r–285v.

strong feelings and their determination to survive, the members of the *reggimento* then focused their attention on the practical problems of defense, finance, and internal security. A striking feature of the *pratiche* in the summer of 1402 is the mood of calm deliberation and (save for one moment, on 27 June) the absence of any sense of panic.[374] The Signoria convened their counselors regularly, to discuss the war and its problems; on some issues, there was unanimity and on others, disagreement.[375] Recommendations were moderate and cautious. The most radical proposals for solving the perennial fiscal crisis were advanced by Piero Firenze, who favored a capital levy of five percent on all property, and Matteo Strozzi, who made the first documented proposal for a *catasto*, or property register, "so that each will pay his due."[376]

In implementing the concrete decisions that touched most directly on their security, Florentine authorities acted quickly and efficiently. Their officials supervised the gathering of the wheat harvest and the storage of grain in Florence and in fortified places in the *contado* and district. Soldiers who streamed back to Florence from Casalecchio were rehired and sent to guard the threatened areas along the northern frontier. Two thousand laborers from cloth factories were also recruited for the defense of the dominion.[377] At many frontier points, the roads were blockaded by Florentine militia as a security measure.[378] Recognizing that the Visconti occupation of Bologna would increase the likelihood of rebellion in the territory, vicars and castellans intensified their surveillance over their jurisdictions.[379] In Barga, Buonaccorso Pitti uncovered a plot of exiles from that border town

---

[374] I concur fully with Herde's judgment, "Politische Verhaltensweisen," 245.

[375] The debate over Faenza was an example of discord; *CP*, 35, ff.131r–137r.

[376] *Ibid.*, f.136v, 14 July. In a *pratica* twenty years later (Nov. 1421), Agnolo della Casa reported that *monte* shares had fallen to 18% of their nominal value after Bologna was occupied by Visconti forces; *CP*, 44, f.158r.

[377] Morelli, *Ricordi*, 397–98. The hiring of the cloth workers was dictated primarily by motives of internal security: "Fu più per tralli della terra che per altra cagione." Similar motives underlay the recruitment of poor laborers into the militia during other periods of crisis, in 1383 and 1417; Brucker, "The Florentine Popolo Minuto," in Martines, ed., *Violence and Civil Disorder in Renaissance Italy*, 173–74.

[378] The war magistracy's instructions to Buonaccorso Pitti, *podestà* of Barga; *Cronica*, 138–40.

[379] A letter written by Matteo Busini, *podestà* of Calenzano, 9 July 1402, *Carte del Bene*, 53, unpaginated: "Mi fu scripto da' Dieci della Balìa s'attendesse a buona guardia e così vi n'aviso. Facciate el dì ed notte però chè Ghino di messer Giorgio Schali con sua compagnia si sono partiti da Bologna e cercharo di torre qualche castellano e accendassi di Calenzano o di Montemurlo. E pero abbiate di dì e di notte buona guardia."

to seize it with the aid of Visconti troops.[380] Pistoia was still unsettled after the Cancellieri uprising of the previous year, and members
of the Guazzalotri family in Prato conspired to gain control of that
town and expel the Florentine garrison.[381] Along the Pisan frontier,
a military force led by Bernardo Mangiadori of San Miniato attempted
to seize the castle of Agliati, but it was repulsed by the Florentine
militia.[382] Had the Visconti army marched into Tuscany after its victory at Casalecchio, these rebellions might have been successful, and
the worst fears of the Florentines could have materialized. But that
army disintegrated when the soldiers' pay did not arrive on schedule,
and the immediate threat of an invasion and siege subsided.[383]

Thrown upon their own resources after Bologna's fall, without allies
or friends, the Florentines pursued a cautious and pragmatic policy,
which focused upon the defense of their territory.[384] Giovanni Orlandini defined the basic objective, "to remain on the defensive without
incurring greater expenses this summer, and then cut our outlays
further in the winter."[385] This mood also dominated the republic's
diplomacy in the weeks following Casalecchio. Florentine statesmen
displayed no interest in bold diplomatic ventures that might attract
potential allies; their negotiations were extremely circumspect. In
early June, Astorre Manfredi of Faenza sent an envoy to Florence to
appeal for help against a rumored Visconti effort to occupy his state.
The strategic and commercial advantages of securing an outlet to the
sea through Romagna were obvious to every citizen who attended the
pratica of 6 July. All spoke in favor of defending Faenza, and some
proposed that the city be occupied by Florentine troops "in the name
of the church."[386] An action so bold and provocative could be justified
only if it were vital to the maintenance of the city's liberty and, after
a week's deliberation, most citizens had concluded that her security
was not yet in such peril as to justify the risk. On 14 July, Maso degli
Albizzi recommended that negotiations with Manfredi be terminated,

---

[380] Pitti, *Cronica*, 140–43. The condemnations of those implicated in that plot are
in *GA*, 97, unpaginated, 24 Dec. 1402.

[381] R. Piattoli, "Di un ignoto tentativo di Giangaleazzo Visconti per far ribellare
la terra di Prato," *Archivio storico pratese*, x (1931), 37–41. The condemnation of
the conspirators is in *ACP*, 2177, ff.17r–20r, 17 June 1402.

[382] Minerbetti, *anno* 1402, ch. 5.   [383] Morelli, *Ricordi*, 397–99.

[384] *CP*, 35, f.139v, 18 July. Filippo Corsini's statement, *ibid.*, f.133r: "Quod limi-
tentur expense et attendatur ad terrarum custodiam."

[385] See Herde, "Politische Verhaltensweisen," 247.

[386] *CP*, 35, ff.133r–133v. Filippo Corsini favored the enterprise, "quia Faventia est
apta dare viam mercantiis," and Antonio Alessandri commented: "Quia si Faventia
perdetur, omnia que habemus in Romandiola perderentur, assumetur defensio."

arguing that the lord of Faenza did not merit Florence's trust. However, the war magistracy continued to discuss an alliance with him, and in late July, presented the draft of a treaty to a *pratica* for comments. Filippo Corsini and Maso degli Albizzi led the opposition to the treaty, and Vanni Castellani and Agnolo Pandolfini recommended its approval.[387] An agreement with Astorre Manfredi was eventually approved; it stipulated that Florentine troops would guard the city of Faenza and its outlying castles for a two-year period.[388]

Throughout the summer of 1402 Florentine diplomats were in Venice and Rome, discussing terms for alliances with representatives of the Serenissima and Pope Boniface IX.[389] These overtures were strongly supported by the citizens who spoke in the *pratiche*, although their public statements did not reveal any strong sense of urgency, or overwhelming need, for an alliance. On 29 June, three days after the Casalecchio disaster, Maso degli Albizzi appealed for an accommodation with Venice and the pope. Antonio Alessandri supported his argument, but attached the qualification that the republic should be accorded equal status, and that her liberty should be guaranteed.[390] Even in those somber times, when the Visconti menace was greatest, the *reggimento* was unwilling to make concessions that were too humiliating or costly. The Venetians were receptive to an alliance, but they were also pressing for a cessation of hostilities. In a *pratica* held on 18 July, counselors welcomed that prospect. Expressing his doubts about a satisfactory agreement with Boniface and King Ladislaus of Naples, Maso degli Albizzi announced his support for a peace agreement with Giangaleazzo, through the mediation of Venice.[391] Two weeks later (7 August), the focus had shifted from peace to the negotiations for a Venetian alliance, which received general though

---

[387] *Ibid.*, ff.136v, 143r–143v.   [388] Minerbetti, *anno* 1402, ch. 11.

[389] For requests to the pope for help against Giangaleazzo, see *SCMC*, 25, f.79r, 30 June; *SCMLC*, 3, ff.41r–41v, 30 June; Herde, 246–47. On papal policy in these weeks, see Esch, *Bonifaz IX*, 370–87.

[390] *CP*, 35, f.129v. Maso: "Et queratur unitas et cum papa et cum rege et cum omnibus aliis prodefensione libertatis et singulariter cum Venetiis"; Alessandri's qualification, "dummodo sit cum equalitate et libertate." Filippo Corsini also favored these negotiations, "sed sub ista spe non stetur sed omnia fiant pro defensione."

[391] *Ibid.*, ff.139v–140r. Maso's statement: "Unio cum papa et rege fiat, cavendo tamen an hoc sit ad sufficientiam, et quia non putat hoc sufficere, pax accipiatur." Others favoring peace were Filippo Corsini, Antonio Alessandri, Vanni Castellani, and Piero Baroncelli. On the next day, *ibid.*, f.141v, Agnolo della Casa spoke for the whole *pratica*, supporting the continuation of peace talks. On this point, concerning Florence's willingness to consider a peace settlement with the duke, cf. Baron, *Crisis*, 2nd ed., 43.

qualified approval from the counselors.[392] Another session was convened on 24 August, to advise the Signoria and the war magistracy on the dual negotiations at Venice and Rome. Speakers were sharply critical of the alliance proposals that were submitted to them. Matteo Tinghi described the Venetian agreement as "too inequitable, too expensive, and too dishonorable" and said he would approve it only if the Venetians contributed one-third of the military expenses in Lombardy and Tuscany. In rejecting the terms of the Venetian pact, Cristofano Biliotti argued that the Adriatic republic was seeking to extend its authority into Tuscany, and thus would be a formidable rival to the Florentines in their own bailiwick. The most forceful argument against a papal alliance was advanced by Filippo Magalotti, who cited the pope's unpredictability, the influence of his brothers, and the nonparticipation of the cardinals in the negotiations, as reasons for opposing the league.[393]

The republic had not concluded an agreement with either Venice or Boniface by 12 September, when a report of Giangaleazzo's death arrived in Florence. The reaction to this news was muted, with no discernible sign of jubilation. Filippo Corsini and Luca del Pecchia offered their gratitude to God for this evidence of divine favor, but their speeches were devoted to practical matters: the defense of Florentine territory; the possibility of a reconciliation with Pisa, Siena, and Bologna; the current negotiations in Venice and Rome. Some of this reserve may be attributed to doubts about the accuracy of the report.[394] Yet, when the demise of their enemy was common knowledge, the Florentines were more concerned with pursuing the war against his successors than with celebrating their liberation from Visconti tyranny. Neither the struggle nor the sacrifices ended with Giangaleazzo's death.

What conclusions about Florentine strategy and the Florentine state of mind can be drawn from the evidence that has survived for these months, between the fall of Bologna and the death of Giangaleazzo? These questions assume a singular importance, since contemporary witnesses and, more recently, historians of this period have regarded the summer of 1402 as a critical moment in Florentine history.[395] The

---

[392] CP, 35, ff.145v–146r. Jacopo Salviati was not enthusiastic: "Quod cum onerosum sit et cum displicentiis liga cum Venetis facere, tamen omnino fiat sicut decem balie videbitur."

[393] CP, 35, ff.148v–149v, 24 Aug., quoted in Herde, "Politische Verhaltensweisen," 247, n.544.

[394] CP, 35, ff.151r–151v; Morelli, Ricordi, 400.

[395] Baron, Crisis, 2nd ed., ch. 2. Cf. Herde's critique of that view, 247–49.

evidence does not support the claim of one contemporary, Gregorio Dati, that the republic had pursued a consistent policy toward Giangaleazzo. For the year 1402, as in previous years, the public records reveal uncertainty and vacillation, doubt and disagreement, and abrupt shifts in attitude and policy that do not relate logically to events or circumstances. One particular calculation that Dati attributes to the Florentines was their assessment of ducal finances, which persuaded them that his current level of expenditure could not be maintained, and that the war could not continue indefinitely. This explained Florence's decision (so Dati argued) to trim their own military expenses, to enable them to outlast their adversary.[396] There is ample evidence of preoccupation with the state of the Florentine fisc in these months,[397] but no reference in the protocols to ducal revenues or expenditures. The sharp concern over excessive costs appears after the loss of 200,000 florins in the aborted German invasion, and after the defeat at Casalecchio, when retrenchment was the order of the day. Was that policy the result of rational calculation, combined with a sublime confidence in their ultimate victory, as Dati argues, or does the evidence suggest a different interpretation?

Throughout the fourteen years of her struggles with Giangaleazzo, the regime's policy had fluctuated between aggressiveness and accommodation. After a lost battle, or an ally's defection, or a strategic decision that misfired, Florentine diplomacy invariably became more circumspect. Her military strategy would shift from offense to defense, and her statesmen would become more amenable to peace discussions. After the failure of the bold initiatives of 1390–1391 and 1396, Florentine statesmen experienced a loss of nerve, perhaps as a reaction to public criticism or doubts about their capacity to make correct decisions. They took no risks and invariably missed opportunities for diplomatic victories, as in Pisa in 1398 and Perugia in 1399. Gradually, this mood of caution and passivity dissolved, as men forgot past failures and regained a measure of their former confidence. Then they launched ambitious projects: the alliance with Charles VI of France in 1396, and with Rupert of Bavaria in 1401. The costly failure of the German invasion, coupled with the loss of Bologna, were the decisive events that, once again, changed the Florentine mood from ebullient optimism to wariness in the summer of 1402. Too much can be read into the patriotic appeals (27 June) for a virile effort against the enemy. Those sentiments did not accurately reflect the mood of the

---

[396] Baron, 173–88.
[397] CP, 35, ff.136v–137v, 139v, 147r–147v.

reggimento, which was chastened, sensitive to criticism,[398] and very restrained. As they had done so often in the past, the Florentines responded to adversity by pulling in their horns. If they sensed that they were living through an historic "moment of decision," their demeanor did not indicate this awareness. Only later, in retrospect, did they recognize the significance of these events, and Gregorio Dati could write that "all the freedom of Italy lay in the hands of the Florentines alone, that every other power had deserted them."[399]

[398] Agnolo della Casa, spokesman for the Sixteen: "Qui locutus contra Decem male et iniuste faciunt et ideo puniantur"; *CP*, 35, f.130r, 29 June.

[399] Baron, *Crisis*, 2nd ed., 188.

CHAPTER IV

Florentine State-Building

THE LIQUIDATION OF THE VISCONTI EMPIRE

GIANGALEAZZO Visconti's death was a significant historical event, and it was so recognized by princes and ruling elites throughout the peninsula. The Visconti drive for hegemony in northern and central Italy had failed; the regents who governed the Milanese state for Giovanni Maria Visconti, the fourteen-year-old heir, were in no position to pursue Giangaleazzo's territorial ambitions. The critical question being pondered in every Italian chancery was the stability of the state the duke had created. Throughout the autumn and winter months of 1402–1403, observers watched for signs of disintegration, but even in those possessions farthest from Milan—Perugia, Siena, Pisa —Visconti officials remained in control of their territories, and the subject populations made no overt gestures of resistance. The ease with which Giangaleazzo's illegitimate son, Gabriele Maria, assumed control of Pisa in November 1402 was a sign that Visconti power in Tuscany was not ephemeral.

The cautious Florentine response to the new political conditions was in sharp contrast to her resolute stance during the summer of 1402, when the city's peril was greatest. Once the danger of conquest had subsided, the regime experienced difficulty in adjusting to the new realities. Uncertainty over the fate of Giangaleazzo's empire and the ability of his successors to hold it together contributed to this indecision. It was difficult to formulate a policy when the political scene was so unsettled.

Though never articulated, the immediate objective of Florentine policy after Giangaleazzo's death was the elimination of the Visconti presence from Tuscany. The republic would accept no peace until Visconti soldiers and officials had departed from Siena and Pisa, and until Florentine merchants were guaranteed access to the sea through a Tyrrhenian port.[1] How could the regime achieve these goals: by diplomacy, force, or some combination of these methods? The strategy

[1] The Florentine objectives are spelled out most clearly in *DBCMLC*, 3, ff.9v–10r, 2 April 1403. The Visconti were responsible for the war, Filippo Magalotti said, "quia illi volunt subjugare nostram libertatem et ob hoc occupaverunt Pisas, Senas et Perusiam et Bononiam; et donec stent effectus et signa huius intentionis, non potest haberi pax"; *CP*, 36, f.7r, 27 Nov. 1402. See also the statements of Cristofano Spini and Anselmo Anselmi, *ibid.*, ff.4v, 10v.

involving the least risk and cost would have been to continue along the course plotted after Giangaleazzo's conquest of Bologna, by deploying Florentine troops in defensive postures while seeking a negotiated settlement through Venetian mediation. By concentrating her troops within her own borders, and limiting their function to the defense of her territory, the republic could resist enemy depredations and, furthermore, she could launch an assault against either Siena or Pisa, if necessary, to break through the blockade on her southern and western frontiers. This defensive policy had some support within the regime. When news of Giangaleazzo's death reached Florence on 12 September, Bartolomeo Valori advised the Signoria to continue peace negotiations in Venice and urged the priors to work for reconciliation with their neighbors.[2] A month later (15 November), Cristofano Spini proposed that the republic terminate all offensive actions and concentrate exclusively on defense. Other counselors referred to the yearning for peace among the citizenry, and the necessity for continuing negotiations, "so that the Signoria will be exonerated in the eyes of the *popolo*."[3] Rich and poor alike were complaining about the fiscal burdens that were depleting their resources, and creating such a dearth of specie that Jacopo Carducci suggested that gold and silver ornaments in the churches be melted to pay the republic's mercenaries.[4]

By year's end, however, the leadership had rejected the arguments for peace and economy and had opted for a major offensive against the Visconti. In early October the Signoria recalled its ambassadors from the peace colloquy in Venice and, on the 19th, Florence's envoys at the papal court signed a formal alliance with Pope Boniface IX; the objective was the explusion of the Visconti from papal territory and from Tuscany. Florence agreed to send troops in support of papal efforts to recover Perugia and Bologna, and for his part Boniface promised to attack Visconti strongholds in the Sienese region.[5] Though not clearly formulated in the official records, the rationale for this policy was a complex mixture of old fears and new expectations. The eagerness with which the Signoria accepted Boniface's offer was possibly a reaction to the anxieties of the past summer. Of more substantive im-

---

[2] *Ibid.*, 35, ff.151r, 169v.

[3] *CP*, 36, f.8r, statement of Antonio Mangioni. See also the comments of Anselmo Anselmi and Filippo Corsini, *ibid.*, ff.10v, 12v.

[4] *Ibid.*, f.15v. For the need to reduce expenses, see the comments of Bartolomeo Valori and Forese Salviati; *CP*, 35, ff.159r, 169r. In 1402, monthly military costs averaged more than 50,000 fl., half of which came from forced loans; Molho, *Florentine Public Finances*, 11.

[5] Mesquita, *Giangaleazzo*, 299; Minerbetti, *anno* 1402, ch. 15; Esch, *Bonifaz IX*, 388–92.

portance, however, was the widely held belief that the Visconti could not be dislodged from Tuscany without help.[6] But if all the potential opposition to the Visconti could be mobilized, it would mean the permanent destruction of the republic's nemesis. Vanni Castellani was so moved by this vision that he urged the Signoria to contract an alliance with Genoa. This would result (so he argued) in the immediate opening of all trade routes and Florence's possession of a port, either Pisa or Piombino.[7] A few warnings were voiced in the councils; Salvestro Belfredelli requested that the decision to continue the war be submittted to a large civic assembly.[8] But Maso degli Albizzi was clearly reflecting majority sentiment within the leadership when he called for a full-scale offensive against the Visconti.[9]

The papal alliance gained a friend for Florence, but the cost was heavy and the advantages dubious. By the terms of the treaty, the republic committed a large portion of her army to the Umbrian campaign which, in terms of her strategic and economic interests, was the least important target in Visconti territory. To support the Perugia offensive with 500 lances, the war magistracy had no choice but to refrain from attacking the Visconti garrisons in Bologna, Siena, and Pisa. Even the rebellious Cancellieri, defiant in their Apennine fortress of Sambuca, could not be coerced into submission. To terminate that humiliating episode, the Signoria and the councils approved a peace settlement with the rebels that provided for the cancellation of their bans and the restoration of their confiscated property.[10] Papal objectives thus took precedence over Florentine priorities. This permitted enemy soldiers to ravage the borderlands on the Sienese and Pisan frontiers, while Florentine cavalry were pursuing the troops of Ottobuono Terzo in the Umbrian countryside.[11] Meanwhile, Florentine merchants were unable to import wool for the cloth factories, which remained idle, or to ship out their merchandise over the blockaded roads.[12] The leadership doubtless realized that the commitment of troops to Umbria and the Romagna would mean sacrificing some

---

[6] Even Boniface's support was not sufficient to defend Florence from the Visconti, so argued Vanni Castellani; *CP*, 36, f.27v. For an official statement of Florence's weakness with respect to the Visconti, see *SCMC*, 26, ff.5r–5v, letter to the king of Castile, 7 May 1403.

[7] *CP*, 36, f.14r.   [8] *CP*, 35, f.169v, 15 Nov.

[9] *CP*, 36, f.18v: "Et non parcentur expensa ita quod tyrannus invadetur"; and *ibid.*, f.58r: "Offendat inimicus; fiant ultima de potentia!"

[10] *Prov.*, 92, ff.153v–158r, 22–23 Oct. 1403.

[11] In Feb. 1403, Florence informed the pope that she would have to withdraw her forces from Umbria to defend her Pisan frontier; *DBCMLC*, 3, ff.3v–4r.

[12] R. Piattoli, "Il problema portuale," *Rivista storica degli archivi toscani*, II (1930), 172–79.

measure of protection for Florentine territory and the continuation, at least temporarily, of the economic blockade. In the judgment of Maso degli Albizzi and Vanni Castellani, however, the destruction of the Visconti empire was worth the sacrifice. But they had failed to consider the limited resources of the pope, who did not contribute his share of the troops needed to liberate Perugia and Bologna.[13] The instructions sent by the war magistracy to the Florentine ambassadors at the papal court were filled with complaints about Boniface's failure to hire the soldiers that he had promised to commit to the enterprise. The officials also complained that papal troops were not attacking the Visconti forces in Sienese territory.[14] The Florentines had mistakenly assumed that the pope shared their determination to destroy the Visconti state in Lombardy; Boniface's more modest objective was the recovery of papal territory under Visconti control.

By committing Florence to this aggressive policy, the regime became inextricably enmeshed in peninsular politics from the Alps to the Tiber. The republic's diplomats visited *signori* in the Lombard plain and in the Apennines, appealing to the latent Guelf sympathies of some nobles, and to the self-interest of others who might profit from the dismemberment of the Visconti state. The Carrara of Padua, the Rossi of Parma, and the Cavalcabò of Cremona were all receptive to the idea of a campaign against the Visconti. To encourage their rebellious impulses, Florentine agents offered stipends to these local lords, promising (for example) Messer Carlo da Fogliano and Bishop Rossi of Parma 2000 florins monthly as long as the war continued.[15] In the Romagna, the major benefactor of Florentine largesse was Carlo Malatesta, lord of Rimini, who had allied himself with Giangaleazzo when the duke's power seemed invincible, but who was now willing to accept a Florentine *condotta*, the initial payment for which was 21,000 florins. Perugian exiles were also on the Florentine payroll, as were members of the Salimbeni, who were fighting to expel the Visconti from Siena.[16] Though no records of the war magistracy's disburse-

[13] Esch, *Bonifaz IX*, 392–407; Partner, *Lands of St. Peter*, 384–85.

[14] *DBCMLC*, 3, ff.7v, 8v, 11r–12v, 14v, 15v. In an angry letter (9 May 1403), the Ten complained that the papal forces were not fighting on any front—in Romagna, Umbria, or Siena—and that the Florentines were bearing the full cost of the campaign: "Facciamo conto che noi abbiamo in Romagna presso a lancie 2000 e per lo santo padre non v'è solo uno cavallo e abbianvi scripto che Polo Asoni [Paolo Orsini] ne vada in Romagna e che si faccia guerra a Siena e a Perugia e di tutte queste cose niuno effeto veggiamo se non parole vane e noi pagiamo"; *ibid.*, ff.17v–18r.

[15] *DBCMLC*, 3, f.17r, 6 May 1403. Payments to these *provisionati* are recorded in *Camera, Uscita*, 341–348.

[16] *DBCMLC*, 3, ff.9v, 43v; *CP*, 37, f.14r; Jones, *Malatesta*, 120.

ments to its clients have survived, the extant evidence does reveal a pattern of subsidy to local lords in a zone that spread from the Genoese Riviera (where the Fieschi were *raccomandati*) across Lombardy, Emilia and the Romagna to the Adriatic, and as far south as Umbria and the Marches.

Once the republic had signaled her intention of redrawing the map of Italy by dismantling the Visconti state, she had to consider—indeed, she solicited—offers from other princes, Italian and ultramontane, to participate in the enterprise and share the spoils. An alliance with Genoa had a particular attraction for those statesmen who dreamed of an Italy totally cleansed of the Visconti.[17] The Genoese accord would also guarantee a port for Florentine merchants and a powerful fleet to protect their trade routes in the Mediterranean. When the possibility of a pact was first discussed (December 1402–January 1403), it was favored by most counselors, including Filippo Corsini and Vanni Castellani, who argued that the resources of Florence and the papacy were not sufficient to defeat the Visconti without additional support. But some were skeptical of Genoa's contribution to the war effort, and Luigi Guicciardini warned that Florence would have to spend 400,000 florins in three years to fulfill her obligations in the projected alliance.[18] Other citizens expressed concern over the role of the French king, whose representative, Marshal Boucicaut, had occupied Genoa with a contingent of Gascon troops. "Under no circumstances should an alliance with the king be signed," one civic group advised the Signoria, "since we are heavily burdened with expenses and it would be difficult for us to fulfill the stipulated commitments. Nor should the commune contribute anything to naval costs; our citizens would never approve that expenditure. . . ."[19] But these objections did not deter Maso degli Albizzi and his associates who argued that the Genoese alliance "would lead either to the destruction of the tyrants or to a genuine peace."[20]

Though the Florentine economy, still deprived of its sea outlets, continued to stagnate,[21] and though officials complained incessantly

---

[17] See *SCMC*, 26, ff.20r, 25r; letters to Jacopo de' Rossi and Giovanni de Vignate.
[18] The discussion is in *CP*, 36, ff.12v–16v, 27r–29r.
[19] *Ibid.*, f.32v. This *pratica* was willing to consider an alliance if the French would provide 2000–3000 lances at their own expense for the assault on the Visconti.
[20] *Ibid.*, f.45v. Others sharing Maso's sentiments were Rinaldo Gianfigliazzi, Matteo Tinghi, and Lotto Castellani.
[21] Francesco Datini wrote to Barcelona (10 June 1403): "Le chose di qua si stano al modo usatto, cho' poco farsi se no' paghare prestanze. Il signore di Lucha per anchora no'ci a modo voglia aprire il paso di Mutrone; menaci pe'lla lungha"; and six months later (3 Dec. 1403), "Dio ci mandi pacie si chè lle merchatantie

about the delinquency of their papal ally, the republic's military strategy appeared to be successful in the summer of 1403. Although Perugia and parts of Umbria were still occupied by Visconti troops, their position became increasingly precarious since they received no money or reinforcements from Milan. In the Romagna a large army was assembling under the leadership of the papal legate, Baldassare Cossa, to attack Bologna. The war magistracy sent a stream of messengers to the legate, imploring him to command the captain general, Count Alberico, to begin his assault on Bologna. In Florence patriotic oratory filled the council halls. Maso degli Albizzi exhorted the war magistracy to prosecute the attack with vigor, so that victory could finally be achieved.[22] From Lombardy came news of riots in Milan and rebellions in Como, Cremona, Bergamo, Lodi, and Alessandria; the Visconti empire appeared to be disintegrating. Writing to their ambassadors at the legate's camp on 12 August, the Ten announced exultantly that the destruction of the enemy was at hand.[23] They pressed for an immediate attack on Bologna, to be followed by an invasion of Lombardy, where the papal-Florentine army would be joined by forces led by the lord of Padua, as well as contingents under the command of the Cavalcabò of Cremona and the Rossi of Parma, who had rebelled against Visconti garrisons in their towns.

Though the public image Florence projected to allies and enemies alike was uncompromisingly bellicose, the republic did engage in a series of diplomatic initiatives concerning Pisa which strongly suggested a readiness to negotiate a separate peace, if she could gain possession of that crucial port. In April 1403 the Ten instructed their emissary, Bartolomeo Valori, to offer to buy Pisa from the Visconti, as part of a general peace settlement.[24] There is no evidence in the protocols that this or any subsequent project for Pisa's acquisition was ever debated in consultative sessions; so delicate was that issue that it could only be discussed in secret conclave. A heavy veil of secrecy shrouded the negotiations conducted in July by Florence's vicar in San Miniato, Bernardo Guadagni, and an agent of an unidentified military captain in Visconti service, to whom the war magistracy offered 100,000 florins

posino andare e venire chome debono, che mil'ani ci pare"; *Datini*, 868, 1067, unpaginated.

[22] *CP*, 36, f.89r. Alessio Baldovinetti, Antonio Mangioni, Nofri Brie, Agnolo Pandolfini, Piero Baroncelli, and Lotto Castellani maintained this aggressive posture.

[23] *DBCMLC*, 3, ff.28v–29r. On the rebellions in Lombardy, *ibid.*, 33r, and *Storia di Milano*, VI, 85–96.

[24] *DBCMLC*, 3, ff.9v–10r, 2 Apr. 1403.

if he took the city and sold it to Florence.[25] But nothing came of this offer and two weeks later the Ten were instructing their envoys in the Romagna to approach Carlo Malatesta, requesting him to facilitate the acquisition of Pisa. The Florentines must have Pisa in order to be secure, the Signoria informed their ambassador who was in contact with Malatesta, "for the politics of the Pisans are so variable that they change regimes whenever the emperor comes, and there is no stability in their government."[26] None of these peace overtures was ever mentioned to Boniface IX, nor did the Ten inform their Lombard allies, who were being incited to attack the Visconti, that they had sent an ambassador to Milan to discuss Pisa's acquisition.[27]

While the Ten were secretly negotiating for Pisa without consulting Florence's allies, the papal legate was pursuing his own diplomatic course. On 1 September, the war magistracy informed its envoys in Rome that a truce had been signed between Baldassare Cossa and the duchess of Milan. The terms called for a cessation of hostilities and the restoration of Bologna to the papacy. "Everyone [in Florence] is grieving over this, and is astonished that the legate has demonstrated so little esteem for our commune."[28] With some justification the Florentines argued that the Visconti state was at the point of disintegration, and that had the allies continued the invasion of Lombardy they would have occupied Milan. Without papal support, however, the Florentine army was not strong enough to continue the offensive, and the Ten agreed to a two-month truce with the enemy.[29] But Florence's diplomatic efforts to foment rebellions in Lombardy had committed her to the defense of the Cavalcabò, the Rossi, and the Carrara.[30] She could not easily extricate herself from the Lombard enterprise without sacrificing these allies or negotiating some settlement with the Visconti that would guarantee their security. This would inevitably complicate any peace negotiations for the removal of Visconti troops from Tus-

---

[25] *Ibid.*, ff.25v–26r, 19 and 20 July 1403: "Faccendogli l'amico signore del luogo e nostro accomandato e dandoci le franchigie nel luogo . . . e levando via gli uficiali del tirrano . . . siano contento prestargli fiorini 6000. . . . Et se per questa via non volesse seguire, siano contento se ci vuole dare la città e cittadella e torri del luogo darli fiorini 100,000." Negotiations with *l'amico* were still continuing on 28 July: *ibid.*, f.27r; thereafter, the sources are silent.

[26] *Ibid.*, ff.28v–29r, 12 Aug. 1403; *SCLC*, 3, f.51r.

[27] *DBCMLC*, 3, f.32v, 9 Sept.

[28] *Ibid.*, f.30r. See also *ibid.*, f.33r, letter of 13 Sept., and *SCMLC*, 3, f.48r, 14 Sept. For the papal point of view, Esch, *Bonifax IX*, 407–14.

[29] *DBCMLC*, 3, ff.37r–37v.

[30] See, e.g., the Signoria's letter to Ugolino Cavalcabò, 20 Nov. 1403; *SCMC*, 26, f.22r; to Giovanni de Vignate of Lodi, *ibid.*, f.25r, 1 Jan. 1404; and concerning Padua, *DBCMLC*, 3, ff.45r–45v, 12 Jan. 1404.

cany, and it explains some of the resentment that Florentines felt toward Boniface IX and his legate.[31]

The papal decision to make peace with the Visconti precipitated a minor crisis within the regime. Though its strategy of grand alliances and offensive warfare had failed to improve the situation in Tuscany, where trade routes remained closed and Visconti garrisons intact in Siena and Pisa, the leadership stubbornly persisted in continuing the war. Tommaso Sacchetti urged the Signoria "to prosecute the war with even greater vigor and increase our strength in Lombardy."[32] Only once in these months did a speaker openly challenge this policy; Niccolò Guasconi argued (November 1403) for an end to all offensive military action. "Reduce the number of our troops," he advised, "and cease all attacks on our neighbors so that it will be obvious that we desire peace." In an oblique criticism of the offensive strategy, Maso degli Albizzi complained (January 1404) about the oppressive cost of the Lombard campaign. "Everyone is calling for more money and for heavier expenditures," he said, "but the situation is intolerable and therefore we should try to have peace by every means possible."[33] Maso may have sensed a rise in popular opposition to the regime and its aggressive policy. A resident of the Albizzi neighborhood, Antonio di Giovanni (alias Cappelletto), was condemned to death for allegedly making this statement: "Don't you see that these priors and the war magistracy and this wicked regime are destroying the city, and they are not doing this for our liberty but to aggrandize themselves and to rob the commune and the poor, and in this way they trick the people? . . . O, you blind Florentines, what prevents you from rising up and killing and burning these evil tyrants who have devastated the city . . . so that good citizens will govern and so that we may escape from this tyranny?"[34]

Guided by Maso degli Albizzi and other prominent citizens who shared his convictions, opinion within the *reggimento* gradually became more receptive to the idea of a negotiated peace. When proponents of a Genoese alliance again placed that issue on a *pratica*

---

[31] Relations between Florence and the papacy deteriorated during the autumn and winter of 1403–1404. The pope accused the Florentines of favoring a rebellion in Bologna against the papal regime and of preferring an independent commune in Bologna; also of occupying some castles in papal territory. Florence denied the charges; DBCMLC, 3, ff.37v, 39v–40r; SCMLC, 26, f.21r.

[32] Sacchetti's statement in CP, 37, f.11v Filippo Corsini, Niccolò da Uzzano, Rinaldo Gianfigliazzi and Lorenzo Ridolfi also supported the war; *ibid.*, ff.5r, 7r–9v, 28r–30r.

[33] CP, 36, f.126r.

[34] AEOG, 1521, ff.93r–93v, 21 May 1404.

agenda in February 1404, the reaction of the counselors was over-whelmingly negative.[35] In March the Signoria sent Maso degli Albizzi's son Rinaldo on a secret mission to the lord of Rimini, Carlo Malatesta, with proposals for an agreement with the duchess of Milan. These stipulated that the Visconti could retain possession of Pisa if Florentine merchants would be guaranteed the privileges previously enjoyed un-der the Gambacorta. Both parties would recognize (and promise not to molest) the allies and clients of the other in their own provinces.[36] So concerned were the priors about the public reaction to this mission that they did not convene a *pratica* to discuss the matter nor, as Rinaldo reported, "did they wish the war magistracy to know anything about it, nor their chancellor, Ser Coluccio [Salutati]. . . ." The priors' decision to send this embassy without consulting the Ten was excep-tional, if not unprecedented, in Florentine political experience. Ex-traordinary, too, was the document containing Rinaldo's instruction, which was signed by all nine members of the Signoria, as evidence of their specific approval of the mission and their acceptance of reponsibility for its implementation.

The most conspicuous failure of the regime's policy had been the prolongation of the military and political stalemate in Tuscany. With Florentine troops scattered from Umbria to Lombardy, the Ten did not have the military strength to support their diplomatic moves in Tuscany; they had been unsuccessful in their efforts to breach the blockade and pry Siena and Pisa loose from their Visconti dependence. Lacking force, they had used money as a lure,[37] and then had resorted to conspiratorial activity. Florentine officials were implicated in a Sienese plot organized by the Salimbeni in November 1403. But the appeals by Salimbeni partisans for a free republic were drowned out by the slogans of their enemies: "Long live the *popolo* and the duke!" The rebellion was crushed by the Visconti troops, and several of the Salimbeni were executed.[38] Another fruitless enterprise was launched

---

[35] *CP*, 37, ff.31r–33r.

[36] *Commissioni di Rinaldo degli Albizzi*, I, 34. The significance of this mission, and of Maso's support for a peace agreement, is noted by A. Molho in *Renaissance Quarterly*, xx (1967), 188–89.

[37] In Feb. 1404, the Ten informed their ambassador in Lucca, Matteo Castellani, that they would pay up to 200,000 fl. for Pisa; *DBCMLC*, 3, f.54r. To persuade Margherita Malaspina to sell the town of Sarzana to Florence (which she had agreed to buy from a mercenary captain, Giovanni Colonna), the Ten informed their agent, Vieri Altoviti, that they had a bag of 8000 newly minted florins ready to transport to Lunigiana to conclude the sale; *ibid.*, ff.73r–73v, 26 Sept. 1404.

[38] *Ibid.*, f.41v, 28 Nov. 1403. Florentine involvement in this plot is proved by a provision cancelling the criminal penalties against two men, "secundum promissa facta . . . occasione cuiusdam tractatus qui per dictum offitium Decem ad finem

against Pisa by the Ten two months later. Encouraged by a report that a section of the Pisan wall was vulnerable to an assault, they sent an armed band to attack the fortifications. However, the engineer's report concerning the wall was inaccurate; the invaders were repulsed and "returned to Florence with little honor."[39] Since neither force nor guile had achieved any of the republic's objectives in Tuscany, the Signoria of March–April 1404 pressed for, and finally obtained, an agreement with the Sienese government.[40] Florentine merchants could use the Sienese port of Talamone for five years without paying tolls, and in a separate agreement with Paolo Guinigi, the lord of Lucca, the port of Mutrone north of Pisa was also open to Florentine commerce.[41]

The signing of the Sienese pact intensified the pressures upon the regime to reduce expenditures and military operations. So insistent were these demands that citizens who favored the proscution of the Lombard campaign found themselves in a minority. Zanobi Ginori, from a mercantile family in the quarter of San Giovanni, called for stringent economies: "The commune should make peace and it should limit its expenditure to words and not become involved in any military campaign or outlay."[42] Maso degli Albizzi warned that the republic could be ruined by uncontrolled spending: "Do not give heed to any proposals that would require the commune to bear the costs of a war, but keep our expenses tolerable."[43] By a large majority, a provision was approved in late June abolishing the Council of Eighty-one and restoring to the legislative councils the authority to elect war

pacis fuit ordinatus in civitate Senarum"; *Prov.*, 93, ff.28v–29r, 13 June 1404. See also an appeal to Pope Boniface IX for his protection of the abbot of S. Gallo, a friend of Florence who was implicated in the conspiracy; *SCMLC*, 26, f.26v, 22 Jan. 1404.

[39] Buonaccorso Pitti was one of the six commissioners; the others were Rinaldo Gianfigliazzi, Filippo Magalotti, Maso degli Albizzi, Bartolomeo Altoviti, and Betto Rustichi; *Cronica*, 143–45. Instructions to these men are in *SCMLC*, 2, f.51v, 15 Jan. 1404: "Anderete chol nome di Dio verso Pisa e ridurretevi alla città e ingegnatevi e per amore e per forza e chon ogni industria d'avere la città o per accordo o per danari. In questo non vi pogniano alcuna limitatione se non che promettiate quella quantità di danari, chon quelli pacti e chonvegne che meglio potrete. . . ."

[40] The peace negotiations are described in *Conc.*, 1856, no. 22 and 27; 1857, no. 2, 10, 12. The treaty was ratified by the councils by a total vote of 317 to 28; *Prov.*, 93, ff.1v–2r, 1–2 Apr. 1404.

[41] *Datini*, 896, unpaginated, letter of 12 Apr. 1404. A letter of the same date was written to the Datini branch in Majorca, *ibid.*, 1067, unpaginated.

[42] *CP*, 37, f.57r, 23 May. Among those favoring a continuation of the enterprise, though with fewer troops, were Niccolò da Uzzano, Matteo Tinghi, Niccolò Guasconi, Cristofano Spini and Filippo Corsini; *ibid.*, ff.55v, 56v–57v.

[43] *Ibid.*, f.53r.

magistracies, impose forced loans, and hire troops.[44] In July, Forese
Salviati and Lorenzo Ridolfi, once ardent supporters of the Lombard
campaign, called for the withdrawal of all Florentine forces from
northern Italy.[45] Another target of the economizers were the *provvisionati* of the republic, whose number had proliferated in the months
following Giangaleazzo's death. Among recipients of Florentine grants
and pensions whose stipends were cancelled in the autumn of 1404
were Carlo da Fogliano, Amerigo Manfredi of Faenza, Piero de' Rossi
of Parma, and the lord of Cortona.[46] There was some sentiment for
discharging the war magistracy before its term expired, and for reorganizing the communal fisc so that no forced loans would be levied
in the future.[47] A proposal for the purchase of the town of Sarzana
north of Pisa for 8000 florins was hotly debated in a *pratica*, with the
opposition arguing that the acquisition was too expensive, and that
it would alienate the other states in the region.[48]

These decisions to terminate hostilities and trim military expenditures won strong popular support. The Sienese ambassador reported
that the artisans and laborers were pleased with the peace treaty and
the end of the blockade;[49] an anonymous Florentine merchant, writing
in August 1404, corroborated that judgment. This observer placed recent events in the broad perspective of Florence's long struggle with
Giangaleazzo. "First and foremost," he wrote, "we do want peace, considering that the world has been in turmoil and that we have been at
war for sixteen years to defend our liberty. . . . Between money well
spent and money thrown away, we have spent between thirteen and
fourteen million florins for Tuscan liberty in the past sixteen years,
and there have been few years when we spent less than 800,000

[44] *Prov.*, 93, ff.57v–58r, printed in F. Pellegrini, *Sulla repubblica fiorentina a tempo
di Cosimo il Vecchio* (Pisa, 1880), v–viii. The council votes: 222–35 and 175–10.
On this provision, see Molho, "Florentine Oligarchy," *Speculum*, XLIII, 51. Cf. the
chronicle of Giovanni Morelli; *Delizie*, XIX, 10.

[45] *CP*, 37, f.72r. Agnolo Pandolfini and Cionaccio Baroncelli supported this view.

[46] *Ibid.*, f.74r; *DBCMLC*, 3, f.71v; *Datini*, 1067, unpaginated, letter of 11 July
1404 from Giovanni Cirioni to Cristofano di Bartolo da Barberino in Majorca:
"Qui si sono levati gl'Ottantuno e non si può porre più prestanze se non pe'chon-
sigli; e i signori anno chasso i provigionati di piazza e levate ogn'altro provigioni
che davano al signore di Cortono e ad altri signori; per levare ogni spesa. Ragionate
d'aghosto in là si spende il Comune il mese fiorini 9000 o circha e pure grazia di
Dio s'aparecchia a ffare. Ogni persona a volontà ghuadagnare, tanto sono stati
sanza potere fare niente."

[47] *CP*, 37, ff.80r–80v.

[48] *Ibid.*, f.77r, statement of Tommaso Sacchetti. On the Sarzana negotiations, see
DBCMLC, 3, ff.73r–73v, 76r.

[49] *Conc.*, 1859, no. 33, 15 Oct. 1404.

florins."[50] He noted that the republic's ordinary revenue had all been consumed by the military budget, that it had been supplemented by sixty forced loans in the past three years, and that "there is not a king or province in the world that could have done the same." Though the fiscal burdens of the war had ruined many citizens, the sacrifices were worth the cost and the Florentines would fight again, if necessary, "to have peace." Writing to a business associate in Majorca (11 July 1404), a merchant named Giovanni Cirioni described the stabilization of relations with the lords of Lucca and Rimini, "who are quiet now and do not bite us, since each is preoccupied with his own security."[51] Lombardy ceased to be a threat: "We need not fear that they will make war on us again." There remained only one area of potential crisis—Pisa—whose Visconti ruler had placed himself under the protection of Marshal Boucicaut, the French captain who governed Genoa for King Charles VI. Though hostilities between Florence and Pisa had ceased after Boucicaut established his protectorate, the situation on the border, and in Pisa itself, remained tense. "I do not know what will happen," Cirioni wrote, "but they are in bad straits; their *signore* has exiled more than 1000 citizens and every day he fleeces them and there is no revenue coming in."

These reports do not touch upon the battles fought within the *reggimento* over this shift in foreign policy; the disagreements had not been fully resolved by summer's end, when the republic finally abandoned the Lombard campaign. Maso degli Albizzi had orchestrated this *volte-face* with a minimum of public quarreling, and with no scapegoats or blighted reputations. But Filippo Corsini, Rinaldo Gianfigliazzi, and others who had supported the continuation of the Visconti struggle were opposed to the new policy of retrenchment and pacification. Rinaldo degli Albizzi noted that the war magistracy were so annoyed by his peace mission to Carlo Malatesta that they refused to pay his travel expenses.[52] The peace settlement with Siena, Giovanni Morelli observed, "was deplored by all of the influential and esteemed citizens and favored by the malcontents, the heavily taxed, and

[50] *Datini*, 1110, unpaginated and dated 10 Aug. 1404. The estimate of 13–14 million florins for military expenditures since 1388 is much higher than Dati's figure of 7½ million florins, or Molho's calculation of 5 million for the period 1390–1402; Molho, *Florentine Public Finances*, 9, n.1.

[51] *Datini*, 1067, unpaginated. Cirioni's correspondent was Cristofano di Bartolo da Barberino.

[52] "Et anche perchè i Dieci della balìa presono sdegno co' Signori della mia andata sanza lor saputa, mai non gli volleno stanziare, benchè i Signori, in verità, ne facesseno ultimo *de potentia*"; *Commissioni*, I, 33. This magistracy had assumed office on 21 Jan. 1404; *Delizie*, XIV, 291.

the ignorant."[53] The legislation abolishing the Council of Eighty-one was an obvious slap at militarists and elitists: "the *popolo* were delighted and the warmongers were furious," Morelli commented.[54] Another provision with partisan overtones was enacted that summer, sponsored by the standard-bearer of justice, Paolo Carnesecchi, who had opposed the invasion of Lombardy. This measure provided for a new scrutiny of the Signoria, the results of which angered some citizens from older families who felt that men of lesser status were gaining offices and honors at their expense. Giovanni Morelli insisted that this accusation was unfounded, and that the only citizens to suffer discrimination in the scrutiny were those who had not served the public interest.[55] Some intransigent members of the ruling group may have entertained ideas of a show of force, or even a coup, to reverse this trend, which (they felt) threatened their own status and the security of the regime. A letter written by a native of Pistoia, Ser Andrea di Ser Niccolò, to his friend Sinibaldo Lazzari (and intercepted by the magistracy responsible for internal security) described the efforts of a member of the Peruzzi family to recruit soldiers in the *contado* to defend the ruling group, or some segment of it, against enemies. According to this source, the Peruzzi and their allies were planning some action, ostensibly against the Alberti but in reality against their rivals for control of, and preeminence in, the *reggimento*.[56]

[53] *Ricordi*, 416. Morelli added: "E quanto che a me, dispiacque, pogniamo che io sia de' gravati, ma io vo' meglio alla città e al bene e onore del Comune che io non voglio alla mia ispezieltà."

[54] *Ricordi*, 427.

[55] *Ibid.*, 427–31. Morelli also noted that Antonio Mangioni and Niccolò da Uzzano were supporters of this scrutiny: "Questi isquittini furono contro alla volontà di molti sono nel reggimento, e spezialmente contro alla volontà delle famiglie; e questo per sospetto di molti popolani i quai e' riputono non essere loro amici." The Sienese ambassador had written (October 1404) that the contentment of the *gente mezzana e minuta* was the result, not only of the Sienese peace settlement, but also "pero chè anno negli onori e uffici più loro dovere non solevano, e ancho aspettano meglio"; *Conc.*, 1859, no. 33.

[56] *SCMLC*, 3, f.58v. Ser Andrea asked Lazzari to inform Bartolomeo Valori of this development, and he also mentioned Paolo Biliotti and Gino [Capponi?] as others who should be informed. A copy of the letter is in *AP*, 4003, ff.44r–46r, as part of a sentence against Ser Andrea for "spreading scandal." He was fined 500 l. Ser Andrea wrote: "Sentio di uno mio intimo e caro amico et huomo da fatti che elli era stato richiesto da alcuno de' Peruzzi che avea bisogna di lui con quella compagnia che poteva, et che stesse in punto colle loro armi, che quando mandasse per lui, fusse presto che tosto serebbe, per chè a Ffirenze si tractava cacciare via quegli della settuccia. . . . Si diceva volere fare contro la famiglia degl 'Alberti qualche cosa, et io credo che sotto questa ombra di intornare contro agli Alberti, quelli della settuccia, se non sono avisati, aranno mal fatto che quello ch'io ti scrivo è la verità. Pregoti segretissimamente li facci sentire."

The disputes over foreign policy which surfaced in these months had their roots in conflicting systems of priorities, and not in factions or cliques. Those citizens who were most eager for peace abroad and economy at home represented the mercantile and artisan interests, which were most sensitive to economic and fiscal conditions. Though this viewpoint was expressed in debates, it was most clearly articulated in mercantile correspondence: "God send us peace so that merchandise can come and go as it should, for it seems like a thousand years."[57] Trade routes, port privileges, and security for merchants and their cargoes were paramount issues for these men, and the argument that peace could be achieved though a vigorous prosecution of the war did not move them.[58] Pragmatic as well as cautious in their approach to foreign policy, they did not favor grand designs nor large-scale enterprises, whether military or diplomatic. Their patriotism and their commitment to civic values were perhaps not so intense as that of Filippo Corsini and Rinaldo Gianfigliazzi, nor of Domenico Giugni who criticized Francesco Datini for leaving Florence to avoid paying his *prestanze*: "Considering that everyone is obligated to his homeland, and should never abandon it, particularly in time of adversity, I tell you that I am one of those who advise you not to forsake yours. If you do, you will be censured by God and the world. . . ."[59] Still recovering in 1404 from the trauma of the Visconti peril, these civic-minded Florentines took great pride in their role as leaders of the defense of Florentine (and Tuscan) liberty against the Milanese tyrant. With the credit gained in that enterprise, they had continued the struggle for two years after Giangaleazzo's death before errors of strategy, heavy expenses, a moribund economy, and war weariness had forced them to abandon that course. Though they could not withstand the pressures for peace and fiscal retrenchment, which became so intense in the spring and summer of 1404, they remained influential in the *reggimento*, and ready at the opportune moment to promote their schemes for Florentine security.

[57] Francesco Datini and Domenico di Cambio in Florence to their associates in Majorca, 3 Dec. 1403; *Datini*, 1067, unpaginated. Similar views in Datini's letter to his partners in Barcelona, *ibid.*, 868, unpaginated, 2 Feb. 1404; "Le chose di qua si stano al modo usatto e pegio se posono. Qua no' si fa nulla se no' dare ordine a paghare danari [al] Chomune. Che Dio ci mandi pacie tosto; bisognio n'abiamo per più caggioni."

[58] The argument that peace could be achieved through intensified fighting was an old theme in Florentine debates on foreign policy; it had been most recently advanced by Tommaso Sacchetti, 16 Feb. 1404; *CP*, 37, f.28r.

[59] *Datini*, 719, unpaginated, letter dated 19 May 1401. It is translated in my *Society of Renaissance Florence*, 82.

The persistence of traditional attitudes, and specifically the aggressive style of diplomacy favored by the imperialists within the regime, is illustrated by the republic's relations with Siena in these months. Though peace was acclaimed by both sides as a restoration of the cordial friendship of past times,[60] relations between the two governments were as tense and prickly as they had been in the 1380s, before Siena's submission to Giangaleazzo. The Florentines insisted upon the settlement of border disputes in their favor, and they were quick to accuse the Sienese of fomenting discord in the frontier areas. Another source of discord was the Sienese port of Talamone which, contrary to the peace agreement, was not used by Florentine merchants, who preferred to ship their cargoes through Genoa or Mutrone.[61] The most prominent figures in the regime participated in these negotiations.[62] The Castellani and Cristofano Spini were identified as good friends of Siena, but in that group were some who, in the Sienese ambassador's words, "speak less than well of you, though these are few in number and they are incited by our own malcontents."[63] Maso degli Albizzi was known to be a friend of those Sienese exiles who had not become reconciled to their city's new government;[64] he was standard-bearer of justice (February 1405) when a band of those exiles was molested by armed men allegedly in the pay of the Sienese republic. Maso angrily berated the ambassadors for their government's complicity in the affair, which threatened to develop into a major diplomatic crisis. Sienese exiles spread the news of the imbroglio in Florence, embellishing the details with stories that the Sienese regime was on the verge of surrendering its liberty to King Ladislaus of Naples.[65] Florentine

[60] For these sentiments, see the letters in the Datini archives, vols. 1067 and 1110 cited above, and *Conc.*, 1856, no. 22; 1857, no. 25.

[61] See the account of these negotiations and of Florentine intransigence from the Sienese perspective; *Conc.*, 1857, no. 64, 66, 69, 71, 74, 85, 88, 89; 1858, no. 28, 51, 81, 84; 1859, no. 32, 65.

[62] References to Maso degli Albizzi, Niccolò da Uzzano, Tommaso Sacchetti in *ibid.*, 1857, no. 64, 66, 74, 83; 1859, no. 32, 33; to Cristofano Spini as a Sienese friend, *ibid.*, 1858, no. 28, and his autograph letter, no. 2; to Messer Lotto Castellani, *ibid.*, no. 81; and to Messer Vanni Castellani, "el quale è nostro buono e perfecto amico," *ibid.*, no. 83.

[63] *Conc.*, 1858, no. 28, 5 July 1404.

[64] *Ibid.*, 1859, no. 85. Maso told the Sienese ambassador that several exiles were "suoi amici e potendoli servire di quello si servono gli amici, il farebbe. . . ."

[65] *Conc.*, 1860, no. 1, 13, 15. Maso spoke to the ambassadors "co' molte pungenti e alte parole"; they continued: "Parleremo con messer Maso e pensiamo riducerlo etc., ma Gaio judeo, che a gran pratica collui per loro fatti . . . ci consiglia per bene del facto si gli donasse una peza di velluto o altro e che sarà buono mezano. . . ."

statesmen had not learned tolerance and magnanimity from their long ordeal with Giangaleazzo. Indeed, their success in resisting the Visconti challenge may have encouraged their arrogance, since they did not feel dependent upon the support of their neighbors.

With the liquidation of the Lombard enterprise and the stabilization of relations with their Tuscan neighbors, Pisa excepted, Florentines were enjoying, in the winter and spring of 1405, their most tranquil period in years. No significant threat to the republic's security existed anywhere in the peninsula, a situation that encouraged parsimonious citizens to reduce the military budget and terminate contracts with *condottieri*. In a series of debates on the appropriate size of the military establishment, the Signoria and their counselors agreed to an army of 250 lances and 800 infantry.[66] This force was quite adequate for the defense of Florentine territory, but not for any incursions outside her borders. In February 1405, a petty Romagnol *signore*, Count Malatesta of Dovadola, seized some goods belonging to Florentine merchants and harassed their subjects. Speeches favoring caution and restraint were made by Piero Baroncelli and Paolo Carnesecchi, the latter urging his audience to resist the lure of military adventures and to concentrate instead on paying the commune's debts.[67] Gino Capponi, who favored the immediate occupation of Modigliana and Dovadola, towns belonging to Count Malatesta, argued forcefully for intervention. Maso degli Albizzi gave qualified approval, and Rinaldo Gianfigliazzi enthusiastic support, for the campaign, while Paolo Carnesecchi and Bartolomeo Valori urged the Signoria to abandon it.[68] Some collegiate groups opposed the Romagna enterprise; others favored annexation of the towns.[69] The imperialist argument that Florentine honor required offensive action did not persuade war-weary citizens who did not favor another military adventure with high risks and dubious benefits.[70]

Pisa, however, was another matter. The eyes of merchants and statesmen had been focused on that port city ever since the death

[66] *CP*, 37, ff.98r–98v, 100r, 107v.

[67] *Ibid.*, f.104v: "Quod in aliquam impresam nichil modo veniatur et solvatur debitum communis."

[68] *Ibid.*, ff.101v, 117v, 122v–123r.

[69] *Ibid.*, ff.123r–124r. The most confusing advice was given by Giovanni di Bicci de' Medici, spokesman for the Twelve: "Quod impresa non manuteneatur nec deseratur; sed presupponatur quod non fiat; fiat quod non possit ibi recepi verecundia."

[70] *Ibid.*, ff.125r, 127r, 128r; *SCMLC*, 3, ff.6or, 63r–66v. The Signoria opted for a negotiated settlement. The republic did attempt to justify its involvement in Romagnol affairs to the new pope, Innocent VII; *SCMLC*, 2, ff.6or–62r, 25 Jan. 1405.

of Pietro Gambacorta had deprived Florentine entrepreneurs of their most expeditious route to the Mediterranean and to the markets of Western Europe, North Africa, and the Levant. Though the issue of Pisa's acquisition was never mentioned in council deliberations, it was rarely absent from the correspondence of the Ten, who persistently sought to persuade the Visconti rulers, their administrators, and their soldiers to turn over the city to Florence. In the last proposal made before Boucicaut established his protectorate, in April 1404, the war magistracy offered to buy Pisa for 200,000 florins.[71] After making peace with Siena in that month, the Ten had intensified military operations against Pisa; in their angry representation to Boucicaut, they claimed that their soldiers were about to conquer the city when he frustrated their plans.[72] Florentine recriminations had no effect on Boucicaut, who seized merchandise valued at 200,000 florins to force the republic to sign a four-year truce with Pisa.[73] That agreement provided for the transit of Florentine goods through the port, but Giovanni Morelli noted that "there was not one Florentine who would have dared to do business there."[74] Only the threat of French reprisals restrained the government from renewing its attack upon the Pisans, who were suffering from the strangulation of their commerce and the misgovernment of their incompetent ruler, Gabriele Maria Visconti. Unable to gain their objective by force, the Florentines resorted to gold. "We offered so much money to Boucicaut, to the lord of Pisa, and to the Duke of Orleans," Morelli wrote, "that they abandoned their hostility and became as sweet as honey, and they listened willingly to the clink of many florins."[75] The official records contain no references to these negotiations, but a secret report despatched to the Sienese government from Florence (1 August) described a meeting held some time in July between Gabriele Maria Visconti and Maso degli Albizzi in

[71] DBCMLC, 3, f.54r. Matteo Castellani had been sent to Lucca to meet a representative of a Roman captain, Giovanni Colonna, who controlled some territory north of Lucca.

[72] CP, 37, ff.44r–45r; DBCMLC, 3, f.58r, 29 Apr. 1404; instructions to Buonaccorso Pitti, ambassador to Boucicaut in Genoa: ". . . essendo nòi col nostro exercito in punto e in ordine per essere intorno alla città di Pisa sperando in brevissimo tempo liberarla dalla tirannia de' Visconti." For other Florentine reactions to Boucicaut's action, see CP, 37, ff.45v–46r.

[73] Pitti, Cronica, 145–48; Morelli, Ricordi, 418–22. The truce was ratified by the councils in September; Prov., 93, ff.90v–91r. For Florentine complaints over Boucicaut's action, see SCMLC, 2, ff.58r–59r, 62r.

[74] Ricordi, 422. On Florentine diplomatic contacts with Pisa, which indicate that some trade did exist between the two cities, see SCMLC, 26, ff.66v, 74r, 82v, 83v, 84v, 89v, 96v–97r.

[75] Ricordi, 438.

Vico Pisano to discuss the matter.[76] Rumors concerning these negotiations spread in Pisa and ignited a rebellion (27 July) of the populace against Gabriele Maria, who escaped into the citadel held by loyal troops. Save for that fortified place, the city was entirely in the hands of the rebels, who taunted their former *signore* with shouts of "Bastard, son of a whore," as he and his mother fled from Pisa for the security of nearby Sarzana.

The Florentine government reacted slowly to this crisis, which had been precipitated by its diplomacy gone awry. Not until three weeks after the rebellion did the Signoria convene a *pratica* to discuss the acquisition of Pisa.[77] Initially, opinions were evenly divided. Matteo Tinghi, Niccolò Cambi, and Tommaso Ardinghelli spoke out against the project, while Rinaldo Gianfigliazzi, Filippo Corsini, and Giovenco della Stufa favored the purchase of Pisa from Gabriele Visconti and Boucicaut.[78] Some speakers hesitated to endorse the acquisition unless the port of Livorno were included in the bargain. With his customary prudence, Maso degli Albizzi did not intervene until he had tested the civic sentiment. Then he delivered his judgment: "In the name of God, let us act!"[79] The evidence in the protocols would suggest that the entire citizenry had been converted to the Pisan enterprise,[80] but this is disproved by a large negative vote (128 of 420) against a provision authorizing the Signoria, its colleges, and an adjunct group of sixty-four citizens to impose levies and hire troops, without any limita-

[76] This report by an anonymous Florentine is in *Conc.*, 1861, no. 62: "Interviene che messer Maso degli Albezi andò a uno suo luogo verso Pisa e aboccassi col signore di Pisa a uno castello che se chiama Vico pisano; et s'intendosi in Pisa questa accozamento et prima avendo posto in Pisa el signore d'una imposta de LXX^M de fiorini, ramaricandosi certi Pisani insieme l'uno coll'altro, vennero a levare el romori a dire: 'Viva el popolo e muoino ei forestieri.'" A different version of events was reported by Sienese officials in Casole; *ibid.*, 1863, no. 69, who stated that the sale of Pisa for 200,000 florins had been settled before the meeting between Maso and Gabriele, which was called by Maso, "o per metter discordia tra Pisani e 'l signore o per qual altra cosa" to inform Gabriele of a Pisan plot against him. Morelli, *Ricordi*, 438, describes the meeting between Maso and Gabriele, as do later chroniclers; see Bayley, *War and Society in Renaissance Florence*, 75, n.48.

[77] There were brief statements by the colleges; *CP*, 37, ff.151v, 152v. The Signoria did pursue negotiations for Pisa's purchase with Gabriele Maria Visconti and Boucicaut; Morelli, *Ricordi*, 442–43.

[78] *CP*, 37, ff.154r–155r.

[79] *Ibid.*, f.157v, 19 Aug. Maso had commented earlier on specific details of the negotiations; *ibid.*, f.156r, 14 Aug.

[80] On 19 Aug., all nine speakers whose views were recorded favored Pisa's acquisition; *ibid.*, ff.157v–158r.

tions, for a six-month period.[81] Though the incorporation of Pisa into the Florentine dominion was clearly favored by a majority in the *reggimento*, and probably in the city at large, a substantial minority cast its white beans against the scheme.

The bargaining between Gabriele Visconti and Boucicaut, on the one hand, and the Florentine ambassadors on the other, focused on the price and also on the legal aspects of Pisa's transfer. The republic finally agreed to pay 200,000 florins for the city and its *contado*, and for the right to use the port of Livorno, with the payments to be made in three stages. To placate Boucicaut and his royal master, the Florentines also accepted the principle of French sovereignty, and the treaty stipulated that they would hold Pisa in fief from King Charles VI.[82] One problem not covered in the treaty was the reconciliation of the Pisan citizenry to Florentine rule. Speakers in the *pratiche* convened in the last days of August apparently did not consider that issue crucial, for they urged the Signoria to conclude the settlement with Gabriele and Boucicaut, and to postpone negotiations with the Pisans until after the legal formalities had been ratified and the citadel occupied by Florentine troops.[83] From a Sienese source, however, came an ominous report that the armed Pisans "had never been so united nor so determined to defend themselves as they are at this moment."[84] Business associates of Francesco Datini wrote their compatriots in Barcelona that "we took the citadel on 31 August and soon we will have the rest [of the city]. They have hired so many troops that it makes one dizzy; and we are pulling a lot of money from our pockets. But it will all be for the best, since we will not need to spend any more in the future. . . ."[85] On 5 September the Ten sent two castellans, Siepe Peruzzi and Alessio Baldovinetti, to join the commander of

[81] *Prov.*, 94, ff.138r–139r. On this, see Morelli, *Ricordi*, 443–44, who also noted that a new war *balìa* was elected. Its members included Rinaldo Gianfigliazzi, Niccolò da Uzzano, Cristofano Spini, Bartolomeo Valori, and Lorenzo Ridolfi.

[82] The negotiations are described by Morelli, *Ricordi*, 441–43; other sources and documents cited by Bayley, *War and Society*, 75.

[83] *CP*, 37, ff.161v–162r, 27 Aug. On 22 Aug., the Signoria informed the Pisans that Florence had acquired the city from Gabriele Maria Visconti; *SCMLC*, 26, f.118v.

[84] *Conc.*, 1861, no. 99, letter from Niccolò di Sozzino, 31 Aug., who also noted that "per quello ch'io sento da chi non parla per affectione, le cose non sono sì grasse [*sic*] chome per lo vulgho si dicha."

[85] *Datini*, 870, unpaginated, letter of Jacopo d'Agnolo to Datini. The republic had earlier requested troops from the legate of Bologna, Carlo Malatesta, and Città di Castello; *SCMLC*, 26, f.118v.

the Florentine garrison, Nencio Raffacani, and to share with him the responsibility for guarding the fortress. The day after they arrived in the citadel (6 September), a small band of Pisans gained entry through a tower gate, subdued the garrison, and occupied the fortress. The news of the disaster reached Florence on the next day. "All true Florentines were grief-stricken," wrote Giovanni Morelli, "and, with their thoughts focused on their honor, they never forgot this disgrace and they will never forget it until they have gained their revenge and Pisa is again in their possession."[86]

The loss of Pisa provided a focus for Florentine energies that had been missing since Giangaleazzo's death. With rare unanimity, citizens demanded Pisa's reconquest; only Matteo Tinghi dared to voice his opposition.[87] To the appeals for peace of an embassy of Pisan citizens, the Florentines turned a deaf ear. "Give the ambassadors permission to depart," advised Cristofano di Giorgio, "and support the war magistracy and never desist until Pisa and all of her territory are in our possession."[88] Francesco Datini informed his partner in Barcelona that the republic was organizing a massive offensive, "and here the sole activity is the hiring of soldiers."[89] The Sienese ambassador reported that an army of 1500 lances and 5000 foot soldiers was being assembled to besiege Pisa.[90] The Ten also hired Venetian galleys to blockade the coast and cut off Pisa's supply routes by sea. To honor its obligations to Gabriele Visconti and Boucicaut, and to pay for these military and naval forces, the regime levied a series of huge *prestanze*. In the calendar year following the loss of Pisa's citadel (October 1405–October 1406), Francesco Datini paid the staggering sum of 6000 florins in forced loans, which was nearly triple his assessment in 1401–1402, before Giangaleazzo's death.[91] The citizens grumbled and some voted

---

[86] *Ricordi*, 444–47. For reactions of Florentine merchants, see R. Piattoli, "Genova e Firenze al tramonto della libertà di Pisa," *Giornale storico e letterario della Liguria*, VI (1930), 221–23.

[87] The *pratica* was held on 7 Sept.; *CP*, 37, ff.167r–167v. Tinghi's statement: "Quod cum minore danno et verecundia fieri potest, discedatur ab inceptis." Five months later, Buonaccorso Pitti proposed that "sub pena capitis nullus audeat consulere pacem cum pisanis nisi commune primo habeat dominium sicut decet"; *ibid.*, f.197r, 21 Feb. 1406.

[88] *Ibid.*, f.172r, 19 Sept. See the earlier discussion on 17 Sept., *ibid.*, f.171r.

[89] *Datini*, 870, unpaginated, letter dated 27 Sept. See also Piattoli, *Giornale storico e letterario della Liguria*, VI, 223.

[90] *Conc.*, 1862, no. 36, 1 Oct. 1405.

[91] Molho, *Florentine Public Finances*, 97. Datini had paid approximately 2200 florins between Oct. 1401 and August 1402. Between Jan. 1400 and Jan. 1407, he paid a total of 15,337 fl.; *ibid.*, 94.

against these fiscal measures.[92] But ultimately they paid, and the military machine which their florins subsidized pressed relentlessly against the Pisan defenses.

At that moment the political situation in Italy was exceptionally propitious for Florence's campaign to subdue Pisa. Her Tuscan neighbors, Siena and Lucca, were too weak and too vulnerable to offer effective assistance to the beleaguered Pisans. Florentine agents were quick to report, and react to, any sign that soldiers were being recruited in Tuscany and the Papal States on Pisa's behalf.[93] In Genoa, Boucicaut could not give help to a city whose sale he had condoned, and from which he had profited. Boniface IX's successor, Innocent VII, was too preoccupied with internal problems to offer any opposition to Florence's campaign. A desperate Pisan effort to surrender to King Ladislaus of Naples was foiled by the adroit diplomacy of Rinaldo degli Albizzi.[94] Their *contado* ravaged by Florentine troops and their food supplies dwindling, the Pisans watched helplessly as the blockade tightened. On 17 July 1406 the town of Vico Pisano, ten miles east, fell to the Florentine army. Still another Pisan embassy came to Florence in search of peace, but Gino Capponi and Bartolomeo Corbinelli, representing the war magistracy, rejected their appeals.[95] Finally, in October, members of the Gambacorta family, whose ancestor Pietro had been a loyal friend of the republic, arranged for the occupation of the city by Florentine troops. On 9 October, an army of 3000 horse and 3000 infantry entered the starving city and took possession of the citadel and the other fortified places. "We do not know and we do not desire to know how much honor and profit we received," Giovanni

[92] For complaints, see a letter from the Datini archives printed in R. Piattoli, *Giornale storico e letterario della Liguria*, VI, 228, n.2; and Domenico di Cambio's letter to Cristofano di Bartolo in Valencia, *Datini*, 989, unpaginated, 24 Apr. 1406: "I fatti di Pisa sono uno nostro cholatoio: quant'io, ne sono disfatto, tante prestanze o a paghare. . . . Questa guera mi chosterà più di f. 400 d'oro. Idio ci dia grazia ch'ella si spacci tosto, sichè noi usciamo di tanta tribolazione." Two measures, one providing for the sale of property of delinquent taxpayers and the other authorizing a *balìa* to impose new levies, were passed by narrow margins (270–119 and 286–142); *Prov.*, 94, ff.165r–166r, 240v–241r. A measure that provided for a new schedule of *prestanze* assessments was rejected eight times before finally passing; *LF*, 48, ff.104r–107r, 127r–136r.

[93] *DBCMLC*, 3, ff.97v–98r, 113v, 114v; *SCMLC*, 27, ff.16r–16v, 18r.

[94] See the Signoria's letter to Ladislaus, *SCMLC*, 26, f.135v, 2 Dec. 1405; and Rinaldo's mission to Ladislaus; *Commissioni*, 1, 90–108.

[95] F. Perrens, *Histoire de Florence* (Paris, 1877–1883), VI, 154, quoting Gino Capponi's memoirs; the records of the war magistracy contain instructions to a Florentine embassy to Pisa demanding the city's submission; *DBCMLC*, 3, f.121r, 4 July 1406.

Morelli observed, "but we paid heavily for it. . . . Our sins and theirs have brought trouble to ourselves and to them, but God has favored us more by his grace and for that we owe him gratitude. . . ."[96]

Problems of Territorial Government

No single event in Florence's history gave more immediate gratification to her citizenry than Pisa's conquest. The public celebrations were the visible manifestations of a great surge of civic pride in that acquisition which had long been a focus of Florentine aspirations.[97] But the leaders of the regime prudently avoided the arrogant stance that had so infuriated the republic's neighbors after Arezzo's annexation in 1384. The tone of Florentine diplomacy in the autumn and winter of 1406–1407 was conciliatory.[98] One group of counselors argued that Florence could not retain Pisa without the cooperation of Boucicaut and the Genoese, and they urged the Signoria to maintain that friendship at all costs.[99] These citizens were acutely aware that Florence's emergence as a maritime power had complicated her relations with Genoa (and thus with France) and with the ruler of the Neapolitan kingdom, Ladislaus. They realized too that the defense of Pisa and her *contado* would be expensive. Beyond these immediate considerations, however, were problems of territorial government, some of long standing, which now became more urgent as a result of Pisa's reconquest.

Of paramount concern to the Florentine authorities was the security of their slippery prize which, a year before, had eluded them. To prevent any repetition of that humiliating episode, the war magistracy picked two trustworthy citizens, Gino Capponi and Bartolomeo Corbinelli, as captain and *podestà* of Pisa, and later chose (by hand and not by lot) the ten members of the magistracy responsible for the city's

---

[96] Morelli, *Ricordi*, 464. Cf. his account of the fall of Pisa, *ibid.*, 459–63.

[97] The festivities are described in *ibid.*, 465–67, 470–72. See M. Mallett's appraisal of the significance of the Pisan conquest; "Pisa and Florence in the Fifteenth Century," *Flor. Studies*, 403.

[98] The Sienese ambassador reported his conversations with Florentine politicians: "Tutti parlano in uno effetto, che non si prenda alcuna onbrosia di questo loro aquisto di Pisa . . . però ch'egli intendono che questa sia in fermamento non tanto di Toscana ma di tutta Italia"; *Conc.*, 1863, no. 98, 28 Oct. 1406. For the Tuscan reaction to the Florentine annexation of Arezzo, see above, ch. III, 105.

[99] *CP*, 39, f.4v, 15 Jan. 1407, statement of Rinaldo Gianfigliazzi. Boucicaut demanded 20,000 fl. from the republic. Most Florentines felt that they did not owe the money, but should pay it to maintain good relations with Boucicaut and the king of France; *ibid.*, ff.3v–4r. For banking arrangements to pay that sum, see *SCMLC*, 28, ff.3v–4r, 6 Feb. 1407; Piattoli, *Giornale storico e letterario della Liguria*, VI, 321.

governance and defense.[100] These officials commanded a military garrison of 1000 lances and 1000 infantry; they also supervised the reconstruction of the citadel and the strengthening of other fortifications in and around the city.[101] Such measures were expensive, and their cost fell upon a citizenry that had subsidized a military enterprise costing one and a half million florins.[102] The Sienese ambassador reported that "there are loud complaints about the taxes and the new assessments, so that it appears that everyone wishes to stop the levy of *prestanze*."[103] Though both colleges (January 1407), advocated the abolition of forced loans, they did not suggest any alternative method of financing the Pisan garrison.[104] Even after the cavalry force was reduced by one-half, to 500 lances, the authorities were hard pressed to pay their wages. The Signoria periodically convened the colleges in the spring and summer of 1407 to discuss means of raising money for the military payroll. Though the counselors encouraged the priors to squeeze more revenue from the Pisans, they finally accepted the necessity of levying several *prestanze* to meet a fiscal deficit of 250,000 florins.[105]

Among the measures proposed to solve the fiscal crisis were the equalization of assessments, the coercion of delinquents, the collection of fees and rents owed to the commune, and the imposition of special levies on *contadini* and clerics.[106] But alongside these traditional

[100] Morelli, *Ricordi*, 464–65, 468–69.

[101] *Conc.*, 1863, no. 98. The Sixteen recommended that all *magistri* working on the cathedral be sent to Pisa to construct the fortress there; CP, 38, f.5r, 18 Jan. 1407.

[102] That estimate was made by Dati: *Istoria di Firenze di Goro Dati dall'anno MCCCLXXX all'anno MCCCCV* (Florence, 1735), 129.

[103] *Conc.*, 1863, no. 98. Several months later, Domenico di Cambio was complaining about the excessive cost of the Pisan occupation; letter to Bartolo da Barberino in Barcelona; *Datini*, 872, unpaginated, 30 Apr. 1407.

[104] CP, 38, ff.2r, 6r. The colleges did press the Signoria to reduce the size of the garrison; *ibid.*, ff.8v, 27v.

[105] CP, 38, ff.18r–18v, 20v–21r, 28v, 37r–37v. The paltry revenues from Pisa, argued Niccolò Barbadori in July 1407, resulted from the lack of trade; neither Pisan nor Genoese merchants had returned to the port; *ibid.*, f.54r. On the depressed state of the Pisan economy in these years, see Silva, "Pisa sotto Firenze," *Studi storici*, XVIII, 20–36, who may have painted too bleak a picture; cf. Mallett, *Flor. Studies*, 405–06, 413–20. Molho, *Florentine Public Finances*, 36, states that only 5000 fl. of 48,000 owed by the Pisans was actually collected in 1407. For a different view, see M. Becker, *Florence in Transition*, II, 243.

[106] The statements of Rinaldo Gianfigliazzi and Maso degli Albizzi, CP, 38, ff.104v, 106r; and the provision concerning delinquents; *Prov.*, 98, ff.34v–35r, 17–18 May 1409. Additional levies on the *contado* were rejected in Dec. 1406, but one was approved in May 1407; LF, 48, ff.155r–162r, 183r.

devices, a new idea appeared in the debates: the rationalization of the fisc. Supervising the collection and disbursement of communal revenues was a large bureaucracy that operated a complex network of separate treasuries, each with specific sources of income—gabelles, *prestanze*, fines—and each responsible for specific expenditures: salaries of judges and professors, stipends of *condottieri*, provisions for the Signoria's *mensa*.[107] In March 1407, Filippo Magalotti proposed a major overhaul of that cumbersome system. Expenditures could be gradually reduced, he argued, if a schedule of priorities were established, so that the most important obligations were met first. "Thus, day by day, let the situation improve, and let the debts be paid little by little, the most pressing ones first [i.e., the salaries of the Pisa garrison], and then the others in orderly progression."[108]

Magalotti's scheme did not gain any support in the *pratiche*, but other reforms were proposed by civic groups appointed to study the fisc. Successive years of deficit financing had so enlarged the funded debt, and the interest charges on that debt, that citizens began to question the republic's ability to satisfy its obligations. Private bankers either did not have the capital, or perhaps the willingness, to make short-term loans to pay the most pressing debts.[109] In September 1407, a fiscal commission appointed by the Signoria calculated that the commune owed some 40,000 florins to its troops, and it proposed an elaborate system of disbursements from various funds to satisfy that commitment. Two months later, another commission drew up a balance sheet of the various *monti* that made up the funded debt and made recommendations for reducing its size.[110] The total funded debt

107 The volumes of the *Camera del Comune* reveal the complexities of the system. In 1384, for example, the revenues came into six separate funds: Introitus generalis, introitus conducte, introitus condempnatorum, introitus castrorum, introitus sexte prestantie, introitus bonorum ecclesiarum; *Camera, Entrata*, 216, *passim*. For examples of the legislation required to transfer funds from one *introitus* to another, see *Prov.*, 76, ff.49v–50v; 100, ff.97v–99r, 124v–126r.

108 *CP*, 38, f.18r: ". . . De die in diem res bene ordinentur et paulatim solvantur debita et primo magis necessaria et sicut successive." Another recommendation on the same day called for the levy of a new *prestanza*; *ibid.*, f.18v.

109 Florentine bankers were an irregular source of credit for the republic in these years; see, for example, *CP*, 37, ff.39v, 69v; and the loan of 2500 fl. from Francesco de' Bardi and company; *CP*, 38, f.85r; and another company, not identified, which was ordered by the Signoria to pay 27,000 fl. to Boucicaut in Genoa; *SCMLC*, 28, ff.3v–4r, 6 Feb. 1407. How extensively private banks were used for short-term loans has not been investigated for this period; for the 1420s and 1430s, see Molho, *Florentine Public Finances*, 153–57, 164–82.

110 *CP*, 38, ff.84v–85r; ff.113r–114v. This is the most elaborate report on the fisc to be found in the protocols to that date.

was then 3,305,000 florins, and the annual carrying charges were estimated at 190,200 florins.[111] An additional sum of 360,000 florins had been received from various *prestanze*; these had not yet been funded. Furthermore, a total of 155,000 florins was still owed to creditors of the *monti* for the years 1403–1407. To satisfy all these claims fully and promptly was beyond the regime's resources, so the commission proposed a series of emergency measures. It recommended that all unfunded obligations be converted into *monti*, but with interest payments postponed for two years. One-fourth of all monies due to holders of *monti* shares (44,423 florins annually) was to be cancelled and used to retire a portion of these obligations. Other sources of income—the salt gabelle, the money assigned to the cathedral building fund, the proceeds from levies on the clergy and the *contado*—were also to be used to reduce the swollen public debt.[112]

The most significant feature of the commission report was its concept of fiscal planning, its vision—still rudimentary—of a budget with future projections of income and expenditure.[113] The commission concluded its report by predicting a budget deficit of 88,000 florins for the nine-month period ending on 1 January 1409.[114] Two months later (16 January 1408), the Sixteen informed the Signoria of their support for measures "to systematize the commune from 1 March [1408] to 1 January 1409," although they disagreed over scheduling the levy of forced loans for those months.[115] The idea of fiscal planning had strong appeal for these citizens who, in their business and personal affairs, were continually involved in this activity. Speaking for the Sixteen (1 March 1408), Giovanni Minerbetti stated that they wished to formulate a budget not merely for the short term, but for a longer period.[116] Responding to these concerns, the civic commission "deputed to put

[111] These figures can be compared with those for 1415, cited by Molho, *Florentine Public Finances*, 72: an annual carrying charge of 185,000 fl. and (Molho's estimate) a total debt of 3.1 million fl.

[112] The university lost its communal subsidy and was closed from 1407 to 1413; Brucker, "Florence and its University, 1348–1434," in *Action and Conviction in Early Modern Europe. Essays in Memory of E. H. Harbison*, T. Rabb and J. Seigel, eds. (Princeton, 1969), 223–24.

[113] Another example of a budgetary projection is the statement of Giovanni Minerbetti, 16 July 1414; CP, 42, f.159r. For a different perspective, see Molho, *Florentine Public Finances*, 89.

[114] "E perchè è di bisogno provedere da kalende di marzo 1407 [1408] in sino a dì primo di gennaio 1408 [1409], che bisogna fiorini 88,000 e più, e questo conviene uscire dele borse de' cittadini"; CP, 38, f.114v.

[115] CP, 38, f.118r.

[116] "Quod ipsi velint ordinare quantocitius fieri potest, commune non solum pro ipsorum tempore sed ulterius etiam"; CP, 39, f.13r.

the commune's finances in order" recommended the imposition of five
prestanze in the ten-month period ending 1 February 1409, specifically
to meet the expenses of the Pisa garrison. That group also proposed
a more rigorous enforcement of the penalties for tax delinquents, a
closer scrutiny of the list of communal creditors in the *libro del banco*,
and the sale of gabelles to tax farmers.[117] It is doubtful whether these
reforms, if fully implemented, would have solved all the commune's
fiscal problems, or even produced a balanced budget. Nevertheless,
they do reflect a more rational approach to the fisc, and particularly
the acceptance of the concept of long-range planning.[118]

With sufficient revenue assured to pay for the salaries of mercenaries and the construction of Pisa's fortresses, Florentine anxieties
did abate slightly. But in the palace of the Signoria, every rumor of
disaffection became a subject for consultation and a pretext for a flurry
of instructions to the magistrates in Pisa.[119] Though apparently re-
signed to the loss of their liberty, the Pisans (so many Florentines
believed) were secretly waiting for another opportunity to revolt.
The trial records of two Pisan citizens accused of conspiracy contained
a prediction that the Pisans were dissembling "by walking with bowed
heads," but that they were determined to rise up and massacre their
oppressors. Officials searched Pisan homes for weapons, and informers notified the authorities of plots allegedly being made in taverns,
churches, and palaces.[120] But these security measures did not satisfy
the regime's leadership; in January 1407, the colleges proposed that
Pisans "who are prone to scandal and rebellion" should be sent into

---

[117] *Ibid.*, ff.18r, 18v: "Rapporto facto a dì iiii del mese di marzo pe' cittadini
diputati a ordinare il comune sopra il bisogno del denaro." The proposal to sell
gabelles was an innovation rejected by the Twelve; *ibid.*, f.19r. Not since the
fourteenth century had gabelles been sold to tax farmers; C. de la Roncière, in
Flor. Studies, 177–83. The last references to the sale of gabelles that I have found
date from 1381 to 1384; *Camera, Entrata*, 204, f.9r; 205, ff.3v–4r; 206, f.2v; 208,
ff.5v, 11r; 214, f.2r.

[118] Molho, *Florentine Public Finances*, 118, wisely cautions against assuming that
plans for fiscal reform were always taken seriously, or implemented. He argues
that serious attempts at fiscal reform did not begin until the 1420s; I suggest that
they began as early as 1407. The ban against *monte* speculators being selected as
officials of the Monte was finally enacted in 1427; Molho, 121, but it was first
suggested in 1407; *CP*, 38, f.114r.

[119] See the letters sent by the Signoria to the captain of Pisa; *SCMLC*, 28, ff.43v–
47v, 50v, 59v–60r; July–Sept. 1407.

[120] The information on the weapons ban, and police searches and informers is in
AEOG, 1611, ff.90r–93r, 4 Nov. 1406, being the trial of Antonio Menicluni and
Nanni Gherardi of Pisa, who were executed for conspiracy. The reference to
Florentine fears of an uprising in *ibid.*, f.91r.

exile. The Signoria approved this project and sent Gino Capponi a list of 108 names of Pisans who were to be sent to Florence for an indefinite period.[121] This rigorous policy continued until the fortifications were completed in the summer of 1407;[122] thereafter, the authorities adopted a more flexible attitude. A civic commission reported to the Signoria (September 1407) that Pisa's defenses should be permanently manned by a large garrison, and that the troops should be paid regularly and their commanders selected with care. The commission did recommend a relaxation of the exile policy, noting that the Pisan economy would not recover until her citizens were free to move without hindrance. Some counselors wished to make distinctions between merchants, artisans, and paupers who were no threat to Florence's rule, and a minority of potential troublemakers who should remain in exile.[123]

The Signoria's decision to renew sentences of exile for some Pisans stimulated a lively debate. The collegiate groups generally supported this policy as essential for the city's security, and their judgment was supported by Piero Baroncelli and, with some reservations, by Vieri Guadagni. But Gino Capponi argued that Pisa was not so gravely imperiled as to justify such measures. "The Signoria should realize that the city [of Pisa] will be destroyed by this policy, that there will be no revenue from gabelles and that our city will be disgraced." Capponi then voiced his concern over the moral aspects of the exile policy. "The Signoria should take care," he warned, "that they do not displease God, who is a much greater lord than this regime."[124] Other critics were more concerned with Pisa's economic recovery. Andrea della Stufa argued that conditions had worsened since the conquest, and that unless Pisans were allowed to return home, the situation would not improve. Though insisting that security should always receive the highest priority, Niccolò Barbadori believed that exiling Pisans contributed not to that objective, but instead to economic stagnation and Florentine dishonor. These critics were publicly raising some basic issues of Florentine policy toward subject communities. Did the requirements of security invariably take precedence over considerations of justice and morality? Would the Florentine citizenry support a repressive policy that guaranteed Pisan security but at the same time damaged her economy? Would a more lenient policy stimulate Pisa's

---

[121] SCMLC, 28, f.9v. The names of the exiles are in *ibid.*, ff.12r–13r. On this policy, see Silva, *Studi storici*, XVIII, 12–16.

[122] Silva, 23–25; CP, 38, ff.25r, 64r–65r.   [123] CP, 38, ff.82v–83v, 86v–87v.

[124] CP, 39, f.1v: "Quod videant domini quod non displiceant Deo, qui est multo maior dominus quam ista dominatio."

economy and thus contribute to a subsidence of hostility and more secure Florentine control? After 1408 the government did mitigate its policy toward exiles, and renewed the sentences only of those judged to be most dangerous.[125] But having once been introduced as a security measure, the policy of exiling potential subversives was later invoked whenever any part of the dominion was felt to be insecure. When signs of unrest appeared in Arezzo in the spring of 1408, the Signoria proposed the introduction of the system there. The colleges, however, objected strongly; they argued that the plan was too severe and that "it would make enemies and would terrorize the citizens of other towns."[126] In periods of extreme crisis, however, these scruples disappeared. When King Ladislaus' army invaded Tuscany in the spring of 1409, civic opinion strongly favored the application of the exile policy,[127] which became a regular feature of Florence's internal security during the next five years.[128]

For the Eight on Security, the Florentine conquest of Pisa was both a challenge and an opportunity. Established in 1378, that magistracy was slow to develop into a powerful office. Its members were initially chosen by the Signoria, who could limit their authority at will and who invariably superseded them in moments of grave crisis—for example, in 1387, 1393, 1398, and 1400. The Eight also shared the responsibility for internal security with the war *balìa* when that magistracy was functioning.[129] The conquest of Pisa greatly enhanced the authority of the Eight. After 1406 its members were no longer elected by the Signoria but were drawn by lot from lists of eligible citizens who had qualified in scrutinies.[130] Since this magistracy was not bound by judicial procedures, it was a more supple instrument for

[125] Silva, *Studi storici*, XVIII, 20–25.

[126] *CP*, 39, f.60v. The Signoria ignored these objections and implemented the plan. On 9 June 1408, the priors reminded the captain of Arezzo of their instructions to draw up a list of 100 Aretini "e quali fossono atti a fare novità," and to send the list under seal to Florence; *SCMLC*, 28, f.82r.

[127] *CP*, 40, ff.11v–12r, 13v, 2–7 May 1409. For implementation of the policy in Pisa, see *SCMLC*, 28, ff.122r–123r, 5 June 1409.

[128] *CP*, 41, f.45v, 10 Oct. 1411; and Buonaccorso Pitti's letter to Forese Sacchetti, 2 Oct. 1409, in which Pitti describes the methods for designating those Pisans to be sent into exile; *Ashb.*, 1842, vol. 3, no. 284.

[129] *CP*, 33, f.22v; 34, f.184v. In 1396, the war *balìa* ordered the Florentine ambassador in Lucca, Bardo Mancini, to hire an assassin to kill a Florentine rebel engaged in subversive activity, Messer Marcello of Arezzo; *DBCMLC*, 2, f.30r.

[130] *Prov.*, 95, f.93r. For provisions authorizing the election of the Eight by the Signoria and the colleges for six-month terms, see *ibid.*, 87, ff.372r–373r; 88, ff.104r–105r.

combating subversion than were the regular courts.[131] The Signoria realized, too, that the incorporation of Pisa into the dominion required greater expertise in security matters. Speaking for the Twelve in October 1411, Ridolfo Peruzzi noted that the responsibilities of the Signoria and the colleges had become so heavy that they could no longer function properly. The solution, he argued, was greater delegation of authority; he proposed that Pisa's governance should be delegated to the Ten on Pisa, and that of the rest of the dominion to the Eight on Security.[132]

The fortuitous survival of one volume of the Eight's deliberations, from August 1408 through June 1409, provides some basis for understanding the scope of that magistracy's authority and functions. Military matters bulked large on its agenda; it regularly exhorted vicars and castellans in the dominion to be vigilant and to keep their troops in good condition and their fortifications repaired. The Eight had the power to levy fines on *contado* towns which did not maintain their walls. They employed spies to travel through the territory and beyond the frontiers to collect information affecting state security.[133] From these and other sources, the Eight obtained intelligence concerning the political temper of the territory. When Tuscany was threatened by Ladislaus' army in the spring of 1409, the Eight informed the captain of Pisa that three Franciscans were suspected of treasonous activity, and ordered him to expel them. Other friars in Arezzo were likewise suspected of disloyalty to the regime, and they too were to be exiled. Acting on information that a native of Arezzo named Ceretta had voiced sentiments "that have generated the gravest suspicions in this magistracy," the Eight ordered the captain to investigate and to arrest him if he were culpable.[134] A Florentine outlaw living in Lucca, Nencio di Piero, was allegedly involved in another conspiracy. Since Nencio visited Pisa regularly, the captain was instructed to seize and interrogate him, and to transmit the results immediately to the magistracy.[135] The Eight apparently found no evidence of disaffection within

---

[131] Martines, *Lawyers and Statecraft*, 135–36. On the expanding jurisdiction of the Eight at the expense of the regular courts, see *ibid.*, 136–43. Cf. G. Antonelli, "La magistratura degli Otto di Guardia a Firenze"; *ASI*, cxii (1954), 3–10.

[132] *CP*, 41, f.46r: "Et quod ob multiplices occupationes incumbentes dominis prioribus et eorum collegiis, impossibile est omnibus providere ut esset opus. . . ."

[133] *Otto di Guardia*, 10, ff.14r, 76r, being payment for salaries and travel expenses for men hired "ad explorandum."

[134] *Ibid.*, ff.53r, 69r, 72v.

[135] *Ibid.*, f.76v. Another reference to seditious activity in the *contado* of Prato, in *ibid.*, f.69r.

Florence itself during these months. But their ears were open and their spies alert. They instructed the *podestà* to investigate reports that an artisan named Miniato Dini had been defamed in posters attached to public buildings. Domenico Ugolini, who carried the image of Christ in the processions that escorted condemned criminals to their execution, was suspected of making seditious remarks. After ordering his detention by the executor, the Eight eventually released him but forbade him to loiter near the prison or to associate with the guards.[136] These petty cases testify to the Eight's preoccupation with public opinion and their sensitivity to any sign of discontent.

Florentine officials had been worried about the possibility of rebellion in Arezzo; they had intensified their surveillance in that area and had sent a hundred Aretini into exile. These measures may have contributed to the exposure of three conspiracies, one in the village of Colle Gringione, and two others in Arezzo. Among the ringleaders were members of the prominent Albergotti and Boscoli clans; their followers included men from various strata of Aretine society—artisans, peasants, and one priest. The focus of their discontent was the crushing tax burden and the exile policy. Giovanni Albergotti noted bitterly that after the Aretini were impoverished by forced exile, the Florentines then levied a forced loan of 4000 florins upon their destitute community. "It will be no cause for wonder if one day this city is destroyed, for the people cannot endure such burdens."[137] Though agents of the Eight may have heard rumors about these plots, an Aretine citizen named Jacopo del Burale gave information to the authorities concerning the identity of the conspirators, one of whom was his own brother Tommaso.[138]

This heightened concern for territorial security was but one aspect of a more general preoccupation with the governance of the dominion, and a more critical appraisal of its shortcomings. In the fourteenth century the commune had viewed its subject territories in a single perspective—as a source of revenue for its burgeoning expenditures.[139] There are no recorded discussions, in the protocols, of the administration of justice, or the recruitment of qualified officials for the *contado*

---

[136] These cases in *ibid.*, ff.9v, 10r, 11v, 12v–13r. Antonelli, *ASI*, CXII, 13, mentions the action against Ugolini.

[137] *AP*, 4207, ff.33r–35r, 24 Dec. 1409. For sentences of other conspirators, see *ACP*, 2395, ff.1r–2r, 78r–79v; U. Pasqui, "Una congiura per liberare Arezzo dalla dipendenza dei Fiorentini," *ASI*, 5th ser., v (1890), 4, n.1. Cf. *CP*, 40, ff.43r, 87r.

[138] *Prov.*, 110, ff.72r–72v. Jacopo petitioned the Signoria in 1420 for permission to bear arms to protect himself from those whom he had denounced in 1409.

[139] De la Roncière, *Flor. Studies*, 156–63, 185–90; Becker, *Florence in Transition*, II, 182–88.

and district. Citizens who served as vicars and castellans habitually viewed their task as burdensome, and the men under their jurisdiction as incorrigible miscreants.[140] Prior to the conquest of Pisa, some Florentines may have drawn a connection between corrupt rule and oppressive taxation in the territory, and outbreaks of unrest and rebellion, but they did not voice these opinions publicly. The evidence for a decisive shift in civic sentiment appears in the protocols after 1410, and for the next decade this theme of maladministration recurred frequently in the *pratiche*.

In a deliberation of December 1411, Ridolfo Peruzzi noted that there had been numerous discussions concerning the prosecution of officials who had extorted money from subjects in Florentine territory. He urged the Signoria to take action against the guilty, "for our subjects suffer cruelly from these depredations, which demeans the honor of the Commune and the city. . . ."[141] At regular intervals in succeeding years, this image of the exploited subject was developed by self-appointed guardians of territorial interests, who used the issue to criticize methods for selecting officials, or to explain why revenues from the subject communities had fallen. Not only the officials but also powerful magnates in these rural areas were guilty of robbery and extortion, Antonio Alessandri claimed. Michele Castellani described the territory (May 1413) as a wasteland populated by subjects who had been robbed of "their pastures, their rights, and their property" by rapacious officials. In July 1414, Giovanni Minerbetti urged the authorities to defend Florentine subjects from the exploitation of their rectors.[142] The government finally, though tardily, responded to these appeals. In July 1415, the councils approved a provision authorizing the Signoria and the colleges to take unspecified action against "the illegal, unjust, and iniquitous extortions, exactions, and bribes that are being imposed at the present time, or at any future time, by any vicar, captain or official . . . in the *contado* and district of Florence. . . ."[143] This law apparently had little effect, and two years later the issue was again on the agenda. The exodus of *contadini* from the territory had increased, Marsilio Vecchietti stated, as a consequence of rectors "who

[140] For two examples, see the letters of Gherardino Gherardini Giani and Franco Sacchetti; *ASI*, cxv (1957), 171–76; and Sacchetti, *I sermoni evangelici*, 238–39. A rare official who sympathized with those under his jurisdiction was Buonaccorso Pitti; see his *Cronica*, 112–14, 230–40.

[141] *CP*, 41, f.60r.

[142] *Ibid.*, f.152v; 42, ff.10v, 159r.

[143] *Prov.*, 105, ff.216v–217r. The vote: 210–46 and 149–26. The Signoria's authority to curb these abuses was given for six months only. For a summary of legislation against these malpractices, see *Statuta populi et communis*, II, 642–57.

are sent there and who do not govern well. . . ."[144] Six years later the Signoria proposed and the councils approved another attempt to curtail the abuses of territorial rectors: a provision describing in precise language the limits of their authority. That power had been exceeded so frequently in the past, the preamble stated, that "it contributed to the audacity of the wicked, to the oppression of the poor and weak, and to the dishonor of the state."[145]

The key problem in territorial government, Antonio Alessandri noted, was "to find a way to select honest rectors who will not devour our subjects and their property."[146] Impeding the attainment of this laudable objective was a massive barrier of self-interest, since offices in the territorial administration were the most lucrative benefits that the regime could grant its supporters.[147] The bickering that surrounded every scrutiny held to select qualified men for territorial posts reflected the sensitivity of this issue. Six months after the conquest of Pisa, the Signoria learned that some ineligible names had been added to the list of those approved for offices in the dominion. In a *pratica* convened to discuss this scandal,[148] Filippo Corsini argued that the irregularities were so serious that the old scrutiny list should be burned and a new election held to choose citizens "who are acceptable to the *reggimento* and who know how to conduct themselves." Francesco Fioravanti challenged this legalist position, contending on pragmatic grounds that the burning of the old scrutiny would exacerbate civic tensions. He and Barduccio Cherichini claimed that no previous regime had ever destroyed a scrutiny list in times of internal peace, and they denounced the proposal as a bad precedent. Although a substantial majority of the counselors agreed with them, the Signoria nevertheless proceeded to nullify the old scrutiny.[149] When, four years later, the priors proposed that a new scrutiny for external offices be held, the measure was rejected six times by the Council of the *Popolo* before it finally passed by five votes.[150] Subsequent provisions calling

---

[144] CP, 43, f.152r.   [145] Prov., 113, ff.144v–146v, 1 Oct. 1423.

[146] CP, 43, f.152r.

[147] Unlike the Venetian republic, Florence did not systematically subsidize its "poor nobles," although vicariates and castellanies were occasionally granted to citizens who pleaded extreme poverty or misfortune; an example in Brucker, *Society of Renaissance Florence*, 22.

[148] CP, 38, ff.9r–12v, 7–19 Feb. 1407.

[149] Prov., 96, ff.47v–49v. For the implementation of that scrutiny, see Lionardo Strozzi's letter to Simone Strozzi, 8 Nov. 1407, in *Strozz.*, 3rd ser., 130, no. 7; *Manoscritti*, 225, f.143r.

[150] LF, 49, ff.121r–125v (1–8 Dec. 1411). The provision finally passed in Jan. 1412; *ibid.*, ff.133r–135r.

for new elections, or for rearranging the electoral pouches, invariably encountered stiff resistance in the councils.[151] No justification was advanced by opponents to explain their votes against measures described by their advocates as "just, rational, and holy."[152] The strongest motivation for casting white beans was more likely to have been private interest than any consideration of the public welfare.[153]

To guarantee that qualified officials would be chosen for important territorial posts, the Signoria would sometimes resort to their selection by hand. When Pisa was finally reoccupied in 1406, the Ten of War appointed three of their own number—Gino Capponi, Bartolomeo Corbinelli, and Bernardo Cavalcanti—to administer the conquered city.[154] But this practice displeased many citizens, ostensibly because it violated communal tradition, but in fact because it discriminated against the rank and file in the *reggimento*. The two sides of the argument were neatly formulated in a debate (January 1418) over the best way to choose the Eight on Security. Antonio del Vigna acknowledged that "by means of the scrutiny, one may hope that all will proceed well, but there is always uncertainty in selection by lot and thus the way of election is superior. . . ." Conceding that better choices were made by election than by scrutiny, Agnolo Pandolfini nevertheless argued that in the absence of an emergency, the traditional method of sortition should be followed since it was more acceptable to the *popolo*.[155] These arguments were repeated a few weeks later (March 1418) when the Signoria sought, and failed to win, legislative approval for a measure substituting election for sortition in the selection of the magistracy responsible for Pisa's administration. Only after prolonged debate was a satisfactory compromise achieved that effectively placed this strategic office in the control of the executive.[156]

The majority of territorial offices, however, continued to be filled by scrutiny. The complaints by territorials against their rectors were so numerous,[157] and doubtless so often exaggerated, that the priors did

---

[151] *LF*, 50, ff.53r–53v, 141r–146v; 51, ff.103r–104v, 125r–139r.

[152] These phrases in *LF*, 51, ff.219v, 222v; 52, f.35r.

[153] "Solo era per ingordigia di chi era nelle borse a non volere compagnia. . . . Era diviso in ogni ufficio, che chi volea e chi non volea, per lo suo proprio utile e non per altro"; Morelli, *Ricordi*, 537–38.

[154] *Ibid.*, 464.   [155] *CP*, 43, ff.165r–165v, 10 Jan. 1418.

[156] Martines, *Lawyers and Statecraft*, 238–41.

[157] See the barrage of accusations and absolutions of vicars and castellans in *AEOG*, 1481, for the year 1403; and in *GA*, 77, for the years 1429–34. The harshest penalties meted out to officials were the death sentences against Andrea Peruzzi, Alessio Baldovinetti and Lorenzo Raffacani, who were blamed for the loss of the Pisan citadel in 1405: "tanquam negligentes femminilles et puxilanimes et

not investigate these charges systematically, nor did they often rep-
rimand culpable officials. When a deputation of citizens from Colle
Valdelsa complained about their *podestà*, Bartolomeo Gherardini, the
Signoria dismissed their allegations as unfounded and ordered them
to obey their rector.[158] In 1418, the Signoria did verify the charges
that the *podestà* of Pisa had organized a linen monopoly and had
engaged in "abominable, odious, and reprehensible" tactics to preserve
it. "We send rectors and officials to maintain justice among our subjects
and to preserve them in peace and unity," the priors wrote, "and not
to engage in violence and extortion under the cover of the offices and
dignities which they hold, nor to prevent our subjects from buying
and selling the necessities of life."[159] Though their language was harsh,
they did not remove the delinquent *podestà* from office, nor prosecute
him for misconduct. Indeed, so few rectors were ever convicted of malfeasance that the prescribed reviews of their tenures must have been
perfunctory. Between 1403 and 1409, only five Florentine officials from
prominent families—Stefani, Falconi, Marchi, Della Casa, Antellesi—
were convicted of malfeasance and fined amounts ranging from 1000
to 2500 lire.[160] Thereafter, patrician rectors were rarely prosecuted
for accepting bribes or extorting money from *contadini*, although
smaller fry—like the collector of the salt gabelle in Arezzo, Giovanni
di Ser Bernardo—were occasionally caught and penalized for lining
their pockets.[161]

Some evidence for the rewards these offices brought, and the powerful temptations to exploit them, comes from the diary of Jacopo
Salviati who, from his own account, appears to have been one of the
more honest and conscientious officials in the territorial bureaucracy.
He noted proudly that after completing his tenure as *podestà* of Montepulciano, no one appeared at his syndication to complain of his
administration; concerning his government of the Apennine region
around Firenzuola, he wrote, "I won the benevolence of that district
because I governed them [the inhabitants] very gently."[162] So fre-

---

homines non avidi, non solliciti, nec actenti ad honorem et statum communis";
AEOG, 1576, ff.19r–20r, 22 Sept. 1405. The penalties were cancelled two years
later; *Prov.*, 96, ff.103r–105r.

[158] *SCMLC*, 29, f.85v, 7 May 1415.

[159] *Ibid.*, f.112v, translated in Brucker, *Society of Renaissance Florence*, 132–33.
For other charges of extortion in Pisa, see Silva, *Studi storici*, XVIII, xx.

[160] *AEOG*, 1521, ff.3r–3v, 31r–32r; 1677, ff.52r–63r; *AP*, 4165, ff.19v–20v; 4183,
ff.17r–19r.

[161] Giovanni di Ser Bernardo's crimes are described in *Prov.*, 105, ff.58v–59v.

[162] Salviati's diary is in *Delizie*, XVIII, 175–361. For these references, *ibid.*, 182, 284.

quently did Salviati fill important territorial offices that he was prac-
tically a full-time administrator: *podestà* of Montepulciano in 1400,
and vicar of the Valdinievole in 1401, Anghiari in 1403, Pistoia in 1406,
Firenzuola in 1407, Arezzo in 1409. The stipends he received from
these offices were an important source of income, which explains the
intense competition for these posts. After paying the salaries of his
retinue, Salviati reported profits ranging from the 200 florins he gained
in six months of service in Montepulciano, to 400 florins from his
Pistoia post. The average, 286 florins for six months of office,[163] was
double the income earned by a prominent lawyer, Ricciardo del Bene,
from his legal practice in these years, and approximately one-half of
the average profits of the Florentine branch of the Medici bank between 1397 and 1420.[164] A substantial portion of his earnings from
Pistoia came, not from his communal stipend, but from gratuities that
he received from the Pistoiese for special services: thirty-eight florins
for holding a scrutiny, twenty-four florins for pacifying the village of
Piuvica, still another gift of a hundred florins for settling disputes between the commune of Pistoia and the Cancellieri.[165] Salviati had no
qualms about accepting these bonuses, which (he implied) were
freely given to him by grateful territorials. A less scrupulous official
might regard such payments as his right, and refuse to perform his
official duties unless he was rewarded liberally for his efforts.

Though difficult to implement, the remedies for bureaucratic incompetence and corruption were obvious: a more careful scrutiny of
qualifications and a more rigorous review of performance. Less
susceptible to any solution was the pressure upon officials to become
embroiled in local feuds and quarrels, and thus to incur charges of
favoritism in the administration of justice and the apportionment of
tax levies. Every rector received a flood of appeals and petitions from
residents within his jurisdiction, requesting the cancellation or mitigation of a criminal sentence, the grant of immunity from prosecution,
the reduction of a tax assessment.[166] Any concession made to one appellant was viewed by his neighbors as a miscarriage of justice. While
serving as *podestà* of Arezzo in the spring of 1419, Forese Sacchetti

---

[163] *Delizie*, xviii, 182, 195, 214, 261, 284.

[164] Martines, *Lawyers and Statecraft*, 103–05. Del Bene's income from his practice
fluctuated between 300 and 500 fl. annually; Medici profits averaged 1100 fl. annually; R. de Roover, *The Rise and Decline of the Medici Bank, 1397–1494* (Cambridge, Mass., 1963), 47.

[165] *Delizie*, xviii, 257–60.

[166] Two rich sources are letters sent to Francesco del Bene, vicar of the Valdinievole in 1381; *Carte del Bene*, 51; and those sent to Forese Sacchetti between
1410 and 1427; *CRS*, 78 (*Badìa*), vols. 323–26.

received an angry letter from a Franciscan friar, Fra Bartolomeo, accusing him of favoring the Ghibellines and ruining the Guelfs in the apportionment of taxes.[167] Strong-minded rectors might resist these importunities, but they could not ignore the appeals of friends and relatives in Florence, seeking to promote the interests of their clients in the dominion. "It appears that you have imprisoned Ugolino di Giorgio of Giova," Giovanni Bucelli wrote Sacchetti in Arezzo [September 1410], ". . . and so I pray you to release him as a favor to me, for he has committed no crime. . . ." Two years later, Cristofano Bagnesi wrote in similar vein to Sacchetti, then serving as *podestà* of Ripafratta: "You are prosecuting in your court Gherardo di Vincilao, a druggist from Pisa. . . . According to what I hear, he is innocent, and so I beg of you to act in Gherardo's case in consideration of my love for you. . . ."[168] Palla Strozzi appealed to his cousin Simone, *podestà* of the *pieve* of Santo Stefano to treat leniently a native of that district, described as "the intimate friend of a close blood relation" who had behaved imprudently "on account of his simplicity."[169]

That these matters were not treated lightly is suggested by a letter sent by Rinaldo Gianfigliazzi to Maso degli Albizzi, which also documents how they could create friction among the great.[170] Rinaldo's client was a poor woman named Margherita, the widow of his "very dear friend from Montevarchi," who had been involved in a lawsuit to recover her dowry. After obtaining a favorable judgment in an Aretine court for the house that was her marriage portion, she was prevented from taking possession by Cristofano Spini, the captain of Arezzo and a man of great authority in Florence. Spini had been ordered by the previous Signoria to desist from interfering with Margherita's possession of her property but "until now he has not been willing to obey, which in my judgment (Rinaldo wrote) is a great crime and sin." Spini had tried to buy the house from Margherita who refused to sell; Rinaldo suspected that he was acting on behalf of his client, the father of a priest who held a benefice from him at Peretola. So the skein of relationships in this case covered a large area of Tuscany: from Florence and Peretola to Montevarchi and Arezzo, forty miles away. Rinaldo asked Maso to see that justice was done to Margherita, "and that the captain of Arezzo does not abuse the civil authority and that he observes the laws. . . ."

Overshadowing all other grievances of the subject communities was

[167] *CRS*, 78, vol. 323, no. 337, 15 March 1419.
[168] *Ibid.*, vol. 323, no. 233; 324, no. 201.
[169] *Strozz.*, 3rd ser., 132, no. 33, 8 Feb. 1417.
[170] *BNF, Fondo principale*, II, III, 434, no. 55, 5 Jan. 1405.

the fisc, a perennial source of resentment that, in the years after Pisa's conquest, became progressively more troublesome. Forced by deficits to exploit every source of revenue to the utmost, the government had increased the tax burden in the territory during a period of demographic and economic regression.[171] The consequences were predictable: an increase in tax delinquencies and private debts, and the departure of thousands of rural subjects from the territory.[172] This phenomenon occurred, in a particularly acute form, during the summer and autumn of 1411, when an epidemic of plague combined with a poor grain harvest to make life intolerable in many parts of the territory. The exodus of peasants was so massive that several citizens warned that if they were not induced, by persuasion or force, to return to their farms, famine conditions would be even worse the following year.[173]

In the past, communal policy toward impoverished and debt-ridden *contadini* had vacillated between rigor and leniency: the harassment of peasants who abandoned their farms, and the granting of temporary tax relief and immunity from prosecution for private debts.[174] But these palliatives no longer satisfied critics, who probed more deeply for the causes of rural distress. For those who believed that tax policy was the key to *contado* prosperity, the solution was simply to reduce assessments to a more tolerable level.[175] A provision

[171] "Le continue e gravi spese le quali la nostra città, costretta per difesa e conservatione della nostra libertà, lungo tempo a portate, anno sì ciascuno stretto e consummato che per nicissità inducono ciascuno a cercare ogni via di trarre danari di qualunque luogo"; SCMC, 27, f.17r, May 1412. Cf. Molho, *Florentine Public Finances*, 23–33.

[172] On the connection between taxes, usury and the abandonment of land, see CP, 43, ff.71r–71v, 4–5 Nov. 1415.

[173] E.g., the statement of Michele Castellani, CP, 41, f.41v: "Provisio adhibeatur erga comitatinos ne cogantur ob necessitatem victualium et timorem patriam relinquere et alienam querere, quibus si non providebitur, fames et carestia in anno futuro speranda maxima est, nam incultus comitatus remanebit." In 1411, the Signoria and the colleges approved a decree granting immunity from prosecution for debt for one year to all "cultivators of land" in Florentine territory; *Merc.*, 1251, ff.511r–512r; 1252, ff.319v–320v, 637v. A similar measure was approved by the councils in Nov. 1415; Prov., 105, ff.215r–216r.

[174] Examples: AP, 3297, ff.125r–125v, 143r–143v (April 1388); CP, 25, ff.184v, 192v; Prov., 74, f.204v; 80, ff.197r–198v. In 1411 civic opinion favored leniency instead of coercion; see the comments of Niccolò da Uzzano and Luca da Filicaia; CP, 41, f.41r, 20 Sept.

[175] For a discussion on reducing *contado* levies, see CP, 43, ff.71v–73v. For legislation reducing or cancelling tax debts owed by communities in the dominion, Prov., 102, ff.15r, 95r, 113r, 138r, 139r, 162r; Molho, *Florentine Public Finances*, 36–37.

abolishing the wine gabelle in the *contado* (April 1416) was motivated (the preamble stated) by the realization that many *contadini*
were reduced to misery by their fiscal obligations.[176] Salamone Strozzi
and Antonio Alessandri argued (June 1417) that exorbitant interest
rates and not taxes were the main cause of poverty in the territory.[177]
Since this touched on the economic interests of Florentine moneylenders (including Salamone's cousin, Strozza di Rosso Strozzi), it was
a sensitive political issue.[178] Though usury, and those who lent at
usurious rates, were targets of civic opprobrium, no one advocated the
prohibition of such loans by Florentine capitalists, nor was any measure
regulating the operations of Christian moneylenders in the *contado*
ever submitted for approval to the councils. On one occasion when the
problem was discussed, counselors were very solicitous of these investments.[179] The government did act obliquely to reduce interest rates in
the territory by authorizing Jewish moneylenders, whose maximum
rates were fixed, to ply their trade in Pistoia, Arezzo, Montepulciano,
and other towns, and thus to compete with Christian usurers.[180]

Speaking in June 1417 on behalf of the captains of the Parte Guelfa,
Matteo Castellani urged the government to be more solicitous of the
welfare of the *contadini* who, he insisted, were as important for the
conservation of the republic as the urban citizenry. Bartolomeo Valori
concurred: "It is only natural to favor and to reduce the burdens of
those who have been most faithful [to Florence]." Valori was puzzled
by the fact that previous recommendations for promoting the welfare of the rural areas had not been implemented, "whether because
of private advantage, or some other reason, I do not know."[181] There
were vague hints in the protocols of disagreement among the priors
and the colleges over territorial policy.[182] But civic concern, though occasionally fervent, was sporadic and haphazard; it did not sustain
pressure on the government to adopt a rational system of taxation in
the dominion. In this, as in other aspects of territorial administration,
a pattern emerges in the years after Pisa's annexation. Demands for

---

[176] Molho, 45, n.48.

[177] *CP*, 43, f.153r, 15 June 1417: "parva sunt onera que comitatini solvunt sed
quidam feneratores substantias consumunt. . . ."

[178] Strozza Strozzi's loans to *contado* towns are described in Molho, 40–41.

[179] See the comments of Niccolò Barbadori; *CP*, 43, f.74v, 20 Nov. 1415. For
denunciations of usury in the *contado*, see Molho, 39, n.37.

[180] Molho, 37–39; and his article, "A Note on Jewish Moneylenders in Tuscany,"
Renaissance Essays in Honor of Hans Baron, 99–117.

[181] These statements are in *CP*, 43, ff.152v, 154v, 15 June 1417.

[182] See Castellani's statement, *ibid.*, f.154v: "sed necessaria est dispositio et unitas
dominorum et collegiorum"; and *CP*, 43, f.71v, 5 Nov. 1415, statement of Luigi
Mannini for the Twelve.

reform were voiced more frequently; commissions to develop proposals for reform were appointed more regularly. Counselors demanded a more efficient and rational—and occasionally a more
humane—policy in the administration of the territory. They did not
hesitate to condemn their officeholding peers for their avarice and
injustice.[183] This impulse for reform was strongest in periods of crisis,
but rarely was it sustained until calmer times might provide a better
context for implementation. And in the years after Pisa's acquisition, the times were never tranquil.

CHALLENGES TO THE FLORENTINE STATE: LADISLAUS AND GENOA

Pisa's reconquest had imposed a heavy burden, both fiscal and administrative, upon the Florentine state. The leaders were so preoccupied with avenging the republic's humiliation that they did not
weigh the costs, current and future, of Pisa's incorporation into the
dominion. Nor did they perceive how her subjection would adversely
affect their relations with other maritime powers in the Tyrrhenian
Sea—Genoa, Naples, Aragon—who were jealous of this new rival. The
first negative reaction to the conquest occurred in France, where two
Florentine ambassadors were imprisoned by order of the Duke of
Orleans, who stated that he had received rights to Pisa from her
former lord, Gabriele Maria Visconti.[184] But the most serious challenge to Florence's precarious base on the sea came from Genoa and
her French ruler, Marshal Boucicaut, whose troops still occupied
fortifications on both sides of Pisa, in Livorno and Sarzana, and also
the towers protecting Porto Pisano.[185] Boucicaut had promised to surrender those towns to Florence within four months of Pisa's acquisi-

---

[183] See, e.g., the statements by Rinaldo degli Albizzi and Matteo Castellani: "Et
quia non solum estimum consumit comitatinos, sed etiam extorsiones que ipsis fiunt
per officiales et alios non servando ordinamenta dominii super iis. . . . Comitatini
multas habuerunt oppressiones propter quod coguntur discedere . . . et nisi . . .
aliquo concessis eis, omnes deserent patriam, et nos cogeremur aut possessiones
incultas tenere aut propriis manibus laborare"; *CP*, 45, ff.55v–56r, 24 Sept. 1422.
For a literary reference to the exploitation of Florentine subjects by officials, see
Vespasiano da Bisticci's life of Ser Filippo di Ser Ugolino; *Vite di uomini illustri
del secolo XV* (Florence, 1938), 413.

[184] Buonaccorso Pitti was sent to Paris to obtain the release of the ambassadors,
Bartolomeo Popoleschi and Bernardo Guadagni; *Cronica*, 150–51; *SCMLC*, 4, ff.1r–
6r. Even before Pisa's reconquest, the Signoria was responding to the king's complaint about the Florentine campaign to recover the city; *SCMC*, 27, f.12r.

[185] On Florentine-Genoese tensions after the conquest, see *SCMC*, 28, ff.16v–
18v, 30r–31v, 38v–39v; Piattoli, "Genova e Firenze," *Giornale storico e letterario
della Liguria*, VI, 322–23.

tion. But the republic's legal rights to Livorno had not been clearly spelled out in the 1405 treaty with the French governor. That agreement had stipulated that Florence was entitled to collect revenues in Livorno, but it had also provided for a permanent French garrison to be stationed there at Florentine expense while Pisa was in her possession.[186]

When, five months after Pisa's occupation, the republic still did not have possession of the fortifications at Porto Pisano, the Signoria sent an embassy to Boucicaut in Genoa, requesting the transfer of the towers, and also Livorno, to Florentine control.[187] Boucicaut rejected the appeals. Fearing retaliatory measures against her merchants in Genoa and in France, the republic did not dare to force the issue, although the Signoria did offer (July 1407) to buy Livorno from its French governor for 50,000 florins.[188] In August, Antonio Alessandri, Gino Capponi, and Marsilio Vecchietti suggested that overtures be made to Boucicaut and those Genoese nobles sympathetic to Florentine interests in the hope of their acquiescence in Sarzana's annexation. Filippo Corsini and Jacopo Salviati, who feared that these tactics would lead to war, spoke out strongly against this proposal.[189] In November a Genoese embassy visited Florence and, after claiming that their government had legal rights to Livorno and Porto Pisano, offered to sell them to Florence. This so infuriated Rinaldo Gianfigliazzi that he advocated an end to diplomatic negotiations and preparation for hostilities. Though the other counselors did not support Rinaldo, and warned specifically against any action that might precipitate war, they did advise the Signoria to reject the Genoese claims.[190] Maso degli Albizzi recommended a posture that neatly combined honor and practicality. The commune should not accept the Genoese offer to buy Livorno, and should continue discussions "not basely but with grandeur, yet not arrogantly. . . ."[191] After weeks of debate, the Signoria decided to send an embassy to Genoa to continue negotiations—which, however, did not bear fruit.[192]

[186] These agreements are published by I. Mancini, "Nuovi documenti sulla guerra e l'acquisto di Pisa (1404–1406)," ASI, 5th ser., XVIII (1896), 227–36.

[187] SCMC, 28, ff.10v–11r, Feb. 1407.

[188] Ibid., f.40r. The possibility of reprisals against Florentine merchants in Genoa was raised by Lippozzo Mangioni in a letter to Francesco Datini, 20 Dec. 1406; Piattoli, Giornale storico e lettario della Liguria, VI, 317–18.

[189] CP, 38, ff.67r–67v, 4 Aug. 1407. The collegiate groups all supported Corsini's moderate position; ibid., ff.67v–68r.

[190] Ibid., ff.92r, 95r–95v.

[191] Ibid., f.108r: "non . . . cum vilitate sed magnifice, non tamen superbe. . . ."

[192] Ibid., f.112v, 17 Jan. 1408.

In this confrontation with the Genoese and their French masters, the spirited rhetoric of the Florentine counselors belied the weakness of the republic's bargaining position. The combination of Genoese sea-power and French military force could undermine Florence's control of Pisa. "If we were to be at odds with the French," the Signoria conceded, "we would lose our outlet to the sea and, with that lost, Pisa would be worth nothing." The Florentines were also troubled by Boucicaut's plan to ally with Piedmontese nobles, with a force of 8000 troops under his command.[193] In their negotiations with Boucicaut and the French court, Florentine diplomats could only appeal to the ancient Guelf ties that had bound them to the Valois for a century and a half.[194] In the southern Tyrrhenian, the naval power of King Ladislaus of Naples was as great, and as threatening, as that of Genoa. In the event of war, Florentine merchants in the Neapolitan kingdom were hostages of the king, as were their counterparts in France.[195] The republic's correspondence with Ladislaus was replete with references to the ancient friendship between Florence and his ancestors.[196] But while French power was declining, as the kingdom under a deranged monarch plunged into civil war, Ladislaus had gained full control of his state and was seeking to expand his authority.[197] The chaotic situation in the Papal States and in Rome itself gave him the opportunity to intervene in central Italy. Preoccupied with Pisa and its maritime problems, Florence was most reluctant to turn her attention southward. Not until Ladislaus' army occupied Rome and much of the Papal States in the spring of 1408 did Florentine statesmen react to this new peril.[198]

Amidst the complexities of Italian politics in these years of Ladislaus' ascendancy, three distinct but connected themes are visible.

[193] SCMLC, 4, f.57r.

[194] Ibid., ff.1r–6r, instructions to Buonaccorso Pitti. For a summary of the Florentine friendship with the French monarchy dating back to Charlemagne, see ibid., ff.55v–56v.

[195] On the danger to Florentine merchants in France, see ibid., f.56v, and the statement of Matteo Tinghi, CP, 38, f.107r; and of those in Naples, the comments of Piero Baroncelli, CP, 39, f.15r.

[196] SCMLC, 4, ff.93v–94r; SCMC, 25, f.2r, a letter to Ladislaus from the captains of the Parte Guelfa.

[197] See Buonaccorso Pitti's reference to the assassination of the duke of Orleans by the duke of Burgundy in Nov. 1407; Cronica, 150–51. On Ladislaus' domination of the Regno, A. Cutolo, Re Ladislao d'Angiò Durazzo (Naples, 1969), 299–308.

[198] For the Florentine response to appeals by the Romans for help against Ladislaus, CP, 38, f.88r; 39, ff.13v, 15r. On the occupation of Rome by Ladislaus, see Cutolo, Ladislao, 336–37.

First was the king's drive to create a strong territorial state in central Italy, and Florence's resistance to that enterprise. The efforts to end the schism and to unite the fragmented church under one pope were closely linked to that issue. For political as well as religious motives, the Florentine republic promoted that scheme, hoping that unification would contribute to the restoration of the papacy's temporal authority in Italy. Ladislaus viewed the end of the schism as a threat to his foothold in Rome and the Papal States, and thus sought to thwart unification. Further complicating these political and ecclesiastical machinations was the old quarrel between rival branches of the Angevin dynasty, and specifically, the claims of Louis II of Anjou to the Neapolitan throne. Though Louis' allies in the Regno had finally been defeated in 1407, the Angevin prince retained a power base in Provence and, with the support of the French crown, was eager to renew the struggle for control of the kingdom of Naples.

The Florentine ambassadors sent to Naples after Rome's occupation were instructed to communicate to Ladislaus "the great joy and satisfaction which we and our people have received from the news of his glorious acquisition."[199] But within the *reggimento*, suspicions of Ladislaus' motives and objectives were being expressed openly in the *pratiche*. "This king is greatly to be feared," Gino Capponi asserted, "for he is seeking to destroy this commune's liberty." A few counselors defended Ladislaus; Giovanni de' Medici called him "the father of this *popolo*" and discounted the rumors that the king intended to subvert the republic. Maso degli Albizzi also based his argument upon Guelf tradition: "We should rejoice in every success of the king, and by our actions and our attitude demonstrate our friendship to him. . . ."[200] But neither Maso nor any other advocate of the king's cause spoke out publicly in favor of a defensive alliance that Ladislaus had proposed.[201] When news reached Florence in mid-June that Ladislaus was planning to visit the council of Pisa, and was requesting a safe-conduct for his escort of 700 lances, the reaction in the *pratiche* was overwhelmingly negative. Rejecting the safe-conduct, Maso degli Albizzi urged the Signoria to adopt a "strong and virile posture" in negotiating with the king. Cristofano Spini called for the election of a

[199] *SCMLC*, 4, f.55r, 28 May 1408. See also *SCMC*, 25, f.2r. This was the typical reaction of other Italian states; Cutolo, 337–39.

[200] *CP*, 39, ff.41r–42r, 45r, 7 and 11 May. Paolo Biliotti and Alessio Baldovinetti supported Ladislaus; Piero Baroncelli and Bartolomeo Valori denounced him. Reports from the Sienese ambassador in Florence indicate that fears of Ladislaus were not intense; *Conc.*, 1868, no. 75, 76, 77.

[201] *CP*, 39, ff.45r–46v.

war magistracy and *prestanze* levies of 100,000 florins.[202] These proposals for war mobilization were too extreme for the Signoria, but the
priors did recruit additional troops in Romagna and Umbria and
signed a pact with Baldassare Cossa, the cardinal legate of Bologna,
for the common defense of their territories.[203]

Not content with controlling Rome and the Campagna, Ladislaus
also coveted portions of the Papal States in central Italy. With the
acquiescence of the impotent Gregory XII, his troops occupied Perugia
and its *contado*, seized control of Cortona (whose lord had been a
Florentine client), and harassed Siena's southern frontier.[204] Meanwhile, ambassadors shuttled between Florence and Naples with messages of friendship and recrimination. Ladislaus again offered the
republic a defensive alliance; it was politely rejected. The Signoria
complained to the king that his incursions into Tuscany violated his
promises to respect Florentine hegemony in that province, and contributed to the turmoil in the region.[205] Ladislaus was hostile to the
church council that had been assembled at Pisa with Florentine support;
he viewed the convocation as a threat to his control of the Papal States,
and also to his possession of the Neapolitan kingdom. The Signoria
insisted that the republic was motivated solely by its concern for
church unity. In a final diplomatic effort to avoid open conflict with
Ladislaus, the republic sent Niccolò da Uzzano and Cristofano Spini
to Naples (March 1409) with specific proposals.[206] There could be no
settlement of their differences, the ambassadors informed the king,
until his armies withdrew from Perugia and until he had severed his
ties with his Tuscan client, Paolo Guinigi, lord of Lucca. Accompany-
ing these proposals was a warning that Florence might accept invitations to ally with Ladislaus' enemies, both foreign and domestic, to
force him to withdraw from central Italy.

The decision to confront Ladislaus with clear options, to retreat or
fight, was extremely painful for many Florentines. Citizens with strong
emotional attachments to Guelfism were reluctant to contemplate a
war with this Angevin prince; others were more concerned about the
republic's vulnerability. French garrisons still occupied Livorno and

---

[202] *CP*, 39, ff.59v–60r, 63r–65r, 15 and 25 June. The Signoria instructed Florence's
ambassadors in Naples to deny the king's request for a safe conduct; *SCMC*, 28,
f.82v.

[203] *SCMLC*, 4, ff.59v–60r, 64r–65r, 69r–70r. Florence sent a contingent of 100
lances to Siena for the defense of that city; *ibid.*, ff.68r–68v.

[204] Partner, *Lands of St. Peter*, 387–88.

[205] *SCMLC*, 4, ff.55r–58r; 77r–80r; *SCMC*, 28, ff.82v–84v; Cutolo, *Ladislao*, 354–56.

[206] *SCMLC*, 4, ff.77r, 91v, 93v–96v.

the fortresses guarding Porto Pisano; the Tyrrhenian was patrolled by Genoese and Neapolitan galleys. If war broke out, Pisa would be blockaded. The situation on land was equally bleak. Florence's allies, the Sienese republic and the legate in Bologna, were too weak and impoverished to defend their territory without support.[207] After the Milanese truce of 1404, the republic had partly dismantled its network of alliances and provisions with nobles and petty *signori* on its Apennine frontier. Some of these barons had sold their services to Ladislaus; others were willing to renew their ties with Florence, for a price.[208] To hire these *condottieri*, and to reconstruct a defensive perimeter on her southern frontier, was an expensive project for a community exhausted by twenty years of war.

The *pratiche* of 1409 reflect these anxieties and the gradual shift of civic sentiment to belligerency. In mid-February, when Ladislaus' ambassador was visiting Florence, the mood among the counselors was still conciliatory and even friendly, as they urged the Signoria to continue diplomatic contacts with the king and to strive for the preservation of their ancient friendship.[209] Maso degli Albizzi, however, sounded a less sanguine note in his speech of 21 February. Military preparedness, he argued, was the key to peace, "so that whoever seeks to harm us will not succeed. . . ." Maso added that the republic's formal response to the king should be reverent, but also "proud and forceful."[210] In March, however, Ladislaus' forces occupied Cortona and ravaged the Sienese *contado*; the prospects for peace declined perceptibly. Those citizens "who controlled the regime" should contribute to a special fund of 100,000 florins, Cionaccio Baroncelli asserted, so that sufficient money would be available for defense.[211] Gino Capponi made a distinction between a campaign to conquer foreign territory—which, he said, he would never advocate—and war for the defense of Florentine liberty, which all citizens should support whole-

---

[207] On subsidizing these allies, CP, 39, ff.140v, 143r, 151v, 153v; 40, ff.4r, 8r. The Sienese could only support the cost of 100 lances, and the legate, 400–500; CP, 40, f.15v.

[208] For the debate on the hiring of an Apennine warlord and former Visconti captain, Ottobuono Terzo, CP, 39, ff.140v–141r.

[209] The statements of Maso degli Albizzi, Jacopo Salviati and Bernardo Guadagni; CP, 39, ff.135v–136v.

[210] *Ibid.*, f.140r: "loquendo magnifice et viriliter et reverenter."

[211] CP, 39, f.160v, 15 March: "Quod fiat quod cives qui habent regimentum, et ipse cum eis optulit, faciant summam C milia florenorum." Several speakers favored the expansion of the army to 1500 or 2000 lances; *ibid.*, ff.151v, 154r, 157r, 161r, 167v.

heartedly. He advocated the creation of a war *balìa*, "under whose aegis the liberty of the Florentine people has so often been secured." To enlist public support for military expenditures, and for resisting Ladislaus' invasion of Tuscany, Alessio Baldovinetti and Piero Baroncelli called for a large civic assembly (*parlamentum*) to hear a report on the crisis.[212] Responding to this pressure, the Signoria chose a war *balìa* in early April. One of its members, Piero Baroncelli, reported to a *pratica* (12 April) on the military and fiscal situation. Reflecting the views of the majority, Antonio Alessandri called for an extraordinary effort to raise revenue for an army of 2000 lances, and an invasion of Ladislaus' territory.[213] A week later the Signoria convened another *pratica* to discuss the king's latest offer for an alliance.[214] Most counselors rejected the proposal, but Agnolo Pandolfini favored an accommodation with the king, insisting that he would rather join a league against the pope than go to war. The banker, Giovanni de' Medici, who believed that an alliance with Ladislaus on the king's terms was the only way to avoid hostilities, supported Pandolfini's position. These arguments did not convince the other counselors, who placed more weight upon Ladislaus' actions—his armies were then threatening Siena, Cortona, and Arezzo—than upon his promises. "The king seeks to deceive us with this league," Pierozzo Castellani asserted, while Vannozzo Serragli scornfully described the proposed league as an instrument for the republic's destruction.

Florentines were thus forced by events to abandon the last vestiges of hope that Ladislaus could be persuaded to abandon his invasion of Tuscany, or that a military confrontation might be averted by a diplomatic *rapprochement*. Though negotiations with the king continued into the month of May, the leadership was now preoccupied not with diplomatic bargaining but with the recruitment of soldiers. On 10 May, Maso degli Albizzi reported that 1900 lances were in Florentine service, and he urged the war *balìa* to hire still more cavalry to defend those parts of southern Tuscany, stretching from the Valdorcia to Cortona and Arezzo, that were being attacked by Ladislaus'

---

[212] *Ibid.*, f.160v.

[213] *CP*, 40, ff.3r–3v. The Florentine determination to resist the king at all costs was noted by the Sienese ambassador: "Non si guarda a spesa nè a denaro e che si soldi e le 1500 e le 2000 lancie e che costui si è gastigato a casa sua"; *Conc.*, 1871, no. 39, 13 Apr. Three days later he wrote: "e diconmi questi X che mai in questa città a trovare il denaro nullo d'essi si ricorda tanta concordia e sono entrati nella spesa di fiorini 50^M ogni mese"; *ibid.*, no. 50.

[214] *CP*, 40, ff.7v–9v: ". . . In magno consilio requisitorum ubi consulabatur si liga et confederatio facienda erat cum rege Ladislao, an non."

army.[215] A fundamental question of strategy confronted the leadership. Should the republic fight a cautious defensive campaign, relying upon her forces and those of her allies to repel Ladislaus' invasion of Tuscany? Or should she adopt an offensive posture and attack the king with all the resources, military and diplomatic, that she and her allies could muster? The ingredients for a grand alliance against the king lay at hand, in Pisa where the council—with Florentine, French, and Venetian support—was moving toward the election of a new pope, and in France, where King Louis of Anjou was eager to launch another invasion of the Neapolitan kingdom. When the Signoria first raised the issue of the Angevin alliance in a *pratica* on 1 June, the reaction of the counselors to this "serious and important matter" was cautiously noncommittal. Cristofano Spini conceded that Florence would need foreign aid to resist Ladislaus, but he argued that the alliance with Louis was fraught with perils.[216] Though he and other skeptics did not explain their reservations about the proposed alliance, they were probably thinking about earlier agreements with foreign princes— Stephen of Bavaria in 1390, the count of Armagnac in 1391, King Charles VI in 1396, Rupert of Bavaria in 1401—which had brought no advantage, but only expense, to the republic. Without publicly stating their doubts about the value of Louis' support, they advised the Signoria to postpone a decision until a new pope had been chosen in Pisa.[217] But proponents of the league insisted that the city's salvation depended upon the alliance; Rinaldo Gianfigliazzi stated flatly that if it did not materialize the republic was doomed. Maso degli Albizzi called for unity, "so that the king cannot say that he had a Florentine faction which opposes the alliance as too dangerous."[218] In Gino Capponi's opinion, the alliance would be the most effective weapon for destroying Ladislaus, and Bernardo da Quarata asserted that "it was as essential as food for sustaining life."[219]

215 *CP*, 40, f.15v. The Sienese had only 100 lances in the field, and the legate, 400–500, against Ladislaus' army estimated at 10,000 horse. On the military situation on the southern front, and the deployment of Florentine troops in that region, see *Conc.*, 1872, no. 1–30. On 9 May, the commander of the Florentine army, Malatesta Malatesta, led his forces through the city gates toward Arezzo, *ibid.*, no. 9.

216 *CP*, 40, ff.23r–24r.

217 See the discussion on 2 June, *ibid.*, ff.25r–26r. The Sienese ambassador reported to his government (4 June) that the proposal for an alliance with King Louis had aroused controversy, and that several secret councils had been convened to resolve the issue; *Conc.*, 1872, no. 37.

218 *CP*, 40, ff.28v–29r, 12 June.

219 The Sixteen opposed the alliance; *ibid.*, f.31r; for the views of Gino Capponi and Bernardo da Quarata, *ibid.*, f.34v.

The league between Louis and the Italian allies—Florence; Siena; Pope Alexander V; Baldassare Cossa, legate of Bologna—was signed on 27 June and published eleven days later. It stipulated that Louis would provide 1000 lances for the defense of Tuscany and the Papal States for one year and that the Italian states would contribute 600 lances, for eight months thereafter, to Louis' campaign to recover the kingdom of Naples.[220] The *balìa* was dominated by citizens who had strongly favored the Angevin alliance and who believed that Louis, from his territorial base in Provence, could recruit a large army. They argued for an offensive campaign against Ladislaus in his own territory to force the king's withdrawal from Tuscany. The recovery of Rome, an invasion of the Abruzzi, a naval assault on Naples: these bold projects excited the counselors, though they were also troubled by the costs of an offensive campaign.[221] Filippo Corsini called for heroic sacrifices, "even our bodies and our lives," to raise money; Messer Rosso Orlandi announced his readiness to pawn his law books as his contribution to the enterprise.[222] These patriotic appeals did not impress the critics of the Angevin alliance, who in August expressed their reservations about the proposed offensive. Matteo Tinghi stated his views with customary bluntness: "Since neither the pope, nor King Louis, nor the cardinal of Bologna have kept their promises, we should attend to our affairs exclusively . . . and fortify ourselves for the defense of our liberty." Recovering Naples for Louis would require a long and arduous struggle, insisted Guidetto Guidetti, and he opposed Florentine participation in that campaign.[223] The supporters of the Angevin alliance defended it on strategic and constitutional grounds. The league was the best means for defeating Ladislaus, Salamone Strozzi argued, and those who expressed doubts about its utility were misinformed. Niccolò Barbadori concurred: "Though the alliance is a heavy commitment, it is not as perilous as some have thought, and I have heard nothing but praise for it while it was being debated, in the regular way, in this palace." The public airing of disagreements over military strategy troubled several counselors and particularly the ten commissioners of Pisa whose spokesman, Gherardo Doni, deplored the discussion "which was not appropriate but destructive and divisive."

In September the focus of the debate shifted from the general

---

[220] Minerbetti, *anno* 1409, ch. 13; Morelli, *Ricordi*, 531. If Louis furnished galleys, his commitment to provide lances was reduced. On the final negotiations, see *Conc.*, 1872, no. 55–57, 21–23 June.

[221] See the comments of the colleges; *CP*, 40, f.37v, 15 July.

[222] *Ibid.*, f.46r, 29 July.

[223] The debate was held on 21 Aug., *ibid.*, ff.51v–52v.

question of offensive versus defensive strategy, to more specific issues of hiring troops for the invasion and finding money to pay them. Maso degli Albizzi presented the arguments for launching a major campaign which would end the war quickly, insure peace, and strengthen the regime. He advised the Signoria and the war *balìa* to hire Giovanni Colonna and the count of Tagliacozzo, which would add only 5000 florins monthly to the military budget, and not 20,000 florins as the Sixteen had estimated.[224] The most persistent critic of the enterprise, Matteo Tinghi, admitted that the invasion might achieve those objectives if sufficient revenue could be raised to pay for the army. But he feared that the campaign would founder for lack of money and that "we might fall into a ditch"; he advised the government to collect the money first, and then hire the soldiers.[225] Several counselors complained about the failure of King Louis and Pope Alexander to provide the troops they had promised; the roseate hopes of June and July were replaced by a pessimistic realization that the republic would be the sole paymaster for the allied army.[226] Though concerned about costs, the majority approved the plan to hire mercenaries to defeat an enemy "who was not a king but a cruel tyrant."[227] On 25 September, 800 lances under the command of Paolo Orsini and the count of Tagliacozzo were hired by the republic to recover Rome and then to invade the Regno.[228]

The fisc was a source of universal anxiety among citizens rich and poor, within and outside the *reggimento*. Half a million florins were spent in 1409 for troops; forced loans for that year totaled nearly 400,000 florins.[229] "It is not possible," exclaimed Antonio Alessandri,

[224] *Ibid.*, f.54r, 3 Sept. The Sixteen had argued that the hiring of these captains would raise the military budget from 60,000 to 80,000 fl. monthly "et quod vident quod non esse possibile quod hic sumptus posset tolerari"; *ibid.*, f.53v. Andrea della Stufa estimated an expenditure of 10,000 fl. monthly; *ibid.*, f.58v.

[225] *Ibid.*, ff.54v, 57r.

[226] As late as mid-August, optimistic reports of an allied force of 3000 lances and 2000 foot were circulating in Pisa; the Sienese ambassador stated that the money for that army had been found; *Conc.*, 1873, no. 29, 17 Aug. But two weeks later, he reported a bitter quarrel among the allies over the payment of 4000 fl. to the marquis of Ferrara, which delayed the army's departure for the Regno; *ibid.*, no. 32 and 34, 28 and 30 Aug. Then Louis left Pisa to return to Provence, to collect more money and troops; *ibid.*, no. 80, 30 Oct.

[227] The quotation is from Francesco Ardinghelli's statement, *CP*, 40, f.58v. Cf. the comments of other speakers, *ibid.*, ff.57r–59v.

[228] Morelli, *Ricordi*, 532–33. Morelli stated that the failure to hire Giovanni Colonna and his 200 lances seriously weakened the effort to recover Rome.

[229] Molho, *Florentine Public Finances*, 61–62. The estimates of monthly expenditures, ranging from 60,000 to 80,000 fl., apparently included all communal outlays, including interest and administrative expenses.

"to continue with this tax system," which he denounced as unjust and an affront to God.[230] In an emotional letter to their ambassador at the papal court, the Signoria stated that each month 70,000 florins were being extracted from the purses of the citizenry, and asked dramatically how long the government could use force "to take bread from the mouths of widows, orphans, and impoverished persons, of whom our population contains a very large number. . . ."[231] The economy was also damaged by the Neapolitan blockade of Porto Pisano. "Commerce is dying," Francesco Ardinghelli asserted in September 1409,[232] and business letters in the Datini archives support that judgment. Six months earlier, in April, a Florentine merchant had complained about the shortage of capital because of diversions from business to fund the war. Giovanni Ciampelli informed the Datini branch in Barcelona in July that the blockade was totally effective, and that no ships were entering or leaving Porto Pisano. "Not in 200 years has this city been in such great travail," Francesco Datini wrote on 23 August, "and if God does not help us, we will soon be in mortal peril."[233] News that a Florentine vessel with a cargo of wool had been seized by a Neapolitan galley stifled hopes that the blockade could be broken.[234] The revival of Florentine trade and the fueling of her economy depended wholly upon the galleys of King Louis, which were assembling in Provençal ports, and the allied army which was slowly moving south towards Rome.

The successful rebellion in early September of the Genoese against their French governor Boucicaut was to have momentous consequences for Florence. Boucicaut had been no friend of the republic, and among the leaders of the new regime were members of Guelf families, like the Fieschi and the Fregosi, with close ties to Florence. But the Signoria made no serious effort to establish diplomatic contacts with the Ligurian republic; instead, they pursued a strategy that

---

[230] *CP*, 40, f.58v. Discontent with the distribution of forced loans was intense in these months; *ibid.*, ff.64r–65v, 24–26 Sept. For a bitter attack on officials responsible for adjusting individual levies, see Matteo Villani's letter to Datini, 27 July 1409; *Datini*, 1104, unpaginated.

[231] *SCMC*, 28, ff.136v–137r, Oct. 1409. On 24 Nov., the Sienese ambassador reported that the Signoria had reduced its cavalry force to 1400 lances "e dicono che vogliono che 'l papa e 'l Re Luigi e legato si caccino mano alla borsa"; *Conc.*, 1873, no. 89.

[232] *CP*, 40, f.58v. On the depressed state of the cloth industry, see *Lana*, 49, f.13r.

[233] Letters of Giovanni Orlandini and Giovanni Ciampelli; *Datini*, 874, unpaginated, 27 Apr.; 1069, 23 Aug. 1409.

[234] *Ibid.*, 874, unpaginated, Bartolomeo di Stefano to the Barcelona branch, 1 Sept.

alienated the Genoese. When the French governor of Livorno offered to sell that port to Florence, Filippo Corsini asserted that the republic had a better legal claim to the city than did the Genoese. Nevertheless, he opposed the purchase as untimely, since it would interfere with the campaign against Ladislaus.[235] The annexation of Sarzana and its *contado* was a more attractive prospect; it would give the republic a fortified outpost in a region of traditional Genoese influence. Filippo Corsini pressed for Sarzana's occupation, to prevent the castle from falling into the hands of "Ghibelline lords"; Niccolò del Bellaccio justified its acquisition by arguing that neither Genoa nor Lucca had any legal rights to possession. "I am an old man and I recall that we have always yearned to possess Sarzana," Andrea della Stufa said as he argued in favor of the enterprise. But Agnolo della Casa did not believe that the republic could muster sufficient force to take Sarzana, and Guidetto Guidetti warned that Genoa would not passively accept this intrusion into her zone of influence. Several citizens wished to defer a decision until the allied army had occupied Rome.[236] Maso degli Albizzi made known his opposition to the Sarzana enterprise, which "was neither praiseworthy nor useful nor timely."[237] Supporting Maso's plea for restraint, Bartolomeo Valori said that the Florentines should not provoke the Genoese but instead should maintain friendly relations with their regime. The Sixteen, however, argued that the Genoese were traditionally hostile to Florence and would adhere to any Ghibelline faction in the Sarzana area. They favored the seizure of the fortress, without regard for the susceptibilities either of the Genoese or the Sienese.

As Maso degli Albizzi and his more astute colleagues realized, these imperialist plans could not be implemented while the war with Ladislaus continued. Only a week after Sarzana's acquisition was discussed, citizens were complaining about a fiscal crisis so grave that it threatened to halt military operations in the Roman area.[238] For weeks, critics of the Angevin alliance had complained about the failure of King Louis and Pope Alexander V to fulfill their treaty obligations; their complaints became even more strident when the pope refused to permit the republic to levy a tax on the Florentine clergy.[239] Matteo Tinghi again raised the question of Florence's ability to fund the war

---

[235] CP, 40, f.66v. Maso degli Albizzi and Lorenzo Ridolfi opposed the acquisition of Livorno.

[236] This debate on 5 Oct., *ibid.*, ff.68v–69v.

[237] *Ibid.*, ff.71r–72r, 11 Oct.

[238] CP, 40, f.73r, 16 Oct. The Sixteen reported that some wealthy citizens were leaving Florence to avoid paying their forced loans.

[239] *Ibid.*, ff.73v, 77r.

from her own resources. Since no support was forthcoming from her allies, the republic must make peace with Ladislaus. Tinghi claimed that many prudent citizens agreed with him. Maso degli Albizzi replied that he too yearned for peace, but that it could only be achieved by fighting. Lorenzo Ridolfi, Filippo Corsini, and Piero Baroncelli agreed with Maso, while others of equal stature—Bartolomeo Valori, Francesco Ardinghelli, Giovanni Orlandini, Antonio Mangioni, Cionaccio Baroncelli—voiced their disenchantment with the alliance and the offensive strategy against Ladislaus, and called for peace.[240] The pervasiveness of that mood among the populace was noted by the Sienese ambassador. He described a conversation with "one of the leading citizens," who regarded the legate of Bologna, Cardinal Baldassare Cossa, as being primarily responsible for Florence's troubles. "This entire region is at war for his aggrandizement," he stated, adding that he had led the pope (Alexander V) to Bologna so that he could "tyrannize that area."[241]

These disagreements over the Angevin papal alliance and military strategy were the sharpest to be articulated in the *pratiche* since the rift over peace with Milan in 1404. As the major architect of that alliance and spokesman for those who viewed Ladislaus as a menace comparable to Giangaleazzo Visconti, Maso degli Albizzi was in a difficult position. The war was universally unpopular; everyone complained about the drain on the city's resources and the broken promises of Florence's allies. With characteristic prudence, Maso did not attempt to silence criticism by exaggerating Ladislaus' threat to Florentine security, or by warning his fellow citizens of the perils of disunity. Instead, he joined the critics in complaining about the intolerable and unjust taxes, and the necessity for equalizing the burdens among the citizens, and also among the allies. While insisting that King Louis and Pope Alexander should pay the major share of the cost of renewing the contracts of Braccio Fortebraccio and Sforza da Cotignola, he proposed that the republic contribute 10,000 florins to support the invasion of the Regno.[242] The occupation of Rome by Paolo

[240] *Ibid.*, ff.73v–78r, 81v–83r, 88r.

[241] *Conc.*, 1874, no. 17, 8 Jan. 1410. The Florentines were angered by the pope's refusal to subsidize the rehiring of Braccio and Sforza; *ibid.*, no. 13, 5 Jan., and by the legate's abandonment of the invasion army to return to Bologna, *ibid.*, no. 14, 6 Jan.: "e gieneralmente tutti lo biasimano per che malegievole sarebbe a trovare le ragione in contrario."

[242] Maso outlined his views in a speech on 23 Dec.; *CP*, 40, f.92v. King Louis was to pay one-half and the pope one-third of the costs of rehiring Braccio and Sforza. For a later appraisal by Maso of military and fiscal problems, *ibid.*, f.96r, 4 Jan. 1410.

Orsini's forces in late December[243] was a partial vindication for Maso and his supporters, who had argued that peace would only be achieved through arms. But they did not indulge in an orgy of celebration after that victory, nor did they speak optimistically of King Louis' project to recruit another army in France for the Neapolitan campaign. By candidly admitting the failures and miscalculations of past strategy, and by avoiding optimistic predictions about the future, the war party had partly disarmed its critics and had created an atmosphere in which peace negotiations with Ladislaus could be rationally debated.

As early as September 1409, Ladislaus had sent a Florentine citizen, Gabriello Brunelleschi, to his native city to initiate peace negotiations. Though the authorities took no official notice of his visit until January, the city was filled with rumors that Brunelleschi had offered peace terms that had been rejected.[244] The debate over this peace initiative was intense and prolonged. Those who, like Agnolo Pandolfini, favored a settlement insisted that Ladislaus genuinely desired peace, and urged the Signoria to act quickly. Cionaccio Baroncelli ridiculed those who were obsessively fearful of the king. "We behave like a cat that raises its tail when touched," he commented, adding that peace was not possible in that fear-laden atmosphere. Citing the pope's refusal to authorize a subsidy by the Florentine clergy and his unwillingness to move his court to Rome as evidence of his uncooperative attitude, Antonio Mangioni advocated a unilateral peace. Paolo Biliotti wished to inform King Louis of the peace discussions, "not because he has any expectations of help from him, but to enable us to withdraw from the alliance."[245]

To refute these opinions, which they considered naive, supporters of the Angevin alliance repeated the arguments for mistrusting a perfidious king, and for relying upon military power for security and, ultimately, for peace. Had he wished to provide counsel that would please his listeners, Rinaldo Gianfigliazzi said, then he would advocate the cancellations of all forced loans, the dismemberment of the army, and a settlement with Ladislaus. But this policy would not achieve a secure peace, which could result only from a strong military posture and the willingness of the citizenry to subsidize it. Filippo Corsini held out hope for victory if the Florentines would reorganize

---

[243] Morelli, *Ricordi*, 533–34; Cutolo, *Ladislao*, 387–88.

[244] Statement of Domenico Corsi, CP, 40, f.102r, 9 Jan. 1410.

[245] These views, *ibid.*, ff.121v, 122v, 127v, 18 and 26 Feb. Supporting the arguments for peace were Strozza Strozzi, Niccolò del Grasso and Giovanni Unghero; *ibid.*, ff.123r, 127v, 128v.

the fisc and continue the war for two months. Gino Capponi insisted that Ladislaus had sent Gabriello Brunelleschi to mislead the citizens and sow dissension. In his judgment, the deleterious effect of internal strife was as dangerous to Florentine security as were the king's troops still deployed on her southern frontiers, in Cortona and Perugia.[246]

Though no agreement was achieved in these deliberations, the Signoria did pursue discussions with Brunelleschi who went to Naples in late January to consult with Ladislaus. He returned to Florence with the king's offer to discuss peace terms with the republic's ambassadors in Naples. On 4 March a lawyer, Messer Giovanni Serristori, received his commission from the Signoria to accompany Gabriello Brunelleschi to Naples, with Florence's conditions for peace. These could not be described as a basis for serious bargaining, since they demanded Ladislaus' total withdrawal from Tuscany and the Papal States, with no concessions by the republic, not even the abridgement of her obligation to furnish 600 lances to King Louis for his projected invasion of the Regno.[247] Ladislaus replied that he would not make peace with the republic unless she agreed to furnish no additional troops to the Angevin.[248] Serristori's report, in early April, on his discussions with Ladislaus precipitated a major debate on foreign policy, in which an exceptionally large number of citizens participated.

During the long debate held on 8 April,[249] the views of most speakers did not change significantly from their earlier ones. Old arguments were repeated, though sometimes refurbished by new evidence and more elaborate logic. Maso degli Albizzi again presented the case for preserving the Angevin alliance and continuing the war. Peace with the king on his terms would not endure; Florence would lose her friends and would have to fight again without allies and with even greater expenses. Even if the republic could legally withdraw from the alliance, it would still be considered a breach of faith by other Italians. The physician Galileo Galilei "warmly praised the keeping of faith and showed that cities could not be governed without it." A unilateral breach of the alliance would alienate the papacy and also the king of France, Filippo Corsini predicted, and would result in the expulsion of Florentine merchants from that kingdom. For Niccolò da Uzzano, the crucial issues were Ladislaus' credibility and his military strength. "If he is capable of attacking Rome, he will reconquer it and

---

[246] *Ibid.*, ff.117r, 121v, 123r.

[247] *SCMLC*, 4, f.123v. For the summary of the ambassadorial instructions, see Cutolo, *Ladislao*, 390–91.

[248] Minerbetti, *anno* 1409, ch. 35; the statement of Paolo Biliotti, *CP*, 40, f.139v.

[249] *CP*, 40, ff.141r–144v.

then he will regain other territory and so we will again be at war with
him. We can never trust his promises since he has broken them before...."

The peace arguments were developed by Matteo Tinghi, an old foe
of the Angevin league, and three prominent merchant statesmen:
Giovanni Biliotti, Francesco Federighi, and Tommaso Rucellai. The
latter recognized the dangers in both options confronting the republic,
but he concluded that a peace settlement was the lesser peril. Biliotti
argued that Ladislaus was genuinely interested in a stable peace,
which was absolutely essential for Florence. Federighi laid particular
emphasis upon internal tensions, and specifically the lack of unity,
which in his judgment was more serious than any threat from abroad.
Of the fifty-eight citizens who were recorded as speaking in this
pratica, only twenty favored the acceptance of Ladislaus' proposals,
and a two-thirds majority rejected them. No business or professional
affiliation distinguished the peace advocates from their more bellicose
colleagues. Representatives from the city's most prestigious families—
Ardinghelli, Bonciani, Rucellai, Altoviti, Strozzi, Peruzzi, Albizzi, Pitti
—favored peace and a disengagement from the Angevin alliance.

Fear was the dominant theme in this debate. Counselors who opted
for continuing the Angevin alliance and the war were afraid of being
duped by Ladislaus, of being isolated, friendless, and dishonored if
Florence abandoned the league against the king. They had no confidence in their ability to defend Florentine territory without support.[250] In balance, these anxieties outweighed concern over popular
unrest arising from the war's prolongation.[251] Still hoping that Ladislaus would modify his terms, several citizens urged Brunelleschi to
return to Naples to explore anew the prospects for peace.[252] No one
could offer much hope that their allies would bring new strength and
vitality to the war effort. The pope languished in Bologna, while Louis
was scouring Provence for troops and money to launch a maritime

[250] This opinion was most clearly stated by Salamone Strozzi, *ibid.*, f.169v, 9
June.

[251] For specific references to concern over popular unrest, see the statements of
Francesco Federighi and Tommaso Ardinghelli; *ibid.*, ff.142r, 154r. An anonymous
letter in the *Carte Strozziane*, dated 18 Feb. 1410, contains this observation:
"Questo popolo grida tutto pacie, e penso che se quello Gabriello Bruneleschi,
che ci s'aspetta, verrà chomandato chon chose che bastino a fare la pace, che ella
si farà. Ogni dì s'aspetta"; *Strozz.*, 3rd ser., 132, f.22r. See, too, *Lettere di un
notaio a un mercante*, ed. Guasti, II, 259–60.

[252] *CP*, 40, ff.145r, 147r–148r, 155r. Brunelleschi was reluctant to go without
formal letters from the Signoria, which he eventually received; *SCMLC*, 4, ff.134r–
135r.

invasion of the Regno. Fighting between allied forces and those employed by Ladislaus continued sporadically in Umbria, the Marches, and in the Campagna south of Rome, with neither side gaining a decisive advantage.[253]

Meanwhile, the republic's relations with Genoa had deteriorated after her occupation of Sarzana in the autumn of 1409. Civic opinion had been divided over the wisdom of that move, but once the fortress was in Florentine hands, counselors advised the Signoria to justify the occupation to the Genoese.[254] In late January 1410, Maso degli Albizzi urged the Signoria to placate the Genoese, though he did not recommend the surrender of the town. The Signoria did send an embassy to Genoa in March but offered no concessions over Sarzana.[255] In a *pratica* of 18 April, Niccolò da Uzzano complained about the perverseness of the Genoese; Cappone Capponi suggested that they were not serious about peace. "The Genoese are making unreasonable demands," Tommaso Ardinghelli complained, "but considering the war and the tribulations of our people, we should make peace with them."[256] In early May, the lawyer Ricciardo del Bene was sent to Genoa with the draft of a peace agreement in which the Signoria made significant concessions. In return for a commitment by both parties to allow the other's merchants to trade in their territory, and a payment of 25,000 florins, Florence agreed to surrender Sarzana and to submit the Livorno issue to arbitration.[257]

But the time for negotiation and compromise had passed; the Genoese had already decided upon war. While Ricciardo del Bene was receiving instructions for his Genoese embassy, the fleet organized by King Louis left Marseille bound for Naples. On 17 May, the Angevin galleys were sunk by a flotilla of Neapolitan and Genoese ships that had attacked them outside Livorno.[258] When news of the disaster reached Florence on the 21st, the initial reaction was, typically, to close ranks and call for civic unity and sacrifice. Matteo Tinghi professed to believe that the Genoese had not formally allied with Ladislaus, and that a peace settlement might still be arranged. But

---

[253] P. Partner, *The Papal State Under Martin V* (London, 1958), 21–22.

[254] See the collegiate response to the Genoese embassy; *CP*, 40, f.91v, 20 Dec. 1409.

[255] *Ibid.*, f.110r, 23 Jan. 1410.

[256] *CP*, 40, f.154r. The undated draft of an agreement between Florence and Genoa, written sometime that spring, is in *SCMLC*, 4, ff.120v–123r.

[257] *SCMLC*, 4, ff.135v–140v, 7 May.

[258] Cutolo, *Ladislao*, 396–97: Valois, *Grand Schisme*, IV, 132–33; Morelli, *Ricordi*, 534–35; H. Finke, *Acta Concilii Constantiensis* (Münster, 1896–1928), IV, 639–42.

most citizens accepted the grim fact that the republic now faced two
powerful opponents, though Vieri Guadagni argued that the Genoese
were not as formidable as some believed. Piero Baroncelli saw two
positive benefits emerging from the disaster: the unity of the citizenry
and divine help for the republic's just cause. He appealed to his fellow
citizens to dedicate themselves, with greater energy and determination
than before, to the defense of their republic.[259]

With its references to unity and patriotism and its neglect of the
political and military realities, Baroncelli's harangue established the
tone of civic deliberations during this crisis. So powerful was the
pressure for conformity that a former critic of the Neapolitan campaign, Matteo Tinghi, and an artisan from the lower guilds, Rosso di
Piero, urged the authorities to prosecute the war with all their resources. Counselors were remarkably unconcerned about the Genoese
threat, and though a few did hope that a settlement could be arranged
they were not willing to surrender Sarzana or to make commercial
concessions to placate the Genoese.[260] Nor did the debates contain
any reappraisal of military strategy in the light of the armada's
destruction. The allied invasion of the Regno remained the highest
priority, although Louis had to beg the republic for 25,000 florins to
recruit more troops. Although some counselors expressed doubts that
this grant would effectively launch the invasion, the majority favored
this contribution, arguing that otherwise the king would abandon the
struggle.[261] "If the king were to withdraw," Filippo Corsini asserted,
"then we would remain alone in the war and our liberty would be
lost."[262] The promoters of the Angevin connection persisted in their
belief that only Louis could save them from Ladislaus. After recruiting
some troops with the Florentine subsidy, the king began his slow
march south toward Rome, stopping frequently enroute for triumphal
celebrations in Siena and Montepulciano.[263] Before reaching Rome, he
asked the republic for more funds to pay his cavalry; the other allied
captains, Paolo Orsini and Sforza Attendola, were also demanding
money for their mercenaries.

The final phase of the domestic controversy over war strategy began
with an oration (10 August) by Maso degli Albizzi, who made another
stirring appeal for civic unity. He deplored the increase of internal

[259] Tinghi stated that he had always been concerned about the possibility of a
Genoese alliance with Ladislaus, and that Louis should have come to Italy by land
and not by sea; CP, 40, f.165r, 20 May. Jacopo Malegonelle also favored peace
with Genoa. Baroncelli's comment; ibid., f.165v.

[260] On the possibilities of peace with Genoa, see ibid., ff.176v–178r, 183v, 186r.

[261] Ibid., ff.169v–174v, 9 and 10 June.

[262] Ibid., f.190v, 10 Aug.   [263] Morelli, Ricordi, 536.

discord, which would make peace more difficult to achieve. That goal would be reached only by pursuing the allied strategy of attacking Ladislaus in his own territory. The citizens must make another heroic effort to raise money for this enterprise, and he would contribute his share although, "as the whole world knows, I have no money and have been heavily burdened by forced loans. . . ." Perhaps sensing that his leader's role, if not his reputation, was in jeopardy, Maso had made a supreme effort to silence critics of the war. But neither his logic nor his rhetoric could quell the peace sentiment that Cionaccio Baroncelli articulated three weeks later: "I see that we must have peace and for the love of God, I appeal to the Signoria to bring tranquility to our people!"[264] Other speakers described the miseries of a populace suffering from oppressive taxation, unemployment, and hunger.[265] Undeterred by these sentiments, the war party called for the expenditure of more money on the invasion of the Regno,[266] and even for the acquisition of the city of Forlì. For the purchase price of 25,000 florins, Rinaldo Gianfigliazzi argued, Florence would establish a secure foothold in Romagna, and contribute to the eventual defeat of Ladislaus. To Rinaldo Rondinelli, however, this imperialist talk was madness: "It appears to me that the pope [John XXIII] . . . is seeking to place another war on our shoulders, and it is not possible for this exhausted *popolo* to bear this burden."[267] Though Niccolò Malegonelle, Barduccio Cherichini, and Niccolò da Uzzano agreed with Rondinelli that the acquisition of Forlì was impractical and dangerous, Rinaldo Gianfigliazzi's viewpoint received support from Giotto Peruzzi, Marsilio Vecchietti, and Giovanni Carducci. Even in this time of fiscal stringency and economic crisis, when the war magistracy had to borrow money from private citizens to pay the salaries of its mercenaries,[268] some citizens could not resist the lure of territorial acquisition.

[264] *CP*, 40, ff.191r, 195v. See also the statements of Francesco Ardinghelli and Matteo Tinghi; *ibid.*, ff.189r–189v.

[265] E.g., the comments of Alessio Baldovinetti and Francesco Federighi, *ibid.*, ff.213r–213v, 5 Nov.

[266] *Ibid.*, ff.198v–200r, statements of Cristofano di Giorgio, Zanobi Rucellai, and Niccolò da Uzzano.

[267] This debate in *ibid.*, ff.209r–211r, 10 Oct.

[268] On 9 Dec. 1410, the bankers Giovanni and Niccolò Barbadori lent 3000 fl. to the ten members of the *balìa* who, as private citizens, promised to repay the loan, plus exchange charges, within two months: "ciascuno di loro come private persone ci si obriganno de rendere i dicti fiorini tria millia per di qui a due mesi proximi che vengano e più in cambi ci costasseno infino seremo interamente pagati e quella provisione che alloro piacerà"; *Merc.*, 1250, f.755r. When that debt was not repaid, the bankers filed suit (29 May 1411) in the Merchants' Court against Maso degli Albizzi, Lorenzo Ridolfi and their associates in the *balìa*; *ibid.*, ff.754v–756r. The membership of that magistracy is in *Delizie*, XIV, 295.

In November, a new Signoria decided to reopen peace negotiations with Ladislaus that had been suspended in the spring.[269] The priors received contradictory advice from the citizens they consulted. Filippo Corsini, Jacopo Salviati, and Salamone Strozzi held firmly to the opinion that only by invading Ladislaus' territory could the republic force the king to sue for peace on acceptable terms. But this argument was challenged by Paolo Biliotti, who accused the war party of being more concerned about the welfare of Florence's allies, King Louis and Pope John XXIII, than that of the republic herself. Many citizens, he reported, were skeptical about the invasion which either would not occur, or would end in disaster. The defensive tone of Filippo Corsini's response, and of others who supported a belligerent stance toward Ladislaus, suggests that their credibility was being eroded, and that pressures for a cessation of hostilities were becoming irresistible.[270] Still, the war party continued to warn the citizenry that by signing a separate peace with the king the republic was acquiescing in the destruction of the Papal States.[271] The Signoria and the war *balìa* did not report on the peace negotiations until Gabriello Brunelleschi's return from Naples on 22 December, with Ladislaus' positive response. On the following day, the colleges gave their tentative approval to the peace settlement, and on 4 and 5 January 1411 the legislative councils approved the election of syndics to sign the treaty.[272] Two days later, the pact was signed and its terms publicized; it was to take effect on 1 February, when the republic's alliance with King Louis was terminated. Both parties agreed to cease all hostile activities against the other; furthermore, Ladislaus promised to withdraw his forces from papal territory, except Perugia, north of Rome, and to sell Cor-

[269] Morelli, *Ricordi*, 537, reported that Gabriello Brunelleschi came to Florence on 29 Oct. with peace proposals; the colleges expressed their support for the negotiations; *CP*, 40, f.216r, 7 Nov. For the Signoria's reaction to Brunelleschi's mission, see *Commissioni di Rinaldo degli Albizzi*, I, 208–09.

[270] *CP*, 40, ff.213v–214r, 5 Nov.

[271] These arguments were made by Vanni Castellani, Filippo Corsini and Cristofano di Giorgio; *ibid.*, ff.216v–217r. Rinaldo Rondinelli and Paolo Biliotti denied that Florence had any obligations to Pope John XXIII.

[272] *Ibid.*, f.226v; *Prov.*, 99, ff.157r–157v. Reporting to his government on 3 Jan., the Sienese ambassador wrote: "Si fè il consiglio di più di mille uomini e stè infino a hore tre di notte dove quello che era fatto per quegli della praticha pare si confirmasse e alloro si desse podestà di quello restasse a fare"; *Conc.*, 1877, no. 79. The ambassador felt that the separate peace was a betrayal of Florence's allies: "e ogni uomo e papa e Re e ancho voi infino a qui anno messo a parte per loro ben proprio, che maggiori inganni non crediano s'avessono. . . . Iddio proveggha a tanta superbia. . . ." For legal opinions by Florentine lawyers on the republic's obligations to her allies, see Martines, *Lawyers and Statecraft*, 334–37.

tona to Florence for 50,000 florins. The settlement reflected the military and political realities of a stalemate, in which neither party could defeat the other, and both had to make concessions to obtain peace.[273]

Though most citizens strongly favored it, a small but influential minority, including some of the most prominent figures in the *reggimento*, opposed the peace agreement.[274] Neither the pressures of economic necessity nor the deteriorating military situation in Rome and the Campagna could persuade these men to accept peace with Ladislaus. Because Luca Pitti had been a member of the commission which drafted the treaty, he became the target of a vendetta (or so his cousin Buonaccorso claimed) instigated by those "who resented the peace," among whom were Rinaldo Gianfigliazzi, Ridolfo and Bindaccio Peruzzi, and members of the Ricasoli, Castellani, and Baroncelli families.[275] Thus the internal divisions over the war, which had begun with the Angevin alliance eighteen months earlier, continued after the peace. One month after the signing of that treaty, the legislative councils approved a measure which sharply curtailed the executive's authority to engage in any military enterprise beyond the republic's frontier.[276] This provision created a special council of 200 citizens which had to ratify, by a two-thirds vote, the launching of any military campaign, the annexation of any territory, or the creation of a war magistracy. This large council, more representative of the guild community than the old Council of Eighty-one had been, was designed to impede aggressive actions, either military or diplomatic, by any Signoria. Experience had shown that the large legislative assemblies could resist the most intense and sustained pressure by the executive to pass legislation desired by the leadership and opposed by the guild community.

This controversy had a long history, extending back to the first Visconti war in the early 1390s. Though fluctuating in intensity and visibility according to events and circumstances, the issue was always near the surface of Florentine politics. Prior to the war with Ladislaus,

---

[273] Terms of the treaty are in *I Capitoli del Comune di Firenze*, ed. C. Guasti and A. Gherardi (Florence, 1866–1893), II, 145ff. See also Cutolo, *Ladislao*, 400–01. The Sienese ambassador also reported on the settlement; *Conc.*, 1877, no. 79, 3 Jan. 1411; and *ibid.*, 1874, no. 18, 8 Jan.

[274] The council vote was 328 to 28 in favor of electing peace syndics. Pitti wrote that "funne contento tutto il popolo e per ispeziale i buoni e veri Ghuelfi"; *Cronica*, 20–21. Morelli, however, wrote that "fu pe' savi biasimato, e meritamente"; *Ricordi*, 538.

[275] *Cronica*, 169–72, 178–80. Maso degli Albizzi was also a member of the peace commission; A. Rinuccini, *Ricordi*, L; *BNF, Magl.*, xxv, 283, *anno* 1411.

[276] *Prov.*, 99, ff.168r–168v. The vote: 177–57 and 141–23.

these differences were neither factional nor ideological in origin, but rather the products of different systems of priorities. Merchants and cloth manufacturers tended to give substantial weight to economic factors in political decision-making, and to judge a policy in terms of cost and utility. Their pragmatism offended the sensibilities of the "patriots" who insisted that the preservation of a free, republican regime took precedence over all other considerations. These two attitudes reflected quite different views of politics and, by extension, of human experience; one, rational, pragmatic, and flexible; the other, rigid and doctrinaire.[277] Accurately reflecting the pragmatic vision was a memorandum sent by the Signoria in January 1411 to its ambassadors charged with justifying the peace with Ladislaus to King Louis of Anjou: "This *popolo* has been oppressed by such heavy expenses, while the war has cut off trade routes and profits, so that it could not survive, nor was it possible for those who governed to lead the mass of the *popolo* farther along that route. . . ."[278] Gino Capponi and Rinaldo Gianfigliazzi were no more patriotic than their pacifist colleagues like Pandolfini, but their political outlook was more dogmatic, and intensely moralistic. Since Ladislaus had once broken his faith with Florence, he could never be trusted. Like Giangaleazzo Visconti a decade earlier, he had become a malignant enemy who must be destroyed.[279] By the same token, the republic could never repudiate its legal obligations or it would incur dishonor and opprobrium by exhibiting the same moral flaw as its enemies did. So Jacopo Salviati stigmatized the Ladislaus treaty as a violation of the republic's faith, since it was contracted while the alliance with King Louis and Pope John XXIII was still in force, "with great shame and humiliation and disgrace to our commune. . . ."[280]

The debate over the acquisition of the papal city of Forlì in October 1410 illustrates more clearly how these two visions of politics clashed. The pragmatists argued that the republic could not afford to engage in this Romagnol adventure while it was fighting Ladislaus in the Roman Campagna. Though Forlì's acquisition might have substantial advantages, and might be considered at a more propitious time, the present circumstances of involvement in a debilitating war dictated a policy of restraint. "If we take Forlì," Niccolò da Uzzano predicted,

[277] This schema borrows heavily from that developed by William Bouwsma, in his conceptualization of the differences between the medieval and the Renaissance views of reality; *Venice and the Defense of Republican Liberty* (Berkeley and Los Angeles, 1968), ch. 1.

[278] *SCMLC*, 5, ff.1r–1v, 11 Jan. 1411.   [279] See above, 137, 152–53, 180.

[280] J. Salviati, *Cronica*, in *Delizie*, XVIII, 352.

STATE-BUILDING 247

"then all of the neighboring states will be disturbed, and he cited many examples to prove that in the past we have been involved in many wars on account of such suspicions."[281] These arguments did not persuade Rinaldo Gianfigliazzi, whose discourse on the Forlì issue reflected a view of politics dominated by categorical imperatives: "The war that is being waged against us in Tuscany, and is being fought in Romagna, is directed by Ladislaus. If Bologna falls, then we will lose all of our Romagna lands. If Forlì falls, Bologna will fall; and if Forlì comes under the domination of the Malatesta or the count of Urbino, it will eventually come into Ladislaus' hands. . . . In the name of God, let us occupy Forlì and loan the pope 25,000 florins, with the stipulation that he go to Rome. . . . And if he goes to Rome, we will have peace in Tuscany and our enemy will have war in his own kingdom."[282] The Malatesta would have no reason to attack Florence if she occupied Forlì, for they had no legal claim to that city. "Moreover, the Forlivesi are the bitter enemies of the Malatesta, and conversely, they desire nothing more than to submit to us. And I am always ready to possess the hearts of men; that is the most solid safeguard for custody."

Gianfigliazzi perceived politics as a system of fundamental, and unchanging, verities: the Forlivesi would always be friends of Florence; the Malatesta would always be enemies. Timing, contingency, even strategy, were scarcely relevant in this view, which stressed the absolute and inexorable aspects of political experience. For Gianfigliazzi—and for Giotto Peruzzi, Michele Castellani, and Marsilio Vecchietti who supported his position[283]—compromise and conciliation with former enemies were painful and difficult choices, because they were founded on a view of reality that emphasized contingency and flux, expediency and pragmatism, and relativity. These characteristics violated, and deeply offended, their perceptions of a world in which policy decisions were dictated by fixed principles, above all by moral and legal absolutes, and not by a rational appraisal of particular circumstances. The disagreements over the nature of political reality exaggerated the tensions within the *reggimento* in the months following the peace with Ladislaus.

---

[281] CP, 41, f.210v, 20 Oct. Rinaldo Rondinelli's reaction to the acquisition was even more negative: "quod non est possibile tollerare hec onera quia populus noster consuntus est et exhaustus; quia nichil lucramur et usus mercantie est sublatus; concludens quod nullo modo attendemus ad istud negotium"; *ibid.*, f.209v.

[282] *Ibid.*, f.209r. If Florence did not move to acquire Forlì, Gianfigliazzi concluded, "quod expendemus nedum florenos 25,000 sed multo plura et quasi infinitum pecunie et veniemus in periculum nostre libertatis. . . ."

[283] *Ibid.*, ff.209v–210r.

CHAPTER V

The Florentine Reggimento *in 1411*

THE SOCIAL COMPOSITION OF THE REGIME

THE structure of the Florentine republic in 1411 had not changed significantly since 1382: in its magistracies and councils, in its electoral and legislative processes. But constitutional stability can mask fundamental alterations in political sytems, as Jacopo d'Appiano, the lord of Pisa, suggested in a conversation with two Florentine ambassadors in June 1396. Jacopo had informed the envoys, Benedetto Peruzzi and Salvestro de' Ricci, that he was concerned about the preservation of Florentine liberty, whose loss, if it came about, would endanger all Tuscany. The Florentine government was friendly to him and to Pisa, he said, except for one citizen, Rinaldo Gianfigliazzi, "who aspires to become a Gambacorta. . . ." The envoys replied that "we intended to preserve our liberty with our lives and with everything we possess, and that neither Messer Rinaldo nor any other citizen was a tyrant, nor did we intend to have one."[1] In response to Jacopo's insinuation that their city was about to succumb to despotism, Peruzzi and Ricci argued that the Florentine government was still a communal regime, in which authority was invested exclusively in the Signoria, the colleges, and the legislative councils.[2] They were reiterating the official view, articulated a few years earlier by Coluccio Salutati when he wrote that in Florence thousands of citizens administered the *rem publicam*, and that short terms of office prevented domination by a select few.[3]

Jacopo d'Appiano's appraisal of Florentine politics was not an isolated opinion. Other critics, both native and foreign, argued that the city was governed by a clique that monopolized the important offices,

---

[1] Jacopo d'Appiano said that "vi piacesse volere conservare la loro e nostra libertà, e che vegnendo meno a voi, vorebbe meno a tutti gl'altri, e che sapea che lla nostra comunità gl'era amica, salvo chè alcuno cittadino che dicieva che se dovesse fare uno Gambacorto; diceva il converebbe fare signore di Pisa, e che questa era Messer Rinaldo Gianfigliazzi, e che niente avea a fare con lui"; *DBRA*, 1, f.19v, 22 June 1396.

[2] "Rispuosesi per noi che la libertà nostra intendevamo mantenere e qui mettere insino alla vita e di ogn'altro che ll'avesse o volesse; e che 'l detto messer Rinaldo nè egli nè niuno altro n'era signore n'entendevamo che fosse; e che qui che potrano e aveanno signoria erano i nostri signori e lloro collegi e consigli opportuni"; *ibid*.

[3] P. Herde, "Politik und Rhetorik in Florenz am Vorabend der Renaissance," *Archiv für Kulturgeschichte*, XLVII (1965), 183, n.225.

and that at the apex of this ruling elite was a handful of citizens whose power rivaled that of *signori* in despotic regimes. Writing in the 1380s, Marchionne Stefani had noted that Florence "has always contained men who were above themselves"; he identified twenty citizens who aspired to preeminence "in the voting, in the granting of dispensations, and in public affairs."[4] In 1391, a Sienese source referred to "thirty *arciguelfi* who in the name of liberty were tyrannizing their own city and were bent on swallowing up the cities of their neighbors."[5] A decade later, a notary from Cesena, Ser Niccolò di Messer Leonardo, claimed that Florence was dominated by sixty men "who tyrannize and exploit this city and keep it in continual ferment and tribulation. . . ."[6] Ser Niccolò's prescription for remedying this situation was to assassinate Rinaldo Gianfigliazzi, whose death, he predicted, would throw the city into such turmoil that the regime would founder.[7] A similar motive may have inspired Agnolo Bastari, grandson of the exiled Filippo, who was convicted in 1401 of spreading tales of Gianfigliazzi's despotic ambitions through an intermediary, Giovanna di Cione. She was identified in the judicial process as a woman who "for more than twenty years, in times of turmoil . . . has gone about the city, inspired by her own thoughts or the suggestions of others, spreading rumors, scandals, and tales of revolutions and upheavals . . . in the style of a possessed woman, to whom many Florentines customarily listen."[8] Agnolo told Giovanna that reports had reached him from Bologna that Rinaldo Gianfigliazzi was the ruler of Florence, and that God wished to inform the Florentines of that fact. During the festival of John the Baptist, the city's patron saint, Giovanna harangued the

[4] Stefani, 923. For earlier complaints, in 1372, about those "qui appetunt . . . esse supra omnes cives," see Brucker, *Florentine Politics*, 253.

[5] Quoted in Herde, "Politik und Rhetorik," 216, n.400. I use Philip Jones' translation, *History*, LIII (1968), 412.

[6] *AEOG*, 1381, ff.51r–52v, 7 Feb. 1400.

[7] Ser Niccolò's condemnation contains a version of his conversation with a prospective assassin, Cola di Giovanni da Francavilla, *ibid.*, f.52r: "E morto miser Ranaldo, tota ista civitas erit in tribulatione et non sit difficille quod presens status subverteretur. Et si hoc sequeretur, dominus Johannes [de Pallatio] veniret in capite balie et moraretur in officio predicto plures quinque annis, cum quo posses superlucrari ultra quingentos florenos et semper toto tempore vite tue haberes bonum tempus. Et deinde, cum sciretur quod tu occidisses dominum Ranaldum, quilibet diceret: 'Iste fuit unus deus pro nobis; nam sumus tot homines in ista civitate et nescivimus hoc facere, et iste solus pro nobis hoc fecit; decens est quod sibi fiat una bona provisio. Nam dabuntur tibi plures centum paghis, et semper toto tempore vite tue bene te haberes.' "

[8] *AP*, 3785, ff.41r–42v, 13 Aug. 1401. Giovanna was sentenced to five years in prison; Angelo was fined 500 l. and exiled for three years.

crowds: "Florentines, take care that you do not lose your liberty to the tyrants, for it is certain that there will soon be a revolution in this city, since Messer Rinaldo intends to become the lord of Florence."

The belief that the regime's viability was dependent upon one or two men influenced the strategy of Florentine exiles who plotted to overthrow it. In 1397, Bastardino de' Medici and Maso di Salvestro de' Ricci had devised a plan to assassinate Maso degli Albizzi and Rinaldo Gianfigliazzi, as a prelude to their efforts to foment a rebellion. When the assassins could not find either of their principal targets, they attacked and killed the son of another prominent statesman, Piero Firenze.[9] In his confession describing another conspiracy in 1400, Sanminiato de' Ricci wrote that a company of armed men led by Stoldo Altoviti was sent to the home of Rinaldo Gianfigliazzi with orders "to break into the house and burn it down and seize Messer Rinaldo and kill him."[10] From Bologna ten years later (August 1411), Bindaccio Alberti devised a plot in which Rinaldo Gianfigliazzi and Neri Vettori would be killed. Bindaccio described Rinaldo and Maso degli Albizzi as the two main props of the regime, "and if either of them falls, the foundations will collapse."[11] Since Maso and Rinaldo were both authorized to carry arms and to grant that privilege to others, they usually chose one of their servants as a bodyguard to protect them from potential assassins.[12]

In his *Istorie fiorentine*, Giovanni Cavalcanti developed his views about the realities of Florentine political life which, he argued, were hidden behind the facade of republican institutions and procedures. He described a *pratica* of 1423 in which citizens were debating the appropriate response to the Milanese invasion of the Romagna, the prelude to the renewal of hostilities with the Visconti. After reading the letters describing these events, the priors appealed to their fellow citizens to advise them on the crisis, reminding them that "if today we hold this office, your turn will come tomorrow when we leave this exalted magistracy." Thus encouraged by the Signoria's invitation, several citizens rose to voice their opinions, which were varied and contradictory. A witness to these proceedings, Cavalcanti reported that Niccolò da Uzzano slept through this debate and then awoke to deliver a brief statement recommending a policy of rearmament.

[9] *ACP*, 2056, f.66v; *AEOG*, 1321, f.20r; Fumi, *Regesti*, II, no. 1803.

[10] Passerini, *Alberti*, II, 278.   [11] *AEOG*, 1759, f.104r. See below, 325–27.

[12] *Tratte*, 315, ff.5v, 38r, 47r. Other prominent citizens entitled to bear arms were Coluccio Salutati, Filippo Corsini, Filippo Magalotti, Vanni Castellani and Gino Capponi.

Speakers who followed Niccolò approved his suggestions unanimously. Cavalcanti concluded that Niccolò had met secretly with other prominent leaders to formulate a policy which would then be ratified in the *pratica*. These men were governing the republic privately "in dining halls and in studies," while the public conduct of affairs in the palace of the Signoria was a sham. While many citizens were elected to communal office, only a few enjoyed the privilege of governing.[13]

Though Cavalcanti was a biased observer, his analysis of Florentine politics was closer to reality than that of apologists like Gregorio Dati and Leonardo Bruni.[14] Cavalcanti focused upon a very significant problem: the discrepancy between constitutional structures and procedures on the one hand, and practice on the other. Those processes— elections, debates, council votes—were not simply facades for the manipulations by a minority, as Cavalcanti suggested. Yet outside this institutional structure there did exist another important level of political activity, involving the *possenti e maggiori*,[15] that cadre of prominent citizens whose power and influence derived not from office-holding, but rather from their status in the *reggimento*, and their continuous involvement in public affairs. These men constituted a ruling elite, or more accurately, a leadership elite. Giovanni Cavalcanti estimated that the "inner circle of the *reggimento*" numbered about seventy men, "who were experienced in affairs of state."[16] Whether in or out of office, they were daily at the palace, absorbing and dispensing information, counseling and advising, persuading and cajoling. Their authority had no constitutional sanction, and no precedent in Florentine republican experience. The analysis of this elite—its

[13] ". . . Mi pareva che nella Repubblica ne dovesse seguire tirannesco e non politico vivere, che fuori del Palagio si amministrasse il governo della Repubblica. . . . Il Comune era più governato alle cene e negli scrittoi che nel Palagio; e che molti erano eletti agli ufficii e pochi al governo"; G. Cavalcanti, *Istorie fiorentine*, ed. G. di Pino (Milan, 1944), book II, ch. I.

[14] Cavalcanti recorded his views twenty years after the event; Rubinstein, "Florentine Constitutionalism and Medici Ascendancy in the Fifteenth Century," *Flor. Studies*, 452–53. On the views of Dati and Bruni on the Florentine constitution, see Baron, *Crisis*, 2nd ed., 205–09; Rubinstein, 450–55; J. Kirschner, "Paolo di Castro on 'Cives ex Privilegio,' " *Renaissance Studies in Honor of Hans Baron*, 263.

[15] Buonaccorso Pitti's phrase; *Cronica*, 135.

[16] ". . . Voi siete in numero di settanta cittadini, tutti usi e anticati al civile reggimento"; *Istorie fiorentine*, III, ch. 2. Cavalcanti also used the phrases "il cerchio del governo" and "il cerchio del bello reggimento"; for other uses of the term, see D. Kent, "Reggimento," *Renaissance Quarterly*, XXVIII, 577–84.

composition, its role in the political process, its style—is essential for an understanding of this regime, which was neither a republic in the classic sense, venerated by traditionalists and idealized by civic humanists, nor yet a despotism.

The image that best describes this regime is a series of concentric circles, in which each circle represents a particular degree of eminence and status within the political community.[17] The outer perimeters represent the largest number of citizens and the inner circles define more exclusive groups with higher status. In the concept of the *popolo*, as the whole guild community, lies the broadest definition of this polity, but the *popolo* did not play a political role save in times of crisis when, assembled as a *parlamento*, it could approve a change of regime. Not all guildsmen, however, enjoyed the right to hold office. That privilege was reserved for those Guelfs of legitimate birth[18] who satisfied certain residence and fiscal requirements. If membership in this polity is thus defined as the right to hold office, the outermost circle would embrace all Guelf citizens and guild members over the age of twenty-five who, or whose ancestors, had lived in the city and had paid *prestanze* for more than thirty years.[19] The scrutiny lists for the Signoria furnish the most solid evidence for the size of this group, since only eligibles were nominated by the guild consuls, the sixteen standard-bearers of the companies, and the Parte captains.[20] That number fluctuated between 5000 and 5500 until 1411; but in the 1433 scrutiny 6354 citizens were nominated for the supreme executive.[21]

Of this large and amorphous body of guildsmen who were technically qualified for communal office, perhaps one-third actually enjoyed that privilege during their lifetimes. A majority of lower guildsmen, those artisans and shopkeepers of modest standing, rarely saw the inside of the palace of the Signoria;[22] their participation in political life was limited to paying their taxes and watching the investi-

[17] The model was first suggested by Martines, *Lawyers and Statecraft*, 388; it is also used by Kent, 578.

[18] The magistracy of the Defenders of the Laws was established in 1429 to weed out officeholders of illegitimate birth; Martines, *Lawyers and Statecraft*, 170.

[19] The residence requirement was enacted in 1379, and the *prestanze* requirement (which was only 25 years for lower guildsmen) in 1404; Kirshner, *Renaissance Studies*, 239–44.

[20] Brucker, *Florentine Politics and Society*, 66.

[21] These figures are from *Delizie*, xvi, 125–260; *Tratte*, 45; and Kent, "Reggimento," 623.

[22] Approximately 130 lower guildsmen sat in the legislative councils in 1411; *Tratte*, 150; or 10% of the 1361 artisans who were scrutinized for the Signoria that year.

ture of each new Signoria in the loggia adjacent to the palace.[23] A republic concerned about broadening its social base and fostering a civic spirit in the populace might have opened up its legislative councils, the least important offices in the government, to all eligible guildsmen. But this regime did not promote or encourage their participation in politics. Even during its most popular phase in the 1380s, when substantial numbers of "new men" qualified for the Signoria, citizens from the old patrician families dominated the councils, as well as the other offices filled by scrutiny.[24] Of eighty councilors from the quarter of Santa Croce who were drawn for the Council of the *Popolo* in February 1382, nearly seventy percent (55 of 80) had qualified for the Signoria held that month.[25] These fifty-five citizens belonged to that minority of 800 eligibles; the other twenty-five were selected from the large mass of 5000 citizens who had not qualified for high office. The pattern of council officeholding did not change significantly during the next three decades. In 1411, a total of 256 citizens from Santa Croce sat in the councils; of that number, thirty-two (13 percent) were lower guildsmen and twelve (5 percent) were magnates.[26] More than two-thirds of the *popolani* councilors (167 of 244) had qualified for the Signoria in that year's scrutiny. Of the 1159 guildsmen from Santa Croce who were nominated, but who failed to qualify, for the supreme executive in 1411, only sixty-seven (6 percent) were seated in a legislative council that year.[27] These statistics suggest that the number of officeholders in any given year was not significantly larger than the number of citizens eligible for the Signoria, and probably never more than 1000 or 1200.[28]

Thus, while the broadest definition of the *reggimento* would include all citizens who filled communal offices at any given time,[29] it seems

[23] The civic militia, to which these artisans belonged, had not been assembled since 1393; above, ch. II, 94.

[24] The personnel in the councils for this decade are recorded in *Tratte*, 142–44.

[25] *Delizie*, XVI, 145–77; *Tratte*, 142, ff.34r–41v.

[26] These statistics are from *Tratte*, 150. In addition to the routine selection of the Councils of the *Popolo* and the Commune every four months, a special council of 200 was chosen on 23 Feb. 1411, for a six-month tenure. Some citizens sat in all three councils during that year.

[27] The data on the 1411 scrutiny from *Tratte*, 45, ff.24r–49r.

[28] This figure is much lower than that suggested by Martines, *Lawyers and Statecraft*, 388–89, and by Molho, "Politics and the Ruling Class," *Nuova Rivista Storica*, LII, 407, who states that some 3000 posts had to be filled annually. Molho's figure may include guild offices and the retinues of the officials in the territorial administration. Many citizens held more than one office in a given year.

[29] For a contemporary identification of the *reggimento* with the entire office-holding group, see the Ridolfi *priorista: Manoscritti*, 225, f.146v: "In questo tempo si fece in Firenze squittino di tutti li officii di drento la città et di fuora, e

already to have comprised only those who qualified for the *tre maggiori*: the Signoria and the colleges. That narrower interpretation was most commonly used in political discourse: by Lorenzo Ridolfi when he spoke of "citizens who belong to the *reggimento*," or Michele Castellani's reference to "the most select citizens who are active in the *reggimento*," or Jacopo Vecchietti's complaint that "many participated in the scrutiny who until now had never been in the *reggimento*."[30] That number varied with each holding of the scrutiny for these offices. In 1411 a total of 1069 citizens gained a two-thirds majority of the votes cast in the balloting, and so were judged worthy of the republic's most important magistracies. The results of that scrutiny show a sharp increase in the number of eligibles, an expansion of the *reggimento*'s size by one-half since 1391, when only 677 citizens qualified.[31] It was larger by one-fourth than in 1382, when so many guildsmen of middling rank had crowded into its ambit.[32]

The incorporation of greater numbers into this "oligarchic" regime was not the result of demographic expansion or an increase in the size of the guild community.[33] It was due instead to a doubling of the ratio of those qualified to those nominated, from one in ten in 1391 to one in five in 1411.[34] This increase was most pronounced in the greater guilds, and particularly among the large patrician families. In Santa Croce, for example, the ten families with the largest blocs of eligibles increased their share of the total from twenty percent in 1391 to thirty-one percent (66 of 212) in 1411. The patrician dominance in the quarter of Santa Maria Novella was even more striking: forty-three percent of the eligibles from the greater guilds belonged to the ten leading

feciono una mescolanza con altre borse, nelle quali messero molta gente nuova, che mai più havevano reggimento." Also, this phrase in a 1400 provision: "cives existentes in regimine et imbursati pro offitiis civitatis"; *Prov.*, 89, f.134r.

[30] "Quod cives sint de regimine et experti"; "civibus electissimis et in regimine consuetis"; "multi intervenerunt ad scrutinium celebrandum qui regimentum hactenus nullum habuerant"; *CP*, 43, ff.37v, 139r; 45, f.54r. Dale Kent argues for this sense of the word as most commonly used; "*Reggimento*," *Renaissance Quarterly*, xxviii, 578–79.

[31] The 1411 scrutiny is in *Tratte*, 45; the 1391 scrutiny in *ibid.*, 397. The statistics in Kent, "*Reggimento*," 633.

[32] In 1382, 752 eligibles have been counted, with two *gonfaloni* missing; Kent estimates the actual total at 860; "*Reggimento*," 613. There may have been a larger number of eligibles in the 1378 scrutiny, for which no records have survived. Between 1343 and 1378, the number of eligibles fluctuated between 300 and 500; Brucker, *Florentine Politics and Society*, 160.

[33] The 1411 plague had reduced the population; the number of nominees declined from 6310 in 1391 to 5265 in 1411; Kent, "*Reggimento*," 633.

[34] *Ibid.*

families in that quarter. The Strozzi qualified fifteen of their seventy-four nominees, or nearly eight percent of the total.[35] In the *gonfalone* of the White Lion in that quarter, the breakdown of the fifty-seven eligibles from the greater guilds reveals this pattern: thirty-six (63 percent) from eleven patrician lineages that had been represented in the Signoria prior to 1378; fourteen (25 percent) from eight families that had first qualified for the priorate between 1382 and 1391; and seven "new men" from four families that had entered the *reggimento* after 1391.[36]

The profile of the regime that emerges from this scrutiny is strongly aristocratic. The old Florentine families that had long been prominent in politics furnished substantial contingents of eligibles, thus insuring their representation in high office for years to come. The Castellani, who had never qualified more than two men in the mid-fourteenth century, and only three in 1391, were represented by nine men in the 1411 scrutiny.[37] In the quarter of Santa Maria Novella, the Altoviti, Rucellai, and Davanzati doubled their representation between 1391 and 1411, while the Gianfigliazzi's delegation increased from one to nine.[38] Many of these family blocs included fathers, sons, and even grandchildren. Among the seventeen Albizzi who qualified were Maso, his two sons Rinaldo and Luca, and three grandsons: Piero, Niccolò, and Ormanno.[39] The size of a family's representation was a rough but useful gauge of its status in the regime, and each man saw himself as a representative of his lineage, and a protector of his kinsmen's interests.[40] The crucial importance of family in determining political status was as clearly revealed by the omissions in this scrutiny as by selection. None of the Alberti, and only two of the Ricci, were among the nominees, while the Bastari, Rinuccini, Del Bene, and Castiglionchio also suffered discrimination if not total exclusion. Several Medici had been declared ineligible for office after the escapade of their kins-

---

[35] In 1391, the ten leading families in S. Maria Novella gained 26% of the total; above, ch. II, n.147. In that scrutiny the Strozzi qualified only seven men.

[36] *Tratte*, 45, ff.69r–72v.

[37] The Castellani representation in the scrutinies of 1348–1363 can be determined from the *Tratte* volumes which record the drawings from the purses for the Signoria and the colleges; see Becker and Brucker, "The Arti Minori in Florentine Politics, 1343–1378," *Medieval Studies*, XVIII (1956), 97, n.32, 33.

[38] Kent, "Reggimento," *Renaissance Quarterly*, XXVIII, 634. The Altoviti representation grew from 5 to 11, the Rucellai from 4 to 10, the Davanzati, from 4 to 8.

[39] *Tratte*, 45, ff.88r–91v. Rinaldo Gianfigliazzi was joined by two sons and three grandsons; *ibid.*, ff.56r–60v.

[40] Kent, "Reggimento," 587–93.

man Bastardino in 1397, and only eight members of that once potent house were among the nominees, of whom three did qualify for the Signoria.[41] The Acciaiuoli were likewise penalized for Donato's disgrace, although four were eligible for the priorate. A substantial number of former magnates who had obtained *popolano* status were nominated, but except for the Gianfigliazzi and the Popoleschi none were selected for inclusion in the pouches.

Although they substantially increased their representation, the aristocratic families did not monopolize the important magistracies, but continued to share them with artisans,[42] and with new families from the greater guilds. In her exemplary analysis of the scrutinies that have survived for this regime, Dale Kent has shown that some new blood filtered into the *reggimento* throughout the fifteen century. The flow was small but remarkably steady: in the quarter of Santa Maria Novella, twenty-one new families in 1391, sixteen in 1411, nineteen in 1433.[43] Among those parvenu families that established themselves firmly in the regime after 1382 were a handful that quickly achieved a measure of political distinction. In this category were the Cocchi Donati, Scambrilla, and Serristori from Santa Croce; the Della Luna and Lenzi from Santa Maria Novella; and the Pandolfini, Fortini, Solosmei, Della Casa, and Ginori from San Giovanni.[44] Some of these new men—Giovanni Serristori, Agnolo Pandolfini, Francesco and Giovanni della Luna, Agnolo della Casa, Zanobi Ginori[45]—were rich; their wealth probably helped them to achieve political recognition. But others—the Solosmei, Cocchi Donati, Scambrilla—possessed neither large fortunes nor distinguished ancestries;[46] no visible merits or distinction set them apart from their peers to explain their prominence in the regime. The Solosmei, Pandolfini, and Della Casa were neighbors of the Albizzi in San Giovanni; the Della Luna resided in

---

[41] *Tratte*, 45, ff.75r–78r.

[42] In 1411, 185 lower guildsmen qualified for the Signoria, compared to 142 in 1391; Kent, "Reggimento," 633.

[43] *Ibid*. For a different view, see Molho, *Nuova Rivista Storica*, LII, 415.

[44] Some of these families, e.g., the Ginori, had been represented in the Signoria prior to 1382, but they did not achieve a solid base, nor build political dynasties, until the 1380s and later. They were well represented among the eligibles in the 1411 scrutiny: Solosmei (4), Della Casa (5), Pandolfini (3), Della Luna (2), Ginori (5), Scambrilla (2), Lenzi (3), Fortini (3).

[45] Martines, *Social World*, 356–57, 369–70, 372.

[46] No member of these families was listed among the 150 wealthiest members of their quarter, except Niccolò di Cocco Donati, who ranked 117th in S. Maria Novella in 1427; *ibid.*, 368. Niccolò was a partner in a banking firm headed by a prominent statesman, Cristofano Spini; *Catasto*, 75, f.155r.

Strozzi territory near the Arno; and the Scambrilla lived adjacent to the Peruzzi in Santa Croce.[47] In return for loyal support, these men may have been backed in the scrutinies by their powerful neighbors.

Success in these elections, however, was not a guarantee that the victors would actually enter the Signoria. Of the twenty-one newly qualified men in the 1382 scrutiny from the Black Ox *gonfalone* of Santa Croce, only six had been drawn for the priorate by 1392; eight others were dead when their names were drawn from the pouches.[48] A wealthy family of dyers from Santa Croce, the Morelli, qualified their first member in 1366, but did not actually gain a seat until 1387.[49] Gregorio Dati recalled that his father Stagio had become eligible for the Signoria but had died in 1374 before his name was drawn. Forty years passed before Gregorio himself was chosen to the Sixteen. Until his selection, Dati wrote, "I had not been sure whether my name was in the purses . . . although I was eager that it should be both for my own honor and that of my heirs."[50] Eventually, the Morelli and the Dati did achieve membership in the Signoria, but the scrutiny lists contain the names of hundreds of obscure men who qualified only once, and then failed to maintain their precarious foothold in the *reggimento*. The statistics collected by Dale Kent show that only one-half of the newly eligible in the quarter of Santa Maria Novella were successful in later scrutinies.[51] Several descendants of once prominent citizens from the Black Ox *gonfalone*[52] failed to qualify in the 1411 election: the sons of Florence's wealthiest resident in 1378, Francesco Rinuccini; the grandsons of the eminent physician Tommaso del Garbo, of the merchant Sandro Barucci, and of a prominent figure in the communal bureaucracy, Ser Piero di Ser Grifo.[53] Other losers in that

[47] The Scambrilla and the Solosmei were partisans of the Albizzi faction in the 1430s; D. Kent, *Rise of the Medici*, ch. 2.

[48] The scrutiny lists are in *Delizie*, XVI, 152–58; the drawings in *Tratte*, 194.

[49] Morelli, *Ricordi*, 158–59, 163.

[50] *Il libro segreto di Gregorio Dati*, ed. C. Gargiolli (Bologna, 1869), 71, trans. in *Two Memoirs of Renaissance Florence*, 125. Dati must have qualified for the *tre maggiori* in the 1398 scrutiny; he polled only 40 votes in 1411, far below the minimum required to qualify; *Tratte*, 45, f.13v.

[51] Kent, "Reggimento," *Renaissance Quarterly*, XXVIII, 617. Of 157 families that qualified in the scrutinies for which records have survived, between 1382 and 1453, one-half were in only one scrutiny; 80 were in two or more; 24 in all seven.

[52] *Tratte*, 45, ff.28r–34r.

[53] On Francesco Rinuccini and his descendants, see Martines, *Social World*, 65–67, 110–12; on Tommaso del Garbo, Brucker, *Florentine Politics and Society*, 162, 176, 182; and Filippo Villani, *Vite degli uomini illustri fiorentini*; on Sandro Barucci, Brucker, *Florentine Politics*, 24, 190, 192; on Ser Piero di Ser Grifo, Brucker, "Ciompi Revolution," in *Flor. Studies*, 332.

scrutiny were sons of men who had qualified in 1382: Paolo di Maffeo de' Libri, the three sons of the cloth manufacturer Giovanni di Francesco di Ser Bartolo, the druggist Berto di Leonardo di Berto, the merchant Maffeo da Barberino. From small families of modest status, these men had failed to capitalize on their fathers' success and so fell back into the anonymous ranks of the *popolo*.[54]

No one outside the perimeters of the *reggimento* was more acutely aware of the privileges of membership than those who (or whose ancestors) had once belonged. When they entered the palace of the Signoria, they could not expect a warm greeting from civic leaders. Instead of listening to requests for help from others, they were themselves appellants for favors. Unless they had friends or relatives in power, they were liable to receive heavy tax assessments and to see their petitions for relief voted down by the colleges or the councils.[55] Members of the Alberti and Rinuccini families, long out of favor with the regime, were among the most frequent petitioners for reductions, alleging that their fortunes had been depleted by forced loans. For example, Simone di Messer Francesco Rinuccini appealed to the Signoria to be released from prison; he claimed that after paying his *prestanze* he could not support his family.[56] Descendants of citizens proscribed by the Parte Guelfa in the 1360s and 1370s were commonly in difficulty with the authorities for unpaid taxes or private debts. Matteo di Piero Petriboni, son of a prominent banker-statesman who had incurred the Parte's wrath in 1373, sent a desperate appeal from prison to Marco di Uberto Strozzi, requesting a personal audience with the Signoria, "even bound with cords and chains," to plead for protection from his creditors.[57] The son of another Parte victim, Vieri

---

[54] Some who qualified in the 1382 scrutiny (Domenico and Francesco di Vanni Chiavaccini; Niccolò di Ser Niccolò, *lanaiuolo*; Francino Tegne, retail merchant; Roberto Naddi, soap-maker) either had no descendants or their children left Florence, since their names do not appear among the candidates in later scrutinies. Thirty-one "new men" who qualified in the 1382 scrutiny from S. Maria Novella did not succeed (nor did their descendants) in any later scrutiny for which records are extant; Kent, "Reggimento," *Renaissance Quarterly*, XXVIII, 634–35.

[55] Some families eventually regained a place in the regime; *ibid*.

[56] *Prov.*, 87, ff.5v–6v, 29–30 March 1398. For other petitions by the Rinuccini, see *ibid.*, 85, ff.241r–241v; 86, ff.313v–314r; 87, ff.47r–48r; and by the Alberti, *ibid.*, 87, ff.237v–238v, 377r–380r; 106, ff.23v–24r. On the Rinuccini, see L. Martines, "Nuovi documenti su Cino Rinuccini e una nota sulle finanze della famiglia Rinuccini," *ASI*, CXIX (1961), 323–32. That the Alberti, Rinuccini, and Monaldi had been ruined by taxation was admitted in 1425 by Averardo de' Medici; *CP*, 46, f.40r.

[57] *BNF, Fondo principale*, II, V, 11, no. 20, March 1408. See also Matteo's petition; *Prov.*, 97, ff.72–73r, 27–28 Aug. 1408. On his father's troubles with the Parte Guelfa, see Brucker, *Florentine Politics and Society*, 263.

di Recco Guazza, was seized by the executor and interrogated, under torture, about the homicide of a usurer. Even though the judges did not convict him of that crime, he was imprisoned by the Signoria, and only released after his petition was approved by the councils.[58] To regain the political status lost by their exclusion from communal offices in 1397, the Mannelli family in 1402 requested the cancellation of that ban. They denied any complicity in the conspiracy, and further cited their antiquity and loyalty to the Parte Guelfa, "which can be proven by chronicles and annals. . . ." Convicted of treason in 1382, Bernardo Velluti successfully petitioned for rehabilitation eighteen years later, claiming that he and his family had always been zealous Guelfs. Even during his years of exile he insisted that "he had defended his city by words and deeds, and had cherished and supported the present regime to the limits of his ability. . . ." Sentenced to death for conspiracy in 1400, Giovanni di Marco Strozzi lived in exile for twenty-eight years, before his friends and relatives in Florence obtained the restoration of his civil rights. "He desires [so his petition read] to return to his native city with his wife and children, and to live in peace and then to die there, so that he can pass on to his descendants the heritage of liberty that he received from his ancestors."[59]

How did Florentines who had never experienced the satisfactions of officeholding regard the government which taxed, policed, and ruled them? Like the views of the urban poor throughout Europe in the pre-industrial age, the political sentiments of this disfranchised group are not well documented.[60] The *popolo* spoke most clearly in anger and outrage, but the ruthless persecution of popular dissent after 1382 eliminated this means of expressing opposition for all but the most courageous.[61] But neither the vigilance of the magistracy for

[58] *Prov.*, 90, ff.281v–282r, 10–11 Dec. 1401. On the father Recco, see Brucker, *Florentine Politics*, 207. Recco and his brother Bernardo also petitioned for tax relief: "ipsi sunt propter infortunia habita quasi in miseria constituti"; *Prov.*, 87, ff.18r–19r, 29–30 March 1398. Other descendants of disgraced or proscribed citizens who were imprisoned for debt or in financial difficulties were: the sons of Giovanni di Luigi Mozzi, Antonio di Paolo Covoni, the sons of Francesco del Bene, the son of Ser Niccolò di Ser Ventura Monachi, the son of Sanminiato de' Ricci; *ibid.*, 86, ff.112v–114r; 87, ff.35v–36v, 62v–64r; 96, f.224v; 109, f.118v.

[59] These petitions in *Prov.*, 91, ff.195r–196r; 89, ff.187v–189r; 119, ff.55v–58v.

[60] But see Brucker, "The Florentine Popolo Minuto," in Martines, ed., *Violence and Civil Disorder in Italian Cities*, 163–65, 176–82, for evidence concerning their mentality; also my *Society of Renaissance Florence*, 233–39.

[61] Brucker, "Popolo Minuto," 180–82; above, 69–70, 93. The *popolo* could be defined constitutionally as the entire group of guildsmen who were eligible for communal office. From the viewpoint of the regime, however, the *popolo* formed the mass of artisans and workers, guildsmen and non-guildsmen, who were effectively excluded from the *reggimento* and could coalesce to form a mob.

internal security, nor the harsh punishment meted out to rebels by the courts, could stifle popular discontent.[62] In 1394 an exasperated Signoria drafted a provision authorizing the payment of rewards, as high as 500 florins, to anyone who identified the authors of scurrilous letters and placards that were posted on buildings at night, "sometimes attacking the whole regime, sometimes certain citizens by name, sometimes the rectors. . . ."[63] It was very difficult, indeed impossible, to repress the malcontents who maligned officialdom in streets and loggias, in churches and taverns, in private homes, wherever men gathered to converse and complain.[64] Much criticism focused on individuals— the "tyrants," Rinaldo Gianfigliazzi and Maso degli Albizzi, the latter's family being described in one report as "rabid dogs" whose flesh would be eaten by their enemies when they returned to power.[65]

The majority of the *popolani* of middling rank and modest aspirations viewed their regime in a different light—with a mixture of patriotic pride, awe, and fear. Many were apparently satisfied with their status as worthy members of their guild, like the goldsmith Matteo di Lorenzo who never qualified for the Signoria but who was elected twenty-two times as consul of Por San Maria, and whose funeral service was well attended by his guild colleagues.[66] The wine merchant Bartolomeo del Corazza was consul of his guild twelve times but was never chosen to a communal office. Bartolomeo's diary emphasized spectacle and ceremony, those dimensions of civic life most accessible to the *popolo*. He described in great detail the jousts and the ceremonial processions honoring such visiting dignitaries as Pope Martin V and Pope Eugenius IV, but he wrote very little about domestic politics.[67] The notary Lapo Mazzei was closer to the centers of power; he proudly informed Francesco Datini that he had more

[62] For example, at the conclusion of the Ladislaus war in July 1414, illegal assemblies and subversive writings spread through the city; *CP*, 42, f.158r.

[63] *Prov.*, 83, ff.206r–207r, 10–11 Dec. 1394; *Panc.*, 158, f.178v.

[64] For examples, see the cases of Giovanni di Matteo Alderotti and Messer Ventura Monachi, above, 139, 171.

[65] *BNF, Fondo principale*, II, III, 434, f.97r; Papi Guidalotti reporting to the Signoria on the statements of Agnolo Bastari. See, too, the bitter diatribe against the regime's leadership by the cloth-worker, Cola di Maestro Piero; below, 325.

[66] The career of this *buono e savio uomo* is described briefly by his cousin, Cambio Petrucci; *Strozz.*, 2nd ser., 10, f.59r. Matteo received 65 votes (of 95 needed to qualify) in the 1411 scrutiny; *Tratte*, 45, f.28r.

[67] The diary was edited by G. Corazzini, *ASI*, 5th ser., XIV (1894), 233–98. Bartolomeo did describe the outbreak of hostilities with Ladislaus in 1413, and the political tensions surrounding the peace with the king in 1414; *ibid.*, 252–53. In 1411, Bartolomeo received 32 votes in the scrutiny; *Tratte*, 45, f.27r. For his economic condition in 1427, see *Catasto*, 80, f.281r.

intimate ties "with those who have the *reggimento* in hand" than other notaries. But those statesmen, he admitted, were masters to be served, and he accepted his lesser role without complaint.[68] Ser Lapo's perception of the political system, of the proper relations between the *maggiori* and their inferiors, is well described in a letter which he drafted for Datini, refuting a charge that the latter had defamed the commune. Why would a *contadino* of humble rank, say anything against his *signore*, the commune of Florence? Datini wrote to the Eight on Security that he treated with honor and deference the lowliest official of Florence, as though he were a father.[69] His home in Prato was open to all of the Florentine magistrates who visited there, and to all worthy citizens, and he kept rooms available for their use and comfort.

This deferential tone was typical of relationships throughout Florentine society, its egalitarian impulses notwithstanding. Sometimes in exaggerated and hyperbolic form, it appears in letters addressed to prominent statesmen by men of high and low station.[70] It appears, too, in the diaries of those citizens who, like Gregorio Dati and Giovanni Morelli, were on the periphery of the *reggimento*, yet not solidly established. When Dati (April 1412) was selected to the Sixteen, he felt unworthy of that honor and frightened by "the insatiable appetites of those in whom success breeds renewed ambition." He vowed that he would not "henceforth invoke the aid of any or attempt to get myself elected to public offices or to have my name included in new purses."[71] Writing a few years earlier, before he had gained any office or political distinction, Giovanni Morelli described his political values:

> He disliked evil things, and particularly those which led to the harm or dishonor of his commune, and those he censured whenever they came up in a discussion. He would have sought to correct those with deeds, if he had been in a position of power. He endeavored to live honestly, without ever opposing . . . those who governed [the commune]. With respect to the regime, with his soul and body and with words and deeds, he always held firm to those worthy Florentines from ancient families. . . . He never had any thought, or desired anything more, than the honor and exaltation of their regime. . . . Up to this time, it has not pleased God to permit him to demonstrate that good will that he has always maintained toward

[68] *Lettere di un notaro a un mercante*, ed. Guasti, I, 64, 15 July 1394.

[69] *Ibid.*, I, 288–89, 23 Oct. 1400: "che a uno minimo famiglio da Firenze io fo onore."

[70] Brucker, *Renaissance Florence*, 99–100.

[71] *Libro segreto*, 71–72, trans. in *Two Memoirs of Renaissance Florence*, 125–26.

the commune and toward its worthy servants and merchants, but it may be presumed that God will grant him that opportunity soon. . . .[72]

Giovanni's loyalty to the regime was finally rewarded, in 1409, by his selection to the Sixteen and, fifteen years later, to the Signoria.[73]

THE POLITICAL ELITE

Buonaccorso Pitti's autobiography suggests a life style, and a temperament, quite different from that of Giovanni Morelli and Gregorio Dati. The latter were parvenus, fearful and insecure, and eager to win the favor of the leadership. Pitti's status within Florentine society and the *reggimento* was much more solid. He was descended from a landowning family in the Valdipesa; his ancestors emigrated to Florence sometime in the thirteenth century and prospered from the manufacture of woolen cloth.[74] A Pitti first sat in the Signoria in 1283, and regularly thereafter; in 1411, seven members of the clan became eligible for the priorate.[75] Buonaccorso's opposition to the popular regime of 1378–1382 had enhanced his reputation as a Guelf conservative; his knowledge of France and the royal court, gained from years of living and trading there, had qualified him for important diplomatic assignments. His political career began in 1396, when he decided to give up his mercantile activities abroad for the sedentary life of a cloth manufacturer in Florence.[76] First entering the Signoria in July 1399, he was thereafter a prominent and active member of the *reggimento*: prior again in 1404; a member of the colleges in 1398, 1403, 1405; standard-bearer of justice in 1422; captain of Pistoia in 1399, vicar of the Valdinievole in 1404, captain of Pisa in 1409, *podestà* of San Gimignano in 1417 and Montepulciano in 1419; ambassador to France in 1396 and 1407, to Germany in 1401, to Rome in 1410, to Venice in 1421.[77] When not abroad on a diplomatic mission or a captaincy in the

[72] Morelli, *Ricordi*, 195–97. Morelli complained that, in the 1393 scrutiny, his family suffered discrimination at the hands of "parecchi nostri vicini cattivi," but he added that "Idio faccia manifesto che è guelfo e chi non è;" *ibid.*, 337.

[73] *Delizie*, XIX, cxi–cxiii.

[74] *Cronica di Buonaccorso Pitti*, 7–10. The classic description of that immigrant group in J. Plesner, *L'émigration de la campagne à la ville libre de Florence au XIIIe siècle* (Copenhagen, 1934).

[75] *Tratte*, 45, ff.6r–7r, 13r–15r.

[76] Pitti, *Cronica*, 93–94.

[77] *Ibid.*, 110–14, 116–30, 135–43, 149–54, 159–61. Pitti's other offices included the Eight on Security (twice), the *operai* of the cathedral (four times), captain of Castrocaro and Pisa, and *podestà* of Prato; *ibid.*, 195ff.

dominion, Buonaccorso was regularly called to the palace to advise the Signoria on policy. The protocols show that he spoke in these *pratiche* regularly. His neighbor, Migliore Migliori, testified to the solid reputation of the Pitti, "worthy and respected merchants of this city," and stated further that Buonaccorso enjoyed a status as high as anyone in Florence, "and that he has achieved more honors in the city, in Germany and in France, than any other citizen. . . ."[78]

Buonaccorso Pitti's colleague on his Roman mission to King Ladislaus in 1410 was Jacopo Salviati, who left a written record of his political career from 1398 to 1411. The Salviati were cloth manufacturers from Santa Croce; they had been represented in the Signoria twenty-seven times between 1297 and 1378. Eight Salviati qualified for the supreme executive in the 1411 scrutiny. Jacopo himself sat only once in the Signoria (May–June 1398),[79] but he played a very prominent role in the *reggimento* as statesman, diplomat, and administrator. Although he was frequently sent abroad on important diplomatic missions, his specialty was military affairs. He was probably the most knowledgeable, and certainly the most trusted, of the citizens sent by the Signoria and the war *balìa* to accompany Florentine armies in the field. Twice, in 1404 and again in 1409, he was himself elected to the war magistracy, a distinction accorded to only a few citizens.[80] The campaign he organized in the summer of 1404 against the Ubertini in their Apennine strongholds was so successful that he was knighted by the republic.[81] Salviati also commanded Florentine troops in the Pisan *contado* prior to the reconquest of that city in September 1406. From the time of his first election to the war magistracy in 1404 until his untimely death in the plague year of 1411, he was a full-time public servant. He was sent on seven important missions to France, Genoa, Lucca, Ferrara, Rome, and Naples; he was vicar of Anghiari and Firenzuola and captain of Pistoia, Pisa, and Arezzo.[82] Most indicative, perhaps, of his status in the *reggimento* and his reputation for integrity was his election in 1406 as *accoppiatore*, responsible for designating those citizens who merited the office of standard-bearer of justice, and

---

[78] *AP*, 4265, f.5r, 5 Dec. 1412. See below, 362.

[79] *Tratte*, 45, ff.45r–46v; *Delizie*, xviii, 185–86. Salviati mistakenly wrote that he had qualified for the Signoria in 1382; he did not become eligible until 1391; *ibid.*, xvi, 174; *Tratte*, 395, f.85v.

[80] *Delizie*, xviii, 218, 311–12.

[81] *Ibid.*, 220–24. The provision authorizing the conferment of knighthood is in *Prov.*, 93, f.93r. See Morelli's laudatory comments about Salviati's conduct in that campaign; *Ricordi*, 412–13.

[82] *Delizie*, xviii, 230, 256, 262, 273, 283–84, 290, 302, 332, 338, 343.

those who qualified for the special pouch or *borsellino* from which some priors were drawn.[83]

Measured by such indices as officeholding, the reception of honors, and public visibility, as well as by the more subjective criterion of civic opinion, both Pitti and Salviati belonged to the regime's "inner circle." They were descendants of ancient Guelf families that had long been prominent in public affairs. In addition to qualifying for the Signoria in 1391 and 1411, and presumably all those held between those dates, they had each received even higher honors as standard-bearer of justice, ambassador, member of the war *balìa*.[84] But the most useful criterion for identifying those citizens who belonged to the ruling elite was participation in the *pratiche*, the special meetings of citizens convened by the Signoria to elicit advice on problems confronting the government. In the thirty-seven *pratiche* that were assembled in the year 1410, a total of 153 citizens were recorded as speakers, though a substantially larger number attended. Most of these *pratiche* were small, averaging about twenty members; only on rare occasions were groups of one or two hundred convened to enable the Signoria to obtain a broad sampling of civic opinion.[85] One-half (79 of 153) of "those who were called" (*richiesti*) spoke only once that year, while eleven citizens made ten or more speeches. Piero Baroncelli spoke thirty times, in nearly every *pratica*; Maso degli Albizzi, Filippo Corsini, Cristofano Spini, Jacopo Malegonelle, and Niccolò da Uzzano intervened frequently enough to indicate that they attended most of these sessions.[86] These six men were all solidly established in the *reggimento*'s inner circle, as were fifty others who, during the twelve-year period from 1403 through 1414, spoke in twenty or more *pratiche*.[87]

[83] *Ibid.*, 250–51. On the office of *accoppiatore*, see Rubinstein, *Government of Florence*, 30–52; on the *borsellino*, above, 92.

[84] That these offices conferred a special distinction, beyond that bestowed on those who were priors, is suggested by a plan submitted in 1502 to create a special council of citizens who had been either a standard-bearer of justice, a member of a war *balìa*, or an ambassador; Rosemary Devonshire Jones, *Francesco Vettori* (London, 1972), 67.

[85] E.g., 21 in the *pratica* of 20 Apr. 1414, 15 on 10 May, 20 on 19 May, 32 on 16 July; *CP*, 41, ff.89r, 92v, 96r, 119v. A very large *pratica* was convened on 17 Feb. 1413; *CP*, 40, ff.175v–177v, in which 66 men spoke. A Sienese ambassador reported a *pratica* of more than 1000; *Conc.*, 1877, no. 79, 3 Jan. 1411; another wrote (April 1430) that he had addressed a *pratica* of 500 citizens; *ibid.*, 1918, no. 21.

[86] Maso spoke 18 times; Filippo Corsini, 20; Spini, 17; Malegonelle, 16; Niccolò da Uzzano, 14. Others who intervened often in these debates were Paolo Biliotti, Agnolo Pandolfini, Antonio Mangioni, Matteo Tinghi.

[87] Although several scholars have suggested that participation in the *pratiche* was a key to defining political status in Florence, Dale Kent is the first to identify the ruling group between 1429 and 1433 by this criterion, and to analyze the social,

These fifty-seven men can tentatively be designated as the elite, the inner circle, of the *reggimento* in 1411.[88] In addition to their qualifications for, and holding of, high office, they received special recognition for their political wisdom and expertise by being invited regularly to participate in the formulation of policy. The number of their appearances in the *pratiche* was a rough but reliable guide to their standing in the *reggimento*. At the apex of the hierarchy were five men who spoke in more than one hundred *pratiche* between 1403 and 1414: Filippo Corsini, Piero Baroncelli, Cristofano Spini, Maso degli Albizzi, and Rinaldo Gianfigliazzi. Just below them was a cluster of fourteen statesmen—including Antonio Alessandri, Gino Capponi, Agnolo Pandolfini, Lorenzo Ridolfi, Niccolò da Uzzano, Bartolomeo Valori—who made more than fifty speeches in these years.

Limiting membership in the elite to those who spoke in twenty *pratiche* is arbitrary, and it excludes some citizens whose political standing, when measured by other criteria, was very high.[89] These additions include twelve citizens who were selected at least once to the war *balìa* between 1395 and 1414, and six whose frequent selection as standard-bearer of justice or ambassador were indications of their high standing in the *reggimento*.[90] The final addition to this political elite is Ser Viviano di Neri Viviani, the notary of the *Riformagione*, who was the most powerful figure in the permanent bureaucracy after Salutati's death in 1406.[91] Ser Viviano's influence extended beyond

economic, and political characteristics of this elite. I acknowledge my debt to her in this analysis of the elite of a generation earlier. She counted 64 citizens who spoke in at least 30 *pratiche* in these years; "Reggimento," *Renaissance Quarterly*, xxviii. Peter Herde has also stressed the significance of the *pratiche* as a source for identifying the political elite: "Politische Verhaltensweisen der Florentiner Oligarchie 1382–1402," in *Geschichte und Verfassungsfüge: Frankfurter Festgabe für Walter Schlesinger*, 178.

[88] The composition of this elite changed continually, as its members died and were replaced. Among the prominent figures in the inner circle who had died by 1411 (and thus are not included in this sample) are: Filippo Magalotti, Tommaso Sacchetti, Leonardo Beccanugi, Bardo Mancini, Lorenzo Machiavelli, Agnolo Spini, Matteo Tinghi, and Andrea Vettori.

[89] Cf. Herde's comments: "Politische Verhaltensweisen," 185.

[90] In this category were: Rinaldo degli Albizzi, Giovanni Aldobrandini, Sandro Altoviti, Francesco and Tommaso Ardinghelli, Filippo Arrigucci, Niccolò Busini, Lotto Castellani, Barduccio Cherichini, Niccolò Davanzati, Neri Fioravanti, Filippo and Jacopo Guasconi, Bartolomeo Popoleschi, Schiatta Ridolfi, Nofri di Palla Strozzi, Giovanni Serristori, and Ubaldo Ubertini. These officeholders all participated in the *pratiche*, but less frequently than some of their colleagues.

[91] See the letters of Sienese ambassadors concerning the prominence of Ser Viviano and Salutati; *Conc.*, 1819, no. 66; 1843, no. 16; 1858, no. 28; 1868, no. 77.

administrative routine to politics and policy, even though he was never qualified for the Signoria.[92]

Sienese ambassadors were very shrewd observers of the Florentine political scene; in their correspondence they identified several members of the inner circle. These envoys had formal audiences with the Signoria and (when it existed) with the war magistracy, but much of their business was transacted with auditors (*uditori*) who were appointed by the Signoria to negotiate with foreign diplomats. Often identified by name in the despatches, these men were largely recruited from "the most prominent and knowledgeable citizens;"[93] of one group of nine *uditori*, "it could be said," a Sienese ambassador informed his government, "that they are the flower of Florence."[94] Official contacts were supplemented by private meetings with citizens who visited the ambassadors in their lodgings, or encountered them in the palace and occasionally in the streets.[95] In October 1406, the ambassador mentioned the names of eight men, all from the elite, with whom he had conversed: Francesco Ardinghelli, Cristofano Spini, Lotto Castellani, Niccolò da Uzzano, Vieri Guadagni, Giovanni de' Medici, Maso degli Albizzi, and Ser Viviano Viviani.[96] They were all considered friends of Siena, promoting that city's interests in the palace, and supplying the ambassadors with information about Florentine politics.[97] The ambassadors also solicited the friendship of Niccolò da Uzzano, "an eminent and worthy citizen," and of Maso degli

---

One ambassador described Ser Viviano as a *buono e valente cittadino*; *ibid.*, 1856, no. 22.

[92] In the 1382 scrutiny, Ser Viviano was nominated for the Signoria "et noluit ire ad partitum, quia retinebat secretum scruptinii"; *Delizie*, XVI, 179. His sons were nominated in the 1411 scrutiny but did not qualify; *Tratte*, 45, ff.51r–52r. One son, Francesco, was a prominent lawyer; Martines, *Lawyers and Statecraft*, 492.

[93] "De' più principali e intendenti cittadini"; *Conc.*, 1887, no. 29; 1911, no. 82. For the identity of these *uditori*, *ibid.*, 1815, no. 12; 1819, no. 66; 1824, no. 20; 1857, no. 66. With one exception (Jacopo di Matteo Ciachi), those identified as *uditori* all belonged to the inner circle. Most of the *uditori* identified for the years 1428–33 also belonged to the elite: 17 of 24 named in *ibid.*, 1914, no. 90; 1930, no. 42, 44, 53; Kent, "Reggimento," *Renaissance Quarterly*, XXVIII, 604–05.

[94] *Conc.*, 1930, no. 44, 30 July 1433.

[95] On visits to hotels, *ibid.*, 1830, no. 47, 13 March 1392; 1843, no. 16; 1856, no. 22. On the contact between a Sienese ambassador and the chancellor, Leonardo Bruni, *ibid.*, 1916, no. 30, 21 June 1429.

[96] *Ibid.*, 1863, no. 98, 28 Oct. 1406.

[97] Niccolò Dardi, a Sienese ambassador, described one of his informants as "uno de' maggiori cittadini di questa città et capo di parte a cui io o parlato più volti de' fatti nostri et truovolo molto bene disposto, il nome di quale io non voglio commettare ala pena"; *ibid.*, 1914, no. 50, 18 Aug. 1429.

Albizzi, "one of the most astute men of this city who understands more than he is willing to reveal. . . ."[98] So exalted was the status of Maso and Niccolò, and a handful of their peers, that they engaged in private diplomacy, by sending personal messages, usually requests for favors for themselves and their clients, to foreign governments.[99]

Those citizens who formed Florence's political elite were thus distinguished by their success in officeholding, by their frequent tenure of important magistracies, and by their prominent role in the consultative, or policy-making, dimension of government. Most were very active and visible in both spheres, although there were some exceptions to this generalization. Piero Baroncelli's distinction as an orator was paralleled by his success in elections: five times a member of the war magistracy, three times standard-bearer of justice.[100] The merchant Francesco Federighi was less eminent though still very influential; he appeared in more than twenty *pratiche*, was twice elected to the war *balìa*, and in 1406 was standard-bearer of justice.[101] Although the merchant Giovanni Orlandini and the lawyer Stefano Buonaccorsi were frequent speakers in the debates, neither achieved any success in the scrutinies, or in any of the important magistracies.[102] Filippo Giugni was four times a standard-bearer, and once a member of the war *balìa*, but he was apparently loath to address the *pratiche*.[103] The elite did furnish most of the personnel of the war *balìe*, as well

[98] *Ibid.*, 1853, no. 83, 20 Aug. 1404; 1860, no. 1, 2 Jan. 1405.

[99] In the archives of the *Concistoro* in Siena are autograph letters written by Buonaccorso di Lapo Giovanni; *ibid.*, 1814, no. 22, 31, 38; Cristofano Spini, *ibid.*, 1877, no. 38, 39; 1880, no. 14, 22; Giovanni di Messer Rinaldo Gianfigliazzi, 1866, no. 69; Ridolfo Peruzzi, 1906, no. 12; Cosimo de' Medici, 1911, no. 93. In the *carteggio* of Paolo Guinigi are replies to letters from Rinaldo Gianfigliazzi, Gino Capponi, Bartolomeo Valori, Niccolò da Uzzano, Matteo Castellani, Rinaldo degli Albizzi, Palla Strozzi and Giovanni de' Medici; *Carteggio di Paolo Guinigi, 1400–1430*, ed. L. Fumi and E. Lazzareschi (Lucca, 1925), 32, 37, 40, 45, 62, 68–69, 72, 93–95, 119, 127.

[100] Lauro Martines has discussed officeholding as an aspect of political distinction; *Social World*, ch. 4; and his profiles of prominent statesmen demonstrate its importance; *ibid.*, 205–10, 224–26, 313–14; and *Lawyers and Statecraft*, 482–84.

[101] Had Federighi not died in 1411, the number of his interventions in the debates would have been much higher. Testimonials to his power and prestige in *Lettere di un notaro a un mercante*, i, 45–46, 49–50, 138, 143, 200, 278, 437.

[102] Orlandini and Buonaccorsi both spoke more than 20 times. They did not qualify in the 1411 scrutiny; *Tratte*, 45, f.82r.

[103] Perhaps Giugni was a poor speaker. Another prominent figure who spoke rarely (7 times in 1403 and not thereafter) was Lotto Castellani, four times elected to the war *balìa*, and standard-bearer of justice in 1404. A professional soldier, Lotto was often away from Florence on military service; *Commissioni di Rinaldo degli Albizzi*, i, 255.

as a substantial portion of the diplomatic assignments. Thirty-five of the seventy-six were chosen at least once to the war magistracy between 1395 and 1414; they filled most of the places that were not reserved for magnates and artisans.[104] And forty-eight held the office of standard-bearer of justice: Filippo Corsini, Lapo Niccolini, and Giovanni Aldobrandini, five times each; Nofri Bischeri, Vanni Castellani, and Filippo Giugni on four occasions.[105] Nearly two-thirds received at least one ambassadorial appointment, but the lack of special skills required of diplomats apparently disqualified some citizens who were otherwise prominent in Florentine politics.[106] Knights and lawyers were especially recruited for embassies, since their titles and status endowed their missions with dignity, and their forensic and legal talents were indispensable for negotiations.[107]

In this cadre of political luminaries were men from sixty-six families, or approximately one-fifth of those constituting the *reggimento*.[108] Only seven lineages had more than one representative in this elite: the Castellani with five; the Guasconi, three; the Ardinghelli (brothers Tommaso and Francesco), Guadagni (brothers Vieri and Bernardo), Albizzi (Maso and his son Rinaldo), Gianfigliazzi (Rinaldo and his son Jacopo), and Strozzi, two each. Considering their size and prominence, the Albizzi, Strozzi, Peruzzi, Rucellai and Baroncelli had meager representation, while other great families—Guicciardini, Vettori, Canigiani, Acciaiuoli, Antellesi, Magalotti—had none at all.[109] The

---

[104] In each *balìa* were two lesser guildsmen and one magnate. The elite occupied 72 places in these *balìe*; only ten other *popolani*, alive in 1411, were chosen to this magistracy in the years 1395–1414; *Delizie*, XIV, 289–96; and *Manoscritti*, 271, unpaginated.

[105] These figures are collated from prior lists in Stefani's *Cronaca*, and the diaries of Ser Naddo di Ser Nepo, Jacopo Salviati and Giovanni Morelli; *Delizie*, XVIII, XIX. Eleven members of the elite were chosen three times to be standard-bearer of justice.

[106] For examples of diplomats and their assignments, see Martines, *Lawyers and Statecraft*, 316ff. Paolo Biliotti, Paolo Carnesecchi, Cristofano di Giorgio, and Jacopo Malegonelle spoke often in the *pratiche* but were never sent on diplomatic assignments.

[107] On the significance of eloquence in Florentine diplomacy, see E. Santini, *Firenze e suoi oratori nel Quattrocento* (Milan, 1922).

[108] Dale Kent has calculated that 325 families from the greater guilds were represented in the group of eligibles in the 1433 scrutiny; "Reggimento," *Renaissance Quarterly*, XXVIII, 589.

[109] Some of these families did have representatives in the elite who died before 1411: Luigi Guicciardini, Andrea Vettori, Filippo Magalotti; and some were soon to be represented again, by Luigi Guicciardini's sons Piero and Giovanni, and by Carlo di Messer Ristoro Canigiani. Two other Strozzi, Marco di Goro and Strozza di Rinaldo, were quite prominent in the *pratiche*; so too was Niccolò di Pepo Albizzi.

group contained no magnates, who were still excluded from the
leadership, and no lower guildsmen, who remained, as they had long
been, a passive element in Florentine politics.[110] Old houses represented in the Signoria for a century or more were very prominent, but
they did not monopolize the inner circle. One-sixth of the membership,
eleven men, belonged to families that first sat in the Signoria between
1343 and 1381, and eleven more entered the *reggimento* after 1382.[111]
Piero Firenze's father Giovanni had been a sword-maker who first
qualified for the Signoria in 1354. Piero later matriculated in the guild
of physicians and apothecaries, qualified for the priorate in 1382 and
repeatedly thereafter. He attended more *pratiche*, spoke more frequently, and held more prestigious offices than any of the Peruzzi. The
physician Maestro Cristofano di Giorgio Brandaglini was also prominent in the debates, if rather less successful as an officeholder; he
participated in more than sixty *pratiche* in these years.[112] In this bloc
of eleven "new men" who had moved into the regime's inner circle
were five lawyers and notaries, one physician, one banker, and two
rich merchants.

The nine lawyers and notaries in the elite constituted just ten percent of the total, but included in that number were three men—Filippo
Corsini, Lorenzo Ridolfi and Bartolomeo Popoleschi—of the highest
distinction in the *reggimento*.[113] Excluding this bloc of professional
men, the elite was drawn largely from the merchants, bankers, and
industrialists who had dominated Florentine politics since the thir-

[110] Messer Bartolomeo Popoleschi was the only descendant of magnates, the
Tornaquinci, in this group; twenty years later, Andrea Pazzi and Francesco Tornabuoni had broken through the barrier that had excluded magnates; Kent, "*Reggimento*," 605. The only artisan who might have qualified for the elite was Rosso
di Piero di Rosso, a tanner from S. Croce, who was thrice elected to the war
balìa. But Rosso died before 1411.

[111] Dale Kent's figures for the 55 families in the 1429–1433 elite: one-half in the
Signoria before 1342; 13 between 1343 and 1382; only eight after 1382; *ibid.*

[112] Cristofano's antecedents are not known. He was one of the few members of
the inner circle without kinsmen to support him; his four sons did not qualify for
the Signoria in 1411; *Tratte*, 45, ff.28r–30v. He had matriculated in the physicians'
guild sometime before 1382; R. Ciasca, *L'arte dei medici e speziali* (Florence, 1927),
705, 709. When a prior in 1399, he was described in these terms: "Egli è il piu, el
meglio e il da più che sia nelo uficio, e quasi il tutto"; *CRS*, 78 (*Badìa*), 315, unpaginated, 20 Dec. 1399.

[113] Besides Ser Viviano Viviani, the other prominent notary was Ser Paolo di
Messer Arrigo della Camera, who intervened in 50 *pratiche*. Other lawyers (Ricciardo del Bene and Alessandro Bencivenni) were on the fringes of the elite,
speaking often in the *pratiche*, or were on the verge, in 1411, of launching distinguished political careers: Carlo di Francesco Federighi, Giuliano Davanzati; Martines, *Lawyers*, 482, 492. The elite identified by Dale Kent for the years 1429–1433
included only five lawyers; "*Reggimento*," 604–05.

teenth century. It is not possible to determine precisely how many were actively and habitually engaged in business.[114] But the evidence —in guild and court records and in merchants' papers—suggests that the majority of these statesmen were also entrepreneurs. Twenty-eight, more than one-third of the total, were engaged in the production of woolen cloth at some times in their careers. Thirteen more were listed in the records of the Cambio guild as partners in banking firms, and another fourteen were identified as merchants in other sources.[115] Those with large investments of time and money in business were among the most active politicians: the bankers Piero Baroncelli, Cristofano Spini, Niccolò da Uzzano, Niccolò Barbadori, and Giovanni de' Medici; the merchants Gino Capponi and Antonio Alessandri; the cloth manfacturers Maso and Rinaldo degli Albizzi and Paolo Biliotti. In this group of seventy-six men, only fifteen were apparently never involved in business enterprises, but gained their livelihood from real estate, investments in the *monte*, and salaries from administrative and diplomatic posts.[116]

Although this elite did include some of Florence's richest citizens, the correlation between wealth and political status was not very close. Of the thirteen households with assessments exceeding 100 florins in the 1411 *novina*, only four were represented in the inner circle: Nofri Strozzi, Giovanni Serristori, Giovanni Orlandini, and Nofri Bischeri. If the sample is enlarged to include the fifty wealthiest households, the elite's portion is twelve, or approximately one-fourth.[117] The correlation is somewhat higher if the lineage instead of the household is the basis for representation, and if the perimeters of the inner circle are widened to include men on the periphery.[118] But even with these adjustments, there remained a large residue of Florentine wealth that did not belong to the governing elite: twenty-two of the fifty richest households were not represented in the *reggimento*, even by kinsmen.

[114] Matriculation lists do not identify entrepreneurs, but election as guild consul, or to the Merchants' Court, would be reserved for men who were actively involved in business.

[115] *Cambio*, 14; *Lana*, 32; *Merc.*, 1250, ff.62r, 225r, 386v, 653v; 1252, ff.134v–135r, 495r, 566r; 1253, 304r; *Catasto*, 65, ff.462v–465r, 471v–475r; 66, ff.76v–81r; 72, ff.211r–214r; 73, ff.141r–143r; 77, ff.383r–389r.

[116] The Castellani were not active in business in the *quattrocento*, nor was Agnolo Pandolfini, except perhaps early in his career; *Catasto*, 80, ff.35r–38v.

[117] The 1411 *novina* is in *Pres.*, 2750–64.

[118] Thus, Niccolò di Buono Busini's brother Nofri, who was not active in politics, had a much higher assessment than Niccolò: 78 fl. to 27 fl. Francesco di Messer Simone Tornabuoni, assessed at 146 fl., moved into the inner circle after 1411, as did Piero di Messer Luigi Guicciardini, assessed at 76 fl.

Of the one hundred wealthiest households in each quarter, as determined by the assessments levied in the 1411 *novina*, only one-fourth qualified for the Signoria in the scrutiny held in that year.[119] Forming the largest bloc of ineligibles were magnates who still, after more than a century, were excluded from high office. In the quarter of Santa Croce, for example, seventy-four households were assessed ten florins or more in the 1411 *novina*. Seven were magnates; ten were from families (Alberti, Rinuccini, Bastari, Covoni) that had been excluded from the *reggimento* for political reasons; a half-dozen others were recent immigrants from the *contado*. These rich men had no voice in politics while, conversely, a surprisingly large number of the most powerful men in the *reggimento* were poor. Sandro Altoviti's assessment was one florin, lower than that paid by many artisans. Alessio Baldovinetti, Paolo Biliotti, Rinaldo Rondinelli, and Francesco Leoni—all in the inner circle—paid just over two florins. Three of the "new men"—Ser Paolo della Camera, Stefano Buonaccorsi, and Cristofano di Giorgio— paid very small assessments that reflected their low economic status, at least by comparison with their wealthy patrician colleagues.[120]

This data suggest that family status was much more important than wealth in attaining the highest levels in the political hierarchy, but that it was not sufficient to guarantee access to the inner circle. As men competed for membership in the elite, personal qualities became increasingly significant, as did particular skills and expertise in the art of government. The recognition of such qualities explains the rise to eminence of Ser Paolo della Camera, Cristofano di Giorgio, and Agnolo Pandolfini—and Niccolò Benozzo Grasso's more frequent membership in the *pratiche* than his neighbors from older and more illustrious houses: Canigiani, Quaratesi, Mozzi, Gherardini Giani, Falconi.[121] The traits these men possessed—or were thought by their peers to possess—were often mentioned in the debates concernnig election to important magistracies or the selection of counselors. Invariably the criteria included loyalty to the regime and to Guelf ideals, a commitment to the public weal greater than any private interest, moral integrity, and wisdom. Men should be chosen for the war magistracy, Antonio Alessandri said in 1417, "who are very knowledgeable;

[119] The ratio is very close to that calculated by Dale Kent for the 1433 scrutiny; "Reggimento," *Renaissance Quarterly*, XXVIII, 597.

[120] These men paid assessments between 3 and 4 fl.; Nofri Strozzi paid 235 fl., Giovanni Serristori, 209. The highest in the city was Gabriello Panciatichi's 1000 fl. For the modest wealth of Piero Beccanugi, see Martines, *Social World*, 81–84.

[121] They all lived in the *gonfalone* of Scala, quarter of S. Spirito. Niccolò was the only member of his small family (5 nominees) to qualify in 1411; *Tratte*, 45, ff.1r–3v.

who possess authority, experience, and prestige; who are affluent; and who in any conflict between public and private interest will always opt for the general welfare."[122] Citizens invited to the *pratiche* should be "prominent in the regime, of ancient Guelf lineage, and experienced," so Filippo Arrigucci defined his civic model, and Dino Gucci stressed the virtues of prudence and judgment as well as expertise.[123] The ideal envisaged by these men was a combination of social distinction, strength of character, and the maturity and wisdom that come from long experience in public affairs.[124] These qualities were summarized neatly by one Signoria in a diplomatic memorandum: "It seemed useful to us to send a man with expertise and good judgment, who would understand what was necessary to do in this serious matter and, moreover, who was held in such repute by our citizens that he would enjoy their trust and would be capable of clearing up doubts in everyone's minds. . . ."[125]

Maso degli Albizzi's career is more visible than those of most of his associates in the inner circle. Born in 1343, he married (1367) Bartolemea di Andrea Baldesi, daughter of a wealthy merchant and Parte stalwart of the pre-Ciompi period. Matriculated in the Lana guild in 1365, he was still operating a cloth-manufacturing shop in 1390, and the records of the guild also reveal details of his investments in fulling mills and stretching sheds.[126] Maso was involved in a large number

[122] *CP*, 43, f.139r. For similar statements, see *ibid.*, 21, f.62r; 25, f.17v; 31, f.58r; 37, ff.18r, 64r; 40, ff.49r, 50r; 42, f.36r; and Gino Capponi's *ricordi*; *Miscellanea di studi offerti a A. Balduino e B. Bianchi*, 35.

[123] "Cives notabiles in regimine, antiqui guelfi et experti"; "una numerum civium non magnum sed discretorum et prudentium et qui ad consulendum sint apti et idonei"; *CP*, 43, f.101r; 44, f.156r. Cf. Cristofano di Giorgio's statement: "ex hominibus status guelfi et ad regimen consuetus et idoneus"; Niccolò di Benozzo Grasso, "cives notabiles, experti, docti et in statu antiquitatis et etate matura"; Antonio del Vigna, "quod domini eligant certum numerum civium, de quo eis videbitur, guelfis et amatoribus status et pacis dominationis, expertis, praticis et doctissimis"; *ibid.*, 43, ff.100v, 104v, 126r.

[124] "Quod domini eligant illos . . . qui non sint passionati"; "qui sint boni et fidei et animosi, tales qui audeant facere et ponere manum ubi oportet"; "eligantur cives non timidi"; "quod cives . . . sint viriles boni [et] non passionem habeant vel affectionem ad ea que non utilia sunt"; *ibid.*, 20, f.113v; 28, f.31v; 39, f.151r; 42, f.36r.

[125] ". . . a noi è paruto utile sopra tanta materia mandare huomo il quale sia experto et prudente et sappia bene intendere et discernere quanto bisogna in sì grave facto, et oltracciò, sta che fusse huomo di tale riverentia che nello nostro popolo gli fusse prestata larga fede, e fusse acto a chiarire le menti di ciascuno"; *SCMLC*, 4, f.127r.

[126] Maso's matriculation is in *Lana*, 20, f.84v. On his partnership, see *ibid.*, 82, f.36v; and his lease of a fulling mill and stretching shed; *ibid.*, 103, f.24v.

of legal disputes with his employees and business associates; one of his debtors went to prison at his instigation, while others had their property seized by guild officials to satisfy his claims.[127] In 1378 he was a defendant in a lawsuit brought by a widow named Cinella who charged that he had illegally occupied her farm. He and his kinsmen petitioned the Signoria (1383) to be separated legally from Francesco di Antonio degli Albizzi, who was forced into bankruptcy just two months later.[128] Maso was a grasping man who, a Sienese ambassador once reported, was not averse to receiving bribes. This combination of ruthlessness and greed doubtless contributed to the building of a large fortune that he bequeathed to his sons, Rinaldo and Luca, at his death in 1417.[129]

Though Maso was recognized as the political heir of his uncle Piero, executed as a conspirator in 1379, he did not immediately achieve a dominant position in the regime established in 1382. He was still quite young, under forty, and he was competing with more experienced politicians: Michele Castellani, Biagio Guasconi, Tommaso Soderini, Bettino Ricasoli, Carlo Strozzi.[130] The political turmoil and uncertainty of those years, when families and factions were competing for control of the regime, may have strengthened his determination to revenge his uncle's death. Though his complicity in the political disgrace of the Alberti cannot be conclusively proved, many Florentines believed that he was responsible for their exile.[131] A letter written by Guido, count of Modigliano, to Maso does implicate the latter in a vendetta against Tommaso Strozzi, who had sought refuge in Ferrara after the 1382 revolution. The Albizzi had asked Marquis Niccolò d'Este to expel Tommaso from his court, but the lord of Ferrara had resisted the pressure. "You know, Guido," the marquis told the count

---

[127] *Lana*, 85, f.32r; 86, ff.9r, 40r; 87, f.3r; 88, f.10r; *AP*, 3394, unpaginated, 1 July 1392; *Merc.*, 1186, ff.115r–118v; 1188, f.165r.

[128] *AEOG*, 818, ff.46v–112r; *Prov.*, 72, ff.26v–27v; A. Rado, *Maso degli Albizzi e il partito oligarchico in Firenze dal 1382 al 1393* (Florence, 1927), 203–05.

[129] Maso's *prestanza* assessment in 1403 was 17 fl., 10 s.; his was the 54th highest in S. Giovanni; Martines, *Social World*, 357. The 1433 *catasto* returns of his sons, Luca and Rinaldo, are in *Catasto*, 499, ff.484v–494v, 655v–661v. Luca had gross assets of 8533 fl. (net: 3677), and Rinaldo had gross assets of 12,803 fl. (net: 3198). Maso's susceptibility to bribery is suggested by a report from a Sienese diplomat, who was informed by Maso's business associate, a Jew named Gaio, that a gift of a piece of velvet would mollify him; see above, 201, n.65.

[130] These aspirants to political leadership were identified by Stefani, 923. Several died in the 1383 plague; *ibid.*, 957.

[131] Nearly 40 years later, Maso's son Rinaldo was accused of emulating his father: "Messer Rinaldo vorrà fare come fece il padre nel MCCCLXXXXIII, che volle fare tutte le sue vendette"; *GA*, 75, f.66or, 12 Oct. 1429.

of Modigliano, "I did not ask Messer Tommaso to come here, nor did I receive him because I had need of him, and he did little enough for me. But I welcomed him because he asked me for bread in such a manner that I could not refuse him."[132] Though Maso's status in the regime improved after 1387, he felt the need to bolster his image by embarking upon a bizzare journey to central Europe to join the Teutonic Knights in a crusade. He desired to participate in that enterprise (so the Signoria wrote to the Grand Master) to learn the arts of war, and to avoid softness and indolence.[133] But his real motive was to win the spurs of knighthood which, a contemporary chronicler reported, he received after killing a Saracen king while fighting, not with the Teutonic knights, but on the island of Rhodes. This account reveals the confusion that surrounded Maso's journey, and the skepticism felt by many Florentines about his military exploits. On the morning after his triumphal entry into Florence, placards appeared in the streets denouncing him as a traitor for pretending that he had fought against the Saracens in Rhodes, when in reality his knighthood was a gift from Giangaleazzo Visconti.[134]

Throughout the 1390s, and particularly after the crisis of 1393, Maso's status in the regime became increasingly secure, though his prestige did suffer temporarily from his alliance with the Avignonese faction.[135] Signs of his eminence appear in diplomatic correspondence, and in letters that he received from abroad. A Sienese ambassador wrote in September 1388 that Maso, "who is a distinguished citizen," had asked him to intercede with his government on behalf of an imprisoned relative. Sixteen years later (1404), another delegation of Sienese diplomats wrote to their superiors that they intended to "inform Messer Maso that we have been sent [to Florence] solely on ac-

---

[132] *BNF, Fondo principale*, II, III, 434, no. 140, 10 Nov. 1385. Tommaso degli Strozzi had just died in Ferrara.

[133] *SCMC*, 21, ff.52r–52v, 24 Sept. 1388. See a similar letter to the duke of Austria, requesting a safe-conduct for Maso; *ibid.*, f.52r. On this mysterious journey, see Rado, *Maso degli Albizzi*, 156–60.

[134] *Panc.*, 158, f.156v. The chronicler described the elaborate celebrations in the Albizzi palace. In a letter dated 20 June 1389, Jacopo di Ser Piero wrote to Manno degli Agli: "Qui si fa oggi una bellissima festa di giostra . . . per la tornata di Mess. Maso degli Albizzi, fatto nuovamente cavalieri in Prussia"; *Datini*, 1112, unpaginated.

[135] The cardinal of Ravenna, an emissary from Pope Clement VII, visited Florence in Sept. 1389: "Si montò a Rovezano a luogo di messer Maso di Lucha degli Albizzi e se gli era bene stato vicitato da cittadini antipapisti a Enpoli molti più era visitato a Rovezano. . . . Molto spiaque a cittadini che voleano vivere in pace l'arienta che fè a Rovezano, e gran biasimo ne seghui a messer Maso di Lucha"; *Panc.*, 158, f.157r.

count of the confidence that you have in him personally."[136] From all over Tuscany, clients wrote to Maso for help. The count of Poppi thanked him for his support and promised him that, like a true son, he was ready to obey his slightest wish. The bishop of Città di Castello appealed to him for assistance in his quarrel with an Aretine magnate, Carlo Tarlati di Pietramala. Seeking the office of Florentine *podestà*, the count of Macerata asked Maso to promote his candidacy, and informed him of his willingness "to demonstrate by my actions that I am totally at your will, pleasure, and command."[137] These letters indicate that Maso could help his friends; others suggest that he could be a formidable enemy. In 1397 some members of the Adimari family had antagonized Maso, who retaliated by picking quarrels with their relatives who lived abroad. From Bologna, Papino Adimari wrote to Maso to refute the rumor that he had slandered him. In another letter sent from Faenza to a kinsman in Florence, Giovanni di Cipolla Adimari expressed his puzzlement over Maso's hostility, and categorically denied the latter's accusation that he had maligned him.[138]

Prior to 1402, Maso's political strategy was a combination of astuteness in recruiting friends and allies, and ruthlessness in destroying his enemies. But after Giangaleazzo Visconti's death his reputation was so great, and his position in the regime so unassailable, that he could play a more benign role in Florentine politics. With his sharp instinct for preserving his authority by avoiding discord and confrontations, he allowed his more opinionated colleagues to speak out on controversial issues, and waited until he could perceive a trend before publicizing his views. But if conflict could not be avoided, he acted decisively to break stalemates. Two letters illustrate his methods. In January 1404, Rinaldo Gianfigliazzi wrote to Maso, who was then standard-bearer of justice, asking him to use his influence to secure the release of his client, one Jacopo di Messer Bertoldo of Montepulciano, who had been sentenced to life imprisonment for some unspecified crime. In a postscript to this letter, Rinaldo expressed his gratitude to Maso for arranging his son Papino's election to the magistracy for internal security. "The time may come," Rinaldo wrote, "when I can do a favor for one of your sons, as you have done for mine."[139] The second letter was addressed to Maso by his son Luca, who was writing on behalf of a political associate identified only as Alessandro. The Signoria was then debating methods for raising

[136] *Conc.*, 1824, no. 4; 1859, no. 85.

[137] BNF, *Fondo principale*, II, III, 434, no. 23, 77, 85.

[138] *Ibid.*, no. 147, 148, 152.

[139] BNF, *Fondo principale*, II, III, 434, no. 38.

money, and Alessandro was soliciting Maso's opinion, so that "together with the others whom you know, an agreement can be reached, so that all will speak with one tongue." Since Maso and his closest relatives were not represented in the magistracies that would vote on these measures, their friends were asking for instructions from their leader and patron. "So write me what, in your opinion, should be done," Luca asked his father, "and by what means a consensus can be achieved."[140]

Rinaldo Gianfigliazzi's status in the *reggimento* was equal to Maso's. A descendant of magnates who had been excluded from the Signoria until 1382, Rinaldo had neither the wealth nor the family support that Maso enjoyed.[141] The Gianfigliazzi, however, were connected by marriage with many ancient lineages, and Rinaldo received some help from these alliances.[142] But his standing in the regime throughout the 1380s and early 1390s was quite precarious. In 1386 he was the target of an anonymous denunciation accusing him of adultery and of Ghibelline sympathies.[143] In March 1394 he committed a serious tactical error by contracting a marriage between his daughter Madelena and the son of Niccolò Alberti, whose family had just been excluded from the *reggimento*. He was criticized by many citizens, the Minerbetti chronicler reported, and particularly those who had joined him in the campaign against the Alberti six months earlier. "For this he was judged a man of little faith, and he was less respected than before."[144] At this low point in his political career he wrote to Donato Acciaiuoli, complaining that he had been publicly maligned by the Signoria and the colleges for pressing Florence's claims to territory in the Apennines adjacent to Castrocaro. He angrily denied the charge that he had a personal interest in the affair, insisting that he was motivated solely by

[140] *Ibid.*, no. 28, 15 March 1408. Alessandro was probably a neighbor of the Albizzi, possibly Alessandro di Ugo Alessandri. He was apparently the spokesman for a group of Albizzi partisans, perhaps their neighbors in the *gonfalone* of Chiave. "Credo che colegi del gonfalone sieno uniti acciò che essi dilibera; pero chè nuovi Dodici sono Luca di Manetto [da Filicaia] e Maso degli Alessandri."

[141] Rinaldo was one of four ex-magnates who received *popolano* status and who was authorized by the 1382 *balìa* to retain his original name and coat of arms; *Balìe*, 17, f.23v. He was not an active businessman and his economic status was quite modest; Martines, *Social World*, 80. For an evaluation of his character, see G. Cavalcanti, *Istorie fiorentine*, ed. Polidori (Florence, 1839), II, 461–62.

[142] On Gianfigliazzi marriages, see *Carte dell'Ancisa*, LL, ff.622r–624r; MM, ff.38v–39r.

[143] *AEOG*, 1014, ff.13v–15r.

[144] Minerbetti, *anno* 1393, ch. 27. Gianfigliazzi did attempt to break up the marriage but the girl refused to consider any other suitor; in 1396, the marriage was consummated; Alberti, *Passerini*, II, 86.

his concern for the republic's honor.[145] Although Rinaldo survived the vicissitudes of these years better than his "greatest friend" Acciaiuoli, he was haled into court (1397) by the Adimari, who were then seeking desperately to placate Maso degli Albizzi, and had to appeal to the Signoria for help in quashing the charges against him.[146] His political recovery was certainly abetted by Maso, whom he could address as an equal in 1403. Two letters sent to him in 1405 by Francesco Datini testify to his eminence. In language that was fulsome and obsequious even by the standards of the time and the genre, Datini appealed to Rinaldo (addressing him as *vostra magnificenza* and *carissimo mio padre*) to protect him from an enemy named Bartolo di Jacopo. He had been reluctant to approach the "magnificent and illustrious knight" with his petty concerns, Datini explained, because he felt unworthy. However, he had been encouraged by Rinaldo's request for a favor. When Gianfigliazzi responded positively to Datini's appeal, the latter wrote: "If I had a hundred tongues and a mouth of iron, I could not do justice to the honor and trust that you have shown me."[147]

Gianfigliazzi's eminence was recognized by friend and foe alike; he was more commonly mentioned as a target for assassination than Maso degli Albizzi. And to a greater degree than was true of his illustrious colleague, his standing in the *reggimento* was a function of his personality. Rinaldo was an aggressive partisan,[148] fiercely loyal to the regime; no citizen spoke more often or more passionately about the supremacy of public over private interest. He was quick to criticize any action by magistrates or councils that, in his judgment, weakened the *reggimento*. Infuriated by the votes of some councilors rejecting the imposition of a forced loan (1411), he said that they deserved to be punished for their intransigence.[149] He was a powerful orator whose eloquence, Cavalcanti wrote, earned him the sobriquet of *il gallo*, the rooster.[150] Blessed with exceptional rhetorical skills, he fre-

[145] *Acquisti e Doni*, 140, part 7, no. 82. Though undated, the letter was probably written in 1395 when the question of annexing Castrocaro was hotly debated in Florence; above, ch. III, 153–54.

[146] *CP*, 32, ff.115r–115v, 2 and 4 Apr. 1397. Speaking for the Sixteen, Niccolò da Uzzano said that the "casus ordinatus contra dominum Raynaldum displicet eis."

[147] *Lettere di un notaro a un mercante*, II, 37–40, 18 and 29 Jan. 1405.

[148] In Buonaccorso Pitti's view, the Gianfigliazzi led by Rinaldo were allied with the Ricasoli, Peruzzi, and Castellani to ruin him and his family; *Cronica*, 165–77.

[149] *CP*, 42, f.35r.

[150] Martines, *Social World*, 249. That phrase may not have been entirely laudatory.

quently assumed the role of spokesman for the inner circle, opening debates with appeals for an aggressive posture in foreign affairs, for large military expenditures, for territorial expansion, and for sacrifices by the citizenry to support these policies. Rinaldo was among the first to advocate war, and the last to accept the necessity of peace.[151] More rigid and inflexible than Maso, less concerned about economic and fiscal realities than most of his colleagues, Rinaldo was the republic's "most noble and renowned knight,"[152] who saw himself as a guardian of those traditional civic values that his ancestors had cherished in the past.

The political career of Niccolò da Uzzano was nearly coterminous with the regime; he made his first recorded speech in a *pratica* in 1387, and he died in 1431. The Uzzano were wealthy bankers from Santo Spirito; Niccolò's father Giovanni was the first member of his small lineage to enter the Signoria in 1363. The money that Niccolò inherited enabled him to marry his daughters to sons of prominent families: the Soderini and the Capponi.[153] But his wealth does not explain his rise to eminence, nor was his small family, so recently integrated into the *reggimento*, a decisive factor. His ascent to the highest levels of the regime was due to his personal qualities and, specifically, his expertise as counselor, magistrate, and diplomat. Five times he was chosen to the war *balìa*; he traveled to every important Italian capital on ambassadorial missions. In 1400 Lapo Mazzei wrote to Francesco Datini that Niccolò was the most useful friend that he could have in the city: "He is a man of courage, wisdom, and integrity; he is powerful and respected."[154] The priors described him in 1406 as "that noble man and our most trusted citizen," when instructing their ambassadors in Naples to investigate a Florentine who allegedly had defamed him.[155] Writing shortly before his death in 1420, Gino Capponi counseled his sons to ally themselves most closely with four prominent citizens, among whom was Niccolò da Uzzano. In 1429 he was described as a "distinguished and noble man and a citizen of great reputation . . . who possesses great authority in that city."[156] The qualities of mind and

---

[151] He was a member of the war *balìa* six times between 1395 and 1414.

[152] The phrase is in a letter addressed by Luigi Guicciardini to Donato Acciaiuoli; *Acquisti e Doni*, 140, part 7, no. 81.

[153] On Niccolò's marriage and early career, see A. Dainelli, "Niccolò da Uzzano nella vita politica dei suoi tempi"; *ASI*, xc (1932), 35–37. In 1427, he was one of the wealthiest men in Florence with gross assets of 50,896 fl.; *Catasto*, 64, ff.65v–75v.

[154] *Lettere di un notaro a un mercante*, i, 257. In another letter, Mazzei wrote: "Niccolò è savio uomo, e molto e oggi riputato che cognosca"; *ibid.*, 431.

[155] *SCMLC*, 3, f.69r, 5 Feb. 1406.

[156] *AP*, 4423, f.iv.

spirit that set him apart from most of his peers are noticeable in his speeches. He was fearless and outspoken, surpassed by none in his ability to analyze the complexities of political issues. He believed more strongly than many of his colleagues in free debate. "It is useful to hear controversy in discussions," he said on one occasion, and later he urged his colleagues in a *pratica* "to speak their minds."[157]

These men—Maso, Rinaldo, Niccolò—all achieved the highest eminence in the *reggimento*: their careers and personalities were exceptional. To observe the political role of a lesser figure like Forese Sacchetti, in the elite but not at its highest levels, provides a different perspective on Florentine politics. Information from hundreds of letters sent to Sacchetti by friends and clients illuminates some obscure aspects of the political system that are not so visible in the public records. Forese's antecedents were respectable, though not so distinguished as several other houses in Santa Croce: Peruzzi, Castellani, Baroncelli, Salviati. The family first entered the Signoria in 1335; in the 1411 scrutiny, Forese was one of five Sacchetti to qualify.[158] His father had been a member of the magistracy responsible for selling ecclesiastical property during the papal war of 1376–1378, and his uncle Giannozzo and cousin Jacopo were executed in 1380 for plotting against the guild regime.[159] Though his uncle Franco had achieved some fame as a poet and *novellista*, Forese's most prominent relative was his cousin, Messer Tommaso, whose political career was cut short by his untimely death in 1404.[160] A year later, Forese entered the Signoria for the first time. A letter from his friend Antonio Gherardini (July 1406) locates Forese's place in the regime with some precision: on the edge of the inner circle. Antonio described the campaign mounted by himself and Forese's other friends to obtain his election to the war *balìa*:

> Since my cousin Ubaldo [Ubertini] is standard-bearer of justice, and out of respect for your virtues, I have appealed to your friends to have you chosen. I have put special pressure on Ubaldo, so that I think he will help us. Three neighbors from your quarter have promised to support you . . . and from others to whom I have spoken, I have received encouraging responses. I have talked to your [friend] Cristofano Bagnesi . . . and also to Ser Piero di Ser

[157] *CP*, 44, ff.61v, 190r.

[158] *Tratte*, 45, ff.28r–29r. Forese's grandfather and namesake was the family's first representative in the Signoria.

[159] R. Trexler, "Who Were the Eight Saints?" *Renaissance News*, XVI (1953), 89; *Diar. anon.*, 402; Stefani, 799, 830.

[160] On Franco, see E. Li Gotti, *Franco Sacchetti* (Florence, 1940). In 1404, the year of his death, Tommaso Sacchetti was a frequent speaker in the *pratiche*.

Mino [the chancellor], and today I will mention this matter to Messer Cristofano Spini who, I believe, has great affection for you. Also I plan to talk to Cappone Capponi . . . who for the sake of kinship will do what he can.[161]

This election, Antonio concluded, would redound to Forese's honor; it would mark him as someone "acceptable to the palace,"[162] deemed worthy of the most exalted magistracies in the republic. Achieving that distinction was not simply a function of merit, but of a sustained effort by relatives, friends, and neighbors[163] to promote their candidate.

Forese was not elected to the war magistracy in 1406; the places for his quarter were filled by two members of that powerful clique formed by the Peruzzi, Baroncelli, and Ricasoli houses that dominated the political world of Santa Croce in these years.[164] Though not hostile to that formidable coalition, the Sacchetti were not closely connected to those great families. Forese was never chosen to the war *balìa*, nor did he ever qualify for the office of standard-bearer of justice. But he did obtain other important offices that (so his friends insisted) redounded to his honor. "I have heard that you are a member of the Ten [on Liberty]," Ser Barone di Michele wrote, "for which I rejoice, as I do for every honor that you achieve."[165] Papi Guidalotti took note of Forese's membership in the Eight on Security: "There are rumors that you are about to enter high estate. Take care of yourself so that you can serve yourself first, and then your friends."[166] Forese spoke in the *pratiche* with increasing frequency, on fifteen occasions in the years 1413 and 1414. Public records—scrutiny lists, the *Tratte* volumes that identify officeholders, the *Consulte e Pratiche*—trace the route by which Forese solidified his place in the *reggimento*.[167] His private correspondence throws additional light upon his status, and the means by which he enhanced it. His closest friend and political ally was his neighbor Cristofano Bagnesi, who saluted him as his "dearest and most

[161] CRS, 78 (Badìa), 323, no. 222.

[162] The phrase is Cavalcanti's; *Istorie fiorentine*, I, ch. 7.

[163] Cf. Tommaso Sacchetti's letter to Forese: "Operate de' parenti e degli amici e de' vicini"; *Ashb.*, 1842, I, no. 169, 3 May 1403.

[164] They were Antonio di Messer Luca da Panzano and Cionaccio Baroncelli; Minerbetti, *anno* 1406, ch. 10. Only one scrutiny list for the war *balìa* survives for these years; *Tratte*, 1160, ff.113r–116v, 25 Oct. 1401.

[165] *Ashb.*, 1842, I, no. 165, undated.

[166] CRS, 78 (Badìa), 323, f.229r, 29 Aug. 1409. Another letter referred to the *nobile uficio* that Sacchetti occupied; *ibid.*, f.230r.

[167] Forese's nephews Niccolò and Filippo, and Niccolò's son Andreuolo, were all in the Signoria; Niccolò was standard-bearer of justice in 1419.

honored and cherished *compare*."[168] Other citizens from prominent families addressed him in language that implied such strong bonds of friendship that they could ask for help. A powerful figure in the inner circle, Giovanni Bucelli, requested a service "for my love"; Maso degli Albizzi's nephew Filippo mentioned "the friendship that has always existed between you and our family." Bernardo Nardi referred to the great affection that Forese had shown toward his father. Papi da Verrazzano sent a plaintive appeal to Forese, for his help in gaining release from prison: "I know of no one, my lord, to whom I can turn in my hour of need with more security and trust than you, who are both able and willing to help your friends and servants. I am one of those who has always been, and always will be, completely devoted to you." Buoninsegna Machiavelli also asked Forese to arrange his release from prison. Neri Vettori wanted to succeed his dead father in a territorial magistracy; Filippo and Niccolò dell'Antella asked for Forese's help in lowering their taxes.[169]

Each of these letters represents a statement about a social and political relationship, in which the status of both parties—the petitioner and the recipient of his plea—was carefully gauged, as was too the precise nature of the bond linking them together. When the relationship was between equals and involved strong mutual obligations, then the appeal would be treated very seriously and a sustained effort made to satisfy the request. But if there was a wide disparity of status, or a weak and tenuous bond between the client and his putative patron, then the appeal would be less compelling and its prospects for success minimal. Piero di Messer Luigi Guicciardini enjoyed a higher place in the *reggimento* than did Sacchetti, so could fend off with placatory words the latter's petition on behalf of an acquaintance: "I excuse my inability to do more since, as you must know, I am always ready to do whatever I can for you and your friends."[170] Jacopo Baroncelli asked Sacchetti to intercede with the *podestà*, Francesco de' Coppoli, on behalf of his brother Gherardo who (Jacopo claimed) was being persecuted by the judge. Forese immediately wrote to Coppoli, with whom he was on intimate terms. The *podestà* replied that he had given Gherardo Baroncelli every consideration, "without violating equity or

---

[168] CRS, 78 (*Badìa*), 324, no. 93, 21 July 1412. For other letters from Cristofano, see *ibid.*, no. 89, 94, 201. Dale Kent places Bagnesi in the regime's inner circle in 1429; "Reggimento," *Renaissance Quarterly*, XXVIII, 604.

[169] CRS, 78, 324, no. 233; 326, no. 43, 335; 323, no. 216; 326, no. 1; 324, no. 59; *Ashb.*, 1842, I, no. 26. For other material on Sacchetti's clients, see my *Renaissance Florence*, 99–100.

[170] *Ashb.*, 1842, I, no. 52, 7 May 1427.

my honor," and added that he and his brother should be grateful for Sacchetti's solicitude. Though promising Forese that "in all of your affairs and those of your friends, I will do everything in my power," he would not quash the case against Baroncelli.[171]

Measuring the gradations of status and the strength of friendships was a fundamental part of a Florentine political education; one expert was Ser Lapo Mazzei, friend and adviser of Francesco Datini. In April 1401, he sent Datini (who was in Bologna) a draft of a petition for tax relief, to be copied and delivered to Niccolò da Uzzano, one of the officials responsible for the *prestanze* levies.[172] The petition began with the salutation, "honorable father," and concluded: "Niccolò, I am writing this with my own hand; keep it to shame me if you find that I have departed from the truth. May Christ give you grace to do His will, and the welfare and honor of your city." Ser Lapo then instructed Datini to write an identical letter to another member of the commission, Domenico Giugni, but to add a sentence which reflected their more intimate relationship.[173] Then, a similar document to Aghinolfo Popoleschi, but with a revision that gave more emphasis to Datini's resentment over his unjust treatment. "Then another to Nofri d'Andrea [del Palagio], similar to Niccolò's. Then in the same style, to Andrea di Messer Ugo [della Stufa], except that at the end of that letter, write as follows: 'Andrea, forgive me if I trouble you about this, which I am not doing without cause. . . .' Then write another to Francesco Federighi. . . . And in each letter, write this salutation: 'To so and so, my honorable father, in Florence.'" Three weeks later, Mazzei advised Datini to send letters to other members of that magistracy, or to their friends. Tommaso Soderini should be asked to speak to his neighbor, Matteo Tinghi, on Datini's behalf. Other letters, "each just a few lines," to Matteo Villani, Tommaso Rucellai, Bernardo and Vieri Guadagni, Domenico Corsi, Andrea della Stufa, Aghinolfo Popoleschi, Niccolò da Uzzano, "but do not write to Matteo Tinghi, to Vanni Rucellai or to Messer Filippo; I don't say that without good reason." Mazzei concluded his letter to Datini by advising him to pause a few days before renewing his campaign; then he should write that he has been pressed by his friends to petition again for relief, so that he would not be destroyed by the oppressive taxation.[174]

---

[171] *CRS*, 78, 324, no. 145, 338, 365. On Sacchetti's friendship with Coppoli, see my *Renaissance Florence*, 148–49.

[172] *Lettere di un notaro a un mercante*, I, 387–88.

[173] On that friendship, see my *Society of Renaissance Florence*, 82–83; and Guigni's letter to Datini, 26 Feb. 1401, *Datini*, 719, unpaginated.

[174] *Lettere di un notaro a un mercante*, I, 389, 4 May 1401.

THE NEW STYLE OF POLITICS

This analysis of the Florentine *reggimento* in the early fifteenth century has emphasized the emergence of a leadership elite that had subtly altered the political system—the ways in which the republic was governed. In 1382 the polity was still predominantly corporate though, as we have seen, the collective ethos and the institutions which embodied that spirit were weaker than they had been a half-century earlier. But policy decisions were still made collegially, and the sporadic attempts of certain groups and individuals to subvert that process were condemned, and sometimes penalized, by the citizenry. Men chosen to civic office regarded themselves primarily as representatives of corporate entities, and in their political behavior they subsumed their identities into that of the group. In the thirty years since the establishment of the regime, the corporate spirit had been further weakened, though never entirely extinguished. But as each year brought a new crisis—either an internal conspiracy to subvert the regime or a foreign effort to conquer it, or both—the pressures to modify the system intensified. How to strengthen the regime and to maintain control by the "good Guelfs" without destroying traditional liberties and customs became a crucial issue. Magistracies with special authority (*balìe*) were created to deal with major crises, but they aroused the hostility of many citizens who viewed them as threats to constitutional government.[175] Very gradually and unobtrusively, the regime was transformed without any major alteration of the institutional framework, through the establishment of a cadre of prominent citizens who formed a kind of unofficial *balìa* to guide the *reggimento* through these difficult years.

The intensity of this elite's commitment to the regime and the republican values that it symbolized distinguished it from earlier forms of civic leadership, which were usually linked to some party based on blood or ideology. These men, whose power depended in some part upon the numbers of their *amici e seguaci*, did not ignore competing claims to lineage, guild or faction.[176] But these claims

---

[175] On civic opposition to *balìe*, see below, 83, 119; Molho, *Florentine Public Finances*, 187, n.10; and the statements of Antonio Mangioni, "populus non libenter ad balias procedit, propter gesta hactenus"; and Rinaldo degli Albizzi, "balie odiose sunt populis"; *CP*, 41, f.109r; 46, f.31r.

[176] See my *Renaissance Florence*, 137–51; and Dale Kent's analysis of factions in the late 1420s; *Rise of the Medici*, ch. 3. See too a report by a Sienese observer in Aug. 1428: "et sia informata la V. M. che . . . l'uficio de' Signori da mezo questo mese in là, sicondo l'usanza dela città, non attenderà se non a cose di loro amici et particulari persone"; *Conc.*, 1914, no. 45.

usually ranked below the public interest in their system of priorities.[177] The strength of an individual's loyalty to the regime was indeed an important criterion for promotion to the inner circle. The pressures to demonstrate their patriotism impelled some citizens to proclaim their readiness to give their lives for the republic, or to announce that they had been impoverished by their sacrifices for liberty. This governing elite was also more stable than any other in the commune's history; no significant change in its composition occurred after Donato Acciaiuoli's exile in 1396. Once distinction was achieved in the *reggimento*, it was not normally surrendered until death; sons frequently replaced their fathers in the inner circle.[178] The stability of this political order would have astonished Dante, whose gibes about the inconstancy of his fellow-citizens were immortalized in the sixth canto of *Purgatorio*. This stablization of civic leadership fostered intimacy and cohesiveness among the leaders and, by comparison with past regimes, a remarkable degree of mutual trust. The trend toward more candid debate and a greater willingness to voice dissent, particularly noticeable after Salutati's death,[179] does suggest that the leaders felt more secure about their status in the *reggimento* than had their predecessors.

The *pratiche* are the key to this regime's methods and values, and to its resilience in the face of adversity. The debates became the institutionalized channel of communication for the elite, and the only legal means by which those statesmen not in office could offer counsel and guidance to successive priorates, whose members might be inexperienced and inept, or immobilized by personal enmities. The number of *pratiche* convened annually by the executive remained constant through the 1380s and 1390s, but then rose significantly after Giangaleazzo's death.[180] Civic representation in the meetings also increased during these years. Salutati identified 193 citizens as speaking in the

---

[177] Bartolomeo Valori's biographer, Luca della Robbia, commented on his refusal to seek a lower tax assessment for his relatives by marriage, the Macinghi; *ASI*, IV (1843), part 1, 251. Such behavior may have been exceptional.

[178] In the inner circle in 1430 were twelve men who had belonged to the elite 20 years before, and 17 others whose fathers or brothers had been members; Kent, "Reggimento," *Renaissance Quarterly*, XXVIII, 604–05. Peter Herde has noted the continuity in this elite as it formed after 1382; "Politische Verhaltensweisen," 178. He identifies some seventy citizens who were very prominent in the *pratiche* between 1382 and 1402. Sixteen were still alive in 1411; four others were the sons of former members of the elite.

[179] Salutati may have sought to minimize discord in his reports. Compare his minutes in *CP*, 26, *passim*, with those written by another notary, ff.188v–197r, whose reports contain more detail and suggest more disagreement.

[180] In 1385, 21 *pratiche* were held; in 1396, 17; in 1403, 34; in 1410, 37.

1385 *pratiche*; his successor as chancellor, Ser Piero di Ser Mino, recorded the names of 464 participants in the 1410 meetings. In the last fourteen months of the second war with King Ladislaus (April 1413–June 1414), 222 speakers are identified in the protocols; they delivered over 1000 speeches, or approximately seventy-five per month, a heavy forensic diet for the citizenry.[181]

The significant expansion, in space and in detail, of the record of these deliberations paralleled this trend toward more frequent *pratiche*.[182] Throughout his tenure as chancellor, responsible for keeping the minutes of these debates, Salutati wrote very brief summaries of the speeches. Usually just two or three lines, his statements were concise recommendations for action, unsupported by a rationale or an analysis of the problem and its context. Without explanation, the speakers recommended (or opposed) the introduction of a statute, the launching of a military expedition, the levy of a forced loan. Salutati's successors, on the other hand, wrote much lengthier and more elaborate reports.[183] An oration delivered by Maso degli Albizzi or Filippo Corsini in 1411 might require an entire page to summarize. While this change may be attributed in part to the different modes of reporting developed by the chancellors,[184] evidence from the protocols suggests that the style of political discourse was becoming more rhetorical. In April 1409, the chancellor Benedetto Fortini wrote that a *pratica* had been convened to hear "a very long oration by Piero

[181] Not everyone who participated in these debates was identified by the notaries who compiled the minutes. They were most scrupulous in reporting speeches by the eminent, and less concerned about those who spoke rarely; see Herde, "Politische Verhaltensweisen," 179. This may explain why the participation of lower guildsmen in debates appears to have been so limited. Only a few were ever invited to a *pratica*; those who were honored by an invitation preferred to listen rather than speak; and if they did address the *pratica*, their opinions might not be recorded by the notary. On this point, see Lapo da Castiglionchio's views; Brucker, *Florentine Politics*, 89.

[182] On the general problem of councils and council minutes in Italian communes, see D. Waley, *The Italian City-Republics* (London, 1968), 64, 107.

[183] The difference in the method of recording debates can be seen most clearly by comparing CP, 37 (Salutati's hand) and 38, written by Benedetto Fortini and Ser Piero di Ser Mino. Printed examples of these more elaborate summaries in *Commissioni di Rinaldo degli Albizzi*, I, 236–37; II, 4.

[184] In their conciseness, Salutati's minutes are similar to those kept by notaries in Dante's time. Two examples may be cited from the *Codice diplomatico dantesco*, ed. R. Piattoli (Florence, 1940), 94–95: "Dante Alagherii consuluit quod capitudines et sapientes cuiuslibet sextus nominent unum in dicto sextu. . . . Dante Alagherii consuluit quod de servito faciendo d. pape nichil fiat." For other examples of this style, see *Le Consulte della Repubblica fiorentina dall'anno 1280 all' anno 1296*, ed. A. Gherardi (Florence, 1896–1898), *passim*.

Baroncelli, a member of the war magistracy who, at great length and in much detail, described the state of the republic and specifically, the financial situation, and the number of cavalry and infantry that were to be hired."[185] Three months later, Fortini noted that Rinaldo Gianfigliazzi had delivered a very elaborate speech which the notary summarized briefly.[186] Lorenzo Ridolfi, Maso degli Albizzi, Niccolò da Uzzano, Jacopo Salviati, and Salamone Strozzi were all identified as orators with a penchant for delivering lengthy harangues. Rarely was a speaker praised by a colleague for his rhetorical skills, although Filippo Corsini once commended the humanist, Roberto de' Rossi for his "elegant" speech, and Giuliano Cherichini made an oblique reference to Agnolo Pandolfini's eloquence which, he noted, was not a talent that everyone possessed.[187] But others found these rhetorical exercises boring and irrelevant. After listening to a parade of verbose speakers, Sandro Altoviti was prompted to say that the issues before the *pratica* required not more long speeches but action. And Gino Capponi once described an oration by Piero Baroncelli as "very pretty but lacking in substance."[188]

The draft of a speech that Palla Strozzi prepared for delivery in a *pratica* on fiscal policy in the early 1420s[189] illustrates the new oratorical style. The minute contains numerous insertions and emendations that Palla had made to clarify his argument. In his opening remarks he took note of the storm of criticism over a new *prestanza*

[185] *CP*, 40, f.3r, 12 Apr. 1409: "Audita longissima oratione Pieri de Baroncellis . . . qui narravit et longe atque late explicavit totum statum rei publice." Two years later, the notary referred to Baroncelli's oratorical style: "post longissimam prolationem verborum"; *CP*, 41, f.1r.

[186] *CP*, 40, ff.33v, 81r, 164v, 191r, 208r, 213v. Strozzi "habuit longam orationem demonstrando qualis erat status noster"; *ibid.*, f.214r.

[187] *CP*, 42, f.124r; 44, f.70v.

[188] "Sermones longos proposita non requirunt sed executionem citam"; *CP*, 43, f.15r; and Capponi's comment, *ibid.*, 39, f.117r: "Consilium Pieri de Baroncellis fuerat pulcrum sed parvum substantie." There may be a connection between these sentiments and those expressed by Cino Rinuccini in his *Invettiva*; see Baron, *Crisis*, 2nd ed., 293; G. Holmes, *Florentine Enlightenment*, 1–3.

[189] The undated minute is in *Strozz.*, 3rd ser., 125, ff.126r–127v. It was probably drafted for delivery sometime between March 1422, when a new assessment was authorized, and Oct. 1424, when it was revised; Molho, *Florentine Public Finances*, 76. Since Palla refers to the *catasto* as a possible solution to inequitable distributions, the draft could not have been prepared after 1427, and certainly not in 1430 as I erroneously stated in *Renaissance Florence*, 140. For another example of this florid rhetorical style, see Giovanni Cavalcanti's account of a speech delivered, not in a *pratica*, but in a private meeting in the church of S. Stefano; *Istorie fiorentine*, book III, ch. 2.

distribution that had passed the bounds of civic propriety and was threatening the public welfare. Palla's speech was a justification of the new assessment, and a critique of the arguments advanced by its opponents. All republics, he said, incur fiscal deficits resulting from ordinary expenses and the costs of defense; these obligations must be met by taxing the citizenry. The appropriate procedure for distributing this tax was to appoint citizens who were knowledgeable about each citizen's wealth and could distribute the levy accordingly. Would the critics prefer (he asked rhetorically) that Florence's neighbors be given the responsibility for making the assessments? Every tax levied upon the citizenry in the past had aroused discontent; this would never change to the end of time. For these assessments were the work of men prone to error; "only God might be able to satisfy us." To abolish the present levy because it contained inequities was both fruitless and dangerous; no scheme for distributing taxes could ever be perfect. That a few individuals paid more than their share was the lesser evil, since the dismantling of the whole tax schedule to correct those flaws would jeopardize the republic's security.[190] Palla then challenged the argument that a tax distribution established by law could be abrogated by executive decree: "That is an act of despots and not of popular regimes." Finally, in his peroration Palla called his audience's attention to the wise practices of their ancestors, who never revised a tax schedule until it had been in effect for several years.

> Do we think that they were less pious and merciful than ourselves? Do we think that they were less prudent? Do we think that they were less expert, less intelligent, less solicitous of the public welfare than ourselves? Such an opinion is untenable! Our ancestors were more prudent and more dedicated to the state than our own generation. Their record proves this, for under their guidance, a puny state was transformed into a great power![191]

[190] "Egl'è stato detto di sopra per me che 'n ognuna n'è stata sempre [disaguaglianze] e in ognuna ne sarà. S'il negassi, a me medesimo mi contradirei. 'Non conciedi tu che sia bene a llevare via le disaguaglianze?': conciedo. 'Dunque è bene a llevar via la distributione presente, che contiene in se disaguaglianze?': questo niegho. La distributione che à in sè disaghuaglianze non si vuole rimuovere: prima, perchè 'gnuna ne può essere sanze chome toccho di sopra; e se 'gnuna ne può esser sanza, 'gnuna n'escirebbe che non s'avesse a tor via. E togliendole tutte el comune non si potrebbe difendere, e non potendo far difesa, la nostra libertà si perderebbe. El minor male si de' preporre al maggiore: minor male a portare un pocho d'ingorda gravezza che a perdere la libertà."

[191] "Crediam noi che fussono men pietosi, men misericordiosi di noi, crediam noi che fussono men prudenti, crediam noi che fussono meno 'sperti e men savi, cre-

The changes in political discourse involved substance as well as form. Some of their implications can be seen by comparing the deliberations prior to the republic's first war with Giangaleazzo Visconti in the winter and spring of 1389–1390 with those that preceded the outbreak of hostilities with King Ladislaus in the spring of 1409. Between December 1389 and April 1390 only seven *pratiche* were convened,[192] and in none of these debates were the diplomatic and military issues discussed thoroughly, although they may have been aired in meetings of the Signoria and the war *balìa*. The records do not trace clearly the evolution of civic attitudes toward the impending struggle, which were probably more discordant than the minutes suggest. In March and April 1390, when the two states were moving toward open conflict, there was no mention of Giangaleazzo or the Milanese threat in the protocols.[193] This reticence was not at all characteristic of the debates stimulated by Ladislaus' invasion of Tuscany in the spring of 1409. Four separate meetings were called by the Signoria in March, when the king's army occupied Cortona. In the *pratica* of 15 March, Alessio Baldovinetti and Piero Baroncelli urged the Signoria to assemble a large group of citizens to make a final decision on war or peace.[194] Though unwilling then to submit the issue to a *parlamento*, the priors did convene a series of *pratiche* in April, one of which (21 April) was described as a "great council" to consider an alliance with Ladislaus.[195] In this debate, civic opinion was sharply divided, and the counselors ranged widely over the spectrum of Italian politics. Some advocated a formal league with the king; others warned of his territorial ambitions, while in the middle stood a large number of uncommitted citizens who favored more discussion. But events, and specifically the incursions of the king's armies into Florentine territory south of Arezzo,

---

diam noi che fussono men teneri dello stato loro? Questo ne è da credere ne è da pensare. E' furon multo più pietosi e molto più prudenti e molto più teneri del loro stato non sian noi del nostro, e l'opere loro el fanno manifesto, che di picchola signoria divennono in grandissima."

[192] The *pratiche* were held on 8 and 9 Dec., 18 Jan., 25 Feb., 3 and 17 March, and 17 Apr.; *CP*, 28, ff.16r–20v, 31r–34r, 41v–42v, 45r–46r, 49v–50v, 53v–55r.

[193] The Milanese crisis was last discussed on 3 March; *ibid.*, ff.45r–46r; and not mentioned again until 30 April, when war had already begun; *ibid.*, ff.60v–61r. There were no references to a possible renewal of hostilities in the *pratiche* that preceded the beginning of the second Visconti war; above, 156.

[194] *CP*, 39, f.161r. Some 50 citizens spoke in these four *pratiche*; *ibid.*, ff.151r–154r, 156v–157r, 160v–162r, 164r–165r.

[195] "In magno consilio requisitorum"; *ibid.*, 40, f.7v: in the *pratica* of 12 Apr., "congregatis ad consultandum mandato dominorum priorum . . . nec non aliis civibus in magno numero"; *ibid.*, f.3r.

overtook these deliberations. "War has already begun between the Florentine people and King Ladislaus"; thus Benedetto Fortini began his summary of the *pratica* held on 1 June.[196] Fortini then observed that the regime was considering an alliance with King Louis of Anjou which, since the two princes were mortal enemies, was a grave decision facing the republic. If that pact were concluded, the war would inevitably expand in scope and cost, so consultations must be held before any decision was taken.

More accurately than any other indicator, this change in the form and content of Florentine political debate reflected the regime's transformation from corporate to elitist.[197] Until his death in 1406, Salutati had remained faithful to the traditional view of the commune as an amalgam of collectivities. The *pratica* was the forum where representatives of corporate bodies delivered their judgments on the issues confronting the republic. Salutati perceived the participants in these debates as spokesmen for their families or guilds or neighborhoods, and not as discrete individuals formulating independent opinions.[198] Eloquence, the ability to present a cogent and persuasive argument, may have been less important for Salutati, and those who shared his values, than the social and political strength of the speaker's constituency. By 1410, however, the *pratica* had been gradually transformed into a forum where prominent citizens might speak on behalf of the leadership, or as individuals whose views carried weight by virtue of their particular expertise or status in the regime. When Rinaldo Gianfigliazzi made the opening speech in a debate, as he often did, he had one of two objectives in mind: either to inform the audience of the elite's position on the issue or, if it were controversial, to argue for his own policy. The vocabulary employed by the chancellors reflected this hortatory aspect of the deliberations. Speakers harangued, exhorted, encouraged their audiences; they sought to arouse and incite them to act. They heaped praise and commendation upon those whose opinions they supported, or they complained about policies or viewpoints they deplored.[199] Among their listeners were uncommitted men

---

[196] *Ibid.*, f.23r.

[197] Cf. M. Becker, *Journal of Historical Studies* (1969–70), 298: "There he [Bruni] would observe what had been in process for over a generation: speakers were appearing not as representatives of a corporate constituency but rather as individuals prone to orate from a civic point of view."

[198] Salutati's views on the crucial role of consultation are stated in *SCMC*, 18, ff.20v–21r, 9 June 1379.

[199] The verbs *hortari, rogare, sollicitare, arguere, conqueri, laudare, commendare,* are introduced into the protocols after 1400; e.g. Matteo Tinghi, "hortatus est ad conservandas pecunias et conquerendis multis verbis de malo statu civitatis"; Gio-

who had to be persuaded and stimulated by these orations, or hostile minds to be converted. The *pratica* became the arena in which the conflicting views of the leaders competed for the approval of the whole *reggimento*. And in those verbal struggles for control of policy, the rhetorical skills of the orator assumed a greater importance than ever before in Florentine history.

The first signs of this new style appear after Salutati's death in 1406; they proliferate after Leonardo Bruni's brief tenure as chancellor in 1411,[200] in the minutes kept by his successor, Ser Paolo Fortini. This notary's records also contain the earliest references to a historical frame of reference in Florentine debates. In a speech delivered in May 1413 a civil lawyer, Piero Beccanugi, expressed the opinion that "to administer public affairs intelligently, it is essential to look into the past, in order to provide for the present and the future."[201] Thereafter, and with increasing frequency, the phrase "we know from experience" prefaced many orations in the *pratiche*.[202] Banco da Verrazzano, Antonio Alessandri, and Antonio Mangioni cited knowledge of the past as the most important element in analyzing current problems and predicting the future.[203] The most extreme claim for the value of history in administering the *res publica* was made by Agnolo Pandolfini, the only humanist to discuss the issue in these debates. "Theoretical knowledge is not valid for the governance of public affairs," he asserted, "since determinations require specific data. But the experience of things judges the past and correctly defines the future."[204] From that principle, Pandolfini derived the corollary that "the conditions and

---

vanni Niccolini, "hortando et rogando dominos"; Piero Baroncelli, "sollicitando et hortando quod proposuit"; Filippo Corsini, "hortando omnes instantissime"; Rinaldo degli Albizzi, "quicumque laudare et commendare debet dominos"; *CP*, 40, f.189v; 42, ff.165v, 176v; 43, ff.11r, 107v.

[200] Bruni's minutes from Dec. 1410 to Apr. 1411 have not survived.

[201] ". . . Ad gubernandam utiliter rempublicam ex preterita recordari presentibus providere et futuris"; *CP*, 42, f.20v.

[202] Examples: Filippo Corsini, "recordari debemus de preteritis"; Rinaldo Rondinelli, "ut multi experti sunt"; Agnolo Pandolfini, "nos experti sumus"; *ibid.*, ff.27r, 44r, 45r.

[203] Verrazzano, "quod preteritum presentium et futurorum scientiam prebent"; Alessandri, "preterita docent quid sit in futurum providendum"; Mangioni, "per experientiam rerum gestarum doctrinam in presentibus et futuris sumere debemus"; *CP*, 42, ff.42r, 79v; 43, f.46r.

[204] "Gubernacula rerum publicarum per scientiam haberi non possunt, cum particulariter requirant determinationes. Sed experientia rerum preteritarum iudicat et futura rite terminat condiciones et voluntates dominorum. Contrarie sunt populis in totum; et cum his similibus populos se ligare et unire utile non est quoquomodo"; *CP*, 42, f.103r.

aspirations of princes and republics are so antithetical that they should never become allies under any circumstances." Florentine history demonstrated the validity of that proposition, he insisted: "Duke [Stephen] of Bavaria who accepted a bribe from the Count of Virtù just as he was about to enter Italy; the count of Armagnac; emperor Rupert; the duke of Athens; the duke of Calabria. . . ."

Once that rhetorical device was introduced, it quickly became popular with speakers and, presumably, with their audiences. The despotic rule of the duke of Athens (1342–1343) was the most frequently cited of the city's past experiences; it was the only time (as Piero Firenze noted) since the Guelf republic was established in the 1260s that Florentines had not been free.[205] Filippo Corsini, who was an inexhaustible fount of historical lore, attributed that temporary eclipse of liberty to civic discord, a malaise that had destroyed many republican regimes.[206] Other events recalled from the very distant past were the wars and alliances that preceded Walter of Brienne's *signoria*,[207] and the struggle with Pisa in the 1360s, cited to demonstrate that excessive parsimony in military expenditures could have disastrous consequences.[208] Filippo Corsini considered himself an authority on the republic's relations with German emperors, whose visits to Italy "were not always detrimental to our interests, as past experience proves." To challenge that idea of imperial benevolence, Paolo Biliotti recalled Charles IV's Italian sojourn of 1368, and his unsuccessful efforts to launch a Ghibelline crusade against the Guelf republic.[209] Apparently, the war with Pope Gregory XI did not loom very large in Florentine

[205] *Ibid.*, f.125r, 14 Apr. 1414: "Semper civitas libera fuit et dominatio a 1268 citra excepto tempore ducis Athenarum." Other references to his dictatorship: Salamone Strozzi, Rinaldo Gianfigliazzi, Filippo Corsini, Niccolò Barbadori, Jacopo Schiatesi; *ibid.*, ff.19r, 24r, 27r, 36v, 147v.

[206] *CP*, 43, f.12r: "Per discordiam multe subverse sunt et annichilate et nos solum ob divisionem tempore ducis Athenarum libertatem amisimus." Corsini was a boy of eight in 1342; Martines, *Lawyers and Statecraft*, 482.

[207] Firenze del Pancia's statement reveals a fine mastery of historical detail: "Quod in 1340 firmavimus ligam cum Venetis contra dominum Mastinum [della Scala], et duravit liga menses XVIII et sine consensu nostro pacem cum eo Veneti fecerunt. . . . Et multa possederunt ab eo data, et Luccam emimus et a rege Roberto auxilia poscendo nobis misit ducem Athenarum, qui auxilio et potentia magnatum et aliquorum popularium dominium acquisiverat civitatis; et in decem mensibus circa 1,000,000 florenos subtraxit"; *CP*, 43, f.39v, 22 June 1415.

[208] Rinaldo Rondinelli and Cristofano di Giorgio; *CP*, 42, ff.71v, 79r. The Florentines failed to hire John Hawkwood, who then fought against them for Pisa.

[209] Corsini's views, *ibid.*, ff.12v, 23r, 143v; Biliotti, *CP*, 41, f.83v; 42, ff.3r, 125r. For other reactions to a possible imperial visit, Roberto de' Rossi and Giovanni Carducci; *ibid.*, 42, ff.122v, 125r.

memory, being mentioned only once by Strozza Strozzi who blamed the Ciompi revolution on the obstinacy of the Eight Saints, "who refused to make peace" with the pope.[210] Though memories of the Ciompi were periodically revived by the conspiracies that employed workers' symbols and slogans, that proletarian revolt was rarely cited in the *pratiche*.[211] The protocols do contain several allusions to Giangaleazzo Visconti,[212] notably his conquest of Padua and Verona, but only one counselor, Lorenzo Ridolfi, referred specifically to the crisis of 1402 and the city's desperate situation after the fall of Bologna.[213]

Thus, with remarkable suddenness, history became a staple of Florentine political discussion: a voluminous source of precept and example, a valid guide for statesmen. Twenty years earlier, Coluccio Salutati had written that "the knowledge of things done warns princes, teaches people and instructs individuals. . . . It is the most certain basis for the conduct of affairs."[214] For Salutati, as for Machiavelli a century later, the classical world provided the most valuable historical examples. Already conditioned by the claims for the relevance of their

[210] "Memorans quod tempore guerre ecclesie gesta fuerunt et quod pacem habere Octo potuerunt et noluerunt ante quam mercantie civium direpte fuissent, unde inter cives hodia creverunt et multa scandala secuta sunt et in manibus vilissimorum hominum devenimus"; *CP*, 43, f.14v. But see Filippo Corsini's comment; *ibid.*, f.67r.

[211] Gino Capponi's statement is well known: "nam melius esset sub Ciompis esse, quam sub thirannide regis"; *Commissioni di Rinaldo degli Albizzi*, I, 237. Another brief reference by Paolo Biliotti, "sic alias per effectum vidimus tempore Athenarum ducis et Ciomporum"; *CP*, 43, f.137r.

[212] Rinaldo Rondinelli, Niccolò da Uzzano, Maso degli Albizzi, Niccolò Barbadori; *CP*, 41, f.128r; 42, ff.13v, 14r, 17v, 36v. Niccolò da Uzzano's comment: "Habemus exempla ducis Mediolani, nam si factum tunc fuisset quod erat facile, concordia inter dominos Veronensem et Paduanum secuta esset; et etiam postea antequam dux Mediolani Peducam occupaverat." A decade later, Giangaleazzo was described by Piero di Messer Luigi Guicciardini as a "homo valens et prudens, et audiverunt dici ipsum solitum dicere quod dominus Coluccius cum litteris suis maius bellum sibi faciebat quam ᶜV lancee"; *CP*, 46, f.144v, 9 May 1426. Guicciardini was spokesman for the Twelve. This is the first documented reference to the famous story of Giangaleazzo's admiration for Salutati's rhetorical skill, later repeated by Pope Pius II.

[213] "Casus gravis est et expensa intolerabilis et alias experti sumus quando Bononie per ducem Mediolani occupata fuit et bis stabat supra, nam omnes mortui videbantur"; *CP*, 42, f.71v.

[214] M. Gilmore, *Humanists and Jurists* (Cambridge, Mass., 1963), 19. In drafting letters sent to foreign princes and republics, Salutati frequently cited events from Roman history, and from Florence's past, to support his arguments; *SCMC*, 18, f.85r, May 1379; 20, ff.30v–31r, Oct. 1384; 21, ff.17v–18r, 24r–24v, March and Apr. 1388; 24, ff.84v–85r, Nov. 1394. For an example of the chancellor's use of a classical source, Cicero; *ibid.*, 21, ff.26v–27r, May 1388.

own past to current problems, citizens who met in the *pratiche* became accustomed to speeches larded with quotations from classical authors, or references to Roman history. Though one might expect that statesmen with humanistic training—Agnolo Pandolfini and Roberto de' Rossi, for example—would have been in the forefront of this vogue, the lawyer Filippo Corsini and the knight Rinaldo Gianfigliazzi were its most active promoters.[215] Corsini's favorite author was Livy, and he cited events from the Punic Wars— the massacre at Cannae and the siege of Saguntum—to bolster his argument for a tough and and uncompromising posture toward King Ladislaus.[216] The old lawyer also quoted from Valerius and Sallust to stress the necessity for decisive action in times of crisis.[217] Gianfigliazzi cited Seneca—"only that which is honest is good"—and the example of the Spartan king Lycurgus who "in promulgating laws stated that public affairs are properly directed by the few with the authority of the many. . . ."[218] The lawyer Alessandro Bencivenni borrowed from Cicero the argument that "it is better to protect one's friend from afar than to [acquiesce in] his destruction."[219] Francesco Leoni approvingly cited Cato's decision to choose death rather than live under Caesar's tyranny, and Agnolo Pandolfini quoted a sentence from the *Gallic Wars*—"si ius violandum est dominandi cupidunt violandum"—to support his argument that princes always violated laws.[220] Rome's fall was a fascinating theme, and also a warning for the Florentines, Lorenzo Ridolfi believed: "Rome was the greatest power in the world and then declined almost to nothing on account of her quarrels, and we are not greater than the Romans once were. . . ."[221]

[215] Martines, *Social World*, does not list either Corsini or Gianfigliazzi in his catalogue of humanists; on the humanistic interests of Pandolfini and Rossi, *ibid.*, 108–10, 256–57, 313–14. Both men delivered several speeches in these months; *CP*, 42, ff.24r, 37v, 45r, 74v, 80v, 93v, 103r, 105r, 121r, 124r.

[216] "Timendum est ne nobis, ut tempore Hannibalis de Sagunto Romanis evenit, recitans illud Livii, 'Dum legationibus tempus teritur, muri Sagunti ariete quassantur'. . . . Quid egerint Romani post conflictum Canne recitando, videlicet, unio inter cives, ut Valerius refert"; *CP*, 42, ff.12v, 36v.

[217] "Ut recitat Salustius in Catilinario, post ornatam orationem Cesaris, Cato dixit: 'Tempus non esse dilationem adhibere, sed cito ad rem, unde salus procedat venire.' Et propter dilationes Romanorum, Anibal Seguntum vincit"; *ibid.*, f.124r.

[218] *CP*, 41, f.175v, 17 Feb. 1413; 42, f.122v.

[219] *CP*, 45, f.1v.

[220] "Et nil carius utilius et honorabilius est libertate, cum in ea bona omnia costet, et Cato mortem constituit ne libertatem amicteret quam Cesar principum omnium gloriosissimus occuparat"; *ibid.*, f.106v; and Pandolfini's comment, *ibid.*, f.124r.

[221] *CP*, 43, f.13v. For similar views, cf. Lippozzo Mangioni, *ibid.*, f.100v.

The refinement of the methodology for examining problems and issues was quite as significant as the introduction of rhetoric and a sense of history into Florentine political discourse. Here, as in other aspects of the deliberative process, Salutati's death in 1406 marks a turning-point, which might have been less abrupt in reality than it appears in the protocols. Coluccio may have chosen to omit the analytical aspect from his summaries, and his successors may have reported the discussion more fully. But the trend toward more complex and sophisticated analysis is very clear. To persuade a knowledgeable and experienced group of citizens of a policy's merits required more than an elegant oratorical style and a talent for quoting Livy and Cicero. As Gino Capponi insisted, the arguments ought to have substance. In the exposition of their viewpoint, Florentine statesmen revealed an increasing talent for analytic thinking, and for grasping the complexities of political issues. As the leading advocate of budgetary planning in the inner circle, Piero Baroncelli displayed his expertise in financial affairs. Few if any statesmen surpassed Agnolo Pandolfini's capacity for mastering detail, and for summarizing the essentials of a problem. The lawyers in the elite—Filippo Corsini, Lorenzo Ridolfi, Giovanni Serristori, Bartolomeo Popoleschi—were all shrewd analysts of political issues,[222] as was Niccolò da Uzzano, who could have taught Machiavelli much about the art of politics. Though Giovanni de' Medici was not noted for his eloquence in debate,[223] the strength of his intellect and his secure grasp of reality is clearly illustrated in the reports of his speeches. When, in May 1413, the republic was starved for money to defend itself against Ladislaus' invasion, the founder of the Medici fortune delivered a characteristically terse speech, excoriating the officials who had made the *prestanza* assessments, and recommending that their schedule of levies be destroyed. Then he commented on the inefficiency of such magistracies; "the larger their number and the more time they have to function, the worse the result."[224] After formulating the maxim that public business was best done quickly by a few, he informed his audience that he had turned over all his business records to the authorities, implying that if such information were provided by every citizen, fiscal inequities would be eliminated.

[222] Martines, *Lawyers and Statecraft*, 239–41, 289–95.

[223] Martines, *Social World*, 249, quotes Cavalcanti's statement about Giovanni: "non era molto eloquente, perchè dalla natura gli era negato la dolcezza del parlare."

[224] *CP*, 42, f.10r: "Cum plus temporis datur et cum plures sunt ad rem gerendam, deterior finis sequatur; et utilius et melius fit per paucos et in brevi tempore ut iam experientia docuit."

These changes in perception and deliberation influenced this regime's *modus operandi*: the ways in which it confronted and solved problems. A good illustration is the Florentine effort to end the Great Schism. Lauro Martines has described the Florentine role in this crisis, and the pressures that forced the regime to abandon its traditional commitment to the Roman obedience by first declaring neutrality, and then accepting the legitimacy of the council of Pisa and its papal nominee, Alexander V.[225] After a projected meeting between Gregory XII and Benedict XIII failed to materialize, the king of France withdrew his obedience from the Avignonese pope, and dissident cardinals from both curias issued a call for a general council, scheduled for the spring of 1409. Joining these cardinals in urging Florence to abandon her allegiance to Rome was the French governor of Genoa, Boucicaut. The question was intensively debated during the winter of 1408–1409; in March, the Signoria decided to withdraw obedience from Gregory XII. The government had earlier given its permission for the council to meet in Pisa, and Florence was one of the first European states to recognize the new pope, Alexander V, chosen by that conclave on 26 June 1409. In his analysis of the deliberations on this controversial issue, Martines emphasized the traumatic nature of this decision to break a thirty-year-old commitment to the Roman papacy. Resistance to this breach came primarily from the rank and file of the guild community, and not from the leadership. Artisans and shopkeepers were frightened by this violation of a traditional bond; they feared for their souls and for the republic. The leadership, on the other hand, was aware of the risks but confident of the regime's ability to surmount them. These statesmen used the *pratica* as an educational forum, where lawyers and theologians justified the shift in ecclesiastical policy and sought to calm the anxieties of the citizenry. Their leadership was thus both political and intellectual. They imported conciliar theories from the outside world, from the universities of Paris and Bologna, and they utilized their political expertise to convert their fellow-citizens to these views.

Though the problem of obedience and legitimacy was the most crucial question confronting the Florentines (and all Christians), a secondary issue, concerning a council site in Florentine territory, was quite as troublesome. As early as March 1407, some citizens were promoting Florence as a site for a meeting between the two popes. The Sixteen had urged the Signoria to work "with the utmost diligence to end [the Schism], and to arrange, if possible, for that union to take

[225] Martines, *Lawyers and Statecraft*, 289–96.

place in Florence."[226] Throughout the spring and summer of 1407, the issue cropped up frequently in council sessions, and the authorities sent embassies to Rome and Avignon, offering their city as a meeting site.[227] During the winter of 1407-1408, it appeared likely that the two popes would agree to meet somewhere in Florentine territory. This prospect aroused the anxieties of some citizens, who believed that a large gathering of foreigners would lead to tumult and disorder, and possibly to revolution. Others feared that this meeting would embitter relations between papal and anticlerical factions in the city. Such concerns prompted Niccolò Barbadori's recommendation (September 1407) that the Signoria refuse permission to Gregory XII to enter Florence or any other town in the dominion.[228] Paolo Biliotti's view (February 1408) was likewise negative; he feared that the papal presence anywhere in the territory would provoke civil strife. Rinaldo Gianfigliazzi agreed that Florence should not be the council site, but he was willing to locate the assembly elsewhere in the territory. To guarantee the council's security, he also proposed that neither cardinals nor secular princes be allowed to bring military escorts, or even a personal retinue, into whichever city was chosen. Responding to these arguments, Antonio Alessandri stated that "he saw no reason to be fearful, since the Sienese had welcomed the pope to their city without any disorders, and that now the lord of Lucca [Paolo Guinigi], whose regime is less stable than ours, is about to receive [the pope]." Nothing would gain greater merit for the city in God's eyes, and greater fame among men, than to assemble a council in Florence to restore church unity. It would be shameful, Alessandri concluded, to withdraw the city's offer of a council site, after so much effort had been invested in that enterprise. The rival popes should be invited to meet either in Florence or in Pisa. Supporting Alessandri's position, Piero Baroncelli argued that the Florentines had already enhanced their reputation by their efforts on behalf of ecclesiastical unity. Their fame would become even greater if they were host to a conclave that would end the schism. Baroncelli preferred Florence to Pisa as a council site; the latter city had too recently been conquered, and was still not adequately fortified.[229]

By the summer of 1408 the moment of decision had arrived. The dissident cardinals had issued a call for a council and were searching

[226] *CP*, 38, f.13v, 2 March 1407. See also *ibid.*, ff.14v, 15r, 25v.

[227] *Ibid.*, ff.58v, 69r-71v.

[228] Ibid., f.80r, 12 Sept. 1407. Guidetto Guidetti and Ricciardo del Bene also opposed any invitations; *ibid.*, ff.71v, 80r.

[229] These arguments in *ibid.*, ff.5v-6v. Gino Capponi also supported that position; *ibid.*, f.6v.

for a convenient site somewhere in Italy. The Signoria convened a *pratica* on 30 July "concerning the problem of granting a location for the cardinals of both curias to hold a council."[230] Matteo Tinghi opposed the concession of any place in Florentine territory, citing the threat of disorder; Niccolò Guasconi and Paolo Biliotti supported his negative stance. In another *pratica* held four days later,[231] Cionaccio Baroncelli warned of a grain shortage if the council met in Tuscany; Luca da Filicaia argued that a new schism might result from this convocation. Jacopo Malegonelle was willing to sanction the council in Florentine territory only if Europe's secular rulers approved of that location. But Cristofano Spini argued that these fears were exaggerated; Jacopo Salviati, Lorenzo Ridolfi, and Piero Beccanugi also spoke in favor of conceding a site in the territory. A majority of the collegiate bodies—the Parte captains, the Eight on Security, the Merchants' Court—also favored this policy, as did the one lower guildsman who ventured to express a judgment on this controversial question.[232] Though civic opinion was clearly divided, the proponents of the council were gaining support for their position.[233] However, they could not overcome the resistance to Florence as the council site, but had to be content with Pisa. That choice received the approbation of a *pratica* held on 21 August, and in September the Signoria ratified the decision by signing an agreement with the cardinals in Pisa.[234]

Underlying this debate over a council site were two contrasting images that Florentines had constructed about themselves and their world. The traditional vision, inherited from the past, was dominated by a sense of vulnerability that reached intense proportions in the decades following the Black Death. One manifestation of this attitude was a reluctance to admit distinguished visitors into the city. Prior to 1343, Florence had welcomed a host of dignitaries: Pope Gregory X in 1273; King Charles I of Naples in the same year; Charles of Valois, brother of King Philip of France, in 1301; King Robert of Naples in 1310; his son Charles of Calabria in 1326. But after the Black Death the city gates were closed to emperors, kings, and many lesser princes. Between 1273 and 1419 no pope set foot in Florence, and only rarely was a cardinal welcomed there. Whenever a German emperor visited Italy, citizens urged the authorities to prohibit his entry into Florence.[235] Three reasons were invariably cited for this reluctance to

---

[230] *CP*, 39, f.78r.   [231] *Ibid.*, ff.79v–80r.   [232] *Ibid.*, ff.78r–79v.

[233] *Ibid.*, ff.80v–81r; see Martines, *Lawyers and Statecraft*, 290.

[234] *CP*, 39, ff.85r, 87v–88r.

[235] See, e.g., T. E. Mommsen, *Italienische Analekten zur Reichsgeschichte des 14. Jahrhunderts (1310–1378)*, (Stuttgart, 1952), 157, 160–61, 171, 189; Brucker, *Florentine Politics*, 143. For reactions to the proposed visit of the duke of Bur-

admit the great. Florentines feared that a prince might be tempted to seize control of the city, as the Duke of Athens had done in 1342. Second, they were concerned about the increase of partisan discord, and finally, they felt that the visit of prominent men might adversely affect the republic's relations with other states. The most recent manifestation of this phobia occurred in 1401, when the republic concluded an alliance with the emperor-elect Rupert against Giangaleazzo Visconti. Some citizens could not bring themselves to trust their ally, to whom they had paid 100,000 florins; they asked the Signoria to reject any plan by Rupert to visit Florence.[236] Though most deeply ingrained in the minds of the *popolo*, these fears of the foreigner were not limited to artisans and small merchants.[237] The more sanguine image of Florence that emerges during these debates over a council site was developed by the leadership; its most ardent propagandists were Antonio Alessandri, Piero Baroncelli, Niccolò da Uzzano, and Cristofano Spini. These men felt greater confidence in the regime's stability, and in their mastery of events, than did many of their fellow citizens. In promoting Florence as a council site, they were motivated by the hope that this conclave would unify the church, and that God would reward Christians who had contributed to the healing of the schism, both in this life and in the hereafter. But the most original feature of their argument was the contention that Florence's reputation would be enhanced throughout the Christian world.[238] This added a new quality to the concept of civic fame that could be achieved not only by the construction of magnificent cathedrals and palaces, or through the exploits of famous sons, but also by being the setting for a major historical event.

In this contest between fearful traditionalists on the one hand and the conciliarists with their ebullient visions of divine favor and temporal glory on the other, the latter scored a qualified victory with the convocation of the council in Pisa on 25 March 1409. But their triumph

---

gundy's son in 1397, see *CP*, 32, f.155v; and of Pope Urban VI, *ibid.*, 25, ff.4r–5r, 128v, 135r.

[236] *CP*, 35, ff.43r, 80r–90v. See above, 176–79.

[237] Writing to Simone Strozzi on 18 Aug. 1407, Veri Rondinelli mentioned the debate over a papal visit: "Tennesi iersera consiglio sopracciò; non so che si diterminasse. Tutti i colegi erano disposti al sì, ma dubito ch'e consigli non sieno così"; *Strozz.*, 3rd ser., 132, no. 2.

[238] Jacopo Salviati, "Quod sit eis concedendis locus pro concilio, quia sequitur honor Dei, utilitas et gloria et firmamentum libertatis nostre"; and Piero Baroncelli, "quod ex hoc sequatur honor Dei, utilitas civium et gloria civitatis et multa beneficia et firmamentum"; *CP*, 39, ff.80r–80v.

was marred by the failure of that conclave to end the schism; those critics had been correct who warned that new divisions might result from this council. That some citizens were still troubled by the prospect of Florence's gates being open to all was evident from a discussion (July 1409) over inviting the newly elected pope, Alexander V, to visit the city. While Filippo Corsini and Giotto Peruzzi were eager to welcome him to Florence, others were less enthusiastic about the visit, and were even more hostile to receiving the republic's ally, King Louis of Anjou, in Pisa. Speaking for the Sixteen, Marsilio Vecchietti could find no valid reason for the royal visit, but feared that the king's presence would incite disorders.[239] In the winter of 1412–1413, the possibility of a coronation trip to Rome via Florence by the emperor-elect Sigismund aroused latent fears of an imperial attack; a few months later, the city gates remained tightly closed against Pope John XXIII, who was seeking a refuge from the armies of King Ladislaus.[240] Not until 1419, when Florentines received Pope Martin V, the newly elected head of a unified church, did the fears subside and the citizenry feel secure with their distinguished guest, who remained with them for eighteen months.

In these debates on Florence's suitability as a council site, as in the related deliberations on war and peace, on finance and justice, one can discern some distinctive elements in this regime's style. It was strongly committed to a thorough study of its problems, and it appears to have been somewhat more tolerant of disagreement, and the open expression of dissent, than was true of earlier regimes. In its handling of controversial issues, it sought to achieve a consensus by frequent deliberations, in which specialists would render their judgments based upon professional competence. By moving slowly and deliberately to allay fears and to convert the undecided, the leadership guided civic opinion along the paths it favored. "Without the leadership and thrust of her top statesmen, lawyers and churchmen," Lauro Martines has written, "the regime could not have broken with the Roman papacy and adopted a conciliar posture in 1408." In seeking to persuade each other, as well as the rank and file, the leaders systematically employed the skills of the logician and the rhetorician. Speeches became longer and more analytical; they were studded with allusions to historical precedents and references to classical authors. These innova-

---

[239] *CP*, 40, ff.39r–42r, 51r, 53v. Justifying their opposition to the king's visit to Pisa, the Signoria wrote "che non era perchè noi non ci fidiamo di lui, ma perchè non suole essere nostra usanza di ricevere simili principi in nostri luoghi"; *SCMC*, 28, f.124v, 17 July 1409.

[240] *CP*, 41, f.185r, and below, 372.

tions were not simply rhetorical gambits, but signs of a basic shift in historical outlook. Florentines were being taught, in these debates, to view their past as a unique experience, filled with challenges and ordeals, but also with triumphs. If they did not yet link their origins directly with republican Rome,[241] as the humanists were beginning to do, they did see the relevance of Roman history to their own problems.[242] Though they still referred to divine grace as essential for Florence's prosperity, they placed increasing emphasis upon themselves as the makers of their destiny. They were proud of their demonstrated ability to maintain their freedom and their republican regime, and they looked with scorn and pity upon their neighbors, the Pisans and the Pistoiese, who had contributed to their own downfall by failing to achieve civic unity.[243] In the midst of a debate (February 1408) over extending invitations to the Roman and Avignonese popes to meet in Florence, Cristofano Spini announced proudly that "not since 1381 has our regime been more stable than it now is, for all those who merit it, belong to it, and there is nothing to fear."[244] This confident mood was to be severely tested in subsequent years, but it did reflect an important element in the Florentine civic mentality of the early *quattrocento*.

The introduction of a hortatory style of political debate, of historical perspective and classical quotations, inevitably raises questions about the relationship between these developments and the rise of civic humanism, which Hans Baron has charted in his classic work, *The Crisis of the Early Italian Renaissance*. The timing of these innovations is particularly important, given the emphasis that Baron has placed upon the 1402 crisis as the catalyst for radical changes in the humanist vision. Not until a decade after Giangaleazzo's death do clear signs of what Baron calls "the new politico-historical outlook"[245] appear in these debates. One can explain that delay as a cultural lag or see the changes as a response not to a single moment of crisis but to a series of events that had a cumulative effect upon the mentality of Florence's governing elite. My reading of the evidence persuades me that internal developments were as important as threats from abroad in changing Florentine perceptions and points of view. And

---

[241] But see, a decade later, Pierozzo Castellani's statement, "a Romanis originem ducimus"; CP, 45, f.44v, 6 Aug. 1422; and Baron, *Crisis*, 2nd ed., 386–87.

[242] Above, n. 221.

[243] The statements of Agnolo di Pino and Gino Capponi; CP, 41, f.132v; 42, f.71v.

[244] "Quod de nichilo dubitat, et quod nunquam vidit statum nostrum firmiorem post 1381, quod omnes qui merentur statum, habent; et quod de nullo dubitat"; CP, 39, f.6r.

[245] *Crisis*, 2nd ed., 445.

in evaluating the impact of foreign perils, one should look—as the Florentines themselves did—at the whole spectrum of these dangers. "We have been able to resist the power of the church, the duke of Milan, and King Ladislaus," Ubaldino Guasconi cried triumphantly in 1412.[246] Filippo Corsini cast his gaze back even further into time, "to recall our achievements in the affairs of San Miniato, the Pisans, the duke of Milan, and King Ladislaus . . . and to recall too what the Romans accomplished after the battle of Cannae. . . ."[247]

The evidence in these protocols, however, does lend support to Baron's major thesis about the emergence in Florence of a new view of history and politics in the first decade of the *quattrocento*. The elements of that vision, which he found in Bruni's *Laudatio* and in Gregorio Dati's history, can also be seen in these debates. The articulation of this new outlook has important implications for what Baron has called "the interaction of ideas and events."[248] The *pratica* was an ideal forum for introducing humanist attitudes to a Florentine audience. Though Salutati apparently did not choose to mediate between the worlds of ideas and experience in this sphere,[249] his successors in the chancellor's office were seemingly more responsive to the new intellectual trends. Leonardo Bruni's brief tenure as chancellor (December 1410–April 1411) may have been a critical phase in this development, although proof is lacking since his records for these months have not survived. Indeed, Bruni may have received some stimuli for the development of his ideology by listening to the debates in the palace. Similarly, the conceptual vision of Gregorio Dati's history of Florence during the Visconti wars may have been inspired by remarks that he had heard in the *pratiche*.[250] The ideas that had been nurtured in private by Salutati and his circle were being spread, though the

---

[246] "Potentie ecclesie, ducis Mediolani et regis Ladislai potenter resistentiam fecimus"; *CP*, 41, f.98v, 29 May 1412.

[247] "Recitans miserias servitutis et gesta nostra tam in factis Sancti Minatis, Pisanorum, ducis Mediolani et regis Ladislai . . . memorans etiam que Romani fecerunt post conflictum Canne"; *CP*, 42, f.60v, 18 Aug. 1413. Cf. Agnolo Pandolfini's statement a decade later: "Per preterita satis aperte videmus que procurant guerre et sub tyrannia venimus ducis Athenarum et ducis Calabrie. Pericula maxima subimus per guerras Ecclesie, ducis Mediolani et regis Ladislai"; *CP*, 45, f.143r, 24 Sept. 1423.

[248] Baron, *Crisis*, 2nd ed., 458. [249] *Ibid.*, 104–20.

[250] Dati may have learned some Roman history in the *pratiche*; see his comments, *CP*, 45, f.166r, 3 Feb. 1424: "Quod Romani pluries ad defensiones permanendo, fere statum amiserunt tempore Gallorum et Annibalis a quo pluries pacem postulaverunt et tunc devicti fuerunt. Demum ad Cartaginem miserunt et Annibal cohactus rediit Carthaginem et noluit pacem per Anibalem petitam consentire. . . . Deberent tamen, ut quidem Romani egerunt, cives aliquid de suo guerram hanc sumere. . . ."

medium of the *pratiche*, to a large group of citizens, whose minds must have been influenced by their exposure to humanist propaganda. Giovanni Morelli may have signaled his absorption of these ideas when, in his diary, he gave this advice to his sons: "Every day for at least an hour, read Vergil, Boethius, Seneca and other authors. . . . Begin your study with Vergil. . . . Then spend some time with Boethius, with Dante and the other poets, with Aristotle who will instruct you in philosophy. . . ."[251]

CIVIC VALUES

The central theme of this analysis has been the transformation of the Florentine republic from a predominantly corporate order in 1382, to one that—thirty years later—was governed by a stable, cohesive elite. This change in the political system was more one of style and mentality than a radical alteration of institutions, or a shift in the social and economic composition of the *reggimento*. That process, moreover, was gradual and incomplete. Its limits were set by, first, the constitutional structures inherited from the past and, second, the conservative mentality of the Florentine statesmen who accomplished it. It is easier to see the nature of the change in retrospect than it was for contemporaries who were so conditioned to think of preserving traditional values and practices. Outsiders were more likely to notice the innovations than were citizens in the *reggimento*, but they were also more prone to wild speculation and exaggeration. No one familiar with Florentine politics could really believe that the regime was, or was about to become, a despotism, but Giovanni Cavalcanti's charge that power had gravitated into the hands of a few was more widely believed, and closer to reality. If one accepts the testimony of Lorenzo Benvenuti, the humanist Niccolò Niccoli believed that the governing elite, whose members he described as tyrants and robbers, had subverted the constitution and embarked upon a series of wars designed to strengthen their authority and to impoverish the citizenry. Comparing Niccoli's perception of the political realities with that of his friend Leonardo Bruni suggests the wide range of opinions on this

---

[251] *Ricordi*, 271-72: "E di poi hai apparato, fa che ogni in dì, un'ora in meno tu istudi Vergilio, Boezio, Senaca o altri autori. . . . Tu potrai istarti nel tuo studio con Vergilio. . . . Tu ti potrai istare con Boezio, con Dante e cogli altri poeti, con Tulio che t'insegnerà parlare perfettamente, con Aristotile, che ti insegnerà filosofia. . . ." A father's counsel to his sons might include "molte cose antiche le quai egli ara vedute o veramente udite o lette ne' libri de' romani o d' altri poeti o valenti uomini"; *ibid.*, 268.

question, and the difficulty of obtaining unbiased judgments from Florentines about their government in these years.[252]

As he lay on his deathbed in 1420, Gino Capponi wrote down (or dictated) a series of observations about Florentine politics, as guidelines for his sons who would no longer have his support and counsel.[253] He was a conservative who believed so fervently in the sanctity of traditional institutions that he once advocated the reimposition of the archaic Ordinances of Justice against the magnates.[254] He favored the strict application of *divieto* legislation that restricted officeholding by the large families; he deplored the fact that "there are more offices than ever before, but power lies in fewer hands." Capponi feared the ambitions of great lineages and prepotent individuals who might aspire to be "more powerful than the Signoria."[255] But he also recognized the advantages, and perhaps even the necessity, of an elitist regime in which the *popolani*, the mass of guildsmen, were kept divided and weak. And he urged his sons "to hold with those who control the state . . . and to support those who rule." He believed that the republic's needs had priority over those of individuals, and he favored the election to the highest magistracies of men "who love the commune more than their own welfare and even their souls." Yet he accepted the validity of traditional bonds of blood, neighborhood, and friendship. "Maintain the closest ties with your neighbors and relatives," he advised his sons, "and serve your friends at home and abroad."[256]

In these epigrammatic fragments, Capponi did not reconcile the contradictions between the imperatives of corporate and elitist politics, nor the rival claims of the state and the individual. His colleagues, with their newly developed analytical skills and historical perceptions, were no more successful in integrating past and present, ideal and reality, into a coherent pattern. Florentine statesmen were too pragmatic to theorize about their government, and too conservative to

---

[252] On Niccoli's views, Baron, *Crisis*, 2nd ed., 326–28; and for Bruni's thoughts on Florentine government; *ibid.*, 205–09, 418–30.

[253] The *ricordi*, first published by Muratori, have been recently edited by G. Folena in *Miscellanea di studi offerti a A. Balduino e B. Bianchi*, 34–39. Capponi died on 19 May 1421; BNF, *Conv. Sopp.*, C, 4, 895, f.104r.

[254] "Magnates nobiscum non concurrunt et sperabant sedere cum dominis . . . et quod Ordinamenta Iusticie ponantur contra magnates"; CP, 42, f.164v, 16 Aug. 1414.

[255] ". . . Non lascerà niuno particulare cittadino o famiglia o congiura essere più potente che la Signoria. . . . Non si dia mai grande condotta o mezzane a niuno cittadino"; *Ricordi*, 34, 35.

[256] *Ibid.*, 37–38.

examine critically the myths by which they lived.[257] They were addicted to vague, moralizing generalizations, exemplified by Marco Strozzi's sententious comment that "there are four things that are important for the city's preservation: peace, prudence, love, and justice."[258] Their debates on civic unity, a staple theme in political discourse, illustrate this inability to move beyond clichés to a clear grasp of the issues. The moral preached incessantly in those secular sermons was the crucial importance of unity for the preservation of liberty. "Where there is unity and love," Niccolò Sacchetti proclaimed in 1415, "there is also God, and every regime that is divided will be destroyed, since through such discord many cities have been conquered and their [inhabitants] enslaved." The evidence lay close at hand, in the context of Florentine experience. "We lost our liberty at the time of the duke of Athens," Filippo Corsini recalled, "solely on account of our differences; and how much evil he did in the short time he ruled will be remembered by those who were there [Corsini was a boy of eight in 1342], and by others."[259] A more recent example was the sorry plight of those former city-states—Pisa, Volterra, Arezzo, Cortona—incorporated into Florence's dominion. "Those whom we rule became subjects through discord," Paolo Biliotti said, and added that their conquest by Florence had been preceded by tyranny, with "a minority seizing power from the *popolo*."[260] The sources of disunity could be traced to the regime's failure to give each citizen his due, or to a moral flaw in some men who aspired to more than they deserved. In prescribing a remedy for civic discord in 1383, Berto Frescobaldi advised the Signoria to "devote attention to unity, giving equitable treatment to each in rewarding and punishing, keeping the regime in the hands of the ancient and virtuous citizens, while excluding the malevolent of whatever condition. . . ."[261] That counsel was repeated again and again in the *pratiche*. The problem remained, intact and intractable; the prescriptions for its solution did not vary in thirty years of debate.[262]

In their consideration of smaller and more concrete problems, the Florentines did provide some useful clues to their notions about their government. The stimulus for the most illuminating discussions was usually some glaring flaw: a rigged election, a violation of some constitutional principle, the use of coercion to gain political advantage.

257 Brucker, *Florentine Politics*, 72–73; D. Weinstein, "The Myth of Florence," *Flor. Studies*, 15–44.

258 *CP*, 43, f.11r.   259 *Ibid.*, f.13v.   260 *Ibid.*, f.15r; 42, f.71v.

261 *CP*, 22, f.90v.

262 E.g., *CP*, 41, ff.7r, 39r (Corsini); 58v (Gino Capponi); 71v–72r.

The discovery of these abuses legitimized criticism and inspired proposals for reform. Such occasions also provided opportunities for reaffirming the validity of institutions that had been corrupted, or conventions that had been violated. One set of problems that aroused discussion, and some dissent, was the location of authority within the constitutional structure: the limits to the Signoria's power; the role of the legislative councils and the *popolo* in policy-making; the integration of a ruling elite into a system designed for corporate government. In a second category were the problems created by the intensification of the state's demands upon the citizenry, and upon the corporate entities to which Florentines still owed allegiance. So powerful was the civic ethos that emerged in these years that men could speak unequivocally of the supremacy of public over private interest, qualified only (and not invariably) by the individual's obligation to God.[263] But this system of priorities was more easily articulated than implemented.

The Signoria's authority was a highly sensitive and complex issue in this regime. As the key magistracy of the republic, the corporeal symbol of her sovereignty, the Signoria possessed broad powers, based on statute and custom, which tended to expand in these years.[264] The manner in which the priors exercised their authority, their sense of opportunities as well as the limits of their power, was an important issue. Citizens desired strong and forceful leadership from the Signoria,[265] but they occasionally reminded the priors of the fine line between persuasion and coercion, between the rule of law and the arbitrariness of tyranny. Most would have subscribed to Guidetto Guidetti's statement that "everyone should agree with the priors and conform to their judgment."[266] When the Signoria was thwarted by a recalcitrant council that refused to approve a provision, the counselors frequently urged the priors to resubmit the measure, and promised to cast their votes in its favor. If conciliar resistance was too strong, however, citizens would urge the priors to be patient and tolerant. Commenting on one council's failure to approve a provision for a scrutiny (April 1417) that had been strongly promoted by the Signoria, Filippo Corsini said that passage of the law would have redounded to their

---

[263] Strozza Strozzi, "Quod post Deum patrie principaliter obligamur"; *CP*, 44, f.45r, 15 Nov. 1420.

[264] Martines, *Lawyers and Statecraft*, 119–29. The Signoria's authority in 1415 is described in the *Statuta populi et communis*, II, 518ff.

[265] E.g., Galileo Galilei, "et gubernantes reipublice timiditatem ostendere non debent"; *CP*, 45, f.128r.

[266] *CP*, 44, f.45r. Also, the statement by Maso degli Albizzi, "ipse paratus est mandatis dominorum obtemperare"; *CP*, 42, f.164r.

honor. But, he added, "we live in a free city and among those things that guarantee our liberty is the freedom of the councils."[267] He warned the Signoria not to violate that principle, a view that was seconded by Bartolomeo Valori and Piero Bonciani.[268] Lorenzo Ridolfi presented the most coherent argument for executive restraint, in a speech made during another controversy over a scrutiny. The provision had been presented to the councils several times while he was a member of the Twelve, and it had never passed. The Signoria then in office decided that any further effort to enact the legislation would tarnish their honor. But the new Signoria had refused to accept this rebuff, and had resubmitted the measure to the councils, "which diminishes the honor of the priors, who now shamefully seek what is unattainable, and not pleasing to the *popolo*; I think they should desist."[269]

The councils were thought to reflect civic opinion, and so their judgments were believed by some to be "the voice of God," as Filippo Machiavelli once asserted.[270] Statesmen often cited the *popolo*'s will as a compelling argument for adopting, or rejecting a policy,[271] but they did not agree on the importance to be assigned to public opinion. A few were inclined to exclude the *popolo* entirely from the decision-making process. The people, Filippo Corsini once said, "should be instructed but not followed." Antonio Alessandri implied that popular judgment was invariably flawed, since the *popolo* always favored peace instead of war. In any large group of citizens, Matteo Castellani thought, there would be a sizeable proportion of unqualified men, those too young or too ignorant to give useful advice.[272] Either the

---

[267] CP, 43, 145r. The statutes of 1415 guaranteed the right of counselors to speak freely; *Statuta populi et communis*, II, 671.

[268] Valori, "Honeste et humane in consiliis domini se gesserunt"; Bonciani, "honestissime domini se gesserunt in propositis consilio factis . . . et si non obtinetur, desistant et dedecorum non est"; CP, 43, f.145r.

[269] ". . . Et si solum domini et collegiis haberent hec deliberare, unum esset; sed ad consilia referri hec debent et quod experientia iam demonstravit quid velint consilia; et ob hoc licet sibi aut aliis videretur quod utilia forent et grata populo et quod obtineri deberet, consuleret ut fieret. Sed contrarium inspiciens et per effectum in diminutionem honoris dominorum quod nunc cum dedecore quererent quod adquesitum est et non gratum populo; et desistendum ab iis putat"; CP, 43, f.116v. Palla Strozzi concurred; *ibid.*, f.117v.

[270] "Vox populi vox Dei est, et dici potest quod heri consilium habitum fuerit approbatum per totam civitatem, quod ex omni qualitate ibi erant cives"; CP, 45, f.45v, 6 Aug. 1422.

[271] Thus, Simone Bordoni, Alessandro Alessandri, Giovanni Biliotti, Maso degli Albizzi; CP, 27, ff.45r, 94v; 32, f.21r; 40, f.96r.

[272] Corsini, "Populus sit docendus et non sequendus"; CP, 43, f.37r. For Alessandri's and Castellani's views, CP, 41, f.161r; 42, f.128r.

peers of these few did not share these elitist opinions or they were unwilling to express them publicly. More common were appeals for more extensive consultation with the citizenry, for larger groups to be assembled in the *pratiche*. Lorenzo Ridolfi's counsel (April 1416) reflects this viewpoint: "So that all might speak with one tongue, and so that greater unity will be achieved among the *popolo*, it seems to me that a larger number of counselors should be assembled." Antonio da Rabatta once proposed that a great convocation be held, "with men of every quality—great, middling, and small."[273] Like Lorenzo Ridolfi, Agnolo Pandolfini was an outspoken advocate of *governo largo*. In a discussion (April 1423) over sending a galley fleet to Atlantic ports, he advised the Signoria to test public opinion before, and not after, the ships had sailed.[274] The regime's willingness to consult the citizenry was perhaps most evident in the decade after 1415, a period marked by the absence of serious crises. In those years a rough consensus may have been achieved on this issue, as formulated by Giovanni Capponi: "The *popolo* ought to concur in all deliberations and in all agreements."[275]

Ridolfi and Pandolfini held that to broaden the consultative process, to canvass public opinion thoroughly, was to guarantee civic support for the regime's decisions. But a price had to be paid for this concession to the popular will: the proliferation of controversy. The reconciliation of diverse opinions was best achieved, Michele Castellani felt, in a "very select group of experienced citizens."[276] When everyone spoke his mind freely, as Bartolomeo Orlandini urged his colleagues to do,[277] the prospects for agreement were less.[278] A minority accepted

---

[273] *CP*, 43, f.86r; 44, f.182r. Cf. Bernardo Guadagni's counsel on behalf of the Twelve: "Quod domini habent consilium requisitorum in magno numero et cuiuslibet qualitatis"; *CP*, 45, f.8r, 2 May 1422.

[274] *CP*, 45, f.101r, 9 Apr. 1423. See Pandolfini's statement; *ibid.*, f.46r: "A consultis tam unite discedere et pro tot non debemus nec convenit et quamvis ostensum sit quod id sequendum, inconveniens sequi posset, tamen peius esse consilium paucorum sequi quam multorum." On the controversy between proponents of a *governo largo* and *governo stretto* in the 1490s, see F. Gilbert, *Machiavelli and Guicciardini* (Princeton, 1965), 19–28, 49–74.

[275] *CP*, 45, f.116r: "Populus concurrere debet ad omnia deliberandam et ad conducendam." Cf. Palla Strozzi, *ibid.*, f.120r: "Persequetur voluntas populi, que habita, ita sequatur."

[276] *CP*, 45, f.54v.

[277] *Ibid.*, f.8v: "Quod opinionis est ut omnia dici et exprimi debeant in numero copioso populi ut ad presens. . . . Suam tandem sententiam expressit, dicens quod etc. . . ."

[278] Jacopo Federighi, *CP*, 46, f.32r: "Nil acceptius Deo et utilius rei publice, sed ut apparet modum in consultis ad presens, sed in consilio populi varie sunt oppiniones. . . ."

this situation as inevitable, and even as a positive feature of republican government. No one should be surprised, Cristofano di Giorgio observed, that there was such diversity of opinion, since Florence was a large and populous city.[279] God and nature have made everyone different, Felice Brancacci noted, and so it is normal for opinions to vary.[280] The mores of a free community, Rinaldo Gianfigliazzi said, permit disagreement, and even criticism of the government.[281] But these liberal views ran counter to a strong conviction that disputes over political issues were a threat to civic unity. Piero Firenze confessed in 1415 that he was frightened by the "various and diverse statements and opinions of the citizens"; Alessandro Bencivenni demanded that criticisms of the regime that were circulating in the streets be suppressed.[282] Within the palace, free debate was tolerated and even encouraged; those who showed any reluctance to express their candid opinions were sometimes criticized for unpatriotic behavior.[283] But once a decision had been reached, then the quarrels must cease and criticism was no longer to be tolerated.

There was more agreement over the need to preserve the Signoria's dignity than to set precise limits to its authority, or to define the *popolo*'s role in the government. The civic impulse to exalt the majesty of the supreme executive appeared to become stronger, or at least more openly expressed, in the early *quattrocento* than before. A decree promulgated in 1420 illustrated this phenomenon; it barred the foreign rectors (*podestà*, captain, executor) from sitting on the same level as the priors in the palace or the loggia.[284] The trend was manifest, too, in the laudatory welcome for every incoming priorate. "To the praise and glory of the Signoria," Michele Castellani dedicated a speech of January 1423, for their efforts on behalf of civic concord; such was their prudence and virtue that their proposals had to be studied with the greatest care.[285] Lorenzo Ridolfi's encomium of 1428

[279] *CP*, 43, f.104v: "Licet aliqui loquantur aliter, non est mirum cum civitas magna sit et civibus plena. . . ."
[280] *CP*, 46, f.76v.
[281] *CP*, 34, f.138r: "Ostendatur dulciter potestati quod de oblocutionibus non curret, narrando ei mores libere civitatis."
[282] *CP*, 43, f.14r.
[283] For examples of such criticism, Niccolò da Uzzano, *CP*, 45, f.115v; Donato Velluti, *CP*, 46, f.40r; Giovanni del Teghia; *ibid.*, f.66r.
[284] The judges and their officials had to sit "in uno gradu inferiori"; *DSCOA*, 34, f.69v, 31 Aug. 1420. On the elaborate ceremony of the installation of each Signoria, see *Statuta populi et communis*, II, 501–04.
[285] See Strozza Strozzi's comment: "Quod cives omnes laudes et commendationes dominorum exhibere debent propter gesta prudentissima et virtuosa"; *CP*, 46, f.48r, 5 May 1425.

was even more enthusiastic: "As only one God should be adored, so you, lord priors, are to be venerated above all citizens, and those who turn their eyes to others are worshipping false idols and are to be condemned."[286] So sensitive were some citizens to any real or imagined affront to the signorial dignity that a minor incident could spark an explosion of outrage. In March 1421, the box for receiving anonymous denunciations (*tamburazioni*) was stolen from the cathedral. The spokesman for the Sixteen, Giovanni Minerbetti, said that he and his colleagues were mortified by that deed, which demeaned the commune and the standard-bearer of justice. For the Twelve, Giovanni Biliotti concurred; the theft was a slur upon the Signoria's dignity that must be removed. Still seething with anger two days later, the Sixteen announced that "they were willing to come and go, according to the Signoria's instructions, from noon until six o'clock at night . . . to obey their commands."[287]

This intense preoccupation with the Signoria's honor and dignity may have been a manifestation of the expanding power of the executive. But Lorenzo Ridolfi's statement suggests that he was concerned about the erosion of the priors' authority, and the possibility of its usurpation by individuals or groups outside the constitutional structure. To confront that issue squarely and to make specific accusations against individuals was to invite retaliation, so civic anxiety was camouflaged by exaggerated obeisances to the executive, or by such statements as Simone Bordoni's injunction that "no one in the city should be above the priors."[288] On rare occasions a citizen might deplore the abasement of the Signoria's prestige,[289] but only once, in the

---

[286] CP, 48, f.51r, cited by Kent, "*Reggimento*," *Renaissance Quarterly*, xxviii, 580. The style of addressing the Signoria became distinctly more obsequious in the late 1420s; the counselors' language (as reported by the notaries) suggests that the priors were the proprietors of the *reggimento*; e.g., these statements by Niccolò Rittafè and Vannozzo Serragli: "Quod proposita facta per dominationem vestram sit honesta et iusta. . . . Dominatio vestra deinde poterit proponi facere inter istos vestros servitores illas societates que videbuntur approbande. . . . Et dominatio, auditis his qui venerint, et examinatis rebus omnibus, poterit cum istis suis servitoribus providere circa approbationem earum societatum que non sunt causa scandalorum civium, ex quo dominationi vestri et vestris collegiis resultabit honor et sequetur unitas"; CP, 46, f.194v, 27 Aug. 1426.

[287] CP, 44, ff.77r–77v. For the reaction to an assault upon a member of the Sixteen, Piero Lenzi, see above, 84–85.

[288] CP, 33, f.134r, 16 Feb. 1399. Cf. the comments of Guccio Gucci and Luigi Guicciardini; *ibid.*, 26, f.32r.

[289] E.g., Piero Firenze; CP, 42, ff.83r, 127r: "Multo tempore citra dominationis reputatio deminuta est"; Gino Capponi, "Quod hec que machinabuntur procedant ex varie locutione . . . civium appetentium ultra debitum, et ex reverentia sublata

summer of 1414, was the problem examined with more than cursory attention. Led by Gino Capponi, a minority within the inner circle had accused certain unidentified citizens, who had promoted the peace treaty with King Ladislaus, of violating the constitution and infringing upon the Signoria's authority. The specific charge against these men was their discussion of public affairs outside the palace, in secret meetings. "We have a Nero in our midst," Gino Capponi cried, "as can be seen from their speeches and the color of their faces!"[290] Filippo Corsini, Marsilio Vecchietti, and Antonio Alessandri also condemned these illegal meetings; the latter proclaimed that only "the priors have the authority to rule and govern, and not private citizens who—by power, presumption or ignorance—involve themselves in these matters."[291] None of these complaints touched upon the crucial issue, which a more astute observer, Paolo Biliotti, perceived as the conflict between republican ideals and a regime permeated with hierarchic and elitist values. To overcome that contradiction, Biliotti argued strongly for the primacy of public authority. Even if a citizen's father or his relatives had been executed by the state, that would not justify any criticism of the republic. Citizens should express their opinions fearlessly, without any concern for their private interest. They should concentrate so intently upon the public welfare that they would never be tempted to use the civic forum to pursue their private quarrels. And they should treat each other not as vassals but as brothers.[292]

This civic ideal—with its emphasis on fraternity and equality, of willing sacrifice for the *res publica*—was much discussed by Florentine statesmen in these years. A profile of the model citizen can be constructed from the records of the *pratiche*. So dedicated was this paragon to the public interest that he gave no thought to private sentiments, nor was he swayed by the importunities of friends and rela-

---

dominis, nam non ut in preteritum devotio et reverentia dominorum adhibentur"; CP, 41, f.53r, 16 Nov. 1411.

[290] *Commissioni di Rinaldo degli Albizzi*, I, 240.

[291] Alessandri, "Quod domini habent regimen et gubernationem et non alii privati qui per potentiam presumptionem vel ignorantiam similia gerunt. . . . Extra palatium publica non geruntur"; CP, 42, f.163r. Corsini's statement, *ibid.*, f.164r.

[292] "Cives omnes esse debent parati ad exequendum quod domini proponunt; et siquis foret cuius etiam pater et maiores occisi fuissent, redarguendus foret si contra publica loqueretur et diabolicus foret. Sed omnes sine passione consulere debent pro bono publico. Et siquis contra loqueretur vel ageret e consortio aliorum eiciendus esse. Omnibus ministretur iusticia; et cives adeo iusti sint, ut aringheria libera sit; et non loquendo secundum voluntatem civium aliquorum inimicentur et contra eos queratur. Et velint alios cives ut fratres et non ut vassalos et sic agendo unitas facta est"; CP, 43, f.15r.

tives. "If we are true citizens," Jacopo Vecchietti said, "we will not consider our personal feelings; Giuliano Davanzati emphasized the need, in assessing forced loans, to suppress "all partisan bias and affection for one's *gonfalone* and quarter."[293] The citizen was ready, indeed eager, to sacrifice everything for the republic: to give all his property in 500-florin installments, as Matteo Tinghi promised; to pawn his law books, as Rosso Orlandi offered; to give all his property and his blood, as Alessandro Bencivenni volunteered.[294] To sharpen this image of sacrifice, some citizens described their own privations resulting from their tax payments or from a communal policy they had supported that had damaged their interests. No family in the quarter of Santo Spirito, Niccolò Barbadori complained, "has been more heavily taxed than my own; I have lost everything."[295] In May 1423 Averardo de' Medici supported a diplomatic policy that would have endangered his mercantile investments in the Regno, "which are greater than those of any other citizen; nevertheless, I favor this action on account of the public good."[296] Speaking in favor of a new scrutiny in 1416, Paolo Biliotti and Matteo Castellani both denied that they were motivated by self interest. In discussing a proposal made that year to tax the clergy, Lorenzo Ridolfi stated that he had no clerical relatives and thus could speak objectively; Matteo Castellani admitted that he did have nephews in holy orders, but said that that fact should not disqualify him from commenting on the issue.[297]

The effectiveness of these exhortations to promote civic virtues and the dramatization of individual sacrifices (or readiness to sacrifice) for the common good is not easily measured. Pressures to conform to this ideal were very powerful, though it would be unrealistic to believe that the public interest invariably triumphed over the desires and passions (*passiones, singularitates, particularitates*) of individuals, even those most strongly committed to the regime. Some pessimistic observers professed to see a decline in patriotic fervor during these years. In 1413 Berardo Berardi compared the singleminded devotion to the commune of earlier generations to the current exploitation of office for private advantage. Similar accusations were made in 1414 by Marco

[293] CP, 44, ff.54r, 136v. Also, Palla Strozzi's statement, "omnes obligantur non ad utilitatem propriam sed rei publice"; and Filippo Mangioni, "singularitates relinquens et ad bonum publicum intendamus"; CP, 46, f.4v.

[294] CP, 26, f.224r; 40, f.46r; 45, f.120v.

[295] CP, 45, f.46v; 46, f.37r. Barbadori voiced his lament in Feb. 1425; two years later, *catasto* records show his net worth, after deductions, at 24,438 fl.; Martines, *Social World*, 375. Cf. Maso degli Albizzi's assertion that "orbi est notum quod non habet pecuniam, et quam enormiter prestantiis sit gravatus"; CP, 40, f.191r.

[296] CP, 45, f.127r.   [297] CP, 43, f.89v.

Strozzi, Antonio Peruzzi, and Michele Castellani; "many are interested only in profit and not in virtue," the latter charged.[298] Those priors who sat in the supreme executive in the spring of 1417 were, Jacopo Vecchietti thought, a very special breed. Unlike their predecessors, "who always attended to their own advantage, and that of their [relatives and friends]," these citizens had put aside their private interests to promote the welfare of the community.[299] Only an innocent would believe that in Florence ties of blood and friendship could ever be excluded entirely from politics. "Everyone thinks about his own advantage," Matteo Castellani admitted, and Piero Guicciardini articulated the corollary, "one desires to favor one's friends and kinsmen."[300] A reasonable goal was to achieve a balance between public and private interest, and to restrain those impulses for self-aggrandizement that were part of every Florentine's heritage.

Though most citizens accepted that reality described by Giovanni Morelli—that in every *gonfalone* or neighborhood existed one or more cliques "in which communal affairs are settled, as happens every day"[301]—these sects aroused much anxiety within the *reggimento*. Factionalism had been the bane of the republic in past times; Agnolo di Pino recalled (1412) the ancient quarrels between Guelfs and Ghibellines and warned that internecine strife might again break out in the city.[302] Two years later (August 1414) Giovanni Soderini was persuaded that the regime's difficulties were due to the proliferation of sects.[303] Religious confraternities had long been viewed with suspicion by the authorities, as centers of illegal political activity. In 1419, the councils approved a provision barring all confraternities and other

[298] *CP*, 42, f.94v.

[299] *CP*, 43, f.139r: "Post commendationes egregias dominorum, qui ut proprias passiones excierunt, ut ad rei publice statum pacificum intendere possint, dixit et consuluit, attento more hactenus consueto in omnibus administrationibus semper ad propriam commodum et suorum attinentium mentes direxerunt, et multi qui merebantur suum debitum non obtinuerunt et iudicia non vera nec iusta data sunt, quoniam multi intervenerunt ad scrutinia celebranda qui regimen hactenus nullum habuerunt...."

[300] *CP*, 44, f.135v; 46, f.37v. Cf. Francesco Machiavelli: "Etiam difficultates esse in regendo vestro populo non est mirandum, quoniam quisque ad commodum suum respicit"; *CP*, 46, f.181r, 6 Aug. 1426.

[301] "... Se nella tua città, o veramente nel tuo gonfalone o vicinanza, si criasse una setta o più, nella quale s'avesse a trafficare i fatti del tuo Comune, come tutto giorno avviene"; Morelli, *Ricordi*, 280. On the structures of these factions, see above, 26–30; and Kent, *Rise of the Medici*, ch. 1, 2.

[302] *CP*, 41, f.71v. For a summary of the legislation prohibiting conventicles and factions, see *Statuta populi et communis*, 1, 275–85.

[303] *CP*, 42, f.165r.

"societies," though providing for the reestablishment of those approved by the Signoria and the colleges.[304] The deliberations that preceded the passage of that legislation have not survived, but the rationale for the dissolution of confraternities was developed in a *pratica* convened in August 1426 to consider another ban on these organizations. If religious societies congregate for the salvation of souls, Francesco Machiavelli said, their purposes are laudable. Instead, "they meet to discuss public affairs, whence the most serious dissensions, hatred and evils arise." Machiavelli advocated the dissolution of all confraternities, good and bad, to insure that "under the guise of virtue, they do no harm."[305] Speaking for the Merchants' Court, Giovanni de' Medici concurred. He and his colleagues had heard that members of these societies had discussed the allocation of offices to unworthy recipients, and the manipulation of tax assessments. That issue had been raised four years earlier, in 1422, when the first debates were held concerning the introduction of the *catasto*. Those who favored that device for achieving fiscal equity cited the proliferation of clandestine meetings that were then being held in several *gonfaloni*, to reduce the tax levies of friends, kinsmen, and clients.[306] Throughout the five-year debate on the merits of the *catasto*, this charge of favoritism in the allocation of the *prestanze* was a key argument advanced by those who believed that fiscal injustice was a malignant disease sapping the vitality of the body politic.[307]

Fueling these debates over the character of this regime—its authority and the limits upon its powers; the obligation to consult and the right to dissent; the tensions between public and private obligations—

---

[304] *Prov.*, 109, ff.160v–161v, 19–20 Oct. 1419, parts trans. in Brucker, *Society of Renaissance Florence*, 83–84.

[305] *CP*, 46, f.184r, 10 Aug. 1426.

[306] Rinaldo degli Albizzi's references to "amicitias et parentelas"; Neri Capponi, "qui fognas posuerunt et conventicula fecerunt"; Ridolfo Peruzzi, "ut dicitur, in pluribus gonfalonis posture facte fuerunt et sic impositiones non honeste processerunt"; Piero del Palagio, "quia inconvenientia multa ex societatibus in civitate secuta sunt . . . offerentes se paratos ut tollantur societates"; Francesco Machiavelli, "exgravationes, ut dicunt, propter parentelas, societates et amicitias non eque fuerunt"; *CP*, 45, ff.43v, 45r, 55r, 96r; 46, f.43r. For a contemporary definition of "fogna," see the petition of Piero and Polda Pazzi, *Prov.*, 105, ff.109v–110r, 28 Aug. 1415: "Quod eisdem redditur impossibile solvere ipsas quantitates sine gratia, cum impositiones que eisdem facte fuerunt ab impositoribus designate fuerunt potius ut fogne, secundum communem usum loquendi, quam ad hoc ut secundum illas onera supportarent. . . ."

[307] Messer Nello Martini, "quod natura gubernande rei publice secundum Philosophum est gubernare ut corpus, et nil relinquatur. Si civitas onerum inequalitate gubernatur, non est utile"; *CP*, 45, f.165r, 3 Feb. 1424.

was a dimly perceived awareness that the polity had changed, was changing, and that new realities required an adjustment of traditional values. Guelfism was perhaps the most emotionally charged of all the concepts that Florentines had inherited from the past, and so a particularly difficult issue to examine objectively. The Parte Guelfa was still part of the constitutional structure, and formal allegiance to Guelf principles a prerequisite to membership in the *reggimento*. But the Parte had been seriously damaged by its struggles with the commune in the 1370s and 1380s; it was no longer an independent force in Florentine politics.[308] By the early years of the fifteenth century, the society had fallen into such low repute, Buonaccorso Pitti reported, that "the Captains had difficulty in recruiting citizens to accompany them on processions. . . ." Rinaldo Gianfigliazzi complained bitterly that he and his sons had been excluded from the Parte captaincy, which had instead been filled by others whose ancestors were Ghibellines and *contadini*.[309] With the approval of their councils and an assembly of other Guelfs, the captains decided (November 1413) to burn all of the old scrutinies for Parte offices and to hold a new election. The objective, so their spokesman Giovanni Vettori insisted, was to rejuvenate the Parte and unite the citizens, "and not for private advantage or any extraneous reason."[310] Though everyone participating in the debate conceded that whatever benefited the Parte must strengthen the regime, several counselors voiced their opposition to these reforms. Michele di Ser Parente feared another purge by Guelf fanatics: "I remember what happened in 1378 and the rumors that have circulated in recent days have frightened me. . . ." Michele's anxieties, doubtless shared by others with long memories and a tenuous foothold in the regime, did not trouble Rinaldo Rondinelli and Piero Baroncelli, who objected particularly to the destruction of the pouches. Since 1378, Baroncelli argued, all Florence's troubles have originated in this nefarious practice, "and it is bringing the city to the brink of disaster." Agreeing with Baroncelli, Lorenzo Ridolfi noted that the Florentines had become the laughingstock of their neighbors because "they were always holding elections"; he warned his listeners that the Bolognese had lost their liberty for indulging in similar frivolities. But these men did subscribe to the principle that the Parte Guelfa was a solid prop for the regime, and that its rejuvenation would promote unity and stability. That myth was so tenaciously held, and

[308] Brucker, *Florentine Politics*, 244-65, 297-308, 336-86; and above, 64-68.
[309] Pitti, *Cronica*, 184; *CP*, 42, f.88r, 16 Nov. 1413.
[310] The debate on this issue is in *ibid.*, ff.87v-89v.

the nostalgia sustaining it was so strong, that it could persist in the face of overwhelming evidence to the contrary.

The decay of Guelfism as a real force in Florentine politics was linked to the disintegration of the Guelf entente in Italy. The keystone of that ideological structure, the Roman papacy, was so badly wounded by the Schism that it could not defend itself effectively, much less provide support for other Guelf states in the peninsula. The papacy's material resources and its authority declined steadily during the pontificates of Urban VI and Boniface IX, reaching its nadir in the first decade of the fifteenth century.[311] Yet the Guelf ideal died more slowly than did the coalition of interests that had supported it. Coluccio Salutati kept the vision alive in his chancery correspondence by praising, among others, Astorre Manfredi, lord of Faenza, for his family's devotion to the Guelf cause.[312] But the concept gradually disappeared from the vocabulary of those participating in debates, as its power to stir emotions dwindled. When men spoke of Guelfism in the *quattrocento*, they usually referred to a past age, as Forese Sacchetti did when he recalled (1421) that the enmity between the Visconti and the Florentine republic had originated in the ancient struggles between Guelfs and Ghibellines.[313] Old men like Filippo Corsini could lament the passing of an age when Guelfism was still a potent force in Florentine, and Italian, diplomacy. Looking back in 1415 over the events of his lifetime, Corsini ascribed the intensification of Florence's difficulties to her war with the papacy in the 1370s. "When there was only one pope," he reminisced, "we were always in good condition, and the church rescued us from many dangers. . . . But when we quarreled

---

[311] Most succinctly described by Partner, in *Flor. Studies*, 381–89.

[312] This and other examples in P. Herde, "Politik und Rhetorik in Florenz am Vorabend der Renaissance," *Archiv für Kulturgeschichte*, XLVII, 182. See the Signoria's letter (written by Salutati) to Carlo Malatesta in Apr. 1399; *SCMLC*, I, f.138v: "Li suoi maggiori sempre sono sute capo di Parte Guelfa in quelli paese come la nostra Signoria di qua. E che se questo segno e nome perisse per forza, converebbe perire elli e la casa sua. E che per questa cagione vedendo li processi di questo signore ghibellino [Giangaleazzo] . . . sarebbe disfacimento del paese, e vedendo che tutti li Ghibellini d'Italia si fanno una cosa e intendonsi con lui. . . ." R. Witt has noted the declining importance of Guelfism in Florentine political thinking at the end of the *trecento*; "A Note on Guelfism in late Medieval Florence"; *Nuova Rivista Storica*, LIII (1969), 134–45. See too Herde, "Politische Verhaltensweisen," *Geschichte und Verfassungsgefüge: Frankfurter Festgabe für Walter Schlesinger*, 165.

[313] *CP*, 44, f.138r. Cf. Roberto de' Rossi's comment, *CP*, 42, f.124r: "Et principaliter guelfi vocare Gebellinum, Italici barbarum et extraneum"; and Guidetto Guidetti, *CP*, 43, f.145r.

with the church, then everything turned against us."[314] Gino Capponi's deathbed statement (1420) exemplified a very different attitude. "A divided church benefits our commune and our liberty," he wrote, but then added that this was "contrary to faith," so the republic should never promote a schism.[315] If the papacy concentrated exclusively on spiritual matters—and, by implication, withdrew from secular politics —then unity would be beneficial to Florence. Then, as if appalled by the radical import of his remarks, he reverted to a more traditional posture: "The friendship of the papacy is useful to our commune, and never for any reason should you [his sons] oppose it, since nothing can succeed for us without the church's friendship."

Capponi's statement can be read as a tentative argument for the supremacy of civic over religious values, and of political realism over Guelf traditionalism. On this issue, as on others, Capponi could not bring himself to resolve the contradictions, as Machiavelli would do so brusquely a century later. Experience was to teach the Florentines that they could survive without papal support, and indeed with little help from any of their former allies. In the leagues that they had formed with other city-states in central Italy—Perugia, Città di Castello, Siena, Bologna, Lucca—during the second half of the fourteenth century, the Florentines had stressed the ideological cement, the commitment to republicanism, that bound them together.[316] During the papal war of the late 1370s, and later in the struggles with Giangaleazzo, this theme was a staple ingredient of Florentine propaganda.[317] The subsidence of this enthusiasm for Italian, as distinct from Florentine, republicanism was the result of bitter experience. One communal regime after another—Siena, Perugia, Pisa, Bologna, Genoa—had accepted the rule of the despot. So vulnerable were these city-states to the stratagems of a Giangaleazzo Visconti, a Jacopo d'Appiano, or a Boucicaut that the Florentines began to doubt the viability of republicanism anywhere except in their own community. When Paolo Guinigi established his control over Lucca in 1400, the republic sent Filippo Corsini to congratulate the new *signore*, whose rule "will provide much more effectively against dangers than the regime of a *popolo*."[318] To appeals for help from neighboring republics, belea-

---

[314] *CP*, 43, f.67r, 2 Oct. 1415.   [315] *Ricordi, op. cit.*, 36.

[316] N. Rubinstein, "Florence and the Despots," *Transactions of the Royal Historical Society*, 5th ser., II (1952), 38–46.

[317] Baron, *Crisis*, 2nd ed., 21–24.

[318] *SCMLC*, 2, f.35v. See also Florence's greetings to the new *signore* of Bologna, Giovanni Bentivoglio; *ibid.*, 3, f.33v, 16 March 1401; and their suggestion to the Perugini that they submit to papal rule; *SCMC*, 23, ff.112r–112v, 17 May 1393.

guered by foreign or domestic enemies, the Florentine government responded after 1402 with encouraging words, but rarely with offers of material aid or an alliance.[319] The Bolognese, Alessandro Bencivenni remarked in 1416, are an unstable people, "and they neither enjoy liberty nor are they able to preserve it."[320] Similar arguments were made about the Genoese, when that republic sought Florentine assistance. They are traditionally prone to revolution, Agnolo Pandolfini said in 1418, and Vieri Guadagni observed (1421) that "for the past thirty years, we have seen the city of Genoa in constant turmoil, and the prognosis for the future is the same."[321]

The major exception to this skepticism about the viability of Italian republicanism was Venice, whose congruence with Florence was mentioned with increasing frequency in the *pratiche*.[322] Like the interest in historical analogies, both contemporary and classical, this preoccupation with Venetian institutions and values began after 1410. Prior to that time, and particularly during the wars with Giangaleazzo, Florentines displayed no serious interest in the Venetian government, but criticized the Serenissima's policies as selfish and shortsighted.[323] The first favorable reference to the Venetian polity was made by Filippo Corsini, who noted (May 1412) that the Venetian commitment to rule by law had contributed to the durability of her regime.[324] Two humanists, Agnolo Pandolfini and Roberto de' Rossi, were most ardent in their praise of the Adriatic republic. There is no community in Italy, Rossi argued, "that is more like ours, since both they and we

---

Florentine ambivalence toward despots and despotic regimes has been noted by Rubinstein, and by Herde, "Politik und Rhetorik," *Archiv für Kulturgeschichte*, XLVII, 190–220.

[319] An example of the rhetoric, *SCMLC*, 6, f.61r, 6 Feb. 1416; and of civic opposition to leagues with Perugia and Bologna; *CP*, 42, ff.178v–180v; 43, ff.6v–85v, 34v–35r, 83v–85v. Florentines did not forget the submission of Siena and Perugia to Giangaleazzo; cf. the comments of Doffo Spini and Giovanni Morelli; *CP*, 42, f.179r; 43, f.85v.

[320] *CP*, 43, f.85r: "Populus ille volubilis est nec suam libertatem gustavit nec apti sunt nec possunt liberatem manutenere." See too the comments of Lorenzo Barducci and Giuliano Davanzati on the mutability of the Bolognese; *CP*, 44, f.155r.

[321] *CP*, 43, f.165v; 44, f.61r.

[322] Two other exceptions: Siena and Città di Castello. Florence gave sustained help to the Sienese republic, to protect her southern frontier. The citizens of Città di Castello were loyal to Florence and their appeals for help always received a sympathetic hearing; e.g., *CP*, 44, ff.76v–78r; 45, ff.34r–36r, 40r–41r.

[323] The Venetians did not respond to Florentine requests for aid against Giangaleazzo; above, 164, 179.

[324] *CP*, 41, f.97v.

enjoy liberty."[325] The notions that Florentines harbored about their fellow republicans in Venice were quite vague and not always accurate. Niccolò da Uzzano, for example, once argued (1422) for an alliance on the grounds that Venetians "are very powerful and do not seek aggrandizement but rather tranquility like ourselves."[326] Though ancient fears and suspicions of Venice dissolved very slowly,[327] the Florentines became increasingly aware of, and sensitive to, the relevance of that community's history to their own problems. Rinaldo degli Albizzi singled out Venice as the model to emulate on electoral legislation, Averardo de' Medici on fiscal reform.[328] In the Venetian republic the Florentines had discovered an elitist regime similar to theirs, whose stability they hoped to emulate, and whose strength they might exploit for their own advantage.[329] The psychological rewards of thus identifying with another republic, even more powerful and durable than their own, were substantial.

[325] CP, 42, ff.103v, 105r (Pandolfini); 121r (Rossi). The theme was picked up in official correspondence: "Non è signoria alcuna in Italia a chui portamo et abbiamo più singulare ne intrinseca affectione et amore che alla loro . . . et in nostro reggimento a loro sono conformi che più alcuno non c'è si governi sotto libertà se non i sanesi"; SCMLC, 6, f.30v, 9 June 1413.

[326] CP, 45, f.24r: ". . . Nova non querunt sed requiscere querunt ut nos." Lorenzo Barducci concurred; ibid., f.25r.

[327] See the debate on the Venetian proposal for an alliance; CP, 43, ff.36v–44v, June 1415.

[328] CP, 42, f.176r; 45, f.48r.

[329] See the comments of Marsilio Vecchietti, Piero Baroncelli, Francesco Machiavelli, Niccolò del Bellaccio and Duccio Mancini; CP, 42, f.157v; 43, ff.36v, 39r; 44, f.131r; 45, f.93v. Averardo de' Medici articulated the vision: "Et est tanta Venetorum et nostra reputatio ut sine expensa et impresa tutari debemus libertatem Italie"; CP, 45, f.24v, 3 June 1422. On the later development of Florentine attitudes toward Venice, see F. Gilbert, "The Venetian Constitution in Florentine Political Thought," Flor. Studies, 472–77.

CHAPTER VI

Crisis, 1411–1414

THE FOUR HORSEMEN

WHEN the Florentine republic made peace with King Ladislaus in February 1411, her leaders could take credit for successfully resisting the Angevin's challenge to their Tuscan hegemony as, a decade earlier, they had survived Giangaleazzo Visconti's assault on their liberty. The conquest of Pisa in 1406 had enlarged her territory by one-fourth, and she had finally gained access to the sea. Internally, the regime was stable. The leaders were united by their common commitment to republican values, and by their sharing of civic rewards. Though resentful of the fiscal burdens and (to a lesser degree) of its loss of power, the *popolo* was placated by the republican propaganda issuing from the palace of the Signoria and by such dramatic events as the conquest of Pisa.

But these strengths and achievements were ignored by Florentine statesmen, who generally shared Alessio Baldovinetti's pessimistic view (January 1411) that the city was in the most desperate condition in its history, "as a consequence of the war, the plague, which is imminent, and business, which is at a standstill."[1] The peace with Ladislaus did not improve civic morale appreciably. The settlement had infuriated the pro-papal faction, whose members viewed its promoters as traitors in the pay of the Angevin king. A badly divided regime was confronted by a set of difficult problems which had not been resolved by the peace. Foremost in this category was the continuation of the Genoese war, which neither force nor diplomacy could terminate. Pisa's blockade by Genoese galleys deprived Florentine cloth factories of wool, and their workers of employment. A bad harvest and a recurrence of plague intensified the sufferings of the poor. The expenditure of public funds for grain to avert starvation and rioting further aggravated a fiscal crisis that had been brewing since Pisa's reconquest in 1406. This conjuncture of disasters encouraged Florentine exiles in Bologna to attack a regime that appeared to be so vulnerable. For three years, from the plague summer of 1411 until the death of the archenemy Ladislaus in August 1414, the regime faced a series of ordeals, each seemingly more dangerous than its predecessor, each taking a heavy toll of resources, energy, and will power.

[1] CP, 40, f.213r, 5 Nov. 1410.

Among the problems confronting the republic in 1411, the resolution of the Genoese conflict was the most intractable. Though both governments professed a willingness to end hostilities, neither was willing to make significant concessions to the other. Initially (March 1411), Florence demanded Genoa's acquiescence in her occupation of Sarzana, as well as recognition of her preeminence in Livorno. When the Genoese balked at these conditions, the Signoria then offered to place Sarzana in the possession of a third party, pending arbitration.[2] The Genoese insisted on the return of two villages, Lerici and Sarzanello, on the Florentine-Genoese frontier, but the Signoria would not surrender them until all Florentine merchandise confiscated by Genoa was restored.[3] Counselors repeatedly denounced the Genoese as faithless Ghibellines and recommended a continuation of the war.[4] In a rare *pratica* appearance, the humanist Roberto de' Rossi excoriated the Genoese for their intransigence: "Never conclude peace with them; it would be more honorable to die and to spend all of our resources. . . ."[5] Piero Baroncelli and Salamone Strozzi echoed these sentiments, but spokesmen for the mercantile community led by Agnolo Pandolfini exerted pressure on the Signoria to continue the parleys with the enemy.[6]

With Genoese galleys blockading Pisa and harassing Florentine trade with other Mediterranean ports, the overland routes received correspondingly greater attention in policy deliberations. "Considering that our city prospers from trade," Rinaldo Gianfigliazzi commented, "we must strive by every means to secure our routes . . . to Genoa, Venice, and Bologna. . . ."[7] The need to control trade outlets was a compelling argument cited by Gino Capponi for acquiring the Romagna city of Forlì, thus securing Florence's control of an important road to the Adriatic.[8] The most important route, however, was

[2] *SCMLC*, 5, ff.7r–8r; 6, ff.1r–3r. On the Florentine determination to have Livorno, *SCMC*, 29, f.3r.

[3] *SRRO*, 2, ff.2r–2v. On the Florentine reaction to this demand, see *CP*, 41, ff.2r–3r, 18 April.

[4] *CP*, 41, ff.9v–10r, 19 May. For Gino Capponi's comment on Ghibelline sentiment in Genoa, *ibid.*, f.43v.

[5] *Ibid.*, f.11r, 23 May. Cf. Martines, *Social World*, 159, n. 74.

[6] For Baroncelli's and Strozzi's views, *CP*, 41, ff.10r, 11r. Pandolfini favored the cession of the two villages, *ibid.*, f.2r. Maso degli Albizzi also wanted peace, f.11v, as did Banco da Verrazzano: "Quicumque pacem negaret, Deum negaret, et ipse pacem affectat et alios cunctos cives idem"; *ibid.*, f.2v.

[7] *CP*, 41, f.12r.

[8] *CP*, 41, f.1r, 13 April. This was a minority viewpoint, rejected by other counselors as too risky.

through Bologna, whose citizens expelled their papal governor in May and restored a republican regime. Though hesitant to alienate Pope John XXIII by giving aid to his rebellious subjects, the Florentines were even more afraid of that city's capitulation to Carlo Malatesta. If Bologna should fall into hostile hands, Filippo Corsini warned, the city's trade route to Venice would be blocked.[9] Though unwilling to make a formal alliance with the Bolognese, the Signoria congratulated them on recovering their liberty and promised to send troops if the aggressions of the Malatesta seriously threatened their regime.[10]

The Florentine economy, and particularly the cloth industry, suffered from the Genoese blockade, though the damage cannot be measured with precision. A biased witness, Agostino Spinola of Genoa, reported that the Florentines "were destitute and the people complain that they cannot earn a livelihood"; the consuls of the Lana guild (October 1412) reported that times were very bad and that neither the cloth manufacturers nor their employees were earning money.[11] The blockade drastically curtailed the supply of raw wool shipped from England and the Low Countries which normally arrived at Tuscan ports.[12] One of Florence's largest importers of Cotswold wool, Nofri di Palla Strozzi, abruptly stopped trading in that commodity in 1410 and did not resume wool purchases until 1414, a year after the peace treaty with Genoa.[13] Some galleys ran the blockade successfully and landed their cargoes in Porto Pisano and Talamone, but others were caught by the Genoese fleet or by pirates. The records of the Merchants' Court for these years are filled with accounts of these losses: fifty bales of Cotswold wool destined for Pisa and seized by the Genoese; a ship laden with merchandise from Palermo bound for Pisa, intercepted and burned; another ship carrying salt taken off the coast

---

[9] *Ibid.*, f.17r.

[10] *SCMLC*, 6, ff.5v–6r, 7v–8r.   [11] *AEOG*, 1759, f.73v, July 1411.

[12] See the petition of several Florentine merchants to use other Tyrrhenian ports besides Pisa, "quod propter guerram inter magnifichum communem Florentie et civitatem Janue, nullus mercator florentinus vel aliunde secure et sine magno periculo potest ad portum civitatis Pisis ponere et conducere . . . mercantias"; *DSCOA*, 30, ff.3v–4r, 5 May 1412. Some English wool was transported to Florence by land; *Merc.*, 1250, ff.251v–253v. The consuls of the Lana guild bought 1000 bales of Cotswold wool from the king of Portugal in Nov. 1411; *Lana*, 49, f.20v.

[13] Between Sept. 1406 and April 1409, Nofri bought 1100 bales of "lana francescha di Chodisgualdo" for 30,000 fl. His profit margin was about 25%; *Strozz.*, 3rd ser., 280, ff.37v–38v, 67v–69r, 90v–91v. Nofri resumed purchases of English wool in May 1414; *ibid.*, f.177r.

of Elba and its cargo confiscated by its captors.[14] These losses were borne by the Florentine merchants who owned the merchandise and by their insurers, who demanded high premiums for assuming part of the risk. Oil and woad were, like wool, in short supply, even though cloth production was below normal.[15] The factories did not shut down completely, as the Lana records show,[16] but continued to produce some cloth for markets that could be supplied by overland routes: by way of Bologna to Lombardy and northern Europe, through Venice to Hungary and Dalmatia, and southward to the Papal States and the Regno.[17]

The plague also contributed to the economic malaise, causing a massive exodus of affluent Florentines (some 3000 by one estimate)[18] who in normal times hired the poor as servants and laborers. With the pestilence, in the summer of 1411, came famine that brought more misery to a weakened and demoralized populace. The market price of wheat increased from 29 soldi per *staio* in February to 50 soldi in November.[19] Before the next summer's crop was harvested, in July 1412, the price had risen another 10 soldi, the equivalent of a week's salary for an unskilled worker.[20] Speaking in a *pratica* in September 1411, Francesco Leoni warned that the famine was a serious threat to the regime; he urged the Signoria to hold the price of flour at its current level, "since the poor are not earning anything."

[14] For these incidents, *Merc.*, 1252, ff.462v–463v; 1254, ff.19v–20r; 1255, ff.153r–153v. For other losses of ships and cargoes, *ibid.*, 1252, ff.462v–463v, 506v–507r; 1253, ff.436r–436v, 509v–510v; 1254, ff.380v–381r; 442r–442v.

[15] *Lana*, 49, ff.29v, 33r; 131, ff.26r–27r, 48v; 132, f.58r.

[16] For evidence of production, of *botteghe* leased and partnerships formed in these years, *ibid.*, 131, ff.45v, 92r; 132, ff.17v, 32r, 34v, 37r; 133, f.66v.

[17] For evidence of Florentine mercantile activity abroad in these years, *Merc.*, 1251, ff.404r–404v (Venice), 549v–550r (Tunis); 1252, ff.506v–507v (Naples); 1253, ff.36v–37r (Hungary); 1255, ff.92r–92v (Venice), 151r–151v (Todi), 152v (Buda).

[18] *Conc.*, 1878, no. 62. Buonaccorso Pitti left Florence with his family for Pisa in April 1411 and did not return until November; *Cronica*, 162–63. On 15 September, Piero Baroncelli advised the Signoria to write to citizens and urge them to return to Florence, "illis presertim quibus statum tangit"; *CP*, 41, f.34v.

[19] *Merc.*, 1251, ff.269v, 399r, 482r–483r. In August, the price was 36 s.; *Conc.*, 1878, no. 62. Goldthwaite's data from S. Maria Nuova does not reflect this increase: "I prezzi del grano a Firenze"; *Quaderni storici*, x, 33.

[20] *Merc.*, 1252, ff.157r (12 Jan. 1412, 55 s.), 568v (29 March 1412, 68 s.); 1253, f.117v (28 May 1412, 60 s.). By late June the price had dropped to 48 s., *ibid.*, f.129r, and in November, to 42 s.; *ibid.*, 1253, f.474v. Throughout the winter and spring of 1412, the price of grain was higher than normal; "valse soldi trenta e più"; *ibid.*, 1254, f.339r. For a general description of grain prices for these years, see Goldthwaite, *Quaderni storici*, x, 5–33.

He also advocated the passage of legislation to stem the exodus of peasants from the land, to avoid another famine in the following year.[21] The grain shortage intensified the fears of a populace that had been reduced to penury by the business recession and terrorized by the plague. The *podestà* and his retinue were insulted in the streets; placards denouncing the authorities were posted at night on public buildings. The Twelve attributed these manifestations of discontent to rumors that grain was being hoarded and exported from the territory. They advised the Signoria to punish both the hoarders and those who criticized the regime, "since these detractors are dangerous, and their words and scrawls are directed toward no good end."[22] The government reacted to the food crisis in customary fashion, by prohibiting grain exports, by imposing a special levy on absentees for food purchases, and by contracting with merchants to buy wheat in Sicily and elsewhere.[23] Some 7500 florins were allocated (August 1411) to a special grain treasury, and an additional 20,000 florins were spent for cereals in the following year.[24]

These extraordinary expenditures were borne by a fiscal system that had been bled by six years of heavy military outlays. In 1411, the total income from gabelles and direct taxes in the *contado* and district was 242,407 florins, a reduction of nearly one-third since 1407. Although the cost of mercenaries had declined since 1409, the fiscal deficit of 1411 still exceeded 230,000 florins, which had to be made up by forced loans.[25] As the number of delinquent taxpayers increased from year to year, the fiscal pressures intensified on those citizens who were still

[21] *CP*, 41, f.35v, 17 Sept. The Signoria and the colleges promulgated a decree that prohibited the prosecution or seizure for debt of any "lavoratore di terre" for one year; *Merc.*, 1251, ff.404r–404v, 511r–512r.

[22] Jacopo Sassolini, for the Twelve, *CP*, 41, f.25r, 12 Aug. The Sixteen commented: "De prolatis potestati per quosdam ex populo se condolent . . . et potestas debet recordari qui ei verba dixit, nam sunt hec importantie." For other references to grain hoarding and speculation, *ibid.*, ff.23r, 32r.

[23] For the special levy, *Prov.*, 100, ff.50v–51r, 13–14 Aug. At least one cargo of Sicilian grain transported by Florentine merchants to Pisa was seized by the Genoese; *SCMLC*, 6, ff.48r–49v. On 13 July, the Sixteen recommended a grant of 1000 fl. as alms for the poor; *CP*, 41, f.20r.

[24] The treasury records for 1411 have not survived, but those for 1412 contain some figures for the previous year; *Camera, Uscita*, 361, *passim*.

[25] Molho, *Florentine Public Finances*, 61–62. The decline in revenue from the *contado* was dramatic, from 154,000 fl. to 70,000 in 1411. Payments to soldiers were two and three years in arrears; *Camera, Uscita*, 361, payments to Paolo Orsini and Sforza da Cotignola. Rectors were complaining about not receiving their stipends; *CP*, 41, f.20r.

solvent.[26] Even an affluent entrepreneur like Nofri Strozzi, who was engaged in profitable exchange operations with Venice after his wool import business collapsed, must have been hard pressed to raise the 10,000 florins for his *prestanze* during the war with Ladislaus.[27] Men like Strozzi and Giovanni de' Medici had ample cause to vote against forced loans, even though they made money from banking during the commercial and industrial recession created by the Genoese blockade.[28] In March 1411, a provision authorizing a new levy and a new procedure for assessments was the subject of acrimonious debate; the disagreements could not be reconciled despite lengthy discussion and frequent balloting. Eventually, a modified version of the original plan for raising revenue passed both councils, but the scheme for reforming assessments was rejected seven times in three months.[29] Quarreling over the fisc did subside during the summer, as the critical problems of famine and plague preoccupied the minds of those citizens who remained in Florence, but it revived again in the autumn.

Public criticism of the fisc did not focus on the basic principles of the system—for example, on the heavy reliance upon gabelles and forced loans, or on the escalating costs of interest charges. Those citizens who had stifled their impulse to flee the hot, plague-ridden city were in no mood to consider basic reforms of a fiscal structure that had long been a target of complaints. The modest effort initiated in 1408 to rationalize the fisc had withered from lack of support; the focus had shifted from the institutional to the personal. Accusing the officials responsible for hiring mercenaries of malfeasance, Strozza Strozzi demanded an investigation of their expenditures.[30] Others grumbled about the poor state (*malus ordo*) of both the fiscal and the military establishment, but complained most vociferously about the flawed procedures for assessing the *prestanze*. In May 1411, Filippo Corsini fixed the blame for the fiscal crisis exclusively on the

[26] *LF*, 49, ff.69r–90r; *Prov.*, 100, ff.1r–2r. *Tratte*, 1095 *bis*, contains the names of some 2000 citizens who had not paid their *prestanzone* assessments, levied in Dec. 1413, by July 1414.

[27] *Strozz.*, 3rd ser., 281, ff.74v, 95r.

[28] Giovanni de' Medici's business operations in Rome and Venice are described by R. de Roover, *Rise and Decline of the Medici Bank*, 40–48, and G. Holmes, "How the Medici Became the Popes' Bankers," in *Flor. Studies*, 361–69. From 1397 to 1420, Medici profits from their cloth factories were much lower, only 1.1 and 4.4% of capital invested, than on their banking operations in Rome (52%), Florence (17%) and Venice (15%); De Roover, 175.

[29] *LF*, 49, ff.69r–90r; *Prov.*, 100, ff.1r–2r.

[30] "Quod ordinem communis et gentium armigerarum pessimum condennandum et inculpandum"; *ibid.*, f.8v.

maldistribution of the forced loans; six months later he repeated that charge, arguing that the inequities of assessment were the primary cause of civic discord. Correcting these injustices, Corsini implied, was not so much an institutional as a moral problem. If citizens who assigned the *prestanze* quotas were honest and virtuous and not greedy and malicious, then each would contribute his fair share to public expenditures, and all would live in peace and harmony.[31]

The debates thus reveal the pervasiveness of discontent in this community infected by plague, weakened and dispirited by unemployment and hunger, agonized by fear. But they did not reflect the intensity of discontent which, by midsummer, had impelled some Florentines to think about rebellion. The accounts of conspiracies contain references to specific feelings and aspirations of disaffected men of high and low status. The poor were the most desperate, and so the most obvious recruits for revolution. "You see," Bindaccio Alberti said to a friend in Florence, "how the *popolo* cries out," and to his relatives in Bologna he reported that "there are many more malcontents than ever before in Florence, and the *popolazzo* complains loudly. . . ."[32] A textile-worker, Cola di Maestro Piero, blamed the food shortage on the government: "These traitorous rulers have taken grain from the poultry and fed it to us; by God, we shall eat the good [grain] in their houses shortly; we don't deserve to be treated like chickens." Harking back to the time when the Alberti were prominent in Florentine politics and business, Cola explained his loyalty to the exiled family: "They were always good merchants and generous men, and they gave good wages to their employees."[33] Bindaccio Alberti testified at his trial that an acquaintance had reported to him that a placard had been posted in the city denouncing Maso degli Albizzi for the exile of his kinsmen. "If the stones could speak," Bindaccio had replied, "they would destroy this regime, and someday the *popolo* will expel him [Maso] and restore us." To the Florentine poor, the Alberti had become (or so Bindaccio was encouraged to believe) folk heroes whose mere appearance in the city would ignite a revolution. Reports of dissension within the leadership over the peace with Ladislaus strengthened Bindaccio's conviction that the regime would collapse easily. Maso degli Albizzi had been responsible for that agreement to win the favor of the *popolo*, so

[31] Cristofano di Giorgio also stressed the importance of choosing assessors "qui sint Deum timentes et passiones non habeant ut unicuique debitum imponant"; *ibid.*, f.53r, 16 Nov. 1411.

[32] *AEOG*, 1759, f.103v, 21 Aug. 1411. The full transcript of the condemnation, *ibid.*, ff.103r–108r.

[33] *Ibid.*, 1763, ff.3r–3v, trans. in my *Renaissance Florence*, 153.

the rumor circulated, and had further antagonized those who deplored the treaty by posting placards justifying his policy. The quarrel between Maso and Rinaldo Gianfigliazzi was so important, Bindaccio believed, because they were "the two principal columns" of the *reggimento*, which would founder if either one fell.[34]

Bindaccio's plot was nearly identical to those organized thirty years before by the Ciompi.[35] It called for the recruitment of a small band of determined men who, after gaining entrance to the palace of the Signoria, would break into the room where the priors were deliberating, shouting "Long live the *popolo* and the guilds!" The conspirators planned to assassinate two priors, Rinaldo Gianfigliazzi and Neri Vettori; the others would be locked in a room under guard. Then the rebels would march through the streets with the flag of the *popolo*, voicing the familiar slogans which, in the folklore of the Florentine conspiratorial tradition, would incite the populace to join the revolution.[36] When Bindaccio outlined the plot to the leaders of the exile community in Bologna, they told him that the risks were too great, and that to capture the palace he would need the cooperation of an official there. Undaunted by these warnings, Bindaccio returned to Florence to recruit his corps of revolutionaries.[37] If his own account may be believed, he enjoyed considerable success in persuading citizens to join the enterprise or, at the least, to promise support once the revolt began. The tenor of his appeal varied: to one, he promised money for a sister's dowry; to another, the cancellation of his criminal penalties; to yet another, the prospect of office in the new regime.[38] In

---

[34] Bindaccio may also have been encouraged by the absence of many citizens who had fled the city to escape the plague. According to a report from Pisa, 3000 Florentines rushed back to the city after the plot was revealed; *Conc.*, 1878, no. 62, 18 Aug.

[35] See my "The Florentine *Popolo Minuto* and its Political Role, 1340–1450," in *Violence and Civil Disorder in Italian Cities, 1200–1500*, ed. L. Martines, 178–79; above, 69–70.

[36] There was some discussion between Bindaccio and his relatives in Bologna concerning the recruitment of soldiers to support the rebellion; Bindaccio feared that the assembly of large bands would be noticed and thus imperil the enterprise; *AEOG*, 1759, ff.105v–106r.

[37] Bindaccio allegedly charged his relatives with cowardly behavior: "Crederisti che quisti captivi [cattivi] de quisti mey consorti non vogliono fare nulla? Ma nui semo iuveni, e faremolo nui francamente"; *ibid.*, ff.105r–105v.

[38] "Ei, fratello mio dolce, tu sai che tu stinti et vive mezzo desperato perchè tu non poi maritare tua sorella. Voresti tu retrovare la su en palagio a fare quello che tu voli? . . . Tu vidi che questa terra grida pane, e viditi i mali contenti. Se se facisse nulla, faresti voi ben niuno? . . . Tu sai che ai delli disdigni e male stato assai; se se facesse nulla, leveresti tu?"; *ibid.*, ff.105r, 106v.

the loggia of the Canigiani, in the piazza de' Mozzi, in the Borgo degli Albizzi, Bindaccio searched for recruits, encouraging those who responded favorably to identify other sympathizers. Inevitably, an informer learned of the plot and revealed it to the authorities. Bindaccio was imprisoned and tortured, and then wrote a lengthy confession implicating his co-conspirators.[39] Among those convicted by the executor were six Alberti, all living in exile, Bartolomeo Scali, Antonio de' Ricci, and three smaller fry. Two other citizens from well-known families, Antonio de' Mozzi and Francesco Mannelli, were also implicated but managed to persuade the authorities of their innocence.[40]

Bindaccio Alberti's execution made him a martyr in the eyes of the Florentine poor, whose hostility toward the regime intensified in the autumn of 1411. The despair born of hunger among these destitute workers was stronger than the fears of discovery and death. In taverns and in public squares, they met to share their grievances, to deplore the death of Bindaccio, "the finest and most chivalric young man in Florence,"[41] and finally to plot another revolution. This conspiracy was characterized by even less planning and leadership than Bindaccio's ill-fated enterprise; it developed spontaneously from random conversations among malcontents.[42] The alleviation of hunger was a primary goal of the leaders, who intended to sack the communal granary. The revolt was scheduled for a Saturday evening, 13 November.[43] Two bands of conspirators were to assemble on the south side of the Arno and move toward the Ponte Vecchio on the way to the palace of the Signoria. One group would stop at the home of Gino Capponi in the parish of San Jacopo Oltrarno, kill him, and sack his house. The converging throngs of revolutionaries would then assemble to storm the palace. If the priors refused to surrender, the rebels planned to seize their families as hostages and kill them if they did not open the palace doors. Once in control of the palace, they planned "to select those priors by hand who merit [the office], and we will burn all of the pouches [with the names of eligibles] of the offices, and we will reform the government as we wish. . . ." Of the fourteen identified conspirators, the majority were residents of the working-class parishes of San Frediano and Santa Maria in Verzaia in the quarter of Santo Spirito.[44] They had made no plans to seek assistance from the exile

[39] Bindaccio's attitude during his last hours is described in *SCMLC*, 6, ff.17v–18r.
[40] *AEOG*, 1759, ff.123r–128v, 13 Sept. 1411; *CP*, 41, ff.25r–26r.
[41] The words of Cola di Maestro Piero of Orvieto; *AEOG*, 1763, f.3r.
[42] *Ibid.*, f.3v; *AP*, 4254, ff.15r–16v.
[43] The fullest description in *AEOG*, 1763, ff.1r–1v.
[44] *AEOG*, 1763, ff.1r, 3r, 13r, 37r, 45r; *AP*, 4254, f.15r. The profession of only one conspirator, the tailor Giovanni di Guccio, was identified.

communities in Bologna and Siena, nor had they given serious thought to the composition of the new regime. To a potential recruit to their cause, one Antonio di Ricco called Magialla, the ringleaders promised that "you will have your part of the profits and honors of the city, and we will persecute those who exploit us daily and who now hold all of the offices within and without, and we will despoil them so that we no longer die of starvation. . . ."[45] One participant in these clandestine meetings, Meo Falconi, informed the authorities of the plot. Four conspirators were seized and hanged, and ten others were condemned to death *in absentia*.[46]

Not since 1400 had the regime been confronted by a serious challenge to its rule, and the leadership reacted quite calmly to Bindaccio Alberti's conspiracy. The counselors did not accuse the authorities of dereliction of duty but urged them to investigate the plot "deliberately and thoroughly," to punish the culpable according to the laws, and to take care that the innocent were not molested.[47] It would not be necessary, Filippo Corsini felt, to establish a *balìa* or to pass extraordinary legislation; "the citizens should unite in harmony and dispel all of their rancors, and thus will liberty and the regime be saved."[48] By minimizing the magnitude of the danger, and by limiting the scope of the inquiry, Corsini and those of like mind hoped to avoid an internal crisis. A minority expressed their disagreement with this strategy. In Matteo Castellani's judgment, Bindaccio Alberti was not lying when he implicated Francesco Mannelli and Antonio de' Mozzi; he wished to identify and prosecute everyone who had knowledge of the plot. Giovenco della Stufa warned that leniency in the past had contributed to this conspiracy and would spawn future ones; he favored a *balìa* to thwart such challenges to the regime's security.[49]

---

[45] *AEOG*, 1763, f.1v.

[46] Some counselors wanted to prosecute Meo, who was technically guilty of joining the conspiracy; others recommended that he be released; *CP*, 41, f.58r. It was suggested that benevolent treatment of Meo would encourage others involved in conspiracies to warn the authorities; *ibid.*, f.64r. Meo was eventually rewarded by the *balìa* created after the second Alberti plot; he received an office in Pisa for one year, and the right to bear arms in perpetuity; *Balìe*, 20, f.9v. Two *prioristi* noted that one of the Buondelmonti, Nanni di Agnolo called Giovanni della Pila, was also executed for treason, but I have not found his sentence in the judicial records; *Manoscritti*, 225, f.146r; *BNF, Conventi Soppressi*, C, 4, 895, f.81v.

[47] E.g., Agnolo Pandolfini and Maso degli Albizzi; *CP*, 41, f.25v, 12 and 17 Aug.

[48] *Ibid.*, f.27v.

[49] *Ibid.*, ff.26r, 27v. Matteo was spokesman for the Eight on Security who wanted to push the investigation. Zanobi Rucellai believed that others were implicated; *ibid.*, f.28r. For a summary of the differences of opinion over managing the investigation, see Passerini, *Alberti*, II, 315–16.

After a week's deliberation, the Signoria finally decided to quash the proceedings against Mannelli and Mozzi and to place the full responsibility for the plot on the Alberti. Only Bindaccio went to the executioner's block, and the councils passed a provision banning the entire family from Florence.[50]

To the news of the abortive revolt by the *popolo minuto* in November 1411, the reaction of the citizens was much less moderate than it had been in August. Speakers in the *pratiche* were incredulous; how could another conspiracy have been hatched so soon after the exposure of the Alberti plot? They excoriated the authorities for failing to take appropriate measures to defend the regime; they suggested, too, that the wretched men implicated in the plot were merely the pawns of prominent citizens. Most counselors agreed that the Signoria and the rectors had been too lax, not only in August, but a decade earlier during the 1400 conspiracy.[51] Leniency had encouraged the malefactors, not only the criminals directly involved in the plots, but those of more exalted condition who had abetted them. Rinaldo Rondinelli was convinced that men of high rank and reputation were implicated in the workers' revolt, and that those who opposed a rigorous investigation sought to protect their guilty relatives. Guglielmo Altoviti supported Rondinelli's contention, arguing that the conspirators had received support from certain unidentified members of the *reggimento*.[52] To ferret out, and to punish ruthlessly these subversives was essential to preserve the regime, but even more action was required, in the judgment of many. The tolerance displayed by the authorities toward the rebels was a symbol of a deeper malaise infecting the polity. Gino Capponi spoke bluntly: "These machinations result from the mouthings of those citizens who are greedy for more than they deserve, and also from a decline of respect for the Signoria." Speaking for the Eight on Security, Lorenzo Ridolfi said that the republic's deplorable state was a consequence of the executive's failure to implement the reforms "concerning which it daily asks counsel." Niccolò da Uzzano agreed that the origins of these evils were deeply rooted in political mores that had become corrupted. "The loose talk of men and the bad state

[50] *CP*, 41, f.30v; *Prov.*, 100, ff.61v–63r; *LF*, 49, ff.102r, 103r. The vote was 178–46 and 104–52. On the demands in the *pratiche* for penalties against the Alberti, *CP*, 41, ff.27v, 28v.

[51] The point was developed by Cristofano di Giorgio, for the Merchants' Court, and by Niccolò Barbadori and Banco da Verrazzano; *CP*, 41, ff.52r, 54v, 16 Nov.

[52] *Ibid.*, ff.52r, 54v, 55r. See Tommaso Popolani's statement: "Cum maturitate et diligentia procedatur in inveniendo radicem tractatus, et culpabiles puniantur; nec putatur ad hoc eos per se motos esse; sed alii multi, quorum ad hic nil dicitur, in his se immiscent"; *ibid.*, f.55v.

of the city are the source, and they provide fuel for conspiracy against the regime. No one should be surprised that so many have become bold in committing atrocities. . . ."[53]

To some citizens, the tone and content of these speeches were as frightening as the subversive activity of the malcontents. They were concerned, first, about the pressures for identifying and punishing those involved in the conspiracies, and, more generally, about the un-leashing of a campaign to purge the regime. To dampen these civic passions without incurring the opprobrium of the zealots became a major preoccupation of Maso degli Albizzi and Rinaldo Gianfigliazzi. The latter proclaimed his great relief and satisfaction (which he invited his listeners to share) upon learning that the conspirators had all been poor men who had not been involved "with any man of reputation or status." Maso also urged restraint: "Justice is the safety of the *popolo*. . . . The innocent should be released and their reputa-tions restored. . . ."[54] In an eloquent defense of government by law, Agnolo Pandolfini contended that "if justice is abandoned, then every-thing will collapse, for it is the only reason why the poor, who are so much more numerous, do not devour the rich."[55] By means of sober argument and soothing rhetoric, the leaders of the *reggimento* sought to calm the anxieties of their more troubled colleagues. Their success can be measured by the subsidence of the more vociferous clamors for vengeance in the *pratiche*[56] and by the rejection of proposals to create a *balìa* reponsible for internal security.[57] To defuse the pressures for institutional reform was a more complex task, since the evidence of maladministration, particularly in the military and fiscal spheres, was too clear to be ignored. In a *pratica* held on 25 November, Jacopo Malegonelle, Marco Strozzi, Niccolò degli Albizzi, and Lorenzo Raf-facani prescribed the remedies for civic unity: a new scrutiny for of-

[53] These statements in *ibid.*, ff.52v, 56v.

[54] *Ibid.*, f.58r, 25 Nov.

[55] ". . . Quia si iusticia cessaret, omnia periclitarentur, cum ea solum sit causa cur divites a pauperibus non deglutiuntur, cum eorum numerus maximus sit"; *ibid.*, f.55r.

[56] For an example of demands for harsh punishment, the statement of Rinaldo Rondinelli: "Quod dolet ex istis Ciompis; fiat vel ostendatur formido et [non] pusillanimitas; et quod pedites omnes qui hic sunt remittantur ad loca et domus eorum, et demum fiat ex culpabilibus executio ut consuetum est; et etiam more Venetorum, qui similes quattuor vel sex ad supplicium mittunt"; *ibid.*, f.58r.

[57] Shortly after the revelation of the conspiracy, the executor was given specific authority to investigate the case and "to conserve the regime"; *Prov.*, 100, ff.88r-88v, 14-15 Nov. 1411. Substantial minorities voted against the measure: 158-76 and 117-55.

fices to reward the meritorious, and a more equitable distribution of the *prestanze*.[58] But Rinaldo Gianfigliazzi and Filippo Corsini warned that instead of reconciling citizens, these measures might stimulate more discord. Gino Capponi delivered the most persuasive argument against any precipitate reform, and specifically against increasing the number of officeholders. Admitting that some citizens of merit had been unjustly denied office, he nevertheless argued that this was not a serious flaw in the political system. Any attempt to correct these inequities would lead inevitably to pressure from others, "and so daily one after the other [will seek his due], for everyone wants honors and profit and in this manner, the city will be destroyed. . . ."[59]

For those citizens who, in these troubled months, bore responsibility for governing the republic, the options must have seemed very limited, and the dangers overwhelming. Within the regime were powerful forces moving at cross purposes: impulses for reform blunted by contrary pressures to maintain the status quo. Any decision to solve an outstanding problem was dangerous in this tense atmosphere, but inaction and drift, the failure to act, were also subject to abrasive criticism. Those who wielded power during the late autumn and winter of 1411–1412, in the Signoria and in the important magistracies, concluded that action was the preferable course in a period of crisis. The public records reflect this decision: to confront the problems of the fisc and officeholding, to act decisively to terminate the Genoese imbroglio, either through negotiation or by force.

The war with the Ligurian republic had intensified in October, when the regime decided to accept the submission of the port town of Portovenere,[60] located on a promontory guarding the gulf of La Spezia, in that frontier zone where Genoa and Florence were competing for jurisdiction. In the *pratiche* held to discuss the acquisition, counselors expressed their frustration over Genoese recalcitrance and the continuation of the blockade which, by impeding grain shipments to Pisa, was an even greater threat to the city's welfare and the re-

---

[58] *CP*, 41, f.58v. Also supporting these reforms were the Twelve, the Parte captains and the Eight on Security; *ibid.*, f.59r.

[59] *Ibid.*, f.58v. Gianfigliazzi: ". . . Dum cupimus ob aliquos non contentos unionem ponere et scrutinia querere, alii demum dissentiunt et sic non sequeretur unitas sed oppositum. . . ." Capponi: ". . . Cum sint aliqui et iuste querentes hec qui merentur; sed infiniti sunt qui hec quererunt et si iuste fieret, extrahendi essent ex his in quibus sunt; nam nunc hec agendo insurgeret gens alia demum idem querens; et sic quotidie unus post alium, cum generaliter omnes appetant honores et utilitates; et taliter agendo, destructio civitatis procedet. . . ."

[60] The provision authorizing the acquisition of Portovenere was approved on 2–3 Oct. by votes of 166–64 and 124–38; *Prov.*, 100, ff.71v–73r.

gime's stability than before. "In the name of God," cried Ubaldino Guasconi, "let us act to occupy Portovenere," whose residents were Guelf and friendly to Florence. Gino Capponi formulated the imperialist argument in its most intransigent form. The Genoese, and particularly those with Ghibelline sympathies, were angered by Florence's acquisition of Pisa, and they would be persuaded to accept peace only by the relentless application of force.[61] Capponi favored the acquisition of Livorno as well as Portovenere, and it was the intensification of hostilities in Livorno that revived anxiety over the war in November.[62] The commander of that port city, Battista da Montaldo, had declared himself an ally of Genoa and an enemy of Florence. Several counselors expressed relief that the period of covert hostility had ended and that, in Tommaso Popolani's words, "it will now be obvious to all that the Genoese are assaulting us, who have continually sought peace." Most counselors felt that the crisis was sufficiently grave to warrant the creation of a war *balìa*. It would relieve the Signoria and the colleges, who were deeply involved in other public matters, of direct responsibility for prosecuting the war, and it would be a signal to the Genoese that, in Antonio del Vigna's opinion, "all of our individual passions and desires have been suppressed, and we are concentrating exclusively on the public interest and are united in our determination to exalt the *patria*. . . ."[63] Throughout his long life (he was seventy-seven), Filippo Corsini asserted, he had always loved peace and hated war, but he could see no alternative to fighting the Genoese with all the commune's resources.[64] Only three men spoke out against the establishment of a *balìa*. Representing the Twelve, Niccolò Benvenuti argued that the Genoese were so nearly invulnerable to attack by land and sea that a war magistracy was not feasible. It was Forese Sacchetti's contention that the commune could not afford a major campaign against Genoa, "since our finances are in disorder and our debts are massive." Agnolo Pandolfini focused on the same issues, with the eloquence that made him, then and later, the chief spokesman in the *reggimento* for a pacific foreign policy. Since commerce and industry were moribund, artisans and laborers idle and hungry, taxpayers drained of their resources, only peace could save the republic. Pan-

---

[61] *CP*, 41, ff.43r-43v, 21 Sept. For other debates on Portovenere, *ibid.*, ff.35r, 40v, 44r, 47r-48v.

[62] *Ibid.*, ff.54v-56v.

[63] *Ibid.*, ff.56r-56v. Cristofano Spini, Rinaldo Rondinelli, Guglielmo Altoviti, Salamone Strozzi announced their support for a *balìa*.

[64] "Sibi cum senex sit et etiam in etate quam fuit, semper guerram odio habuit et pacem optavit"; *ibid.*, f.54v.

dolfini vehemently opposed the election of a war *balìa*, "since these always involve us in military campaigns and expenses," and instead proposed the creation of a magistracy charged with finding ways to achieve peace.[65]

Even though the republic did not mount a full-scale offensive against Genoa in the winter of 1411–1412, military expenditures increased as fighting intensified in the Livorno area.[66] A growing number of citizens could not, or would not, pay their *prestanze*; many expressed their dissatisfaction with the regime's fiscal policies by voting against every tax measure presented to the legislative councils.[67] The most outspoken supporters of the war minimized the role of the economy in the commune's fiscal dilemma. They either assumed, like Filippo Corsini, that the citizenry would always be able and willing to subsidize liberty or, like Michele Castellani, that they could be coerced into paying their assessments.[68] But the economic realities intruded, with greater force and frequency, into the fiscal debates, as did criticism of the regime's failure to take appropriate measures to correct abuses and inequities. Changes in the method of assessment had been recommended for two years, Bartolomeo Valori noted, "in large and small councils," but no reform had ever been adopted. Valori now demanded action, as did the Sixteen, who claimed that the regime's survival depended upon the implementation of fiscal reforms.[69] With some sense of urgency, therefore, the Signoria and the colleges approved a provision for revising the assessments. First proposed to the Council of the *Popolo* on 17 October, it was rejected four times before passing by a single vote on 9 November. Twenty citizens were authorized to draw up a new schedule of assessments, "having respect for God and for justice . . . and so that an equitable distribution will be achieved and that peace and concord will reign in the city. . . ."[70]

Conflict over the fisc did not subside, but rather intensified, as the Signoria and the councils fought bitterly over a provision imposing six forced loans. Opposition to this measure may have been due to the retention of the old schedule of assessments, or possibly to the amount of the levy. After three rejections the measure did pass the Council of

---

[65] *Ibid.*, f.55r–55v, 56v. Pandolfini and his allies were able to thwart the election of a war magistracy.

[66] *CP*, 41, ff.50v, 69r–69v, 6 Nov. 1411 and 11 Jan. 1412.

[67] *Prov.*, 100, f.126v; *SCMLC*, 6, ff.14r, 16r.

[68] *CP*, 41, ff.39r, 44r. Castellani's statement: ". . . totum in pecunia consistit que a civibus extorquenda est. . . ." See also Antonio Alessandri's recommendations for coercing delinquents and those who criticized the tax system; *ibid.*, f.42r.

[69] *Ibid.*, ff.47r, 48r.

[70] *LF*, 49, ff.110r–118r; *Prov.*, 100, ff.84v–86r. The vote: 153–71 and 117–55.

the *Popolo*, which traditionally was more obdurate than the Council of the Commune in resisting fiscal measures. But the latter fought this provision with unusual determination. On four successive days, from 9 through 12 December, that council voted against the new levies, and on the 12th the Signoria convened a *pratica* to discuss the crisis.[71] Every counselor emphasized that the regime's survival depended upon the enactment of this legislation. "For many it is hateful to pay forced loans," conceded Niccolò da Uzzano, "but it is better to pay than to lose [liberty]." The priors were fulfilling the responsibilities of their office by submitting a provision that had been thoroughly debated and approved; no better system for raising money could be devised. These speeches were conciliatory,[72] but Rinaldo Gianfigliazzi "deplored the failure of the Council of the Commune to pass the provision that had been formulated for the security of the city's liberty and the preservation of the *reggimento*." The councilors deserved to be reprimanded, and he would have approved his son's punishment if he had not voted for the provision.[73] Fortified by this vote of confidence, the Signoria reconvened the Council of the Commune late that evening and called for one vote after another, refusing to allow the councilors to leave the hall to eat or drink, until they finally succumbed to this pressure and voted, 133 to 57, for the measure.[74] "If they have done well," one observer commented, "God will reward them, but it was judged to be a shameful thing by a majority of the people, for nothing like this had been seen or done in our times."[75] Though coerced by the Signoria on this issue, citizens who sat in the councils persisted in casting their white beans against fiscal legislation.[76] To show their resentment of the Signoria's tactics, several councilors voted against the provision (30 December) that approved payment for the priors' living expenses. An anonymous source noted that this measure, which normally received automatic approval, was voted down ten times before a two-thirds majority could be mustered.[77]

---

[71] *LF*, 49, ff.121r-124r, 126r-129r; *CP*, 41, ff.60v-61r. The vote was 177-55.

[72] Thus, Cristofano Spini: "Quod nulli voluntarie ad solvendas pecunias accedunt, cum unicuique onus suum et grave attributum sit"; and Vanni Castellani, who complained about the size of his assessment; *ibid.*, f.61r.

[73] *Ibid.*, f.60v.   [74] *Prov.*, 100, ff.97v-99r.

[75] *BNF*, *Magl.*, xxv, 283, at the priorate of Nov.-Dec. 1411. For other negative comments, see *BNF*, *Conventi Soppressi*, C, 4, 895, f.81v; *Manoscritti*, 225, f.146r.

[76] Examples: *LF*, 49, ff.140r, 141r, 142r-144r, 147v, 148r, 151v-152r, 155r.

[77] ". . . E'nanzi la vincissono, la missò X volte e vinsela per quartura [sic: quartiere] e grandissima pena che questo non si vide mai più fare"; *BNF*, *Magl.*, xxv,

In a *pratica* convened on 18 January 1412, Filippo Corsini made a report on the progress that had been made, since the conspiracy of the previous November, toward achieving that degree of civic unity which would prevent future crises. Legislation to equalize the tax burden had been enacted during the tenure of the previous Signoria, "and now nothing remains but to distribute offices and honors appropriately," a task which Corsini assigned to the current priorate.[78] Other participants in the discussion favored electoral reforms to eliminate injustices that exacerbated relations between citizens. Agnolo di Pino compared these dissensions to earlier quarrels between Guelfs and Ghibellines, "the consequences of which are known to all." Giotto Peruzzi, Marco Strozzi, and Cristofano Spini urged the Signoria to act decisively to eliminate these sources of rancor. The simplest method for correcting inequities in officeholding was to hold new scrutinies, a course advocated by Niccolò degli Albizzi, from an ancient Guelf family, and by Giovanni Unghero, a parvenu whose antecedents were obscure. Rinaldo Rondinelli complained that the entire administration was in a deplorable state; he assigned first priority to reforming the distribution of the *prestanze* which, he implied, was still not finished, and then to the holding of new scrutinies for all offices.[79] While giving lip service to the principles animating the *pratica*, the conservative defenders of the status quo sought to cool the enthusiasm for electoral reform. Antonio Alessandri agreed that unity was a laudable goal, "for which our ancestors labored," but he did not believe that new scrutinies would achieve it. Encouraging his colleagues to look to the past for guidance, Alessandri reminded them that "under the pretext of unity, the regimes of other cities have been overthrown."[80] The efforts to achieve unity through a more equitable distribution of civic honors were thwarted by what Giovanni Morelli described as "the avarice of those who were qualified for office and who did not wish to have companions."[81] The provision finally approved in the councils did author-

---

283, priorate of Nov.–Dec. 1411. The vote on this provision: 130–59 and 115–49; *LF*, 49, ff.131r, 132r.

[78] *CP*, 41, f.71v.

[79] *Ibid.*, f.72r. Jacopo Malegonelle also noted that fiscal reforms had not yet been implemented; *ibid.* A letter from Niccolò de' Biffoli to Forese Sacchetti, 27 June 1412, contains this statement: "Questi della ventina chiegono termine ancora 6 mesi: credo partorirà buono frutto, perchè sento truovano a uno de' nostro gonfalone fiorini 8000 contati et più, ed a di prestanza f. due o circa. Pensa quello debbe essere altrove"; *CRS*, 78 (*Badìa*), 324, no. 179.

[80] ". . . Nam preterita in futurum omnes docendum debent, cum alii gubernantes olim civitatem sub pretextu unionis regimen amiserunt"; *CP*, 41, f.72r.

[81] *Ricordi*, 537.

ize new scrutinies for territorial offices, and stipulated that the names of newly qualified citizens would be inserted directly into the pouches for those posts in the *contado* and district.[82] But no new opportunity was granted to the worthy and meritorious to qualify for the highest executive offices: the Signoria and the colleges. Those who had been qualified in the 1411 scrutiny were to be distributed in the pouches of previous scrutinies according to age, but this privilege, which greatly enhanced their prospects for being selected to the Signoria, did not apply to citizens whose forbears had not qualified for the priorate before 1381.[83] This proviso limited the flow of new blood into the Signoria, since those new men would have to wait a decade or longer before their names would be drawn.[84]

The passage of this measure did not improve civic morale during the spring of 1412. Speaking for the most conservative elements in the regime, Antonio Alessandri attributed the persistence of the malaise (May 1412) to the immoderate thirst for change, and, specifically, the demands of outsiders for admission to the *reggimento*. "Many ignorant men and Ciompi are demanding the earth," he lamented, and he urged the Signoria to resist these egalitarian pressures.[85] Others, however, argued that the responsibility for civic unrest lay with the executive, which had neglected to insert the names of newly qualified citizens into the old pouches. Several counselors suggested that the Signoria was deliberately sabotaging the January law. Though he had always opposed the mixing of the pouches, Strozza Strozzi said, nevertheless the reform had been thoroughly debated by prominent citizens and approved by the councils. There could be no justification for failing to execute a provision that had been discussed so thoroughly, Piero Beccanugi insisted, and its revocation would do great harm. His opinions supported by sixty-three years of political experience, Filippo Corsini spoke to the larger issues raised by this problem. "Nothing is more important for those in authority than to obey the laws and to be constant in everything; the Venetian regime follows this [prin-

[82] *Prov.*, 100, ff.114v–117r, 27–28 Jan. 1412. The vote: 168–80 and 132–48.

[83] This restriction had been proposed by Rinaldo Gianfigliazzi and Maso degli Albizzi, speaking for the *pratica* on 21 Jan.; *CP*, 41, ff.73r–73v.

[84] The names of these parvenus remained in the 1411 pouches, but they would be drawn only after the earlier ones had been emptied. For example, the 1411 pouch for the office of the Sixteen from the *gonfalone* of Curris, quarter of S. Croce, was not touched until 25 March 1428, seventeen years after the scrutiny; *Tratte*, 197, at date.

[85] The debate was held on 29 May; *CP*, 41, ff.97r–97v. Alessandri's phrase: "multi ignorantes et Ciompi appetunt omnia." The January law stipulated that the mixing of the pouches must be completed by Oct. 1412.

ciple] and it has survived for a long time." The legislation that provided for the integration into older pouches of those who were eligible in the 1411 scrutiny had been formulated after long and careful deliberation, and approved in a constitutional manner. It should be implemented speedily, Corsini argued, to dampen civic discontent.

While the regime was considering measures to strengthen itself, a major conspiracy was being organized in Bologna by the leaders of the Alberti family. This plot, described by Filippo Corsini[86] as "the most ambitious and most dangerous" assault on the republic, was similar to those organized by exiles in the 1380s and 1390s. It was motivated by identical aspirations; it attracted a similar clientele, it pursued the same strategy, and it was foiled, as all the others had been, by betrayal. Of all facets of Florentine political experience in these decades, the style of revolution was seemingly most impervious to change.

The Alberti hoped to gain support from every level of the social hierarchy. Cionettino Bastari, who later revealed the plot to the authorities, reported that he had seen, in the Bologna headquarters of the conspiracy, "a room in which several tailors were sewing a great banner of the *popolo*, and then a trunk was opened which contained shirts marked with the arms of families: Ricci, Adimari, Alberti, Strozzi, Rucellai, Pagnini, Bastari, Scali, and many others.[87] These symbols were designed to stimulate the oldest and strongest loyalties of the Florentine *popolo*: their commitment to the guild regime established in the thirteenth century, and their allegiance to particular families which these armorial insignias might arouse. The slogans of the conspirators—"Long live the *popolo* and the guilds; down with the forced loans and the taxes and the gabelles!"—were aimed at the poor. If the Alberti had built up a following within the city, its size and importance is unknown,[88] since their plans were revealed to the Signoria as they rode into Florentine territory with their band of 150 cavalry. Forty-eight conspirators (including eight Alberti, two Strozzi, two Ricci, and two Scali) were condemned to death *in absentia* for participating in that expedition, but only three of their associates within the walls were

[86] *CP*, 41, f.107r, 14 June.

[87] The most detailed source for this conspiracy is a letter from Niccolò de' Biffoli to Forese Sacchetti, 6 June 1412; *CRS*, 78, 324, no. 175. For an official version, see the Signoria's complaint to the commune of Bologna; *SCMLC*, 6, ff.20r–20v, 27 June 1412.

[88] Paolo della Camera to Forese Sacchetti: ". . . Son arivati poi alchuni sbanditi, i quali erano colla brighata che venivano. Riafermano el tractato eglino avevano qui grande apoggio, secondo ch'era dicto lor da principali del tractato, ma chi sieno, nollo sanno"; *CRS*, 78, 324, no. 279.

convicted of treason.[89] Two members of prominent families, Meo di
Bartolo Altoviti and Antonio d'Albizzo de' Medici, were interrogated
under torture, but then were released from custody.[90]

In contrast to the intensive appraisal of origins that resulted from
the conspiracies of the year before, the civic response to this affair was
more narrowly focused on the problem of security. Only one counselor, Banco da Verrazzano, referred to the need for civic unity; the
rebels were counting on support from the disenfranchised "plebeians
and paupers," as well as from other malcontents who should be reconciled with the regime "for the public good."[91] But for Verrazzano's colleagues, the lesson of this third abortive coup within a year was clear:
repression and vigilance were the sole antidotes to revolution.
Speakers vied with each other in their denunciations of the Alberti and
in prescribing the most extreme penalties for the traitors. Rinaldo
Gianfigliazzi deplored the breakdown of internal security that had
permitted the rebels to organize another conspiracy. The regime was
saved by Cionettino Bastari's betrayal of his accomplices, which suggested to Gianfigliazzi, and to others, that the regime's main hope for
survival depended upon rewarding him so lavishly that future conspirators would be tempted to emulate him.[92] To make decisions about
punishments and rewards, and to enact legislation that would prevent
recurrences of these uprisings, the counselors approved the creation
of a special *balìa* for internal security. That magistracy, comprising
eighty-one officials and citizens, was authorized by a provision of
17 June to promote the security and welfare of the citizenry, and to
repress all "seditions, conspiracies, and plots" against the regime.[93]

Responding to the tone as well as the content of the debates on the
Alberti conspiracy, the *balìa* authorized a reward for Cionettino
Bastari that was unprecedented for a Florentine citizen. He received,
first, an outright gift of 400 florins, then a military provision of five
lances for his lifetime, plus the privilege to bear arms for himself and
his descendants, and, finally, an immunity from all communal taxa-

[89] The condemnation of the 48 in *AEOG*, 1785, ff.14v–16r, 22 July 1412, and of
the three accomplices, one identified as a taverner and another as a soap-maker;
AP, 4261, ff.32r–33v, 41r–42r, 83r–85v. Only the taverner Giorgio di Ser Francesco was hanged.

[90] The Biffoli letter, cited above; *DSCOA*, 20, f.27r.

[91] *CP*, 41, f.109v, 15 June. A summary of the debate concerning this conspiracy
in Passerini, *Alberti*, II, 321–23.

[92] Filippo Corsini: "Procedatur accerrime et sine remissione aut misericordia";
Maso degli Albizzi: "Rigide adversus culpabiles procedatur, ut ceteris transeat in
exemplum"; *CP*, 41, f.105v, 13 June; Gianfigliazzi, *ibid.*, f.107r.

[93] *CP*, 41, ff.109r–112r; *Prov.*, 101, ff.121v–122r.

tion.[94] Toward the Alberti, on the other hand, the *balìa* prescribed the bitter medicine appropriate for losers. They were all declared rebels of the commune; their assassins would receive rewards of 1000 florins if they were killed within 200 miles of Florence. The unusual feature of the *balìa*'s vengeance on the Alberti was its extension to the innocent. All male members of the family had to leave Florence and live more than 200 miles away, or suffer the confiscation of their property. Their houses in Florence were to be sold; their wives and daughters were ordered to evacuate them. Any citizen who married into the family had to pay a special tax of 1000 florins; none could have any business relations with them in Italy.[95] These provisions were designed to weaken the economic power of the Alberti so they could not subsidize another campaign against the regime and, by cutting their marital and business ties with other patrician families, to isolate them from the main reservoirs of Florentine wealth and power.[96]

In addition to enacting this punitive legislation, the *balìa* took other steps to carry out its mandate. Each member of the *balìa* was authorized to carry arms, for himself and one companion, during his lifetime. A special police officer (*bargello*) was appointed for a six months' term to apprehend suspected criminals; the guard responsible for public order was expanded by 250 men.[97] With its grant of authority to enforce the measures against the Alberti, and with a budget of 6000 florins assigned for that purpose, the Eight on Security enjoyed greater authority to engage in counterrevolutionary activity.[98] Though the *balìa*'s jurisdiction had been strictly limited to the area of internal security,[99] it did enact one significant decree concerning officeholding. For a one-year period, the membership of the legislative councils was restricted to those citizens who had previously served in the Signoria,

---

[94] *Balìe*, 20, ff.6v–8v. See also *CRS*, 78, 324, no. 289. The military provision gave Bastari an annual income exceeding 200 fl.; *Camera, Uscita*, 361, *Capse Conducte*, 13 July 1412. Bastari was assassinated by an unknown assailant in 1432; *Prov.*, 124, ff.245v–246r.

[95] Passerini, *Alberti*, II, 324–28. Rewards would also be paid for the killing of the two rebel Strozzi, Bernardo and Giovanni, Nanni di Silvestro, and Antonio di Bernardo de' Ricci, and Bartolomeo di Agnolo Scali; *ibid.*, 335.

[96] These provisions were not as severe as those recommended by Marco Strozzi and Gino Capponi, who proposed that all property owned by Alberti women for their dowries should be sold, and only the amount stipulated in their marriage contracts be given them in cash; *CP*, 41, ff.107r, 108v.

[97] *Balìe*, 20, ff.18r–21r, 31r–33r; Pagolo della Camera to Forese Sacchetti, 2 July 1412; *CRS*, 78, 324, no. 281.

[98] Passerini, *Alberti*, II, 327–28, 335–37.

[99] Biffoli to Sacchetti, 18 June 1412; *CRS*, 78, 324, no. 177.

the colleges, or the other important magistracies.[100] This may have been inspired by the determined opposition, in the Council of the Commune, of some citizens to the fiscal provisions of the previous December.[101] Whatever the immediate circumstances and motives inspiring the promulgation of this decree, it had another, more basic objective: to strengthen the elitist forces and to thwart the pressures for broadening the regime's social composition.

THE GENOESE WAR

In the *pratica* of 14 June that discussed the second Alberti plot, Antonio Mangioni placed the event in a broad historical context. "Much has happened in the city during this past year: plague, famine, war, and three conspiracies. The epidemic was a judgment of God, and so outside human control. Everything possible was done to avoid the famine, and likewise to achieve peace, even with the commune's dishonor. But our enemies were filled with pride and they did not desire peace. . . ."[102] When Mangioni spoke, the latest revolutionary threat had been foiled; the plague had run its course and the new harvest was filling granaries and stomachs. Only the Genoese war, now in its third year, cast its shadow over city and countryside.

During the year 1412, a succession of Florentine embassies traveled to Pietrasanta, to meet their Genoese counterparts, to submit the offers made by their respective governments for peace, and, regularly, to reject those tendered by the other side. Early in the year, the general of the Dominican order, the Florentine Leonardo Dati, played a mediatory role in peace negotiations, but with little positive effect.[103] The key issue dividing the belligerents was control of Livorno which, from Florence's viewpoint, was necessary for the defense of Pisa, and which Genoa considered as crucial for maintaining her hegemony in

[100] *Balìe*, 20, f.33v; Pagolo della Camera to Sacchetti, 2 July; *CRS*, 78, 324, no. 281.

[101] On 21 Jan. 1412, Rinaldo Gianfigliazzi and Maso degli Albizzi, speaking for the *pratica*, had proposed that one-half of all councilors should have previously sat in the Signoria or the colleges, or have been captains of the Parte Guelfa; *CP*, 41, ff.73r–73v.

[102] Antonio Mangioni: "In presenti anno multa concursa sunt in civitate, videlicet: epidimia, caristia, guerra et conspirationes tres. Dei iudicio, infectio acris evenit et provideri per homines nequit; pro evitanda caristia possibilia quelibet facta sunt; et pro habenda pace omnia, etiam cum dedecore communis"; *CP*, 41, f.107r.

[103] *Ibid.*, ff.75v–76r, 121v, 144v. Niccolò del Grasso called Dati a Ghibelline for, presumably, favoring the Genoese position; *ibid.*, f.144v. On the peace negotiations, see *Le croniche di Giovanni Sercambi*, ed. S. Bonghi (Lucca, 1892), III, 191, 203–04.

the Tyrrhenian Sea.[104] In a memorandum sent to Florentine ambassadors in Pietrasanta on 22 May, the Signoria again insisted on their rights to Livorno, and also to Portovenere that had been acquired the year before. But the Signoria was willing (or so the instructions read) to concede Livorno to the Genoese, if they in turn accepted Florence's possession of Portovenere and adjacent towns.[105] But Genoa insisted on Florence's withdrawal from Portovenere, Sarzanello, and Lerici, and adamantly refused to make any concessions over Livorno.[106] So resistant to compromise was the Genoese posture that the Florentines, who in the past had made their reputations as tough bargainers, became increasingly exasperated with their inflexibility. One counselor proposed a truce in lieu of a peace; another, the occupation of the disputed towns by neutral parties as a preliminary step to arbitration. But either these suggestions were never discussed at the peace parleys, or they were rejected by the Genoese.[107]

The Florentines were so frustrated in these peace negotiations because they could not apply military pressure on the Genoese to gain diplomatic concessions. Without a naval force to challenge Genoese galleys, or threaten her commerce, or attack her coastline, they were experiencing the disadvantages of their situation as a maritime state without a navy. Occasionally, an angry counselor would remind his listeners that the surest way to peace was through waging relentless war, or that in the past the appointment of a war magistracy would so frighten enemies that they would immediately sue for peace.[108] But more thoughtful men perceived that the old clichés did not apply to this conflict. The peculiar quality of this war, Antonio Mangioni noted, was that so much was spent for so little result; Maso degli Albizzi

---

[104] Gino Capponi's statement about Livorno's crucial importance for Pisa's defense; CP, 41, f.75v, and the comments of Banco da Verrazzano on Genoese objectives; ibid., f.100v.

[105] SCMC, 29, ff.17v–18r. The Signoria's attitude was quite conciliatory in this memorandum. The concession of Livorno had not been discussed in a pratica, but some counselors did indicate a willingness to give up Portovenere in exchange for Livorno; CP, 41, f.100v.

[106] Maso degli Albizzi's statement, CP, 41, f.100r. Filippo Corsini commented: "Nimium sunt superba et inhonesta postulata per Januenses, et nullus princeps vel dominus condictiones imponit in pacem ut ipsam, nisi victores et imperantes"; ibid., f.99r.

[107] Maso degli Albizzi and Filippo Corsini; ibid., f.100r.

[108] Buonaccorso Pitti, Pierozzo Castellani and Ser Paolo della Camera, ibid., ff.76r, 87r, 126v, 18 Apr. and 3 Aug. 1412. See, too, the comments of Ubaldino Guasconi, ibid., f.98v. Florence was allegedly implicated in one conspiracy against the "Ghibelline" regime in Genoa, organized by the Guelf Fregosi; Sercambi, Croniche, III, 190–91.

admitted that it was not possible to mount an offensive against the Genoese.[109] The awareness of these limits on Florence's capacity to harm her enemy, reinforced by growing anxieties over costs, persuaded a majority of counselors to oppose plans formulated by the five commissioners of Pisa: first to besiege Livorno, and then to harass the Genoese littoral.[110] Unable to sustain the expense of such enterprises, the communal treasury was so depleted that several counselors opposed, on fiscal grounds, a proposal for sending an embassy to King Ferdinand on his accession to the Aragonese throne, to persuade him to attack the Genoese.[111] But civic morale had sunk too low, and the prospects of Aragonese support were too faint, to stimulate any genuine enthusiasm for continuing a fruitless struggle. When Maso degli Albizzi and Filippo Corsini conceded that Florence could not wrest control of Livorno away from the Genoese, or challenge their supremacy on the sea,[112] they were acknowledging a painful reality that in other wars at other times, they had refused to accept.

The Genoese war had so immobilized the republic that she could not intervene effectively in other spheres affecting her interest. Her statesmen and diplomats were eager to mediate between Pope John XXIII and King Ladislaus, but they could claim no real credit for the peace settlement that was signed in June.[113] Rinaldo Gianfigliazzi recalled the days when Florence was the keystone of the Guelf alliance that maintained peace in the peninsula; in a more realistic vein, Cristofano di Giorgio somberly invited his colleagues to consider the dangers which would confront Florence if the papal state disintegrated, and if the pope were forced to abandon Italy. Niccolò Barbadori spelled out the grim prospects: if Ladislaus subdued the pope, he would become master of Italy.[114] No one expressed any enthusiasm for the king's proposal for a league; Jacopo Malegonelle argued that Florence should never become allied to princes more potent than herself. The consequences of every alliance, Filippo Corsini warned, were military

---

[109] CP, 41, ff.98v, 100r, 29 and 30 May. For details of the fighting; Sercambi, Croniche, III, 187, 194, 201, 203.

[110] These proposals were made in February and April; CP, 41, ff.74v–75r, 86r–88r.

[111] Ibid., ff.122v–123r, 27 July. Others favored the despatch of the embassy; ibid., ff.121v, 124r–124v.

[112] Ibid., ff.134v, 142v, 5 Sept. and 10 Oct. Cf. Corsini, ibid., f.145v: "Januensibus in potentia maris nec pares nec equales sumus."

[113] Instructions to Florentine ambassadors sent to Rome and Naples; SCMLC, 6, ff.17r–18r, 8 June. News of the peace agreement was lauded in Florence; CP, 41, ff.112v–113r.

[114] CP, 41, ff.92r, 103r.

adventures and expenditures; the treaty that Ladislaus sought would be directed against the emperor-elect Sigismund, who was then publicizing his intention of visiting Italy to defend the papacy against its rebellious Angevin vassal. This alliance against Florence's sovereign lord, the Holy Roman emperor, would be a violation of her faith, and, Corsini concluded, "we would lose all of the territory which our ancestors have acquired in the past."[115]

A thread of anxiety concerning Ladislaus' aggressive intentions did run through the debates for these months,[116] but no one yet considered the German as a potential ally against the king of Naples. Sigismund was, initially, a source of vague anxiety mixed with a measure of contempt. Paolo Biliotti recalled that Sigismund's father, Charles IV, had sent his imperial insignia to Florence in 1368 "so that our city would submit to his authority"; experience had shown, he added, that no emperor had been able to invade the peninsula without Italian money.[117] Though the republic could not afford to subsidize the emperor-elect's journey, she could at least send an embassy to greet him. In a *pratica* held on 16 July, twenty counselors favored the despatch of the embassy, while eight opposed it.[118] Though ambassadors were elected to visit Sigismund in Budapest, they did not actually depart,[119] a fact that later provided ammunition for critics of the regime's foreign policy.

Thus, the arguments for terminating the Genoese war became more compelling, as statesmen who worriedly scanned the Italian scene now allied themselves with merchants and guildsmen, who focused on economic difficulties, to find a formula for peace. Always sensitive to the political realities, Maso degli Albizzi publicly announced (30 May) his conversion to peace, "for the city is being destroyed and devastated."[120] Supporting him were two confederates, Filippo Corsini and Rinaldo Gianfigliazzi, who in times past had been among the most passionate defenders of civic honor, and the most willing to make

---

[115] *CP*, 41, f.129r, 13 Aug. See also *ibid.*, f.77v.

[116] Giovanni di Bicci de' Medici's statement: ". . . inspiciendo quod rex Ladislaus querit dominium Italie"; *ibid.*, f.129v. See also comments by Niccolò Barbadori and Cristofano di Giorgio; *ibid.*, f.103r.

[117] *Ibid.*, f.83v, 7 Apr. See also Gianfigliazzi's statement, *ibid.*

[118] *Ibid.*, f.119v. Niccolò del Bellaccio, *ibid.*, f.116v, opposed the embassy on the grounds that it would result in great demands on Florence and would incur Venetian enmity.

[119] *Ibid.*, ff.130v, 132r.

[120] *Ibid.*, f.100r. Maso, however, did not articulate Paolo Biliotti's sentiments, "pax suscipiatur . . . etiam cum dedecore," but the import of his speech was clear.

sacrifices to uphold it.[121] Yet despite all these pressures, from the populace[122] and now from a frustrated leadership, the regime could not reach a settlement with the Genoese. In early September, the peacemakers inaugurated an intensive campaign to break the impasse, which continued for six months before an agreement was finally hammered out.

The *pratica* convened by a new Signoria on 5 September provided a forum for the peace party to renew its appeals for an accommodation with Genoa, and indirectly to criticize the leadership for its failure to achieve that objective. Speakers emphasized two themes: the catastrophic effect of the war on the economy, and the impregnability of Genoa's—and Livorno's—defenses.[123] Luca da Filicaia deplored the paralysis of commerce and industry, which had forced many honest merchants "to engage in usury and other illicit business. . . ."[124] There was no money anywhere, neither in the city nor the territory, Paolo Biliotti asserted, and without money it was impossible to fight a war. Conceding that a few citizens still possessed some wealth, he warned that their resources were limited and their numbers few: "they ought to be protected lest they be ruined." He bitterly attacked the republic's imperialist policy, her insatiable thirst for war, and her profligate waste of resources in pursuit of territorial conquest. Comparing Florence to a man who consumed his estate by gluttony, Biliotti suggested that by pursuing the Genoese war to absurd lengths, the republic was jeopardizing her control of her state. He estimated a loss of a million florins in communal revenue and mercantile profits during each year of that conflict. "Our city was feared by all," he recalled, "before we possessed Arezzo, Pistoia, San Miniato, the Valdinievole, the Valdarno, Colle, San Gimignano, and other places. We were in a better condition than now, after we have gained all of those cities and Pisa too!"[125]

---

[121] Corsini's strongest peace statement; *ibid.*, ff.134v, 145v, 5 Sept. and 13 Oct.; Gianfigliazzi, *ibid.*, f.151v, 5 Dec.

[122] As early as February, Lorenzo Ridolfi and Bartolomeo Popoleschi were expressing concern about the popular clamor for peace; *ibid.*, ff.74v, 75v.

[123] *CP*, 41, ff.134v–136v. Speaking on Genoa's power were Vieri Guadagni, Maso degli Albizzi and Piero Baroncelli.

[124] *Ibid.*, f.135v. Filippo Corsini and Maso degli Albizzi also mentioned the poor state of the economy; *ibid.*, f.134v.

[125] *Ibid.*, f.135r. Biliotti's statement: "Et nobis dici potest quod vulgariter fatur: 'Va che gli manichi in sul letto in zuchero et confetti,' et perseverando ut facimus, nobis dici idem poterit, cum terra et loca non multo tempore citra habuerimus; et notum est quanta damna perpessi sumus ob guerram Januensibus; nam quolibet anno de redditibus communis et utilitatibus mercatorum florenorum mille milia amittemus; et dominus Pierus Gambacurta optime providit quod palam civitas Pisarum se omnibus; et omnes civitatem nostram formidabant antequam Aretium,

In the range of its historical vision and in the boldness of its judgments, Biliotti's outburst had few precedents in Florentine political discourse. We do not know if his opinions were shared by many citizens, or if he spoke only for a small minority. None refuted or challenged his arguments; counselors evaded the issue by speaking in vague generalities, and by encouraging the Signoria to pursue diligently its quest for peace.[126] But the abrasive tone of Biliotti's address, and his attack upon civic myths about war and territorial expansion, may have alienated those citizens who believed that the republic fought only for just causes. Biliotti's speech sharpened the internal quarrels that had been smoldering for months, fed by economic pressures, resentment over tax inequities, and suspicions unleashed by the abortive conspiracies. Henceforth, debate on the war would become increasingly partisan, as citizens accused each other of malfeasance, disloyalty, and even treason.

Speaking in a *pratica* (10 October) called to consider the current state of peace negotiations, Filippo Corsini repeated the familiar arguments: "We need peace desperately, since our merchants and guildsmen are idle and this city nourished on trade is dying. . . . On the sea the Genoese are all-powerful and we cannot attack them there. . . ." Corsini, who was presumably speaking for Maso degli Albizzi and Rinaldo Gianfigliazzi, was now willing to abandon Florentine claims to Livorno and its environs, in order to have peace.[127] This admission of Florentine impotence, and of the concessions that the leadership was apparently willing to make, infuriated those citizens who could not face these realities, and who were determined to continue hostilities until Florentine honor was vindicated. Their counterattack took two forms. They argued, first, that Genoa's bargaining position had been strengthened by their knowledge of Florence's peace proposals, which had been publicized by unpatriotic citizens who had violated their oath of secrecy. In a bitter denunciation of these revelations, Matteo Castellani said that the Genoese had learned that some citizens had proposed the restitution of Portovenere and Sarzana to Genoa, and so were even more determined to have those towns. Ser Paolo

---

Pistorium, Sanctum Miniatem, Vallem Nebulis, Vallem Arni, Collem, Sanctum Geminianum et alia multa haberemus et melius stabamus quam nunc; postquam omnia hec et Pisas et alia habuimus."

[126] Typical was the statement of Michele Castellani, speaking for the Eight on Security: "Quod grave sunt que proposita et narrata fuerunt; et quod ipsi, dulcitudine pacis capti, eam nullatenus deserere volunt. De modis adhibendis differentia aliqua inest; ad quos capiendos domini deputent . . . cives"; *ibid.,* f.136r.

[127] *CP*, 41, f.142v.

della Camera believed that the enemy received encouragement from the pacifist opinions broadcast in public streets and squares, where critics complained that "we cannot fight any more and we are dying for an unworthy cause. . . ."[128] To stop this flow of crucial information to the enemy, Buonaccorso Pitti proposed that knowledge of the negotiations should be restricted to a few, and Agnolo di Pino recommended that only "those who favor the exaltation of this regime and this *popolo*, and not the opposite" should be invited to participate in the *pratiche*.[129]

The zealots went beyond this sharp but essentially futile criticism of unpatriotic behavior to attack specific concessions to the Genoese that the leadership had proposed. Reporting on behalf of a *pratica* (11 October) convened to debate clauses in the peace settlement pertaining to Livorno, Vieri Guadagni approved a plan for giving the republic temporary jurisdiction in a fortified place (*bastia*) outside Livorno's walls, where her merchants could store their wares, with a final decision on the legal rights to Livorno and its environs postponed for twelve years.[130] Three days later (13 October), Francesco Leoni reported that he and his colleagues of the Twelve "were sick at heart over the recommendations of that *pratica*, with respect to both public honor and also the advantages accruing to citizens and merchants." The collegiate group demanded that the republic insist unequivocally upon Florentine control of Livorno and its fortified places, and furthermore that she honor her commitment to the citizens of Portovenere by refusing to surrender that town to Genoa. Leoni impugned the motives of those who had advocated concessions to the Genoese: "Considering the qualities and the status of these citizens who made those recommendations, they [the Twelve] are stupefied!"[131] No one should be surprised by the behavior of those citizens in the *pratica* who did not insist on Florentine rights in Livorno and Sarzana, Lorenzo Ridolfi said, "for this is the consequence of the actions of . . . those who value their own advantage and not the commune's honor."[132] The targets of this opprobrium, who had participated in that *pratica*, tried to justify their position. Peace and prosperity were every citizen's goals, Piero Baroncelli said, but there could be legitimate differences over their achievement. He defended the compromise that

---

[128] *Ibid.*, ff.143r–143v, 146v.   [129] *Ibid.*, ff.143r–143v.

[130] *Ibid.*, f.144v. That fortified stockade had recently been constructed by a Florentine armed force; Sercambi, *Croniche*, III, 203–04.

[131] *CP*, 41, f.144v. The Twelve were particularly incensed by the report that the Genoese were now opposing the grant of any site in Livorno for Florentine merchants.

[132] *Ibid.*, f.147r.

had been accepted by the *pratica*; so did Filippo Corsini, who urged his colleagues to accept this delay in Livorno's ultimate disposition, "since after twelve years we will be stronger and more capable of resisting Genoa's power."[133] Corsini admitted that the fate of Porto-venere, and the other towns in that region which had voluntarily ac-cepted Florentine rule, did involve the commune's honor. To abandon them would destroy faith in the republic's promises, Ser Paolo della Camera argued; Michele Castellani predicted that their restoration to the Genoese would enrage the king of France and endanger Floren-tine merchants who lived and traded there.[134]

This *pratica* exposed the complex and delicate relationship between concepts of honor and considerations of utility that surfaced in every Florentine debate on foreign affairs. It also explains why those debates were so lengthy and arduous, and often so agonizing, before any resolution could be achieved, or stubborn convictions either changed or neutralized. The October debates did not reconcile divergent opin-ions on the peace negotiations; these still persisted, with even sharper edges and more personal overtones, through December and January. In a *pratica* held in early December, the main focus of the debate was the destructive effect of civic discord upon peace negotiations. Coun-selors generally praised the priors for their efforts to reconcile the quarreling citizens,[135] but some expressed fear that the pressures for unity might become so powerful that none would dare to speak out against the policies of the executive, in foreign or in domestic af-fairs. Thus, Piero Baroncelli opposed the grant of any authority for peace negotiations to the magistracy that had been created to pacify the citizens. The attainment of peace should be voluntary and genuine, he insisted, "for it cannot be truly called peace if it is achieved by coercion."[136] Antonio Alessandri charged that a cabal had been formed by certain prominent men who had imposed their will upon the city, and who were prepared to accept a peace without honor.[137] The prolif-eration of discord was the consequence of the unbridled defamation and calumny of "worthy citizens," by whom Alessandri presumably meant those zealots who, like himself, had always defended the

---

[133] *Ibid.*, f.145v.

[134] *Ibid.*, ff.143r, 146r. Leoni had made a similar argument about the French problem; *ibid.*, f.145r.

[135] *Ibid.*, ff.151v–152v.

[136] *CP*, 41, f.151v: "Quod nulli danda est auctoritas ad aliquos arcendum per vim ad pacem; cum pax voluntaria dulciter et ex animo provenire debet; nam aliter pax dici non posset cum ad eam quis cohactus veniret."

[137] *Ibid.*, f.152v: ". . . cum aliqui primates quasi thyrannidem assumpserunt dicte civitatis." Alessandri specifically charged these "tyrants" with usurping the author-ity of the magistracy responsible for Pisa's security.

republic against those who "would surrender completely to the Genoese."

Though ultimately doomed to failure, the dogged efforts of these imperialists did postpone the peace settlement until the late spring of
1413. In October, they were still talking about the possibility of
Aragon's intervention in the war; two months later, they seized upon
the prospect of using the good offices of their old enemy Ladislaus to
induce the Genoese to be more flexible in the negotiations.[138] In a
pratica held on 5 December, Cristofano Spini called for a final heroic
effort against Genoa, including the creation of a war *balìa* and the
hiring of 2000 infantry.[139] Rinaldo Gianfigliazzi assumed the responsibility for educating his colleagues about the brutal realities of Florence's condition: a city dying from economic strangulation, her revenues shrunken, her soldiers hungry and unpaid.[140]

The gravity of the fiscal crisis is documented by the extraordinary efforts to raise additional revenue that were discussed, and
in part implemented, during these months. A commission established
in April 1412[141] recommended the imposition of new gabelles upon
rents, upon silk and woolen cloth, and upon money deposited in banks
or involved in exchange operations. In two *pratiche* convened in
September, counselors approved the imposition of gabelles on flour
and rents but rejected those proposed for cloth and monetary exchanges and deposits, "to avoid a scandal."[142] These levies were to be
collected only for a three-year period, and their yield used exclusively
for paying the salaries of mercenaries. A similar time limit was attached to another provision (4-5 October) authorizing the Signoria
to impose six *prestanze* in three years, the revenues from which would
not be repaid by the commune or credited to any of the *monti*.[143] Only
a fiscal crisis of unparalleled gravity would have induced the councils

---

[138] Gregorio Dati, *ibid.*, f.143v; and on the role of Ladislaus as peacemaker, *ibid.*,
ff.155r-155v, 19 Dec.

[139] *Ibid.*, f.151v.

[140] *Ibid.*, f.160v, 9 Jan. 1413: ". . . cum introitus pisarum ad nichilum reducti sunt,
et civitas nostra et pisarum in diminutionem maximam pervenisse; et stipendarii
nostri ubicumque constituti fame et egestate periclitantur; et in communi penuria
pecunie est. . . ." On the poor condition of Florence's army, see also the statement
of Niccolò del Bellaccio, "cum stipendarii a XIIII mensibus citra non scripserunt vel
mostram fecerunt"; *ibid.*, f.135v, 5 Sept. 1412.

[141] *Prov.*, 101, ff.35r-35v, 13-18 Apr. 1412. The majorities were paper-thin: 150-
72 and 115-56.

[142] *CP*, 41, ff.136v, 139v, statements by Niccolò Barbadori and Maso degli Albizzi.

[143] *Prov.*, 101, ff.185r-185v: ". . . Dicte prestantie solvantur . . . ad perdendum et
nichil exinde propterea restituantur . . . sed ad lucrum communis omnes intelligantur
et integre solvantur. . . ."

to accept this radical innovation which, if perpetuated, would have eliminated an important source of income for Florence's moneyed citizens.

Of all the pressures bending the regime toward an accommodation with Genoa, the influence of public opinion was less important than fiscal, strategic, or mercantile considerations. Like the war with Ladislaus, and unlike those with Giangaleazzo Visconti, the Genoese conflict was waged without any significant reference to public sentiment. The popular desire for peace was frequently cited as a compelling reason for pursuing a settlement,[144] though without any discernible effect upon the progress of the negotiations. Lorenzo Ridolfi reminded his audience that "the war is not being waged solely by the priors and the colleges, but also by the masses (*multitudine*)," who provide the wherewithal for the fighting.[145] But the zealots were not swayed by any argument that the populace had a legitimate role in the formulation of policy. The clamor for peace in the streets, they insisted, encouraged Genoese recalcitrance in negotiations; the enlargement of the *pratiche* impeded negotiations and increased the danger of vital secrets being leaked to the enemy.[146] Antonio Alessandri commented that "in every war that we have ever fought, the populace has always opted for peace, and so they do in this one"; their judgment, he implied, was not to be trusted.[147] This elitist viewpoint was too extreme for the majority of counselors who, by early 1413, were becoming more fearful of popular dissatisfaction over the delay in achieving peace.

These anxieties were evident in the debate (12 January 1413) over the occupation of a fortified bastion in Livorno, which would give Florence control over the port, or so the proponents of the plan believed. Formulated in discussions between the magistracy responsible for Pisan security and Livorno's governor, Battista da Montaldo, this plan was enthusiastically supported by those who had so stubbornly

---

[144] "Quod commendandi sunt cives pacem appetentes. . . . Quod summe affectat pacem . . . cum ea populus optet. . . . Quod omnes appetunt pacem in civitate. . . . Clare conspicitur per consulta per omnes quod pacem egemus et eam populus affectat"; *CP*, 41, ff.133r, 146r, 146v, 159r.

[145] *Ibid.*, f.152v, 5 Dec.

[146] On loose talk in the streets and the leaking of secrets, above, 346; and *CP*, 41, f.143v, statement of Matteo Castellani. On the desirability of a small negotiating committee, the statements of Rinaldo Gianfigliazzi and Piero Baroncelli; *CP*, 41, f.151v. The latter's comment: ". . . Nam si publice pax tractaretur et non concluderetur, animi dissidentium fortius animarentur et sequiretur oppositum eius quod queritur." See also Paolo della Camera's comments; *ibid.*, f.146v.

[147] *CP*, 41, f.161r, 9 Jan. 1413.

resisted peace, and also by some prominent statesmen, notably Rinaldo Gianfigliazzi, who had previously abandoned any hope of taking Livorno. With the port in Florentine hands, Francesco Leoni argued, the Genoese would be more willing to make peace; he argued further that the Florentine *popolo* would approve of Livorno's acquisition. Gino Capponi was primarily interested in the strategic aspects of the occupation that would guarantee access to the sea.[148] Opponents of the project argued that it would impede, and indeed might rupture, peace negotiations with the Genoese, and that it would further alienate a war-weary populace. Paolo Carnesecchi said that he would rather have Livorno in Genoese hands and a speedy peace, than in Florentine possession with the war continuing. Giovanni de' Medici argued that Livorno's acquisition would delay peace, intensify popular resentment, and contribute nothing to the promotion of Florentine trade. Cristofano Spini concurred in that judgment: "We will never have peace with the Genoese and the port will be useless since no one will come there if we are at war." Spini urged the Signoria to abandon its consideration of this proposal; otherwise the *popolo*, "which yearns for peace as we know from the debates, will say that we do not want peace and will revolt."[149] These arguments persuaded the Signoria to resist the alluring prospects of Livorno's acquisition, with its grave risks, and to continue negotiations with the Genoese.

Accurately reflecting the comparative strength of these opposing viewpoints on the Genoese war, this debate also furnishes some clues to the mentalities of the protagonists. An unlikely coalition of patrician conservatives and new men whose voices had only recently been heard in debates joined together to resist any concessions which would brand Florentines as pusillanimous traitors.[150] Antonio Alessandri, Gino Capponi, Ubaldino Guasconi, Matteo Castellani, and Salamone Strozzi were representatives of the old Guelf aristocracy whose patriotic feelings sometimes obscured their political judgment.[151] Elitist in their political outlook, narrow and doctrinaire in their views on foreign policy, they tended to blame Florence's difficulties on the ineptitude and lukewarm patriotism of their opponents. Their prejudices were articulated by Lippozzo Mangioni (17 January) who denied that Florence's poor bargaining position with the Genoese was due to her im-

---

[148] *Ibid.*, ff.162v, 163v, 165r. Ubaldino Guasconi also insisted that the *popolo* would welcome this move, f.162v.

[149] For these negative opinions, *ibid.*, ff.162v, 165r.

[150] Ubaldino Guasconi, "quod florentini, qui quotidie per universum sunt, proditores non reputentur et ab omnibus non offendantur"; *ibid.*, f.161r.

[151] For their contributions to the debate on Livorno, *ibid.*, ff.162v-163v, 165r.

potence for, he argued, effective punitive measures could have been taken against the enemy at very little expense. The villains were those traitors who leaked secrets to the Genoese and who favored them at the expense of their own city.[152] The pattern of these arguments fits into the context of Florence's political experience, and of the traditions of its oligarchic component, but the adherence to these principles of Francesco Leoni, Niccolò del Bellaccio, Ser Paolo della Camera, and Berardo Berardi is not easily explained.[153] So deviant in their political attitudes from the vast majority of citizens of middling rank, they were either aberrants who belonged to no recognizable category, or perhaps they had become clients of their aristocratic allies whose opinions they repeated. Though their outspoken patriotism was tolerated, and may even have been admired, by their peers, they did obstruct the peace efforts of Maso degli Albizzi and his associates. After weighing the risks and potential benefits of the Livorno enterprise, these statesmen chose the more cautious if less heroic course. "We have no aptitude for waging a conflict on the sea," was Filippo Corsini's rejoinder to those who still believed that the Genoese could be coerced into a settlement.[154] Representatives of the business community—Giovanni de' Medici, Paolo Carnesecchi, Piero Firenze, Antonio da Rabatta, Bartolo Banchi, Giovanni Orlandini—whose sense of the futility of the war was sharpened by their awareness of its deleterious effect upon their own fortunes, supported this conservative view.[155]

The peace treaty with Genoa was signed on 27 April 1413.[156] The final phase of the negotiations was complicated by political disturbances in Genoa, which raised doubts about who there was authorized to conclude a settlement. Battista da Montaldo claimed to represent the Genoese republic; so did Messer Luca Fieschi and Messer Tommaso Campofregoso, scions of prominent Genoese families who were jostling for power.[157] The Florentines resisted the temptation to take advantage of Genoese disorders by prolonging negotiations: "a certain peace is preferable to an expected victory," observed Antonio

---

[152] Ibid., f.167r.   [153] For their views, ibid., ff.163v–164r.

[154] Ibid., f.165r, 17 Jan. Also Piero Firenze, "per mare Januenses multa possunt et nos minime"; ibid., f.167r.

[155] Their demands for peace; ibid., ff.160v, 162v–164r, 166r–167r.

[156] It was announced publicly three days later; SCMC, 29, f.48r, 29 Apr.

[157] For references to these men, ibid., ff.45r–45v; CP, 41, ff.167v, 175r, 182r. The statement by Piero Bonciani, ibid., f.166r, is particularly relevant: ". . . quod unusquisque suum querit honorem; nam Baptista qui est de popolo querit, et generalis [Leonardo Dati] praticat cum nobilibus. . . ." On the role of these families in Genoese politics, see J. Heers, Gênes au XVe siècle (Paris, 1961), 585–89, 598–600, 609–11.

Mangioni.[158] In early April there were increasing signs in the *pratiche* of Florentine exasperation over Genoese perversity, and several counselors pondered the advantages of breaking off negotiations.[159] But the ominous news of Ladislaus' assault on the Papal States, and the prospect of emperor-elect Sigismund's invasion, intensified the pressures on the diplomats at Pietrasanta to conclude peace. The final settlement was a victory for the Genoese, who kept possession of Livorno though the Florentines did receive port privileges.[160] The coastal towns north of Pisa—Portovenere, Lerici, Porto Pino, and Sarzanello—were restored to Genoa, despite the feeling of some citizens that Florentine honor was compromised.[161] The republic did receive 10,000 florins as compensation for the surrender of these towns, and also an indemnity for merchandise that had been confiscated by the Genoese. Though the treaty was ratified by large majorities in the councils, its proclamation sparked no celebrations in the streets, and no rejoicing in the palace of the Signoria. Only the staunch pacifist Agnolo Pandolfini publicly lauded the peace as "just and praiseworthy," and expressed the hope that it would inaugurate a new era of prosperity, and an end to war.[162]

The Polarization of the Regime

During the final phase of the Genoese war and the subsequent confrontation with King Ladislaus, the regime was more visibly fragmented, and its leaders more openly at odds, than at any time since 1382. It is possible that civic discord was no more intense in these months than in the past, but rather that the articulation of dissent had become more common, reflecting the confidence of citizens that they would not be penalized for expressing their opinions, however negative or critical. This feeling of security, of immunity from reprisal, may explain the exceptionally sharp tone of Francesco Leoni's attack on members of a *pratica*, or Paolo Biliotti's denunciation of the imperialist

[158] *CP*, 41, f.182r, 26 March.

[159] *Ibid.*, f.187v, statements of Lorenzo Ridolfi and Francesco Leoni.

[160] Bayley, *War and Society*, 79, but with the date (27 April 1414) of the peace treaty wrong. Cf. Sercambi, *Croniche*, III, 206.

[161] On civic concern about Portovenere, *CP*, 41, ff.172r–173r, 186r, statements of Salamone Strozzi, Piero Bonciani, and Piero Baroncelli. Citizens of Portovenere who were unwilling to live under Genoese rule were offered sanctuary and provisions for their livelihood in Florentine territory; Sercambi, *Croniche*, III, 206.

[162] *Prov.*, 102, ff.25r–26r; *CP*, 42, f.2v, 4 May. The comment of Maso degli Albizzi—". . . Quod superfluum videtur commendationes dominorum recitare vel de pace cum Januensibus loqui. . . ."—was more typical.

nature of Florentine foreign policy. Still, the debates reflect a recrim-
inatory spirit that had not been evident before, and that was apparently fostered by the frustrations of two wars in which the republic
had been unable to subdue her enemies, by either force or diplomacy. Instead of explaining these failures in terms of economic and
strategic realities, or blaming themselves for errors of judgment, some
citizens preferred to seek scapegoats among those who, in Rinaldo
Gianfigliazzi's words, "look to their own advantage and not to the public good. . . ."[163]

This squabbling began in February 1413 with an election scandal.
In the scrutiny for the treasurer of the *monte* and *provveditori* of the
fisc, the electors (unidentified by name) had voted only for themselves
and had not approved any other citizens for these lucrative offices.[164]
A storm of criticism prompted an embarrassed Signoria to convene
a large *pratica*, in which eighty-two citizens registered their opinions.
Attesting to official concern over this affair was the rare spectacle of
artisans—the glove-maker Lorenzo di Francesco and the potter Piero de
Bartolomeo—speaking in this *pratica*.[165] No one denied the illegality
of the scrutators' behavior, but opinions differed about the remedy.
Rinaldo Gianfigliazzi proposed that the scrutiny lists be burned and
a new election held, supporting his argument with a reference to
Seneca—"only that which is honest is good."[166] A majority of counselors agreed with Gianfigliazzi that the scrutiny could not be salvaged.
But Piero Baroncelli objected in principle to any interference with the
electoral process; he suggested that the list of eligibles certified in the
disputed election be expanded by a supplementary scrutiny. This
would avoid the destruction of the electoral pouches, which he called
on odious practice. Antonio da Panzano noted that he had consistently
opposed revisions in the scrutinies that had been made during the past
year, since the original errors could not be remedied without committing new mistakes. The most pessimistic judgment was registered by
Giovanni Soderini, who claimed that a new scrutiny would not be an
improvement over the old, "for each scrutator will nominate another."

[163] *CP*, 42, f.24r.
[164] For the prefatory statement to the *pratica*, *CP*, 41, f.175v, 17 Feb. Salamone
Strozzi, *ibid.*, f.176v, noted that the offices were lucrative.
[165] *Ibid.*, ff.178r–178v. Recorded as speaking for the first time in a deliberative
session were Bivigliaro di Andrea Raugi, Piero di Jacopo Bini, Francesco di Bon-
aiuto Rimbe, Ridolfo and Guccio da Sommaria, Francesco di Ser Andrea, Cille di
Neri Viviani, and Giovanni di Pazzino Cicciaporri.
[166] *Ibid.*, f.175v: ". . . Quia scrutinatores non honestatem servaverunt in scruti-
nando, scrutinium dici bonum non potest, cum quasi nulli obtinuerunt partitum,
domini novum celebrent scrutinium. . . ."

He proposed that the offices of treasurer and *provveditori* be filled through direct election by the Signoria and the colleges.[167] Salamone Strozzi's solution was to eliminate any personal profit from the holding of these offices, "so that the commune might receive this advantage, let the officials of the *monte* . . . buy [shares] and take other actions which will redound to the public benefit." If this proposal were enacted into law, Strozzi implied, these fiscal posts would be filled only by worthy candidates.[168]

The increasing frequency with which scrutinies were challenged was profoundly disturbing to those Florentines who invested these civic ceremonies with a quasi-sacral character. Niccolò Sacchetti paraphrased, and elaborated on, a principle enunciated by Gino Capponi, when he said that every revision made in a scrutiny or a tax assessment inevitably produced negative results.[169] But beyond their undermining of traditional institutions and practices, these challenges impugned the integrity of the Signoria, which was ultimately responsible for the proper functioning of the commune, and of the other magistracies whose failures and shortcomings were revealed by the periodic crises. Three months after the flare-up over these irregularities, the commission appointed to reform the *prestanze* assessments notified the Signoria that it was unable to complete its task.[170] In the *pratica* convened on 20 May to discuss this crisis, the counselors wrestled with the question of responsibility. All agreed that the new schedule was as inequitable as the old. Salamone Strozzi noted that assessments varied sharply, from five to twenty florins, among members of one family possessing similar patrimonies.[171] Some critics felt that the tax commissioners should be charged with criminal negligence, but Gino Capponi and Piero Firenze absolved them of deliberate fraud.[172] One problem troubling the commissioners was the decline in the number of residents whose wealth justified their inclusion in the *prestanze* rolls; thus, to achieve the total of 24,000 florins established for the whole city, the rates of other taxpayers had to be increased.[173] But instead of accepting the reality of a shrunken tax base, angry citizens charged the

---

[167] *Ibid.*, ff.176v, 178r.   [168] *Ibid.*, f.176v.

[169] *CP*, 42, f.9v. For Capponi's comment, above, 331.

[170] *CP*, 42, f.8r, statement of Mariotto della Morotta, spokesman for the Twelve: "Inspectis gestis per illos de ventina super nova distributione iam tanto tempore expectata, dolorem summunt tam ex predictis quam ex querelis que fiunt per omnes, et de passione per dominos sumpta. . . ."

[171] *Ibid.*, f.10r. Cf. Antonio Mangioni's comment; *ibid.*, f.9v.

[172] *Ibid.*, ff.9r–9v: ". . . Sed malicia dolus vel defectus per eos non est commissus ut putat et videtur. . . ."

[173] *Ibid.*, f.9v, Piero Firenze: ". . . Nec mirandum est si partite diminuite sunt cum in prima ventina fuerunt multi in s. 6 et d. 8 descripti; in secunda et tertia,

officials with a lack of diligence or, more seriously, with being concerned with their own interests. Antonio Alessandri accused them of failing to scrutinize the economic resources of the citizens, so that some assessments were based upon concrete evidence and others on guesswork or rumor.[174] Marco di Goro Strozzi and Giovanni Peruzzi suspected that quarrels among the officials had produced the inequities. These men did not merit commendation or gratitude, Peruzzi concluded, "but as John the Evangelist said, 'Their works will follow them.' "[175]

So, after eighteen months of labor, the errors in the *prestanze* assessments were still uncorrected and, as the debates made clear, there was no agreement on a remedy. Salamone Strozzi proposed an extreme cure: the abolition of *prestanze* and the total reliance upon gabelles and direct taxation in the territory.[176] But this idea was judged to be impractical by realists who knew that the commune could not subsist on those revenues. Banco da Verrazzano criticized those "who say that there will be no troubles this year, since it cannot be denied (though some assert the contrary) that their beginnings are already visible, especially in Italy."[177] The majority concluded that there was no viable alternative to forced loans; an increase in revenue from the territory was not feasible, nor could salaries be substantially reduced.[178]

---

pauciores et nunc etiam pauciores aliis." On increasing the levy to 24,000 fl., the counsel of Antonio Alessandri and Salamone Strozzi; *ibid.*, ff.9r, 10r.

[174] "Quod resistentia facta per illos de ventina in non assumendo in principio onus eis commissum, fuit solum ad preheminentias proprias quas volebant; et non ob aliam causam; negare tamen non possunt quod errores varios non commiserint in distributione, et multo plures quam ipsi dicunt; sequendum non est quod per aliquos dicitur, ut fiant impositiones secundum examinationes et scripturas factas per illos de ventina, cum aliquibus fuerit adhibita fides ut ipsimet voluerint, et aliis in nichilo, et multi de suis substantiis nil ostendere voluerunt; et sic inequalis foret impositio que fieret secundum scripturas predictas"; *ibid.*, f.9r. Giovanni di Bicci de' Medici asserted that the commission scrutinized his business records: "Ipse statum suum clare et limpide illis de ventina ostendit per libros suos et aperte gesta per eum a multo tempore citra"; *ibid.*, f.10r.

[175] *Ibid.*, ff.10v–11r.

[176] *CP*, 42, f.10r. Cf. the comments of Francesco Ardinghelli, spokesman for the Merchants' Court: "Provideatur ut iura communis et redditus et omnia pertinentia in commune redeant; et de terris et locis fructus habeantur; corrigantur delinquentes et res communis non bene gerentes. Et sic agendo cum gabellis et residuiis sufficiet ad presens pro exigentiis communis"; *ibid.*, f.11r.

[177] *Ibid.*, f.10r.

[178] These were suggestions by Banco da Verrazzano, *ibid.*, f.10r. Lapo Niccolini also argued that the territory could be mulcted for more revenue, but Michele Castellani insisted that Florence's subjects had been bled white by rapacious officials; *ibid.*, f.10v.

Civic opinion was sharply divided over the value of the old assessments. Should these, with their errors and omissions, be preserved as the basis for a revised schedule, or should a new catalogue be drawn up by a more conscientious group of assessors?[179] Niccolò Sacchetti thought that the work of the old commission could still be utilized if the assessments were checked by twelve worthy men whose own levies were "equitable and fair." Cristofano Spini was very perturbed by the proposals for destroying the old schedule which, he insisted, "would set a very bad precedent and [would lead] to grave dangers." He supported Sacchetti's plan for revising the lists, using documents furnished by individual taxpayers. Though sharply critical of the assessors' performance, and skeptical about improving their work, Antonio Alessandri was still not willing to sanction the burning of the lists.[180] Underlying this conservative position was the premise, which applied to electoral as well as fiscal reform, that efforts to eliminate inequities were always futile because, in Alessandri's words, "the powerful always have the means to gain advantage, while others do not."[181] But if Paolo Biliotti's poll of the counselors from his quarter was an accurate measurement of civic sentiment, a strong majority favored the destruction of the old assessments and the compostion of a new schedule.[182] However, the war scare that followed Ladislaus' reoccupation of Rome (June 1413) forced the Signoria to place a higher priority upon obtaining revenue than upon rectifying these inequities. The clamor for fiscal reform gradually subsided, as the newly created balìa, given full authority in fiscal affairs, began its intensive search for money to subsidize another war.[183]

The revival of the Ladislaus peril was the spark igniting all the

[179] In Forese Sacchetti's words, "cives quosdam praticos bonos et prudentes et qui passionem non habent"; *ibid.*, f.11r.

[180] These arguments in *ibid.*, ff.9r–9v.

[181] "Exgravatio fienda non est, cum potentes commoditatem haberent et alii non"; *ibid.*, f.9r.

[182] *CP*, 42, f.11v. Twenty-six from the quarter of S. Spirito wanted to burn the old assessments, "ut nil remaneat ex ea"; eleven preferred to give the Signoria and colleges authority to formulate policy. The Eight on Security and the Merchants' Court also favored the destruction of the old schedule, as did Giovanni di Bicci de' Medici: ". . . Nam cum plus temporis datur et cum plures sunt ad rem gerendam, deterior finis sequitur; et utilius et melius fit per paucos et in brevi tempore, ut iam experientia docuit"; *ibid.*, f.10r.

[183] For collegiate demands that the Signoria act "cum celeritate ut equalitas detur in distributione noviter facta," *ibid.*, f.23r, 31 May. The councils approved (12–13 June 1413) a provision creating a fiscal balìa for one year, comprising the Signoria, colleges, Merchants' Court, Eight on Security and 21 guild consuls; *Prov.*, 102, ff.33r–33v.

smoldering discontents over the administration of public affairs. The council halls reverberated with barbed criticisms of past policies and practices, and denunciations of those judged responsible for the republic's debilitated condition. Had we built up our military force to 1000 lances before the king occupied Rome, Niccolò da Uzzano grumbled, then we would not now be threatened with another war.[184] That statement ignored the limitations on rearmament imposed by the prolongation of the Genoese conflict and the city's economic crisis, but no excuse, in Michele Castellani's view, could justify the failure of six successive priorates to send an embassy to the emperor-elect Sigismund. "A thousand times in the past year, it was recommended that ambassadors . . . be sent to the emperor, and these were never despatched." Paolo Carnesecchi also deplored the executive's refusal to implement this policy, "which had been advocated in councils, both large and small, for ten months and longer."[185]

Those allegedly responsible for thwarting the civic will were private citizens, not public officials, who were suspected of being secret friends of Ladislaus. By sabotaging this diplomatic overture to Sigismund, they were effectively nullifying any prospect of his crossing the Alps with an army to defend the papacy (and also Florence) from Ladislaus' attack. In a *pratica* held on 22 May to discuss the crisis, Piero Guicciardini criticized those who "covertly defended" the king's violation of his treaty with Florence and his occupation of Rome. Those who had brought about this deplorable state, Gino Capponi charged, "acted either from ignorance or from malice," and he warned his colleagues of potential traitors "like Buonaccorso di Lapo Giovanni," who might sell their city to the enemy. Niccolò Barbadori said publicly that some citizens were receiving pensions from Ladislaus.[186] Though reluctant to speak out on a matter which others "of greater authority" had not mentioned, Michele Castellani voiced his concern over a report that a citizen, "and not the lowliest in the city," had accepted an office in the king's government, thereby setting a deplorable example that the Signoria should correct.[187] The king's friends in Florence were also accused of leaking information to Naples, and specifically details concerning military and diplomatic policy. In

---

[184] CP, 42, f.14r: ". . . recitans que sibi Ciuccius de Aretio dixit de pessima nostra ordinatione; nam si lanceas mille habuissemus, tunc nobis guerram non intulisset; hec asserens et demonstrans ut propter expensas evitandas parvas, maximas incurrimus."

[185] *Ibid.*, ff.2r, 4v, 4 May. Cf. Strozza Strozzi, f.4r.

[186] CP, 42, f.14v, 19v, 36v, 40r.

[187] *Ibid.*, f.35v. That citizen was probably Luigi Pitti; see below, 363.

demanding the enforcement of the regulations prohibiting the revelation of state secrets, Gino Capponi hoped that the news of those deliberations would not become public knowledge "in the Crown Inn."[188] The king is advancing more rapidly than he would have done, Antonio Alessandri said, because he knows that he has influential friends in Florence. He is privy to our secrets, and particularly those provisions for defense that have not been implemented. "Whoever has spoken out strongly and effectively for liberty," Alessandri charged, "has been defamed by certain citizens, by writings, and by other means." He urged the Signoria to appoint members of a war *balìa* "who are loyal to the regime and not supporters of the king, and who neither possess nor seek any gifts from him."[189]

These accusations obscured an important policy issue which, in this tense atmosphere, could not be debated fully on its merits. The *reggimento* was divided into cliques: those who, in Marco Strozzi's words, "favored the pope, others who supported the emperor, and others, King Ladislaus."[190] In the papal camp were citizens who were eager to fight the king to defend John XXIII and papal territory; opposing them was a peace group whose members did not believe that Ladislaus was an enemy of the republic, or that an independent papal state was necessary for Florentine security. Only the spokesmen for the philopapal group could express their genuine feelings: "We must do everything to conserve the pope in his territory. . . . If Rome falls, our liberty is in peril."[191] Filippo Corsini was appalled by the prospect of John XXIII fleeing Italy for Avignon, "for then we will be all alone." Antonio Alessandri formulated an early version of the domino theory: "Much more will be lost than Rome itself, for if Rome falls, then the duchy [of Spoleto], the Patrimony, the Marches, and many of the church's provinces and her soldiers, will all be lost."[192] Though many, perhaps most, citizens did not subscribe to this view, none dared to refute these arguments publicly. Even the outspoken Paolo Biliotti, who

---

[188] *Ibid.,* f.17r: "ut que consuluntur non sint prius nota in hospicio Corone quam in loco presenti."

[189] *Ibid.,* f.36r. Niccolò da Uzzano's comment: ". . . nam contra eis qui bene consulerunt, multi conati sunt calumnias inferre et dare in civitate"; *ibid.,* f.37r.

[190] *Ibid.,* f.16v, 23 May: ". . . Dummodo cives requisiti sint sine passione, cum multi ad dominum papam, alii ad regem Romanorum et alii regem Ladislaum afficiantur; et de bono publico non curant." Also the statement of Messer Domenico di Ser Mino: "Multi videntur dubitare de adventu regis Romanorum; aliqui ex apparatibus regis Ladislai"; *ibid.,* f.14v.

[191] *Ibid.,* ff.16v (Cristofano Spini and Antonio Alessandri), 19v (Gino Capponi), 26r (Vieri Guadagni).

[192] *Ibid.,* ff.24r, 36r.

had challenged the imperialists in his speech of the previous September, did not directly refute the contentions of the papal faction, or express any sympathy for Ladislaus. Possibly chastened by his conviction (which may have been instigated by his political enemies)[193] for misconduct while serving as a treasury official, Biliotti maintained a low profile in the debates. He did speak out strongly for peace in two *pratiche* of 20 and 22 May, warning his colleagues that some citizens, manipulated by the pope, were seeking to embroil the republic in a war with Ladislaus. Denying that he had "received any gift or horse from the king," Biliotti urged his colleagues to speak honestly and objectively. He was not alone in favoring peace; many other counselors had spoken of the destructive effects of war on the citizens, whose fortunes had been consumed by military costs.[194]

Biliotti's call for a free debate on these issues was not supported by those who agreed with his views; they were unwilling to challenge the war party openly, and risk persecution for their candor. Betto Rustichi did touch gingerly on the sensitive issues when he pointed to the large debts owed the republic by Pope John and King Louis of Anjou, and thus indirectly of the disastrous consequences of Florence's last alliance with the papacy.[195] In his private diary, Buonaccorso Pitti presented the opposition's viewpoint that was not formulated in the *pratiche*.[196] Papal partisans, he wrote, had always resented the peace with Ladislaus and had done everything in their power to undermine it. War was about to break out with the king "as a result of the ruthless machinations of the papal faction within our city. . . . They have persuaded the citizenry that the king's capture of Rome and other papal possessions portends his doing the same with our own territory and liberty, and have generally aroused a mood of suspicion and unrest." Known as friends and clients of Ladislaus, the Pitti were primarily targets of the papal faction's hostility. Buonaccorso's account of his

---

[193] *AEOG*, 1785, ff.32r–33r, 7 Nov. 1412. On the discussion about this case, *CP*, 41, f.141v, 5 Oct.; *Prov.*, 101, ff.181r–181v. Biliotti's conviction did not ruin his political career, although he was barred from communal office. He continued to participate in the *pratiche*; e.g., *CP*, 41, f.155v; 42, ff.3r, 9v, 11r, 13r.

[194] *Ibid.*, ff.13r–25v: ". . . Examinandum est an per pacem vel guerram libertas servari debet; et clarum est quod per guerram status multorum adhichilatum est; et quia per alios locutum est quam sit damnosa guerre et sine passione quicumque loqui potere; et ipse beneficium non habet nec equum habuit a rege. . . ."

[195] *CP*, 42, f.14v. The pope's debt was 118,000 fl. Rustichi also referred to the provisions that had been enacted to limit the commune's involvement in military enterprises, a reference to the establishment of the Council of 200 in 1411.

[196] *Cronica*, 181–82.

family's ordeal is a fascinating story of the connectedness of private and public conflict that reveals with unusual clarity the persistence, in Florentine politics, of traditional habits and mentalities.

The affair began innocuously enough, in a friendship that developed between Buonaccorso's brother Luigi and an elderly monk, Benedetto, abbot of the Camaldolese monastery of San Piero a Ruota, in the Valdambra district west of Arezzo. The abbot needed protection from "certain mighty personages who had taken advantage of his age to molest him," and the Pitti seized the opportunity to help a man who could repay them with the gift of his monastery. But that benefice was located in the heart of Ricasoli country, and those "mighty personages" were angered by this poaching in their domain.[197] The Ricasoli campaign against the abbot began with an insinuation of treason, followed by a judicial process in the Roman curia to deprive him of the monastery. By this time the Pitti were acutely aware of the powerful forces arrayed against them, not only the Ricasoli but the Peruzzi, one of whom was to replace Abbot Benedetto in Ruota. Prudence would have dictated a withdrawal from this unequal struggle, but, motivated either by greed or by their sense of honor, the Pitti persisted in defending the abbot. The Ricasoli and the Peruzzi had the ear of Pope John XXIII, whose judge delegate, Cardinal Orsini, deprived Benedetto of his abbey and sentenced him to life imprisonment. In Florence, the Pitti tried vainly to persuade the Ricasoli to abandon their vendetta, and they also failed in their efforts to persuade the Signoria to write the pope on the abbot's behalf.[198] Undaunted by these rebuffs, the Pitti then devised a risky plan to implicate the Ricasoli in a fake attack on Abbot Benedetto outside of their Florentine palace. The scheme backfired and Buonaccorso revealed all of the details to the *podestà*. Though not as potent and influential as the Ricasoli clique, Pitti's friends in the *reggimento* were able to quash the criminal charges against him, and to moderate the penalties imposed on his son Luca and others who had participated in that bungled plot.[199]

Only that bizarre trick to deceive the authorities, and to foil their enemies, distinguished this squabble between the Pitti and the Ricasoli

---

[197] *Cronica*, 165–67. On the antiquity of the Ricasoli, see L. Passerini, *Genealogia e storia della famiglia Ricasoli* (Florence, 1870).

[198] *Cronica*, 168–72. The captains of the Parte Guelfa did write to the pope, urging him not to listen to the "detractores et calumniatores" of the abbot; *SCMC*, 25, ff.10r–11r, 16 Dec. 1411.

[199] *Cronica*, 173–77. Buonaccorso was absolved; his son Luca was fined 800 l. and exiled for three years. Four other accomplices received smaller penalties; *AP*, 4272, unpaginated, 17 Dec. 1412.

from dozens of similar disputes.[200] This quarrel, however, had an unusual political dimension, the consequence of a twist of fortune that
had placed Luigi Pitti in the Signoria which, in December 1410, had
negotiated the peace treaty with Ladislaus. The papal faction identified Luigi as the prior who was most responsible for the settlement,[201]
so the Pitti became the focus of their hostility. When Buonaccorso in-
terceded with Cardinal Orsini on behalf of the abbot of Ruota, Pandolfo Ricasoli, a papal chamberlain, denounced him as an enemy of the
church and the pope. "Our opponents," Buonaccorso wrote in his
diary, "keep harrying and hounding us and never miss a chance to
humilitate us or do us an ill turn."[202] That campaign was motivated as
much by political considerations as by a desire for personal or family
revenge. If the Pitti could be driven out of the *reggimento*, or reduced
to silence and impotence, the foreign policy they had espoused—accommodation with Ladislaus and neutrality towards the pope—would
also be discredited.

Though biased, Buonaccorso Pitti's account of his family's ordeal,
and of the motives and machinations of his enemies, does tally closely
with information from other sources. Those citizens whom he identified as his persecutors were all prominent men in the *reggimento*
and, more important, they were the strongest advocates of an aggressive posture in foreign affairs. They consistently displayed a willingness—indeed an eagerness—to rely on force as an instrument of
policy, and they were also committed to close ties with the papal
curia. Buonaccorso identified the leaders of that clique as Rinaldo
Gianfigliazzi, Gino Capponi, Bartolomeo Valori, and Niccolò da Uzzano; among their "henchmen and satellites" were (besides the Peruzzi
and Ricasoli) Michele Castellani, Piero Baroncelli, Betto Busini, and
Niccolò Barbadori.[203] The political and ideological affinities of this
clique were reinforced by bonds of blood and geography, for many of
these families—Ricasoli, Peruzzi, Castellani, Baroncelli, Busini—were
neighbors in the quarter of Santa Croce.[204] Prominent among the defenders of the Pitti were friends and neighbors in the Oltrarno quarter: Guidetto Guidetti, Francesco Machiavelli, Nofri Bischeri, Gio-

[200] Brucker, *Renaissance Florence*, 178–80; and "An Unpublished Source on the
Avignonese Papacy: the Letters of Francesco Bruni"; *Traditio*, XIX (1963), 351–70.

[201] Since Luigi was the brother-in-law of Gabriello Brunelleschi, Ladislaus' agent
in the peace negotiations, he would have had an additional incentive to promote a
settlement; Pitti, *Cronica*, 20–21, 180, 191.

[202] *Cronica*, 180.

[203] *Ibid.*, 169–70, 172–73, 175–76.

[204] Dale Kent has emphasized the importance of neighborhood in the formation
of the Medici faction in the late 1420s; *Rise of the Medici*, ch. 1, v.

vanni Carducci, Migliore Migliori, and the humanist Roberto de' Rossi, "my trusty friend . . . whose help was invaluable. . . ." In the process arising from the fake assault on the abbot of Ruota, Machiavelli, Guidetti, Carducci, and Migliori testified to Buonaccorso's good reputation. So, too, did Sandro Altoviti, who declared under oath that Buonaccorso was "a most worthy man who, were he not so esteemed, would never have received the honor that he has won in the city. . . ." Altoviti also testified that "among those unaffected by partisanship (*non passionatis*)," it was generally believed that Buonaccorso was innocent of any participation in that plot, that he was not a vindictive man.[205] Buonaccorso's marriage to Maso degli Albizzi's niece was probably the crucial factor in persuading Maso's son Rinaldo and his cousin Piero di Luca to support him. Though Buonaccorso did not identify Maso himself as an ally, he may have worked in private to protect a beleaguered relative whose brother had been his supporter in the controversy over the Ladislaus peace.

In the fiasco involving the abbot of Ruota, the roles of the protagonists are clearly defined, their actions and motives described in full detail in the criminal records and in Buonaccorso's diary. The next scene in the Pitti melodrama, however, is more obscure.[206] A letter written by Ladislaus' ambassadors to the king was intercepted by officials of the war *balìa*; it allegedly implicated Luigi Pitti as the source of official secrets that the diplomats were transmitting to their master.[207] Upon receipt of this document, the executor instituted a process against Luigi, who was then on his way to L'Aquila to renew his service with Ladislaus as captain of that city. To guarantee that Luigi would return to face trial, the executor imprisoned Buonaccorso and his brother Bartolomeo. Responding to the desperate appeals of Buonaccorso's nephew, Neri di Piero, a crowd of 200 friends assembled to pledge

[205] *AP*, 4265, ff.5r–6r. Migliori testified that Buonaccorso was "de meliori condictione quam aliquis alius civis civitatis Florentie quem ipse testis cognoschat, et qui fecit plures honores civitatis predicte in Alamannia et in Francia quam alius civis. . . . Ipse et sue fuerunt semper de bonis mercatoribus huius civitatis. . . ."

[206] The details in Pitti, *Cronica*, 177–81, are corroborated by the reports of the Sienese ambassador; *Conc.*, 1882, no. 64, 75, 76, 79, 86.

[207] The letter was read to a *pratica* of 200 citizens, according to the Sienese ambassador: ". . . e in esso consiglio pare che si leggiessero lettere le quali infra l'altre cose doveano continere che dappoi che Luigi Pitti si parti di qui, non avevano potuto sentire dele cose come sentirono primo si partisse, pero chè lui dicieva era disposto di porre di continuo la testa in mano per fare cosa piacesse al Re, e così senza rendare consiglio o prendare altro partito, uscì il consiglio. Bene pare vi fusse dette dele parole a grido: 'Faccisi ragione se ci è comisso defetto'"; *Conc.*, 1882, no. 75, 25 July.

their support, and to petition the Signoria and the executor to release the hostages. Though the colleges were shocked by these revelations, "by the mores of those citizens who betray the *patria*," they were reluctant to punish the Pitti.[208] The executor finally released Buonaccorso and his brother, but he prosecuted the case against Luigi with great vigor. The latter was on his way back to Florence to defend himself against the charges of treason when, in Perugia, he learned that he had been outlawed and his property confiscated.[209]

Buonaccorso Pitti insisted that the Ricasoli and the Peruzzi were the villains of this plot to discredit Luigi and ruin his family; there is circumstantial evidence to corroborate that opinion. When petitioning the Signoria for the cancellation of his ban, Luigi declared that he had not been a member of any magistracy or council where he could have learned about official secrets.[210] His intention to defend himself personally against the charges of treason gives some weight to his protestations of innocence, just as the publication of his ban while he was en route to Florence raises some doubts about the executor's impartiality.[211] The evidence against Luigi was not so conclusive as to sway civic opinion against him or his family.[212] Whatever the verdict on Luigi's treasonous activity, he was guilty of irresponsible behavior in accepting office from Ladislaus. To disregard the accusations of improper relations between the king and his Florentine friends after the king's occupation of Rome, and when war fever was spreading in Florence, was foolhardy.[213] Buonaccorso himself was not an apologist

---

[208] *CP*, 42, ff.53r–53v, 24 and 26 July, 1 Aug.

[209] Pitti, *Cronica*, 179–81; *AEOG*, 1808, ff.68r–69r. The sentence was cancelled a year later; *Prov.*, 103, ff.54v–55r.

[210] *Prov.*, 103, f.54v. Luigi had been an official in L'Aquila and had returned to Florence before being reappointed by Ladislaus; Pitti, *Cronica*, 179–80.

[211] *Prov.*, 103, f.54v: "Affines ipsius Loysii Florentie existentes sine ulla dilatione miserunt litteras, nullis parcendo expensis, ad dictum Loysium. Sciens innocentiam suam dimissis omnibus suis negotiis, ascendit equum et iter arripuit non subsistendo sed de die et de nocte equitando et pervenit Perusium. . . ." The executor published the ban against him, "ut pessime informatus et etiam sollicitatus per aliquos. . . ."

[212] *CP*, 42, f.53v, Paolo Rucellai for the Sixteen: "Omnes dolore debemus de quocumque infortunio quod evenit civibus guelfis bonis et fidis et quomodo sic reputant illos de Pittis et etiam insontes, licet sine culpa detenti cum dedecore sint et non culpa dominorum. . . ." Rinaldo Gianfigliazzi, whom Buonaccorso considered an enemy, and Filippo Corsini led civic delegations to the Signoria and the executor to plead for the Pitti; *Cronica*, 179.

[213] The Sienese ambassador reported: "Al tempo de' Signori passati di qui, fra quali era Bartolomeo suo fratello, esso Luigi dimandò licentia d'andare al suo offitio, pensando da quelli di mai non poterla avere e obtenerla, e poi al tempo di

for Ladislaus, even in his private diary. He conceded that the king may have planned to conquer Florence, but, he added, "if he has, the fault lies with the provocative and bellicose behavior in which the papal clique in Florence has indulged ever since peace was signed against the pope's will."[214]

The Florentine promoters of curial interests were motivated not by patriotism, Pitti argued, but by greed. John XXIII had bought their allegiance "with gifts of benefices and promises of more," and to earn these rewards they labored to align Florentine policy in accordance with his goals.[215] By borrowing money from his supporters, the pope had further strengthened their adherence to his cause.[216] When John XXIII stopped outside Florence after his flight from Rome (July 1413), many citizens visited him to request benefices for themselves, relatives, and friends.[217] This traffic was so heavy that an alarmed Signoria drafted a provision to prohibit such activities. That measure imposed a five-year moratorium on any petition for a benefice by a Florentine citizen; it also stipulated that no foreigner could hold an ecclesiastical office within Florentine territory without the consent of the Signoria and the colleges.[218] According to the Sienese ambassador, the pope was "scandalized" by the proposal, and announced his intention of going to Avignon if it were enacted. The pope's friends in the *reggimento* mobilized their forces to defeat the provision. In a *pratica* held on 3 August Cristofano di Giorgio expressed his fear that the pope would react to this infringement on his prerogatives by abandoning Italy. Gino Capponi said that the provision had some merit, but that the time was not propitious for its enactment. "We should do nothing," he concluded, "that would harm the pope's authority in England, France, Germany, or any other province, for his state is ours."[219] Agreeing with Capponi that the proposed law was both useful and popular, Forese Sacchetti nevertheless opposed its passage if it dis-

---

questi [Signori], senza parlarlo nulla, partì di qui e andasene nel Reame, della quale partita qui s'è sparlato fortemente per gli uomini del reggimento, e lui e tutti i suoi ne sono venuti anco più in disgratia e potrebono passar le cose in modo che anco pegio n'andarebono"; *Conc.*, 1882, no. 64, 15 July.

[214] *Cronica*, 181.   [215] *Ibid.*, 182.

[216] Two papal creditors who strongly supported his cause in the *pratiche* were Antonio Alessandri and Bernardo Guadagni; *Merc.*, 1252, ff.727v–728r, 779r.

[217] *Cronica*, 182–83. Gino Capponi commented on the swarm of Florentine petitioners around the pope; *CP*, 42, f.55r.

[218] *Conc.*, 1882, no. 86, 3 Aug. There is no record of this provision in the official sources.

[219] *CP*, 42, ff.54v–55r.

pleased the pope. Only the war *balìa* and one segment of the Sixteen unequivocally approved its adoption.[220] But their support was not sufficient to counteract the pressure from those who argued that a benevolent pope and an independent papal state were essential for the regime's security.

Among those Florentines who had business with the pope and his entourage in these months were, besides the seekers of ecclesiastical office, the humanists and the bankers. George Holmes has traced these connections, and has described their impact upon the cultural life of the two communities, urban and curial,[221] and also upon the fortunes of the Medici. Among John XXIII's many talents, Holmes has shown, was a particular ability to raise money from the clergy within his obedience. From 1411 onward, he spent money lavishly, if unsuccessfully, to defend his territory from Ladislaus' depredations. To collect and disburse these sums, the pope selected a coterie of Florentine financiers—notably the Medici, the Spini, the Carducci, and the Bardi—to replace those bankers, largely recruited from exiled families (Alberti, Ricci, Del Bene) which had been most heavily involved in papal finance in earlier pontificates.[222] At the time of John XXIII's sojourn outside Florence, Giovanni di Bicci de' Medici was the leading curial banker, and papal business accounted for a large part of his profits.[223] The shift in Giovanni's political loyalties, from Ladislaus, "the father of this *popolo*,"[224] to John XXIII may not, of course, have been influenced by his fiscal ties to the curia. Still, the metamorphosis in his opinions, as revealed in the *pratiche*, is striking. Prior to John's election in 1411, Giovanni had advocated peace, restraint, the settle-

[220] *Ibid.*, f.56v, 4 Aug. Speaking for the war *balìa*, Piero Baroncelli commented that "si per evangelistas ordinata provisio foret, iustius aut sanctyus fieri non potuisset. . . ." The pope should not be angry, Baroncelli continued, "quod omnibus papa posset beneficia concedere ut voluerit, dummodo florentini ea acceptare non possunt; et alienigene debeant approbari per dominos et collegia et consilia ne lex fraudetur, multas et varias rationes adducendo ad hortationem legis et provisionis ordinate."

[221] G. Holmes, *The Florentine Enlightenment*, 57–105.

[222] Holmes, "How the Medici Became the Pope's Bankers," in *Flor. Studies*, 357–80 and esp. 360–73. One banker who may have been displaced by the Medici was Aldigerio Biliotti, *ibid.*, 361, brother of Piero Biliotti, whose antipapal attitude may have been influenced by this shift. See A. Esch, "Florentiner in Rom um 1400," *Quellen und Forschungen aus Italienischen Archiven und Bibliotheken*, LII (1972), 497–98.

[223] R. de Roover, *Rise and Decline of the Medici Bank*, 38–47, 202–03.

[224] See above, 228, where Giovanni agreed with Pandolfini on peace with Ladislaus. Giovanni did have a branch of his company in Naples; De Roover, 254–56, which may explain his initial sympathy for Ladislaus.

ment of disputes by negotiation; thereafter, he denounced Ladislaus as an implacable enemy of the republic. As early as August 1412 he warned his colleagues that the king was intent upon the conquest of Italy; in May 1413 he expressed the hope that war with the king would be publicly declared, to end the uncertainty, and to force the republic to fight before Ladislaus had become invincible.[225] The fortunes of Giovanni de' Medici were as closely linked to John XXIII as were those of the four Ricasoli, who were papal chamberlains and knights, or Leonardo Bruni and Poggio Bracciolini, who were secretaries in the curia.[226]

In an atmosphere so heavily charged with partisanship, in which public and private interest were so inextricably linked that everyone's motives were suspect, the prospects for constructive solutions to the problem of civic discord were remote. Antonio Alessandri, Rinaldo Gianfigliazzi, and their conservative allies viewed political conflict as essentially a moral question that was susceptible to correction not by legislative action, but only by the purgation of unworthy elements from the *reggimento*. Alessandri castigated those who banded together in secret colloquy to defame "patriots" and whose disruptive activities had gone unpunished for too long.[227] The motives of these malcontents were envy and greed, and a perverted sense of priorities. Such men, Niccolò Barbadori believed, were responsible for the general decline in respect for communal authority, and specifically a contempt for the office of the Signoria.[228] Bartolomeo Valori denied that tax inequities were at the root of civic discord, "but before that, one could see the work of those who so directed the affairs of the republic that they fell into great disarray."[229] Coercion and punishment were the essential remedies for these ills. Rinaldo Gianfigliazzi approved the grant of police powers to the magistracy charged with settling quarrels, "since

---

[225] CP, 41, f.129r; 42, f.20v: ". . . Si ad guerram venire debemus, in conspectu Dei et mundi iustificari debemus et populus in unitate quod potentia nostra ibi est. . . . Sperandum sit quod guerra publice geretur, et uno vel alio in eam veniemus; et quotidie res devenirent ad scandala maiora et nullus est modus nisi nos . . . et forte accidere poterit ut rex aliqualiter acquirat vel agat et quod nunc fieri potest, tunc non poterit. . . ."

[226] The four Ricasoli who were curial officials are identified by Pitti; *Cronica*, 168; the benefits accruing to humanists in John's court noted by Poggio; Holmes, *Flor. Studies*, 374.

[227] CP, 41, f.152r: ". . . Advertentia maxima adhibenda est ut odia que occulte inter cives simul colloquentes sunt tollerentur et ad reprimendum calumniatores et infamatores contra bonos cives . . . cum propter non datam talibus penam in preteritum inconvenientia orta multiplicia sunt. . . ."

[228] CP, 41, f.152v.   [229] CP, 42, f.35r. .

few or none can be persuaded by words alone. . . ." Salamone Strozzi
proposed that those who defamed other citizens be severely punished,
since their slanderous comments fueled civic hatred.[230] Bernardo
Guadagni and Antonio di Niccolò Alberti suggested that an official
(*capitaneus balie*) be appointed with authority to punish calumnia-
tors, a category that included, in Piero Baroncelli's judgment, anyone
who spoke publicly in favor of either the pope or King Ladislaus.[231]

This conspiratorial view of politics was not embraced by all, and
perhaps not even a majority, of the citizens in the *reggimento*. Maso
degli Albizzi, Lorenzo Ridolfi, and Filippo Corsini did not indulge in
public tirades against "the malevolent ones," though Corsini, in a rare
censorious mood, did say that "if our fathers were to rise [from the
dead], they would consign us to hell for our misdeeds. . . ."[232] The
political attitude of these men was more open and flexible, and less
partisan, than that of the zealots. They believed that the injustices and
inequities stimulating civic discord could be corrected if not eliminated by legislation and administrative decisions.[233] Like Leonardo
Bruni and the civic humanists, they preferred persuasion to coercion
as a means of reducing tensions and achieving unity. Less concerned
about calumny, and more receptive to free and open debate, than their
more conservative peers, they subscribed to Filippo Corsini's dictum
that "everyone should speak truly and honestly, even in disagreement. . . . We live in a free city and that which, among other things
promotes liberty is freedom [of speech] in the councils."[234] Lorenzo
Ridolfi was probably the strongest advocate, in the inner circle, of a
governo largo, a regime with a broad popular base. His political views
were thus akin to the republican ideals espoused by Leonardo Bruni
and his circle. "Nothing is more pernicious than to act against the
wishes of the citizenry," he reminded his colleagues, "and conversely,
nothing is more useful than to implement the will of the *popolo*. . . ."[235]

[230] *CP*, 41, f.141v, 153r.

[231] *CP*, 42, ff.36v, 40v, and Baroncelli's statement, f.37r: "Et potens est dominatio
punire cives et subditos loquentes de defensione pape et de rege Ladislao . . . et
siquis contra ageret, puniatur. . . ."

[232] *CP*, 42, f.36v: "Quod si patres resurgerent, nos in locum vilissimum facerent,
inspectis nostris gestis. . . ."

[233] Corsini had long insisted that inequitable tax assessments were the main cause
of internal discord; in agreement were Francesco Tornabuoni, Mariotto della
Morotta, Barduccio Cherichini, and Andrea Buondelmonti; *ibid.*, ff.14r, 15r, 24r,
32r.

[234] *CP*, 42, f.10r; 43, f.145r. On this issue, see above, ch. v, 306–08.

[235] *CP*, 42, f.23v. For his earlier statement on the *popolo*'s role in policymaking,
above, 349.

As the danger of war with Ladislaus increased in the spring of 1413, the quarreling among factions, families, and individuals abated. Even such zealous partisans as Strozza Strozzi and Michele Castellani concluded that "the time is not propitious for quarrels but for remedies; private passions and advantages should be subordinated to the public interest."[236] The appeals for unity and sacrifices were possibly more intense than during previous crises since, in Filippo Corsini's judgment, the republic had not been in greater peril in his lifetime.[237] Piero Guicciardini's speech of 22 May is a dramatic example of the genre: "Everyone should do all in his power to defend liberty, offering both life and property. Though nearly ruined by taxes, I am prepared to offer the rest of what I possess, and my body and soul, so that we may live as free men." Bartolomeo Valori's exhortation was couched in similar terms, but he offered a more modest sum of 500 florins as his initial contribution to the republic's defense.[238] "The *patria* is more important than our children," Rinaldo Gianfigliazzi said, "and everything should be done for its protection, so that we bequeath to our posterity what we have inherited from our ancestors."[239] That death would be preferable to servitude was a common theme in these orations; so too was the argument that, once lost, liberty would never be recovered. "Some think that if we are subdued, we could expel our conqueror with the aid of our friends," Rinaldo said, "but that hope is vain."[240] In a speech that could have been written for him by Leonardo Bruni (who was indeed then residing in Florence), Rinaldo made the most extreme claim for preserving republican liberty: "Without freedom, Florence cannot survive, and without Florence, liberty cannot survive!"[241]

THE SECOND WAR WITH LADISLAUS

The news of Rome's seizure by Ladislaus' troops, and of the pope's flight, reached Florence on 11 June 1413.[242] The Signoria immediately proposed the creation of a war *balìa*, the election of a police official

---

[236] *CP*, 42, f.37r.

[237] *Ibid.*, f.63r. Others who believed that the peril was the greatest in the regime's (or even the commune's) experience were Bernardo Guadagni and Gino Capponi, *ibid.*, ff.40v, 71v. "Libertas nostra est in maiori periculo quam unquam fuerit. . . ."

[238] *Ibid.*, ff.14v, 35r.   [239] *Ibid.*, f.17v.

[240] *Ibid.*, f.60v. For similar statements by Gianfigliazzi, Antonio Alessandri, and Niccolò da Uzzano, *ibid.*, ff.17v, 23v, 36v.

[241] *Ibid.*, f.79v: "Quod sine libertate, Florentia durare non potest ac libertas sine Florentia, cum multe patrie servabunt dominis et tirannis. . . ."

[242] *CP*, 42, ff.36r–37v.

(*capitano di balìa*) to repress internal dissent, and a fiscal magistracy to raise money. Reporting these developments to his government, the Sienese ambassador commented that "in this popular regime, there has emerged a unity, a conformity of spirit, and a determination to pursue those courses that will promote their and our liberty . . . that is almost incredible, in the light of the variety of opinions expressed since this morning." As evidence of this unity, the ambassador noted that the three provisions proposed by the Signoria had been approved unanimously by the colleges, and also by the special council of 200 that was convened to vote on legislation pertaining to war and peace. "So, my lords," the ambassador concluded, "you may be confident that . . . liberty, which is the highest good in this life, is triumphant here. . . ."[243]

The division of opinion between those citizens who saw Ladislaus as the republic's archenemy and those who perceived him as the victim of papal duplicity continued throughout the summer and autumn of 1413, and indeed for the duration of the war. Both sides used rational arguments, as well as polemic and invective, to gain support for their viewpoints and to denigrate their opponents. The war faction favored a military offensive against the king, similar to the campaign of 1409–1410. When Michele Castellani learned that Rome had been occupied by Neapolitan troops, he told the *pratica* that "we must elect citizens, who are not partisan, to levy 100,000 or 150,000 florins; it is deplorable that we have been placed in this situation by the actions of certain [men]. It is also necessary, though regrettable, that a war *balìa* be established; it would be a greater misfortune to lose our liberty. The citizens must be coerced to conform, and those who do wrong should be punished."[244] Antonio Alessandri was perhaps the most eloquent spokesman for the war party during these months. Convinced that Ladislaus was determined to conquer Florence, he saw no advantage in diplomatic parleys with the king: only by a show of force could he be persuaded to abandon his aggressive plans. He favored the despatch of troops to Rome and to Bologna to defend those beleaguered cities.[245] He placed the responsibility for that fiasco directly on the king's friends in Florence, who had kept Ladislaus informed of political developments, and who had sabotaged the efforts of those who had

---

[243] *Conc.*, 1882, no. 32 and 33, despatches of the envoy Ardinghieri, 11 June. The text of the three provisions are in *Prov.*, 102, ff.31v–34v; the record of voting in *LF*, 50, ff.78r, 79r, 80r. Contrary to the Sienese diplomat's statement, one-third of the votes were cast against the *balìa*.

[244] *CP*, 42, f.37r, 11 June.

[245] *CP*, 42, f.23v. For previous statements of his opinions, see *ibid.*, ff.16v, 18r, 23 and 24 May. On the legal problems involved in sending military aid to these cities, see Martines, *Lawyers and Statecraft*, 337–38.

sought to bolster the republic's defenses.[246] The triumphal progress of the king's armies through papal territory, and the pope's flight, strengthened his conviction that the day of reckoning had finally arrived. "Our procrastination, both past and present, has brought us to this perilous state," he said in mid-September, "and if we continue along this path, we will finally achieve our ruin." So bleak was the military situation at that moment, with the Papal States almost entirely occupied by the king's armies, and John XXIII cowering outside Florence's walls, that Antonio's resolution momentarily wavered. On 26 September, he asked if the papal connection were still a Florentine asset; if not, "then it is stupid to continue to spend as we have done and are doing."[247] But he quickly reverted to his earlier convictions, and in October he worked hard to promote an alliance with the pope.[248]

Agnolo Pandolfini was the most consistent advocate of a peaceful settlement with Ladislaus. He had initially proposed (31 May) that the republic offer to guarantee the implementation of any peace agreement which Florentine diplomats could arrange between the king and the pope. Although conceding that the loss of Rome would endanger the republic's security, he argued nevertheless that Florence was too weak to undertake a serious military effort to defend the city.[249] Rome's conquest by Ladislaus shook his faith in diplomacy, and he joined his more bellicose colleagues in exhorting the Signoria to take all appropriate measures to defend Florentine territory. He rationalized his prior advocacy of moderation toward the king by saying that he had not believed that Rome would surrender so easily.[250] But

---

[246] CP, 42, f.36r: "Consuluit quod nil gravius iam diu accidit nostre civitati, considerato quod statui nostre libertatis importat amissio Rome . . . et ne in aliud provideat, infra mensem rex ad janua nostra veniet; et ipse eam novit quod sit hec agere, nam nunc citius veniet quam alias quia melius noscit vel quod multos sub hic facientes habuerit. . . ."

[247] Ibid., ff.69r, 74v.   [248] Ibid., f.79v, 10 Oct.

[249] CP, 42, f.24r: "In rebus magnis premeditatio diligens habenda est; et que proponuntur gravissima sunt, cum sint ut in pace conservemus vel in guerram vivamus. . . . Si [Roma] amittitur, libertas nostra perdita est; sed quoniam difficile est propter consumptionem civium et preteritas guerras et non equalitatem onerum; libertatem tamen hortatur; et alia via utilior videtur, videlicet, quod promissionem faciamus de observantia quam querunt rex et papa, eos in concordiam ponendo, et hec sine expensa procedit, allegans: 'ferre minores volo ne graviora feram;' et eligenda sunt que minoris sint periculi et jacture, ut est promissio postulata aut liga. . . ."

[250] Ibid., f.37v: "Quod casus presens terrorem cunctis afferre debet et omnes animare ad hortandum dominos et alios ad omnia remedia summenda pro salute nostre libertatis et status; et si in preteritum alter erat opinionis, videlicet, ut temperate ad hec procederetur, non putabat Romam adeo de facili amitti posse. . . ."

after the fears aroused by Rome's fall had subsided, Agnolo reiterated his belief that the republic should try to avoid war with the king. By remaining at peace, he said, "we will be stronger than the pope or the emperor, or any other power that confronts us; but if we become involved in war, then everyone will watch us and none will give us help. . . ."[251] Pandolfini urged the Signoria and the *balìa* to take seriously their discussions with Ladislaus' ambassadors, who had brought the king's latest proposals for a settlement.[252] After these negotiations broke down in August, Agnolo was still unwilling to concede that conflict was inevitable. In October, he opposed an alliance with the pope, claiming that it would make a settlement with Ladislaus more difficult, and that it should be signed only after the last flicker of hope for peace had been extinguished.[253]

The supporters of the papal cause, and of a strong response to Ladislaus' invasion, monopolized the debates on military and diplomatic strategy. Agnolo Pandolfini's position, and particularly his relatively benign view of the king, received no support in these discussions, since the expression of such opinions would be labeled unpatriotic by the war party.[254] Yet, despite the predominance of these bellicose views in the *pratiche*, the priors and the war *balìa* pursued this conciliatory policy. "My conclusion is this," the Sienese ambassador wrote on 14 June, "that they [the Florentines] are afraid of war because they realize that if it begins, it will be very costly and they want peace if they can have it. . . ." Three weeks later (4 July), the Signoria informed the ambassador that they were biding their time until the harvest was completed and the republic's defenses were strengthened.[255] The war *balìa* did hire more cavalry and infantry, and sent a contingent of 300 lances into the Patrimony to defend those towns that remained loyal to the pope.[256] By maintaining this defensive

---

[251] *Ibid.*, f.45r, 3 July: "Guerram evitare omni modo debemus, nam difficillimum est pacem demum habere; et nos experti sumus alias; et donec guerram non habemus, maiores erimus papa imperatore et aliis omnibus qui ad nos nunc veniunt et mittunt; et si guerram haberemus, ad nos omnes inspicerent et pro nostra tuitione nil afferetur. . . ."

[252] *Ibid.*, f.46v, 7 July.   [253] *Ibid.*, f.80v, 10 Oct.

[254] In the streets, however, vocal support for Ladislaus was more common; see the comment of Sala Marsili, *CP*, 42, f.97r.

[255] *Conc.*, 1882, no. 36, 58.

[256] According to the Sienese ambassador, the Florentine army in mid-June comprised only 400 lances in poor condition; by mid-July 1120 lances were under contract; *ibid.*, no. 36 and 66. On the 300 lances sent into the Patrimony, *Dieci di Balìa, Carteggi, Missive Interni*, 1, f.13r. The republic also accepted, as *racco-*

posture, and by carefully limiting their support for John XXIII, Florentine officials obviously hoped to induce Ladislaus to avoid a military confrontation in Tuscany, and to negotiate seriously for a peace settlement. Diplomats continued to shuttle between Florence and Rome (and later Naples), carrying proposals and counter-proposals from the two chanceries. But the Signoria received little encouragement from these contacts, since Ladislaus insisted that the republic's fortresses be turned over to his troops, and that her soldiers swear allegiance to him.[257]

The presence of Pope John XXIII in a monastery outside Florence intensified the political struggles then being fought within the *reggimento* over foreign policy. The Signoria had sent an embassy to Siena, where the pope had stopped on his way north, to urge him to bypass Florence on his way to Bologna. "If he says that he would like to visit our city, then inform him that for good and sufficient reasons, and to avoid any scandal, His Holiness should decide not to come here. . . ."[258] The pope ignored this advice and brought his entourage to the city gates;[259] he may have hoped that his friends in the *reggimento* would arrange for his triumphal entry into the city. On 20 August the Sienese ambassador reported that the pope would be housed in Santa Maria Novella, the Dominican convent, but that rumor proved to be unfounded.[260] Though he did not receive the welcome and the honors which he considered his due,[261] John XXIII was

---

mandati, three papal mercenaries: Count Guidantonio of Montefeltro, Lodovico degli Alidosi and Ugolino Trinci; *I Capitoli del Comune di Firenze*, I, 545-47, 550.

[257] The details of Ladislaus' proposals are described in *Conc.*, 1882, no. 50, 62; 29 June and 8 July. Ladislaus also insisted that the Florentines deposit 100,000 fl. in Venice, to guarantee that they would fulfill their obligations.

[258] *SCMLC*, 6, ff.31v-32r, 15 June. The text is printed in H. Finke, *Acta Concilii Constanciensis*, I, 171. The issue of a papal visit was never raised in a *pratica*.

[259] The pope arrived at S. Antonio del Vescovo on 21 June; the Signoria, the war *balìa* "e molti altri cittadini" visited him on the 22nd; "Diario di Bartolomeo di Michele del Corazza," *ASI*, 5th ser., XIV, 252. The Sienese ambassador (15 July) reported the pope's arrival at the monastery, but said that he was planning to go directly to Bologna; *Conc.*, 1882, no. 64.

[260] "Costoro tenghono ragionamento di mettere il papa dentro in Firenze; credesi starà in Santa Maria Novella. Che seguirà, saprete"; *Conc.*, 1882, no. 68, 20 Aug. The issue was not mentioned again in the Sienese diplomatic correspondence.

[261] The pope departed from S. Antonio del Vescovo when he went to Bologna in mid-November; K. Eubel, "Das Itinerar der Päpste zur Zeit des grossen Schismas," *Historisches Jahrbuch*, XVI (1895), 564. He never entered Florence as Perrens, *Histoire de Florence*, VI, 188, and Cutolo, *Ladislao*, 443, asserted.

able to influence Florentine policy and to gain the military alliance that was his primary objective.

His first concern was to preserve some portion of his disintegrating state before it was completely occupied by Ladislaus. He appealed to the Florentines and the Sienese for a subsidy to pay his troops in Umbria and the Patrimony and to strengthen his control of Bologna, which was challenged by Niccolò d'Este, lord of Ferrara. Mindful that Bologna's capitulation might result in a blockade as total as that envisaged by Giangaleazzo Visconti in 1402,[262] the Signoria hired Niccolò d'Este and thus relieved the pressure on that key city.[263] But the war *balìa's* proposals to subsidize Paolo Orsini's defense of papal territory encountered stiff resistance from those who viewed this as a ploy by John XXIII to dump his military responsibilities upon Florentine shoulders. In addition to her own expenses which are so heavy that many citizens have been ruined, Francesco Ardinghelli complained, the pope now wants the republic to pay for 1000 lances that he has hired.[264] The solution to the fiscal crisis actually lay in papal hands, Cristofano Spini insisted. "The pope should authorize the sale of ecclesiastical property worth 300,000 florins, as was done before, and this would be a legitimate expenditure for defending the church. . . ."[265] That proposal gained strong support from the colleges, and also from members of the Merchants' Court and the Eight on Security.[266] But when collegiate representatives sought an audience with the pope to recommend this scheme, they were kept waiting for hours outside the monastery gates.[267] The colleges voiced resentment over this treatment and the pope's adamant refusal to consider the alienation of church property which, so Bartolomeo Corbinelli argued, "was uni-

[262] Cf. Lorenzo Ridolfi's statement: "Et nunc adhitus omnes reclusi nobis sunt per mare et per terram"; *CP*, 42, f.71v, 13 Sept., and earlier, Ridolfo Peruzzi, *ibid.*, f.36r, 11 June.

[263] On the conclusion of the agreement with the lord of Ferrara, *ibid.*, ff.74v, 77v; and Partner, *Papal State*, 27.

[264] *CP*, 42, f.60v; also the comments of Banco da Verrazzano and Francesco Machiavelli, *ibid.*, ff.63v–64r. The war *balìa* finally agreed to pay 30,000 fl. to hire Orsini for six months; the pope was to contribute 10,000 fl.; *Conc.*, 1882, no. 73, 23 Aug. See also *ibid.*, no. 68, 20 Aug. On papal revenues in these months, see G. Holmes, *Flor. Studies*, 373.

[265] *CP*, 42, f.60v, 18 Aug. [266] *Ibid.*, ff.72v, 73v, 75v, 76v, 77v.

[267] Lapo Corsi: "Dolent vehementer quod dominus papa ad se non intromicti illico fecerat [illos] ex collegiis ad eum transmissos qui per horas ad hostium mora traxerunt aliis multis et sassolino intrantibus et exeuntibus; ac etiam de responsionibus domini pape ipsis collegiis factis representantibus maxime dominationem; et quod non tamen deseratur postulatio, sed prosequatur donec licentia obtineatur"; *ibid.*, f.77v, 30 Sept.

versally judged to be honest and reasonable, since it was to pay for expenses incurred in defending the church."[268]

The project to subsidize the war with church lands was as obviously attractive to an overtaxed citizenry as it was repugnant to John XXIII and his Florentine supporters, who could recall the expropriation of ecclesiastical property during the war of the Eight Saints. Though the colleges sought to keep the issue alive, as a bargaining point in negotiations for an alliance, the Signoria and the war *balìa* were not so intransigent and the plan was eventually scuttled.[269] Neither that controversial issue, nor any other problem, should thwart the immediate conclusion of a papal alliance, so argued John XXIII's staunchest friends—Antonio Alessandri, Rinaldo Gianfigliazzi, Filippo Corsini— who insisted that Florentine liberty could not be preserved without it.[270] Agnolo Pandolfini and Maso degli Albizzi waged a determined fight against the papal party; the latter suggested a postponement in signing the treaty until news arrived from the Florentine ambassadors at Ladislaus' court in Naples.[271] Persisting in these delaying tactics a week later, the opposition suggested (21 October) that the specific terms of the alliance should be entrusted not to the war *balìa*, but instead to an assembly of citizens.[272] This strategy, Piero Firenze insisted in an angry speech delivered on 24 October, violated the conventions of decision-making. In the past, those holding minority opinions had eventually submitted to the majority will, but on this issue the op-

---

[268] *Ibid.*, f.72v.

[269] The colleges insisted on this point as late as 21 Oct.; *CP*, 42, f.83r, but the treaty contained no reference to the sale of church property; *Conc.*, 1883, no. 35, 7 Nov.

[270] *CP*, 42, ff.79r–79v. Cf. Gianfigliazzi's statement: "Si liga non fit cum domino papa, que necessaria est et quam ipse consulit et hortatur, perdimus auxilia et reputationem; licet non habemus subsidia que vellemus; et ubicumque papa est et nos iam amissimus provincias multas et ceteras amittemus. . . ." Gregorio Dati strongly supported the alliance; *ibid.*, f.80v.

[271] *Ibid.*, ff.79r, 80v. Lorenzo Ridolfi also advised delay, *ibid.*, f.80r. The colleges were divided, as were the citizens called to attend the *pratica*: an even division in S. Spirito and S. Giovanni; three-fourths from S. Croce favoring Gianfigliazzi's counsel; the majority from S. Maria Novella supporting Maso degli Albizzi; *ibid.*, f.81r.

[272] *Ibid.*, ff.82r–83r. A poll of the Sixteen illustrates the civic division on this issue: the philopapal position supported by Amerigo da Verrazzano, Pierozzo Castellani, Adoardo Acciaiuoli, Battista Arnolfi, Tommaso Pazzini, and the furrier Francesco di Cristofano. Supporting Pandolfini's position were Agostino di Francesco, Lapo Corsini, Antonio Lorini, Bernardo Fagni, Salvi Dietisalvi, Giovanni Carducci, and the harness-maker Michele di Salvestro. Patricians tended to be philopapal; artisans and merchants of lesser status, antipapal.

ponents of the papal alliance insisted on being consulted on every detail of the treaty. Such demands were unreasonable and perverse, and they demeaned the honor and reputation of the priors, "who know everything and have deliberated prudently. . . ."[273] If the republic rejected the pope's offer, Agnolo della Casa predicted, he would abandon Italy and all his territory would be seized by Ladislaus, "and we will be beseiged and will not dare to place one foot outside [our territory]." These arguments effectively silenced those who had so firmly resisted the papal alliance. A poll taken of the councilors "after the space of several hours" indicated that the treaty's approval was guaranteed, with only two of twenty-one guild consuls still intransigent in their opposition.[274] After two more weeks of negotiations, the treaty was finally signed on 6 November, and shortly thereafter John XXIII and his court left San Antonio del Vescovo for Bologna.[275]

The terms of this alliance were uncharacteristically vague and ambiguous, a fact that reflects both the hastiness of its composition[276] and the controversy that surrounded its ratification. The one precise feature was its duration, for one year only. Neither party committed itself to a specific military or fiscal contribution, but promised only to assist the other in the defense of its territory. The treaty specifically authorized each signatory to make a separate peace with Ladislaus, if he desired to.[277] Although the Sienese had been a valuable if minor partner in the earlier resistance to the king, they were not included in this treaty. When the Sienese ambassador protested against that

[273] "Quod omnes boni admirationem summere debent prospiciendo dominationem per varios modos et extraneos, nec sic per tempora preterita gestum est, cum fides dominis per omnes dabatur; sed mores presentes aliter se habent et dilationem tribuunt omnibus bonis negociis et dum contentiones in principio habentur, sic in medio et fine durant; sed finaliter ad bonum omnia reducuntur"; *ibid.*, f.83v.

[274] *Ibid.*, f.84r. Those favoring the alliance were Ridolfo Peruzzi, Bartolomeo Bartolini, Antonio da Verrazzano, Maestro Antonio di Maestro Guccio, and Filippo di Firenze del Pancia, *ibid.*, ff.83v–84r.

[275] Rinaldo Gianfigliazzi: "Bene deliberatum est ut liga cum domino papa firmetur, et super ea aliud dicendum non est nisi quod Decem prudenter et bene concludent, et fructus ex ea utilis sperandus est"; *ibid.*, f.85r.

[276] The Sienese ambassador described the papal pressures to conclude the treaty; *Conc.*, 1883, no. 29 and 30, 17 and 25 Oct. The pope was angry over the delay in the treaty's approval by the Florentines; *ibid.*, no. 35, 7 Nov. Some issues were still unresolved when the treaty was publicized; *ibid.*, no. 36, 8 Nov.

[277] The terms are summarized in *ibid.*, no. 35, 7 Nov. I have been unable to find a draft of this treaty in the Florentine *Archivio di Stato*. Theiner's documentary collection, *Cordex Diplomaticus Temporalis S. Sedis*, 3 vols. (Rome, 1861–1862) does not include the text.

exclusion, the Signoria informed him that his government could negotiate a separate alliance with the pope. But John XXIII had already departed for Bologna, leaving no one behind to tie up loose ends.[278]

The Signoria did not consider this alliance as a declaration of war aganist Ladislaus.[279] Florentine ambassadors continued to discuss a peace settlement in Naples, though the prospects for an agreement had been diminished by the king's imprisonment of merchants in Rome and the confiscation of their property.[280] The prolongation of these negotiations gratified Agnolo Pandolfini and Filippo Corsini, who still clung to the hope of reconciliation, and angered Betto Busini and Francesco Leoni, who viewed these overtures as evidence of Florentine credulity and weakness.[281] After months of prodding by the papal faction, the Signoria finally sent an embassy to the emperor-elect Sigismund, who was then in Italy to promote interest in a council to end the schism, and to consider ways of defending the Papal States from Ladislaus. Even before the king had occupied Rome, some citizens— and notably Filippo Corsini—had urged the Signoria to consider an alliance with Sigismund who could muster, according to some reports, as many as 15,000 cavalry for an Italian expedition.[282] One Florentine embassy had visited him in July, but had been given no authorization to conclude an alliance.[283] The newly chosen envoys, Stefano Buonaccorsi and Antonio Alessandri, met Sigismund in Lodi in late November. They were instructed to listen to his views on bringing peace to Italy, and to obtain specific information about the size of the army he proposed to recruit. But the tone of these instructions was very cautious: the diplomats were asked to judge how much credence to

[278] *Conc.*, 1883, no. 39–42, 15 and 19 Nov. The pope's hasty departure for Bologna was prompted by the news that Sigismund had announced that Constance would be the seat of the council; Cutolo, *Ladislao*, 445.

[279] See the instructions of the ambassadors to Sigismund; 16 Nov., *SCMLC*, 6, f.34v, printed in Finke, *Acta*, I, 249: "Noi per nostra singularità niuna nimicizia o guerra avere col re Ladislao, perchè con lui vivevamo in buona pace. . . ."

[280] The Florentine embassy had arrived in Naples on 13 Sept. and did not leave until December; *SRRO*, 2, ff.20r–21r. On the diplomatic contacts between Ladislaus and Florence after the imprisonment of the merchants in Rome, see *Conc.*, 1882, no. 65; 1883, no. 4 and 19.

[281] *CP*, 42, ff.90r, 92v–93v.

[282] On the possible size of the invading army, see *SRRO*, 2, f.18r. The failure to send an embassy to Sigismund had prompted a mini-crisis in the spring; above, 357. For Corsini's arguments for an imperial treaty, see *CP*, 42, ff.12r, 79r, and those of Agnolo della Casa, *ibid.*, f.70r.

[283] *SRRO*, 2, ff.17v–19r.

place in Sigismund's proposals, and "whether they are merely thoughts and fantasies . . . or whether they might be realistic. . . ."[284] This wariness, so characteristic of Florentine diplomacy in these months, was prompted by skepticism of German promises, which had so often deluded the Florentines in the past, and possibly the realization that the republic could not afford to subsidize a German invasion.

The papal alliance had not significantly improved Florence's position, either militarily or diplomatically, nor did it bolster civic morale. Rarely if ever had the citizenry felt so frustrated and vulnerable, and so angry with their government and each other, as in the weeks following the ratification of that treaty. Wherever men gathered, they criticized the regime.[285] In the palace of the Signoria, the king's enemies monopolized the debates, denouncing those who opposed the war and the papal alliance. The war *balìa* had been so intimidated by the peace faction, Niccolò Barbadori believed, that they had not taken adequate measures to defend the republic. Gino Capponi, Francesco Leoni, and Dino Gucci also blamed the purveyors of subversive opinions for sabotaging the efforts of patriots to achieve civic unity and to raise money.[286] "In every magistracy," Rinaldo Rondinelli said, "justice is violated and is for sale. . . ."[287] In a searing indictment of the administration, Berardo Berardi developed this theme. Either by divine judgment or through fortuitous circumstance, he said, the Florentines are rushing headlong toward their destruction. In past times, citizens sought office for the glory and reputation of the republic, but now men were intent only on their personal advantage. They viewed public office as an opportunity to exploit those under their jurisdiction. The citizens were so preoccupied with their quarrels and their denunciations of each other that they could devote no thought to the public welfare. Praising the work of the war *balìa*, Berardi proposed that a special magistracy be established to suppress all criticism of their activities.[288] This proposal to silence critics gained some support in

[284] *SCMLC*, 6, f.35r; Finke, *Acta*, I, 249.

[285] See the references to "oblocutiones" and "susurrones" in the statements of Francesco Leoni, Dino Gucci, Simone Salviati, and Piero Firenze; *CP*, 42, ff.92v, 94v–95r.

[286] Barbadori's comment; *ibid.*, f.93v, 6 Dec.: "Dolendum est quod decem ob dicta aliorum non honesta res communis deserverunt. . . ." Statements by Capponi, Leoni and Gucci in *ibid.*, ff.92v, 94r, 94v.

[287] "Non est mirum si in terminis peximis sumus, nam nichil in civitate fit et coram quocumque preside et officio nisi contra ius et iustitia et ob preces et munera"; *ibid.*, f.92v.

[288] *Ibid.*, f.94v.

the *pratiche*. Sala Marsili deplored all partisan talk in public places, but singled out as targets for punishment only those "who spoke well of King Ladislaus."[289]

On 11 December, the Signoria learned from Florentine ambassadors in Naples that negotiations with Ladislaus had finally broken down and that the envoys were returning home. For those who had never placed any credence in the king's protestations of peace, the news was a welcome relief. Gino Capponi advised the Signoria to convoke a large assembly of citizens to hear the report, "so that the *popolo* will give its counsel publicly concerning what should be done for our security and the defense of our liberty." Filippo Corsini proposed a declaration of war against Ladislaus; he also suggested that Florentine agents be sent into the Regno to foment rebellions. Marco Strozzi called upon his fellow citizens to suppress their selfish impulses and offer their property and their lives for the defense of the republic. Whoever is unwilling to give up body and soul for freedom, Bernardo da Quarata declared, "is a bad citizen and indeed no citizen at all." The goldsmith Domenico Dei appealed for a suspension of all complaints about tax inequities, so that the total energy of the Florentine people could be devoted to the enemy's destruction.[290]

These patriotic harangues may have stimulated some popular enthusiasm for the war (though this is doubtful), but they did not enhance the republic's prospects for victory. The regime faced a powerful enemy with its citizenry divided and angry, its resources taxed to the limit, its mercenaries unpaid and restive, and its papal ally weak and unreliable. In the deliberations over the rehiring of the troops commanded by Braccio Fortebraccio and Paolo Orsini, who still defended the papal cause in Umbria and the Patrimony, there were no more complaints about John XXIII's inability or unwillingness to pay them. The issue was moot, since the pope was obviously penniless.[291] In his negotiations with Sigismund at Lodi, he had received no concrete help for the defense of the Papal States. The only portion of his territory to remain under his direct control was Bologna and its environs, and even that enclave was threatened by a coalition of rebellious Romagnol barons led by Carlo Malatesta.[292] Painfully aware of

---

[289] "Dolendum est quod multi in locis publicis loquantur; hi sunt amici domini pape aut regis; et quod ordinetur ut bene loquentes de rege Ladislao puniantur"; *CP*, 42, f.97v, 14 Dec. See also the statement of Piero Firenze, *ibid.*, f.95r.

[290] Capponi's statement in *ibid.*, f.96v; the others in *ibid.*, ff.97r–98v.

[291] *Ibid.*, ff.101v, 102r, 103r, 104r. Maso degli Albizzi once expressed the hope that the pope could pay something; *ibid.*, f.101v.

[292] *Ibid.*, ff.112r–114r, 14–15 March 1414.

their vulnerability, and of Ladislaus' superiority in arms and resources, Florentine statesmen realized that they must either sue for
peace or, in Forese Sacchetti's words, "we must seek [to ally ourselves]
with princes and lords against Ladislaus, for we are not strong enough
to defend ourselves alone."[293] A peace overture did come from Naples
in early February, brought by Gabriello Brunelleschi who had played
a key role in peace negotiations three years before. So strong was the
civic desire for peace, and so fearful were the authorities of angering
the *popolo*,[294] that they scrutinized Ladislaus' proposals very carefully.[295] A typical response was that of Rinaldo degli Albizzi, who was
not sanguine about the prospects for peace, but who did favor the
renewal of diplomatic contacts with the king. Rinaldo Rondinelli
angrily proposed that Brunelleschi be expelled from the city "so that
he cannot sow discord as he . . . seeks to do."[296] The Signoria's decision to reject Ladislaus' overture was made only after lengthy debate
in which, the Sienese ambassador reported, "there was much argument and disputation, and some had one opinion and some another."[297]
With the failure of Brunelleschi's mission, Florentine statesmen renewed their search for allies with more vigor and a greater sense of
urgency.

Months before Ladislaus had renewed his assault upon the papacy,
when the republic was trying to extricate itself from the Genoese
imbroglio, a few citizens had identified the German prince, Sigismund,
as the city's potential savior. King of Bohemia and Hungary, lord of
the Luxembourg lands in Germany, the emperor-elect looked from
a distance like "a powerful prince who rules over many [territories].
. . ."[298] Angered by the failure of successive priorates to negotiate with
Sigismund, these men ignored the practical difficulties of a German
alliance. Filippo Corsini, Maso degli Albizzi, and Rinaldo Gianfigliazzi
were all persuaded that Sigismund was able and willing to cross the
Alps, to recover the Papal States for the pope, and to protect but not
subjugate the Florentines, who were legally his subjects.[299] The authority of these leaders, however, was not sufficient to overcome civic op-

---

[293] *Ibid.*, f.103v, 21 Jan.

[294] See the comments of Niccolò Davanzati and Ricovero Ricoveri; *ibid.*, ff.105v, 106v.

[295] The Signoria's report to the Florentine ambassadors at the papal curia in Mantua; *SCMC*, 29, f.56r, 21 Feb.; and the reports of the Sienese ambassadors; *Conc.*, 1883, no. 74, 85, 89, 91.

[296] *CP*, 42, ff.106v, 107v, 17 Feb. [297] *Conc.*, 1883, no. 89, 18 Feb.

[298] Riccardo Borgognone, *CP*, 42, f.118v, 23 March.

[299] *Ibid.*, f.102v, 21 Jan. See too the statement of Nanni Unghero; *ibid.*, f.106v.

position. Some feared that the cost of subsidizing Sigismund's invasion was too great; others expressed doubts about his ability to recruit a large and potent army. The emperor had no money and can do nothing, Paolo Biliotti said scornfully, and he reminded his colleagues of the huge sums squandered in the past on German princes. "And if this one comes," he warned, "we will pay 500,000 or 600,000 florins!"[300] In Agnolo Pandolfini's judgment, an alliance between Florence and the emperor was not feasible because of their different political systems. He proposed Venice as an alternative to Sigismund; the Venetians "are strong and they are like us in the possession of liberty."[301] But Lorenzo Ridolfi saw Venetian strength and aggressiveness as threats to Florence, and he warned of the perils that might arise from an alliance with a superior power.[302] The theory that republics had a special affinity for each other appealed particularly to the humanist Pandolfini, but not to his colleagues who saw little in Venice's past to support that conclusion.

The critical moment in the debate over an imperial alliance occurred in mid-April. With spring weather heralding the onset of the fighting season, Ladislaus' armies prepared to attack the castles and towns that still remained loyal to the papacy, and then to move against Florence.[303] From Bologna, the pope sent urgent appeals to the Signoria for help against Carlo Malatesta, whose troops were assaulting papal forces in the Bolognese *contado*. But the republic could not spare even a token contingent of lances for Bologna's defense, nor could she risk a war with the Romagnol lords in their Apennine lairs.[304] If the pope's position in Bologna became untenable, he might be tempted to abandon Italy for France or Germany. That prospect so frightened some citizens that they were willing to offer asylum to him in Florentine itself.[305] This was the historical context for the *pratica* of 14 April,

[300] *Ibid.*, f.120v, 13 Apr. Concurring in this negative judgment of imperial power was Marsilio Vecchietti; *ibid.*, f.112r; Guidetto Guidetti was more fearful of Sigismund; *ibid.*

[301] *Ibid.*, f.103r, 21 Jan. Cf. Pandolfini's statement, *ibid.*, f.105r: "Et nos debemus libertatem Venetorum concupiscere et ipsi nostram. . . ."

[302] *Ibid.*, f.103v: "Veneti potentes sunt et prerogativam volunt et nos experti sumus." Also opposing the Venetian alliance were Filippo Corsini and Riccardo Borgognone; *ibid.*, ff.115r, 120v.

[303] On the situation in the Papal States, Partner, *Papal State*, 28.

[304] *CP*, 42, ff.112r–113r, 114r, 119v, 121r–123r. Rinaldo degli Albizzi's statement was typical: "Si contra dominos Romandiole guerram moveremus, expensa maxima insurgeret nobis, cum per LX miliaria confinia habemus simul"; *ibid.*, f.122r.

[305] The statements of Rinaldo Gianfigliazzi and Ser Paolo della Camera; *ibid.*, ff.119v, 121v.

which the Signoria called to test civic sentiment on the imperial alliance.[306] Several speakers commented on the sharp disagreements over policy revealed by the discussion, which Filippo Corsini deplored as a malady that would destroy the republic, but which was lauded by Dino Gucci as evidence of the strength of the Florentine commitment to liberty.[307] The tone was set by the humanist Roberto de' Rossi, who presented a lucid, closely reasoned analysis of the dilemma confronting the republic.[308] Neither Roberto nor those who followed him indulged in any personal recriminations against their opponents; they concentrated on the substantive issues.

Three particular nodes of disagreement emerged from these deliberations: the necessity for an alliance to save the republic, Sigismund's value and suitability as an ally, and the appropriate procedure for making policy decisions. The two assumptions upon which the proponents of the German alliance based their presentation were, first, the republic's inability to defend herself alone, and, second, Ladislaus' record as a perfidious tyrant with an insatiable appetite for conquest. The king crushed everyone who opposed him, Banco da Verrazzano argued, and without help Florence would be his next victim. He was prepared to join forces with any power, even the Turk, to avoid that fate.[309] Filippo Corsini could see no workable alternative to an alliance with the Luxembourg ruler. Though he agreed with Roberto de' Rossi's point that the Venetians would be more appropriate allies, he dismissed that prospect as chimerical. He predicted that if Florence failed to reach an accord with the emperor-elect, Ladislaus would dominate all central Italy, and that Paolo Orsini would desert the republic to fight for the king,[310] As so often in the past, Agnolo Pandolfini led the opposition to these prophets of doom. In a sanguine appraisal of the republic's situation, he argued that Florentines should

---

[306] This *pratica* was noteworthy for candor and eloquence. See the comment by Filippo Corsini, "et eleganter Robertus [de' Rossi] oravit"; and Maestro Cristofano di Giorgio, "quod cum passione loquuntur perspicaces cives"; *ibid.*, ff.124r, 125r. Carlo Tinghi admitted that he agreed with Niccolò da Uzzano who favored the alliance, but then was persuaded by the speeches of Rossi and Agnolo Pandolfini to oppose it; *ibid.*, f.127r.

[307] *Ibid.*, ff.124r, 127r. Cf. Piero Firenze's comment, *ibid.*, f.125r: "Si cives uniti essent, ut deberent, ad bonum publicum, tot practice non forent."

[308] *Ibid.*, f.124r.

[309] *Ibid.*, f.126r. Cristofano di Giorgio, Piero Firenze, Paolo Carnesecchi, Simone della Fioraia and Rinaldo Gianfigliazzi supported these arguments; *ibid.*, ff.125r–126r.

[310] *Ibid.*, f.124r. Corsini's predictions were quite accurate; Partner, *Papal State*, 28.

pursue an inexpensive defensive strategy, eschewing any offensive action or alliance with a foreign power. Recalling that many princes had tried to conquer the Florentines, he predicted that Ladislaus would be no more successful than Giangaleazzo Visconti, and that his treasury would be empty before the republic ran out of money.[311]

While Agnolo's optimistic evaluation of Florentine strength did not assuage the anxieties of his listeners, his criticisms of the imperial connection struck responsive chords in them. Guidetto Guidetti agreed that Sigismund was too weak to help Florence, and that money given to him would be thrown away. It would be an insult to offer Sigismund the paltry sum of 25,000 florins for confirming Florence's possession of Pisa and Cortona, Roberto de' Rossi observed, and a larger amount was beyond the citizens' ability to pay. Vanni Castellani drew a very different picture of Sigismund as a valiant warrior whose desire for fame and glory would impel him to vanquish his enemies. This image of Sigismund as invincible conqueror troubled Marsilio Vecchietti, who feared that the emperor-elect would use the subsidy from the Florentines to dominate them.[312] Paolo Biliotti reminded his colleagues that Sigismund's father was Emperor Charles IV who twice, in 1354–1355 and in 1368, had invaded Tuscany to establish imperial authority over that province. Charles had violated his pledge to respect the privileges of Tuscan cities by entering first Pisa and then Siena; he had fomented uprisings in the Florentine dominion. From these experiences Paolo drew the conclusion that "it is not true what others have said, namely, that a promise of any prince can be trusted. . . ."[313] With this history lesson and with references to the Ghibelline barbarians, the opponents of the German alliance conjured up visions of imperial ruthlessness and aggrandizement in Florentine minds. Sigismund's friends labored to correct the misconceptions of this propaganda. It was more than a century ago, Giovanni Carducci noted, "that an emperor [Henry VII] came and occupied a few castles and then withdrew"; he was confident that Sigismund would keep his promises.[314] To refute stories about Sigismund's past that apparently had circulated in Florence, Riccardo Borgognone denied that the emperor-elect had been responsible for the death of his brother, John of Gorlitz, or that he had tried to poison his brother Wenceslaus, the king of Bohemia.[315] He was a "good and humane" prince who treated gently those

---

[311] CP, 42, f.124v.   [312] Ibid., ff.124r–124v, 125v, 126r.

[313] Ibid., f.125v.

[314] Ibid., f.125r. Carducci conveniently forgot the forays of Charles IV.

[315] Ibid., f.126v. Borgognone had witnessed Sigismund's rule in Hungary: "Ipse fuit et vidit."

Hungarian barons who had conspired against him. Filippo Corsini suggested that the Ghibelline epithet no longer had any significance, and he pointed to the impeccable Guelf lineage of Florence's arch-enemy, the Angevin prince Ladislaus.[316]

One ardent supporter of the German alliance, Simone della Fioraia, noted that the proposal had been exhaustively debated "in many councils large and small" for the past six months, and that every consulative group had favored it. This statement was an implicit criticism of the Signoria's reluctance to implement the civic mandate. But Marsilio Vecchietti used a similar argument to oppose the alliance: "The voice of the *popolo* is the voice of God; and three-quarters [of the citizens] are not pleased by his coming."[317] Agnolo Pandolfini also warned of popular discontent and, specifically, opposition to any military expenditure outside Florentine territory. "If we spend money against the will of the citizenry," he concluded, "it will be difficult to raise taxes."[318] With sentiment in the *pratica*, and throughout the city, so divided on the German alliance, some counselors saw but one solution: to place the decision in the hands of the war *balìa*. Even Roberto de' Rossi, who had made a strong argument against the alliance, was willing to accept that judgment, "considering the dignity of those in that office . . . and the quality of their character and deportment." But Roberto urged his audience to support that decision "so that there will be unity in the palace and no rumors of dissension outside."[319]

The war magistracy, whose members were charged with the resolution of this vexing issue, could not have gained much comfort from a debate that revealed such sharp divisions. Still, the discussion had clarified some issues, and had suggested which alternatives would be most palatable to the citizenry. As a potential ally, Sigismund did not win much favor in the *reggimento*; he was too weak for some, too dangerous for others, and too expensive for everyone save his most committed partisans. The testimony on the state of the economy and the fisc indicated clearly that Florence could not afford to pay Sigismund, or any ally, a large subsidy.[320] So the discussion with the emperor-elect may not have been serious, but rather designed to warn Ladislaus

---

[316] *Ibid.*, f.124r. Rinaldo Gianfigliazzi also examined Ladislaus' genealogy; *ibid.*, f.126r.

[317] *Ibid.*, f.125v–126r.

[318] *Ibid.*, f.124v. Guidetto Guidetti also commented: "Sic expendendo, pecuniam jacimus; et patientes non erunt cives ad sic solvendum"; *ibid.*, f.125v.

[319] *Ibid.*, f.124r. For opinions favoring a *balìa*, *ibid.*, ff.126v–127r.

[320] Pandolfini mentioned the figure of 100,000 fl. which, he argued, neither the Florentines nor the pope could raise; *ibid.*, f.124v. Guidetto Guidetti stated that "nil lucrantur cives, mercatores et artifices"; *ibid.*, f.126r.

against attacking Florence, and to encourage him to negotiate seriously.[321]

For these tactics to succeed, Ladislaus and other Italian powers had to be convinced of Florence's determination to defend her liberty at all costs and by whatever means. The evidence of discord in this *pratica* certainly did not promote that impression, nor did the vote, a week later, of the Council of 200 in rejecting a provision for the renewal of the war *balìa*.[322] This vote dramatically revealed the strength of peace sentiment, not only in the larger community, but in the inner councils of the *reggimento*, from which the membership of that assembly was drawn.[323] Stunned by this rebuff, the leadership made a strong appeal to the councilors to reconsider their decision. Amid dire warnings that such irresponsible behavior would lead the republic to ruin, the council eventually passed the measure, though by less than a two-thirds margin.[324] Neither critics nor sympathizers labeled this gesture accurately, as a protest against the regime's war policy.[325] But that message was not lost on Maso degli Albizzi, who assumed the office of standard-bearer of justice on the first day of May.

For Maso and his colleagues in the Signoria, the situation was even more desperate, and the options fewer, than in April. Sigismund had left Lombardy for Germany, to prepare for the council scheduled to meet at Constance in October. In Bologna, John XXIII maintained a precarious hold upon that city, which had twice before rebelled against his rule. Some of the cardinals and curial officials had left the city, while rumors circulated that the pope was considering flight to Ferrara or some other refuge.[326] In the south, Ladislaus had persuaded Paolo Orsini to abandon his former employers and join the Neapolitan army that was moving up the Tiber valley toward Perugia. Orsini's

---

[321] It was important to build up Sigismund's reputation, Filippo Corsini argued, for if the rumor spread that there would be no alliance, then all central Italy would fall to Ladislaus; *ibid.*, f.124r.

[322] *LF*, 50, ff.116r–117r. That provision had also been rejected twice in March; *ibid.*, ff.112r, 113r; *CP*, 42, f.117r, 29 March.

[323] This council, selected by the Signoria and the colleges, was more exclusive in its composition than the other councils: "Sunt in regimine. . . . Sunt notabiles cives"; as Paolo Biliotti and Matteo Castellani noted; *CP*, 42, ff.127v–128r.

[324] The vote was 118–69; in the other councils, 171–82 and 133–64; *LF*, 50, ff.119r, 120r; *Prov.*, 103, ff.4r–4v. For the discussion, *CP*, 42, ff.127v–128r.

[325] Piero Firenze attributed it to the decline in respect for the Signoria; Matteo Castellani to the presence of "iuvenes et alii non cum matura discretione" in the council; *CP*, 42, ff.127v–128r.

[326] Finke, *Acta*, I, 255–56; Partner, *Papal State*, 28. See Neri Ardinghelli's statement on 15 May: "Cardinales ultramontani iam de Bononia discedunt"; *CP*, 42, f.132r.

defection eliminated a major barrier to Ladislaus' complete mastery of central Italy, and left only Braccio Fortebraccio's band as a small node of resistance. To this somber news from the southern front, Florentine statesmen reacted predictably by appealing for courage and steadfastness in the face of adversity.[327] But this patriotic rhetoric lacked the fervor of that of earlier times. Had Paolo Orsini remained loyal, Vieri Guadagni said bitterly, we could have resisted Ladislaus. Piero Firenze disassociated himself from those who had claimed that peace with the king was feasible; "but if it is possible, let the Signoria try to give peace to the *popolo*."[328] On 14 May, the priors listened to concrete proposals for a settlement which Gabriello Brunelleschi had brought from Ladislaus's camp in Umbria.[329] The king was willing to make peace with Florence and her allies, Siena and the pope, if they would unite with him in an Italian league that might also include Venice and Genoa, and if they accepted his possession of the papal territory occupied by his army. In return for his payment of an annual *censo*, he demanded from the pope the vicariate of those church lands, and from Florence, a commitment to support him if John XXIII violated the peace. He also promised to release all Florentines whom he had imprisoned, and to restore their property.[330]

In the *pratica* held on 15 May to consider these proposals, civic sentiment was overwhelmingly in favor of peace on the king's terms. Though a minority led by Gino Capponi and Vanni Castellani repeated the standard objections to any agreement with Ladislaus,[331] their warnings were ignored. The most eloquent argument for continuing the war was made by a goldsmith, Domenico Dei,[332] whose views certainly did not reflect the mood of the guild community. Those who had favored peace during the past thirty years, Domenico argued, have been responsible for the endless succession of wars, while those who resisted these lures were promoting Florentine security. "Let us fight the king so that we can live as free men and not be forced into exile, or see our children enslaved!" These warnings failed to persuade

[327] Matteo Martini, for the Sixteen: "et in adversis virtus dominorum cognoscetur"; Filippo Corsini, "in adversis animus virtuosi cognoscitur"; Lorenzo Ridolfi, for the new war *balìa*, "virilem animum omnes assumere debemus"; *ibid.*, ff.128v–129r. Cf. the statements made during the crisis of June 1402; Baron, *Crisis*, 2nd ed., 43.

[328] *CP*, 42, f.128v.

[329] *Ibid.*, f.131v, 14 May; Cutolo, *Ladislao*, 453.

[330] *Commissioni di Rinaldo degli Albizzi*, I, 244; *SRRO*, 2, ff.19v–20r.

[331] *CP*, 42, ff.132r–132v. Others resisting the peace movement were Cristofano di Giorgio, Michele Castellani, and Francesco Leoni; *ibid.*, ff.132v, 133r.

[332] "Ipse artifex est et de pace vivit et de guerra consummitur"; *ibid.*, f.133v.

conservative patricians like Salamone Strozzi, Sandro Altoviti, and Giotto Peruzzi, who had formerly supported the papal alliance and a strong military posture.[333] Francesco Machiavelli noted that Ladislaus' army of 6000 lances was nearly double the size of the republic's force. With the king's superior strength, Giovanni Vettori concluded, the Florentines could not prevent him from going wherever he wished. Given the heavy expenses, inequitable taxation, and a stagnant economy, Florence must accept peace. Marsilio Vecchietti feared that disorders would erupt in the city if peace negotiations failed.[334] While recognizing that Ladislaus might try to dupe the Florentines after a settlement was achieved, these men decided that a prolongation of hostilities was the greater peril facing the republic. In their public statements, they said nothing about the fate of the pope who, unable to defend himself or help his ally, had become a minor factor in Florentine diplomatic calculations.[335]

To negotiate with the king's emissary, the Signoria appointed a committee of ten prominent citizens, among whom were Maso degli Albizzi, Rinaldo Gianfigliazzi, Niccolò da Uzzano, and Lorenzo Ridolfi. The priors also informed the Sienese and John XXIII of their discussions with Brunelleschi, and the terms offered by the king. On 19 May, Vieri Guadagni and Giovanni Serristori were sent to Bologna to urge the pope to consent to the peace, which the republic had been forced to accept.[336] A week later (27 May), the Signoria convened another *pratica*, to test the civic mood. In even greater numbers than before, and with even greater fervor, the counselors favored an immediate settlement.[337] Agnolo Pandolfini was most optimistic about the benefits of peace; he recalled earlier experiences when negotiations to end wars had been resisted by some citizens later proved wrong by events. He urged the Signoria to make peace even if the pope did not accept the

[333] For their views, *ibid.*, ff.132r, 133r.

[334] Machiavelli estimated that the republic had 3700 lances in its employ; *ibid.*, f.132v. For the statements of Vettori and Vecchietti, *ibid.*, ff.132v, 133r.

[335] Cristofano di Giorgio feared that the pope would leave Italy; Strozza Strozzi wanted papal approval of any peace treaty; *ibid.*, ff.132v, 133r.

[336] "Veduti i pericoli che soprastanno a lui e a noi, i grandissimi apparechi e exercitii del Re per terra e per acqua . . . e che sanza sospetto si può il Re dirizzare contro a Senesi e a noi et ancora in Romagna con mandare parte della sua brigata dove e come gli piacesse e non cognoscendo essere possibile a riparo a questa per potentia che abbia la sua Sanctita, i sanesi e noi . . . e noi veggiamo i nostri cittadini per le lunghe e gravissimi spese . . . essere stracchi e de' loro substantie molto diminuite et i loro traffichi e mercatantie non potere exercitare di che solevano trarre utilità et supplire alle spese"; *SCMLC*, 6, ff.35r-35v.

[337] The debate continued for two days, 27 and 28 May; *CP*, 42, ff.138r-142v. Some of the speeches are printed in *Commissioni*, i, 235-37.

terms. Only if John XXIII could show the Florentines that he could reduce their expenses or obtain more advantageous conditions, would he favor a postponement. Conceding that Ladislaus might violate the peace, he did not believe that Florentine security would be enhanced by asking the duke of Milan, or anyone else, to guarantee the treaty's enforcement. "The states of *signori* are not as secure as those of communes," he said, "for death does not destroy a community as it does a *signore*."[338]

Supporting Pandolfini's arguments were merchants who were rarely invited to participate in a *pratica*, and men from the inner circle: Antonio Mangioni, Ridolfo Peruzzi, Marsilio Vecchietti, Niccolò degli Albizzi.[339] They were less afraid of Ladislaus than of the possibility of internal disorders if peace did not come quickly.[340] A handful of dissenters led by Gino Capponi and Filippo Corsini opposed this surge of peace sentiment; their numerical weakness was partially offset by their reputations and the intensity of their convictions. Abandoned by Maso degli Albizzi and Rinaldo Gianfigliazzi, and receiving only lukewarm support from Niccolò da Uzzano and the Castellani,[341] these men scorned the pragmatic arguments of the peace party, while bearing witness to their political ideals. Filippo Corsini could not accept a peace without the pope's approval; that would violate Florence's obligations to her ally and would cover her with infamy. If John XXIII received promises of Florentine aid to defend Bologna, he might accept the peace terms and remain in his corner of the Papal States as

---

[338] *CP*, 42, f.140r; *Commissioni*, I, 236. The printed text should be emended to read: "Et semper paces quas firmavimus, licet in principio oppugnate fuerunt, tamen fructus in processu temporis dederunt." The same point was made by Francesco Machiavelli: "Tres paces fecimus que a principio non laudate fuerunt; una cum Senensibus, aliaquam cum rege Ladislao fecimus, que necessarie fuerunt et fructus parturierunt optimos; alia que cum Januensibus firmata fuit que necessaria et utilis summe fuit"; *CP*, 42, f.138v.

[339] *Ibid.*, ff.140r–141v. For mercantile opinion, see *ibid.*, ff.141r–142v. Typical was the statement of Luigi Aldobrandini, *ibid.*, f.142r: "Quod numquam audivit quod libertas nostra amissa sit nisi per expensas superfluas; et nunc in eas sumus et intramus maiores. . . ."

[340] Pandolfini alluded to the danger: "et populus etiam, qui pacem affectat, multa gerere"; *ibid.*, f.140r; so did Piero Firenze, *ibid.*: "quod si pax non concluditur, cives aliqui disponiti sunt ad mala multa peragendum"; and Bartolomeo Carducci, *ibid.*, f.142r: "quod in civibus unitas non est et contrarium dici non potest; et ut pericula guerre evitetur, pax concludatur. . . ."

[341] As standard-bearer of justice, Maso did not speak in the *pratica*. Gianfigliazzi favored a peace settlement; *ibid.*, f.141r; so did Niccolò da Uzzano, *ibid.*, f.141v, although he took issue with some of Pandolfini's statements about the papal alliance. For the views of Vanni Castellani, *ibid.*, ff.138r, 140v.

a useful ally.[342] The angry rhetoric of the archpatriot Gino Capponi contrasted sharply with the moderate views of the venerable lawyer. Gino had hoped for death, he said, after the conclusion of the previous peace with Ladislaus, because he saw that Florence's liberty would be lost, and so it happened. To prove that his opposition to peace was not motivated by self-interest, he reported that he had lost 1200 florins when Ladislaus confiscated Florentine merchandise in the Regno, which he would recover if a treaty were signed. Gino echoed Filippo Corsini's argument that a peace without the pope's consent would be an abomination "in the eyes of God and men." Ladislaus would never abandon his ambition to conquer Florence; his peace overtures were more dangerous to her liberty than the king's armies. "Better to live under the government of the Ciompi," he cried, "than under the tyranny of that king!"[343]

Two days after this acrimonious debate, Pope John XXIII sent an embassy to Florence with a message rejecting the peace terms.[344] But this rebuff did not deter the Signoria. Without convening a *pratica* to discuss the papal reaction, the priors sent Agnolo Pandolfini and a lawyer, Torello Torelli, to Ladislaus with a mandate to conclude peace.[345] The main points in the king's original proposals were acceptable to the Signoria, although the ambassadors were instructed to bargain for better terms. Hoping to placate the papal faction in the *reggimento*, Maso degli Albizzi and his colleagues wanted to extract a promise from Ladislaus that he would not attack Bologna, and that the league uniting the former antagonists should not be contingent upon the pope's acceptance of the peace treaty. After a week of negotiations, the ambassadors informed the Signoria that the king was still disposed to make peace, but that some issues, and specifically the clauses

---

[342] *Commissioni*, I, 235–36. Lorenzo Ridolfi called for a committee of lawyers to advise the Signoria on Florence's legal obligations in the papal alliance; *CP*, 42, ff.138v, 141r; Martines, *Lawyers and Statecraft*, 339.

[343] Capponi's speeches are printed in *Commissioni*, I, 236–37; see Baron, *Crisis*, 2nd ed., 368, 543.

[344] *Conc.*, 1884, no. 55, 30 May. In earlier reports, the Sienese ambassador had noted the pope's indecision; *ibid.*, no. 50, 26 May; it was also noticed by Agnolo Pandolfini on 27 May: "Dominus Papa in suspenso permanet, et non consentit neque negat"; *Commissioni*, I, 236.

[345] *SCMLC*, 6, ff.36r–36v, 1 June: "V'ngegnerete con ogni industria . . . conchiudere secondo l'effetto della nota capitoli infrascripti portate con voi, et vantaggiano in ciascuna parte quanto vi sarà possibile. . . . Voi avete piena e chiara notitia della volontà nostra et di tucte le particularità di questa materia." On the lawyer Torelli, see Martines, *Lawyers and Statecraft*, 499.

concerning the pope, were not yet resolved. When that message reached Florence on 13 June, rumors that peace was imminent spread through the city.[346] The Sienese ambassador was cautiously optimistic about the prospects for a settlement, since so many Florentines were favorable, but he did admit that "there are some who are of the contrary opinion."

Those negative views were aired in the two days of debate (14–15 June) on the specific points that Ladislaus now proposed. The king insisted upon clauses that would require Florence to assist him against all potential foes, including the pope and the emperor. In the words of an outraged Piero Firenze, he wanted the Florentines "to seek out his enemies, to violate their pledges, and to be vile and pusillanimous." Filippo Corsini declared that if Florence joined a league that might require her to fight her sovereign, the Holy Roman Emperor, she would be guilty of infidelity and would accomplish her own destruction. Describing the king's demands as unjust and dishonest, Vieri Guadagni said that his intent was to drive a wedge between the Florentines and the pope. He would only approve a treaty that contained solemn guarantees that John XXIII would not be molested in Bologna, and that Florence would never have to fight her spiritual lord.[347] Gino Capponi viewed the king's demands as irrefutable proof of the king's duplicity; under the guise of peace, Ladislaus was methodically eliminating his enemies in the Regno and elsewhere, and eventually Florence would be his target. Gino's thoughts leaped from war and diplomacy to economic matters: "We will forfeit the money in our *monte*, which is a most precious resource for our wives and children and descendants and others."[348] These speeches aroused latent anxieties and guilt feelings that had been lulled by the arguments of the peace faction. Niccolò degli Albizzi, Francesco Machiavelli, and Dino Gucci withdrew their previous support for a settlement and now insisted on treaty guarantees that the pope would be secure in Bologna. Others said that they would accept the original proposals but not the later emendations, and particularly the commitment (under certain conditions) to make war on the pope and the emperor.[349] Strozza Strozzi noted that he had favored the terms originally published, but that he viewed the revised proposals with fear and

---

[346] *Conc.*, 1884, no. 63, 13 June.   [347] *CP*, 42, f.143v, 14 June.

[348] *Ibid.*, f.144r, printed in part in *Commissioni*, I, 238.

[349] *Ibid.*, f.144r. Others who qualified their support of the peace treaty were Niccolò da Uzzano, Vannozzo Serragli, Marsilio Vecchietti and Berardo Berardi; *ibid.*, ff.144v–145v.

trembling, when he considered the perils and the infamy. Did these tribulations mean (he wondered) that God was punishing the Florentines for their sins? That idea also occurred to Zanobi Rucellai; it explained to his satisfaction the civic quarrels, the failure to provide adequate defenses, and now the king's proposals that would "violate honor and justice and transform our friends into enemies."[350]

To the pragmatists, these exhortations to resist Ladislaus and thus prolong negotiations were irresponsible. Paolo Bordoni spelled out the political and military realities: a city hemorrhaging from years of heavy taxation, a rebellious subject population, a king so powerful that he could move freely against any opponent. The *popolo* is clamoring for peace, Nofri Bischeri said, and he warned that many citizens, unable to pay their *prestanze*, were planning to flee. In Lorenzo Ridolfi's judgment, the republic was in a worse condition than when negotiations began, and he called for an immediate settlement.[351] This view was supported by several counselors—Inghilese Baroncelli, Giovanni Peruzzi, Antonio da Panzano, Sandro Altoviti—from patrician families with strong Guelf and papal sympathies, who now were persuaded that extreme necessity required the sacrifice of Florence's traditional ally. On the day following this debate (16 June), the Signoria wrote to their ambassadors, identifying the disputed issues but furnishing no precise instructions for their resolution.[352] Acutely aware of the political storm that was brewing, Maso degli Albizzi and his colleagues placed a heavy responsibility on the ambassadors, who were willing to accept the burden.

The results of their bargaining with Ladislaus could be seen in the text of the treaty signed on 22 June. Most of the king's demands were met: a league with Florence and Siena for six years (which the pope was invited to join), with the parties obligated to help each other against any power that attacked them; the republic's recognition of Ladislaus' possession of the church's territory that he had occupied, and the obligation to help him maintain control of those lands. The only concession won by the ambassadors was the king's promise to refrain from attacking Bologna and its *contado*, or to interfere with the pope's possession of that enclave. However, if John XXIII sought to recover his lost territories from Ladislaus, then he could be attacked in his Bolognese sanctuary. Florence could not assist him in this contingency, although she was not specifically obligated by the treaty to

---

[350] *Ibid.*, ff.147v, 149r, 15 June.

[351] *CP*, 42, ff.144v, 145v, 146r. Similar views were expressed by Averardo de' Medici, Betto Rustichi, and Simone da Quarata; *ibid.*, ff.145v, 147v.

[352] *SCMC*, 29, ff.60v–61r.

fight against him.[353] The ambassadors had accepted a peace which, if its terms were implemented, guaranteed Ladislaus' hold upon Rome and most of the Papal States until 1420. The treaty also required Florence to repudiate the alliance with John XXIII that had been signed eight months before.

On 26 June, the ambassadors brought the treaty home[354] to a city divided between those who felt relief, and others who felt outrage and humiliation. In the latter category was Berardo Berardi, who described how his mood had changed from exaltation, upon first hearing the news of peace, to grief and despair when he learned about the terms.[355] In the debate held on the 26th to consider the pact,[356] two lawyers, Lorenzo Ridolfi and Francesco Machiavelli, presented the case for ratification, with support from Marsilio Vecchietti, Sandro Altoviti, Nofri Bischeri, Niccolò degli Albizzi, and Niccolò Davanzati. Four men—Gino Capponi, Filippo Corsini, Vieri Guadagni, and Vanni Castellani—argued for rejection; they consistently opposed any accommodation with Ladislaus. They insisted that the ambassadors had exceeded their mandate: by not incorporating a clause stating that Florence would not go to war against the pope or the emperor; by failing to guarantee Bologna's security against the Malatesta; and by excluding Braccio Fortebraccio from the treaty as a Florentine client. While admitting that the ambassadors may have exceeded their instructions on some points, Lorenzo Ridolfi nevertheless argued that the treaty should be ratified. "In the populace there are various opinions and judgments," he said, "and many are ignorant who, if they vilify the regime, could cause much trouble by saying that we did not intend to make peace." Francesco Machiavelli denied that the ambassadors had erred; he noted that the language of their instructions was quite general and imprecise, and subject to various interpretations.

[353] The text of the treaty is in Cutolo, *Ladislao*, 479–86. Florence was obligated to try to persuade the pope to desist from aggression against Ladislaus and his *raccomandati*; if after twenty days he refused, then "licitum sit Maiestatis Regie prefatisque confederatis et aliis supradictis movere guerram contra dictum papam et dictam civitatem Bononie"; *ibid.*, 482. Assistance from allies could be invoked "contra omnes et singulos homines et personas qui possunt vivere et mori cuiuscumque Status et conditionis existant, et quacumque dignitate sint positi spirituali vel temporali"; *ibid.*, 481.

[354] The ambassadors reported on their mission; *SRRO*, 2, f.21r, 26 June. Vespasiano da Bisticci described that embassy in vivid detail in his biography of Pandolfini; *Vite di uomini illustri*, 313–17.

[355] *CP*, 42, f.152r.

[356] The debate is in *ibid.*, ff.151r–152r; selections are printed in *Commissioni*, 1, 239. On the disagreements among the lawyers on the legal issues raised by the treaty, see Martines, *Lawyers and Statecraft*, 340–42.

Pope John XXIII had consistently violated the alliance, so that Florence was not legally bound to observe its conditions. Machiavelli saw nothing in the treaty that would allow the Malatesta to attack Bologna; as for Braccio, the republic would no longer have any need for his services, now that peace had been declared.

Shortly after this debate, the Signoria presented the provision ratifying the treaty to the Council of 200 which, two months earlier, had so resolutely opposed the reelection of the war magistracy. The *Libri Fabarum* record only the final tally on the measure, which passed by a narrow margin, but the wine merchant Bartolomeo del Corazza described the dramatic prelude to this vote.[357] So fierce was the opposition, he reported, that ratification would never have been approved if Maso degli Albizzi had not exerted his influence, and his talent for persuasion and intimidation, to push the treaty through the recalcitrant council. Bartolomeo also mentioned a rumor, unverified by any other source, that Maso was prepared to call a *parlamento* of the guild community "to see who favored it and who opposed it." In the Councils of the *Popolo* and the Commune, the treaty also passed by narrow margins.[358] Then, on 30 June, it was publicly announced to the citizens, and bonfires were lit in the streets to celebrate peace after five years of war.[359] A week later, a new Signoria sent Niccolò da Uzzano and Bernardo Guadagni on a thankless mission to Pope John XXIII in Bologna, to justify the republic's treaty with the king.[360]

After ratification of the peace treaty, the regime was under intense pressure to reduce military expenses. The leadership sought to moderate the demand for disarmament by reminding the citizenry of the perils still threatening their security. Even though Florence was at peace with Ladislaus, Antonio Alessandri warned, "the appetite for domination is still rampant among many, as experience has demonstrated. . . . Many regimes have been destroyed—for example, [those of] Messer Bernabò [Visconti] and Messer Pietro Gambacorta, the city of Lucca—by their failure to provide for their security. . . . Look at Lombardy and the cities of that province which have been ruined and their women placed in brothels. . . ."[361] It was better to hire one

---

[357] *LF*, 50, f.125r; *ASI*, 5th ser., XIV, 253. The vote was 126 to 63.

[358] *LF*, 50, ff.126r, 127r, 27 and 29 June. The votes: 189–89 and 137–66.

[359] *ASI*, 5th ser., XIV, 253.

[360] *SCMLC*, 6, ff.37r–37v. The ambassadors reported on their mission; *SRRO*, 2, ff.21v–22r. The pope complained that the treaty was made too hastily "e con poco riguardo di lui."

[361] *CP*, 42, f.160r, 3 Aug. Cf. Alessandri's earlier statement, *ibid.*, f.154v, 3 July: "Et fortiores esse debemus nunc quam in preteritum, ob vicinitatem quam habemus

hundred lances more than is required, Francesco Machiavelli argued, than two fewer than are necessary.[362] Some suggested that the army be reduced from 3700 to 1500 lances; others felt that 1000 lances would be adequate.[363] But provisions imposing forced loans to pay for these troops were systematically voted down, in late July and through the month of August, in the Council of the *Popolo*.[364] With an army of 1000 lances and 2000 infantry, the republic would be able to defend her territory from small predators, if not from her new ally, and also provide modest assistance to Pope John XXIII in Bologna.[365] But she was too weak and exhausted to play a larger role in Italian affairs, to involve herself, for example, in Lombard politics where Ladislaus, Sigismund, the duke of Milan, and the Venetian republic were maneuvering for advantage. Soon after their alliance was formalized, Ladislaus had proposed that Florence join him in a league with Venice, but this suggestion elicited very little enthusiasm. Venice's good friend, Agnolo Pandolfini, either was not invited, or prudently refrained from speaking in these debates; only Marsilio Vecchietti favored the alliance, arguing that "the government of the Venetians is very similar to ours."[366] Recalling that Venice had often deceived Florence, Filippo Corsini warned that the Serenissima was not trustworthy. The Venetians, he said, "live according to their desires and not by law." Giovanni di Ser Nigi agreed with Corsini's judgment, though he conceded that others had a different opinion of Venetian reliability.[367] Antonio Alessandri's opposition to the Venetian connection was based on prac-

---

regis Ladislai qui potissimus est, licet in pace sumus, nam libidinis dominandi contra fidem multa geruntur, ut apparet ex gestis a quadriennio citra. . . ."

[362] *Ibid.*, f.160r.

[363] Cf. the opinions of Filippo Corsini, Rinaldo Rondinelli and Marsilio Vecchietti; *ibid.*, ff.154r–154v. The size of the army was fixed at 1000 lances and 1500 footsoldiers; *ibid.*, f.162r, statement of Giovanni Minerbetti.

[364] The first provision was rejected on 26 and 27 July; *LF*, 50, ff.128r–129r. After three other measures were defeated in August, one was finally approved on 6–7 Sept.; *ibid.*, ff.130r–137r; *Prov.*, 103, ff.69v–71r.

[365] While urging the pope to make peace with Ladislaus, the Signoria also advised him to retain Braccio's services and to maintain his military strength; *SCMLC*, 6, ff.37r–37v; Cutolo, *Ladislao*, 457. Several citizens were worried about Bologna's security; *CP*, 42, ff.154r–154v.

[366] *Ibid.*, f.157v: "quia status Venetorum nostra satis est conformis." On Pandolfini's pro-Venetian views, see above, 317.

[367] Corsini's statement: "secundum voluntatem vivunt et non secundum iura"; *CP*, 42, f.157r. Others opposing the Venetian alliance, in addition to Giovanni di Ser Nigi, were Giovanni Soderini, Matteo Castellani, and Gino Capponi; *ibid.*, ff.157v–158r.

tical grounds. If Florence joined that league and hostilities broke out between Venice and Sigismund, Florence's merchants in Hungary would be in jeopardy. Nor did Antonio favor Venice as a guarantor of the peace with Ladislaus, "for she could always hurt us . . . and it is better to be free than to submit to the judgment of another."[368]

As these debates show, the civic temper after the peace with Ladislaus was very troubled. Doubts about the king's motives for making peace, and uncertainty about his objectives, heightened the sense of anxiety.[369] Being so nebulous, the perils which loomed over the city seemed greater than the more concrete dangers of war. No one in Florence appreciated the significance of Ladislaus' abrupt return to the Regno, and the illness which struck him at Narni. As the king lay dying in the church of San Paolo *fuori le mura* outside Rome, the Signoria instructed Gabriello Brunelleschi to visit him and complain about the ravages of his soldiers in the Sienese *contado* and the Foligno area, and to expedite the release of Florentine merchants in Rome.[370] The initial reaction to the news of Ladislaus' death was quite subdued. It was deplorable, Bartolomeo Valori said, that Florentines must rejoice over this event, when their forebears had grieved over the demise of his ancestors. The priors should inform the *popolo* of the king's death, but with restraint and dignity, since he was Florence's ally.[371] Two days later, however, the proprieties were ignored as those citizens who hated and feared Ladislaus expressed their true feelings. God had saved the city once again, as he did at the time of Giangaleazzo's death, Strozza Strozzi said, expressing an opinion that was shared by many. Feelings of relief and exultation were expressed by the king's enemies who had resisted him to the bitter end, and others like Maso degli Albizzi, Marsilio Vecchietti, and Francesco Machiavelli who had favored the peace settlement.[372] Gino Capponi could not resist the temptation to throw barbs at those friends of the king whose words and gestures betrayed their sorrow at his death.[373] But Cap-

---

[368] *Ibid.*, f.157r.

[369] Those anxieties were expressed more candidly after Ladislaus' death; see the statements by Vecchietti, Capponi, and Minerbetti; Cutolo, *Ladislao*, 488-89, n. 200.

[370] *SCMLC*, 6, ff.38v-39r, 27 July. The king's itinerary is traced by Cutolo, 458. Ladislaus fell ill in mid-July.

[371] CP, 42, f.162r, 14 Aug.; partially printed in *Commissioni*, I, 239-40.

[372] For their identity, CP, 42, ff.162v-165v; Cutolo, 488.

[373] Capponi's famous comment: "Nam hostem exterius habebamus, et Neronem intus, ut apparet ex locutione diversa multorum et colore faciei"; *Commissioni*, I, 240; also, CP, 42, f.164v: "Et nobis necessaria fuit talis mors, nam aliqui de suo obitu tristabantur et de vita letabantur."

poni's vindictiveness was atypical; most citizens would have concurred
with Strozza Strozzi's assessment: "In the past, the actions of citizens
were motivated by their sense of what was best [for the republic] or
by ignorance. Now, thanks be to God, the problem is resolved and no
one was beheaded, exiled or suffered the loss of property, for which
we must rejoice."[374] With the removal of their heavy burden of fear,
Florentines could look forward to a time of peace and prosperity.
They were indeed at the beginning of a peaceful era, but there would
be shadows to mar their enjoyment of those halcyon years.

[374] *CP*, 42, f.162v.

CHAPTER VII

The Ordeal of Peace and the Ordeal of War:
1414–1426

PEACE WITHOUT PROSPERITY

I N his diary written sometime in the late 1450s, Giovanni Rucellai
recalled the years after Ladislaus' death as a time of exceptional
prosperity. "From 1413 to 1423," he wrote, "we enjoyed a tranquil
peace, without any fear; the commune had few expenses for troops,
and few taxes were levied, so that the region became wealthy."[1] As
evidence of that prosperity, Rucellai cited the high prices quoted for
monte shares, and the two million florins that Florentine merchants
possessed as investment capital in 1423.[2] Scarcely had news of the
king's death reached Florence when Rinaldo Gianfigliazzi spoke of the
bright prospects of a business revival, and the garnering of profits
abroad. "Now we live in peace and quiet," Piero Baroncelli said a year
later (August 1415), "and our citizens are scattered all over the world
occupied with their affairs. . . ."[3] Filippo Corsini, whose memory went
back eighty years to the 1340s, expressed the opinion in 1420 that
the city had never enjoyed such felicity.[4] Even the impulse to expand
the dominion, to control another seaport or Apennine pass, was muted
if not extinguished. "We have enough territory for our needs," Palla
Strozzi insisted in 1420, "and we should give thanks to God and to the
Signoria for placing us in this state of security."[5] This decade provided the Florentines with a unique opportunity to replenish their
fortunes, to restore the fabric of their polity and social order, and
to enjoy a respite from the grinding pressures of war.

But this prosperity was neither permanent nor universal, and the
regime did not take full advantage of these peacetime years to
strengthen itself and to promote the welfare of its citizens. The most
striking feature of Florentine politics after 1414 was the elite's failure
to provide effective leadership, in sharp contrast to the time following
the death of Giangaleazzo Visconti in 1402. Florentine statesmen were

---

[1] *Giovanni Rucellai ed il suo Zibaldone*, ed. A. Perosa (London, 1960), I, 46;
trans. in Brucker, *Renaissance Florence*, 82; also in Molho, *Florentine Public
Finances*, 1.

[2] *Zibaldone*, I, 46, 62. *Monte* shares varied between 62% and 96% of their
nominal value; Rucellai wrote: "sono d'oppenione che solo di danari contanti e
merchatanti e' cittadini avessono il valore di due milioni di fiorini. . . ."

[3] *CP*, 42, f.164r; 43, f.6or.   [4] *CP*, 44, f.76v.

[5] *Ibid.*, f.37v.

disoriented by the unexpected death of their nemesis, and their will
and determination appeared to falter. They did not reform the fisc, the
military system, or the territorial government.[6] The dominant mood
was passive, almost indolent. It was epitomized by Matteo Castellani's
statement in 1421, when he congratulated his fellow-citizens on their
prudent administration of public affairs. He believed that this idyllic
state might continue indefinitely if the Florentines "would never seek
anything that might provoke a change."[7]

One unfortunate legacy from the wars with Ladislaus was partisanship, which had been particularly intense at the time of the peace in
June 1414, and which did not subside completely after the king's
death. The persistence of civic animosities and their corrosive effect
upon the regime were dramatized by the trial and execution of Sandro
da Quarata in the early months of 1415. A small but politically influential family from Santo Spirito, the Quaratesi had been affiliated
with the Ricci faction before the Ciompi revolution and, though
stigmatized as antipapal and Ghibelline, its members were not purged
by the Parte Guelfa nor excluded from the *reggimento* after 1382.[8]
While visiting Bologna in December 1414, Sandro da Quarata allegedly heard about a plot organized by a group of prominent Florentines to assassinate Maso degli Albizzi. His informant, a certain Andrea
Fighineldi, said that he would be willing to identify the ringleaders if
he received a safe conduct to Florence. Sandro then reported this news
to several citizens, among whom were leaders of the peace party,
Paolo Biliotti and Luigi Pitti.[9] They informed Maso and the priors,
who issued a safe conduct for Andrea to come to Florence. So ex-

---

[6] The last references in the *pratiche* to the need for "ordo et provisio" were in
1414: Filippo Corsini, "provisio et ordo necessarius est in omnibus et non per
fortunam se gubernare"; CP, 42, f.160r; Lippozzo Mangioni, "quanto plus de
ordine communis loquitur, inordinatio sequitur"; *ibid.*, f.184r; Michele Castellani,
"semel videndum est ut res nostre stabilitatem habent, et non de die in diem nova
querantur"; *ibid.*, f.176r. Perhaps the most important contribution to the rationalization of administration was the codification of the statutes, begun in 1409 and
completed in 1415; D. Marzi, *La cancelleria della Repubblica fiorentina*, 165.
See the rationale for this work in the *proemio* of the *Statuta populi et communis
Florentiae*, 1.

[7] CP, 44, f.128v: "Si consideramus pacem . . . et expensam parvam quam habemus, nova querere non debemus. . . . Qui sunt in statu bono non debent querere
ea que possint mutationem dare. . . ."

[8] Brucker, *Florentine Politics*, 199–200, 317, 348–49. In 1411, five Quaratesi
qualified for the Signoria; *Tratte*, 45, ff.1r–2r; Sandro received only 40 votes of
90 required to qualify.

[9] These details in Sandro's conviction; AP, 4288, ff.29r–30v, 19 Feb. 1415.
Sandro also told his story to Alamanno Salviati, Bernardo Fagni, and Maso
dell'Antella.

plosive were his revelations that the judicial records do not identify those who were accused of planning Maso's death. Hints were dropped in the *pratiche*, however, that Gino Capponi, Rinaldo Gianfigliazzi, and Niccolò da Uzzano had been implicated.[10] Giovanni Cavalcanti reported that Gino allegedly "had sworn in the hands of the most worthy citizens that he would humble Messer Maso, and others who had favored the peace," when he was chosen standard-bearer of justice in March.[11]

The motives of the participants in this drama are not fully clarified by the evidence. Sandro da Quarata had apparently hoped to convince Maso, and those who had supported his peace campaign, that their lives were in jeopardy. But Maso refused to launch a vendetta, insisting that the Signoria should conduct the investigation and determine the truth of the charges. "Don't tell me anything about any citizen," he was quoted as saying to Sandro, "because any small report linked to me is blown up out of all proportion. Go to the Signoria, because it demeans the republic when state affairs are treated by private citizens."[12] The authorities took their cue from Maso, and also from those who, like Piero Baroncelli, pointed out that the accused "were loyal, worthy, and prudent citizens who led honest lives and who enjoyed status, money, and property."[13] They tortured Sandro and questioned Andrea intensively to extract more information,[14] but they did not interrogate those accused of plotting Maso's death. Two members of the Eight on Security went to Bologna to question Florentine exiles suspected of inventing the story about Maso's assassination.[15] That version of events was accepted by the *podestà* and the Signoria, and Sandro was condemned to death for spreading seditious information that he

[10] Carlo Federighi: "Ut tollantur scandala, respondeatur domino Rainaldo, Nicolai et Gino, quod debent esse contenti quod domini et alii ad quos pertinet sequatur super negociis ut eis utile videbitur, nam sui honoris et fame consideratio habeatur ut requiretur et ad sufficientiam, et de hoc exitare non debent"; CP, 43, f.2v, 6 Jan. 1415.

[11] *Istorie fiorentine*, Polidori ed., II, 519.

[12] *Ibid.* Sandro did not speak directly to Maso but through Paolo Biliotti, who was instructed by Maso to tell Sandro "quod vadat ad dominos priores et dicat eis et narret dictum factum prout dixit vobis"; AP, 4288, f.30v.

[13] CP, 43, f.11r. Also, Giovanni de' Medici: "consideratis qualitate civium nominatorum et eius qui eos nominabat"; *ibid.*, f.12r.

[14] *Ibid.*, ff.4v–5r, statements of Filippo Guasconi for the Sixteen. Since Andrea had come to Florence with a safe conduct, he could not legally be imprisoned and tortured, but there was some sentiment to violate those guarantees; *ibid.*, ff.9r–10r.

[15] SCMLC, 6, ff.45r–45v; SRRO, 2, ff.25v–26r. The papal legate did apprehend four men but did not allow the Florentine officials to be present at their interrogation; CP, 43, ff.2v, 9v.

knew to be false.[16] While the investigations continued through January, citizens were anxious and tense, "fearing that there was some substance to the reports," as Filippo Corsini confessed in a *pratica*.[17] He was profoundly relieved to learn that Gino Capponi and Rinaldo Gianfigliazzi had been absolved, for their implication in that crime might well have doomed the regime.

The lesson taught by the Quarata episode was spelled out by Corsini, in a *pratica* held on 8 February.[18] Cities flourish through unity and they are ruined by discord. He recalled that the duke of Athens had exploited divisions within Florence to establish his rule in 1342, and had then been expelled by a unified citizenry. Rinaldo Gianfigliazzi warmly supported Corsini's sentiments, and urged the Signoria to continue its efforts at pacification, for which its members would gain divine approval as well as the enhancement of their wordly reputations. Lorenzo Ridolfi commented: "A city is the unity of its citizens, and where there is not unity, there is no city but a fortress." Maso degli Albizzi quoted a verse from Psalm 118: "This is the day which the Lord hath made; we will rejoice and be glad in it." Some counselors saw their personal experiences and feelings as relevant to this issue. Lorenzo Ridolfi described himself as a man without rancor, "and if anyone has a contrary opinion, I stand ready to demonstrate that fact." Insisting that he had been maligned by others, Luigi Pitti nevertheless offered to turn the other cheek, and to pardon those who had offended him. Giovanni de' Medici said that he bore no grudges and he urged others to follow his example. Niccolò da Uzzano made the sensible observation that every citizen who held office committed some acts that displeased others. He suggested that, although this reality could not be changed, its negative effects would be minimized if citizens did not view such political decisions as inspired by malice.

Though it cannot be proved, it seems likely that Sandro da Quarata's sensational accusations were concocted by Florentine exiles in Bologna to embarrass the regime. The ruse failed because Maso degli Albizzi

---

[16] "Cum dictus Sander in animo suo cognosceret que verba sibi dicta per Andream Fighineldi erant fabulatoria et veritate carentia sed erant acta ad semindandum zizanias scandala discordias et turbationem inter cives florentinos"; *AP*, 4288, f.29v. Sandro's informant, Fighineldi, and Nanni de' Ricci were convicted of seeking to persuade Carlo Malatesta, lord of Rimini, to warn Maso of the plot, which was allegedly instigated by Pope John XXIII: *ibid.*, ff.33r–34v.

[17] "Diebus preteritis in maxima amaritudine permansit, dubitando ne alia fundamenta que dicebantur haberent, cum nil gravius cogitare possit, sed audita veritate rerum, letatur cum solum ab exititiis procedant, ut scandala inter cives semant, et cives nominati boni et legales sunt"; *CP*, 43, f.11r, 2 Feb. For another reference to civic anxiety, "in civitate multa varia locuntur"; *ibid.*, f.1v.

[18] *Ibid.*, f.13v. The full debate, *ibid.*, ff.13v–15v.

refused to precipitate a crisis, either because he did not believe the allegations, or because he knew that the regime could not survive a purge of its leadership. How fragile were the bonds holding it together was vividly revealed by these events, whose repercussions extended well beyond the inner circle to the whole community. That many Florentines believed the charges against Gino Capponi and Rinaldo Gianfigliazzi is clear from the references to "the varied opinions of the citizens" and "the ignorance of the multitude." The Twelve were so fearful of public reaction that they warned the Signoria against convening any *pratiche* to discuss this lethal issue.[19] The *popolo*'s disenchantment with the regime's leadership surfaced in other ways: in rumors of a scheme, allegedly promoted by leading politicians, to replace lower guildsmen in the Signoria with magnates;[20] in the tendency of legislative councils to vote against the provisions submitted for approval; in their occasional refusal to authorize payment for the Signoria's living expenses.[21] The leadership had lost some measure of credibility, and thus of its capacity to govern. Never again during the regime's lifetime would its elite command the allegiance and support that it had enjoyed in the years after Giangaleazzo's death, before the wars with Genoa and Ladislaus had soured the political climate.

Combining, then, to create that mood of lethargy and passivity which pervaded the regime in the postwar years were, first, the absence of any serious threat to Florentine security and, second, the temporary discomfiture of the elite, plagued by internal rifts and mistrusted by a resentful, uncooperative *popolo*. Another element in this political setting, which has not been properly understood,[22] was the limited nature of Florence's economic recovery after the second Ladislaus war. The testimonials left by Giovanni Rucellai and Tommaso Mocenigo[23] concerning Florence's prosperity must be qualified by other evidence which, though fragmentary, depicts an economic

[19] Statements by Simone Ginori and Francesco Canigiani, *ibid.*, f.1v, 4 Jan., and by Banco da Verrazzano, *ibid.*, f.3r.

[20] *CP*, 42, ff.164v, 166v, statements by Gino Capponi and Giovanni Minerbetti.

[21] Giovanni Barbadori, for the Sixteen: "Tempore preteritorum dominorum si que expense eorum in consiliis obtente non fuerunt, quod cum dedecore dominationis procedit"; *CP*, 43, f.125r, 14 Jan. 1417. See also *LF*, 51, ff.229r–231r, 27 Oct. 1419.

[22] For a more positive valuation of Florence's economy in these years, see my *Renaissance Florence*, 82, and Molho, *Florentine Public Finances*, 1–5.

[23] In 1423, Mocenigo stated that Florentine merchants brought goods valued at 840,000 fl. each year into Venice, including 16,000 bolts of cloth for the Levant; Mallett, *Florentine Galleys*, 7.

landscape with much darker hues. The years between 1414 and 1423 were not, as Rucellai alleged, uniformly prosperous. In 1417, a plague struck, killing as many as 150 souls daily, from April until the following January.[24] In a *pratica* held (June 1417) to discuss the crisis, counselors referred to the desperate condition of the poor who, unemployed and destitute, "were dying of hunger" as well as from plague. Fearful that their misery might lead to disorder, Antonio Alessandri recommended that foreign troops be recruited to guard the city, and Buonaccorso Pitti suggested that potential troublemakers be hired and sent into the dominion to garrison fortresses there.[25] In order to conserve public funds for giving alms to artisans, "who in these times have earned little or nothing from their labors," the authorities took the unprecedented step of prohibiting oblations to churches, monasteries, and hospitals.[26] That epidemic struck the countryside as well as the city, decimating the population of many villages and disrupting a rural economy that had long been depressed.[27] Three years later (1420), a poor harvest created famine conditions that persisted into the spring and summer of 1421[28] and may have contributed to a temporary but very sharp decline in the economy. In their frequency and intensity, the complaints about business conditions in that year were reminiscent of wartime laments about the effects of severed trade routes and exorbitant taxes.[29] These statements suggest that the economy was far from robust in 1421, even after seven years of peace.[30]

[24] Rucellai, *Zibaldone*, I, 45. Filippo Rinuccini's estimate of 16,000 deaths in the city seems too large; *Ricordi storici*, ed. G. Aiazzi (Florence, 1840), liv–lv.

[25] *CP*, 43, ff.150v–153v, 15 June 1417, excerpts trans. in my *Society of Renaissance Florence*, 230–31.

[26] *Prov.*, 107, ff.154r–154v, 28–29 Aug. 1417.

[27] *Ibid.*, ff.312r–313r; 108, ff.84r–88r. On the territory's economy in these years, see Molho, *Florentine Public Finances*, 42–45; G. Morelli, *Ricordi*, 102; *Prov.*, 108, ff.107v, 109r–111r; *CP*, 43, ff.134r, 151v–153r.

[28] *Prov.*, 110, ff.55v–58r, 112v–113r, 187v–188r, 194v–195r, 201r; *SCMLC*, 6, ff.111v–115r; *CP*, 44, ff.13v–14v, 37r, 43v, 48v–49r, 54v, 114r.

[29] On the specific character of their complaints, see below, 405. In Oct. 1421 a provision was enacted authorizing officials to lease communal property at lower rates, on account of the depression; *Prov.*, 111, ff.142v–143r. This evidence forces me to revise my statement that Florence was enjoying great prosperity in 1420, "Florence and Its University, 1348–1434," in *Action and Conviction in Early Modern Europe*, ed. T. Rabb and J. Siegel (Princeton, 1969), 224. It helps to explain why the subsidy for the Florentine Studio was reduced from 3000 fl. to 1500 fl. that year, and two years later, to 600 fl.

[30] Cristofano di Giorgio: "Sumus in pace et sine expensa vel minima"; *CP*, 44, f.128v, 2 Oct. 1421. The most solid evidence for prosperity is the high level of gabelle revenues for the years 1416–20; Molho, *Florentine Public Finances*, 54.

While the whole economy fluctuated in response to the imperatives of weather and disease, each segment was influenced by such factors as market demand, competition, and the cost and availability of labor and raw materials. The bankers prospered most, being the least affected by wartime restraints on trade and industry, and accustomed to those "dishonest gains"—Strozza Strozzi's phrase—with which they had filled their coffers while endangering their souls.[31] The silk industry also flourished in these years, as demand for velvets and brocades rose in European and Levantine markets.[32] But the fortunes of Florentine merchants who traded abroad varied greatly from region to region. The Levant was becoming more accessible to Florentine traders, or so Tommaso Mocenigo's estimate of their involvement in that commerce would suggest. But many parts of Europe that had once attracted hordes of Florentine merchants—the Regno, Rome, Dalmatia, Hungary, France—were suffering from political disorders that diminished the opportunities for profit.[33] The most depressed sectors of the Florentine economy were agriculture and woolen cloth-manufacturing, which employed the largest number of workers and fed the largest number of stomachs. The countryside had long been suffering from heavy taxation and from the exploitations of usurers and officials; the value of property owned by residents of the *contado* and district had declined by twenty-eight percent between 1404 and 1414, and again by that ratio from 1414 to 1427.[34] Grants of tax concessions and immunity from debts, which were promulgated in 1415,

---

[31] "Ob preteritas expensas maximas, propter quos ad non honesta lucra cives deducti sunt"; *CP*, 42, f.162v, 14 Aug. 1414. Cf. Luca da Filicaia's statement, "cum ars lane et artes nil faciant et artifices se consummunt; et ob hoc omnes ad usuras et inlicita lucra se tradunt"; *CP*, 41, f.135v, 5 Sept. 1412. On the role of Florentine bankers at the papal curia in these years, see G. Holmes, "How the Medici Became the Pope's Bankers," *Flor. Studies*, 357–80.

[32] Molho, *Florentine Public Finances*, 4; G. Corti and J. da Silva, "Note sur la production de la soie à Florence au XVe siècle"; *Annales*, xx (1965), 309–11. For a comparison of profits in the wool and silk industries, see my *Renaissance Florence*, 85–86. The Florentine silk industry benefited from protectionist legislation that prohibited the manufacture of silk cloth in the dominion; *Prov.*, 109, ff.39v–40r, 24–25 May 1419.

[33] Brucker, *Renaissance Florence*, 83–84. In France (for example), 20 Florentine merchants were killed, and others imprisoned, when the Burgundian army occupied Paris in May 1418; *BNF*, II, IV, 380, pp. 433–34; the diary of Alamanno di Luigi Mannini.

[34] Molho, *Florentine Public Finances*, 26–28. The colleges expressed concern (5 March 1421) about the exodus of usurers from the *contado*; "Ex feneratoribus habeantur aliqui olim exercitium illud agentes, et cum eis praticentur ut mutuent et fenerentur et causas notas faciant cur se retrahunt, et modus detur utilis et talis unde effectus sequatur quod pauperibus subveniantur mutuo super eorum rebus"; *CP*, 44, f.66r.

1420, and 1422, did not stem the exodus of the peasantry, which was further intensified by the series of poor harvests between 1417 and 1420.[35] Either these hungry, impoverished rustics left the territory altogether, or they came into the cities in search of work and a livelihood. Formerly, the woolen cloth industry had absorbed this migrant labor, but the *botteghe* were not operating at full capacity in these years. In their 1427 *catasto* reports, several *lanaiuoli* noted that they were not making cloth, and that their shops had been closed for several years. Florence's largest industry, which nourished thousands of unskilled laborers, and hundreds if not thousands in subsidiary occupations (dyeing, fulling, stretching, trimming, mending) was experiencing lean times.[36]

These trends may have contributed to a fundamental reshaping of the Florentine social and economic order, towards that pattern David Herlihy has described for Pistoia in these years: "great concentrations of wealth, an extension of fiscal pauperism and a weakened middle class."[37] By 1427, when the first *catasto* records provide concrete evidence of the distribution of wealth, the pattern is clear: a tiny minority of very rich citizens (86 with property exceeding 10,000 florins; 202 above 5000), a preponderant majority of poor residents (82 percent or 8340 households paying less than one florin), and a small and probably shrinking "middle class" with modest affluence: 1525 households that paid between one and ten florins.[38] Most of the great fortunes—Medici, Strozzi, Tornabuoni, Bardi, Peruzzi, Pazzi, Uzzano, Borromei—were built from the profits of banking and exchange operations.[39] Other forms of entrepreneurial activity—international trade, cloth manufacturing, real estate investments—were less profitable than

[35] Molho, 27, n. 11; CP, 44, f.114r, 30 July 1421: "Quod casus grani gravis est et remedium exigitur festinum, nam quod pretium creverit mirum est; et licet recollectus non sit excessivus, tamen melior est quam annis tribus elapsis. . . ."

[36] For data on cloth *botteghe* that had been closed since 1417 and 1418, see *Catasto*, 64, f.24r; 69, f.65v; 74, f.170r. The shops operated in these years by Giovanni de' Medici, Simone Strozzi, and Andrea Fortini made only modest profits; De Roover, *Medici Bank*, 42, 47; Goldthwaite, *Private Wealth*, 42; Brucker, *Renaissance Florence*, 86.

[37] *Medieval and Renaissance Pistoia*, 191.

[38] The data from Martines, *Social World*, 106, 365–78; De Roover, *Medici Bank*, 28–31; Herlihy, "Some Psychological and Social Roots of Violence in the Tuscan Cities," in L. Martines, ed., *Violence and Civil Disorder*, 151, who notes that the richest 99 households controlled one-fourth of the city's wealth after deductions.

[39] See the *catasto* returns of Niccolò da Uzzano, Ridolfo di Bonifazio Peruzzi, Giovanni Giugni, Francesco and Niccolò Tornabuoni, Palla di Nofri Strozzi, and Andrea de' Pazzi; *Catasto*, 64, ff.65v–75v; 72, ff.110r–116v, 211r–214r; 76, ff.169v–202v; 77, ff.383r–390r; 80, ff.586r–593r.

banking, and seemingly more depressed in these years. The manufacture and sale of woolen cloth had long been an important source of income for the middle strata of Florentine society: the reduction if not elimination of these profit margins damaged an economy already weakened by the drain of military expenses. Concrete details of this process of impoverishment are recorded in the flood of petitions for tax relief in these years, and in the 1427 *catasto*, which indicate that investments in cloth factories and trading companies, and indeed in entrepreneurial activity of every kind, was quite modest by comparison with the sums invested in real estate and the *monti*. Of the twenty-two Medici households recorded in the *catasto*, only five had any capital investments in business companies; for the Strozzi, the ratio was seven to thirty-three.[40] The wealthiest members of these families still invested a portion of their capital in cloth *botteghe* and mercantile companies, but their poorer cousins now bought real estate and shares of the public debt with assets that, a generation before, they might have invested in business.[41]

Florence's "middle class" was thus apparently declining in size and in wealth in the early *quattrocento*. According to one estimate in 1421, the number of households assessed one florin or more in the *prestanze*

[40] The Medici returns in *Catasto*, 75, ff.668v–680r; 78, ff.111v–113r, 481r–488v, 532r–532v; 79, ff.29r–30r, 33r–33v, 55r–56r, 87r, 160v–163r, 255v–258r, 311v–312r, 347r–347v, 462v, 472v, 474r, 483r–485r, 565r, 605r; 81, ff.29v–32r, 111v–118r, 271r–271v; the Strozzi, *Catasto*, 72, ff.197r–201r; 75, ff.131r–132r, 196v–197v; 76, *passim*.

[41] In 1427 many rich Florentines had invested most of their assets in real estate and *monte* shares; e.g., these residents of S. Spirito:

name	real estate	*monte*	business	source
Lippaccio and Francesco di Benedetto Bardi	4792 fl.	10,452	2950	*Cat.* 64, ff.54r–58r
Giovanni di Barduccio Cherichini	11,620	16,560	5520	*Cat.* 64, ff.77r–84r
Jacopo di Filippo Guidetti	7600	17,870	0	*Cat.* 65, f.108v
Messer Giovanni di Messer Luigi Guicciardini	9360	10,000 circa	1450	*Cat.* 65, f.483r
Donato di Ugolino Bonsi	5000	14,500	5960	*Cat.* 67, f.49r
Bernardo di Ugolino Bonsi	2100	10,400	1540	*Cat.* 67, f.77r
Francesco di Messer Tommaso Soderini	9040	6882	0	*Cat.* 67, f.79v

had fallen to 1700, a substantial decline since 1411.[42] This group of moderately affluent—merchants and industrialists (and some rentiers) with assets of 3000–5000 florins—had been hurt by the fiscal demands of the state and the constriction of business opportunities. Andrea di Bartolo Manni had once operated a woolen cloth factory with his father but (he reported in 1422) his patrimony had been devoured by taxes and the depression of the cloth market. Baldassare di Arrigo Simone's fortune had been reduced by 5000 florins, as a result of the flooding of the Arno, which ruined his farm near Settimo, and of losses incurred in the silk trade. Antonio di Niccolò Castellani owed (June 1422) 508 florins in unpaid *prestanze*; so meager was the return on his investments that he could not pay his living expenses from current income. Antonio's cousin, Jacopo di Stefano Castellani, insisted that he would have to go into exile if he could not obtain a reduction of his tax obligation (231 florins) and his assessment. Business reverses were cited by Bernardo di Alderotto Brunelleschi as the explanation for his inability to pay a tax obligation of 194 florins; he petitioned for the cancellation of that debt and a reduction of his assessment. The sons of Messer Carlo Cavalcanti had their entire patrimony of 7900 florins tied up in real estate from which, they claimed, they received little revenue. Giovanni di Antonio Berti suffered heavy losses from the bankruptcy of business associates, as well as from his taxes "which are beyond his ability to pay, and also from the depression in the leather trade in which he had once been active and was now forced to abandon."[43] Bernardo di Messer Biagio Guasconi, who in 1403 was ranked among the fifty richest men in his quarter, petitioned (August 1421) for the cancellation of his tax debt of 110 florins, stating that "he was not only poor but living in the most extreme misery, as a result of the misfortunes that have befallen him . . . from which not only his own but his wife's patrimony (which was ample) has been consumed. . . ."[44]

<hr />

[42] *CP*, 44, f.137r, 22 Oct. 1421, statement of Giuliano Davanzati, "maxime attento quod impositiones totius civitatis, viz., particularium civium a floreno supra non ascendit ad summam 1700 impositarum. . . ." Those whose assessments were 1 fl. or less could elect to pay one-third "ad perdendum"; which substantially reduced the cash flow into the treasury; *Prov.*, 103, ff.69v–71r; 104, ff.40r–42v. The lowest assessments, 6 s., 8 d., or less paid nothing, but these men could not hold communal office. In 1424, Paolo Petriboni calculated that only 1600 households of 7000 were assessed at 1 fl. or more; *BNF, Conventi Soppressi*, C, 4,895, f.112v. In 1411, there were over 800 households assessed more than one fl. in the quarter of S. Croce alone; *Pres.*, vols. 2754–2757.

[43] *Prov.*, 111, f.146r; 112, ff.40r, 104v, 105v, 119v; 113, f.113v; 116, f.125r.

[44] *Prov.*, 111, ff.130v–131v. Bernardo may have exaggerated his plight; in 1427 he had 4005 fl. in gross assets, and 2205 fl. in taxable assets; *Catasto*, 78, ff.50v–53r.

This reshaping of Florence's socio-economic structure—with its small elite of the very rich, its middle echelons depleted and impoverished, and its huge concentrations of the poor and the marginally poor—had important political repercussions. The decline of the "middle class" had enlarged the category of the *poveri vergognosi*, men of respectable families whose fortunes had declined and (in many cases) whose unpaid tax obligations made them ineligible for office.[45] As the number of these poor "gentlemen" grew, so did the intensity of their thirst for salaried offices, the stipends from which could supplement their meager incomes from *contado* farms, urban real estate, and *monte* investments. Those who did not succeed in the scrutinies flooded the Signoria with petitions for appointments to a vicariate or a castellany, often citing their poverty and their inability to earn a living from their trade.[46] These men were seeking to recoup their losses, or at least avoid falling deeper into poverty; those whose fortunes were intact were concerned about the preservation of their wealth. Paolo Biliotti spoke for this group when he noted that many citizens had already been ruined by taxes, and that the regime should take care to preserve the survivors.[47] Whether rich or poor, whether rising or falling on the economic scale, every citizen in the *reggimento* was acutely concerned about the fisc. To reduce expenses to the barest minimum, and to avoid any enlargement of the budget, was a primary goal of every Signoria in these years.

Peacetime Problems and Anxieties

The regime's first priority after Ladislaus' death was the dismantling of the expensive military force that had been recruited to defend the territory. From an initial reduction to 500 lances, first proposed in August 1414, the mercenary army was further cut to 400 by year's

---

[45] On this general problem in Florence, and its worsening in the 1420s and 1430s, see R. Trexler, "Charity and the Defense of Urban Elites in the Italian Communes"; in F. Jaher, ed., *The Rich, the Well Born and the Powerful* (Urbana, Ill., 1974), 64–109, and esp. 79, 86–87.

[46] Examples: *Prov.*, 113, ff.113v, 132r, 178v–179r; 115, ff.28r–28v. Many of these petitions, approved by the Signoria and the colleges, were rejected in the councils; e.g., *LF*, 53, ff.170v, 231r–231v. For a list of private petitions (which had to be approved by two *uditori* before they could be presented to the Signoria) for the years 1419–1428, see *Tratte*, 23, *passim*. Some Florentines, like Pazzino di Messer Palla Strozzi, sought offices abroad, in the Papal States, or like Donato dell'Antella, in the service of a *signore; Strozz.*, 3rd ser., 111, f.25r; *CRS*, 78 (*Badia*), 324, f.57r.

[47] *CP*, 41, f.135r: "si aliqui sunt potentes, conservandi sunt ne consummantur, quia numerus parvus est, et cito ad nichilum venerent. . . ."

end.[48] In November, the commune's monthly outlay had been reduced by nearly one-half, from 37,000 to 22,000 florins, but the fiscal deficit was still nearly 100,000 florins.[49] After six months of living in "peace and tranquillity," the citizenry felt secure enough (March 1415) to reduce the military establishment to 200 lances, which, Piero Baroncelli estimated, would cost only 3000 florins monthly, and could be borne without resort to forced loans. Although these expenditures continued to decline, the fiscal situation did not become as healthy as Baroncelli predicted. In November 1416, he estimated that the commune's annual deficit was 60,000 florins, which would require either a forced loan or an increase in the gabelles on food.[50] In 1417, the authorities were hard pressed to find money for the salaries of the Pisan garrison and to buy grain for a hungry, plague-stricken populace. Two forced loans were imposed to make up the deficit, which, in January 1418, was still 20,000 florins, thus necessitating additional levies in that year.[51] After a year's respite from these burdens, the situation again deteriorated in the summer of 1420, provoking a spate of grumbling and recrimination over the inept management of the fisc. The Sixteen were displeased to learn, Antonio Benizi said (19 September 1420), that the commune could not subsist on its ordinary revenues; they saw no alternative to the imposition of another forced loan, appropriately entitled "the third *dispiacente*." Speaking for the *pratica* a day later, Piero Beccanugi agreed that the *prestanze* were necessary, but he called for the appointment of a commission to suggest ways to cut expenses and increase revenue.[52]

The regime's failure to balance its budget, in these peacetime years when conditions were most propitious for fiscal reform, was due as much to political as to economic factors. During a fiscal debate held in November 1416, Piero Baroncelli expressed the hope that the commune would be able to liquidate all its *monte* obligations, "and then it will be free of debt and will be able to meet its expenses without taxing the citizenry."[53] How visionary Baroncelli's statement was can

[48] CP, 42, ff.162v, 166v, 167v, 183v.

[49] *Ibid.*, f.183v. In May the commune was spending 37,000 fl. monthly; in July the fiscal deficit was estimated at 220,000 fl.

[50] CP, 43, ff.22v–23r, 102v, 113r.

[51] *Ibid.*, ff.136r–138r, 169v–171r, 177r; *Prov.*, 106, ff.340r–340v; 107, ff.122r–123v; 108, ff.121v–122v, 171v–173v.

[52] CP, 44, ff.33v–34v; see also *ibid.*, ff.22v–23r; *Prov.*, 110, ff.55v–57v, 114r–115r. A special magistracy was elected in 1418, with one year's tenure, to reduce the administrative expenses in the *contado; Balìe*, 21, *passim*.

[53] ". . . Solidentur ordinamenta montis. Nam in parvo tempore si illesa permanent, commune suis creditoribus solvet montis et sine debito permanebit et sine onere civium de suo commune necessitatibus subveniet"; CP, 43, f.113r, 6 Nov. 1416.

be seen from the fiscal data collected by Anthony Molho: a funded debt in 1414 exceeding three million florins, which was reduced by only 175,000 florins (5.6 percent) during the seven years following Ladislaus' death. The interest charge on that debt averaged 180,000 florins annually, or nearly one and one-half million florins for the years 1415–1422; it constituted more than one-half of the total communal budget.[54] Here was the crux of the regime's fiscal problems, which could have been alleviated only by a massive effort to reduce that debt to manageable proportions. But Florentines were unwilling to confront an issue that, in retrospect, seems more fundamental than the inequity of tax assessments, which was eventually solved by the *catasto*. One obstacle to the liquidation of the *monti* was the importance of those interest payments, the *paghe*, in the budgets of Florentine families, rich and poor.[55] To diminish that "precious resource"—Gino Capponi's phrase—would complicate investment patterns, and where but from the "purses of the citizenry" would come the money to amortize the debt? Gabelle revenues were as high as in wartime; any increase in the rates would have worsened the plight of the city's poor, particularly during the lean years between 1417 and 1420. Income from direct taxation of the *contado* had declined by nearly forty percent between 1416 and 1419, reflecting the deteriorating conditions in the countryside.[56] The only sector of the Florentine economy that had not been heavily taxed by the state was the clergy, but the leadership was more reluctant to tap that resource than previous regimes had been.[57] Although the issue had lost some of its ideological coloration of the past, it had become more enmeshed in private interest, as was illustrated by a debate (November 1416) on

[54] Molho, *Florentine Public Finances*, 72–73, and table 4, 61. The money to reduce the debt came primarily from the retention of one-fourth of interest payments on *monte* shares, a practice begun in 1404 and continued in 1415 and 1419; *Prov.*, 105, ff.262v–267v; 109, ff.217v–222r; Molho, 71–73. In 1421, 50,000 fl. of that reserve was used for the acquisition of Livorno; see below, 430.

[55] The importance of the income from the *monte* can be seen in private account books, e.g., those of Matteo Palmieri and Nofri di Palla Strozzi; *Acquisti e Doni*, 7; *Strozz.*, 3rd ser., 281; and in the *monte* investments recorded in the *catasto*. Cf. Becker, in *Flor. Studies*, 125–27.

[56] Tax revenues from the dominion declined from 133,360 fl. in 1416 to 81,827 fl. in 1419; Molho, *Florentine Public Finances*, 61.

[57] For example, in the expropriation of church property during the war with Pope Gregory XI; Brucker, *Florentine Politics*, 304–05, 317–19; Trexler, *Spiritual Power*, 161–64. The argument against taxing the clergy was formulated most clearly by Antonio Alessandri and Piero Carnesecchi; *CP*, 43, f.136r, 10 March 1417. On the general problem, see my *Renaissance Florence*, 184–85.

the Signoria's proposals to disqualify from civic office the close relatives of clerics who had not paid their taxes.[58] Lorenzo Ridolfi, a canon
lawyer, sharply criticized the scheme, declaring that it was unjust and
discriminatory, and that it would strain relations between clerics and
their lay kinsmen. Conceding that the plan was unjust, "since it penal-
izes one for another's defect," Piero Baroncelli nevertheless favored
the proposal as being justified by the state's need. This debate revealed
how important the revenue from benefices had become for some
Florentine families. Ridolfi alluded to the common practice of laymen
paying the tax obligations of their clerical brothers or sons, and
Bartolomeo Valori stated bluntly that "many laymen share in, and live
on, ecclesiastical revenues." Economic necessity was forcing many
Florentines to ignore the advice that Buonaccorso Pitti gave to his
sons, to avoid any "meddling in squabbles over church benefices and
getting involved with priests."[59]

The fate of any legislative proposal to amortize the *monti* rapidly,
or to reform the fisc in substantive ways, was predictable, given the
stubborn opposition in the councils to several fiscal measures proposed
by the Signoria in these years. In October 1418, a provision imposing
a forced loan for the payment of mercenary salaries was repeatedly
defeated in the Council of 200 and the *Popolo*, amid complaints that
the money spent on defense was being wasted. When the Signoria
endeavored to meet that criticism by proposing the establishment of
a commission to reduce expenditures, that provision was also rejected.[60] The priors who entered office in November were no more successful than their predecessors had been. Finally, on 21 November,
the Council of the *Popolo* did approve the provisions by narrow
margins, but the Council of the Commune resisted them so strenuously
that one angry counselor spoke of the obstinacy, "and perhaps even
the depravity," of the dissenting minority.[61] Paying soldiers fifty soldi
for services worth only fifteen was one source of civic dissatisfaction

[58] *CP*, 43, ff.116v–117r, 19 Nov. 1416.

[59] Pitti, *Cronica*, 177, trans. in *Two Memoirs of Renaissance Florence*, 95. Cf.
Gino Capponi's comment: "Non v'impacciate con preti, che sono la schiuma del
mondo, nè di pecunia nè di chiesa"; "Ricordi," *Miscellanea di studi offerti a A.
Balduino e B. Bianchi*, 35.

[60] The controversy over these provisions in *LF*, 51, ff. 226v–240r, 21 Oct.–28
Nov. 1418. Particularly critical of fiscal administration was Antonio del Vigna,
spokesman for the councilors of S. Maria Novella: "quod est verecundia communi
se non aliter gubernare, et quod vicini se aliter gubernant et bene et cum maiori
ordine"; *ibid.*, f.227v.

[61] *Ibid.*, f.240r, 26 Nov.

with the fisc, but Filippo Salviati also complained about the mismanagement of the gabelles and inequities in the assessment of forced loans.[62] Similar criticisms were voiced two years later (September 1420) when another *prestanza* measure foundered in the councils for two weeks before it was finally approved. After witnessing (November 1421) three negative votes against a measure to reform these assessments, the Signoria abandoned its efforts, thus perpetuating an outmoded schedule that had not been changed since 1411.[63]

In another sphere where the commune had exerted itself forcefully in the past, the promotion of the Florentine economy, these years mark a low point of activity and concern. No significant legislation affecting trade routes or tariffs was initiated by the Signoria, nor did the councils pass any protectionist legislation favoring Florentine merchants and industrialists. The leadership apparently felt that entrepreneurs would prosper without the government's assistance, so long as peace continued and taxes were moderate. Florentine ambassadors did exert pressure upon Queen Joanna of Naples to indemnify those citizens whose property had been despoiled by Ladislaus in 1414. The government also sent diplomatic missions to Genoa on behalf of merchants who were involved in disputes over the shipment of Florentine cargoes in Genoese galleys, and the gabelles that were levied on that merchandise in Genoa.[64] But these sporadic interventions can hardly be defined as a policy of "proto-mercantilism" which, Marvin Becker has argued, was an important feature of Florentine policy in these years.[65]

One issue that did engage the leadership's attention, and generated intense and prolonged controversy, was officeholding. To every proposal by the Signoria that a new scrutiny be held, or a change instituted in the method of filling offices, opposition was registered in the councils, sometimes so strongly that it could not be overcome by executive pressure. The basic problem seems to have been the size and composition of the regime's membership. Conservatives were seeking to raise the standards for officeholding, to accept only Guelfs from the oldest and most prominent families, and to stem the flow of new blood that continued to seep into the *reggimento*. These elitist pressures

---

[62] *Ibid.*, ff.233r–233v. The two provisions finally passed on 26 and 28 Nov.; *ibid.*, ff.240r–241r.

[63] *LF*, 52, ff.53v–61r, 118v–120r; Molho, *Florentine Public Finances*, 75–76.

[64] *SCMLC*, 6, ff.52r–53r, 55r–56r, 60r–60v, 72r–74v; *SCMC*, 29, ff.80r–89r, 98r–103r.

[65] M. Becker, *Flor. Studies*, 111–17. Becker states that the Lana guild sought protection from the import of foreign cloth; *ibid.*, 116, n. 3, but provisions designed to furnish that protection were rejected in the Council of the *Popolo*; *LF*, 51, ff.203r, 206v, 30 May and 9 June 1418.

were resisted by guildsmen who sought to keep the regime open and flexible, and to preserve a share of offices for men of middling status.[66]

Though never developed into a coherent program, the conservative position was articulated, if only fragmentarily and sporadically, in the *pratiche*. That only the meritorious should be chosen for office was a cliché frequently heard in debates, but the achievement of that objective was difficult. Rinaldo degli Albizzi did suggest (October 1414) that the *reggimento* was too large, and, in particular, that the number of eligibles for territorial offices should be reduced.[67] The Castellani were especially critical of the quality and performance of these officials, and they implied that the worst offenders were men of dubious antecedents and little merit, who had somehow wormed their way into the group of qualified officeholders.[68] Almost certainly in this category were the baker Lorenzo di Giunta, who was selected as *podestà* of Antella in 1413; the linen-maker Leonardo di Tommaso da Careggi, *podestà* of Pescia in that year; Lorenzo di Santi, old-clothes dealer, *podestà* of Figline in 1414; Lorenzo di Boldro, butcher, *podestà* of the league of Avene; Lorenzo di Giovanni, armorer, *podestà* of the Chianti district in 1415.[69] To keep such men from positions of authority and responsibility, the procedure for selecting the scrutators should be reformed, Marsilio Vecchietti and Cristofano di Giorgio argued, so that only men with impeccable credentials would pass on the merits of candidates for these magistracies.[70] They should be chosen, Giotto Peruzzi insisted, from the most exalted "optimate" families.[71] Perhaps the most radical suggestion made in these debates was the abolition of the *divieto*, which had been instituted in the fourteenth century to restrain the tendency of large families to monopolize offices. But so deeply ingrained in the civic mentality was this principle that it could

[66] Dale Kent argues persuasively that during the 1420s, the Medici gained many adherents from this group by systematically promoting their candidacy to communal offices; *Rise of the Medici*, ch. 1, vi, vii.

[67] *CP*, 42, f.176r. Matteo Castellani also noted that "nunquam preteritis temporibus tantus numerus in bursis fuit ut nunc"; *CP*, 43, f.116v.

[68] See above, ch. IV, 217, and *CP*, 42, f.186v, statement of Matteo Castellani: "Inspectis quod querele multe provenient a subditis ob non honeste gesta per rettores. . . ."

[69] *Tratte*, 134, under "L" at date. Artisans and "new men" were well represented in these territorial magistracies, not in the most important posts (Arezzo, Pisa, Cortona, Valdinievole) but in the lesser offices. On territorial administration, see Martines, *Lawyers and Statecraft*, ch. 6.

[70] *CP*, 43, ff.105v, 139r.

[71] "Eligi deberent ad scrutinandum in quolibet gonfalone et familia optimates et meliores et non ad placitum"; *ibid.*, f.127r.

not be touched.[72] Even with the *divieto*, Lippozzo Mangioni complained that smaller houses were being squeezed out of office, while
powerful families were becoming stronger.[73] To defend their position
in the *reggimento*, Mangioni and other conservatives favored the concept of the *rimbotto*, the mixing of eligibles from different scrutinies,
to give some advantage in the drawings for office to older men of
distinguished ancestry and social eminence.[74] The *rimbotto* was
designed to minimize the adverse effects of *divieto* regulations on
prominent aristocratic families whose members, by the normal process
of sortition, would be disqualified more frequently than citizens with
few or no relatives in the pouches. It provided for the inclusion of
those gaining majorities into old pouches, where the more eminent citizens would accumulate slips (*polizze*), and thus be eligible more frequently when sortition occurred.[75] Moreover, the younger members
of these aristocratic lineages were included in more recent pouches,
so that they would be eligible for office when they reached the proper
age.[76] This elitist principle underlying the *rimbotto* explains the resistance that proposals for reconstituting the pouches often encountered
in the councils.[77]

The most intense and protracted struggles over officeholding involved not the scrutinies or *rimbotti* for the Signoria, but the selection of personnel for territorial offices. Although less prestigious than the

[72] For the sharp reaction to one proposal for modifying the *divieto*, see *ibid.*,
f.92v, 19 July 1416. Gino Capponi was strongly opposed to any change in these
controls; "Ricordi," *op. cit.*, 35. They are summarized in *Statuta populi et communis*, II, 732ff.

[73] "Iniquum esset ut qui in bursis sunt vel extracti non intrarent noviter, nam hoc
contra populares venit, et familie potentes semper crescunt; et ex eis quando sex
vel X mittuntur qui non erant, quoniam multe sunt familie ex antiqua prosapia in
numero parvo et non introirent nec ullum beneficium obtinerent quod iniquum
foret"; *CP*, 43, f.100v, 25 Sept. 1416.

[74] Matteo Castellani, Jacopo di Messer Rinaldo Gianfigliazzi, Luca di Messer
Maso degli Albizzi, Bartolomeo Valori, Niccolò di Pepo degli Albizzi and Piero
Baroncelli supported the principle of the *rimbotto*; *CP*, 42, ff.186v, 188r; 43, ff.89v–
90r.

[75] The *rimbotto* reinforced the aristocratic predominance that the work of the
accoppiatori also promoted; see above, 92; Rubinstein, *Government of Florence*,
46–47. For a different perspective on the *rimbotto*, see Cavalcanti's summary of
Rinaldo degli Albizzi's views in *Istorie fiorentine*, III, ch. 2.

[76] A *rimbotto* provision of June 1416 stipulated that eligibles over 25 would be
placed in the 1391 pouches; those between 15 and 25 in the 1393 and 1398 pouches,
and those under 15 in the 1400 pouches; *Prov.*, 106, ff.32v–35r. "New men" would
not normally qualify for the Signoria until they were much older.

[77] The *rimbotto* provision of June 1416 was rejected three times before it passed:
196–81 and 137–60; *LF*, 51, ff.76v–78v.

priorate, the vicariates and castellanies were sources of profit (*utile*) for their incumbents.[78] Gino Capponi focused on these offices, rather than the unpaid domestic magistracies, when he recalled (November 1416) a prediction made a decade before, at the time of Pisa's conquest by a Florentine notary identified only as Ser Benedetto. "Now we are lords of the Pisans, which I never believed would happen," Ser Benedetto exclaimed, "but I fear that it will result in the destruction of Florence, on account of the scrutinies that will be held for territorial offices."[79]

In the first campaign (October–November 1414) to hold a new election for these posts after Ladislaus' death, the enabling provisions were finally passed after several rejections in the Council of the Commune.[80] Two years later, resistance in the councils to another scrutiny was much greater. A provision authorizing the election was first voted down in the Council of the *Popolo* on 12 August, and on two successive days thereafter. Revived again on 30 September, the measure quickly gained the approval of that council on 1 October, but then failed in the Council of the Commune after eleven ballots. In the *pratiche* convened to discuss the impasse, counselors were unanimous in their support of the measure, which, they argued, would contribute to civic peace by giving offices to the worthy.[81] Those casting negative votes either did not believe that propaganda, or they feared that they—or their kinsmen and friends—would not be successful in the scrutiny. To intensify the pressure on the dissidents, some speakers suggested that failure to pass the law would be an insult to the Signoria; others, however, rejected that argument, and instead warned the priors against coercing the council.[82] In January 1417, their successors tried again

---

[78] Rubinstein, *Government of Florence*, 57–58. For evidence of this preoccupation, see the testimony of an unidentified elector in a 1417 scrutiny: ". . . Ci siamo trovati a rendere le fave; ed esendo tra noi chi dubitava che noi non vi mettiamo ogni huomo ordinatissamamente, siamo stati guardati e bociati per lo squittino di molte cose di veduta, delle quali nulla n'anno potuto vedere, avegnia chè di molte per immaginazione si sieno forse aposti. Potrebbe essere il fruto forse migliore che io nonne imagino, ma nollo credo uno bene"; *CRS*, 78 (*Badìa*), 325, f.67r, Nov. 1417, letter addressed to Forese Sacchetti.

[79] *CP*, 42, f.117v, 19 Nov. 1416.

[80] *LF*, 50, ff.141r–146r; 51, ff.5r–8v, 11–17 Oct., 12–21 Nov. 1414; *Prov.*, 104, ff.32r–39r. One reason cited for opposing the scrutiny was a plan for a *rimbotto* of the pouches: "albi dicunt quod inmistio '93 et '98 esset dissidia civium"; *LF*, 50, f.146v.

[81] *LF*, 51, ff.86v–104v; *CP*, 43, ff.104v, 107v.

[82] Ser Bonifazio di Messer Coluccio Salutati: "quod honor dominorum et collegiorum et pax et unitas civium requirit ut obtineatur scrutinium"; *ibid.*, f.105v; and the comments of Lorenzo Ridolfi, Niccolò Benvenuti and Palla Strozzi, who criticized the Signoria for their excessive zeal; *ibid.*, ff.116v–117r.

and failed to gain approval for a territorial scrutiny.[83] Opponents were influenced neither by the unanimity of the priors and colleges nor by Piero Bonciani's contention that Christ himself would favor the holding of that election.[84] One final and unsuccessful effort was made in late March and early April, before the onset of plague distracted the attention of the citizenry to the more serious problem of survival.[85]

The plague decimated the urban population and drove large numbers of Florentines into temporary exile. In these abnormal conditions, the Signoria was able to muster majorities in the councils for a new scrutiny, which was held in late October.[86] That election aroused intense controversy, since many citizens had not yet returned to Florence. These absentees were not included among the scrutators nor, apparently, were they considered as candidates for territorial magistracies. Thus, "worthy citizens" who should have qualified for vicariates were barred from these posts, which instead were filled by men of lesser status and experience.[87] The Signoria in office during September and October 1418 attempted to amend the results of that scrutiny, but their proposals were consistently rejected in the councils. Every speaker in the *pratiche* favored the measure, deploring the intransigence of the opposition and even suggesting that "those who are governed should abide by [the decisions of] the governors."[88] In January 1419, a new Signoria tried again to push a scrutiny provision through the recalcitrant assemblies, but with no more success than before. Modified versions of the original measure were sent to the councils in April, and again almost a year later (January 1420), but neither

[83] It did pass the Council of the *Popolo* but not that of the Commune; *LF*, 51, ff.125r–126v.

[84] Bartolomeo Valori: "et nunquam audivit dici quod omnes XXXVII, videlicet domini et collegia, sint uniti; et presumptio maxima esset siquis contradiceret"; and Bonciani, "quod inspiratio Jhesu Christi esse debet ut reformetur officia extrinseca"; *CP*, 43, ff.127r–127v, 29 Jan. 1417.

[85] *LF*, 51, ff.136r–139r, 29 March–4 Apr. 1417. On this occasion, too, counselors cautioned the Signoria about coercing the councils; *CP*, 43, f.145r, 5 Apr. 1417.

[86] *LF*, 51, ff.173r–175r, 12–21 Oct. 1417. The size of the majorities was impressive: 146–66 and 132–44; 173–37 and 144–27; 194–47 and 139–38.

[87] These complaints are recorded in certain *pratiche* held in 1420; the records of debates for the preceding two years are lost. See Giovanni Carducci's statement: "Memorant propter locutiones que fiunt in civitate de scrutinio celebrato in 1417 tempore epidemie in quo dicitur esse defectus et multi cives optimi non obtinuerunt"; *CP*, 44, f.41v, 5 Nov. 1420.

[88] Statements of Niccolò da Uzzano and Galileo Galilei; *ibid.*, f.221v. Several councilors described the provision as "iusta" and "sancta"; *ibid.*, ff.221v, 222v, 226r. The voting: *LF*, 51, ff.216v–226v.

threats nor cajolery could break down the resistance.[89] The motives of the dissidents are not clear, since no one spoke out against the scrutiny in these debates. The introduction of the principle of the *rimbotto* into territorial offices may have alienated some councilors who perhaps feared that they would be excluded from these magistracies by aristocrats.[90] Certainly, the key issue in the conflict, the most protracted dispute between the executive and the legislature in this regime's history, was access to its patronage. It crystallized the resentment of patricians, who felt that they were being deprived of their proper share of the spoils, and the fears of their social inferiors that they would be entirely excluded from civic offices.

The frustrations arising from the leadership's failure to enact this legislation reached a climax in 1420. Regularly each month of that year (the only exceptions were February, September, and October), the Signoria and the colleges approved a scrutiny provision, and the councils rejected it.[91] After each vote, members of the inner circle—Rinaldo degli Albizzi and Giovanni de' Medici, among others—would propose some variation in the provision to placate the councilors who had opposed the legislation. Speaking to the issue in a July *pratica*, Rinaldo degli Albizzi expressed his puzzlement and chagrin: everyone condemned the 1417 scrutiny, he said, but the votes to reform it could not be found.[92] In November, counselors were voicing their fears that civic unity would be jeopardized unless the crisis were resolved. Matteo Castellani and Rinaldo degli Albizzi spoke for a *pratica* that recommended the annulment of the 1417 scrutiny, but that scheme terrified Filippo Corsini, who believed that the burning of electoral pouches was tantamount to destroying the regime. Those who defended the 1417 scrutiny, Vieri Guadagni said, were falsifying the truth, "for it was held at an inopportune time, and its participants should be blamed for setting a bad precedent for the future." Guidetto Guidetti and Rinaldo Rondinelli raised the issue of legislative recalcitrance; it would be better to abandon the consultative process, the latter argued,

---

[89] *LF*, 51, ff.246r–249r, 260r–264r; 52, ff.21r–25r.

[90] Cf. the summaries of these provisions; *LF*, 51, ff.216v, 217r; and the letter sent by Antonio di Ser Michele to Forese Sacchetti, 25 Jan. 1419, *CRS*, 78 (*Badia*), 324, f.60r: "Qui si cerca di fare rimbocti ma per insino a ora non è vinto nel consiglio del Popolo, che più dì s'è ragunato per dicta cagione. Il modo del rimbocto è questo: che ci octinesse sia imborsato nello squittino del 1407 e in sul 1417 e in sul quello del septe, non obstante che altra volta avesse vinto il partito. . . ."

[91] *LF*, 52, ff.21r–25r, 33r, 35r–39r, 47v–49r, 68v–73r.

[92] *CP*, 44, ff.10r, 11r, 15v–18r, 20v. On those debates and particularly the role of lawyers, see Martines, *Lawyers and Statecraft*, 208–09.

if the advice of the citizens was ignored.[93] The Signoria then sent a proposal for a scrutiny to the Council of the *Popolo* which, after one rejection, approved the measure on 20 November. The Council of the Commune then surrendered, ending its three-year campaign of resistance; the final ratification came on 23 November.[94] In addition to authorizing a new scrutiny, to be completed by February 1421, this law also provided for a reconstitution (*rimbotto*) of the pouches; those obtaining majorities in the forthcoming election would also be included in the bags for earlier scrutinies.[95]

The rebuffs suffered by the leadership in fiscal and electoral policy were hardly conducive to the formulation and implementation of a dynamic foreign policy. So powerful were the civic pressures against "expenses and adventures"[96] that no one, not even Gino Capponi or Rinaldo Gianfigliazzi, dared to advocate any territorial acquisition or any intervention in peninsular politics. The impulse to take advantage of the power vacuum created by Ladislaus' death and the disintegration of the Papal States was dampened by a feeling, articulated by Antonio Alessandri, that Florentine "insolence" had so alienated her neighbors that they would never join her in a defensive alliance.[97] To avoid any suggestion of prepotence, the government rarely intervened in the disputes between nobles and *signori* that were so common in the anarchic conditions prevailing in central Italy. The regime was even hesitant to discipline one of its own subjects, Carlo Tarlati di Petramala, who had been accused of supporting Ladislaus' military offensive against the republic in 1409. When the issue was raised in a *pratica* of December 1416, Piero Baroncelli advised the Signoria to forget the matter. Any attempt to punish Carlo would strain relations with Florence's neighbors, "who would say that we are accustomed to war and cannot remain at peace." Other counselors agreed with Baroncelli that any attempt to confiscate Carlo's estates would be expensive and disruptive, and that the rewards were too small and uncertain to justify the enterprise.[98]

---

[93] *Ibid.*, ff.42v–43r, 44r–45r.

[94] *LF*, 52, ff.68r–73r. Three provisions had to be passed to hold this scrutiny: the first two suspended provisions of 1404 and 1407 that prohibited new legislation concerning scrutinies.

[95] *Prov.*, 110, ff.177r–180v; Rinuccini, *Ricordi*, lix.

[96] E.g., Piero Firenze, "prudentis est aufugere expensa et impresa"; Niccolò da Uzzano, "domini se abstineant a rebus novis"; Filippo Corsini, "nollet impresa vel expensa"; *CP*, 42, f.180v; 43, ff.8r, 83r.

[97] "Propter insolentiam nostram vilipendimur a vicinis nostris"; *CP*, 42, f.180v.

[98] *CP*, 43, f.121v, 10 Dec. 1416. For details of the case, *ibid.*, ff.120v–121r. Eighteen months later, Carlo was convicted of treason; *ACP*, 2672, ff.1r–2v, 2 July 1418.

To the chaotic situation in the Papal States, where every vestige of a political order had disappeared with Pope John XXIII's departure for the Council of Constance,[99] the regime responded by doing nothing. This mood of indifference was so pervasive that the Signoria did not once raise the issue of the Papal States in a *pratica*. Florentines showed little concern over the pope's difficulties at the council, to which the republic had not sent any official representatives. Only once, in July 1415, did counselors even discuss John's problems, and then only to concede that the republic was powerless to obtain his release from custody. Filippo Corsini and Antonio Alessandri, who had been strong supporters of the former pope, now agreed that Pope John's position was hopeless, and that Florentine efforts to help him might be counterproductive. "It is strange," Corsini admitted, "that we do nothing for Pope John's liberation, since he was a friend of the commune though he did have strange habits."[100] To justify the commune's inaction, Corsini pointed out that the pope had not supported the republic's efforts to acquire Pisa or to resist Ladislaus: "and much was done for him, both as pope and as friend." In October 1415, an embassy from the council visited Florence, asking the Signoria to send official representatives to the council, to participate in the great enterprise of ecclesiastical unity. For a community that had been so eager to end the schism eight years before, Florence's response to this invitation was very cool.[101] While expressing their pleasure over the council's achievements and reiterating their devotion to "Holy Mother Church," counselors were unanimous in opposing the despatch of an embassy to Constance. Even after the council's election of a pope, Martin V, the republic delayed several months before sending ambassadors to congratulate the new pontiff.

Florentine statesmen displayed no more concern over the deteriorating political situation in the Papal States than over the fate of their erstwhile ruler. With the exception of Bologna, whose status directly affected her interests,[102] the regime was unmoved by appeals

---

[99] See Partner, *Papal State*, 30–40; Jones, *Malatesta*, 144–57.

[100] *CP*, 43, ff.53r–53v. Guidetto Guidetti said that only the French king could help John; Bartolomeo Valori suggested that letters supporting the pope be sent to Venice and the emperor-elect, as well as to the king of France.

[101] *Ibid.*, ff.66v–69v, 2 Oct. 1415.

[102] Thus, Giovanni Morelli: "Visis quod Bononienses sunt conformes cum statu vestro et hec conformitas videtur quasi quedam unio et quod in vestris necessitatibus vobis pluries subvenerunt, et quod magis tristatus est hic populus ob mutationem status Bononie tempore ducis Mediolani quam Senensium aut aliorum"; *CP*, 43, f.85v, 10 March 1416. To protect Bologna, the republic did send ambassadors into the Apennines east and south of Bologna to settle the conflict between the

for help from former allies in the papal territory. Florentines responded negatively to a request from Perugia (January 1415) for an alliance that would strengthen her republican regime. For the Twelve, Francesco Canigiani spoke against a federation with Perugia, "since they are not strong, and a league would alienate the pope, and we would be involved in expenses and war."[103] When Bologna was threatened by the Malatesta in June 1415, the Florentine reaction was more positive, but nevertheless fell short of a commitment to send troops for her defense.[104] The republic's posture of non-involvement did not change after John XXIII was deposed, and the Papal States were without a temporal lord. Civic opinion was not sympathetic to an offer by the lord of Forlì to become a Florentine client, nor to proposals that the republic send troops to defend the newly established communal regime in Bologna.[105] In the spring of 1416 a Perugian embassy visited Florence to appeal for help against Braccio Fortebraccio, who was then embarking upon a campaign to carve out a state for himself in Umbria. Rinaldo Gianfigliazzi summarized the arguments for and against a Perugian alliance. The two communities had formerly been allies, he admitted, but the Perugini had also fought against Florence.[106] Though support might keep them out of the hands of an unfriendly power, it could also alienate Braccio, who had fought for the republic in the past. If Florence could forge a league of central Italian republics—Bologna, Perugia, Siena—then she would indeed be impregnable, Lorenzo Ridolfi calculated. But, from past experience, he did not believe that the Perugini could be trusted, and he was prepared to sacrifice them to Braccio, to remain in the latter's good graces. Both Ridolfi and Bartolomeo Valori alluded to another reason for opposing intervention in the Umbrian crisis: the *popolo's* determination to avoid any diplomatic move that might lead to war. Deprived of support from Florence or any other Italian state, the Perugini surrendered to Braccio in July 1416.[107] The fragmented state of Italian politics in these years lent some justification to this isolationist policy. The kingdom of Naples had again fallen into that chaos from which Ladislaus had temporarily rescued it. From the straits of Messina to the headwaters of the Tiber, there existed no

---

Malatesta and Braccio Fortebraccio; *SCMLC*, 6, ff.50v–53v, 68v–69r; *SCMC*, 29, ff.118r–120r; *SRRO*, 2, ff.26v–28v; Jones, *Malatesta*, 145–46.

[103] *CP*, 43, ff.6v–8r. See also the discussion in Oct. 1414; *CP*, 42, ff.179r–180v, and later when the argument cited against an alliance was that the Perugini "liberi non sunt sed ecclesie subditi"; *ibid.*, f.83v, 27 Feb. 1416.

[104] *CP*, 43, ff.34v–35r, 53v–54v, 56r.   [105] *Ibid.*, ff.83r, 84r–85v.

[106] *Ibid.*, ff.86r–86v, 13 Apr. 1416.   [107] Partner, *Papal State*, 36–37.

political force capable of threatening the republic's security.[108] Although the political order in northern Italy was more stable, its two main components—the Venetian republic and the Milanese state, ruled by Filippo Maria Visconti—displayed no interest in expanding their boundaries southward. The French monarchy might have been tempted to fill the vacuum in central and southern Italy, but it was preoccupied by foreign invasion and civil war. The emperor-elect Sigismund was deeply involved in conciliar politics and in a losing effort to preserve his Friuli lands from Venetian occupation. Officially and publicly, the regime continued to adhere to the principle enunciated by Alessandro Alessandri in 1415: "We have always done everything possible to conserve the Papal States, and we are disposed to continue that policy in the future.[109] In practice, however, the republic appeared to condone, or at least to tolerate, the breakdown of papal government; the leadership had become accustomed to chaos on its Apennine frontiers. So long as Florence (to paraphrase Filippo Corsini) continued to bask in divine favor, "so that we have nothing to fear from our enemies,"[110] that pragmatic strategy was workable. If, however, conditions were to change either in the peninsula or beyond the Alps, Florentines might have second thoughts about the wisdom of their diplomacy.

Only once in these peacetime years did the regime seriously consider a different policy. The occasion was a Venetian offer for a defensive alliance (June 1415) aimed at Sigismund, who, the Serenissima's envoys insisted, was planning to invade Italy. The ambassadors were very clear about the nature and immediacy of the German threat, and they warned the Florentines that Bologna would be particularly vulnerable to an invasion.[111] The responses of the counselors to the Venetian proposal was conditioned by their assessment of Sigismund's resources, and the likelihood of his crossing the Alps. A minority— Niccolò Barbadori, Doffo Spini, Giovanni Carducci, Rinaldo Gianfigliazzi—were inclined to consider the Venetian overture seriously. But Paolo Biliotti, who had never disguised his contempt for the Luxembourg dynasty—from Henry VII to Sigismund—insisted that the latter was penniless and did not represent a genuine danger to Flor-

---

[108] The conditions of the Papal States and the peninsula generally are graphically described by Partner, *Papal State*, 30–40; see too his article, "Florence and the Papacy," in *Flor. Studies*, 388–90. See also Jones, *Malatesta*, 149–52.

[109] *CP*, 43, f.66v, 2 Oct. 1415.   [110] *Ibid.*, f.121v, 10 Dec. 1416.

[111] See Piero Baroncelli's summary of their proposals; *CP*, 43, f.41v, 26 June. A Sienese embassy reported on the arrival of the Venetian diplomats; *Conc.*, 1887, no. 30, 10 June 1415.

ence or Italy.[112] While few citizens dismissed the emperor-elect as
casually as Biliotti did, the majority did not perceive the threat as immediate and compelling.[113] After two weeks of intensive debate, the
leadership decided to reject the Venetian offer, but to hold out the
prospect of participating in a larger federation that would include all
of the major Italian states.[114]

These debates reflect the somber, anxious mood that pervaded the
reggimento in the months after Ladislaus' death. There was no trace
of the ebullience that had characterized the debates of the 1407–1409
period; the Florentines had not yet recovered from the traumas of the
intervening years. The opinions expressed about Venice, and Florence's relations with the Serenissima, are particularly instructive in
this context. Francesco Machiavelli and Matteo Castellani did comment positively on the greatness of Venetian power, her long experience as a free republic, and the congruity of her institutions with Florence's.[115] Yet they were reluctant to ally Florence with Venice, whose
superior strength would establish her as the dominant partner in the
league, and whose impregnability would minimize her commitment to
Florentine security. The Venetians are so situated, Machiavelli argued,
that "if we were to contract an alliance with them, they would have
one-third of our citizens in their hands, and we would have to follow
their wishes and not ours." Rinaldo degli Albizzi concurred: "If any
power were to invade Italy, the Venetians are much better equipped
to defend themselves than are we; even if they were to lose Padua,
Verona, and the rest, they would never lose Venice itself."[116] Other
counselors recalled Venice's behavior in the past, when she had formed
an alliance with Florence and (so they alleged) had callously violated
her obligations. Firenze del Pancia cited the league contracted by
the two republics against Mastino della Scala in 1340, "when the Vene-

[112] *CP*, 43, ff.36v, 41v, 42r, 44r, 47r. The most positive assessment of Sigismund
was made by Nanni Unghero, who had lived in Hungary when the emperor-elect
was ruler of that kingdom: "Ut audit et audivit, magnanimus et munificus est; et
verba iam protulit: 'Germanus meus Cesar [Wenceslaus] non curavit nec curat de
meliori membro imperii; sed si vita michi comes est; ego multa faciam'; nominando
Pisas, quod civitatem illam in pristino statu ponere volebat aut vicarius imperii vel
aliter. . . ."

[113] The *popolo*'s hostility to alliances and war was cited by several counselors—
Andrea Peruzzi, Guidetto Guidetti, Piero Firenze, and Ugo della Stufa—as a reason
for rejecting the Venetian proposal; *ibid.*, ff.37v, 39r, 39v, 44r.

[114] *Ibid.*, ff.48v, 49v. Filippo Rinuccini commented: ". . . Non si fece: che sa-
remmo stati gran tempo in pace, avendolo fatta"; *Ricordi storici*, liii.

[115] *CP*, 43, ff.39r, 40r.   [116] *Ibid.*, f.44r.

tians made peace without our consent."[117] Antonio Mangioni focused on a more recent time, when the Florentines appealed to the Serenissima for support against Giangaleazzo Visconti. "They did not wish to give us any help," he said bitterly, "alleging their past expenses, and even after the loss of Bologna, they contributed nothing to our defense."[118] Venice had displayed no more concern for Florence's predicament when Ladislaus embarked upon his imperialist adventures. Not surprisingly in view of that record, the leadership concluded that in proposing an alliance against Sigismund the Venetians were motivated primarily by self-interest, and not by any larger concern for Florentine, or Italian, security.

The delayed visit of Pope Martin V to Italy, and his eighteen-month sojourn in Florence (February 1419–September 1420) did not alter the regime's foreign policy. Florentine statesmen viewed calmly the strife that convulsed every part of the papal territory, involving *signori* (Malatesta, Varani, Feltreschi, Orsini), clerics (the cardinals Stefaneschi and Isolani), and *condottieri* (Braccio, Sforza, Tartaglia) who fought each other for control of cities, fortresses, and rural populations. Though publicly the regime urged Martin V to return to Italy, and sent two embassies to Constance to hasten his departure,[119] some citizens may have secretly hoped that Martin would never cross the Alps, since he might disturb a situation advantageous to Florentine interests. As the pope's entourage moved into northern Italy in the early months of 1419, another Florentine embassy was sent to welcome him, even though one witness reported that many citizens were not eager to invite him to their city.[120] A detailed account of the papal entry into Florence (26 February 1419) has been left by two diarists, Paolo Petriboni and Bartolomeo del Corazza, who both stressed the ceremonial grandeur of the occasion. The priors went to the Porta San Gallo to greet the pope, Petriboni wrote, "accompanied by a great concourse of notable citizens who (one might say) constituted the flower

[117] *Ibid.*, f.39r. See also Paolo Carnesecchi's criticism of Venetian tactics; *ibid.*, f.37v.

[118] *Ibid.*, f.42r. On Venice's reaction to Ladislaus, the statements of Giovanni de' Medici and Antonio Fronte; *ibid.*, ff. 39r, 39v.

[119] *SCMLC*, 6, ff.78r–78v, 90r–92r; *SRRO*, 2, ff.47v–48r; *Commissioni*, 1, 291–309.

[120] The embassy was sent to Mantua on 7 Jan. 1419; *SCMLC*, 6, ff.95r–97r. See Neri di Gino Capponi's letter to Forese Sacchetti; *Ashb.*, 1843, II, no. 175: "Credo si darà in comessione che qui possa venire, che non so se sia bene, ma per quello io ne conosscha, a me non parrebbe per più ragioni metterlo drento, ma ssì in ogni altra nostra terra. E anche ci sono molti di questo parere; ma veduto quanto è stato proferto e quanto da più è disiderato, non ci è chi ardischa a negarlo."

of the city, all dressed in very elegant clothes, which was a magnificent sight."[121] This was only the first of many spectacles that the Florentines witnessed in subsequent months, as the pope left his quarters in Santa Maria Novella to visit churches and monasteries, to dedicate the cathedral, and, in one particularly grand ceremony, to bestow a golden rose upon the city. The citizens obviously enjoyed these occasions, for they flocked in large numbers to watch the processions and religious celebrations in which so many dignitaries participated. If any resented the drain on the treasury that resulted from the papal visit, they took pains to hide their annoyance.[122] Outwardly, the regime treated Martin with the respect that was due to the titular head of the Guelf party. Behind this facade of devotion, however, were profound disagreements that poisoned relations between the pope and his hosts.

Neither the pull of Guelf ideology, nor the material advantages that might accrue to Florentine bankers and clerics through papal patronage,[123] could move the regime to support Martin's efforts to regain control of the Papal States, almost totally governed by usurpers.[124] Since the *Consulte e Pratiche* records are missing for the first year of Martin's stay in Florence, there is no information about the papal requests for help from the church's erstwhile ally, nor of the debates that must have followed these appeals. But the rationale for Florentine policy was obviously based upon two considerations: the *popolo*'s resistance —so strong as to be tantamount to a veto—to any substantial expenditures, and the close friendship that had developed between the republic and Braccio, the most powerful of the pope's subjects. He had built a *signoria* in Umbria; from that base he was able to resist all challenges to his authority, and to move with impunity through the papal dominion, ravaging the countryside and extorting ransom from cities. Braccio did not violate Florentine territory in his campaigns; he remained loyal to the republic that paid him an annual subsidy.[125]

---

[121] *BNF, Conv. Sopp.*, C, 4, 895, f.101v. Cf. Bartolomeo del Corazza's account; *ASI*, 5th ser., XIV (1894), 256–57.

[122] The commune spent 1000 fl. to redecorate the papal quarters in S. Maria Novella; and gave 50 fl. each to 19 cardinals; Petriboni, f.99r; on the lavish gifts of wax and food, see Bartolomeo del Corazza, 258.

[123] See the lists of requests on behalf of Florentine clerics, in the instruction to the ambassadors sent to Martin V: *Commissioni*, I, 300–01. On the role of Florentine bankers in papal finances after 1419, see Holmes, *Flor. Studies*, 377–78.

[124] The story of that recovery, immensely complex in its detail, is well told by Partner, *Papal State*, ch. 2.

[125] See Averardo de' Medici's statement, "et Braccius magnus est dominus et strenuus capitaneus et nobis fidissimus"; *CP*, 43, f.188v, 16 Apr. 1418; also, on Braccio's contract of service to Florence, concluded in 1413 for a ten-year period,

By comparison with the enormous sums that had been spent on direct subventions to Alexander V and John XXIII, this outlay was a small price to pay for security. Braccio would be available to fight for the republic; he could even be used to intimidate neighbors—the *signore* of Lucca, for example—who were unfriendly to Florence.[126] Moreover, he was strong enough to prevent the emergence of any rival power in central Italy. But Florentine Guelfs could not admit publicly, or even to themselves, that they were supporting a policy inimical to papal interests; they rationalized their behavior by insisting that Braccio was a loyal servant of the pope who was fighting to recover his master's territory from "tyrants." The realities were publicized, however, in February 1420 when Braccio visited Florence to sign an agreement with Martin, that invested him as papal vicar in his lands and guaranteed him a large subsidy for maintaining an army in the papal service.[127] Crowds of urchins ran through the streets singing "*Papa Martino non vale un quattrino!*" Leonardo Bruni, then an official in the papal court, tried to appease the pope's anger by reminding him that the song was chanted by children, but Martin replied: "If the men had not agreed with it, the children would not have said it."[128]

Only once during the eighteen months of Martin's stay did the public facade of friendship crack to reveal the true feelings of the pope and his hosts. The occasion was a visit by a Bolognese embassy to Florence, requesting assistance for a newly created communal regime. Martin was seeking to reestablish his direct control over the Emilian city and was infuriated by the Signoria's reception of the envoys.[129] Placing the city under an interdict, he instructed the bishop (10 April 1420) to "notify all of the churches within Florence that they should neither celebrate mass nor ring their bells nor open their doors. . . ."[130]

---

see Partner, *op. cit.*, 47, n. 2. For references to money owed to Braccio, statements by Lorenzo Benvenuti and Piero Baroncelli; *CP*, 43, ff.97r, 102v.

[126] On Braccio's punitive campaign against Lucca, which was made possible by a Florentine safe-conduct through her territory, see Partner, *Papal State*, 47; *Carteggio di Paolo Guinigi*, 407–14, 434. Florence was accused of instigating Braccio's attack on Lucchese territory.

[127] Partner, *Papal State*, 62–63.

[128] The story in Bruni's *Commentarii*, *RRIISS*, xix, cols. 931–32, and repeated by Vespasiano in his life of Bruni; *Vite di uomini illustri del secolo XV*, 454–55. Additional details in the life of Bartolomeo Valori; *ASI*, 1st ser., iv, part 1 (1843), 263–65. Cavalcanti repeated the story, *Istorie fiorentine*, ii, ch. 21, and added this line to the song: "Braccio valente che vince ogni gente."

[129] Partner cites the references to this interdict in the papal sources; *Papal State*, 65–66. Cf. R. Trexler's notice of the affair in *Spiritual Power*, 166.

[130] Petriboni, *BNF*, *Conv. Sopp.*, C, 4, 895, f.101v.

In a large *pratica* convened on 10 April, counselors denounced the papal action, which they interpreted as an attack upon Florentine liberty.[131] "We are not subjects of the church, nor of anyone else," Rinaldo Gianfigliazzi proclaimed, and he encouraged the Signoria to follow a policy that would guarantee "that we live in freedom, and that neither the pope nor any cardinal should be the supreme lord in our city!" Never had he seen anything so outrageous as this papal affront to the Signoria, Manetto Scambrilla said; it was so inexplicable because Martin had received more honors from the republic than any other pope. Francesco Machiavelli likewise stressed the benefits the city had showered upon their visitor and, with some exaggeration, insisted that the reunification of the church had been due primarily to Florentine efforts. Though the rhetoric in this debate was often heated, the prevailing mood was conciliatory. The Bolognese envoys could not be expelled because, Niccolò Barbadori insisted, that would be tantamount to surrendering Florentine liberty. The ambassadors resolved that issue by voluntarily leaving the city on 14 April, but the reimposition of the interdict was still a possibility a week later when another *pratica* was convened.[132] Civic sentiment in this session was somewhat more moderate and pacific, but no speaker recommended that the Signoria capitulate to papal demands. By a process that has left no trace in the documents,[133] relations between the pope and the Florentines were sufficiently repaired so that the two could resume their public roles of benevolent father and obedient sons. Yet, though Martin continued to make amicable gestures toward his hosts until his departure for Rome in September, he never forgot the slights and humiliations that he had received at Florentine hands.[134]

As the pope and his court were making preparations for their journey to Rome, the citizens forgot their anger over the interdict and their amusement over Martin's impotence. Their main concern was to provide a magnificent setting for the papal departure, hoping perhaps to mollify the Colonna pope, whose fortunes had prospered in spite of their unwillingness to help him. Matteo Castellani recalled that Martin V had responded graciously to Florentine petitions for benefices; he

---

131 *CP*, 44, ff.3v–5v. Petriboni said that 200 citizens attended the *pratica*.

132 *CP*, 44, ff.7v–8v, 22 Apr. The interdict was apparently lifted on the 11th; Bartolomeo del Corazza, *ASI*, 5th ser., XIV, 269; Petriboni, f.101v. But the counselors on 22 April were very concerned about its reimposition.

133 The records of the *Consulte e Pratiche* are very thin for the spring and summer of 1420; *CP*, 44, *passim*. On the pope's relations with Bologna, which came under his rule in July, see Partner, *Papal State*, 66–67.

134 Bartolomeo del Corazza, 269–73; Giovanni Morelli's comment, "et andossene a Roma a dì 9 di Settembre et poco amico della Comunità"; *Delizie*, XIX, 43.

predicted that the republic would remain in the pope's good graces. Filippo Corsini was even more sanguine: "Never have we been in a more favorable situation with the church than we are now." Francesco Machiavelli commended Martin and his entourage for the "minimum of scandal" that had resulted from their stay.[135] Whatever reservations Florentines may have had about the pope's feelings, his residence had apparently dissipated their fears that the city would suffer from visits of the great. When, a year later (9 August 1421), a *pratica* was held to consider a plan to offer Florence as the site of the next church council, civic opinion was generally favorable, though some vestiges of the old anxieties persisted.[136] It would be necessary to guard against potential dangers, specifically, by limiting the size of the escorts that secular princes could bring into the city. It seemed to Alessandro Bencivenni that the council would promote the "honor and exaltation" of Florence and, furthermore, that it would benefit the city's ailing economy by stimulating trade and increasing gabelle revenues. Economic considerations were paramount in Guidetto Guidetti's mind: "Our city is exhausted and we should search for anything that would contribute to our advantage." Averardo de' Medici "sees that florins are the means by which we preserve our liberty . . . and so we should investigate every possibility for gaining those florins." Recalling how the city had prospered from Martin V's visit, Simone Tornabuoni argued that the economy desperately needed the stimulus that it would receive from a large convocation of clerics and laity.[137] Speaking in a *pratica* of 12 November, Vieri Guadagni said that never before in his experience had Florence's reputation been so great, nor the economy—and the condition of the citizens—so weak.[138] Some drastic measures would have to be taken, he insisted, to remedy the situation.

THE REGIME'S RECOVERY

The note of urgency in these debates signalled a decisive change in the civic mood, from the complacency of the postwar era to a more anxious feeling, in which awareness of the city's peaceful existence was mixed with vague fears of dangers that could not be clearly perceived and confronted.[139] Within the *reggimento* and in the community at

---

[135] *CP*, 44, ff.24r–24v, 26 and 27 Aug. 1420. The ceremonies for the papal departure are described by Bartolomeo del Corazza, 270–71.

[136] *CP*, 44, ff.114v–115r. Cf. Martines, *Lawyers and Statecraft*, 296–97.

[137] *CP*, 44, ff.128v–131r, 2 Oct.   [138] *Ibid.*, ff.144v–145r.

[139] Matteo Castellani reflected this mood in a *pratica* of 2 Oct. 1421: "Si consideramus pacem . . . et expensam parvam quam habemus, nova querere non debe-

large, there was strong sentiment for continuing the policy of détente, which minimized the risks of war and expense. Though not strongly represented in the *pratiche*, this viewpoint was consistently expressed in the legislative assemblies: in the negative votes cast against provisions for stimulating the economy, for strengthening the republic's defenses, for levying taxes to subsidize these enterprises. In 1421 the leadership began to pursue a more dynamic policy, in domestic as well as foreign affairs. In addition to promoting Florence as the site for a church council, the inner circle drafted legislation authorizing the purchase of Livorno, the construction of a galley fleet, and the support of local industry. Alarmed by events that seemed to threaten the peace of Italy, Florentine statesmen became more active in peninsular diplomacy, more preoccupied with the security of their dominion. This revival of civic energy was partly a response to events, partly a result of efforts by the leadership to recover its authority and prestige within the *reggimento*. Gregorio Dati alluded to these motivations when, arguing in favor of Livorno's acquisition, he said that its possession would dampen acquisitive impulses that might otherwise focus upon other targets. "Our citizens do not rest until they obtain their desires," he said, "and if they do not gain Livorno, they may do something worse. . . ."[140] Giovanni Cavalcanti also commented on this Florentine trait, most pronounced in the *reggimento*'s inner circle. "The great citizens are always eager for new enterprises," he wrote, "because they gain more wealth and a prolongation of life, in that they enjoy more fame and authority."[141]

The skein of motives influencing Florentine political behavior in these years is not easily unraveled. The thrusts of personal and civic aggrandizement were well hidden, rarely exposed in the *pratiche*, and then only in the guise of concern for the republic's honor and reputation. The interlocking issues of security and prosperity were most sharply defined (being the most fully comprehended). In the debates of 1421 and 1422, counselors expressed a persistent concern over the sluggish economy, that had not responded well to the stimuli of peace and lean budgets. Neither merchants nor artisans were earning a

---

mus et unde expensa veniat, sed etiam vidimus res omnes stabiles non esse, et prudentis est providere omnia que emergere possent"; *CP*, 44, f.128v.

[140] "Quod populus noster ortus in libertate si in omnibus eam concupiscit non obtinet, requiem non summit, et sic non habendo Liburnum, agit quilibet parvus sit"; *ibid.*, f.70r.

[141] "I grandissimi cittadini cercavano attizzare nuova impresa, perchè a loro era accrescimento di ricchezze e prolungamento di vita, in quanto gli ampliavano fama e grandigia"; *Istorie fiorentine*, I, ch. 11; Di Pino ed., 14.

decent livelihood, Rinaldo degli Albizzi complained in April 1421.[142] Business conditions did not improve significantly during the next eighteen months, if the negative appraisals by Salamone Strozzi and Paolo Carnesecchi (November 1421), Mariotto Baldovinetti (February 1422), and Palla Strozzi (September 1422) can be accepted as valid.[143] This worry was aggravated by events in northern Italy, where the young and ambitious lord of Milan, Filippo Maria Visconti, had launched an attack against Genoa. If the Ligurian port fell into Visconti hands, her commercial fleet—which carried a large part of Florence's overseas trade—would then be controlled by a potential adversary. Even more ominous was the prospect of Milan's possession of Livorno and Porto Pisano, which remained under Genoese control by the terms of the 1413 treaty. These strategic considerations weighed as heavily in Florentine calculations as did the prospects for improving her position as a maritime power.

The issues involved in the Livorno debate were sufficiently complex and controversial to bring out those analytical skills that Florentine statesmen had previously displayed in their arguments over foreign policy between 1410 and 1414, and that had rarely been exercised since then. Florentine eyes had intermittently focused upon Livorno ever since Pisa's conquest in 1406. The regime had sought to gain the port, first by conquest and then by negotiation, in the long and inconclusive war with Genoa (1411–1413). But the civic mood after Ladislaus' death dampened the acquisitive impulses that might have persisted in some Florentine minds. In June 1419, the Signoria sent an embassy to Tommaso Campofregoso, the Genoese doge and a friend of Florence,[144] with an offer to buy Livorno for 60,000 florins.[145] Genoa was then experiencing one of its periodic crises, with a pro-Florentine Guelf faction headed by the doge challenged by a coalition

---

[142] "Civitas disposita male est, cum nil lucratur per mercatores et artifices"; CP, 44, f.79v.

[143] Salamone Strozzi, "Utile est ut populus noster lucra suscipiat; nil lucrantur mercatores et artifices. . . . Subditi etiam ut apparet pauperes et male contenti [sunt]"; Carnesecchi, "civitas in pessima ordine est et nil lucratur"; Baldovinetti, "per artes nil fit ubi lucratur cum in pessimo statu sit"; Palla Strozzi, "civitas in malo ordine est"; CP, 44, ff.146v, 147r, 172v; 45, f.52v. For differing views, see above, 396.

[144] See the comments of Niccolò da Uzzano and Piero Beccanugi about the doge: "Nullum amiciorem habere possumus in civitate illa. . . . Attento quod hic a nobis servitia et emolumenta accepit, si a iustitia et via grata non recidet, benivolus nobis esse debet"; CP, 43, f.165r, 10 Jan. 1418.

[145] SRRO, 2, f.57v, 17 June 1419. The Genoese demanded more than 100,000 fl.; the Florentines made a counteroffer of 80,000; SCMC, 29, ff.119r–119v, 23 June.

of "Ghibelline" clans, which opposed Livorno's sale.[146] In the first
significant debate for which records survive (5 January 1421), political considerations—the instability of the Genoese regime and uncertainty about the doge's legal right to sell Livorno—were cited as
frequently as were economic and fiscal problems.[147] Palla Strozzi enu-
merated the benefits that would accrue to the republic from Livorno's
acquisition: her reputation enhanced, her revenues enlarged, Pisa's
security bolstered. Casting an anxious eye at the first signs of the
revival of Visconti power in Lombardy, Francesco Machiavelli argued
that Livorno's purchase would guarantee Florence's access to the sea.
Public opinion was apparently favorable to the scheme, although the
colleges did insist on guarantees that the transaction was legal.[148] Paolo
Biliotti thought that the purchase price—between 60,000 and 80,000
florins—was excessive and should be reduced by one-half.[149] An outlay
of 100,000 florins would not be too great, Agnolo Pandolfini said, if
the acquisition did not create any problems for the regime. But he
feared that the Genoese were so divided that Livorno's sale would
bring the anti-Florentine party into power, and thus increase the
risk of another war. Agnolo disputed Vieri Guadagni's contention that
Livorno was essential to Florentine security in the event that the Visconti conquered Genoa. He compared Filippo Maria's situation to that
of his father Giangaleazzo: "He does not have Siena nor Pisa nor
Bologna . . . and if he should obtain Genoa, he still could not move
against us." Eventually, he argued, the situation in Genoa would
deteriorate to a point where "we can have Livorno without expense
or danger."[150]

In these debates over Livorno, which continued through the end
of March, echoes of past controversies reverberated. The issues at
stake, and the arguments for and against the purchase, were developed with greater clarity than in any previous discussion on territorial
expansion. Avoiding polemics, several counselors mentioned the complexity of the issue, and the dangers they saw in either seizing or
rejecting the opportunity to have Livorno.[151] A coalition of mercantile

[146] Mallett, *Florentine Galleys*, 11. Piero Bonciani commented in Jan. 1421 that
"quasi civitas Janue derelicta est et in statu peximo"; *CP*, 44, f.51r.

[147] *CP*, 44, ff.51r–52r. There is no reference to Livorno in the protocols between
1415 and Apr. 1418; from that date until Apr. 1420, no records of debates survive.

[148] Messer Giovanni Bertaldi and Messer Carlo Federighi both mentioned the
popolo's approval; *ibid*., ff.52r, 54r.

[149] *Ibid*., f.51v. The Genoese had demanded as much as 160,000 fl.; Mallett, *Florentine Galleys*, 11.

[150] *CP*, 44, f.61r, 15 Feb.

[151] The statements of Forese Sacchetti, Filippo Corsini, Matteo Castellani, and
Giovanni de' Medici; *CP*, 44, ff.68r–69r, 13 March.

interests, whose spokesmen emphasized the commercial advantages, supported the acquisition.[152] They were joined by statesmen who viewed with growing alarm the efforts by Filippo Maria Visconti to occupy Genoa and thus gain a foothold on the Tyrrhenian Sea. If Visconti forces occupied Livorno, Niccolò da Uzzano warned, they could blockade Pisa and cut off Florence's access to its overseas markets. "We must consider two things: whether to accept Livorno if we can obtain it from the doge and the Genoese, and, second, whether the cost is worth the acquisition, in terms of Pisa's prosperity and security." Giovanni Guicciardini and Rinaldo degli Albizzi viewed Livorno as contributing to both Florentine honor and utility, "the two things for which we strive most in this world." Giuliano Davanzati and Agnolo Pandolfini led the opposition. Davanzati rejected the argument that the republic would be imperiled if Filippo Maria Visconti acquired Genoa and Livorno. "He is not as powerful as was his father, who possessed Vicenza, Padua, Verona, and other territory; if he were to attack us, we are ready and able to resist him, as we did his father."[153] Agnolo Pandolfini deprecated Livorno's value to Florence either commercially or militarily; the port was too easy to blockade, and it could not hold a large military force. Its acquisition would increase the likelihood of Florence's involvement in a war with Genoese exiles, who might recover their city from their Guelf rivals. Agnolo understood the dynamics of imperialism. "If we obtain Livorno," he argued, "then each will think that we are avidly seeking his territory." Precipitating the first war with Giangaleazzo, he recalled, was the republic's occupation of Montepulciano, which infuriated the Sienese. Similarly, Florentine appetites had been stimulated by the occupation of towns on her frontier—Pisa, Arezzo, Cortona—by her enemies. We have had much experience with wars and their burdens, he concluded, and we should avoid any gesture that would ignite the embers of conflict.[154]

Civic opinion gradually shifted toward approval of Livorno's acquisition, despite the forebodings of a dissident minority.[155] Elder statesmen like Antonio Alessandri and Matteo Castellani were enthusiastic promoters of the scheme, but others—Strozza Strozzi and Giovanni de' Medici, for example—were more reluctant to favor a policy so fraught with uncertainties. The head of the Medici bank was not impressed by arguments that Livorno was vital to Florentine interests, nor did he believe that the port could compete with Pisa as an *entre-*

[152] Among the strongest proponents of acquisition were Betto Rustichi, Niccolò Barbadori, Francesco Tornabuoni, and Giovanni Bucelli; *ibid.*, ff.62r–63r, 69v.
[153] *Ibid.*, ff.61v, 62v, 63r, 15 Feb.   [154] *Ibid.*, ff.68r–68v, 13 March.
[155] Giovanni Morelli wrote that Livorno's purchase "in Firenze fu da molti contradetto"; *Delizie*, XIX, 50.

pot. On the other hand, he noted that public sentiment favored its purchase, and that future dangers might be avoided if the town were incorporated into the dominion. He did feel that the price of 120,000 florins demanded by the Genoese was inflated; he urged the Signoria to consider Florentine honor, as well as cost, in their negotiations with the doge.[156] On 24 May, a provision authorizing the Signoria and the colleges to buy Livorno for that sum was first defeated, and then approved, in the Council of 200. Within three days, the bill had passed the other councils by narrow margins; its enactment inaugurated a new chapter in Florence's maritime history.[157] The provision authorized the appointment of syndics to negotiate for the purchase of Livorno and Porto Pisano, for a sum no larger than 100,000 florins. To finance this purchase, the Signoria was authorized to levy *prestanze* of 40,000 florins, and also to tap the reserve created to reduce the funded debt.[158]

Livorno's acquisition signaled the beginning of a campaign, unprecedented in its scope and intensity, to strengthen the Florentine economy by means of subsidy and supervision. The key piece of legislation was a provision approved on 13 December 1421, creating a new and powerful magistracy, the Sea Consuls. This office was designated to become the regime's agent for launching a commercial offensive that would enable the republic to compete with other maritime powers—Genoa, Venice, the kingdom of Aragon, Naples—for Mediterranean trade. The Sea Consuls were given broad authority to stimulate the economy, even to intervene in matters that had formerly been under the jurisdiction of the guilds.[159] But their specific mandate was to construct a galley fleet, modeled upon the Venetian system, that would end Florentine reliance upon foreign shipping and promote the interests of her merchants who, so the Signoria claimed, "are inferior to no others in their involvement in commerce throughout the world. . . ."[160] The establishment of this magistracy was never

[156] *CP*, 44, f.63v.

[157] *LF*, 52, ff.91r–93r. The votes: 128–61, 89–43, 157–71, 102–49. The debate in *CP*, 44, ff.72v–73r, 85v–86r.

[158] *Prov.*, 111, ff.31r–35r. A maximum of 50,000 fl. from the retirement fund was to be applied to the purchase price; the remaining 10,000 fl. was to be paid by crediting the doge, Tommaso Campofregoso, with 16,500 fl. in the *monte*. Cf. Molho, *Florentine Public Finances*, 145, n. 71.

[159] Michael Mallett has discussed this provision in his article, "The Sea Consuls of Florence in the Fifteenth Century," *Papers of the British School at Rome*, XXVII (1959), and his book, *Florentine Galleys*, 21–23.

[160] *SCMLC*, 7, ff.1r–3r, 13 June 1422. Not mentioned in this debate was the need to end Florence's reliance upon Genoese shipping for transporting wool from

debated in any *pratica*, but an apprehensive Signoria did ask for civic support (4 February 1422) to fund the galley project.[161] Unanimously and enthusiastically, the counselors urged the priors to continue the building program, since it would enhance the republic's reputation and benefit the citizenry.[162] Great enterprises are launched with difficulty, Paolo Carnesecchi observed, and they always require more money than was originally estimated. News of this enterprise, he reported proudly, had spread "throughout the world." With this fleet, Michele Pagnini believed, the Florentines could gain as much glory at sea as they had previously won on land through territorial acquisition. Both he and Francesco Machiavelli alluded to the fleet's importance for stimulating a weak economy.[163] Averardo de' Medici spoke to those citizens, in the *pratica* and in the city, who did not share his enthusiasm for the galleys. They should realize the benefits—in profits, fame, and honor—that would flow from the project. In a campaign to gain support for the fleet from an apathetic public, the Signoria organized a celebration on 24 March 1422, when the first galley sailed on its maiden voyage. When news reached Florence a year later (11 February 1423) that it had returned from Alexandria, the priors ordered the church bells to be rung, and proclaimed a holiday to commemorate the event.[164]

While the Florentine fleet was growing as fast as the shipbuilders at Pisa could construct the galleys, the regime was also promoting a mercantilist policy in the industrial sector, though with less tangible results. The law establishing the office of Sea Consuls had granted that magistracy wide authority over the whole economy, but it did not

---

England and the Low Countries. By the terms of the Livorno purchase, Florence agreed to ship merchandise from English and Flemish ports exclusively in Genoese ships; Bayley, *War and Society in Renaissance Florence*, 84. See Salamone Strozzi's comment: "Lana nutritur civitatem, populum et communitatem et ut tute veniant, omnia fienda sunt"; *CP*, 45, f.28r, 19 June 1422.

[161] The provision authorizing construction of the galleys provided specifically for a subsidy of 600 fl. for each galley from the funds of the Florentine Studio; Mallett, "Sea Consuls," *op. cit.*, 166. It did stipulate that *monte* revenues could also be spent on the fleet, if the Signoria and the colleges approved the expenditures; G. Müller, *Documenti sulle relazioni delle città toscane con l'Oriente cristiano fino all'anno MDXXXI* (Florence, 1879), 279.

[162] *CP*, 44, ff.172r–173r.

[163] Machiavelli: "Necessitas nos urget propter diminutionem civitatis ut augeatur"; Pagnini: "sicut in terris gloriosi sumus, sic in mari efficientur, necessaria quidem propter diminutionem civitatis et lucrorum defectum; et deficientibus lucros nova sunt querenda ut utilitas multorum sequatur"; *ibid.*, ff.172r–172v.

[164] Bartolomeo del Corazza, *ASI*, 5th ser., xiv, 277. On these galley voyages, see Mallett, *Florentine Galleys*, 35–39.

formulate specific guidelines for exercising that power. Initially pre-occupied with building the nucleus of a fleet, the consuls apparently did not devote much attention to the trades and métiers under guild control. In December 1422 the Signoria drafted, and the councils passed, a law that reflected official concern over the stagnant econ-omy.[165] The Sea Consuls were instructed to draw up an inventory of every craft and manufacture in Florentine territory, and to find out why they were not flourishing. The clear intent of this legislation was to marshal the state's resources to stimulate old industries, and also to encourage new ones. To protect these enterprises from foreign competition, the consuls were authorized "to prohibit the importation of any or all merchandise into this city and territory. . . ."[166] This mer-cantilist response to economic malaise was not limited to Florence; in Venice, for example, similar legislation had been enacted to protect native merchants from competition by foreign traders.[167]

We do not know enough about the Florentine economy in the 1420s, or indeed in subsequent decades, to hazard a judgment about the ef-fect of these policies upon the city's commercial and industrial enter-prises.[168] But the political achievement of those who had promoted this legislation was altogether remarkable. They had induced a parsimonious *reggimento*[169] to disgorge 100,000 florins for a small and undeveloped port and, furthermore, to accept a permanent charge on the treasury for a galley fleet. These successes in the economic sphere encouraged the statesmen most concerned about Florentine security to press for a more dynamic foreign policy and for a stronger military force. The deliberations over the state's role in the economy were a prelude to a more fundamental controversy between the advocates of preparedness and détente, between the spenders and the misers, be-tween the proponents of reform and the defenders of the status quo.

[165] In Sept. 1422, the Sixteen reported that the city was "in malo ordine" and that many trades were depressed; *CP*, 45, ff.52v, 53r.

[166] *Prov.*, 112, ff.245v–246v, printed in Molho, *Florentine Public Finances*, 127, n. 34.

[167] In Jan. 1422, Buonaccorso Pitti was sent to Venice to protest against these restrictions on Florentine merchants; *SCMLC*, 6, ff.136v–137r. Doge Tommaso Mocenigo warned the Venetians about Florence's challenge to their commercial prosperity; W. C. Hazlitt, *The Venetian Republic* (London, 1915), I, 840–43. On efforts to reduce the gabelles paid by Florentine merchants in Milanese territory, see *SCMLC*, 6, f.125r, 26 June 1421; *SRRO*, 2, f.89r, 13 Aug. 1421.

[168] For some opinions, see Becker, in *Flor. Studies*, 117, 127–29, and Molho, *Florentine Public Finances*, 128–30.

[169] Just before the approval of Livorno's purchase, the Council of 200 had re-jected a provision authorizing the despatch of a small contingent of lances to de-fend Città di Castello; *LF*, 52, f.88r, 14 Apr. 1421.

The Italian scene was, in 1421, more confused and unsettled than at any time since the 1380s. Florentine statesmen were beginning to realize that the chaos, which they had tolerated if not encouraged after Ladislaus' death, might become a nightmare for their city. No foreign power was yet able to take advantage of the power vacuum, but in the Papal States, in the kingdom of Naples, and above all in Lombardy, political realignments and crystallizations were threatening the *pax Italiana*.[170] The emergence of Filippo Maria Visconti as a dynamic force in peninsular politics coincided with Florence's ratification of a peace treaty with the Milanese despot in February 1420.[171] That agreement terminated a technical state of war that had existed between the two powers since 1400. Filippo Maria had already begun his campaign to recover territories lost after his father's death: Como, Vercelli, Cremona, Bergamo, Piacenza, Parma, Brescia. With pacifist sentiment so strong in the city, Florentine statesmen apparently viewed the peace treaty as the only feasible response to Visconti imperialism. The treaty established a demarcation line between Lombardy and central Italy, with the signatories promising to refrain from intervention in each other's zone of influence. The pact gave Filippo Maria freedom to continue his war with the Genoese, who could not legally be assisted by Florentine arms. On the other hand, the duke was barred from any involvement in Bologna, or any part of the Papal States. The republic sought to mediate between the Visconti ruler and his enemies in Genoa and along his southern frontier, where he was embroiled in quarrels with Niccolò d'Este, lord of Ferrara, and Pandolfo Malatesta. In the first Florentine embassy to visit Milan (October 1419), the ambassadors were instructed to greet the duke "as a very special and good friend" and to urge him to settle his disputes with his neighbors. In pursuing this peacemaking role, the Signoria was motivated (so its instructions read) "by divine commandments, as well as by the obligations of friendship and our traditions, since we are aware of the dangers that war brings, and the fruits and advantages of peace. . . ."[172] This cordial tone soon disappeared, however, in the diplomatic exchanges between the two states. Giuliano Davanzati

---

[170] On the situation in the Papal States, Partner, *Papal State*, 67–73; on Florentine anxiety about the Neapolitan kingdom, see *Commissioni*, II, 313–20.

[171] *Prov.*, 109, ff.182v–183r, 28–29 Nov. 1419. That provision had been rejected a month earlier; *LF*, 52, ff.10v–11r, 12v–13v. The debates on this peace treaty have not survived. The treaty was not signed until 8 Feb. 1420; Bayley, *War and Society*, 83. Its text is in *Commissioni*, II, 232–40; its key points are summarized in *Storia di Milano*, VI, 196–97.

[172] *SCMLC*, 6, ff.120v–123r, 30 Sept. 1419. An earlier embassy had been sent (June 1418) to Genoa and Milan; *ibid.*, ff.84r–85r.

and Astorre Gherardini Giani were sent to Milan two years later (July 1421) to warn Filippo Maria to desist from his attacks on Genoa and his machinations in the Lunigiana area, which violated (so the Signoria claimed) the 1420 treaty. In their instructions to the ambassadors, the priors took note of Florentine suspicions concerning the duke's objectives. If he continued to refuse the Florentine offer of mediation with Genoa, then he should be reminded that in the past the republic had frequently been invited by his enemies to join them in attacking the Visconti.[173]

Fears of a revived Visconti threat were first voiced in the *pratiche* early in 1421, when Livorno's acquisition was a burning issue. Palla Strozzi mentioned Filippo Maria's "appetite for conquest," and particularly his designs on Genoa; Rinaldo degli Albizzi said that he had always feared the duke, "who is young and eager to do great things." He was spending more money on arms than his father and, like Giangaleazzo, he was not unduly concerned about breaking his promises.[174] The greatest anxiety about ducal objectives were expressed by veterans of the wars with Giangaleazzo: Antonio Alessandri, Vieri Guadagni and Strozza Strozzi. The latter reminded his fellow-citizens that "the Visconti of Milan have always been our enemies and have pushed us to the extremity of peril."[175] Agnolo Pandolfini and Giovanni de' Medici tried to assuage these fears; they professed to see no Visconti threat to Bologna or to Florentine interests in central Italy.[176] In October 1421, the papal legate in Bologna asked the republic for troops to defend his shaky regime, which prompted speculation that Filippo Maria's agents were plotting a coup.[177] The news of Genoa's surrender to the ducal army (3 November) sent shock waves through the *reggimento*.[178] Forese Sacchetti interpreted that event as a clear sign of Filippo Maria's determination to conquer Italy: "That family has always been our enemy for they favored the Ghibelline party and we the Guelfs." Palla Strozzi agreed that Genoa's fall was a very serious matter; he feared that the duke's success would inspire him to emulate his father. Other counselors were worried about Pisa's security; they

[173] *Ibid.*, ff.123v–125r. For Filippo Maria's reply, *SRRO*, 2, ff.89r–92r. For instructions to an earlier Florentine embassy to Milan, *ibid.*, ff.108v–109r.

[174] *CP*, 44, ff.54r, 79v.

[175] *Ibid.*, ff.61v, 68v, 79v. Strozzi added that "putabat per ea qui iam audivit ducem Mediolani non multum vivere debuisse; nunc videt propter nostra demerita in vita preservatum esse. . . ."

[176] *Ibid.*, ff.68v, 80v. Speaking for the Merchants' Court, Luca da Filicaia did not view the Visconti as a serious threat; *ibid.*, f.110r.

[177] *Ibid.*, ff.133v–135r. Florence had no troops to spare for Bologna.

[178] *Ibid.*, ff.138r–140r.

cited the poor condition of the Florentine garrison and Filippo Maria's popularity among the Pisans. Criticizing the regime's failure to support the Genoese against the duke, Lorenzo Lenzi and Guidetto Guidetti warned their fellow-citizens that they would have to pay dearly for their liberty. "Many would like to spend after the fact, which is impossible," Lenzi said, and Guidetti repeated the cliché about the Florentines being so sluggish in reacting to danger. Justifying the regime's cautious policy, Sandro Altoviti argued that the fears expressed by these men were exaggerated. Paolo Carnesecchi was more outspoken in his criticism of those who "under a cloud of rhetoric seek to involve us in an alliance that will lead to war. . . ."

Two prospective allies, the papal legate in Bologna and the Venetian republic, had already made diplomatic overtures to the regime; the implications of these alliances were debated intensively in November 1421. Being the more threatening the Venetian league aroused the greatest concerns among the citizens, many of whom saw that connection as more dangerous than the peril it was designed to avert. In a *pratica* (12 November) convened to debate the issue, only Vieri Guadagni favored a Venetian alliance which, he argued, would guarantee that Florence would be immune to any Visconti assault.[179] Although several counselors expressed some sympathy for Guadagni's position, they were not willing to conclude a formal pact with the Venetians. Lorenzo Ridolfi repeated the arguments about Venetian duplicity and her overweening power, which would place Florence in the role of junior partner in any alliance. Averardo de' Medici minimized the danger of a Milanese assault; he believed that Filippo Maria was too preoccupied with domestic enemies, in Genoa and elsewhere in his dominion, to attack Florence. Giovanni Guicciardini estimated that the duke had only one-half of his father's resources and that, unlike Giangaleazzo, he possessed no foothold in Tuscany that could be used against Florence. Paolo Carnesecchi contended that the Venetian alliance would violate the peace treaty with Filippo Maria; he could not believe that anyone would favor that course, when the ink on the document was not yet dry. Civic opposition to an alliance with the papal legate was weaker, though still substantial.[180] Bartolomeo Valori and Simone da Filicaia cited evidence to support the theory that the duke was plotting to gain control of Bologna; Nic-

---

[179] *CP*, 44, ff.144v–147v. The Venetian alliance was proposed by the papal ambassador, Leonardo Dati, general of the Dominican order, but apparently with the Serenissima's consent; see the comments of Piero Bonciani and Guidetto Guidetti; *ibid.*, ff.144v, 146v.

[180] The debate on 21 and 22 Nov.; *ibid.*, ff.154r–159r.

colò del Bellaccio stressed that city's value to the republic and to Florentine merchants. They should not have signed a treaty with Filippo Maria, Vieri Guadagni said, since his objective was not peace but the opportunity to conquer Lombardy. Unless the course of Visconti aggression were not stopped at Bologna, he predicted that Florence would have to fight for survival against the tyrant. Two merchants (Giovanni Vettori and Piero Bonciani) and two lawyers (Giuliano Davanzati and Lorenzo Ridolfi) opposed the Bolognese league, arguing that it was both expensive and dangerous, and that the papal regime was not seriously menaced by the Visconti. The councils, however, voted for an alliance with the legate, stipulating that it had to be approved by Pope Martin V, and that it could not be directed against the republic's *condottiere*, Braccio Fortebraccio.[181]

These *pratiche* revealed sharp divisions over foreign policy within the *reggimento*. More openly than was customary, speakers referred to "the varieties of opinions" over these projected alliances; several also mentioned the reluctance of some counselors to voice their true judgments.[182] Several representatives of the old Guelf aristocracy— Rinaldo degli Albizzi, Palla and Salamone Strozzi, Vieri Guadagni, Michele Castellani, Ridolfo Peruzzi, Antonio Alessandri—supported a policy of containment; they were willing to risk war to keep the Visconti in check.[183] They were joined by merchants and professional men from less prominent families: Lorenzo Lenzi, Niccolò del Bellaccio, Alessandro Bencivenni, Lorenzo Barducci, Galileo Galilei, Agnolo della Casa, Cristofano di Giorgio. Michele Pagnini, from a small and obscure family in San Giovanni, was more hostile to the Visconti, and more willing to confront him directly, than his patrician neighbors.[184] These men all shared the conviction that the lord of Milan was bent upon Florence's destruction. Supporting a con-

---

[181] *Prov.*, 111, ff.194r–195r, 26–27 Nov. 1421. The votes: 148–73 and 115–54.

[182] See the statements of Lorenzo Ridolfi, Sandro Altoviti, and Galileo Galilei; *CP*, 44, ff.144v, 145v, 147v, and particularly the collegiate opinions voiced by Zanobi Arnolfi and Dino Gucci; *ibid.*, f.156r.

[183] For their views, *ibid.*, ff.139r, 139v, 145v, 155r, 158v, 159r, 177v. Antonio Alessandri expressed his grave concern over the Visconti threat to Bologna, where he was then staying, in a letter to Simone Strozzi, a member of the Signoria: "Simone mio, tu sai quanto lo stato di questa terra [Bologna] importa a chotesta terra [Florence], e che vegniendo questa terra a le mani del ducha di Milano, in che spese e pericholo ameterebe il nostro stato e la nostra libertà. . . . E per tanto abi a buono riguardo a lo stato di questa città"; *Strozz.*, 3rd ser., 132, no. 50, 2 Nov. 1421.

[184] Pagnini argued that if Florence had allied with Venice, she would have destroyed Filippo Maria's state and, earlier, would have prevented his occupation of Brescia, Cremona, Parma, and Genoa; *CP*, 44, f.177v, 2 March 1422.

tinuation of the policy of détente, on the other hand, was a coalition that included rich merchants (Averardo de' Medici, Paolo Carnesecchi, Giovanni Guicciardini, Schiatta Ridolfi), lawyers (Giuliano Davanzati, Lorenzo Ridolfi), statesmen (Agnolo Pandolfini, Sandro Altoviti) and a large group of artisans and small merchants who were more influenced by their sense of the city's economic difficulties than by strategic considerations. Though largely anonymous and inarticulate, these *popolani* did express their opinions in the councils, by voting against provisions to recruit troops and to raise money for military purposes.

The dilemma confronting this divided *reggimento* in the autumn of 1421 was neatly summarized by Lorenzo Ridolfi: "We have 145 lances and we want to govern the world." Those who, like Niccolò de' Nobili, were frightened by Filippo Maria's "power, character, and appetite" appealed to the citizenry to support a program of rearmament, to narrow the gap between Florence's meager force and the ducal army of several thousand soldiers.[185] The republic's defenses were in disarray; so too was the fisc. "For public and private affairs," Niccolò del Bellaccio announced, "order and structure are necessary!"[186] Capitalizing on the fears aroused by Genoa's surrender, the Signoria was able to secure approval of two provisions: to hire 500 foot soldiers, and to impose another forced loan.[187] But the efforts to improve the fiscal system by equalizing assessments and developing a rudimentary budget were consistently rejected in the councils. After two negative votes by the Council of the *Popolo*, a scheme designed to balance the military budget for a two-year period was abandoned by the Signoria.[188] That council also defeated a proposal to reform *prestanze* assessments,[189] the need for which had long been recognized by the

[185] Nobili's statement, *CP*, 44, f.150r. The estimate of the Visconti army by Lorenzo Ridolfi: "Dux Mediolani plurima equitum et peditum millia habet et de suis redditionibus solvit omnibus"; *ibid.*, f.144v.

[186] "Quod ad conservandum nedum publicum sed privatum, ordo forma et modus est necessarium"; *ibid.*, f.150v. Giuliano Davanzati concurred: "Quod satis patet si utile est honor et quasi necessarium ut cum ordine et forma vivatur"; *ibid.*

[187] *Prov.*, 111, ff.190r–192r; *LF*, 52, f.117r. Two weeks before (24 Oct.), the Council of the *Popolo* rejected two provisions to impose forced loans; *ibid.*, f.113r.

[188] Though precise details of the plan are not known, it did provide for the levy of a forced loan each year, and for monthly disbursements from the salt gabelle to pay for military expenses; *LF*, 52, ff.118v, 120r, 18 and 20 Nov. 1421. See the comments of Lorenzo Ridolfi: "Super ordinatione communis pro futuris duobus annis et unde omnia intelligantur, pratica habeatur"; *CP*, 44, f.149r. The Merchants' Court and the colleges all supported the scheme; *ibid.*, ff.151r, 152r.

[189] *LF*, 52, ff.118v–120r, 122v–123r, 18–20 Nov., 2 Dec. 1421.

leadership. A decade of wars and plagues had so altered the fortunes of the citizens, Paolo Rucellai and Forese Sacchetti had argued in July, that the creation of a new tax schedule should have the highest priority.[190] But this issue stimulated waves of anxiety in the community; each citizen feared that his neighbors, who might be chosen as assessors, would protect themselves by ruining him. Every plan devised to insure justice and equity was opposed by large blocs of councilors, who preferred known evils to the uncertainties of a new assessment.[191] Early in March 1422 the Signoria again tried to equalize the levies. After each defeat in the councils, the priors and their colleges revised the provision, first by increasing the number of citizens who could pay a reduced assessment *ad perdendum*, then by lowering the total amount of the levy.[192] After nine rejections in the councils, the measure was finally approved on 19 March 1422. It provided for a new schedule, valid for a five-year period, to be compiled by a nine-man commission (*novina*) whose members were instructed "to have concern for God, justice, and the conservation of the republic" in their labors.[193]

During the year 1421, Florentine politics had been partly revitalized by a combination of domestic and external stimuli, with significant consequences for the republic's diplomacy as well as for economic and fiscal policy. The program initiated to strengthen the regime continued into the next year, but with no greater unity of purpose than before. Though fears of the tyrant's ambitions had not abated, Florentine statesmen were puzzled by his strategy. So they tended to avoid any diplomatic or military initiative, but instead reacted to specific threats and provocations, real or imagined. They responded, for example, with consternation to the news (28 February 1422) that the duke had signed a non-aggression pact with the legate of Bologna. Speaking for the Twelve, Donato Barbadori advised the Signoria to convene a very large *pratica*, "since civic opinion is so divided, and unity is so necessary."[194] That assembly (2 March) confirmed the rift

---

[190] *CP*, 44, f.113v. Matteo Castellani made the same point: "Cum divites pauperibus et ex pauperibus divites facta sunt"; *ibid.*, f.135v, 12 Oct. 1421.

[191] On controversies over the assessments, see *CP*, 44, ff.110v–111r, 135v–137r; Brucker, *Renaissance Florence*, 143–44; Molho, *Florentine Public Finances*, 74–75.

[192] For these debates, *LF*, 52, ff.139r–146r, 4–19 March 1422. Cf. *CP*, 44, ff.180v, 182r, 184v. The provision to raise the minimum levy, from 1 to 2 fl., for those qualifying for a reduced payment *ad perdendum*, was eventually rejected by the councils.

[193] *Prov.*, III, ff.331v–334r. The votes: 152–76 and 110–53.

[194] *CP*, 44, f.176r.

between those who, like Francesco Tornabuoni, described their feelings of terror when they contemplated the duke's successes and others like Averardo de' Medici, who was quite sanguine about the regime's ability to defend itself.[195] "All citizens know," Lorenzo Lenzi said with some exaggeration, "that the duke of Milan is our enemy, determined to destroy our liberty." Lenzi favored the recruitment of 500 lances, which would cost 50,000 florins annually. Conceding that this was a large outlay, he nevertheless argued that if the duke were to conquer Florence, he would use their resources to dominate Italy. "We should spend for our liberty while we can," he said, adding that his own contribution would not be given freely, but only with the conviction that it was for his—and his city's—salvation.[196]

Those who shared Lenzi's views achieved the passage of legislation (7–8 April) that authorized the Signoria, with the consent of several collegiate groups, to increase the size of the Florentine army to 1000 lances and 1000 foot soldiers.[197] Though still concerned about Milanese pressure on Bologna, the leadership was even more worried about Visconti penetration into the Lunigiana district north of Sarzana, on the Genoese frontier. To shore up Florence's defenses in that hilly region, the Signoria hired the services of Tommaso Campofregoso, the former doge, and Giovanni Fieschi, who possessed estates and clients in the area.[198] The weakness of the republic's military position was most dramatically revealed by events in the south, where Braccio Fortebraccio had received the vicariate of Città di Castello from Pope Martin V, and launched a campaign to occupy the city. As Florence's most loyal allies in that part of Umbria, the Castellani naturally turned for help to their Tuscan friends. Rarely had the Florentines been placed in a more agonizing dilemma. Rinaldo degli Albizzi con-

---

[195] *Ibid.*, ff.177v–179r. Tornabuoni's statement: "Quod in numero eorum est qui non solum ligam factam cum cardinale Bononie per ducem Mediolani terrorem sumit, sed multa per eum tentata et facta; iuvenis hic est, potens in armis, nutritus et semper victoriosus in omnibus, et Januam acquisivit in parvo tempore quam pater in longo tempore habere non potuit et nostrum claudat Pisarum aditum"; *ibid.*, f.178v. Averardo de' Medici: "et immo non est demonstrandus pavor et terror"; *ibid.*, f.178r. Giovanni Cavalcanti described the Florentine reaction to the league; *Istorie fiorentine*, I, ch. 4.

[196] *CP*, 44, f.189r, 4 Apr. Others voicing similar views were Dino Gucci, Niccolò Niccoli and Niccolò Barbadori; *ibid.*, ff.178v, 179r, 189r.

[197] *Prov.*, 111, ff.2r–3r. The votes: 154–70 and 103–48. Later efforts to hire more troops were rebuffed; *CP*, 45, ff.11r–12v, 18r–20r.

[198] The provision authorizing these *accomandagie* in *Prov.*, 112, ff.26v–28r, 5–8 June 1422. The votes in *LF*, 52, ff.152v–154v. The debates on this controversial issue in *CP*, 45, ff.30r–30v, 32r.

ceded that the citizens of Città di Castello had legitimate claims on Florence, even though "there was no written obligation."[199] But the Signoria had no troops to spare for the Castellani. Counselors denounced the pope for betraying his loyal subjects, and criticized Braccio for his greed. But eventually the citizens accepted the sage if unpalatable counsel of Niccolò da Uzzano, who said that since they could not save the Castellani, they should make the most advantageous possible bargain with Braccio.[200] By the terms of a provision approved on 1 August, he was hired, with 1000 lances and 300 foot soldiers, for a two-year period, thus providing the republic with a substantial military force. This agreement sealed the fate of the Castellani, who surrendered to Braccio's army two months later.[201]

The regime's diplomatic responses to the Visconti threat were as vacillating as its program for rebuilding its military arm. In late April, ambassadors from Filippo Maria visited Florence to reaffirm the duke's friendship with the republic, and to deny any violation of the treaty.[202] Fearing that the envoys would become aware of the rifts within the *reggimento*, Giovanni Bertaldi advised the Signoria to dismiss the embassy forthwith.[203] In a disputatious *pratica* assembled to discuss Filippo Maria's overture, counselors could not agree about the duke's culpability, nor about the appropriate response to his moves.[204] Among those who placed the worst construction on his intentions were Francesco Viviani, Guaspare Accorambuoni, Bartolomeo Orlandini, Niccolò del Bellaccio, and the goldsmith Domenico Dei. Agnolo Pandolfini and Averardo de' Medici employed more conciliatory language in recommending that the Signoria treat the ambassadors with respect, and listen sympathetically to their presentation. "We should do everything in our power," Agnolo said, "to avoid war with the duke of Milan." Niccolò da Uzzano's views on foreign policy had become less bellicose than formerly; his comments on the Milanese embassy re-

---

[199] ". . . Devotio Castellanorum nota est, licet obligatio nulla per scripturam sit; tamen omnia nostra mandata et beneplacita adimplencia et pro nostra parte interveniret ut adherentes et nil contra nos unquam egerunt; per statum tamen sua habuisset ne aliunde possint potestatem eligere nisi hinc; et propter gratitudinem dolere de suis casibus debemus ultra quam de nostris"; CP, 45, f.35r, 9 July.

[200] *Ibid.*, f.40r. See the comments of Palla Strozzi, Stefano Buonaccorsi, Jacopo Vecchietti and Gregorio Dati; *ibid.*, ff.39r–40v.

[201] LF, 52, ff.162v–164v. Partner, *Papal State*, 73, stated that the Florentines helped Braccio to subdue Città di Castello.

[202] The ambassadors' arguments were summarized by Matteo Castellani and Alessandro Bencivenni; CP, 45, f.5v, 26 Apr.

[203] *Ibid.*, f.6r. Forese Sacchetti noted that "in consultis varietas est"; *ibid.*

[204] *Ibid.*, ff.5v–7r, 8v–10r; 26 Apr., 4 and 5 May. Cf. Cavalcanti's account of this *pratica*, I, ch. 7.

flected his moderate position. That Filippo Maria represented a threat to Florentine security could not be doubted by reasonable men; any sign of weakness or fear would incite the duke's ambition and increase the danger of hostilities. But Niccolò realized, too, that the Visconti prince might be provoked to fight by a display of Florentine arrogance. "Do not show either fear and timidity, or bravado," the old banker advised his fellow-citizens, "and by pursuing that route, we can have peace."[205] Whether dictated by necessity—a sense of their weakness and disunity[206]—or by the conviction that restraint was the best policy, the Florentine response was propitiatory but not obsequious. Florentine suspicions *had* been aroused by the duke's conquest of Genoa and his interventions in the Lunigiana and the Papal States. A genuine peace between the two communities could be achieved only if Filippo Maria would desist from these provocations, which violated the spirit if not the letter of their treaty.[207]

If, in sending an embassy to Florence, the duke's objective had been to immobilize the regime, his strategy was a brilliant success. Though the mission did not calm the fears of his bitterest foes, it had blunted their arguments and strengthened the position of moderates who sought to avoid war. Rinaldo degli Albizzi could arouse no enthusiasm for an alliance with Martin V;[208] few could see any advantage in a league with a weak and impecunious pope.[209] But when Giovanni Strozzi, a Florentine citizen in the service of the marquis of Mantua, visited the city with a proposal for a Venetian alliance, the response was quite favorable.[210] Rinaldo degli Albizzi and Palla Strozzi called for negotiations with the Serenissima; they were joined by Niccolò da Uzzano, Buonaccorso Pitti, Bartolomeo Valori, Averardo and Giovanni de' Medici, Francesco Machiavelli, and Gregorio Dati. Niccolò's

[205] *CP*, 45, f.6v.

[206] Alessandro Bencivenni noted that Florence was not prepared for war: "nec in ordine sumus"; *ibid.*, f.5v. Agnolo Pandolfini, however, stressed the republic's military strength: "Et talis est potentia et reputatio nostra quod apti sumus ad exterminium suum non minus quam ipse ad nostrum"; *ibid.*, f.6v.

[207] The response summarized by Lorenzo Ridolfi and Rinaldo degli Albizzi; *ibid.*, f.10r, 5 May. Cf. Cavalcanti, *Istorie fiorentine*, I, ch. 9.

[208] *CP*, 45, ff.13r–13v, 15 May. Only Giovanni Guicciardini and Salamone Strozzi supported Rinaldo's position.

[209] Manetto Scambrilla commented that "fides minima haberi potest in papa et legato Bononie"; *CP*, 45, f.19v. See also the statements of Agnolo Pandolfini; *CP*, 44, f.183v; 45, f.14r.

[210] *CP*, 45, ff.23v–25v, 3 June. On the next day, the colleges, "quasi omnes unite," expressed their approval of the alliance; *ibid.*, f.26r. Only Paolo Carnesecchi opposed the league: "Ligari velle non debemus cum sumus liberi et salvi et status civium in pecuniis debilis est"; *ibid.*, f.23v.

advocacy of the alliance was characteristically lucid and forceful. If Florentines did not have legitimate anxieties about Visconti aggression, he said, they would not join any league. But their experience with Giangaleazzo and Ladislaus has taught them about princes and their avarice. From Genoa come reports that the duke was intent upon war; he probes constantly for vulnerable spots in central Italy: in the Papal States, in Lunigiana, in Lucca and Siena. The Venetians are powerful, with an army of 1000 lances that would be employed in our defense if the duke were to attack us. But Niccolò did not believe that he would be so foolhardy; he considered the alliance a solid guarantee of peace and Florentine security. This surge of interest in, and support for, a Venetian entente did not lead to concrete results, possibly because the doge and the Senate had not formally approved the Mantuan initiative. Except for indicating a shift in Florentine attitudes toward her Adriatic neighbors, the debate had no practical significance.[211] The sole agreement concluded by the republic in the summer of 1422 was a defensive alliance with the lord of Lucca, Paolo Guinigi, whose state was particularly vulnerable to Visconti pressure in northwestern Tuscany. The enabling provision was approved on 22 August after several rejections, and only after the Signoria's authority to conclude the pact was narrowly restricted.[212] Some citizens were as suspicious of their leaders as of Filippo Maria Visconti.

By summer's end, the republic had strengthened her military force by her pact with Braccio, and had taken some tentative steps to recruit allies against the duke. Filippo Maria may have been deterred by these measures, at least temporarily, or he may have been waiting for a more favorable moment to renew his offensive. For whatever reason, the tensions between the two states slackened abruptly, giving hope to some Florentines that war was not inevitable. Between August 1422

[211] There is no record of any embassy sent to Venice, although historians of Venice have stated that the Florentines urged the Serenissima to federate with them and were rebuffed. The rejection was the occasion of Tommaso Mocenigo's famous oration in the spring of 1423; W. C. Hazlitt, *Venetian Republic*, 1, 839–46.
[212] *Prov.*, 112, ff.93v–94v, 26 Aug. On the voting, *LF*, 52, ff.165r–170v, 12–26 Aug. Some opposition to this alliance was ideological, e.g., Salamone Strozzi: "Quod congruum dici non potest, quod dominus Lucanus semper fuit inimicus quia ghibellinus et sic hortatus est et operam dedit et semper nostris inimicis adhibuit"; *CP*, 45, f.50v. Niccolò da Uzzano favored the league: "Dominus Lucanus non fuit conformes nostris voluntatibus et sic apparet, non tamen totaliter ad nostras offensas venit. Et licet cum rege Ladislao querit, non tamen offendit. Alii tamen nostri vicini offenderant. Et facilius est veniam dare non offendentibus quam offendentibus. Et si nunc veniret ad ea que alia non consensit, non est mirandum. Omnes querunt adherire potentioribus. . . ."

and May 1423 the leadership had an opportunity to scrutinize the political order and to consider how it might be strengthened in the event that war did come.

On the surface, the regime had never been more stable. No cases of treason or sedition were prosecuted in the criminal courts since Sandro da Quarata's execution in 1415. The communities of exiles in Bologna and Modena were too weak and disorganized to threaten the republic.[213] The miseries of the subject populations in the territory did not ignite rebellions.[214] The cancellation of bans against outlaws who had been convicted of political crimes was an indication of the regime's confidence; even some of the Alberti were thought to merit rehabilitation.[215] There were no serious challenges to the regime from outside, but within its ranks criticism grew more intense. Jacopo Vecchietti deplored the exclusion from territorial offices of those citizens who had been too young to qualify a decade before, when the last scrutiny was held. "If they cannot be integrated into the regime now," he said, "they will never have another opportunity."[216] But these arguments on behalf of a young patrician generation did not persuade the rank and file, nor did warnings that new scrutinies were necessary to preserve civic unity. This battle between the executive and the legislative councils began on 9 July, with the rejection by the Council of the *Popolo* of a law authorizing scrutinies for all territorial offices. The measure did not pass after four more ballots that month, five in October, seven in November and December. A new Signoria waited until the end of January 1423 to launch another unsuccessful effort to pass this legislation.[217]

[213] There were rumors in 1417 of plots by exiles, but they did not materialize; *SCMLC*, 6, ff.76r–76v; *SCMC*, 29, f.105r.

[214] The one significant case of violence in the dominion was touched off by the murder of the count of Moncione, a Florentine subject, in May 1421; see Martines, *Lawyers and Statecraft*, 155–61; also *AEOG*, 1966, ff.48r–51r, 4 Aug. 1421. For details of an abortive plot to seize the fortress at Prato in June 1422, see *Prov.*, 116, ff.83r–83v.

[215] Beneficiaries of these cancellations were Simone di Messer Bindo Altoviti, Michele di Messer Lapo da Castiglionchio, Valorino Valorini, and Bernardo di Giovanni Strozzi; *Prov.*, 108, ff.221r–222r; 111, ff.124v–125r; 112, ff.32r–33r, 46v–49r. An unsuccessful attempt to cancel the bans against Antonio Alberti and his brothers is described by Paolo Petriboni; *BNF, Conv. Sopp.*, c, 4, 895, f.105r, Dec. 1421.

[216] *CP*, 45, f.54r, 23 Sept. 1422. See also the statements of Giovanni Barbadori, Fruosino da Verrazzano and Giuliano Davanzati; *ibid.*, ff.33r–33v, 81r. Vecchietti was suggesting that for some territorial offices, no scrutiny had been held since 1407.

[217] *LF*, 52, ff.159v–162r, 175v–179r, 188r–193r.

By emphasizing so strongly the civic benefits of electoral reform, its proponents implied (although they did not state openly) that the opposition was motivated by selfishness. The critics of the *prestanze* assessments were not so reticent; they announced publicly that the new levy was the most unjust in the regime's history. And the flaws were the result, not of ignorance or incompetence, but greed and malice. The most prominent figures in the *reggimento*—Rinaldo degli Albizzi, Lorenzo Ridolfi, Bartolomeo Valori, Salamone and Palla Strozzi, Bartolomeo and Giotto Peruzzi, Francesco Machiavelli, Niccolò del Bellaccio—deplored the "secret plots and machinations" which had created this travesty of an assessment.[218] The remedy was the *catasto*, first proposed by Rinaldo degli Albizzi in a *pratica* convened on 6 August 1422.[219] Only by scrutinizing lists of every citizen's possessions—real estate, *monte* credits, business investments—could equity be restored to the fisc. "Let us make a *catasto*!" Francesco Machiavelli cried. Alessandro Bencivenni concurred, noting that it was the only way to achieve fiscal justice, "without which no regime can survive." If these inequities were not eliminated, Francesco Tornabuoni warned, the republic would not be able to raise money for the emergencies that the future might bring. The *catasto*, Jacopo Gianfigliazzi believed, would achieve unity, "so that citizens would tend to their affairs, conventicles would dissolve, and money would always be on hand. . . ." No other *prestanza* assessment had stimulated so much dissension, Giotto Peruzzi observed in recommending its annulment. "The *catasto* should be established by citizens elected for that purpose, as the Venetians do." Salamone Strozzi sketched an image of a stricken community whose citizens had been forced to flee abroad, and whose revenues were consequently depleted by the loss of income from gabelles. Lorenzo Lenzi could see no merit in the current assessment; he suggested that the records of that levy be burned, "and that the tree and its evil fruit be completely destroyed. . . ."[220]

---

[218] Rinaldo degli Albizzi stated that the *novina* assessments had been influenced by "amicitias et parentelas"; Francesco Machiavelli, "in vexillo suo multe sunt inequalitates . . . quia in eo sunt cives qui eque et bene vivere nolunt"; *CP*, 45, f.43v. Giovanni Cherichini, "per conventicula videt ad impositionem deventum esse"; *ibid.*, f.44v. Neri Capponi: "Qui fognas posuerunt aut conventicula fecerunt, corrigendi sunt"; *ibid.*, f.45v. See too the comments of Bartolomeo Peruzzi and Lorenzo Ridolfi; *ibid.*, f.49r, 8 Aug.; and above, ch. 5, n. 342. Alamanno di Luigi Mannini identified and excoriated the *novina* officials who had calculated his assessment; *BNF*, II, IV, 380, pp. 445-46.

[219] *CP*, 45, f.43v.

[220] Several counselors, in the regime's inner circle and on its fringes, complained about their excessive levies: Taddeo dell'Antella, Jacopo di Piero Baroncelli,

So massive was the antipathy to the *novina*, and so universal the clamor for a *catasto*, that several counselors argued for its immediate adoption, as an implementation of the civic will. Francesco Machiavelli claimed that citizens "of every condition" had approved the *catasto* and that "the voice of the *popolo* is the voice of God."[221] During the second day's debate, however, serious objections were raised to the scheme. Though supporting it in principle, "because he sees that the rich favor its adoption," Averardo de' Medici recognized that it could not be implemented for two years, and that some interim system would have to be employed until the property inventories had been filed and evaluated.[222] But not every wealthy Florentine approved of the *catasto*. A rich banker from Santo Spirito, Niccolò Barbadori, argued that it would ruin the poor and, furthermore, that it would have an adverse effect upon business by restricting the supply of credit. Giovanni Minerbetti also predicted that money would flow from the city and thus limit the amount of capital available for investment in commercial and industrial enterprises.[223] Enthusiasm for a *catasto* waned as citizens realized that its adoption would not be a quick panacea for fiscal abuses, but its proponents continued to argue for that reform. Fiscal inequity was the most pernicious evil in any political order, Francesco Machiavelli said, because it ruined widows and orphans and fomented hostility between father and son, and between brothers. "Let us not say that we cannot emulate the Venetians," he cried, "for we are men and we can and ought to live and govern

---

Giuliano Ginori, Bernardo Manetti, Niccolò Barbadori; *CP*, 45, ff.43v, 45r, 46v. See the comments on this debate in the diary of Alamanno Mannini; *BNF*, II, IV, 380, pp. 446–47.

221 *Ibid.*, f.46r. Others who argued that the judgment of that *pratica* could not be ignored were Bartolomeo Corbinelli, Salvestro Ceffini, Agnolo Pandolfini, Niccolò Serragli, Dino Gucci and Giovanni Salviati; *ibid.*, ff.46r–46v, 47v–48r.

222 *Ibid.*, f.48r. "Pro futuro laudaret catastum quin videt divites illum petere; et ipse etiam possessiones et Montem habet; et de pecunia numerata faciliter potest provideri; nam non est octava pars substantie. . . . Veneti sic agunt et per annos DCCCC regent; et ut ipsi agunt et nos facere debemus, nec debemus cum dedecus reputare ab ipsis notitia. Et infra duos annos erit facile fieri."

223 Barbadori: "De possessionibus et pecunia montis fieri potest, et si fiet possessiones urbis etiam, nec equitas ulla esse potest ad eum qui habet possessiones et qui pecuniam. Et sine credito agere non possumus, et guerras passi sumus maximas et longo tempore. Et exercicia terram nostram salvaverunt, et nunc in partibus orientis et cum nostra pecunia agere non possemus. Ipse his ad nichilum venit et cum credito lucratus est; et si fit catastus, exercicia diminuntur et destructio civitatis. . . . Pauperes destructi essent ex catastu et non divites." Minerbetti: "Et civitas nostra cum exercitio gubernetur et si fit catastum, habentes pecunias numeratas ex civitate portaverunt et sic exercitia minuentur"; *ibid.*, f.46v.

ourselves as they do!"[224] A week after Machiavelli's appeal (30 September), the first provision to "establish a *catasto* in the city of Florence" was rejected by the Council of the *Popolo*, as was a companion measure to reform the assessment of the *prestanzone*. After a second attempt failed the next day, the Signoria concluded that legislative resistance was then too strong to be overcome. Nor did the leadership succeed in gaining approval for more modest efforts to provide some relief for individuals whose assessments were unconscionably high.[225]

In a debate (18 December 1422) over the refusal by the Council of the *Popolo* to approve a levy of two forced loans based upon the discredited *novina*, a lower guildsman named Bartolomeo Angelini made a patriotic appeal for the enactment of that measure. He warned his colleagues that by refusing to raise money for defense they were encouraging their enemies to attack the republic, and thus would incur a much heavier expense.[226] That judgment would certainly have been corroborated by Rinaldo degli Albizzi and his confederates, who had so often raised the alarm about Filippo Maria's imperialist goals. But Rinaldo also realized that neither eloquence nor logic would convince a citizenry so distrustful of the leadership and so reluctant to tap their money chests unless the threat to the republic was immediate.[227] Throughout the winter and early spring of 1422–1423, Florentine statesmen watched their northern borders for signs of Visconti aggression. In December, the focus of concern was the Lunigiana; by February it had shifted to the Romagna and, specifically, the possibility of a Milanese attack on Forlì, then governed by the widowed Lucrezia Alidosi for her young son, Teobaldo Ordelaffi.[228] Forlì was weak and vulnerable, and so an ideal target for Visconti intrigues. Florentine of-

---

[224] *Ibid.*, f.55v, 24 Sept. Machiavelli argued that unjust taxation stimulated more discontent than did inequities in the distribution of offices.

[225] *LF*, 52, ff.173v, 174v. The rejection of provisions authorizing *sgravamenti*, in *ibid.*, ff.170r, 177v, 202v, 203r. For the leadership's reaction to these rebuffs, *CP*, 45, ff.69v–70r, 74v–75r, 18 Dec. 1422, 14 Jan. 1423.

[226] About his own condition, Angelini, a seller of leather scraps (*pezzaio*), said: "Tenuis sibi est substantie et onus leve portare potest, sed maiores sui onera grava supportaverunt"; *CP*, 45, f.69v, 18 Dec. Everyone who spoke in that *pratica* said that he had voted for the measure except Jacopo di Piero Baroncelli, "quia tam enormiter est gravatus ipse et frater. . . ." For the votes, *LF*, 52, f.198v, 21 Dec.

[227] A provision authorizing the hiring of 333 lances and 1000 infantry was approved by the councils with difficulty, even though it reduced the maximum size of the army; *Prov.*, 113, ff.1r–2v, 8–10 Apr. 1423; *LF*, 52, ff.214r–216v.

[228] *CP*, 45, ff.65r, 79r, 83v, 91r–91v; Partner, *Papal State*, 76–77. See Simone Strozzi's report of his embassy to Imola and Forlì (March 1423); *SRRO*, 2, ff.111v–113v.

ficials were particularly concerned about Visconti penetration into the Romagna, since the republic's ally, Braccio, was then preoccupied with his possessions in Umbria and the Marches. Florence could expect no help from Martin V, who indeed encouraged the duke to meddle in the Romagna; her efforts to revive Venetian interest in an alliance were unsuccessful.[229] Some citizens were so reluctant to avoid any provocative gesture that they counseled the Signoria to postpone the launching of a galley fleet to Provence and Catalonia, because the Genoese had threatened to sink the ships. But Niccolò da Uzzano and Giovanni de' Medici argued that to abandon these voyages would bring ridicule and ignominy to the republic.[230]

WAR

A rebellion of Visconti sympathizers in Forlì (14 May 1423) provided the duke's enemies in Florence with concrete evidence of his violation of the 1420 treaty.[231] On two successive days, 17 and 18 May, the regime's leadership discussed the appropriate response to this provocation. In several respects, the debate followed predictable patterns. There were the customary harangues about liberty and freedom, and calls for sacrifices to secure that precious heritage and to preserve it for future generations. The duke was excoriated as a faithless tyrant whose actions proved that Visconti leopards never changed their spots.[232] Those who had depicted Filippo Maria as a dangerous foe criticized the regime's flaccid response to his previous aggressions. If Florence had not made peace with the tyrant, Vieri Guadagni said, then he would not have become so powerful. Particularly disturbing, in Bartolomeo Orlandini's view, was the effect of the Forlì affair upon Florence's reputation, "which used to be the highest in Italy."[233] Few believed, however, that this crisis was comparable to those of 1402 and 1414, or that war was inevitable; a solid majority supported a cautious and temperate response to Visconti intervention in Romagna. They reasoned, first, that Filippo Maria was not the menace to Florentine security that his father had been, and that his aggression could be

[229] Partner, *Papal State*, 76–77; *CP*, 45, ff.93v–94r. Rinaldo degli Albizzi's mission to Venice in March; *Commissioni*, I, 384–98.

[230] *CP*, 45, ff.99r–101v, 9 Apr.

[231] Partner, *Papal State*, 77; Bayley, *War and Society*, 85. The events are described by Cavalcanti, *Istorie fiorentine*, I, ch. 3–5. For a summary of ducal strategy and objectives, in the context of peninsular politics, see *Storia di Milano*, VI, 202ff.

[232] Michele Castellani, Alessandro Bencivenni, Niccolò da Uzzano, Guaspare Accorambuoni, Niccolò del Bellaccio; *CP*, 45, ff.120v–121v, 125r.

[233] *Ibid.*, ff.120v, 125r.

more easily contained.[234] Another potent argument for restraint was
the sluggish economy and the notorious reluctance of the citizenry to
spend money on soldiers.[235] Francesco Tornabuoni believed that
Filippo Maria was a future—but not a present—threat; the *popolo*
should be apprehensive, but not terrified, of the tyrant.[236] The representatives of the *popolo* in the councils were sufficiently worried to
vote for the creation of a war *balìa* (21–23 May) with a six-month
tenure of office, to organize the republic's defenses.[237] The establishment of that magistracy was construed by the leadership not as a
belligerent gesture but rather as a warning to the duke. Heretofore,
Rinaldo degli Albizzi noted, Florentines have not responded to his
provocations. Now he will realize that they are determined to resist
him; knowing that his own subjects are discontented, he will abandon
his plans for aggrandizement.[238]

This limited response to the duke's occupation of Forlì was dictated
by necessity: the regime was not strong enough to send a military
expedition into Romagna immediately, nor did it yet enjoy enough
civic support to wage war openly. The *balìa*'s first priority was the
recruitment of troops and the strengthening of the garrisons of Florence's Apennine frontier and in the Livorno-Pisa-Sarzana region.[239]
Braccio was so preoccupied with his affairs in the Marches that he refused to come north to help his Florentine ally, so the republic hired
Pandolfo Malatesta, with 500 lances. On the diplomatic front, Florentine ambassadors made the rounds of the republic's clients among the
Apennine nobility, and negotiated a defensive alliance with the new

[234] Rinaldo Rondinelli believed that Filippo Maria was more dangerous than his
father; *ibid.*, f.126r; those favoring a policy of restraint were Neri Capponi, Dino
Gucci, Bartolomeo Valori; *ibid.*, ff.120v, 122v, 126r. Cavalcanti identified the leaders
of the "peace party" as Agnolo Pandolfini, Giovanni de' Medici and Simone da
Filicaia; *Istorie fiorentine*, II, ch. 5.

[235] Guaspare Accorambuoni's comments on the economy: "Nemo vellet guerram
vel expensam cum lucra non fecerit populus. . . . Mercatores pecuniis extenuati
sunt et nil lucrantur"; *CP*, 45, ff.121r, 138v. Giovanni Bertaldi would have liked
to attack the Visconti state "sed non videns civitatem nostram aptam"; *ibid.*, f.125r.
On the necessity for popular support for the war, see Giovanni Capponi's statement, *ibid.*, f.116r.

[236] "Temperate incedere ut populus noster terreatur utilius est quam eum expa-
vescere"; *ibid.*, f.122v.

[237] *Prov.*, 113, ff.30r–31v, printed in *ASI*, 4th ser., XI (1883), 23–24. The *balìa* was
strongly supported in the *pratica* of 20 May; *CP*, 45, f.123v.

[238] *CP*, 45, f.124v, printed in *Commissioni*, I, 442.

[239] Details in Palla Strozzi's diary of his service in the war *balìa*; *ASI*, 4th ser.,
XII (1883), 25–48. The Ten had heard that the duke was plotting a revolt in Pisa;
ibid., 28.

legate of Bologna, Giovanni Condulmer (later Pope Eugenius IV), in September.[240] A Milanese embassy came to Florence in July, proclaiming the duke's sincere desire for peace. The Sixteen advised the Signoria to divulge their message to an assembly of citizens, "so that a unified *popolo* will become more fervent, and more willing to pay taxes."[241] In August, two Florentine ambassadors, Bartolomeo Valori and Nello Martini, journeyed to Milan with instructions to inform the duke that the republic insisted upon the withdrawal of his troops from Forlì, and the cessation of his interference in the Papal States. Refusing to consider any compromise, the Signoria insisted upon strict compliance with the terms of the peace treaty.[242]

September marked the turning-point in this bloodless duel. During that month, the leadership's mood and behavior had shifted from the cautious vigilance of the summer to a more aggressive stance, following the prescription of Francesco Machiavelli who counseled his fellow citizens to be "virile . . . and not timid or craven. . . ."[243] The duke had made no further gestures to provoke the republic, either in the Romagna or elsewhere, but Florentine nerves were strained, not relaxed, by the prolongation of the stalemate. Neither the city nor the territory was immediately threatened by Visconti troops, as Rinaldo degli Albizzi admitted. But some citizens feared that his tactics were so designed to weaken the republic that she would succumb without fighting. Lorenzo Lenzi was enraged by the Signoria's reception of a ducal embassy, whose sole purpose was "to create a schism within the *popolo* so that we will neglect our liberty."[244] Florentines were vexed by the realization that Filippo Maria was able to exert pressure on the republic without spending much money, while their expenses were soaring. "We are heavily burdened," Piero Beccanugi complained, "while he uses only his ordinary revenue."[245] Responding to

[240] Partner, *Papal State*, 77–78; *Commissioni*, I, 462–63, 486; Palla Strozzi, *ASI*, 4th ser., XI, 30, 146–49, 293–94. For Pandolfo's career in Lombardy prior to this election, see Jones, *Malatesta*, 154–57.

[241] *CP*, 45, f.133r, 26 July. On that embassy, Strozzi, 45–47.

[242] *SCMLC*, 7, ff.29v–30r. The duke was to promise that he would abandon his league with the legate of Bologna, and to engage in no warlike acts on the sea; *ibid.*, ff.31r–31v.

[243] "Prosequi debemus viriliter et in reputacione nostra non deficere et viles et timidi non esse"; *CP*, 45, f.147r, 5 Oct.

[244] *Ibid.*, ff.130v, 135r.

[245] *Ibid.*, f.143v: "Ipse ultra consuetum nil expendit"; *ibid.*, f.143v, 24 Sept. Matteo Castellani: "Dux nil ultra solitum expendit et nos iam mense singulo florenos 25,000 et ultra iam expendimus. Adeo ipse sua negotia gerit, et incomportabile veniet expensa nostra"; *ibid.*, f.134r, 5 Aug.

these pressures, the war *balìa* sent two commissioners, Rinaldo degli Albizzi and Francesco Tornabuoni, to the army then being assembled in Romagna by Pandolfo Malatesta, with instructions to attack Forlì and drive the Visconti forces from the region. To pay for that campaign, the Ten had borrowed 36,000 florins on their own signatures and then requested the levy of two forced loans to cover that obligation. Speaking for his colleagues in the war magistracy, Niccolò da Uzzano urged the councils to approve the legislation authorizing these levies. He told them (Palla Strozzi reported) "how many lances and foot soldiers the commune had hired, and the extraordinary expenses, and the additional costs . . . and then the forced loans that had been assessed during their term of office. He concluded by saying that if we were to continue the enterprise [in Romagna], we had to have money. . . . He urged them to act forcefully, because then we would be successful in preserving our liberty."[246] After several rejections, and more oratory by Matteo Castellani and Palla Strozzi, the provision was finally approved. The votes cast against this levy were the most concrete indications of popular opposition to the confrontation with the Visconti, that was not articulated in the *pratiche*.[247]

The republic's incursion into Romagna did not dislodge Filippo Maria's partisans, who remained in control of the city (though not the fortress) of Forlì. A skirmish on 6 September between Florentine and Visconti mercenaries was indecisive, though it inspired rumors that Pandolfo Malatesta's force had been badly mauled.[248] Reports also reached Florence that Pisa and Livorno were threatened by a Genoese armada, and that 2000 additional troops were needed to protect the Tuscan littoral.[249] From Milan, Florentine ambassadors wrote that the duke was determined to retain control of Forlì, and that he charged the republic with committing the first violation of the peace treaty.[250] Although a few citizens persisted in the hope that war might yet be averted, the contrary view was expressed more openly

---

[246] *ASI*, 4th ser., XII, 149–50. See too *Commissioni*, I, 480–81. For another example of the war *balìa*'s borrowing money as private individuals, see above, ch. IV, 243.

[247] For other fiscal measures rejected by the councils, *LF*, 53, ff.5r, 6r, 23 Oct. Cavalcanti presented the arguments of the *meno possenti* outside the *reggimento* who opposed the moves toward war: "Tutta la città si doleva di questa così fatta impresa"; *Istorie fiorentine*, II, ch. 7.

[248] *Commissioni*, I, 468–70, 478, 483; Jones, *Malatesta*, 158.

[249] *Commissioni*, I, 475, 480, 486. The armada was reported to be the largest seen in the Tyrrhenian Sea in thirty years. For the reinforcement of the Pisan garrison, *Prov.*, 113, f.197r, 27–28 Nov. 1423.

[250] *Commissioni*, I, 517–19. On the return of that embassy to Florence, Palla Strozzi, *ASI*, 4th ser., XI, 294–96.

and frequently. Even Agnolo Pandolfini conceded that the duke's posture was bellicose, and that prospects for peace were dim. But he could not refrain from warning his fellow citizens about the pernicious effects of war, however just: "We know from experience that by engaging in hostilities we succumbed to the tyranny of the duke of Athens and the duke of Calabria, and that we endured the gravest perils in our struggles with the church, the duke of Milan and King Ladislaus." He did not regard Forlì's occupation as a serious threat to Florentine security; a more cautious policy in Romagna, he implied, might better serve the republic's interests. But the leadership had formed an image of Filippo Maria as a master of deceit who, like his father before him, spoke words of friendship while scheming to destroy his victim. The style of tyrants, Gregorio Dati said, was to stimulate an eagerness for peace while preparing for war.[251] Filippo Maria reminded Pierozzo Castellani of the monster Geryon, described by Dante in the *Inferno*, who with a smiling visage lured travelers into his den before killing them.[252]

We are unusually well informed about the events (and Florentine reactions to those events) that culminated in full-scale warfare between the republic and the duke in February 1424. In addition to the *pratiche*, there has survived Palla Strozzi's account of his service with the war *balìa*, and Rinaldo degli Albizzi's correspondence with that magistracy from the Romagna, where he served as liaison with the mercenaries commanded by Pandolfo Malatesta. From their respective vantage points—the war magistracy in the palace responsive to public opinion, and the commissioner in the field frustrated by military deficiencies and ineptitude—emerged quite different views about the strategy that the republic should pursue. The *balìa*'s posture was conservative and defensive, reflecting the mood of a citizenry that had not been aroused to patriotic fervor[253] and that was most reluctant to subsidize military campaigns. Though the *balìa*'s diplomatic activities blanketed the entire peninsula, from the Angevin court in Naples to the duchy of Savoy in Piedmont, its achievements were very modest. The republic's envoys could not persuade Braccio to abandon the seige of L'Aquila in the Marches to attack Forlì, nor did they reach

[251] Pandolfini and Dati; *CP*, 45, ff.143r, 151r.

[252] *Ibid.*, f.151r. Either Castellani or the chancellor Fortini misquoted Dante: "quod dicere possumus cum Dante: 'Ecco colei che colla coda aguza.'" The reference is in *Inferno*, canto XVII, lines 1 and 3: "Ecco la fiera con la coda aguzza. . . . Ecco colei che tutto il mondo appuzza." Galileo Galilei quoted the same lines correctly in Feb. 1424; *CP*, 45, f.169v.

[253] The councils spurned an attempt by the Signoria in October to reappoint the war *balìa* for one year; *LF*, 53, ff.5r–5v; *CP*, 45, ff.148r, 150r; *Commissioni*, 1, 523–24.

an agreement with the duke of Savoy or the Swiss cantons for a concerted attack against Visconti territory.[254] Meanwhile, the military campaign in the Romagna was foundering. Pandolfo Malatesta's troops were slow to assemble; one contingent suffered heavy casualties in a skirmish near Forlimpopoli; and the army did not receive enough support from Florence to besiege Forlì. To calm a populace frightened by rumors of a Genoese armada descending on Pisa and the other Tuscan ports, the war *balìa* sent troops destined for Romagna into that area. Writing apologetically to Rinaldo about that diversion, Palla Strozzi reported that "here everyone is shouting Pisa, Livorno, Piombino, and Sarzana, because of the armada." His colleague Vieri Guadagni wrote that officials in Pisa were demanding 2000 troops to defend that territory from a potential attack that had spread panic among the populace and had disrupted the *balìa*'s military strategy.[255]

After the initial hopes for a rapid conquest of Forlì had evaporated, Rinaldo degli Albizzi found himself embroiled in the murky world of Romagnol politics: encouraging reluctant captains to fight aggressively, placating friends and potential allies, seeking to isolate the Visconti garrison in Forlì and thus weaken its ability to resist. Everywhere he saw waste and incompetence: in the hiring of unqualified troops, in the evasive tactics of their captains, in the failure to provision Florentine castles on the frontier.[256] Rinaldo's initial enthusiasm for Pandolfo's energy and aggressiveness ebbed as he observed his reluctance to fight. Though loath to criticize "the magnificent captain" openly, he did suggest that by these defensive tactics Pandolfo had missed the opportunity to accomplish "useful and honorable things." If Braccio were here with only 100 cavalry, he wrote (26 October) to Vieri Guadagni, we might have achieved victory. But without the overwhelming force that would have solidified Romagnol support for the republic, the Florentine position deteriorated as mercenaries defected and local nobles vacillated in their allegiance. The army was so weak and demoralized, Rinaldo wrote to the *balìa* on 30 October, that he feared it would not survive the winter.[257] The frustrations of this campaign transformed Rinaldo's thinking about the war. Defen-

---

[254] On the *balìa*'s efforts to persuade Braccio to move north, *ASI*, 4th ser., XI, 146–49; and the mission to Savoy and Switzerland, *ibid.*, 30–31, 153; *Storia di Milano*, VI, 212.

[255] *Commissioni*, I, 501–02: "Qua ognuno grida Pisa, Livorno, Piombino e Serezana, per rispetto dell'armata; e conviensi pure provedere, e fassi quanto si può. . . . Questa armata di Genova ha messo a questo popolo tanto sospetto, che se portassimo Firenze a Pisa, non parebbe loro fossi sicura. . . ." Florence was also suffering from a plague epidemic, which drove many citizens away; *ibid.*, I, 544.

[256] *Ibid.*, I, 499, 505, 521–22, 530–31.   [257] *Ibid.*, I, 535–36; 547, 553.

sive tactics should be abandoned, he believed, in favor of an offensive thrust into Lombardy. "If the duke has difficulty in raising money now," he wrote to Vieri Guadagni (12 October), "consider what will happen in the future, and particularly if the Swiss or the duke of Savoy or you [the *balìa*] would launch an attack against him, as you could do. If you crossed the Po river, his state would collapse." If Florentines would be willing to take this risk, he concluded wistfully, they would gain more fame than the Romans had ever achieved.[258]

This argument for a more aggressive strategy was the first move in a struggle between advocates of offensive and defensive warfare that dominated the debates over military policy in the winter of 1423–1424. In early November, Battista Campofregoso came to Florence with a proposition for a joint assault on Genoa and the Riviera by an Aragonese fleet, supported by Florentine mercenaries and Genoese exiles. If the enterprise succeeded, Battista said, Genoa would rebel against the duke. This project created a sharp cleavage within the *balìa*, Palla Strozzi reported. Opponents argued that the republic's participation would be an open declaration of war, and would thus endanger her forces in Romagna and also on her northern frontier. Moreover, the outcome of this enterprise was not certain, given the winter season and the strength of Visconti forces in Genoa.[259] Niccolò Sacchetti, spokesman for the Twelve, argued for the naval attack, insisting that Genoa was the duke's Achilles' heel. With very little expense or danger, he said, Florence could gain as much advantage as the conquest of two cities in Lombardy.[260] After several consultations with the newly elected war *balìa*, and with other magistracies, the Ten decided to pursue negotiations with the Campofregosi and the Aragonese, and to give limited support to the armada. However, they were not willing to join King Alfonso of Aragon in a formal alliance that would commit the republic to providing men and money for the war's duration. Although negotiations with an Aragonese embassy were renewed in late December, the *balìa* failed to reach an agreement with this potential ally.[261]

On 30 November Rinaldo degli Albizzi returned to Florence from his unproductive mission; two days later he made a speech advocating a Lombard invasion. Peace is a fantasy, he insisted; the Florentines must accept the inevitability of war. A defensive strategy would

---

[258] *Ibid.*, 1, 523, cited by Baron, *Crisis*, 2nd ed., 376.

[259] "Udito messer Battista, si paticò tra noi che fosse da fare. Furono e pareri diversi"; Palla Strozzi's diary, *ASI*, 4th ser., XI, 303–04.

[260] *CP*, 45, f.153v, 10 Nov.

[261] Palla Strozzi, *ASI*, 4th ser., XI, 307–09; XII, 9–12.

eventually ruin them, because their resources will dwindle while the duke's territory is unmolested. Carlo Federighi, Salamone Strozzi, and Lorenzo Lenzi joined Rinaldo in supporting an offensive against Filippo Maria. The latter noted that military costs were rising from 30,000 to 50,000 florins monthly, a burden that could not be sustained by the citizenry. Lenzi predicted that the republic was doomed if she remained on the defensive.[262] Rinaldo's viewpoint prevailed in that pratica, whose members advised the balìa to take offensive action against the duke, and to raise the money for supporting this enterprise.[263] But civic support for this policy was tenuous;[264] many continued to hope that the duke might still be persuaded to negotiate rather than fight. When the marquis of Ferrara sent Nanni Strozzi to Florence with a message suggesting that Filippo Maria was amenable to a settlement, that hope grew stronger. Urging the Signoria to pursue the peace initiative, Agnolo Pandolfini said bluntly that the republic was too weak to invade Lombardy. Even such inveterate foes of the Visconti as Vieri Guadagni and Francesco Machiavelli agreed with him, the latter arguing that the city's economy could not support an offensive campaign. Employing a religious theme rarely brought up in these debates, Niccolò del Bellaccio said that "no good citizen would reject peace if it could be achieved, since our Lord Jesus Christ gave his life for peace, and in death he left that inheritance, which cannot be denied by a true Christian. . . ."[265] The Signoria sent ambassadors to Ferrara with instructions to respond positively to the marquis's offer, but Florence's terms for peace were still the withdrawal of all Visconti forces from Romagna and Lunigiana.[266] Meanwhile, the tempo of military recruitment intensified. By late January 1424, the Florentine army had grown to 1200 lances and 2800 infantry, and the war balìa was planning to enlarge it (so Francesco Machiavelli reported) to 2600 lances.[267] The troops for a Lombard invasion were thus being assembled, although the decision to launch that offensive had not yet been made.

[262] CP, 45, ff.155v–156r. Cf. the argument of Francesco Viviani: "Stando ad defensionem quia minor est expensa, conservamus tantum; si ad offensionem venimus, duplex erit expensa et in statu sumus epidemie et sine lucris"; ibid., f.156r.

[263] Ibid., f.157r, 3 Dec., printed in Commissioni, II, 3.

[264] Giovanni Cavalcanti, Istorie fiorentine, III, ch. 10: "Sapete che nel principio i potenti furono gl'inventori di questa guerra; e il popolo, con assai uomini, a nulla voleano se non che alle difese si stesse da quella parte dove il Comune fusse più debole."

[265] CP, 45, ff.158r–158v, 162r.   [266] Commissioni, II, 7–9, 31 Jan.

[267] CP, 45, f.164r, 22 Jan.

While the Florentine ambassadors were traveling north to Ferrara, a Visconti army occupied Imola, whose *signore*, Francesco Alidosi, was a client of the republic.[268] This coup dispelled any hope for an accommodation with the duke, who was characterized by angry citizens as equaling if not surpassing his father in the arts of treachery. The civic reaction to this event, as measured by the oratory in the *pratiche*, differed little from the responses of previous crises. Every speaker made the traditional appeal for unity and sacrifice, while emphasizing the republic's innocence in provoking hostilities. Comparing the Florentines to the Romans in their reluctance to begin wars, Galileo Galilei also noted their perseverance in the face of adversity, citing the battle of Cannae during the second Punic War as an example of Rome's determination. Gregorio Dati used other examples from Roman history to support his contention that defensive strategy in warfare was ruinous; Carlo Federighi pointed to Philip of Macedon's conquest of Greece to demonstrate that tyrants and free cities could never cohabit in peace.[269] These debates provided opportunities for displaying rhetorical skills and patriotic fervor; they also inspired realistic appraisals of Florence's situation. In Giovanni de' Medici's judgment, the war would be decided in the treasuries of the combatants: "whoever obtains the most money will be the victor."[270] Inhibiting the flow of coins into the Florentine treasury was, first, the economic depression that troubled Niccolò da Uzzano, and, second, the unwillingness of citizens to subsidize a war.[271] Cristofano Bagnesi suggested that money would be difficult to collect: "Many citizens are in a rebellious mood and do not wish to pay."[272] Little consolation was to be gained from Rinaldo degli Albizzi's assertion that Filippo Maria was himself having difficulty in raising money;[273] Florentines were convinced that, as the weaker power, they would need help to defeat the duke, particularly

---

[268] *Commissioni*, II, 18–19.

[269] For these references, CP, 45, ff.166r, 168v, 169v. Cf. Guglielmo Tanagli's statement: "Quod dulce est nomen pacis ut in XII Filippica Cicero scribit, alia recitans et de Marcantonio etc."; *ibid.*, f.170r.

[270] *Ibid.*, f.170r.

[271] *Ibid.*, f.165v. See Giuliano Manovelli's letter to Simone Strozzi, 29 Feb. 1424: "E' si dà a credere pel volglio del nostro popolo che non vogliamo ghuera, e parli posto che assai chiaro vede per l'opere l'oposito che no' dobiamo durare. Il perchè fatele chome e buo' Romani, cho' la'nsegna in su ghabia reale, e se no' basterà cho' l'avere, si facci chole persone, e Idio n'aiuterà"; *Strozz.*, 3rd ser., 132, no. 84.

[272] CP, 45, f.172v, 4 March.

[273] "Et eius subditi pessime sunt dispositi quia gentes armorum eos consummunt et devorant, quia ipse florenos solum VIII per lancea solvit"; *ibid.*, f.172r.

if they opted for the offensive strategy that, it was generally agreed, would be most effective against him.[274]

Though urged by Rinaldo degli Albizzi to resurrect the scheme for an Aragonese alliance and a naval assault on Genoa,[275] the war *balìa* continued to pursue a very cautious policy. Its diplomatic posture was wary and hesitant; it seemed reluctant to take any step that would commit the regime irrevocably to hostilities.[276] An invasion of Lombardy was not feasible, Palla Strozzi wrote in his diary on 6 March, adding that the *balìa* would limit its hiring of mercenaries to 1900 lances and 6000 infantry, sufficient for defending the republic's territory.[277] Paying those troops created a monthly deficit of 20,000 florins, so Palla informed a council that had balked (9 March) at approving another forced loan. He and his colleagues were loath to ask for this money, Palla said, but those expenditures were essential for their security. "If our enemy were to see us unprepared, he could harm us more easily, and would be more willing to continue fighting. . . ."[278] Employed so often and so successfully in the past, this argument had lost some of its power to persuade the citizenry. Antonio Acciaiuoli informed his brother Neri in Athens (February 1424) that two forced loans were being imposed each month; he expected an even higher levy in the future. "I do not know how you can survive without help," he wrote, and then added that Palla Strozzi was in similar difficulties with his assessments.[279] In the *pratiche*, counselors renewed their complaints about the inequitable distribution of the fiscal burden, which was forcing some despairing citizens into exile. "We cannot defend our liberty with this schedule," Filippo Mangioni cried, but his colleagues

[274] Francesco Machiavelli, for the Sixteen: "Potentes non sumus per nos contra ducem et querere socios debemus"; *ibid.*, f.171v; Rinaldo degli Albizzi, "et soli non sumus ad offensam apti"; *Commissioni*, II, 6.

[275] "Felix est et prospera cuncta gessit et contra ducem Mediolani voluntarie venit, quem proditorem vocat in omnibus. Et nemo eo melior est, utilior aut potentior"; *CP*, 45, f.172r. On the *balìa*'s negotiations in February with the Aragonese envoy, see Palla Strozzi's diary; *ASI*, 4th ser., XII, 14–15.

[276] This can be seen from Palla Strozzi's diary for these months; 12–22. On 6 March the councils passed a provision that was, in effect, a declaration of war against the duke; *Commissioni*, II, 47–49.

[277] Palla Strozzi, 20: "Non potavamo offendere el nimico a casa sua; a nostra difesa bastavano lance 1900 e fanti 6000."

[278] *Ibid.*, 20–21. The total expenditure for military purposes was 50,000 fl. monthly.

[279] *Ashb.*, 1830, vol. I, no. 3–5. On Palla's financial difficulties, see Molho, *Florentine Public Finances*, 109, 157–60. Piero Strozzi wrote to Matteo Strozzi (15 Apr. 1424) about the difficulty in raising money for *prestanze*; *Strozz.*, 3rd ser., 132, no. 86.

feared that a revision would intensify the fiscal crisis.[280] Every member of the inner circle was aware of the resentments fed by these forced loans; that realization cooled the ardor of those who, like Rinaldo degli Albizzi, had been so eager to launch an offensive against Milan. No more talk was heard in the *pratiche* about a Lombard invasion, or the destruction of the Visconti state.

Throughout the spring and early summer of 1424, the war *balìa* continued its defensive policy of limited risk. The Ten did not actively seek an alliance with Aragon or Venice, nor did they challenge Visconti forces in the Romagna. Though troubled by the news of Braccio's death in battle, and by rumors of an agreement between Martin V and the duke of Milan, these officials were content to prolong a stalemate that cost the republic 45,000 florins monthly.[281] When, in mid-July, the Signoria convened a *pratica* to discuss an incursion into Lombardy, civic opinion was very cool to the scheme. Salamone Strozzi was the only counselor to favor an offensive; Niccolò da Uzzano, Giovanni de' Medici, and Palla di Novello Strozzi expressed serious reservations about an enterprise that was both costly and unpredictable.[282] Just two weeks later (30 July) the Florentines were stunned by the news that their Romagna army had suffered an overwhelming defeat at Zagonara near Faenza.[283] This disaster furnished Giovanni Cavalcanti with an opportunity to vent his rage on the ruling elite which, ever since the war with Ladislaus, had "continued to search for new wars." Cavalcanti spoke for the disenfranchised citizens who (he argued) had been ruined by the "great citizens"; they had nothing left to give the state. Where will the leaders turn now for aid: to the Angevin rulers of Naples to whose ruin they have contributed? To Pope Martin V whom they maligned? "Go now and fight your wars and appoint your *balìe* and say that you are going to terrorize the enemy. You have begun this war without any justification, and without any consideration for the counsel of good citizens, whom you have ridiculed by saying 'They are from the [council of] forty-eight.' "[284]

Similar thoughts may have been entertained by men within and

---

[280] CP, 45, f.175r, 2 May. For the whole discussion, *ibid.*, ff.174v–176r. Cf. Bartolomeo Corbinelli's statement: "mercatura quasi nulla fit in civitate"; *ibid.*, f.176r.

[281] CP, 45, ff.178r, 179v, 180r–182v, 2 and 3 June. See also Partner, *Papal State*, 78–79.

[282] *Ibid.*, ff.184r–186v, 15 July.

[283] G. Morelli, *Delizie*, XIX, 64. Morelli estimated that 5000 horse and 2000 infantry were lost in that battle; *ibid.*, 68.

[284] *Istorie fiorentine*, II, ch. 21. The "forty-eight" were members of the council of 131 chosen from the 16 *gonfaloni*, and not *ex-officio*. That council had frequently rejected provisions for rearmament and its financing.

outside the *reggimento*, but no trace of recrimination appears in the minutes of the *pratica* of 3 August, assembled to discuss the crisis. The debate was monopolized by that inner circle identified and pilloried by Cavalcanti: Rinaldo Gianfigliazzi, Giovanni de' Medici, Niccolò da Uzzano, Palla and Salamone Strozzi, Michele and Matteo Castellani, Francesco Machiavelli, Niccolò Barbadori. In its organization as in its deliberations, the *pratica* signified the closing of ranks by the inner circle, and a reaffirmation of its commitment to its principles—republican and elitist.[285] No one sought to minimize the magnitude of the disaster or the dangers that imperiled the regime. But adversity is the seed-bed of virtue, and Florence's tribulations were perceived as an opportunity to develop those qualities for which the Romans were immortalized.[286] The physician Galileo Galilei noted that "among the other great and laudable things recorded of the Roman people two are unforgotten: their refusal either to lose courage in adversity or to be flushed with success. The greatness of the Roman mind showed itself more in misfortune than in good fortune. The wood of the tree is an image of hope: wounded, it bursts into leaf and is covered again."[287] These exhortations had a practical purpose: to motivate the citizens to endure the sacrifices that would now be required and to raise the money for hiring mercenaries to replace those killed and captured at Zagonara. The paramount concern was the defense of Florentine territory: the provisioning of fortresses on the frontiers, the recruitment of troops to fend off the expected invasion. Some counselors proposed that the republic seek an accommodation with Pope Martin V; Niccolò Barbadori also suggested that an embassy be sent to Venice.[288]

Perhaps no civic assembly in this regime's history had ever displayed its spirit more impressively than did this *pratica*, with its combination of lofty idealism and a sharp sense of reality. These citizens attached the highest value to the benefits they derived from belonging to a republican regime, and they were prepared to pay heavily for that privilege. To sustain that commitment, however, was more difficult than to articulate it; as Bartolomeo Orlandini observed, it is easy to say that it is necessary to raise money and defend our territory, but

[285] The full debate is in *Commissioni*, II, 145-49. See Rinaldo Gianfigliazzi's statement: "Et finaliter cum sententia Ligargi [Lycurgus] concludens, ut per paucos ordinetur quod per multos deliberetur"; *ibid.*, 145. Cavalcanti's account of Gianfigliazzi's speech differs from that recorded by the chancellor Fortini; *Istorie fiorentine*, II, ch. 23.

[286] See the statements cited by Baron, *Crisis*, 2nd ed., 385-86.

[287] *Commissioni*, II, 149, trans. by Baron, 386.

[288] *Ibid.*, 146, 148.

harder to implement those goals.[289] The economy was still depressed, and "merchants are crying because they cannot trade."[290] Giovanni de' Medici and Strozza Strozzi both hinted at waste in the hiring and deployment of mercenaries.[291] Instead of pressing the *balìa* to spare no expense in fortifying the territory, some counselors recommended restraint so that (as Niccolò del Bellaccio said on 9 October) "we will be prepared in summer as well as in winter."[292] To a greater degree than in any previous conflict, the costs of this war were being borne by the citizens in the inner circle of the *reggimento*, and particularly its wealthiest members. Giovanni Cavalcanti certainly exaggerated when he wrote that those excluded from the regime had been so impoverished by taxation that they could contribute nothing to the treasury.[293] Yet the statement does contain a kernel of truth. A *prestanza* levy that once yielded 120,000 florins now brought only one-tenth of that sum to the treasury, according to Niccolò del Bellaccio.[294] On the pretext of fleeing the plague, some citizens had left the territory without paying their assessments.[295] Others, no longer deterred by the ignominy of the *speculum*, simply refused to pay.[296] Filippo della Fioraia noted that the clergy and *contado* residents could not

[289] *Ibid.*, 146.

[290] Guaspare Accorambuoni, *CP*, 46, f.13v. Cf. Strozza Strozzi and Galileo Galilei, *ibid.*, ff.5r, 10r.

[291] *Ibid.*, ff.4v–5r.

[292] *Ibid.*, f.14r. See also Marcello Strozzi, *ibid.*, f.13r. But Dino Gucci insisted that "nulla parsimonia fienda est, sed substantiam et vitam exponere, cum si casus sinister eveneret, odio vitam quisque haberet"; *ibid.*, f.4r.

[293] *Istorie fiorentine*, III, ch. 1.

[294] Though a gross exaggeration, that statement did point to the trend of declining *prestanze* revenues from a shrinking urban populace. More accurate was Guglielmo Spini's statement, 22 Feb. 1425: "Per impositionem prestanzonis, pecunia obculata fuit, nam solùm 40,000 florenos in sigillo reperti sunt et 10,000 in occulto in feminis et similibus"; *CP*, 46, f.41v. In that *prestanzone* of 50,000 fl., only 1600 households were assessed more than 1 fl.; 3200 households, between 6 s. 8 d. and 1 fl. (and so paid a reduced rate *ad perdendum*); and 2300 households were assessed 6 s. 8 d. or less and paid nothing; *BNF, Conv. Sopp.*, c, 4, 895, f.112v. Petriboni, who recorded these statistics, wrote that "insino a tutto quello mese d'ottobre 1424 si fe' pagare prestanze quarante cinque di questa novina che sono flor. M^M per la guerra del ducha."

[295] Betto Busini, "multi cives discesserunt sub colore epidemie ut non solvant"; *CP*, 45, f.176r, 2 May. Paolo Petriboni reported that Giovanni Panciatichi was ordered by the Signoria to return to Florence from Siena, or he would be banned and his property confiscated; *BNF, Conv. Sopp.*, c, 4, 895, f.111r.

[296] "Contra illos qui speculum non formidant, fiat provisio. . . . Pro iis qui non timent speculum, provisio data est ut solvant"; *Commissioni*, II, 145. A provision of Oct. 1424 authorized the election of a magistracy to sell the property of tax delinquents; *Prov.*, 114, f.35v.

contribute as much as in the past, a judgment that is corroborated for the *contadini* by Anthony Molho's data.[297]

The grim mood within the *reggimento* was not lightened by diplomatic developments after the disaster at Zagonara. To rebuild the shattered Florentine army, the war *balìa* had appealed to Martin V for permission to hire troops under his control, specifically those commanded by Niccolò Piccinino and Oddo Fortebraccio, Braccio's illegitimate son. By refusing his consent, Martin V forced the Florentines to calculate whether their military requirements outweighed the risk of alienating a potential friend, who might still be persuaded to join them against the duke. So inhospitable was their reception at the papal court, Rinaldo degli Albizzi and Vieri Guadagni reported, that they felt like Jews.[298] In a *pratica* of 16 September, counselors agonized over the Florentine predicament, without reaching a conclusion. "We must be careful to do nothing to displease the pope," Bartolomeo Corbinelli warned, but then added that the military situation was so grave that mercenaries had to be recruited. If Florence could survive without these soldiers, Salamone Strozzi said, then she should not incur the additional expense. But he was persuaded that Piccinino's band was needed to fend off the four-pronged offensive that the duke was planning to launch against the republic.[299] Perhaps mindful of his large investment in papal banking operations, Giovanni de' Medici was particularly concerned about curial sensibilities; he warned his fellow-citizens that Florence's survival depended upon maintaining her friendship with Martin V.[300] The *balìa* eventually decided to risk the pope's anger by hiring Piccinino and Fortebraccio.[301] "The lord

[297] CP, 46, f.14v. Income from the direct taxation of the *contado* in 1424 was 83,840 fl., a decline of 37% since 1416. In 1426 it had fallen to 74,000 fl.; Molho, *op. cit.*, 61. Income from all gabelles in 1424 was 159,000 fl., a decline of 23% since 1416; *ibid.*, 54.

[298] *Commissioni*, II, 172, letter of 2 Sept. Rinaldo had been at the papal court since June; *ibid.*, 87–89. On 2 Aug., the war *balìa* instructed him to ask the pope for soldiers; *ibid.*, 144.

[299] CP, 46, ff.9r–10v. The Visconti offensive was to include a naval attack against Florentine ports and land assaults via Firenzuola, Lunigiana, and Arezzo; *Commissioni*, II, 188. Florentine agents were attempting to persuade the duke's captains to leave his service and fight for the republic; *ibid.*, 222–23.

[300] CP, 46, f.9v. Giovanni added that "satis facile deliberaret si amictere trafficum curie deberet vel solvere ut cogitur, quia cunctus trafficum amicteretur. Et omnis mercantia que fit in Florentia, Rome portatur et venditur, et alibi nil fiat mercature."

[301] On Piccinino's hiring, see *Commissioni*, II, 186, 272; on Fortebraccio, Partner, *Papal State*, 80.

pope is lukewarm and timid, and we cannot hope for anything from him," Palla Strozzi said on 29 October. From his fruitless conversations with Martin V during the summer and autumn of 1424, Rinaldo degli Albizzi had also concluded that the pope was unwilling to support the republic.[302] Martin was now exacting his payment for the insults he had suffered in Florence five years earlier.

The recruitment of new troops, and their disposition along the northern frontier, was a stopgap measure that strengthened Florentine defenses to a degree but did little to modify the military balance that was heavily weighted in Filippo Maria's favor.[303] Beginning in October, the war *balìa* canvassed Italy for other sources of help, now that the pope had demonstrated his indifference to their fate. Giovanni de' Medici and Palla Strozzi were sent to Venice to solicit support from that republic under her new doge, Francesco Foscari. The failure of that mission was a severe blow to Florentine morale, which reached a low point in the *pratica* held on 19 October.[304] "We are in such grave peril with heavy expenses and a debased reputation," Sandro Altoviti said, "that I do not see how we can resist and survive." So pervasive was the mood of vulnerability, of imminent doom, that several counselors proposed that an invitation be sent to the emperor-elect Sigismund, who, fourteen years after his election, had not yet traveled to Rome for his coronation. Some citizens feared that Sigismund's journey would create such turmoil in the peninsula that Florence would be hurt rather than helped; her complicity in the invasion, Lapo Niccolini believed, would turn every Italian power against her. That risk should be taken, Luca degli Albizzi and Dino Gucci argued, because the republic was in such dire peril. "If the emperor comes," Luca reasoned, "he will come with maximum force, and if he should be defeated we will still be secure, not for a day but for a year. And if he wins, we will be the masters of Italy!"[305] The *balìa* did send agents to Sigismund to discuss an Italian journey, but those negotiations did not

---

[302] *CP*, 46, f.16v; *Commissioni*, II, 185–87, 290–92, 307–09, 311–15.

[303] On Piccinino's movements, *Commissioni*, II, 276–77. Florence had 1500 lances under contract in late October; Filippo Maria was estimated to have 4000 lances; *ibid*. The Malatesta had joined the duke; Jones, *Malatesta*, 162–63.

[304] On that mission, see *Commissioni*, II, 247–48; *SCMLC*, 7, ff.40r–41v. See Nerone Dietisalvi's lament: "A Venetis sperabamus ut a fratribus et civibus et in dominio et moribus paribus"; *CP*, 46, f.18v. See Palla Strozzi's account of that mission; *ASI*, 4th ser., XIV, 15–16.

[305] *CP*, 46, ff.17r–17v. Francesco Machiavelli and Filippo Arrigucci opposed an invitation to Sigismund, but a majority in the leadership (Palla Strozzi, Rinaldo Gianfigliazzi, Niccolò Barbadori, Vieri Guadagni, Ridolfo Peruzzi) supported it.

bear fruit.[306] In December, the proposal for an Aragonese alliance and a joint assault on the Genoese Riviera was again suggested in a *pratica*. Once a strong supporter of that scheme, Rinaldo degli Albizzi was not sanguine about its prospects, though he did not wish to terminate discussions with the Aragonese ambassador.[307]

From the Florentine point of view, this war was an experience of unrelieved adversity. Never before within memory, Tommaso Ardinghelli observed somberly (13 February 1425), had the republic been in such extremity, without friends or allies and (he might have added) without an army to defend it.[308] The mercenary force led by Niccolò Piccinino, which had been recruited with such difficulty, was routed in early February by a Visconti army near Faenza; Piccinino and Niccolò da Tolentino were taken prisoners, Oddo Fortebraccio killed in battle. Having returned to Florence from his frustrating mission to Rome, Rinaldo degli Albizzi assumed the role of chief spokesman for a troubled leadership. He did not gloss over the magnitude of that defeat, nor did he hold out any hope for salvation from other sources. The choice, he said, was simple if unpalatable: to continue the struggle, recruit more troops, and find the money to pay them.[309] The war *balìa* scoured the peninsula for soldiers to replace those lost in battle.[310] The monthly outlay for the military rose above 50,000 florins; in early May, Niccolò Barbadori estimated that it had reached 60,000 florins, which, he claimed, was more than was ever spent during the wars fought against Giangaleazzo.[311] A rich and prominent banker, Barbadori was most concerned about Florence's economic troubles that would affect her ability to fight. "Our enemy watches us, and in

[306] Florentine agents sent to Sigismund are identified by Rinaldo degli Albizzi as Messer Bartolomeo Montegonzi and Ser Antonio Salvetti; *Commissioni*, II, 322–23. Their mission apparently was not a formal embassy. Bernardo Guadagni said (13 Feb. 1425) that "spes omnis pacis et transitus imperatoris ad nostra subsidia sublata est"; *CP*, 46, f.35r.

[307] *Commissioni*, II, 320–21, 26 and 27 Dec. 1424.

[308] "Quod non est memor tante extremitatis ut ad presens, nam semper hactenus cum amicitia et fide vicinorum aliqua fuimus salvo quam nunc"; *CP*, 46, f.34v.

[309] G. Morelli, *Delizie*, XIX, 64. Rinaldo's speeches of 2 and 9 Feb. are printed in *Commissioni*, II, 321–22.

[310] *CP*, 46, f.34r, Averardo de' Medici for the Sixteen. Niccolò Barbadori said that a force of 2000–2400 lances was planned; *ibid.*, ff.34v–35r. The *balìa* also decided to subsidize Catalan galleys to attack the Genoese Riviera; Palla Strozzi's diary; *ASI*, 4th ser., XIII, 154–55.

[311] *CP*, 46, f.49v, 5 May. Barbadori made a reference to Boethius: "Et cum Boetio, tempus est medicine potius quam querele si opus medicantis expectas ut vulnus detegas." Other references to monthly expenditures by Averardo de' Medici (57,000 fl.) and Rinaldo degli Albizzi; *ibid.*, ff.45v, 46v.

the Roman curia they make calculations about our money. Neither the wool nor the silk industries are producing, as is well known; and no revenue is coming in from outside." The economy was weaker than during the Giangaleazzo wars, Filippo del Pancia said, "because in 1400 money flowed into Florence from abroad, but now everyone has returned home." In the opinion of Giovanni di Michele di Ser Parente, the city's population and wealth had been reduced by one-half since the turn of the century: "It was easier to pay 60,000 florins in the time of this duke's father than 30,000 now."[312]

That florins were the sinews of war, and the foundation of the regime's security, was an axiom whose truth was not doubted by any citizen.[313] If money ceased to flow into the treasury, the republic was doomed. These convictions explain the extraordinary attention paid to the fisc—and particularly to the unequal assessments—in these months. Unsuccessful in its military and diplomatic enterprises, the leadership hoped to gain some merit (if not honor or prestige) by equalizing the tax burden and so removing a perennial source of discord. Efforts to achieve civic peace through fiscal equity were as old as the regime itself; the new factor in this campaign was the strength of the leadership's commitment, and its embrace (the word is apt) of a radical solution. During the previous October, a new schedule of levies had been approved by the councils;[314] its proponents hoped that the assessors would not conspire to manipulate the assessments, as other officials had done in the past. It may have been true (as Niccolò del Bellaccio argued) that eight men would not have as many motives for commiting fraud as the 144 officials who drew up the *novina*.[315] But Rinaldo degli Albizzi's correspondence with Vieri

---

[312] *Ibid.*, ff.49v–50r. See the comments of Giovanni Minerbetti, 22 Feb. 1425: "Cives non erunt aliter quam in preteritum, et ordinatio novarum gabellarum etiam demonstrat. . . . Possessiones et res propter multas pecunias necessarias communi non erunt pretii ut nunc sed multo minor"; *ibid.*, f.40v.

[313] Thus, Francesco Machiavelli: "Quod omnes putant certo res esse quod pecunia nostra est defensio et in ea consistit nostra salus"; *ibid.*, f.37r.

[314] Molho, *Florentine Public Finances*, 76, n. 16. This was not a reform of the *prestanza* levy, as Molho states, but of the *prestanzone*, a different schedule with larger assessments. A *prestanzone* was designed to yield 50,000 fl., a *prestanza* only 15,000. For example, Cederno Cederni was assessed 10 fl. in the *prestanza*, and 23 fl. in the *prestanzone*; he estimated his wealth at 1900 fl.; *CP*, 46, f.38r. For the voting on this reform, see *LF*, 53, ff.36r–39r, 4–14 Oct. 1424.

[315] "Nam octo cives passiones non multas habent ut CXL cives et equaliter imponetur quod oppositum fuit in novina, quia cum conspirationibus occultis et cum passione imposuerunt"; *CP*, 46, f.14r. In the *novina* system, nine citizens in each *gonfalone* drew up the schedule. Alessandro Alessandri proposed that the assessors "clauderentur ita quod parentele et rogamina non deviaverent eos a iusti-

Guadagni reveals that these ardent patriots had no compunction about pulling strings to reduce Rinaldo's assessment.[316] The new schedule had made more enemies than friends among the citizens, who expressed their resentment by voting against every fiscal measure submitted to the councils, including petitions by individuals for a reduction of their debts and their levies.[317] In February 1425, the Signoria tried to raise money quickly by authorizing a commission of 151 citizens to arrange for the payment of tax obligations at a reduced rate; it was rejected three times by the Council of the *Popolo*.[318] So many voted against these provisions, Rinaldo degli Albizzi explained, because they believed that the commissions had made arbitrary and unjust decisions in the past, and had permitted rich Florentines to evade their obligations. As the tax burden increased, so did anger over these alleged inequities.[319] If those families that had been ruined and driven into exile by fiscal persecution were still living in the city, Averardo de' Medici observed, they would now be contributing their share of the war's cost.[320]

In the vanguard of the campaign to persuade the *reggimento* to adopt the *catasto* was Rinaldo degli Albizzi, who argued that its implementation would pacify the citizens, encourage them to pay their taxes, and fortify their determination to resist the Visconti. Together with Francesco Machiavelli and Niccolò Barbadori (the latter a recent convert), Rinaldo cited Venice as a model for Florence to follow.[321] That these arguments had persuaded many citizens—rich and poor; of high, middling, and low estate—is evident from the roster of those who announced their support for the scheme. Members of the inner circle—Piero and Giovanni Guicciardini, Palla and Strozza Strozzi, Francesco Tornabuoni, Donati Velluti—were most enthusiastic, but they were supported by some artisans and retail merchants from the

---

tia"; *LF*, 53, f.37r. Cf. the statements of Francesco Machiavelli and Guaspare Accorambuoni; *CP*, 46, ff.13r–13v.

[316] Rinaldo to Vieri, *Commissioni*, II, 249: "Vieri mio, aiutami tu della graveza; che sai com'io sono tratto nelle vecchie; e io ne scrivo a'miei, che ne sieno teco; aiutagli, e consigliagli per modo che io possa stare a Firenze con voi altri alle percosse. . . ." The issue recurred in later correspondence; *ibid.*, 278, 285, 289.

[317] *LF*, 53, ff.42r–48r, 5–13 Dec. 1424.

[318] *LF*, 53, ff.52v–56r, 6–12 Feb. 1425. For the arguments in favor of this measure, which would grant clemency to tax delinquents, see *CP*, 46, ff.31v–32v, 9 Feb.

[319] *Commissioni*, II, 322, speech of 9 Feb. 1425.

[320] Averardo was speaking for the Sixteen; *CP*, 46, f.40r, 22 Feb. As examples of ruined families, he mentioned the Alberti, Rinuccini, Monaldi, and Cocchi Donati.

[321] *Commissioni*, II, 322–24.

lower guilds.[322] Among the handful of dissidents willing to criticize the *catasto* publicly was Filippo della Fioraia, who pointed out that the scheme had been debated for twenty years. Its implementation would be expensive and time-consuming; it would require a minimum of two years to collect the data, and another three to correct errors. Establishing a *catasto* would drive money and trade from Florence; *monte* investors would sell their shares and weaken the economy further.[323] The *catasto* would frighten merchants and artisans, Guglielmo Spini argued, and diminish the revenues coming into the treasury. Gherardo Gherardi did "not believe that the men who would administer the *catasto* would be different in their attitudes and desires from those who have made other assessments; it would be unrealistic to hope that anything except hatreds and enmities would arise from this. . . ."[324] Gherardi pictured a city devoid of capital, its trade reduced to a trickle, and its citizens in dire poverty. Such fears were still too strong and pervasive to be overcome by the logic of the *catasto*'s promoters, who did not even succeed in getting a provision before the councils.

Thwarted by this opposition to fiscal reform, Rinaldo degli Albizzi and his allies attacked the problem from other directions. They achieved the passage of a law creating *ragionerii straordinari* (December 1424) who discovered, so the colleges reported, more than 100,000 florins of communal property in private hands.[325] They also obtained passage of legislation that encouraged delinquents to settle their accounts with the treasury by paying a fraction of their obligations.[326] In October 1425, the councils approved a measure granting authority to the Signoria and collegiate bodies to increase gabelles in the city and territory, and to levy new taxes on merchandise and banking.[327] Three

[322] The discussion is in *CP*, 46, ff.37r–43v, 19 and 22 Feb., and 15 March; see Molho, *Florentine Public Finances*, 77, n. 17. In addition to individuals called to these *pratiche*, each member of the colleges was asked to give an opinion on the *catasto*; ibid., ff.40r–41v. Among the lower guildsmen who favored the *catasto* were a carpenter, gilder, brazier and harness-maker.

[323] "Alias super catastu fuit habita pratica annis iam XX exactis, et conclusum fuit per prudentes quod fieri iuste non poterat"; *ibid.*, f.41r.

[324] *Ibid.*, ff.40v, 41r.

[325] *Prov.*, 114, ff.70r–72r, 9–10 Dec. 1424. The office was renewed a year later, as was that of the magistracy charged with selling the property of tax delinquents; *Prov.*, 115, ff.170r–175v. On collegiate opinion concerning the *ragionerii*; *CP*, 46, f.81v, 26 Sept. 1425.

[326] *Prov.*, 115, ff.120r–120v, 223r.

[327] *Ibid.*, ff.178r–179r. The gabelles of the gates, the gabelles on food, and the *contado estimo* were not to be increased. Taxes on trade and banking had been proposed before, in 1412, but rejected; see above, ch. VI, 348.

new *monti* were created in one year (December 1424–December 1425), the most important being the *monte delle doti*, which encouraged citizens to invest their money in a fund that would eventually provide dowries for their daughters and business capital for their sons.[328] A special magistracy of eight citizens (December 1425) was created with authority to cut salaries, eliminate or reduce pensions, and abolish offices.[329] This legislation, however, had no impact upon military expenditures, which by summer's end had risen to 80,000 florins monthly. Niccolò Sacchetti believed that this outlay was the greatest in the city's history; Giuliano Davanzati calculated (November 1425) the war's cost at two million florins.[330] Even though forced loans were being levied every month, the treasury could not pay the salaries of Florentine mercenaries. The war magistracy was forced to borrow money from private bankers to make up the deficit, at interest rates that sometimes reached forty and fifty percent annually. These charges were denounced as exorbitant in the *pratiche*,[331] but critics could not suggest any feasible alternatives. After several banking companies had failed as a result of the *balìa*'s inability to repay these loans, the Signoria drafted a provision that funded the outstanding obligations (estimated at 180,000 florins) and fixed the interest rate at fifteen percent.[332]

Despite warnings that the level of expenditure, if sustained, could destroy the regime, the war *balìa* continued to hire mercenaries and

[328] *Prov.*, 114, ff.90r–93v, 143r–144v; 115, ff.263v–268r. On the *monte delle doti*, see Molho, *Florentine Public Finances*, 138–41.

[329] The provision authorizing this reduction of expenses in *Prov.*, 115, ff.176v–178r; the decrees of this magistracy in *Balìe*, 22 and 23. On this *balìa*, see Molho, *Florentine Public Finances*, 116–18.

[330] *CP*, 46, ff.78v, 93r. Sacchetti's statement: "expensa gravior est quam nunquam nostra civitas habet et soli ad expensam sumus et mercatura nil aut parum agit." The Sienese ambassador estimated the monthly expenditure at "95 migliaia di fiorini o più"; *Conc.*, 1908, no. 16, 2 Aug. 1425.

[331] The statements of Lippozzo Mangioni (for the Twelve): "Audiverunt Decem ducentes 180,000 florenos super cambiis tenere . . . ad XL vel L pro cento"; Antonio Albizzi, "teneantur ad cambium tot milia florenorum et costat 40 pro cento"; Palla Strozzi, "et domini avertere debent successores ad interesse excessivum, nam si via non datur utilis, ad dextructionem nos perducet ut notum"; *CP*, 46, ff.76r, 78v, 87r. Cf. the comments of Piero Bonciani and Bartolomeo Carducci; *ibid.*, 88r, 88v. Though reduced temporarily, interest rates rose as high as 46% in the 1430s; Molho, *Florentine Public Finances*, 174–75.

[332] Molho, 153–54, 165–66. Among the bankrupts were Giovanni di Matteo Corsini, Salamone and Palla di Messer Palla Strozzi, and Niccolò Serragli.

to spend large sums on military operations.[333] The Florentine army in Romagna was estimated at 3000 cavalry in early August, and new contingents were being recruited to strengthen it.[334] These troops, however, remained on the defensive, and the *balìa* placed its hopes for victory on a fleet of Catalan galleys carrying Genoese exiles that raided the Ligurian coastline. After some initial successes, the armada suffered a defeat at Rapallo in late April and had to suspend operations until it received supplies and reinforcements.[335] Rinaldo degli Albizzi and Ridolfo Peruzzi had enthusiastically supported the naval action; Guglielmo Tanagli argued that it had been "useful" because it forced the duke to double his military expenditures.[336] On 7 November the Signoria convened a *pratica* to discuss the renewal of a subsidy for that operation. Palla di Novello Strozzi and Guidaccio Pecori wished to continue the naval attacks on the Riviera which, the latter insisted, had inflicted serious damage on the enemy and had brought honor to the republic. But Giovanni de' Medici described the Genoese operation as a costly failure.[337] Other counselors joined him in criticizing the naval campaign and, more generally, the *balìa*'s conduct of the war. Guidetto Guidetti and Giovanni Corbinelli deplored the poor discipline and ineptitude of the Florentine mercenaries "who do not fight and . . . who are paid too much." Niccolò Barbadori's judgment was even harsher: "We are spending 76,000 florins each month, and in two years of fighting we have done no harm to the duke."[338] In Giuliano Davanzati's opinion, the offensive strategy pursued by the *balìa* was both expensive and futile. The republic's territory could be defended, he argued, with a much smaller army of 900 horse and 4000 infantry, at a monthly cost of a mere 30,000 florins.[339]

These muted expressions of discontent did not accurately reflect

[333] Speaking for the Sixteen, Mariotto Baldovinetti: "Attenta gravissima expensa in qua sumus, non videant quod durare possumus"; *CP*, 46, f.52r. See also *ibid.*, f.62r. The war *balìa* made frequent pleas to the Signoria, the colleges and the *pratiche* for more money; *ASI*, 4th ser., xiv, 6, 10–12.

[334] *Conc.*, 1908, no. 16, 2 Aug. For negotiations concerning the hiring of more troops, see *Commissioni*, ii, 361, 370–71; *ASI*, 4th ser., xiv, 4–5, 8–10. In November, the army was estimated at 2000 lances; *CP*, 46, f.98v.

[335] *ASI*, 4th ser., xiii, 164–68; xiv, 5–6, 8.

[336] *Commissioni*, ii, 325; *CP*, 46, f.57r, 72v.

[337] *CP*, 46, f.93v: "Imprensa Janue aggressi sumus cum maximo apparatu maritimo et terrestri et quasi nil factum est." The armada cost 20,000 fl. per month; *ibid.*, ff.68v, 92v; statements of Morello and Palla Strozzi.

[338] *Ibid.*, ff.94r–94v. See the comments of Bernardo Guadagni; *ibid.*, f.101v, 6 Dec.

[339] *Ibid.*, f.93r. Agnolo Pandolfini made a similar argument six months earlier; *ibid.*, f.47v.

the civic mood outside the palace, where citizens were seething over "this accursed war."[340] That this anger was not directed solely at the enemy, but also at the leadership, was suggested by Lippozzo Mangioni, a spokesman for the Twelve, who complained about the slanders directed at public officials by the *popolo*.[341] In his diary Giovanni di Jacopo Morelli recorded his judgment of the war leadership: "Make war, begin war; give nourishment to those who live off war. Never has Florence been without war, nor will that ever change until we behead four of our leaders every year."[342] The Sienese ambassador reported that "seditious talk" was commonplace, and that wealthy citizens reacted to the crisis by indulging in an orgy of pleasure.[343] Lorenzo Ridolfi complained that some Florentines reported to their Venetian acquaintances that "our commune and our city are in the worst possible condition."[344] The first serious conspiracy since the Quarata affair in 1415 was uncovered in the spring of 1425; the leaders belonged to a mercantile family of San Giovanni, the Pagnini. Recruiting supporters in Bologna and in Florence, they planned to assemble secretly near the church of San Lorenzo, and then "go to the Mercato Nuovo and there kill everyone of the *reggimento* whom they found there, while shouting, 'Long live the *popolo* and the guilds!'" When the plot was discovered, the Pagnini fled to avoid capture; one of their followers, a resident of the parish of San Frediano named Lamberto di Piero, was executed.[345]

The autumn of 1425 marked the nadir of the republic's fortunes. On 9 October, at Anghiari near Arezzo, Florentine mercenaries were defeated by a Milanese army; eight days later, another battle was lost at Fagiuola in the Romagna. Six defeats without a single victory, so Giovanni Morelli summed up the results of two years of fighting: "First at Ponte a Ronco in Romagna; the second at Zagonara, a catastrophe;

[340] The phrase, by the lawyer Giovanni Bertaldi, is part of a comment on civic alienation: "Quod non miratur si ferventes non sunt cives ad consulendum, attentis propositis factis gravibus, et populo odiosus. . . . Actenta afflictione populi exausti pecunia pro hac maledicta guerra et pluries memoravit ut aliqui auxilia tribuerent populo in solucione"; *CP*, 46, f.66r, 4 Aug. 1425.

[341] *Ibid.*, f.81v, 26 Sept.

[342] "Fate guerra, inducete guerra, date poppa a chi nutrica la guerra. Mai è stata Firenze senza guerra, nè stara perinsino non taglia la testa ogni anno a 4 de' Maggiori"; *Delizie*, XIX, 73.

[343] *Conc.*, 1908, no. 16, 2 Aug.: "Le case de' povari sono senza uscia e [sono] vuote. Grande piata è a vedere questi richi attendono a diletti quaxi come disperata. Per tutta la città si giuca come cosa rotta."

[344] *CP*, 46, f.89v, 26 Oct.

[345] *ACP*, 2898, ff.23r–23v, 19 June; 2918, ff.13r–13v, 19 Sept. On this plot, see *CP*, 46, ff.24r, 52v.

the third defeat in Valdilimona, 600 horse and 1500 infantry lost; the fourth at Rapallo on the Genoese Riviera; the fifth at Anghiari, 300 horse and 500 infantry; the sixth at Fagiuola, 1000 infantry."[346] Then, in November, the Florentine captain, Niccolò Piccinino, switched his allegiance to the Visconti, and at the head of a large army of 3000 horse and 4000 infantry, ravaged the Aretine *contado* and seized several castles in that area.[347] The leadership reacted stoically to this tide of bad news. Speaking for his quarter of Santa Croce, Ridolfo Peruzzi mentioned these military failures, while urging the Signoria to act decisively "to remove this shame and humiliation from us."[348] Some used the occasion to flay the *balìa* for its failure to build a more efficient army;[349] the majority, however, accepted the losses as due, not to human failure, but to the fortunes of war. The leaders focused their attention on the one resource—money—that could preserve their regime and their fortunes.[350] They had no illusions about the difficulties of extracting still more florins from the citizenry; Rinaldo degli Albizzi warned that the internal strife generated by these exactions could be more perilous than a Visconti invasion. "Let us follow the counsel of those who are the foundation of the *reggimento*," Lippozzo Mangioni said, "and everyone should accept their decision." Giovanni Guicciardini was not concerned about the "scandals" that certain men might provoke. If they are unwilling to follow the guidance of their superiors, he said, the Signoria will instruct them in the behavior appropriate to citizens of a free republic.[351]

The war's turning-point occurred at that moment when Florence's prospects were bleakest. On 8 December 1425 a courier from Venice brought the news that, four days earlier, an alliance between the republics of Florence and Venice had been signed.[352] That pact was the culmination of months of negotiation, and of shifting relationships among the major Italian powers: Florence and Venice, the papacy and Filippo Maria Visconti. While professing his sincere desire for peace, Martin V had skillfully worked against any resolution of the conflict

---

[346] Morelli, *Delizie*, xix, 68. See also Cavalcanti, *Istorie fiorentine*, iii, ch. 26; *Commissioni*, ii, 425–26.

[347] Morelli, 69; Cavalcanti, iii, ch. 27–28.

[348] *CP*, 46, f.102v, 6 Dec.

[349] Thus, Bernardo Anselmi, Francesco Machiavelli and Felice Brancacci for the Sixteen; *ibid.*, ff.101v, 103r.

[350] On fiscal needs, the statements of Giovanni Bischeri and Giovanni de' Medici, and the collegiate spokesmen, Felice Brancacci and Cambio Salviati; *ibid.*, ff.101r, 103r–103v.

[351] *Commissioni*, ii, 552–53; *CP*, 46, ff.111v, 113r.

[352] *Commissioni*, ii, 510–11.

between the republic and the duke of Milan.[353] Florentine ambassadors in Rome were unable to win over the pope to the republic's side or induce him to play a peacemaking role. The impasse was broken by Venice, whose diplomats began (July 1425) to participate more actively in peace discussions.[354] When Filippo Maria refused to accept a Venetian offer to mediate between the combatants, the Serenissima's ambassadors in Rome became more friendly to the Florentine envoys, Rinaldo degli Albizzi and Agnolo Pandolfini.[355] That shift in mood and purpose also created a more cordial atmosphere in Venice, where Florentine ambassadors had been laboring for months to conclude an alliance.[356] In Rome, meanwhile, Filippo Maria's ambassadors told Rinaldo degli Albizzi of the duke's willingness to make peace, if the Venetians were excluded from the negotiations. Rinaldo wrote to his friend Vieri Guadagni, urging him and his colleagues in the war magistracy to consider that proposal seriously: "For God's sake, give peace to your *popolo* and you will be adored as saints!" For his pains, Rinaldo was chided by Guadagni for being too credulous and rebuked by the Ten for his presumption in writing about state affairs to one citizen, instead of to them.[357] Though tempted to pursue this peace initiative, the *balìa* finally decided against any parleys with the duke's agents that might alienate the Venetians.

As Martin V railed at the Florentine ambassadors for their refusal to negotiate with the Milanese envoys,[358] notaries in Venice were drafting the text of the alliance between the two republics. The purpose of the federation, so the preamble read, was "to conserve the status [of the signatories] against the lord Filippo Maria Visconti"; it was to remain in effect for ten years, even if peace were made with the duke.[359] To Venice was given responsibility for achieving that objective, and Florence was obliged to accept the terms obtained by her ally. However, the signatories promised that, if a peace or truce had not been signed by the end of February 1426, to recruit an army of

---

[353] For an assessment of papal policy, see Partner, *Papal State*, 86–89.

[354] *Commissioni*, II, 337–38, 344, 358. On these diplomatic developments, see *Storia di Milano*, VI, 216–19.

[355] *Ibid.*, II, 362–63, 384, 390, 396, 428, 442.

[356] See Ridolfi's letters of 14 Aug. and 19 Sept., *ibid.*, II, 375–76, 402–03. The instructions to Ridolfi, when he departed on his mission in Apr. 1425, are in Palla Strozzi's diary; *ASI*, 4th ser., XIII, 156–60.

[357] *Commissioni*, II, 436, 440–41. Rinaldo noted, *ibid.*, 442, that "la moneta sciema a lui come a voi. . . . Il Duca è in mancamento di danari. . . ."

[358] *Ibid.*, II, 480–83, 486–87, 492–93.

[359] The text in *ibid.*, II, 541–51.

16,000 horse and 6000 infantry, each to pay for one-half of that force and to share equally all military expenses. Territory held by the duke in Tuscany and Romagna that came under allied control was at Florence's disposition; that conquered in Lombardy belonged to Venice.

The historical significance of this alliance has long been recognized. It signaled a decisive shift in Venetian foreign policy, from detachment and disinterest to a sustained involvement in Italian politics. For the Florentines, the treaty ended a decade of debate over the wisdom of an alliance with that "congruent regime," whose stability and durability they admired while fearing its superior power. Though the signatories contributed equal portions of men and money to the war, Venice had demanded, and received, the dominant role in achieving a peace settlement, and thus a critical advantage over her partner in determining the future course of the war. The Serenissima could also hope to profit more from territorial conquest than Florence, whose rights over papal territory would be challenged by Martin V. But these considerations did not trouble those citizens who praised the officials responsible for contracting the Venetian alliance which, Agnolo Acciaiuoli believed, was the best guarantee of the regime's security.[360] They worried instead about finding the money to subsidize an army of 8000 cavalry and 3000 infantry, which would raise the military budget to new heights, possibly exceeding 100,000 florins monthly.[361] The leaders of the *reggimento* had purchased a mortgage on their estate, but they could not be sure that the shareholders could meet the payments. That issue was at the center of Florentine politics for the war's duration, and beyond.[362]

---

[360] *CP*, 46, f.105r, 2 Jan. 1426. There was no recorded debate on the Venetian alliance before its conclusion, and very little thereafter. No meetings of the colleges or the *pratiche* are recorded between 8 Dec. 1425 and 2 Jan. 1426; *ibid.*, ff.103v-104r.

[361] Rinaldo degli Albizzi's estimate was 92,000 fl.; *Commissioni*, II, 553. Giovanni Minerbetti reported the *balìa's* estimate of 95,000 fl.; *CP*, 46, f.127r, 20 March 1426.

[362] That issue has been well analyzed by Molho, *Florentine Public Finances*, ch. 6.

CHAPTER VIII

The Regime's Climacteric, 1426–1430

THE REVIVAL OF THE FACTIONS

THE Venetian alliance may have been Florence's salvation in her struggle with Filippo Maria Visconti, but it did not lighten the civic mood appreciably, nor did it dampen criticism of the leadership's conduct of the war.[1] Never have tax inequities been so great, nor have so many quarrels arisen from them, Messer Francesco Viviani observed somberly.[2] Nicola di Messer Vieri de' Medici thought (August 1426) that civic discord had reached the highest levels in the regime's history.[3] The citizens were so financially exhausted, and so resentful over their burdens, that they were reluctant to discuss fiscal problems in the *pratiche*.[4] "We have no more money," Rinaldo degli Albizzi said with some exaggeration, "and what never happened before in any of our previous wars is now occurring: robberies and extortions, the flight of our subjects from the territory, many acts of treason. . . ."[5] Conceding that the administration of the republic was becoming increasingly difficult, Francesco Machiavelli attributed that development to each citizen's preoccupation with his own interests.[6] Filippo Mangioni criticized those in the *reggimento* who wished to lord it over their peers, and who were more concerned with their own status than with the public good.[7]

Giovanni Cavalcanti reported that the old, intractable problem of *prestanze* assessments crystallized these discontents in the summer of 1426.[8] These payments were so heavy that even wealthy citizens now feared that their patrimonies would be dissipated. Their influence in

---

[1] For evidence of dissatisfaction with the war *balìa*'s activities, see *Commissioni*, II, 552–53; CP, 46, ff.112r–113r, 23 Jan. 1426.

[2] CP, 46, f.105v, 2 Jan. 1426. Cf. Giotto Peruzzi's comment: "Quod inequalitates maxime sunt et maiores quam unquam fuerint post hedificationem Karoli Magni citra"; quoted in Molho, *Florentine Public Finances*, 80, n. 24.

[3] CP, 46, f.194v, 28 Aug.

[4] Paolo Carnesecchi, "Excusando tarditionem consiliariorum, quia materia odiosa est et cives pecuniis sunt exhausti"; Bartolomeo Valori, "Facta excusatione tarditas ad consulendum propter expensa excessiva et oblocutiones multorum"; Jacopo Federighi, "quod odiosa est materia que tractatur et displicibilis, quia populus noster expensis fessus est"; *ibid.*, ff.111v, 139v, 150v.

[5] *Commissioni*, II, 553. Cf. Rinaldo's statement of 6 Sept.: "Addita etiam dissensio inter cives quam nunquam maior fuit"; CP, 47, f.4r.

[6] CP, 46, f.181r, 6 Aug. 1426.   [7] *Ibid.*, f.111v, 23 Jan. 1426.

[8] *Istorie fiorentine*, III, ch. 2.

the regime had not protected them from arbitrary and excessive levies; they hoped to gain some modest relief by the passage of a law revising the assessments. But that measure was repeatedly rejected in the Council of the *Popolo* by "artisans and citizens of low condition." In Rinaldo degli Albizzi's opinion, some voted against this measure because the tax relief was so small, but others "because they wished to cause scandal."[9] The frustrated leadership then considered ways to overcome the opposition. According to Cavalcanti, a group of prominent citizens obtained permission from the standard-bearer of justice, Lorenzo Ridolfi, and a sympathetic prior, Francesco di Messer Rinaldo Gianfigliazzi, to meet secretly to discuss the issue. Three members of the war *balìa*—Matteo Castellani, Niccolò da Uzzano and Vieri Guadagni—allegedly participated in this meeting, which was held, so Cavalcanti reported, in the church of Santo Stefano sometime in August 1426. Rinaldo degli Albizzi was the choice of these "most powerful men in the *reggimento*" to deliver the keynote speech.

According to Cavalcanti's account of this Santo Stefano meeting, Rinaldo delivered a scathing attack upon the artisans who had voted against the law providing tax relief, and who had gained a foothold in the *reggimento* with the connivance of their social superiors. They regularly voted against all legislation that was designed to promote the welfare of aristocratic families. Since they had little money or property, and their taxes were minimal, they readily voted for wars and for the levies that subsidized military campaigns. In wartime, Rinaldo believed, money flowed steadily from the wealthy citizens to these artisans and retailers, who sold goods and services to the soldiers hired by the republic. These artisans were the descendants of those radicals who "for forty accursed months [1378–82] held this *popolo* in servitude." In language that Cicero might have applauded, Rinaldo invited his audience to visualize the tombs of ancestors martyred by that regime: the bloodstains on the parapets of the captain's palace where they had been executed; the sights and sounds of widows and orphans grieving for their dead husbands and fathers. These men who sat in the Signoria were descendants of serfs. Many came into the city from Empoli or the Mugello, where they had been dependents of Florentine citizens. Their bestial nature will never change; they were incapable of love or civilized behavior. Who can deny, Rinaldo asked, the right of a Bardi to be superior to the nephew of Piero Ramini, or to the son of the baker Salvestro? Was it not appropriate for a Rossi [a distinguished family of magnates] to be above someone called Stucco, or for

[9] *CP*, 46, f.181r, 6 Aug.

a Frescobaldi to hold civic office in place of a Stuppino? Those "mechanics" who worked with their hands, or who sold soap and pork and wine in retail shops, were unfit for membership in this *reggimento*.

Rinaldo's speech (as summarized by Cavalcanti) was the clearest statement of the elitist viewpoint articulated by any Florentine statesman of this regime.[10] Arguing from the premise that the interests of aristocrats and artisans were irreconcilable, he urged his audience to act decisively to protect themselves and their state. "You are the commune; you are the embodiment of honor; you guide the destiny of this city. . . ." To recover their rightful place in the polity, they must cease their fratricidal quarreling, since conflict had been the means by which the "mechanics" had gained office and influence. In his more extreme statements, Rinaldo appeared to advocate the total expulsion of the artisans and shopkeepers from the regime. His specific recommendation, however, was more moderate: the reduction of the number of lower guilds from fourteen to seven, and the halving of their representation in communal offices. Though he favored the cancellation of all restrictions on officeholding by magnates, he did not make a concrete proposal for this reform. His proposals could not be implemented by legislation, Rinaldo admitted, but only by force. The war *balìa* was the key to success, since that magistracy could bring troops into the city under the pretext of military necessity. "In the last analysis, the sword is decisive." With loyal troops defending the palace, the elite could reform the regime and suppress any opposition by the lower guildsmen. "Then worthy men will have the honorable posts in the commune, and these upstarts (*veniticci*) will stay in their shops and labor to earn the wherewithal to feed their families and, as promoters of scandal and discord, they will be excluded entirely from the administration of the republic."

Since no other contemporary source mentions the Santo Stefano meeting, Cavalcanti's account must be treated with great caution.[11] The records of the *Libri Fabarum* do show that a provision to revise *prestanze* assessments had been voted down several times by the Council of the *Popolo* during July and August 1426, when Lorenzo Ridolfi and Francesco Gianfigliazzi were members of the Signoria.[12]

[10] For similar views, attributed to Niccolò da Uzzano, see the anonymous poem printed in *ASI*, 1st ser., IV (1843), part 1, 297-300.

[11] That the meeting did occur is accepted by C. Gutkind, *Cosimo de' Medici Pater Patriae* (Oxford, 1938), 56-57. Bayley, *War and Society*, 111-12, is skeptical of Cavalcanti's report. D. Kent, *Rise of the Medici*, ch. 3, is uncertain about the meeting, but accepts the chronicler's account of Rinaldo's speech as an accurate statement of the aristocratic viewpoint.

[12] *LF*, 53, ff.121v–123v, 130r.

There was, moreover, an uproar in the *pratiche* that summer concerning reports that secret meetings had been held in Florentine churches. Though not conclusive, this evidence gives some credibility to Cavalcanti's assertion that a group of prominent statesmen had met privately to discuss political issues. Less persuasive, however, is the chronicler's attribution of the proposed reforms to Rinaldo degli Albizzi. Though echoes of his known opinions do appear in the Cavalcanti version, Rinaldo's political style was not as aggressive or conspiratorial as this reported speech suggests. That he would advocate a violent revolution in response to a council's rejection of a fiscal measure is scarcely credible. Even more fanciful is Cavalcanti's statement that Rinaldo's analysis of the crisis, and his prescription for its solution, were unanimously accepted by these statesmen, "who raised their hands to heaven, praising God and Messer Rinaldo." And his account of the sequel to this colloquium was either a figment of his imagination or a report that he had heard in that gossip-filled city. Rinaldo was allegedly sent by the group to tell Giovanni de' Medici of the plan to reform the republic; they hoped that this "patron and leader of the guildsmen and merchants" would approve the scheme. Instead, the old banker criticized Rinaldo for repudiating his father's policy of favoring the *popolo*. He would not give his blessing to the enterprise, and he urged Rinaldo to leave the regime as his father had bequeathed it to his son's generation.

Though Cavalcanti's account of the Santo Stefano colloquium is not accurate in all respects, some parts can be verified by other sources. The councils were indeed rejecting provisions that would reduce some *prestanze* assessments, as Cavalcanti noted. But despite his statement that artisans and shopkeepers always supported military enterprises, the fact is that the councils voted consistently against legislation pertaining to the Milanese war, its management, and its funding. In January 1426, the Signoria fought and won two prolonged battles with the councils over the passage of fiscal legislation that, in the leadership's judgment, was necessary to meet the republic's obligations in the Venetian treaty. A key feature was the creation of a fiscal magistracy authorized to impose forced loans at its discretion, without any limits, for a one-year period.[13] One sign of the intense hostility to that commission and its labors was an attempt (August 1426) to burn down the house of Niccolò Carducci, a member of that magistracy.[14] The debates on fiscal reforms in the summer of 1426, when the Santo

---

[13] For the votes and the deliberations on this legislation, *LF*, 53, ff.98r–101r; *Prov.*, 115, ff.274r–281r, 283r–288r, 295v–297r; *CP*, 46, ff.111v–113r.

[14] Molho, *Florentine Public Finances*, 108.

Stefano colloquium was allegedly held, were noteworthy for their tone of desperation. Without significant revisions in the assessments, the priors argued, revenues would fall, and citizens with excessive levies would flee to avoid ruin.[15] The councilors were not moved by these pleas, nor by the arguments of Giovanni de' Medici, nor by those of Luca degli Albizzi (Rinaldo's brother) who, speaking for the Eight on Security, reported their profound disappointment over the council's refusal to support the Signoria.[16] Quite as important for the war effort as the revision of assessments was the reelection of the war *balìa*, also resisted in the councils. Initially proposed in August, the provision to extend the *balìa*'s authority for six months was finally approved by the narrowest of margins in mid-October, after several rejections. This magistracy's authority was limited by a clause stipulating that it could not engage in any new wars or campaigns without the approval of the Signoria and the colleges.[17]

In his summary of grievances, Cavalcanti did not mention office-holding, beyond noting Rinaldo's complaint that too many lower guildsmen had been allowed into the *reggimento*.[18] He did not discuss the feuding over the holding of scrutinies and *rimbotti*, which had been as bitter and divisive as the controversies over the fisc. In June 1426, the councils had rejected a provision authorizing a *rimbotto*: the insertion of newly qualified citizens into pouches from past scrutinies.[19] Several men from aristocratic families—Francesco Machiavelli, Guglielmo Altoviti, Lorenzo Ridolfi—spoke in favor of that provision; Ridolfi argued that the law would benefit "the young men whose fathers and older brothers had died." He cited his own situation—"of my five sons, only one is now alive"—to demonstrate the merits of this legislation. It would be a grave miscarriage of justice, Leonardo Fantoni argued, if descendants of old and distinguished

---

[15] See the comments of Giovanni Minerbetti and Antonio dell' Antella; *LF*, 53, ff.123r–123v. Earlier, in February, the authorities were concerned about the massive outflow of capital from Florence "ad alienas partes per viam cambiorum"; *Prov.*, 115, f.297r.

[16] *CP*, 46, f.182v, 6 Aug. Rinaldo degli Albizzi, *ibid.*, f.181r, made an impassioned plea for the enactment of that provision.

[17] *Prov.*, 116, ff.174r–175v. For the controversy over this measure, *LF*, 53, ff.143r–145r; *CP*, 46, ff.189r–190r, 17 Aug.

[18] "Per dispetto de' nobili e degli antichi popolani ciascuno ha fatto nuovo rimbotto, e aggiunti tanti novissimi e meccanici nelle borse, che ora le loro fave è tal numero che le vostre non ottengono"; Cavalcanti, *Storie fiorentine*, book III, ch. 2.

[19] *LF*, 53, ff.112v–116v, 12–25 June 1426. After two rejections, the bill was approved by the Council of the *Popolo*, only to be rejected in the Council of the Commune.

Guelf families, which had sacrificed so much for Florentine liberty, were now to be deprived of those benefits. Fantoni also repeated the argument that offices should be allocated in proportion to the size of the individual's contribution to the fisc.[20] Rinaldo degli Albizzi publicly admitted that he preferred to associate with citizens of high status and exalted lineage and, by implication, argued that such men were more deserving of office than men of lower status.[21] "Offices should be granted either to the virtuous," Niccolò da Uzzano said, "or to those who deserve them on account of family and kin."[22]

Such expressions of the elitist mentality within the leadership must have antagonized guildsmen and strengthened their determination to resist every legislative proposal for a *rimbotto*. By voting against the leadership on this issue, artisans may have been expressing their resentment over a provision, enacted in December 1425, which limited their access to the salaried offices in the dominion. During the war's early stages, four castellans from the lower guilds had surrendered their fortresses to Visconti troops; they were subsequently convicted of treason and sentenced to death *in absentia*.[23] Taking note of these incidents, the 1425 provision suspended the normal procedure of sortition for territorial offices and, for a one-year period, gave authority to the Signoria, the colleges, and the war *balìa* to elect castellans to these posts.[24]

Though he took liberties with the facts when he wrote his account of the Santo Stefano conclave, Cavalcanti did portray quite accurately the political climate in 1426, and specifically the aristocratic point of view. He realized that the primary source of conflict was the rift between the regime's elitist leadership and the guild community. He was dimly aware, too, of the historical context of the rivalry between corporate and aristocratic values that for more than a century had pitted ancient families against artisans and shopkeepers, cloth-manufacturers and merchants, upwardly mobile parvenus. With exceptional clarity and vigor, he voiced the aristocratic conviction that the regime

---

[20] *CP*, 46, ff.162r–162v, 20 June. See also *LF*, 53, ff.114v–115r.

[21] ". . . Unum magis quam alium secundum gradum et parentelam diligatur"; *Commissioni*, III, 506, *pratica*, of 26 Apr. 1430.

[22] ". . . Dentur dignitates vel virtutibus vel merentibus propter domum et parentes"; *CP*, 49, f.33r, 16 Apr. 1430.

[23] Nanni Dei, Niccolò Delli, shirt-maker; Bartolo di Lorenzo di Francesco, blacksmith; Domenico di Romolo; *AP*, 4363, ff.37r–37v, 49r–49v, 71r–71v; *AEOJ*, 2045, ff.23r–24r. Cf. Cavalcanti, *Storie fiorentine*, III, ch. 20.

[24] *Prov.*, 115, ff.219v–220r. The major castellanies in Pisa, Pistoia, Arezzo and other important cities which were reserved for prominent citizens were exempt from this provision.

was rightfully the exclusive property of the great families, and that it no longer needed its corporate chrysalis. The views attributed to Rinaldo degli Albizzi were certainly not his alone, but an amalgam of elitist opinions and prejudices, including those of Cavalcanti himself, a magnate who was hostile to the aristocratic leadership, but also resentful of the "mechanics" who sat in offices that he could not hold.[25] Rinaldo may not have voiced (or even consciously felt) the hatred for the artisans and peasants that Cavalcanti ascribed to him, but those sentiments were part of the Florentine aristocrat's psychic baggage.

Cavalcanti had portrayed Giovanni de' Medici as the upholder of constitutional government, and Rinaldo degli Albizzi—with his oligarchic associates—as the promoters of revolution. This division between constitutionalists and conspirators was never so neat as the chronicler suggested. While some citizens with oligarchic sympathies may have dreamed of using force to gain their political objectives, they could not have persuaded many of their colleagues to participate in a scheme that would not have guaranteed their control of the councils. Every member of the political elite was publicly committed to the preservation of the republic's institutions and values, while at the same time joining secret societies. Such associations had long been a feature of Florentine political life. Normally, they operated so quietly and unobtrusively through private contacts and agreements that their existence and influence was hardly noticed. When the regime distributed its largesse to the satisfaction of its membership, these "societies" played only a minor role in lubricating the machinery that dispensed offices, honors, and benefits. But when the system was malfunctioning, as in the 1420s, and men felt that their interests were not being protected by officialdom, they sought help "outside the palace" by expanding their circle of friends and allies, and by strenghtening those personal ties which linked Florentines to each other.

The sudden surge of civic interest in these societies was probably the result of the Santo Stefano meeting, or the circulation of rumors about such gatherings, in which, so Francesco Machiavelli reported, "public business is transacted, whence arises dissension, hatred, and evil."[26] The first reference to these conventicles occurred in a report by Bartolomeo Valori and Uberto del Palagio, speaking for a *pratica* on 4 July 1426. These counselors had considered the pernicious growth of these societies; they recommended that punitive legislation be

[25] On Cavalcanti's political opinions, see Marcella T. Grendler, The *"Trattato Politico-Morale" of Giovanni Cavalcanti (1381–c.1451)* (Geneva, 1973), ch. 1, 4.
[26] *CP*, 46, f.184r.

enacted to eliminate this threat to the regime.[27] The issue, however, remained dormant for several weeks, until mid-August, when civic anxiety over clandestine organizations became so intense that war-related problems were pushed from the agenda of the *pratiche*. Cities were destroyed by divisions, Rinaldo degli Albizzi solemnly told one group of counselors. He had heard that many citizens were meeting in illegal assemblies, and he urged the authorities to act decisively to dissolve them. On 12 August, Rinaldo and Ridolfo Peruzzi counseled the Signoria to launch a campaign against all confraternities.[28] Officials should be sent to every church and monastery where these groups met, to collect and burn their records. The entrances to the meeting-places should be sealed; the rectors of the churches should be warned that they would be punished severely if they permitted the disbanded societies to meet on their premises. The legislation passed in 1419 to regulate confraternities had authorized the Signoria to approve those they considered beneficial; that authority should be withdrawn, "so that every one of these societies is totally disbanded, and so that they do not commit evil under the guise of virtue." Anyone suspected of membership in these organizations could be denounced to the priors who, with their colleges, would vote on the merits of the accusation. Those convicted of belonging to an illegal group would henceforth be ineligible for communal office.[29]

These recommendations received the support of every counselor who participated in these debates. No one dared to defend the societies, although some collegiate groups expressed the pious hope that confraternities with genuine spiritual concerns might be salvaged from the wreckage.[30] Yet these harsh proposals were never enacted into law, which suggests that the leadership did not favor a ban on the societies. A provision dissolving the confraternities had apparently been drafted and discussed by the Signoria, but either it did not win the priors' approval or it was rejected by the colleges.[31] Instead of approving legislation curbing the societies, the priors and their colleges promulgated an executive decree which authorized the Eight on Security to scrutinize each confraternity and to determine whether it

[27] *Ibid.*, f.169r. See also the statements made in another *pratica* of 17 July; *CP*, 46, ff.172v–173r.

[28] *CP*, 46, ff.184r, 187r.

[29] Cf. the statement of Stefano Bencivenni; f.184r.

[30] Niccolò Rittafè for the Twelve, and Vannozzo Serragli, for the Parte captains; *CP*, 46, f.194v, 28 Aug.

[31] For references to the provision, the statements of Piero Beccanugi and Vannozzo Serragli; *ibid.*, f.194r.

was involved in political activity. The Company of the Magi received a clean bill of health from the Eight on 19 September: "They declared the said confraternity and the men of the said confraternity to have been, and be, good men, and men of good condition, morals, and fame, and of this quality likewise the works and activities of the said confraternity; and that the men of the said confraternity . . . occupy and have occupied themselves with things divine and not with any mundane or material business of the Republic of Florence. . . ."[32]

The issues involved in this political furor were not defined clearly by the protagonists, who disguised their sentiments behind clouds of civic rhetoric. Rinaldo degli Albizzi and Giovanni de' Medici, the leaders of the rival factions, insisted that they "had never belonged to any society."[33] They could deplore the illegal meetings of their rivals: evil, grasping men concerned only with their selfish interests. But they were not eager to promote legislation or enforce regulations that would eliminate all private associations. While the civic ethic required them to denounce such groups as pernicious, they could not conceive of a polity so austere that private interests were totally subsumed into the *res publica* or friendships did not play a role in public affairs. The system which they manipulated, and from which they profited, was deeply rooted in their customs and their consciousness.[34] Six months after the debate on the societies, Luca di Matteo da Panzano wrote to his friend and neighbor, Forese Sacchetti, offering his services in the revision of the *prestanze* schedule that had finally been approved by the councils.[35] If he should be chosen assessor, Luca promised to have such concern for Sacchetti's interests that he and his kinsmen would be satisfied. In exchange for that commitment, Luca wanted Forese's support in the reconstruction (*rimbotto*) of the pouches that was imminent. If that bargain were actually con-

---

[32] R. Hatfield, "The Compagnia de' Magi," *Journal of the Warburg and Courtauld Institutes*, XXXIII (1970), 110, 145–46. No provision concerning confraternities was submitted to the councils during that summer; *LF*, 53, ff.133r–134r. For an illustration from the Medici period of a confraternity's involvement in politics, see Rubinstein, *Government of Florence*, 119.

[33] Rinaldo: "Ipse de nulla societate fuit vel est, et amplo loqui potest"; *CP*, 46, f.184r. Speaking for the Merchants' Court, Giovanni de' Medici: "Ipse de nulla societate sit"; *ibid.*, f.185r.

[34] Nicolai Rubinstein has demonstrated the survival of this system, and this way of perceiving politics, through the Medici period; *Government of Florence, passim*. See too the comments of L. Martines, "A Way of Looking at Women in Renaissance Florence," *Journal of Medieval and Renaissance Studies*, IV (1974), 23–26.

[35] *CRS*, 78 (*Badìa*), 324, f.17r, 5 Feb. 1427.

summated, it could hardly be described as a conspiracy. But it was one strand in a complex network of private relationships that existed alongside the state and encroached upon its jurisdiction. While reporting to his cousin Forese about a political mission that he was about to make to Duccio Mancini, a neighbor in their *gonfalone*, Andreuolo Sacchetti made a very revealing statement. "You know that everyone is concerned with his own interests in these matters," he wrote, "so that one does not work very hard for those to whom one is not bound by some obligation."[36]

DISINTEGRATION

Florentines customarily viewed civic discord as a moral issue that was susceptible to treatment by exhortation and, more pragmatically, as a problem that could be solved or alleviated by legislation. The leadership launched a massive campaign to stimulate patriotism, and by its adoption of the *catasto* it hoped to eliminate a major source of strife. Only after these efforts had failed did the regime adopt, in 1429, more drastic measures to save itself from disintegration.

Between 1426 and 1429 Florentines witnessed a veritable orgy of civic celebration; public festivities were more frequent and more elaborate than at any time since the papal war of the 1370s. Processions moved through the city's streets for three successive days in February 1426, to celebrate the ratification of the Venetian alliance. A month later, bonfires were lit when news arrived that Venetian troops had breached the outer circle of Brescia's walls. The fall of the citadel in Brescia (September 1426) was marked by the ringing of bells and the lighting of bonfires; on five separate occasions during that autumn the good news from the Lombard front prompted the Signoria to organize celebrations.[37] The tempo of these festivities slackened in 1427,

[36] *Ibid.*, f.19r, 22 Feb. 1427: "A Duccio farò vostra inbasciata, e credo che essendo toccho la sorta dell'essere rimaso e tratto al fratello, n'arebe fatto il possibile, ma non essendo, ad altri n'è rimasta la faticha, e questo vi basti. Perchè, come sapete, di simili cose ongnuno n'à la spezialtà sua, in modo che per altri che non gli sia congiunto non troppo si travaglia. Pure mi rendo certo che per l'amore che sempre v'à portato, se io l'avessi richiesto più d'una chosa che d'un' altra, v'arebe volentieri servito; ma di questo no'll'ò richiesto, non mi parendo suo istreto bisongnio, e massime essendoci gli sgravatori istati pure assai amici." On the exploitation of these bonds by the Medici in elections, see the letters of Giuliano de' Medici and Antonio Serristori; D. Kent, *Rise of the Medici*, ch. 3, n. 53 and 60.

[37] Morelli, *Delizie*, XIX, 69-70, 73; Petriboni, *BNF, Conv. Sopp.*, C, 4, 895, f.117v.

but an allied victory near Mantua in October of that year was signaled by another round of "festivals, fires, and solemn processions."[38] To mark the conclusion of peace with Filippo Maria Visconti in May 1428, the Signoria ordered the venerated portrait of the Virgin from Impruneta to be carried through the streets at the head of a large procession.[39] In the loggia of the Signoria, the priors and their entourage listened to the proclamation of peace delivered by the chancellor, Leonardo Bruni. A witness, Pietro Petriboni, reported that on that occasion, Bruni presented the Signoria with a copy of his works, and then delivered a formal oration.[40] In this celebration, secular and sacred rituals, themes, and personalities were combined to glorify the republic, as they were every year on the feast day of Saint John the Baptist. There was also official encouragement and patronage of the festivities held annually on Epiphany when the Company of the Magi and other confraternities reenacted Biblical scenes on a platform erected in front of the Signoria's palace. Those performances had apparently been suspended after 1419, as a result of the ban on confraternities enacted in that year. They were revived in 1429 by decree of the Signoria and the colleges, "desirous that those things which customarily were done for the magnificence of the people of Florence, not be lacking to the city on account of negligence. . . ."[41] There were no traces of religious ritual or symbolism in the tournaments, which were becoming so popular in these years. Their significance as manifestations of the aristocratic ethos has already been noted, but they were also civic celebrations. The judges who selected the victors were chosen, like the priors, from each quarter of the city; a fifth member was added from the lower guilds. These men belonged to the regime's inner circle; their sons and nephews participated in the competitions to win honor and prizes.[42] In April 1429, for example, the Signoria announced that a joust would be held to honor the visit of a Portuguese prince. To insure that it would be held as scheduled, and without cost to the republic, the priors levied fines of 1000 florins upon five citizens —Lorenzo di Messer Palla Strozzi, Filippo Tornabuoni, Domenico Lamberteschi, Cionettino Bastari, and Giovanni di Tommaso Giovanni—

[38] Morelli, *Delizie*, XIX, 77.

[39] On the history of these processions, see R. Trexler, "Florentine Religious Experience: the Sacred Image," *Studies in the Renaissance*, XIX (1972), 11–16.

[40] Petriboni, f.112v: "Detta hora in sulla ringhiera detto dì, Messer Leonardo detto donò a' signori uno libro delle opere sue et fece una diceria et poi sonarono le trombette et pifferi et incominciò a passare la processione."

[41] Hatfield, "Compagnia de' Magi," *Journal of the Warburg and Courtauld Institutes*, XXXIII, 110–11, 146.

[42] Petriboni, ff.121r–122r, 124v; *Strozz.*, 2nd ser., 16, ff.4r, 4v.

but with the proviso that the fines would be cancelled if "they come into the arena upon horses in armor, as is customary, to participate in a joust at their own expense. . . ."[43]

In the streets and squares, processions and tournaments; in the loggia of the Signoria and within the palace, an effusion of oratory, to encourage the "good citizens" and to deter those whose motives and actions were evil. But the leadership was not so naive as to believe that pageantry and speeches alone could improve civic morale, without some concrete action to correct the flaws in the political system. During the debate on the societies in August 1426, Rinaldo degli Albizzi and Palla Strozzi had both insisted that these phenomena were spawned by inequities in the allocation of forced loans.[44] This argument was repeatedly made by proponents of the *catasto*, who renewed their campaign for the adoption of the scheme in the summer of 1426, and with even greater urgency in the spring of the next year.[45] The *catasto* would reveal every citizen's wealth, Matteo Castellani asserted; he questioned the motives of its opponents "who wish to hide their property and defraud the commune. . . ." In an eloquent speech, Niccolò Barbadori described the manifold benefits that would derive from the *catasto*: "It will reveal [everyone's] property; it will bring unity to the *popolo* and eliminate discord; it will encourage citizens to speak freely in debates and provide for the commune's necessities. . . ." Had the *catasto* been instituted twenty-five years before, the lawyer Guglielmo Tanagli said, his own fortune would not have been dissipated.[46] Biagio Niccolini was persuaded of the *catasto*'s merits by its Roman precedent; Rinaldo degli Albizzi noted that Venice had long employed a similar system, "and that city, compared to all others, is the best governed. . . ."[47] These arguments, so eloquently presented in the debates, did not persuade skeptics who stubbornly voted against the *catasto* because, their spokesmen argued, its implementation would

---

[43] *GA*, 75, ff.201r–201v, 22 Apr. 1429.

[44] Strozzi, "Omnis discordia oritur propter onerum inequalitatem"; Albizzi, "Provenit omne dissensio per onera non iuste distribuita, et per societates qui ad ea vigebant"; *CP*, 46, f.184r; 47, f.4r.

[45] For discussion of, and votes on, the *catasto* legislation, *LF*, 53, ff.140v–151v (Oct.–Dec. 1426), 176v–181r, 188v–190v (March–May 1427). See, too, *CP*, 47, ff.23r–23v, 52v–53r; being *pratiche* not published by G. Berti, "Documenti intorno al catasto," *Giornale storico degli archivi toscani*, IV (1862), who did transcribe the two most significant debates, on 7 March and 12 May; 42–52, 54–59.

[46] Berti, 44, 50.

[47] "Et Veneciis forma hec servatur, et dicitur civitatem illam pre ceteris melius regi et gubernari. . . . Et Cesar, ut tributa haberet, unite machinam universam describere fecit: et per hoc clare apparet utilem esse viam Catasti"; *ibid.*, 43, 51.

drive capital from the city, and would depress the value of *monte* shares.[48] Eventually, however, the *catasto* law was approved by the Council of the Commune by a single vote, after it had been accepted by the Council of the *Popolo* with two beans to spare.[49]

So, after five years of sporadic but intense debate, the *catasto* became an integral part of the fiscal system. Some contemporaries recognized its historical significance, and so too has every serious student of the period, from Machiavelli to the present.[50] There still remain unresolved questions, specifically the identity and motivations of the advocates and the opponents of the *catasto*. The dispute was not primarily economic in character, not a fight between rich and poor. Neither was it a factional quarrel between Rinaldo degli Albizzi's oligarchs and the Medicean party of merchants and guildsmen.[51] Though it was, in one sense, a victory of the regime's leadership over the guild community, it can best be understood as the triumph of bureaucracy and statism, and of the principle of order in public affairs. It was a step toward the realization of Piero Baroncelli's dream: a rational system of allocating the tax burden.[52] Among its most fervent partisans were men with oligarchic inclinations—Rinaldo degli Albizzi, Niccolò Barbadori, Matteo Castellani—and also a large cadre of lawyers: Francesco Machiavelli, Giuliano Davanzati, Francesco Viviani, Guglielmo Tanagli, Biagio Niccolini, Nello Martini, Guaspare Accorambuoni. These men of law favored the *catasto* because, in Tanagli's words, it was a contribution toward perfecting the administration of the republic.[53] Who, then, opposed the *catasto*? Among those casting white beans were doubtless some who, through luck or chicanery, paid less than their fair share of the *prestanze*. But a more fundamental motive for this resistance was a vague fear of change: a reluctance to abandon

[48] Cf. the opinions of the standard-bearers of the companies; *LF*, 53, ff.180v–181r, 4 Apr. 1427. Some counselors agreed that the *catasto* should be approved eventually, but that the times were not then propitious, "propter carestiam pecunie et guerram vigentem"; *ibid.*, f.181r.

[49] The votes: 144–70 and 117–58; *ibid.*, ff.190r–191v. For the law's text, O. Karmin, *La legge del catasto fiorentino del 1427* (Florence, 1906); and for analyses of its contents, C. Bayley, *War and Society in Renaissance Florence*, 91–93; Molho, *Florentine Public Finances*, 84–87.

[50] For a summary of those views, U. Procacci, "Sulla cronologia delle opere di Masaccio e di Masolino," *Rivista d'arte*, XXVIII (1953), 17–24.

[51] Cf. Gutkind, *Cosimo de' Medici*, 58–62.

[52] See above, 210–12, 407–08; and the comments of Matteo Castellani and Stefano Bencivenni; Berti, *Giornale storico degli archivi toscani*, IV, 54, 55.

[53] Berti, 59.

a familiar method, which did involve neighborhoods in the assessments,[54] for a new and untested system that might be more coercive, and perhaps more arbitrary, than the old ways.[55] Giovanni de' Medici was perhaps reflecting this parochial, traditionalist viewpoint of the guild community when he voiced his reservations about the *catasto*.[56]

Francesco Machiavelli had predicted (March 1427) that civic strife would cease with the introduction of the *catasto*: "The societies will disband; there will be an end to [tax] evasion, and to the power of the cliques, and to the complaints of the multitude who are constantly clamoring at the doors [of the Signoria's palace]. . . ."[57] This utopian vision did not materialize, although the *catasto*'s implementation did reduce internal tensions, by minimizing (without eliminating completely) the opportunities for evasion and favoritism.[58] Fewer complaints about fiscal injustice were registered in the *pratiche*, and the number of petitions for tax relief declined significantly in the autumn of 1427.[59] But the *catasto* did not solve the regime's most serious fiscal problems: it did not alter its reliance on forced loans and deficit financing, nor did it reduce the interest charges on the communal debt.[60] Scholars have argued that, under the new method of distribution, the poor paid less, and the rich more, than before; but this has not been proved.[61] Nor did the introduction of the *catasto* persuade absent citizens to return home, or achieve the prosperity that its

[54] See, on this point, Molho, *Florentine Public Finances*, 85–86.

[55] This sentiment can be detected in the ambiguous statements opposing the *catasto* by spokesmen for the *gonfaloni*; *LF*, 53, ff.180v–181r.

[56] See his statements in Berti, 47–48, 57.

[57] "Cessabunt societates et simulaciones et potencium civium clientela et querele multorum qui ad hostium continue clamant"; Berti, *op. cit.*, 45.

[58] De Roover has shown that the Medici were guilty of tax evasion in the 1450s; *Rise and Decline of the Medici Bank*, 73–74; C. Klapisch suggests that evasion increased progressively during the *quattrocento*; P. Laslett, ed., *Household and Family in Past Time* (Cambridge, 1972), 267–81.

[59] For a positive assessment of the *catasto*'s contribution to civic peace, see the statement of Galileo Galilei in Feb. 1431; F. Pellegrini, *Sulla repubblica fiorentina a tempo di Cosimo il Vecchio*, xxxvi–xxxvii, quoted in Molho, *Florentine Public Finances*, 84. On the decline in the number of petitions for tax relief, see *LF*, 53, ff.221r–235v.

[60] Molho, 84–87.

[61] Cf. Bayley, *War and Society*, 92–94; Procacci, 30–31; Molho, 122. To prove this hypothesis, a systematic comparison would have to be made of assessments and payments, by economic category, before and after the *catasto*'s implementation. The data I have seen suggest that the *catasto* did not change assessments of wealthy citizens significantly; see Procacci, 30–31.

advocates had envisaged.[62] The economic benefits accruing to the citizenry, in the months following the *catasto*'s adoption, were due primarily to the end of hostilities and a consequent reduction in military expenditures.[63]

Neither fiscal reform nor the conclusion of a peace treaty with Filippo Maria Visconti (April 1428) reduced civic tensions. Though men complained less about their tax assessments, they continued to fight over the distribution of offices, and their portion of "profit and honor," the twin causes (so Luca degli Albizzi believed) of factionalism.[64] The war's drain on fortunes, and the paucity of investment opportunities in these years, doubtless intensified the competition for the material benefits of office. But the search for the honor attached to these dignities was as intense as that for profit, and seemingly stronger in these months than ever before in the regime's experience.[65] Members of old families in economic difficulties were most fearful of derogation: for example, certain Strozzi and Serragli who had suffered bankruptcy; and the Castellani, Mangioni, Antellesi, and Giugni, whose fortunes had declined since 1400.[66] Marcello Strozzi voiced the hope that no citizen who had ever held civic office would henceforth be deprived of that privilege; Lippozzo Mangioni favored the selection of scrutators who would preserve the political patrimony of those who "had

[62] For these predictions, see the statements of Niccolò Barbadori, Francesco Viviani, and Giovanni Minerbetti; Berti, 50, 55, 57. That the economy did not revive substantially after 1427 is suggested by Molho's data on communal revenues; 54, 61.

[63] Giovanni and Cosimo de' Medici's payments to the treasury declined substantially from 1427 through 1429; Molho, 101.

[64] "Due sunt cause settarum, videlicet, utilitas et honor"; *Commissioni*, III, 165. Cf. Dino Gucci's comment: "Divisio est inter eos, qui pro recuperando statu subierunt damna; et querunt dare status illis qui intulerent eis illa damna"; *ibid*.

[65] The colleges reacted very positively to the suggestion that worthy citizens be knighted by the republic. Speaking for the Sixteen, Luigi Vecchietti said: "Quod dominatio erat commendanda et etiam illi cives apud illam moverunt militum creationes, et hortantur ad hoc faciendum propter honorem civitati. Addunt tamen quod dominatio inspiciat et provideat quod hec dignitas militie detur potius et conferatur dignitati personarum quam divitiis"; *CP*, 48, f.90v, 5 Oct. 1429.

[66] On the bankruptcies, Molho, *Florentine Public Finances*, 152. Though the proof is at hand, in the *catasto* records, it has not yet been established that "the overwhelming majority of Florentines were losing entire patrimonies during these years because of the oppressive tax burden"; *ibid*., 176. The decline of the economic status of the Castellani, etc., is suggested by a comparison of the richest households in each quarter, in 1403 and 1427; Martines, *Social World*, 351–78. Dale Kent has concluded that the fortunes of many aristocrats in the Albizzi faction were declining in the 1420s, while those of the Medici party were improving; *Rise of the Medici*, ch. 2.

the state."[67] The passage of a provision (February 1428) authorizing a new scrutiny for most offices did not assuage these anxieties.[68] Before a year had elapsed, critics were complaining that the scrutators had arbitrarily reduced the number of candidates nominated for office; others deplored the trend toward filling posts by hand instead of the customary method of sortition.[69] Giovanni Morelli and Ridolfo Peruzzi were fatigued by the perpetual tampering with the electoral process. "It disgraces us in front of our neighbors," Morelli complained, "that this issue of scrutinies is so frequently debated. . . ."[70]

The fragmentary records of the *pratiche* provide little evidence to document the course of sectarian politics in these months.[71] Letters in the Medici archives contain oblique references to the two large factions: a "popular" party headed by Cosimo and Averardo de' Medici in the quarter of San Giovanni, and an aristocratic coalition based upon the Peruzzi, Baroncelli, and Ricasoli families in Santa Croce.[72] Not since the rise of the Albizzi and Ricci factions in the 1360s, or those led by the Albizzi and the Alberti in the 1380s, had such large "sects" formed in the city. It was their abnormal size and power which aroused so much anxiety, and which prompted some citizens to seek ways to weaken, if not to destroy, them. In 1426, the sectarian menace had been denounced in the *pratiche*, but not energetically attacked by the authorities. The year 1429, by contrast, witnessed an unprecedented number of debates "concerning unity" in January and February, in September, and again in December.[73] The mood of these

[67] CP, 48, ff.40v, 62r. See, too, the comments of Giovanni Morelli, "Provideatur quod guelfi et populares non habent deficientiam in honoribus," and Lorenzo Lenzi, "Provideatur quod illi qui sunt qui habent regimen et multos filios et fratres mictantur ad partitum omnes, ita non visi sunt visi"; *ibid.*, ff.40v, 41r.

[68] *Prov.*, 118, ff.187r-193r, 6-7 Feb. 1428. The provision was approved with great difficulty; LF, 53, ff.250r-261r. It provided for a *rimbotto* of the *tre maggiori*, but not a new scrutiny for those magistracies. On these scrutinies and the *rimbotto*, see D. Kent, *Rise of the Medici*, ch. 3.

[69] E.g., the statements of Ridolfo Peruzzi, Lorenzo Lenzi, Giovanni Morelli, and Francesco Bucelli; CP, 48, ff.41r, 85v.

[70] *Ibid.*, f.40v.

[71] From the passage of the *catasto* (May 1427) until Dec. 1428, the records of the debates are sparse and uninformative. During this interval Ser Paolo Fortini was replaced as chancellor by Leonardo Bruni who may have been reluctant, in the first months of his office, to reveal the existence of civic discord; CP, 48, ff.40v-41r.

[72] On the formation and composition of these factions, see D. Kent, *Rise of the Medici*, ch. 1-3. References to the factions have been culled from the Medici correspondence by Dale Kent; e.g., MAP, II, 32, 57, 95. I must acknowledge my great debt to Dr. Kent, upon whose analysis of Florentine politics in these years I have relied very heavily in this chapter.

[73] These debates have been published in part in *Commissioni*, III, 164-72.

deliberations was somber; citizens realized that their political patrimony was in grave jeopardy. Counselors pleaded with their audiences to eschew discord and live in harmony. They praised civic unity as the highest temporal good; they condemned secret societies. They called upon the good citizens—those not infected with sectarian passions, who were willing to speak the truth and to sacrifice everything for the public good—to save the city from ruin. Prayers to God and the Virgin, and gifts of alms to the poor, would foster that spirit of love and charity which revealed God's presence in human communities.[74] Finally, they invited every loyal member of the regime to take an oath that he would support the republic and that he would "divorce himself completely from every sect or faction."[75] Not for two centuries had the sworn oath been used in this fashion to bolster a Tuscan regime.[76]

Except for that moment in 1426 when (if we may believe Cavalcanti) some Florentines considered the use of force to reform the regime, the leadership had consistently relied upon persuasion to gain its domestic objectives. This policy was based upon the conviction that reason and exhortation were more effective than coercion in a republican polity.[77] The introduction of the *catasto* was a victory for this moderate viewpoint as was, too, the successful campaigns to rehabilitate political exiles, and notably the Alberti, who regained their civic rights in 1428.[78] The regime's unwillingness to move deci-

[74] See the comments of Lorenzo Ridolfi, Giovanni Morelli, Luca degli Albizzi, Niccolò da Uzzano, Battista Arnolfi, and Niccolò del Bellaccio; *Commissioni*, III, 165–66. Niccolò da Uzzano's statement was particularly poignant: "Et ipse me offero ad omnia pro pace et concordia habenda, etiam si expediret vitam et statum ponere pro illa." See, too, the comments of Stefano Bencivenni and Bartolomeo Peruzzi; *CP*, 48, ff.51v, 52r. Dale Kent has identified those prominent statesmen who were not associated with either major faction, and whose political posture was independent: Lorenzo Ridolfi, Giovanni Morelli, Guglielmo Tanagli, Carlo Federighi, Piero Beccanugi; *Rise of the Medici*, ch. 2, iii.

[75] *Commissioni*, III, 166.

[76] The oath of allegiance to a specific regime was not a common Florentine practice in the medieval period; for its use in other Tuscan towns, see D. Herlihy, *Medieval and Renaissance Pistoia*, 73. The oath was later employed by the Medici; Rubinstein, *Government of Florence*, 156–58. Another anachronistic proposal was made by Luca da Filicaia: "Si nos non sufficientes per nos ad faciendum unionem, scribatur Papa ut mictatur nobis unum cardinalem"; Pellegrini, *Sulla repubblica fiorentina*, 51. The suggestion was perhaps inspired by Cardinal Latino's peace mission of 1280.

[77] The controversy over this issue can be traced back as far as 1379; see above, ch. I. It was revived in 1411–12 after the Alberti conspiracies; above, ch. VI.

[78] Petriboni's chronicle; *BNF*, *Conv. Sopp.*, C, 8, 395, ff.122v, 123v–124r. In addition to the Alberti, members of the Giani, Baroncelli, Tornaquinci, Bardi, and Biliotti families were pardoned.

sively against the clandestine societies was another example of this attitude; a group of counselors advised the Signoria in November 1429 to be gentle and restrained in their attempts to eliminate dissension, so that the citizenry would not become fearful and suspicious.[79] But the voices of moderation were being challenged by those who called for a more coercive policy to restore unity to a disintegrating regime.[80] Those aristocrats who had voiced their resentments in the Santo Stefano conclave now believed (or professed to believe) that the societies were the creations of the regime's enemies, and particularly those parvenus—the Ghibellines of an earlier generation—who had wormed their way into the *reggimento* by deceit and fraud.

The campaign to purge the regime of its corrupt members achieved its first success in February 1429, with the enactment of legislation creating the Defenders of the Laws (*Conservatores Legum*). That magistracy received a mandate to scrutinize the qualifications of office-holders, and to exclude minors, bastards, bankrupts, malfeasants, tax delinquents, and anyone who (or whose father and grandfather) had not paid *prestanze* for at least thirty years. The provisions' objective (so its preamble read) was to enforce the laws and restrain ambition, but its opponents viewed it as another instrument of proscription, like the Parte Guelfa in the 1360s and 1370s.[81] In December 1429, another scheme of civic pacification was debated in a series of *pratiche*, and finally enacted by narrow majorities. To eliminate the "societies" and the sectarian spirit that promoted them, the provision authorized the Signoria to assemble eighty citizens twice a year, in March and again in September. The purpose of this convocation was defined in these terms:

To restrain wars, their campaigns and their beginnings, and to eliminate the occasions for waging them; to reduce the expenses of the commune and to eliminate all superfluous outlays; to remove all sects and divisions whatsoever; to repress the boldness and the power of all prepotent individuals whomsoever; to extirpate the title, effect, and name of such prepotence and power; to mete out justice to great and small alike in this city; to preserve the liberty of

[79] ". . . Che a volere levar via queste discordie fra i cittadini . . . pare che e' si debba provedere e procedere per modo dolcie et habile et che desse meno pavento e sospetto alla cittadinanza"; *CP*, 48, ff.106r–107r.

[80] For opposing opinions on this issue, see the statements of Luca degli Albizzi, Marco Strozzi, and Carlo Federighi; *CP*, 48, ff.51r, 51v, 53v.

[81] After several rejections, the law was finally passed on 11 and 12 Feb.; by majorities of 170–83 and 135–57; *Prov.*, 120, ff.7v–11r. For the voting, *LF*, 55, ff.1v–5r.

this good, peaceful and tranquil regime . . . and so that whoever does not wish to live in peace will do so and will not exceed reasonable limits through fear of penalties. . . .[82]

To achieve these goals, each member of this assembly was to search his conscience, "having put aside hatred, love, envy, and any other sentiment," and then identify any citizen who promoted scandal, sedition, and faction, or who sought to be greater than the commune, or whose behavior was arrogant or prepotent. Anyone identified by at least six members of the assembly as fitting the aforementioned categories was then scrutinized by the entire group. Those receiving a two-thirds majority were publicly branded as *scandalosi* and, by votes of the group, could be barred from communal office for one, two, or three years, or sent into exile for similar periods.

Ever since the guild republic was first established in the 1280s, its successive regimes had made sporadic attempts to achieve internal peace and unity through coercion. This campaign to enforce a strict code of civic morality was no more successful than the others,[83] but it did provide more opportunities for settling scores against enemies and rivals, for expressing those feelings of hatred and envy that good citizens were expected to eschew. While only a few were caught in the machinery for identifying *scandalosi*, hundreds were denounced to the Defenders of the Laws as unworthy to hold office in the republic.[84] Someone who was (or had been) a neighbor or relative of Antonio di Piero Migliorotti, selected to the Merchants' Court in 1429, informed the Defenders that Antonio was illegitimate; the magistracy fined him 500 lire and permanently excluded him from communal office. Pagolo di Agostino di Pagolo, a baker, and Pazzino di Ser Cristofano were also denounced as bastards; the latter was alleged to be the son of a priest from Quaracchi in the *contado*. A belt-maker, Giovanni di

---

[82] *Prov.*, 120, ff.430v–432v, 29 and 30 Dec. 1429. For the debate on the provision and a summary of its contents, see *Commissioni*, III, 169–72; Kent, *Rise of the Medici*, ch. 3. This law was to be in effect for three years.

[83] While attempting to enforce its regulations concerning membership, the regime was also seeking to control civic mores more rigorously, by electing officials to enforce sumptuary legislation, the laws against sodomy and gambling, and those safeguarding convents; Brucker, *Society of Renaissance Florence*, 178–84, 203–07.

[84] Kent, *Rise of the Medici*, ch. 3. Only Neri di Gino Capponi was identified in the official records as having been declared a *scandaloso* and exiled, in March 1432; the penalty was cancelled two months later; *Prov.*, 123, ff.98r–99r. Three others—Averardo de' Medici, Giovanni Guicciardini, and Ser Martino Martini—received a minimum of six votes, but not a two-thirds majority of the assembly; Pellegrini, *op. cit.*, xlvii.

Miniato, had been selected to fill a territorial office in Arezzo when he was too young (so his accuser charged) to hold that position. About to be chosen a member of the Twelve, Filippo di Giovanni da Ghiaceto was accused of malfeasance by an anonymous informer.[85] A lawyer from Pistoia, Messer Tommaso Salvetti, was charged with violating the law that officeholders must have paid *prestanze* in Florence for at least thirty years. Messer Tommaso was described by his accuser as a presumptuous usurper, a onetime subject of the marquis of Ferrara, and a man whose professional career was marred by "a thousand betrayals and deceits."[86]

The tone of Salvetti's denunciation reveals the aristocratic impulse behind this effort to discredit men of modest status, and to exclude them from the *reggimento*.[87] But calumny was a game that everyone could play, as several prominent Florentines discovered to their sorrow. Neri Capponi, son of the illustrious Gino, was a victim of the *scandalosi* law, despite his protestation that he was a peace-loving man, "who has always sought to unite the quiet and unassuming citizens."[88] Bernardo di Filippo Salviati was fined 500 florins for accepting membership in the Eight on Security when he was only twenty-seven years old. Gherardo di Jacopo Baroncelli had been sentenced to death for malfeasance while serving as an official in the Lunigiana; his sentence was canceled after his appeal for mercy, "having consideration for the works of his ancestors and particularly his father, and compassion for his young children. . . ."[89] The most notorious cases of powerful men humbled by these methods occurred during the Lucca war. Appointed a war commissioner to serve with the Florentine army that had invaded Lucchese territory, Jacopo di Luca Ridolfi had been condemned by the Defenders of the Laws for committing numerous crimes against the natives of that region.[90] Also serving at the Lucca

[85] *GA*, 75, ff.446r–449r, 487v; 77, part, 1, ff.251r–252r; 79, ff.116r–117r.

[86] *GA*, 75, ff.626r–628v. See also Kent, *Rise of the Medici*, ch. 3, n. 99. On Salvetti, see Martines, *Social World*, 67–69.

[87] "Notificasi a voi, signori dieci delle leggi etc., è di bisognio, signori conservatori, avere diligentia che voi non siate ingannati nel facto di messer Tommaso da Pistoia. Sapete con quanta diligentia siete stati electi . . . et spetialmente acciò che vostri uffici e degli altri antichi et buoni cittadini non sieno occupati dagli indengni. Et se niuno è indegnio, sono questi presuntuosi frategli esupratori, sarebbe inpossibile poter exprimere le loro usurpationi e rubaria"; *GA*, 75, ff.626v–627r. Salvetti's brother, Ser Antonio, was also denounced by the informer.

[88] *Prov.*, 123, f.98v. For the background to Capponi's disgrace, see Bayley, *War and Society*, 114–15.

[89] *GA*, 75, f.491r; *Prov.*, 119, ff.247v–249v. Salviati's sentence was later cancelled; *Prov.*, 120, f.370r.

[90] *Prov.*, 125, ff.229r–230r, being the cancellation of Ridolfi's conviction.

front, Giovanni Guicciardini was accused of malfeasance, but the charges were eventually dismissed by the Signoria.[91] The most prominent victims from the inner circle were Giovanni di Messer Donato Barbadori and Francesco di Messer Rinaldo Gianfigliazzi. Barbadori was penalized 1500 florins for his delicts as *podestà* of Montepulciano; Gianfigliazzi was fined 200 florins for a series of illegal acts while serving as *podestà* of Librafatta.[92] His brother Giovanni was later accused of illegal conduct while vicar of San Miniato, but the Defenders quashed that charge.[93]

This purge of citizens both great and small did not extinguish the sectarian spirit. Those who had been penalized for their misconduct were not motivated to become better citizens; instead, they intensified their efforts to gain friends by adhering more closely to a faction. Guildsmen without ties to a powerful aristocratic lineage like the Peruzzi or Baroncelli tended to gravitate toward the Medici "society," with its large complement of parvenus. So too, apparently, did some scions of aristocratic houses like Bernardo di Gherardo Canigiani, who was accused of belonging to "the gang that runs to the Medici and their crowd. . . ."[94] In November 1429, the Defenders of the Laws received a deposition from an anonymous informant who claimed that he had been coerced into joining a secret society with an oligarchic coloration.[95] He identified four other members—Roberto dell' Antella, Bernardo Portinari, Bernardo Bischeri, and Francesco Bucelli—all associates of the Peruzzi and Ricasoli, of whom three (Dell' Antella, Bischeri, Bucelli) were later penalized by the Medici after their return to power in 1434.[96] With two other recruits, the informer was taken to Portinari's house for supper; then, he wrote, "we swore an oath between their hands, and they made us sign our names to a document, but they would not allow us to read the rules [of the society]." They would be given instructions each day by either Portinari or Bischeri, who in

[91] M. Moriani, *Giovanni Guicciardini ed un processo politico in Firenze (1431)* (Florence, 1954), ch. 5.

[92] *GA*, 77, part 1, ff.77r–85v, 103r–106r; part 2, ff.334r–336r. Andrea di Niccolò Giugni, vicar of Pescia, was fined 100 fl. for baratry; *ibid.*, part 1, f.142r.

[93] *Ibid.*, part 2, ff.229r–229v. Other prominent citizens absolved of similar charges were Giovanni Biffoli, Alessandro d'Ugo Alessandri and Mariotto Baldovinetti; *ibid.*, 77, part 2, ff.303r–304v; 78, ff.170r–170v.

[94] ". . . Perchè egli è della compagnia che corrono a chasa e Medici e loro concurrenti"; *GA*, 75, f.495r, 21 May 1429. The informer contrasted Canigiani's sectarianism with the civic spirit of Bernardo Salviati: "Egli è huomo di se e non è schiavo di quegli che anno sempre cerchato novità del ghoverno. . . ."

[95] *Ibid.*, 75, ff.724r–724v, 18 Nov. 1429.

[96] Kent, *Rise of the Medici*, Appendix II.

turn received orders from their superiors. The society was well supplied with money, the recruits were told, and they would be defended and supported "in everything." Although he was not privy to all of the secrets of this conventicle, the informer believed that its leaders were conspiring to subvert the regime.[97] But after interrogating Portinari concerning these charges, the Defenders concluded that they were unfounded, and terminated their investigation.

Was this accusation fabricated, or were the Defenders unwilling to probe deeply into that sectarian milieu where they would have encountered relatives, friends, perhaps some of themselves? There can be little doubt that this fear inhibited the regime's prosecution of Tommaso Soderini, scion of a prominent Santo Spirito family, who was accused (December 1429) of plotting to assassinate Niccolò da Uzzano, the most eminent survivor of that cadre of political leaders that had guided the regime since the 1390s. In the *podestà*'s court, Tommaso was accused of hiring two assassins—one an outlaw from a magnate family, the Lamberti—and sending them to Florence to stay in his house on the Lungarno.[98] From that hideout they planned to go to the Ponte Vecchio to await Niccolò's return from the palace of the Signoria, where he was involved "in the arduous affairs of state and the commune of Florence. . . ." There, if the plot had succeeded, they would have assaulted Niccolò with poisoned swords, and then fled in the darkness. But an accomplice of the assassins revealed the plan to Bernardo di Antonio da Uzzano, who warned his kinsman and the authorities.[99] Summoned to discuss the case by the Signoria, the colleges reported that they were confused by Niccolò da Uzzano's accusation, and by Soderini's denial. They urged the priors to discover the truth and punish the guilty.[100] But those officials decided that truth

---

[97] In December, the informer submitted another accusation; *GA*, 75, f.747r, 7 Dec.: "Ricordovi, signori governatori, quello vi scripsi più dì fà di quelle compagnie di Ruberto dal Antella e Bernaba Bischeri e Francesco Bucelli e da lloro, sentì quello cercavano. E ancora fui avisato da loro come la brigata da Brolio de' Ricasolessi e dipoi furono a Prato. In ogni luogo furono grandi ragionamenti di fare ora grandi fatti. E mi è paruto che voi n'abiate fatto stima d'una de' magiori case avesse questa città mai. Se Idio non ci pone le mani, io dubito d'un grande pericolo a questa città quanto avesse mai." Though no evidence exists to document this theory, the subject of the *grandi ragionamenti* might have been the Lucca war, which was begun in December.

[98] *AP*, 4423, ff.1r–4v, 17 Dec. 1429.

[99] *AEOG*, 2145, ff.41r–41v.

[100] Speaking for the Twelve (3 Nov.), Piero del Benino said: "Per ritrovare la verità di quello che si fa querela per Niccolò da Uzzano, et se e si trova essere vero, quello che dice Niccolò da Uzzano, che e' si punischa chi a errato. Et se e si

and justice must be sacrificed, on this occasion, for a higher goal: civic peace. With the concurrence of their colleges, the Signoria ordered the *podestà* to quash the case against Soderini.[101] To justify their interferences with the judicial process, the priors noted that the two protagonists had long been enemies. If the case against Soderini were to continue, "it might generate the most grave and irreparable scandals and quarrels among an infinite number of worthy and cherished citizens. . . . ." One of the killers hired by Soderini, Donato di Tommaso alias Barba, was treated less gently than his alleged employer; he was sentenced to death *in absentia* for conspiring to kill Niccolò da Uzzano.[102]

This episode must have been demoralizing to members of the regime's inner circle. To what state had the republic fallen when its most distinguished statesman was threatened by assassination, and his integrity doubted by his fellow-citizens?[103] The crisis had erupted at a critical moment, when the subject city of Volterra had rebelled against Florentine rule,[104] and just before the outbreak of the Lucca war. The evidence does not survive (if it ever existed) that would prove a connection between fears of the regime's disintegration and the decision to attack Lucca, which was made in the first week of December 1429. Since neither the advocates nor the opponents of the war cited the domestic crisis as a motive for launching that campaign, the link can only be suggested as an unproved and unprovable hypothesis, which does help to explain an otherwise puzzling development. It would not have been the first, nor the last, time in the republic's history that a military adventure was launched to solve, or to alleviate, a domestic crisis.

Just a month before the assault on Lucca, a *pratica* debated a request from that city's *signore*, Paolo Guinigi, for an alliance. Though cool

---

trovasse che Niccolò da Uzzano fingesse questo per calumniare, che essa punischa lui come la cosa merita"; *CP*, 48, f.99r. On this case, see *ibid.*, ff.98v–99v, 103v–104r.

[101] *AP*, 4423, f.3v.

[102] *Ibid.*, ff.16v–17r, 12 Jan. 1430. The text of the accusation against Donato was identical to that formulated against Soderini. For other allegations concerning the political aspects of this plot, see Niccolò Tinucci's confession, in Cavalcanti, *Istorie fiorentine*, Polidori ed., II, 402–03. Cf. Kent, *Rise of the Medici*, ch. 3.

[103] It is instructive to compare the collegiate suspicions of Niccolò (see note 114 above) with the confidence expressed in his probity, and that of Gino Capponi and Rinaldo Gianfigliazzi, in 1415; above, ch. VII, 398. The accusation made against Niccolò da Uzzano was still troubling Niccolò Barbadori eighteen months later; Pellegrini, *Sulla repubblica fiorentina*, 33.

[104] News of the Volterra rebellion reached Florence in mid-October; *CP*, 48, ff.94v–98r.

to the proposal, counselors appeared to be satisfied with Guinigi's posture; they gave no hint of any plan to attack their neighbor.[105] Indeed, in a *pratica* convened the year before to discuss the republic's relations with Siena, counselors had urged the Signoria to promote friendly relations with their southern neighbor and other Tuscan states. Nothing was more dangerous, Neri Capponi said, "that to harbor suspicions about one's neighbors." Even though the Sienese had not been the best of allies in the recent war with Filippo Maria Visconti, they had not harmed the Florentine cause.[106] Paolo Guinigi had been less friendly and, indeed, had allowed his son to fight for Filippo Maria Visconti. But his behavior was condoned by Giovanni Morelli, who pointed out that Paolo had first offered his son's service to Florence, before turning to Milan.[107] Why, then, were Guinigi's efforts at reconciliation rebuffed, at precisely the moment when internal divisions within Florence were most acute, and when the Volterra rebellion threatened control of its dominion?

The sources do not indicate clearly the process by which an overburdened and war-weary citizenry was converted to belligerency overnight, without any external provocation. If the chieftains of the Medici party were responsible for this development, as their enemies charged in 1433,[108] they disguised their role very effectively. Though the civic temper (as revealed in the *pratiche*) was generally pacific in 1429, there are occasional hints of frustration over the republic's situation, and signs of latent pressures for a more aggressive posture in Italian diplomacy. Even before peace was signed with Milan in April 1428, Neri Capponi was deploring the fact that, with Florentine help, the Venetians had acquired much territory in Lombardy, while "we have gained nothing."[109] When Carlo Malatesta, lord of Rimini, died in September 1429, the prospect of gaining territory in the Apennines

---

[105] *CP*, 48, ff.90v–91r, 5 and 7 Oct. 1429. Antonio da Rabatta said that a league with Lucca could not obtain the approval of the councils; Simone da Filicaia proposed that Guinigi be made a *raccomandato* but not an ally.

[106] *Ibid.*, ff.29v–30v, 11 Oct. 1428. Capponi: "Nichil est magis pericolosum paci vestre quam tenere vicinos in suspicione. Et licet senenses non fecerunt omnia, tamen etiam non fecerunt illud mali quod poterant." Lippozzo Mangioni: "Teneantur senenses in bona amicitia quia fecerunt satis in hoc bello. . . . Inimici aut vicini possunt multum nocere et multum potuissent nobis nocere in hoc bello si aperte tenuissent cum duce Mediolani dum erant eius gentes in territoris nostris."

[107] *Commissioni*, III, 192.

[108] See Molho, *Florentine Public Finances*, 188–89; Bayley, *War and Society*, 97. Dale Kent discusses this issue, and the general background of the war, in *Rise of the Medici*, ch. 4.

[109] *CP*, 48, f.3v, 21 Jan. 1428.

whetted some Florentine appetites. Antonio da Rabatta advised the Signoria to be prepared to occupy Malatesta lands on the frontier, since the republic would incur infamy "if we didn't take what we could. . . ." Averardo de' Medici, Piero Guicciardini, and Lippozzo Mangioni were likewise avid for pieces of the Malatesta state, but their more cautious colleagues—Piero Beccanugi, Felice Brancacci, Mariotto Baldovinetti—warned the executive against any precipitate action that might lead to hostilities.[110] A few days after this debate, on 7 October, Giovanni di Piero del Teghia denounced Paolo Guinigi of Lucca as an enemy of the republic and urged the Signoria to rebuff his ambassadors, who were requesting an audience. Those Florentines who defended Guinigi's crimes were probably receiving money from him, Del Teghia said; he believed that the time was propitious to consider punishment for the Lucchese tyrant.[111]

Thus, within the leadership and possibly among the rank and file in the *reggimento*, there was a faint but discernible current of bellicosity nurtured by feelings that Florence's reputation had been tarnished by the Milan war and its unsatisfactory conclusion. While no one dared to contemplate a renewal of hostilities with "the great power of the duke," some would have agreed with Francesco Viviani, who argued that the republic should settle accounts with its neighbors, as Filippo Maria Visconti was then preparing to do with his local enemy, the marquis of Montferrat.[112] The invasion of Lucchese territory in late November by Florence's captain, Niccolò Fortebraccio, may have been done on his own initiative, although he was certainly aware of the strong antipathy toward Lucca among the Florentine populace and in certain segments of the leadership.[113] When news of the attack reached Florence (25 November) counselors denied the republic's complicity in the enterprise and advised the Signoria to apologize to Paolo Guinigi. Within a week, however, the mood had changed decisively; citizens vied with each other in denouncing him and calling for a massive attack on his territory.[114] With the exception of Rinaldo degli

[110] These views were expressed in a *pratica* of 19 Sept. 1429; *ibid.*, ff.86r–88r.

[111] *Commissioni*, III, 191.

[112] Filippo Maria had complained of harassment by the marquis, who had been an ally of Florence and Venice during the recent war. Viviani's statement: "Provideat dominatio ut assecuret se de vicinis dum habet tempus, ut vult facere dux de marchione"; *CP*, 48, f.122r, 5 Dec.

[113] For the suspicion that Fortebraccio had been encouraged by some citizens to attack Lucca, see Lippozzo Mangioni's statement of 26 Jan. 1430; Moriani, *Giovanni Guicciardini*, 98–99. Leonardo Bruni blamed the *popolo*'s hostility toward Lucca for the war; Bayley, *War and Society*, 99.

[114] The debates are summarized in *Commissioni*, III, 195–205.

Albizzi and Neri Capponi, the majority of those advocating war were not known for their partisanship; instead they represented that large middling bloc of civic-spirited men whose commitment to the regime and the republic was very strong.[115] They were persuaded by arguments that the campaign against Lucca would be quick and inexpensive, and that the Visconti would be deterred from attacking the republic by this example of Florentine aggressiveness.[116]

From the beginning, the Lucca war was a very controversial issue. Six men spoke out strongly against it in the December deliberations; three of them (Palla Strozzi, Felice Brancacci, Giovanni Guicciardini) were leaders of the aristocratic coalition.[117] Conservatives, who had been the most ardent supporters of the Visconti war, now formed the core of the opposition to the Lucca campaign.[118] They complained that the decision to wage war had been made hastily, without a careful appraisal of the dangers and the costs. Warmongers had promised the Florentines that Lucca would fall quickly; those who attacked their arguments could not make their voices heard in the councils.[119] Niccolò da Uzzano was particularly incensed by the war party's incitement of popular feelings against Lucca. Ser Paolo Fortini, the former chancellor who had been deprived of his office by Medici partisans, made an oblique reference to the extra-legal machinations of the war's promoters.[120] Speaking for the counselors of Santa Croce (the Peruzzi quarter), Duccio Mancini asked the Signoria to consider the enactment of a law that would keep the republic out of such enterprises,

[115] Among the "warmongers" were Piero Bonciani, Lorenzo Lenzi, Francesco Viviani, Bernardo Anselmi, Niccolò Rittafè, Manetto Scambrilla, Giovanni del Teghia, Bartolo Bartolini, and Giovanni Torsellini. Scambrilla was an ally of the Albizzi and Peruzzi; Medici partisans who were probably active in promoting the war included Puccio Pucci, Giuliano Davanzati, and Agnolo Acciaiuoli.

[116] See Neri Capponi's argument: "In facto lucano, non deseratur ista impresa propter metum ducis, quia sequatur reputatio huic dominationi et etiam melius erit in punto de gentibus et per consequens dux magis se abstinebat a bello"; CP, 48, f.123r, 5 Dec.

[117] Giovanni Morelli, Alberto di Recco Capponi and Guglielmo Tanagli, a lawyer, also voiced their opposition; Commissioni, III, 196–98. Niccolò da Uzzano was identified by Cavalcanti, Storie fiorentine, v, ch. 6, as the leader of the opposition, but his statements were not recorded in the pratiche.

[118] Other aristocratic critics of the war were Lippozzo Mangioni, Giovanni di Messer Rinaldo Gianfigliazzi, Messer Palla di Messer Palla Strozzi, Luca degli Albizzi, Ridolfo Peruzzi, and Giovanni Minerbetti; Moriani, Giovanni Guicciardini, 98–99; CP, 49, ff.47r, 51v, 53r, 55r; Commissioni, III, 510.

[119] See the statements of Niccolò da Uzzano, Lippozzo Mangioni and Giovanni Gianfigliazzi; Moriani, 104; CP, 49, ff.39v, 47r.

[120] Moriani, 104, 109. See Fortini's other comments on the war; CP, 49, ff.38v, 55r.

"which lead to the loss of liberty."[121] So loud was this chorus of recrimination that the Twelve (1 March 1430) recommended to the Signoria that the Eight on Security be authorized to punish anyone criticizing the war in public places.[122] But nothing could stem the growing tide of discontent, as the Lucca campaign dragged on without any prospect of victory, and as pestilence and hunger contributed to the miseries of a populace which had quickly lost its taste for war.[123]

To counteract this torrent of criticism and obloquy, the war's supporters argued, first, that it was (in Galileo Galilei's words) "just, reasonable, and, above all, beneficial and honorable," and that no constitutional principle had been violated during the debates on the issues. The decision to attack Lucca was proper, Rinaldo degli Albizzi insisted, and he added that its goal was not primarily the acquisition of that city, but the defense of Florentine liberty.[124] Once the decision to fight had been made by the appropriate authorities, Fruosino da Verrazzano said, then it was every citizen's duty to support the action.[125] Repeating a common cliché, Giovanni Capponi exhorted his fellows to give up their property and their lives, if necessary. To the limit of his capacities, he would sacrifice everything for the republic, but he added, "I am not fit for military service on account of age and inexperience, and I have no money and a nubile daughter who needs a dowry."[126] Though he possessed no ready cash to subsidize the treasury, Mariotto Baldovinetti was willing to sell his property and give the proceeds to the state. Giorgio Serragli offered his *monte* shares, the income from his small cloth factory, and even the clothing on his back.[127]

Neither this patriotic rhetoric nor threats to punish dissent created that degree of civic unity that was a prerequisite (so Averardo de' Medici believed)[128] for a successful military effort against Lucca. In a *pratica* held on 26 April 1430, Lorenzo Ridolfi once again appealed for internal peace. Citizens should treat each other like brothers; each should "open up his heart and state how he feels that he has been offended. . . ." Admitting that the legislative efforts to curb factionalism had failed, Rinaldo degli Albizzi claimed that nearly every citizen now belonged to one of the partisan groups. Using a medical metaphor that

---

[121] Moriani, 99.

[122] Parigi Corbinelli, spokesman for the Twelve; *CP*, 49, f.6r, 1 March 1430.

[123] For references to these perils, the statements of Gregorio Dati, Paolo Fortini, and Giovanni Vettori; Pellegrini, *Sulla repubblica fiorentina*, 36; *CP*, 49, ff.55v, 66r.

[124] Moriani, 105; *Commissioni*, III, 509.

[125] Moriani, 99.   [126] Pellegrini, 52.

[127] *Ibid.*, 105–06. See too the comments of Francesco della Luna and Giovanni Morelli, *ibid.*, 54, 152.

[128] "Si fuisset unio inter cives, bellum esset finitum"; 38.

was becoming popular, Rinaldo described sectarianism as a disease (*morbum*) that required strong medicine for its cure.[129] This *pratica* witnessed the first documented attempt by conservatives to blame the Lucca war on the Medici faction.[130] The decision to attack Lucca was made privately, not publicly, Felice Brancacci charged, "by sects and factions. . . ." The men "who wish to be greater than the Signoria, in gaining honors and waging wars" were known to the priors, Antonio della Casa said ominously. Who but these sectaries, Andrea Rondinelli asked, have filled the important offices, the war *balìa* and the fiscal magistracies, for the past six or seven years? "If you wish medicine to be effective," Andrea del Palagio said, "you must lance the infected parts." Worthy citizens had been maligned by partisans; no one could speak in the *pratiche* except those thieves who usurped offices and involved the city in war and expense.[131] With heavy irony, Giovanni Minerbetti apologized for his unwillingness to speak on military matters, "since I was waiting for one of those who had promoted the Lucca war. . . ." The lawyer Guglielmo Tanagli spoke more bluntly: "I say that it would be good to demand money from those who got us into this war; let them extract us from this mess, just as they got us into it!"[132]

Despite the urging of civic-spirited men like Lorenzo Ridolfi that the war not become a partisan issue,[133] the Medici and their supporters were pilloried as warmongers and sowers of discord. They did not defend themselves publicly against these charges, but in their private correspondence they gave vent to their resentment. Even before the Lucca campaign a Medici partisan, Doffo Arnolfi, had written to Averardo de' Medici describing their rivals, the men who had controlled the regime in the past, as "horses without bridles" whose arrogance should be curbed.[134] The Medici were convinced that the failures of the Lucca campaign were due to the stupidity and malevolence of

[129] *Commissioni*, III, 506. For other examples, Pellegrini, *op. cit.*, 33, 38, 43.

[130] Dale Kent has noted the conservative orientation of this *pratica*; *Rise of the Medici*, ch. 4.

[131] *CP*, 49, ff.34v–35r, cited in Kent, ch. 4, n. 106. See too the comments of Niccolò degli Albizzi and Mariotto Baldovinetti; *ibid.*: "Ambitio et invidia causa sunt discordie civium, quia multi non merentes se mereri credunt officia. . . . Esse bonum gastigare et ammonire illos qui requisaverunt homines et fecerunt adunatas."

[132] *Commissioni*, III, 509–10.

[133] "Nemo reprehendit verbis imprehensam Luce quia non est utile et producit scandale"; Moriani, *Giovanni Guicciardini*, 106. See too his statement of 24 May; *CP*, 49, f.51r.

[134] "Questi nostri che ci anno governato per lo paxato non restano di fare del pazzie e vero temerità loro uxate; soleano essere cavalli sanza freno"; *MAP*, II, 32, cited by Kent, *Rise of the Medici*, ch. 3, n. 64.

their enemies.[135] That "gang" (*brigata*) continued to spread false reports, Cosimo wrote to Averardo (August 1431); "You can imagine what they would do if we gave them any ammunition."[136] Another Medici ally, Niccolò Valori, criticized those "who do not wish to spend a soldo in defense of liberty. . . ."[137] So intense was the feuding between the factions that the regime was threatened with paralysis. Alamanno Salviati reported to Averardo about conditions in the city in December 1431: "Here there is nothing new, except anger, confusion, ignorance, sadness, lies, and indolence. . . ."[138] Gradually but inexorably partisan postures hardened and battle lines were drawn. "Our friends are ready to fight to defend us," Giovanni da Panzano wrote Averardo in February 1432, "and conversely, our enemies do the same, with their falsehoods and their trickery. . . ."[139]

By 1430, the factions of the Medici and their rivals had become the most important groups in the *reggimento*: overshadowing guilds and *gonfaloni* if not *consorterie*; exerting a powerful and often decisive influence in the selection of officeholders and the formulation of policy. Dino Gucci invested them with a quasi-official status when he proposed (April 1430) that a commission of twenty-four citizens be created to consider the domestic crisis, "twelve of whom should not be partisan in any sense, and the other half comprising partisans, in equal numbers from each faction. . . ."[140]

THE BALANCE SHEET

In contrast to its condition in earlier periods of crisis—in the 1390s, in 1402, in 1411–1414, the Florentine *reggimento* in the 1420s appeared to be very strong and stable. It had survived a series of major challenges and confrontations, from within and without. Until the outbreak of the Lucca conflict in 1429, internal dissent had been sporadic and disorganized, limited mostly to grumbling over fiscal inequities and maladministration of the Milanese war. Florentine exiles no longer considered the prospect of overthrowing the regime by force; instead they humbly petitioned the Signoria to cancel their bans and restore

[135] See, for example, the comments of Niccolò Tinucci and Alamanno Salviati; Pellegrini, cxlv, clxi.

[136] *Ibid.*, clxvii.

[137] *MAP*, III, 196, cited by Kent, *Rise of the Medici*, ch. 4, n. 108.

[138] Pellegrini, clxxxv.   [139] *MAP*, II, 95.

[140] *CP*, 49, f.32r, 26 Apr. 1430: "Fiat nunc per dominos deputatio civium numero 24, eligendo 12 de civibus nullo modo passionatis, et totidem de passionatis in hac divisione que dicitur esse et sint pari numero ex utraque parte et hoc videtur melius." Gucci was spokesman for the two colleges.

their political rights. The countryside was quiet. This regime had been strengthened by the enlargement of its bureaucracy; by the concentration of authority in key magistracies like the Eight on Security; by the stimulation of civic pride.[141] The process of statebuilding was still far from complete in the 1420s, but the trend toward political centralization had been firmly established. The institution of the *catasto* in 1427 was probably the most significant event in this development: a bureaucratic dream which, despite many imperfections and inadequacies, became a reality.[142]

A major source of strength for this regime was its longevity, its durability. Florentines could proudly claim, in the 1420s, that their government had survived longer, without significant alterations in its constitution or leadership, than that of any other republic in the peninsula save Venice. The inner circle was made up of experienced statesmen, recruited largely but not exclusively from the great families, who had devoted much of their adult lives to government service. These leaders were not oligarchs; they did not "rule" Florence. They were the most influential figures in a large and socially diverse electorate. Hundreds of Florentine citizens—artisans and shopkeepers, notaries and physicians, merchants and rentiers—filled the magistracies, the territorial offices, and the legislative councils. They had to be persuaded to support the policies favored by the leadership, or a majority of it. Though the members of the elite were naturally concerned with preserving their political and social status, and their economic interests, they had to be responsive to the needs and concerns of the larger community, the *popolo*. Even the welfare of the disenfranchised—the poor urban workers and the residents of the territory—claimed their attention. These statesmen realized that Florentine security was dependent upon the labor and the fiscal contributions of those groups without representation in the *reggimento*.[143]

The political style of this elite is revealed most clearly in the record of its deliberations. These statesmen were intensely patriotic: they

---

[141] Cf. Martines, *Lawyers and Statecraft*, 464–75; Becker, "The Florentine Territorial State," *Flor. Studies*, 109–39; Tenenti, *Florence à l'époque des Médicis*, ch. 3.

[142] Molho's account of the trend toward "a greater measure of efficiency in taxation," *Florentine Public Finances*, 113–25, can be supplemented by evidence from criminal court records for the 1430s, which reveal a close inspection of the books of communal treasurers, and penalties for any shortages; e.g., *AEOG*, 2191, ff.16r–17r, 55r–56r, 59r–60r, 77r–78r; 2202, ff.15v–17r, 27r–32r, 39r–40r.

[143] See, e.g., my *Society of Renaissance Florence*, 229–31; and "The Florentine *Popolo Minuto*," in *Violence and Civil Disorder in Italian Cities*, ed. Martines, 172–77. For a different perspective on this problem, see Martines' comments in *Violence and Civil Disorder*, 13–17.

believed that their government was the best that could be devised by men, a worthy successor to the Roman republic. They willingly accepted the need to make sacrifices—of time, energy, and money—to preserve that liberty which so many other Italian communities had lost. Their debates were an essential feature of their political system: the means by which diverse viewpoints could be articulated, and either a consensus achieved or the dissenters induced to accept the will of the majority. By the 1420s, Florentine statesmen had learned how to argue forcefully and eloquently, and to discuss political issues analytically. They were able to unravel the intricacies of a political problem and to perceive the connections among its various aspects. They realized, for example, that superior resources of money and manpower were necessary for victory in war, but they also appreciated the importance of the human element: the ambitions, hopes, and fears of leaders; the morale of citizens and subjects. The evidence from their deliberations suggests that they had a firmer grasp of political realities than their fathers and grandfathers had had, particularly in their perception of limits. Experience had taught them that Florence's wealth was not inexhaustible, that they could not wage war indefinitely, that they had to restrain their imperialist ambitions. This generation of Florentine statesmen had received an excellent political education.

How then does one explain the foundering of a regime with substantial resources, a strong base of civic support, and an intelligent and experienced leadership? The fiscal burdens of the Milanese war were most apparent, if not most fundamental, in this scenario of political disintegration. When hostilities began in 1423, the Florentine fisc was in a precarious state, requiring a steady influx of forced loans to meet its obligations. But revenues declined progressively, and fiscal authorities were forced to borrow money from private sources at high rates of interest, thus increasing the charges on the fisc.[144] By every means available to them, the authorities sought to extract more revenue from citizens.

They even imposed the death penalty upon certain delinquents, hoping to persuade others to pay their tax obligations.[145] But these draconian measures were as ineffective as appeals to patriotism, or the sporadic efforts to increase revenue by canceling or reducing

---

[144] Molho, *Florentine Public Finances*, ch. 6, 7.

[145] The law authorizing the death penalty for nonpayment is in *Prov.*, 116, ff.23r–24v, 11–12 Apr. 1426. For examples of capital sentences against Niccolò Tornaquinci, Agnolo Biliotti, Jacopo de' Bardi and Piero Fracassini, see *AP*, 4380, ff.35r–36r; *ACP*, 2933, unpaginated, 1 July 1426. Several of these condemnations were later cancelled; *Prov.*, 118, ff.22r–23r; 119, ff.341v–342r; 120, ff.22v–24r.

penalties for nonpayment. The records of the criminal courts from 1427 to 1434 are filled with sentences against hundreds of Florentines, rich and poor, who were unable to pay their *catasto* assessments and so were subject to fines and the confiscation of their property.[146]

The costs of the Milanese war depleted Florence's wealth at a time when a stagnating economy could not restore these outlays. Only a handful of wealthy bankers—Cosimo de' Medici and Andrea de' Pazzi, for example—increased their fortunes in these years; the majority of affluent citizens, like Palla Strozzi, saw their wealth declining: through forced loans and *catasto* assessments, bad debts, the devastation of their estates on the Lucchese frontier.[147] Investment capital was scarce and expensive, since so much money was requisitioned by the state. There was widespread unemployment in the cloth *botteghe* and in the construction industry, as civic, ecclesiastical, and private building declined. Many artisans and laborers were destitute, like the painter Mariotto di Cristoforo who wrote to the tax authorities (1432): "There is no work in my profession and I want peace and not war, and I have six mouths to feed and I cannot do any more. . . ."[148] Like other poor residents, Mariotto would have had difficulty in obtaining credit from pawnbrokers: even the lifting of the ban against Jewish moneylenders in 1430 did not immediately alleviate the shortage of consumer credit.[149]

Two political developments of the late 1420s can be linked directly to this economic crisis: a rising tide of criticism against the regime's leadership for its failure to end the Milanese war (and, later, the Lucca conflict); and the intensification of the competition for salaried offices. The struggle for success in the scrutinies, which had been a perennial source of discord in Florentine political life, now became even more bitter, as profits and patrimonies shrank. This frenetic competition for office contributed significantly to the formation of the factions after 1426,[150] and it may also have strengthened the solidarity of lineages, whose members needed, more desperately than ever before, the support of kinfolk as well as of *amici* and *vicini* to obtain

[146] E.g., *ACP*, 3113, ff.14r, 19v, 23r, 39r; *AP*, 4465, unpaginated, 25 Oct., 3 and 26 Nov. 1432; *AEOG*, 2227, ff.45v–46r, 59v–60r, 66v–67r, 81v–84r.

[147] Molho, *Florentine Public Finances*, 157–60, 172–82; Brucker, *Renaissance Florence*, 83–84. For specific cases involving heavy losses by Giannozzo Gianfigliazzi, Francesco Tornabuoni, Andrea Borgognone and Donato Adimari, see *Prov.*, 123, ff.262v–267r, 391v–392r.

[148] U. Procacci, *Rivista d'arte*, XXVIII, 31–34.

[149] Molho, *Florentine Public Finances*, 151–52.

[150] See D. Kent, *Rise of the Medici*, ch. i, vi, vii; 3.

majorities in the critical scrutinies.[151] In addition to promoting relatives, friends, and clients for office, politicians also sought to damage the candidacy of rivals before the scrutinies were held, and thereafter. Many accusations of ineligibility and malfeasance submitted to the Defenders of the Laws were inspired by factional rivalry. Officials found guilty of illegal conduct, or of being delinquent in paying their taxes, or of being too young or illegitimate, were excluded from all magistracies.[152] They were thus deprived of income and honors that might instead be garnered by their political rivals.

Throughout its history, this regime was plagued by two kinds of internal conflict: first, a persistent tension between the Signoria (influenced if not dominated by the elite) and the legislative councils, which reflected the political interests of rank-and-file guildsmen; second, a struggle within the inner circle, and among families represented there, for preeminence. Quarreling between the leadership and the guild community invariably became more intense in wartime. It was most precisely measured by legislative resistance to the imposition of forced loans, or measures to implement fiscal or electoral reforms. Councilors could express their negative feelings about the administration of the Milanese war, and later the Lucca campaign, only by casting white beans against every provision that imposed a new levy or sanctioned some bureaucratic intrusion into their lives. At some critical moments—for example, in the winter and spring of 1433—this opposition could not be worn down by appeals from the priors and the colleges, who had to wait until the seating of a new group of councilors to enact important legislation.[153] This resistance to the leadership was so tenacious that some statesmen may indeed have contemplated a fundamental reform of the constitution, as Cavalcanti believed, to reduce the representation of those dissidents in the councils and the magistracies.

Frustrated by their inability "to put the commune in order,"[154] the regime's leaders vented their anger upon each other. Some criticized their colleagues for involving the republic in the Visconti war in 1423: "If our affairs had been administered prudently, we would not have

---

[151] *Ibid.*, ch. 2, iii; F. W. Kent, *Family Worlds*, ch. 4. The same argument is made for an earlier period, by R. Witt, in an unpublished article, "Florentine Politics and the Ruling Class, 1382–1407."

[152] Youths would be qualified as soon as they became of age; tax delinquents, when they had paid their obligations to the treasury.

[153] See *LF*, 56, ff.48r–52r, 59r–84r, 89v–91r, 102r–105r, 111r–116v.

[154] Niccolò del Bellaccio, "In omnibus est habendus ordo et precipue in gubernatione rei publice"; *LF*, 54, f.24v, 23 Nov. 1428.

had [to fight] it," so argued the Medici partisan Doffo Arnolfi in 1426.[155] The disasters of the Lucca war convinced many that the republic was governed by traitors. The minimum of trust needed to enable this polity to function dissolved in this poisonous atmosphere. Citizens came to rely more heavily upon their private connections, because they no longer trusted the leadership to govern intelligently and to protect either the community's welfare or their own. While the factions increased in numbers and strength, the unaligned and independent citizens were losing influence and prestige. No one in the regime possessed the authority and the astuteness of Maso degli Albizzi, who had been instrumental in preserving the regime in 1414 and 1415. Rinaldo had inherited his father's role as its titular head, but he did not possess Maso's political skills: his ability to reconcile divergent viewpoints, his fine sense of timing. Except for Cosimo de' Medici and Neri di Gino Capponi, the sons who had replaced their fathers in the inner circle—Giovanni di Rinaldo Gianfigliazzi, Jacopo di Piero Baroncelli, Carlo di Francesco Federighi, Niccolò di Bartolomeo Valori—were not endowed with exceptional talents. Nor did the survivors from Maso's generation—Niccolò da Uzzano, Lorenzo Ridolfi, Agnolo Pandolfini, Niccolò Barbadori, Piero Bonciani—provide strong leadership, perhaps because they were old and tired, or because their reputations had been tarnished by their alleged mismanagement of the Milanese war.

Yet the regime might still have been able to surmount its difficulties if it had not embarked upon the Lucca campaign. That decision proved to be fatal. The rebellion of Volterra in 1429 was the first of a series of uprisings that erupted throughout the territory: in Arezzo, along the Sienese frontier, in the Pisan *contado*, and in the region adjacent to Lucca. The records of the criminal courts from 1429 to 1434 contain a score of convictions against residents of the territory who had planned, or participated in, a rebellion.[156] There are an equal number of capital sentences against Florentine officials who had been in charge of fortified places that had been captured by, or abandoned to, enemy

---

[155] *CP*, 47, f.5r.

[156] So numerous were these uprisings that a special magistracy was created to investigate them; *Prov.*, 122, ff.216v–217v, 16–17 Oct. 1431. Examples of conspiracies: *ACP*, 3113, ff.28r–29r, 36r–36v, 47r–47v; U. Pasqui, "Una congiura per liberare Arezzo," *ASI*, 5th ser., v (1890), 1–19; *GA*, 102, part 2, ff.47r–50v, 67r–68r, 93r–95r, 258r–258v. In the last cited case a Pisan rebel, Tinaccio Bernardi, described his motives: "Io sono vecchio et niuna utilità aspetto di questo che se venisse fatto; ch'io vedessi Pisa libera, morrei pisano contento."

forces.[157] The priors were deluged by petitions demanding that certain individuals be declared magnates for allegedly committing crimes against *popolani*.[158] Rich bankers were denounced for hiding their wealth to avoid taxes, and for gaining enormous profits from their short-term loans to the treasury.[159] Accusations of malfeasance were made against scores of vicars and castellans in the territory, even against the Eight on Security and the Signoria for July-August 1433.[160] The expulsion of the Medici in November of that year did not deter the critics of officialdom. When a silk manfacturer, Francesco Buti, learned that Bernardo Guadagni, a leader of the anti-Medici faction, had received the captaincy of Pisa, he cried: "Robbers! Those [members of the reform *balìa*] are doing very well for themselves, and they can even share the revenues of the Ponte Vecchio, just as they divided up Christ's garments!" A butcher named Andrea di Francesco was fined 100 lire by the Eight on Security (November 1433) for uttering these prophetic words: "If Cosimo were still among us, we should send for him and give him a double stipend instead of exiling him; that would be the lesser evil. This regime cannot survive, and it will not. You will see that before a year has passed things will be different. The merchants should govern, not those [who are now in power]. . . ."[161]

Many guildsmen like Francesco Buti and Andrea the butcher were sympathetic to the Medici, but neither at the time of their expulsion, nor during the disorders following their restoration, did they participate actively in the events which determined Florence's political future. The old battle-cry, "Long live the *popolo* and the guilds," was not heard in the city during these crises; the corporate spirit, which had animated guildsmen and *gonfalone* residents in the fourteenth century, was moribund. The dynamic elements in Florentine politics in the early 1430s were the factions. After the recall of the Medici in September 1434, the leaders of the Albizzi party assembled their supporters in the piazza of Sant' Appollinare. From an initial cadre of 150 armed men, that band had grown to 500 and then (if the testimony of Ugolino Martelli may be believed) to more than a thousand. Instead

157 Examples: *ACP*, 3113, ff.5r–5v, 12v–13r, 36v–38r; 3125, ff.44v–47r; *AEOG*, 2211, ff.36r–37r.

158 On legislation pertaining to magnates, *Prov.*, 122, ff.349r–350r; 123, ff.256r–256v. For examples of these petitions, *DSCOA*, 39, *passim;* 40, ff.47r–47v.

159 *CP*, 49, f.92r, statements of Marco Strozzi and Lorenzo Ridolfi, for the colleges: "Castigentur isti qui faciunt mercaturam super pecuniis communis. . . . De pecuniis illorum de Peruziis, putamus quod providebitur et tamen compellantur illi ad solvendum. . . ." Cf. *CP*, 50, ff.8r–8v, 9v.

160 *GA*, 75, 77, *passim*; *AEOG*, 2227, ff.3r–4r, 17r–18r.

161 These cases in *GA*, 77, part 2, ff.380r–380v.

of attacking the palace of the Signoria, where the priors were guarded by a contingent of 500 soldiers, the Albizzi *brigata* attacked the house of the Martelli, who were fervent partisans of the Medici.[162] When that assault failed, the triumph of the Medici faction was assured.[163]

The regime which Cosimo and his allies established in 1434 was modeled closely upon its predecessor. Except for some changes in electoral procedure to guarantee Medici control of offices, the constitutional system of the old regime was preserved intact.[164] Another element of continuity was the social foundation of the Medici government: the same coalition of old and prominent lineages, purged of its Albizzi-Peruzzi partisans, and with a leaven of parvenu families that had actively supported the Medici prior to 1434. Cosimo and his close associates formed an inner circle within the *reggimento*, although Cosimo's influence in policy-making, particularly in foreign affairs, was greater than that enjoyed by any statesman in the past. But the methods and techniques of government were very similar to those developed by Maso degli Albizzi, Rinaldo Gianfigliazzi, Niccolò da Uzzano and their colleagues in the early years of the *quattrocento*. They had created the polity that was to govern Florence for a century.

[162] L. Martines, "La famiglia Martelli e un documento sulla vigilia del ritorno dall' esilio di Cosimo de' Medici (1434)," *ASI*, cxvii (1959), 41–42. The *brigata* contained a "grandissima fanteria di villani armati," according to Cavalcanti, *Istorie fiorentine*, x, ch. 7. The condemnation of an Albizzi partisan, Domenico Lamberteschi, identifies the ringleaders of that assault, many of whom had recruited *garzoni* from their estates; *ACP*, 3212, ff.16v–17v, 18 Nov. 1434. See too *ibid.*, ff.18r–27r.

[163] These events and those preceding them are analyzed by D. Kent, *Rise of the Medici*, ch. 5.

[164] N. Rubinstein, *The Government of Florence under the Medici*, part i.

Index

Abruzzi, 233

Acciaiuoli, family, 29, 146, 256, 268;
Adoardo, 374n; Agnolo, 471, 497n;
Alamanno, 45, 72n; Antonio, 456;
Donato d'Albizzo, 29; Leone, 27;
Lodovico d'Adoardo, 29; Michele di
Zanobi, 29, 97; Neri, 456
Messer Donato di Jacopo, 18, 27,
103n, 127, 129n, 138, 144, 174, 256,
276-77, 278n; character of, 98; exile
of, 29, 39, 95-100, 155, 284; political
role of, 98-99; political views of,
118n, 128n, 149, 152, 154-55

accoppiatori, 80, 92, 263, 412n

Accorambuoni, Guaspare, 440, 447n,
448n, 459n, 464n, 484

Adimari, family, 31, 93, 100, 171, 275,
277, 337; Amedeo, 27, 86n; Andrea,
95; Donato, 503n; Messer Filippo, 27,
157; Giovanni di Cipolla, 275;
Leonardo, 68; Papino, 275

Agli, family, 31; Ceffo, 41; Manno,
274n

Agliati, castle of, 182

Agnolo di Pino, 300n, 312, 335, 346

Albergotti, family, 216; Giovanni, 216

Alberico, count, 192

Alberti, family, 20-21, 28, 31n, 75-76,
78-79, 82, 86-87, 88n, 89-92, 95, 97-99,
104, 150, 173, 199, 255, 258, 271, 273,
276, 325, 327, 329, 337-39, 365, 443,
464n, 487-88; Alberto di Bernardo,
90-91; Messer Antonio, 91n, 173,
367, 443n; Benedetto, 47n, 48n, 50-51,
53, 54n, 55, 57, 78-79, 102n, 104, 107,
124-25; Bindaccio, 250, 325-29;
Cipriano, 79, 90-91, 106; Francesco
di Messer Jacopo, 21; Giovanni di
Cipriano, 91; Jacopo, 95; Leon
Battista, 23, 37n; Nerozzo di
Bernardo, 91; Messer Niccolò di
Jacopo, 21, 91n, 276; Piero di
Bartolomeo, 91; Riccardo, 96, 99,
174; Simone, 73

Albizzi, family, 25, 41, 62, 81n, 92,
95-96, 117, 137, 139, 240, 255-56,
257n, 268, 276n, 487, 497n, 507;
Alberto, 77n, 115; Andrea di
Francesco, 82, 114n; Antonio, 466n;
Filippo, 281; Francesco di Antonio,
273; Luca di Messer Maso, 255, 273,
275-76, 412n, 461, 476, 486, 488n,
489n, 497n; Niccolò di Pepo, 255,
268n, 330, 335, 387, 389, 391, 412n,
499n; Ormanno, 255; Piero di Luca,
42, 56, 255, 273, 362
Messer Maso di Luca, 87n, 89, 92n,
112n, 124, 149n, 159n, 160, 164, 174,
176n, 178, 180n, 182, 189, 196, 198,
203, 209n, 222, 232, 234, 245n, 255,
260, 264n, 265, 277-78, 281, 285,
306n, 311n, 320n, 328n, 336n, 338n,
341, 344-45, 348n, 352n, 362, 378n,
390, 505; assassination plots against,
97, 100, 250, 397-98; business activities
of, 270, 272; diplomatic career of,
157, 159, 178, 203; political role of,
151, 156, 160, 163, 170, 194, 201,
237-38, 250, 264, 266-68, 272-76, 279,
286, 325-26, 351, 367, 384, 386, 388,
392, 398-400, 507; political views of,
117, 149, 152, 155, 163, 167-68, 169n,
173, 183, 190-92, 194, 202, 204, 225n,
226, 228, 230-31, 236-37, 239, 241-43,
292n, 305n, 330, 340n, 341n, 342-43,
374, 379, 387, 394
Messer Rinaldo di Messer Maso, 195,
207, 225n, 255, 265n, 273n, 290n, 318,
362, 380n, 427, 429, 434, 444, 446,
447n, 448, 456-57, 463, 465, 467, 469,
471, 477-78; business activities of,
270; diplomatic career of, 450-53,
460, 470; political role of, 267n, 268,
462, 473-76, 480, 505; political views
of, 198, 283n, 313n, 379, 411, 415,
420, 436, 439-41, 449, 452, 461-62,
464, 472, 479, 483-84, 496-99

Alderotti, Giovanni di Matteo, 171,
260n

Aldobrandini, Giovanni, 265n, 268;
Luigi, 387n

Alessandri, Alessandro di Ugo, 100n,

Alessandri, Alessandro di Ugo (*cont.*)
107n, 112n, 120n, 123, 124n, 128n,
131-33, 134n, 137, 146n, 149n, 150-51,
153, 154n, 155-56, 165n, 275-76, 463n,
492n
Antonio, 182n, 183, 217, 224, 234,
265, 333n, 347, 355-56, 364n, 388n,
370, 393-94, 401, 408n; business
activities of, 270; diplomatic career
of, 376; political role of, 264, 350,
374; political views of, 184, 218, 226,
231, 271-72, 290, 296, 298, 306, 310,
335-36, 346, 349, 358, 366, 392, 416-17,
419, 429, 434, 436
Alessandria, 136, 192
Alexander V, pope, 233-34, 236-37, 240,
299, 423
Alexandria, 431
Alfonso, king of Aragon, 348, 453
Alidosi, Francesco, lord of Imola, 455;
Lodovico, 372n; Lucrezia, 446;
Messer Obizzo, 60
Altoviti, family, 25, 27, 40, 88n, 240,
255; Bartolomeo, 196n; Bindo, 27;
Giovanni, 172; Guglielmo, 329, 332n,
476; Meo di Bartolo, 338; Messer
Palmiero, 27; Sandro, 265n, 271, 286,
362, 386, 390-91, 435, 436n, 437, 461;
Simone di Messer Bindo, 443n;
Stoldo, 66n, 73, 121n, 137, 143, 250;
Vieri, 195n; Zanobi, 68
Ambrogio di Meo, 138
Andrea di Ser Niccolò, Ser, 199
Angeli, Andrea di Giovanni, 141
Angelini, Bartolomeo, 446
Anghiari, 112n, 221, 468-69
Anselmi, family, 24; Anselmo, 187n,
188n; Bernardo, 469n, 497n; Filippo
d'Anselmo, 24; Gino di Bernardo,
24, 104, 111n, 128n, 131n
Antonio di Giovanni, alias Cappelletto,
194
Antonio di Maestro Guccio, Maestro,
375n
Antonio di Niccolò d'Ancisa, Ser, 25
Aragon, kingdom of, 225, 430, 453, 457,
462
Ardinghelli, family, 25, 240; Francesco,
27, 132n, 151n, 178n, 234n, 235, 237,
243n, 265n, 266, 268, 355n, 373;

Giovanni di Bernardo, 25; Jacopo,
171-72; Neri, 384n; Tommaso di
Neri, 28n, 204, 240n, 241, 265n,
268, 462
Arezzo, 75, 104-05, 109, 112, 121, 173,
208, 214-16, 220-22, 224, 231, 232n,
288, 304, 344, 411n, 429, 460n, 491,
505
aristocracy, conflict with guild
community, 39-42, 49-50, 55-57,
64-68, 72-74, 80-83, 87, 124-25, 200,
415, 473-78, 484-85, 491; ideology of,
8, 10n, 20, 30-39, 74, 245-46, 283,
318, 473-78; political role of, 6-9,
39-42, 51, 60-75, 78-101, 137-38,
151-52, 163-64, 220, 248-302, 501.
See also elite
Aristotle, 302
Arnolfi, Battista, 374n, 488n; Doffo,
499, 505; Zanobi, 436n
Arrighi, Cambio, 24n; Matteo di
Jacopo, 67n, 111n, 149n, 169
Arrigucci, Alessandro, 130, 131n, 133n,
149, 153, 154n, 163; Filippo, 265n,
272, 461n
Asini, family, 48; Matteo, 180n
Asti, 163
Athens, 456
Austria, duke of, 274n
Avignon, 116-17, 156, 163, 296, 358, 364

Bagnesi, Cristofano, 22, 222, 279-80,
281n, 455; Rinieri di Bagno, 25
Baldesi, family, 88; Andrea, 272;
Bartolomea di Andrea, 272
Baldovinetti, Alessio, 67n, 106n, 172,
178, 180n, 192n, 205, 219n, 228n, 231,
243n, 271, 288, 319; Francesco, 172;
Mariotto, 427, 467n, 492n, 496, 498,
499n; Niccolò, 119; Piero, 22n
balìa, 44, 53, 60, 62-63, 65-68, 72, 74n,
78-79, 81, 83-84, 91-94, 129, 147, 165,
263-65, 267, 268n, 280n, 283, 288, 328,
333-34, 338-39, 348, 356, 362, 368, 371,
373n, 374, 377, 383-84, 448, 450,
452-53; of 1387, 86; of 1393, 99n
Banchi, Bartolomeo, 351
Bandini, Agnolo, 71
Barbadori, family, 20n; Donato, 47, 55n,
58, 438; Francesco, 486n; Giovanni

di Messer Donato, 243n, 400n, 443n, 492; Niccolò, 209, 213, 224n, 233, 243n, 270, 291n, 292n, 296, 311, 329n, 342, 343n, 348n, 357, 361, 377, 419, 424, 429n, 439n, 445, 458, 461n, 464, 467, 483-84, 494n, 505

Bardi, family, 34, 39, 365, 413, 488n; Aghinolfo, 34; Alessandro, 103n; Francesco di Benedetto, 210n, 404n; Jacopo di Bindello, 34n, 502n; Lippaccio di Benedetto, 404n

Barducci, Lorenzo, 317n, 318n, 436

Barga, 181

bargello, 339

Barletta, 98

Baron, Hans, 7, 9, 300-01

Baroncelli, family, 245, 268, 279-80, 361, 487, 488n, 492; Cionaccio, 174, 197n, 230, 237-38, 243, 280n, 297; Gherardo di Jacopo, 281-82, 491; Giovanni, 130; Inghilese, 390; Jacopo di Piero, 281, 444n, 446n, 505 *Piero di Jacopo*, 183n, 192n, 202, 213, 228n, 265, 294, 318n, 322n, 344n, 347, 352n, 353, 365n, 367, 396, 423n, 484; business career of, 270; political role of, 264, 267, 285-86, 361; political views of, 227n, 231, 237, 242, 288, 290n, 296, 298, 314, 320, 346, 349n, 398, 407-09, 412n, 416, 419n

Barraclough, Geoffrey, 10

Bartoli, Francesco di Piero, 27

Bartolini, Bartolino, 27, 209n; Bartolomeo, 375n; Domenico, 124; Guccio, 74; Meo, 27

Bartolomeo del Corazza, 260, 392, 421, 424n, 425, 431n

Barucci, Sandro, 257

Bastari, family, 84, 89, 255, 271, 337; Agnolo, 249, 260n; Cionettino, 337-38, 482; Filippo, 41, 52, 57, 73n, 82, 95-96, 100, 104-06, 107, 109, 112n, 124n, 129-30, 132n, 133n, 135, 138n, 249; Giovenco, 84

Battista da Montaldo, 332, 349, 351

Bavaria, 133

Beccanugi, family, 67; Leonardo, 169, 265n; Moscone, 66; Piero, 290, 297, 336, 407, 427n, 449, 479n, 496

Becker, Marvin, 7-9, 410

Bellaccio, Niccolò del, 318n, 348n, 444, 446, 447n, 454, 463, 488n, 504n

Belfredelli, Salvestro, 189

Belletri, district of, 44, 70n

Bencivenni, Messer Alessandro, 269n, 293, 308, 311, 317, 425, 436, 440n, 441n, 444, 447n; Stefano, 479n, 484n, 488n

Benedetto, abbot of S. Piero a Ruota, 360-62

Benedict, XIII, pope, 295

Benini, Michele, 172

Bentivoglio, Giovanni, 176-77, 179-80, 316n

Benvenuti, Lorenzo, 302, 423n; Niccolò, 332, 412n

Berardi, Berardo, 311, 351, 377, 389n, 391

Bergamo, 192, 433

Bernabucci, Ser Biagio, 130, 137

Bernardone da Serra, 170, 180n

Bertaldi, Messer Giovanni, 428n, 440, 448n, 468n

Berti, Giovanni di Antonio, 405

Biffoli, Giovanni, 492n; Niccolò, 335n, 337n

Biliotti, family, 488n; Aldigerio, 365n; Agnolo, 502n; Biliotto, 97; Cristofano, 184; Giovanni, 114, 118, 153, 156n, 163n, 167-68, 240, 306n, 309; Giovannozzo, 169n; Paolo, 199n, 228n, 238, 239n, 244, 264n, 268n, 270-71, 291, 292n, 296-97, 304, 310-11, 343-45, 352, 356, 358-59, 380, 382, 384n, 397, 398n, 406, 419-20, 428n; Piero, 365n

Bischeri, family, 25; Bernardo, 492; Giovanni, 469n; Nofri, 268, 270, 361, 390-91

Black Death, 4, 12, 30, 72

Boccaccio, Giovanni, 3

Boethius, 302, 462n

bollettini, 143n

Bologna, 90, 100, 129-30, 136, 166, 171, 175, 181-82, 184-85, 188-90, 192-93, 194n, 237, 240, 247, 292, 316, 317n, 319-20, 322, 326, 328, 337, 369, 372-75, 376n, 378, 384, 386-93, 398, 419, 421, 428, 433-34, 439, 443, 468; Florentine relations with, 98n, 109, 111-12, 115,

Bologna (*cont.*)
120, 148-50, 153-55, 159, 162n, 176,
179-80, 317, 321, 380, 418, 423-24,
435-36. *See also* papacy, Roman
Bombeni, Filippo, 27
Bonaiuti, Bartolomeo, 118
Bonciani, family, 240; Gagliardo, 129n;
Piero, 306, 351n, 352n, 414, 428n,
435n, 436, 466n, 497n, 505
Boniface IX, pope, 135, 140n, 153, 155n,
156n, 157n, 159, 169, 175-76, 183-84,
188, 189n, 190, 193-94, 196n, 315
Bonsi, family, 87; Bernardo di Ugolino,
404n; Donato di Ugolino, 404n
Bordoni, Giovanni, 306n; Paolo, 390;
Simone, 92n, 104, 123, 129, 132n, 134,
167, 309
Borgognone, Andrea, 503n; Riccardo,
379n, 380n, 382
borsellino, 81n, 92, 93n, 264
Borromeo, family, 403
Boscoli, family, 216
Boucicaut, Marshal, French governor
of Genoa, 160n, 191, 198, 203-08,
210n, 225-27, 235, 295, 316
Bracci, Inghiramo de', 140
Bracciolini, Poggio, 366
Brancacci, Felice, 308, 469n, 496-97, 499
Brandaglini, Maestro Cristofano di
Giorgio, 137-38, 206, 243n, 244n, 268n,
269, 271, 272n, 291n, 308, 325n, 329n,
342, 343n, 364, 381n, 385n, 386n, 401n,
411, 436
Brescia, 177-78, 433, 436n, 481
Brie, Nofri, 138, 192n
Brunelleschi, Bernardo di Alderotto,
405; Gabriello, 238-40, 244, 361n,
379, 385-86, 394
Bruni, Messer Francesco, 74n, 103n,
106; Leonardo, 9, 31n, 98n, 251,
266n, 290, 301-02, 303n, 366-68, 423,
482, 487n, 496n
Bucelli, Francesco, 487n, 492; Giovanni,
222, 281, 429n
Budapest, 343
Buonaccorsi, Giovanni di Simone, 26;
Stefano, 267, 271, 376, 440
Buonarroti, Simone, 25
Buondelmonti, Andrea, 367n;

Francesco, 56n; Gherardo, 56n,
115, 120n, 143; Nanni di Agnolo, 328n
Buoninsegna, Lorenzo, 78-82
Burgundy, duke of, 227n, 297-98
Busini, family, 361; Betto, 361, 376,
459n; Niccolò, 37n, 265n, 270n;
Nofri di Buono, 270n
Buti, Francesco, 506

Camaldoli, district of, 44, 69
Cambi, Giovanni, 60; Niccolò, 204
Campagna, Roman, 229, 241, 245-46
Campofregoso, Battista, 453; Messer
Tommaso, 351, 427, 430n, 439
Cancellieri, family, 173-75, 182, 189,
221; Riccardo, 173
Cane, Ruggero, 140
Canigiani, family, 20n, 268, 271;
Bernardo di Gherardo, 492; Carlo di
Messer Ristoro, 268n; Francesco,
400n, 418; Luigi, 92n, 129n, 151;
Piero, 55n
Cannae, battle of, 293, 301, 455
capitano di balìa, 82n, 100n, 165n,
367, 369
capitudini of the guilds, 46, 51n
Capponi, family, 278; Alberto di Recco,
497n; Cappone, 39, 241, 280;
Giovanni, 448n, 498; Neri di Gino,
313n, 421n, 444n, 448n, 490n, 491,
495, 497, 505; Simone, 16n, 111n,
113n, 125n, 129n, 154n, 163n, 167n
Gino di Neri, 6, 199n, 219, 228, 239,
250n, 265, 267n, 278, 286, 292n,
296n, 304n, 307, 327, 329, 331, 339n,
341n, 354, 387, 408, 409n, 412n, 494n;
business career of, 270; political role
of, 207-08, 264, 350, 361, 398-400;
political views of, 40-41, 170, 178,
202, 213, 226, 230, 232, 246, 294, 300n,
303, 309n, 310, 316, 320, 332, 338n,
357-58, 364, 368n, 377-78, 385, 388-89,
391, 393n, 394-95, 413, 416
captain of the *popolo*, 60, 66n, 71, 84n,
140, 308
Carducci, family, 365; Bartolomeo,
387n, 466n; Giovanni, 243, 291n,
361-62, 374n, 382n, 414n, 419; Jacopo,
188; Niccolò, 475

Carlo da Fogliano, Messer, 190, 197
Carnesecchi, Paolo, 199, 202, 268n,
   350-51, 357, 381n, 421n, 427, 431,
   435, 437, 441n, 472n; Piero, 408n
Carrara, family, 190, 193; Francesco da,
   lord of Padua, 130, 136, 148-49, 192
Casalecchio, battle of, 181-83, 185-86
Casini, Francesco, 51
Castellani, family, 137, 201, 245, 255,
   268, 270n, 277n, 279, 361, 387, 411,
   439-40, 486; Antonio di Niccolò,
   405; Berto, 163n; Giovanni, 144;
   Jacopo di Stefano, 405; Lotto, 111n,
   127n, 129n, 158, 161, 174, 176, 178n,
   191n, 192n, 201n, 265n, 266, 267n;
   Matteo, 195n, 203n, 224, 225n, 267n,
   306, 311-12, 328, 345, 349n, 350, 384n,
   393n, 397, 411n, 412n, 415, 420,
   424-25, 428n, 429, 438n, 440n, 449n,
   450, 458, 473, 483-84; Michele, 72,
   217, 223n, 247, 254, 273, 307-08, 312,
   333, 347, 355n, 357, 361, 368-69, 385n,
   397n, 436, 447n, 458; Pierozzo, 231,
   300n, 341n, 374n, 451; Vanni, 160,
   167, 183, 189-91, 201n, 244n, 250n,
   268, 334n, 382, 385, 387n, 391
Castiglionchi (Da Castiglionchio),
   family, 31-32, 255; Albertaccio, 32;
   Bernardo, 31-32; Guido, 56n; Messer
   Lapo di Albertaccio, 31-33, 42, 141,
   285n; Michele di Messer Lapo, 141,
   443n; Paolo, 141; Rinaldo, 56n;
   Ruggiero, 32
Castrocaro, 114, 153-55, 276, 277n
Catalonia, 447
catasto, 181, 286n, 313, 403-04, 408,
   444-46, 464-65, 481, 483-86, 487n,
   488, 501, 503
Cato, 293
Cavalcabò, family, 190, 192-93; Ugolino,
   193n
Cavalcanti, family, 27, 29; Amerigo, 62;
   Bernardo, 219; Messer Carlo, 29, 405;
   Francesco d'Agnolo, 25; Giovanni,
   250, 302, 398, 426, 450, 457-59, 472-78,
   484, 504; Giovanni di Messer
   Amerigo, 29; Guido, 35n; Otto di
   Messer Mainardo, 29; Ridolfo, 35n
Cavalli, Cavallino, 140-141

Cavicciuli, Jacopo, 56n; Vieri, 106n,
   146n, 150n, 169-70
Cederni, Cederno, 463n
Ceffini, Salvestro, 445n
Cenni di Marco, innkeeper, 38, 62, 151n
Cerchi, family, 29
Charles of Calabria, 291, 297, 451
Charles of Durazzo, king of Naples,
   56, 76-77, 102-04, 114n, 124, 297
Charles IV, emperor, 291, 343, 382
Charles VI, king of France, 102, 152,
   155-56, 158-60, 163, 185, 198, 205,
   208n, 232, 347
Cherichini, Barduccio, 147, 172, 218,
   243, 265n, 367n; Giovanni di
   Barduccio, 404n, 444n; Giuliano, 286
Chiavaccini, Domenico di Vanni, 258n;
   Francesco di Vanni, 258n
church, Florentine, 119n, 211, 311-12,
   360-61, 373-74, 408-09, 422-25, 478-80
Ciachi, Jacopo di Matteo, 266n
Ciampelli, Giovanni, 235
Ciardi, Morello, 139n
Cicero, 292n, 293, 294, 473
Cirioni, Giovanni, 172, 197n, 198
Città di Castello, 119, 205n, 316, 317n,
   432n, 439-40
civic ideology, 9-11, 30, 180-81, 185,
   248, 302-18, 354, 367-68, 374-75, 378,
   415-16, 428-29, 447, 455, 458-59, 481-83,
   498, 501-02
civic unity, in Florence, 47-48, 52, 62,
   75, 78, 86, 99, 101, 180-82, 242-43,
   283-84, 302-10, 369, 377, 399, 462,
   488, 490, 498
Clement VII, Avignonese pope, 103,
   116-18, 274n
Cocchi Donati, family, 256, 464n;
   Niccolò, 256
Cola di Giovanni da Francavilla, 249n
Cola di Maestro Piero, 260n, 325, 327n
Colle, 61n, 220, 344
Colonna, Giovanni, 195n, 203n, 234
Como, 192, 433
Company of the Magi, 480, 482
conspiracies, involving Alberti, 77-80,
   90-92, 250, 319, 325-31, 337-40, 488n;
   of Ciompi, 49, 56, 64, 69-71, 139-40,
   327-29; in the dominion, 140-43, 165,

conspiracies (*cont.*)
174-75, 182, 212-16, 495, 505; internal,
55-61, 75n, 77-80, 90-101, 139, 165,
171-74, 199, 249-50, 259, 325-31, 397-99
Constance, 376n, 384, 421; council of,
417
Coppoli, Francesco de', 281, 282n
Corbinelli, Bartolomeo, 207-08, 219,
373, 445n, 457n, 460; Giovanni, 467;
Parigi, 498n
Corbizzi, family, 20, 79, 84, 87, 89
Corsi, Domenico, 238n, 282; Lapo,
373n
Corsini, family, 38n, 117; Giovanni di
Matteo, 466n; Lapo, 374n; Cardinal
Piero, 37, 117, 156
Messer Filippo di Tommaso, 104, 124,
127-28, 144, 146n, 156, 178, 180n, 182n,
188n, 191, 194n, 196n, 250n, 265, 268,
285, 292n, 299, 305, 317, 321, 324-25,
333, 345, 347, 380n, 384n, 389, 396,
397n, 415, 425, 428n; diplomatic
career of, 316; political role of, 137,
264, 267, 269, 294, 363n, 367, 374;
political views of, 100n, 108n, 111n,
113n, 115, 117, 127n, 130-33, 149-50,
152, 154-55, 158, 183-84, 198, 200,
204, 218, 226, 233, 236-39, 242, 244,
286, 290n, 291, 293, 298, 301, 304,
306, 310, 314-15, 328, 331-32, 335-37,
338n, 341n, 342-44, 346, 351, 358,
367-68, 376, 378-79, 381, 387-88, 391,
393, 399, 416n, 417, 419
Cortona, 111n, 197, 229-31, 239, 288,
304, 382, 411n, 429
Coucy, Enguerrand de, 104-05
Council of the Commune, 14, 38n, 72n,
85n, 86-87, 94, 334, 340, 392, 409,
413, 416, 476n, 484
Council of Eighty-one, 147, 151, 156n,
157, 176, 196, 199, 245
Council of Forty-eight, 457n
Council of the *Popolo*, 14, 55, 67-68,
73-74, 75n, 83-84, 94, 100, 113, 129,
147n, 161, 165n, 218, 333-34, 392-93,
409, 413, 414n, 416, 437, 443, 446,
464, 473-74, 476n, 484
Council of Two-Hundred, 384, 392,
409, 430, 432n
Covoni, family, 24, 64, 87, 89, 174n,

271; Antonio di Paolo, 259n; Messer
Bettino, 51, 55n; Jacopo, 174; Jacopo
di Paolo, 24n; Jacopo di Sandro, 25;
Matteo di Lodovico, 28n; Niccolò di
Messer Bettino, 180n; Piero, 68
Cremona, 192, 433, 436n
Curiani, Valorino, 89

da Filicaia, family, 25; Luca, 223n,
276n, 297, 344, 402n, 434n, 488n;
Simone, 435, 448n, 495n
da Ghiaceto, Filippo di Giovanni, 491
Dalmatia, 322, 402
Da Mezzola, Ermellina, 25; Messer
Zanobi, 25, 26
Dante, 3, 4, 285n, 302, 451
da Panzano, Antonio di Messer Luca,
280n, 353, 390; Giovanni, 500;
Giovanni di Ciampino, 28n; Luca
di Matteo, 29n, 480; Matteo di
Messer Luca, 68
d'Appiano, Jacopo, lord of Pisa, 149,
152, 158, 164-65, 167-68, 248, 316
da Rabatta, Antonio, 307, 351, 495n, 496
Dardi, Niccolò, 266n
Dati, family, 257; Gregorio, 15, 185-86,
251, 257, 261-62, 301, 348n, 374n, 426,
440n, 441, 451, 455, 498n; Leonardo,
general of the Dominican order, 340,
351n, 435n; Stagio, 257
Datini, Francesco di Marco, 22n, 78-80,
138, 161n, 171-72, 176n, 177n, 191n,
200, 205, 277-78, 282; letters by, 171n,
207n, 235; letters to, 133n, 139, 163n,
164n, 169-70, 172, 226, 260; views of,
162, 168, 206, 261
Davanzati, family, 21, 22, 255;
Bartolomeo, 22; Bernardo, 170;
Chiarino, 21-22; Messer Giuliano,
269n, 311, 317n, 405n, 429, 433, 436-37,
443n, 467, 484, 497n; Marco, 151-52;
Niccolò, 265n, 379n, 391, 466; Piero,
101, 151, 170
Davidsohn, Robert, 4
Davizzi, Francesco, 171-72
Defenders of the Laws (*Conservatores
Legum*), 489-93, 504
Dei, Domenico, 378, 385, 440
del Bellaccio, Niccolò, 236, 351, 435-37,
444, 459, 488n

del Bene, family, 21n, 26-29, 86-87, 171, 255, 365; Berto di Tano, 26; Borgognone, 27; Francesco di Jacopo, 21, 26-28, 80, 87, 89n, 221n, 259n; Giovanni d'Amerigo, 21, 26, 27n, 80, 87; Jacopo di Francesco, 86n, 89n; Messer Ricciardo di Francesco, 27, 86n, 221, 241, 269n, 296n

del Bugliasse, Cristofano, 25

del Caccia, Caccino, 27

del Garbo, Tommaso, 257

del Grasso, Niccolò Benozzo, 238n, 271, 272n, 340n

de' Libri, Maffeo di Ser Francesco, 116, 118; Paolo di Maffeo, 258

della Fioraia, Simone, 381n, 383; Filippo, 456, 465

dell'Antella (Antellesi), family, 220, 268, 486; Alessandro, 102n; Antonio, 476n; Donato, 406n; Filippo, 281; Leonardo, 27, 176n; Maso, 397n; Niccolò, 281; Nofri, 48; Piero di Masino, 26n; Taddeo, 444n

della Camera, Ser Paolo di Messer Amerigo, 269n, 271, 337n, 341n, 346-47, 349n, 351, 380n

della Casa, family, 220, 256; Agnolo, 181n, 183n, 186n, 236, 256, 375, 376n, 436; Antonio, 499

della Luna, family, 256; Francesco, 256, 498n; Giovanni, 256

della Robbia, Luca, 284n

della Scala, Mastino, 291n, 420

della Stufa, Andrea di Messer Ugo, 39, 149n, 213, 234n, 236, 282; Giovenco, 204, 328; Ugo, 420n

del Palagio, Andrea, 499; Guido, 38, 62, 96, 103n, 131n, 133, 155n, 158, 159n, 168n; Nofri d'Andrea, 282; Piero, 313n; Uberto, 478

del Pancia, Filippo di Firenze, 375n, 463; Firenze, 291, 420

del Teghia, Giovanni, 308n, 496, 497n

del Vigna, Antonio, 219, 272n, 332, 409n

Dietisalvi, Nerone, 461n

Dini, Giovanni, 51, 59; Miniato, 216

divieto legislation, 303, 411-12

Domenico di Cambio, 133n, 139, 177n, 200n, 207n, 209n

Domenico di Ser Mino, Messer, 358n

dominion, administration of, 75n, 142, 208-25, 323, 402, 408, 411-14, 477n, 491-92; expansion of, 104-12, 120-23, 131, 192-93, 202-08, 235-37, 246-47, 276, 320, 344-48, 396, 416, 426-31, 495-97

Donati, family, 29

Doni, Gherardo, 233

economy, Florentine, condition of, 4-5, 7, 10, 19, 69-70, 170, 191, 223-24, 235, 322-23, 325, 344, 396, 400-06, 426-27, 455, 463; regime's policy concerning, 52, 63n, 410, 430-32; war's effect on, 138, 142, 148, 158, 162, 179-80, 182, 200, 203, 227, 243, 319, 321-22, 401, 473

Eight on Security (Otto di Guardia), 54, 57, 59, 70, 90n, 94, 96, 170n, 171, 199, 214-16, 219, 262n, 280, 297, 339, 373, 398, 479-80, 491, 498, 501, 506

Elba, 322

elite, governing (of 1382-1433 regime), 8-12, 61-62, 72, 79-80, 87-89, 92-94, 124, 248-318, 361-62, 396-97, 400, 411-12, 457-58, 501-02. See also aristocracy

Emilia, 119, 191

England, 321

Este, Alberto d', lord of Ferrara, 130; Niccolò, lord of Ferrara, 148, 150-51, 166, 234, 273, 373, 433, 454, 491

estimo, 53-55, 146, 148n, 465n

Eugenius IV, pope, 260, 449

executor of the Ordinances of Justice, 308

exiles, Florentine, 26-29, 49, 56-57, 69, 74n, 86-87, 90-91, 94-95, 97-100, 171, 175, 212-14, 259, 325-28, 337-39, 488, 500-01

factions, in Florence, 26-30, 40-42, 50, 57-61, 110-11, 116-18, 124, 164, 248-52, 283, 312-13, 352-68, 444, 463, 478-81, 487-500, 503-05

Faenza, 100, 151, 171, 175, 181n, 182, 457, 462

Fagni, Bernardo, 374n, 397n; Guido, 47n

Falconi, family, 220, 271; Meo, 328

family (lineage), concept of, 18-26, 30-39; marriages, 21, 24-26, 95-96; political role of, 19-21, 26-30, 84, 245, 254-59, 268-69, 303, 359-64, 412, 487, 503. *See also* factions

Fantoni, Leonardo, 476-77

Federighi, Messer Carlo di Francesco, 269n, 398n, 428, 454-55, 488n, 489n, 505; Francesco, 163, 240, 243n, 267n, 282; Paolo, 307n, 472n

Ferdinand, king of Aragon, 342

Ferrara, 120n, 151, 153, 159, 384, 455

fidei commissum, 18

fideiussori, 29n

Fieschi, family, 191, 235; Giovanni, 439, Messer Luca, 351

Figinaldi, Andrea, 397, 399n

Figliopetri, Filippo, 141

Filippo di Ser Ugolino, Ser, 225n

Fioravanti, Francesco, 169n, 218; Neri, 265n

Firenze, Giovanni, 269; Piero, 181, 250, 269, 291, 308, 309n, 351, 354, 374, 377n, 378n, 381n, 384n, 385, 387n, 389, 416n, 420n

Firenzuola, 220-21, 460n

fisc, Florentine, 185, 197-98, 206-07, 222-24, 230, 323-25, 348, 404-05, 465-69, 502; budgets, 209-12, 324, 397, 407-08, 462, 466-67; complaints concerning, 138, 142-43, 161, 188, 207-08, 234-35, 333, 373, 459, 472-73; political conflict concerning, 53-55, 145-47, 161-62, 197, 237-38, 286-87, 311, 333-34, 354-56, 409-10, 437-38, 444-46, 459-60, 463-66, 472-76, 483-86; regime's policy concerning, 63-64, 146, 175-76, 181, 212, 373-74, 465-66. *See also estimo*, forced loans, *monte*

Foligno, 394

forced loans (*prestanze*), 55, 64, 148, 160, 165, 176, 200, 206, 230, 238, 243, 252n, 282, 313, 331, 335, 348, 354, 355, 459; assessment schedules of, 143, 146, 170, 294, 324-25, 333-34, 354-56, 410, 438, 444-46, 456-57, 463-65, 472-73, 476, 483-86; delinquencies for payment of, 143, 146, 161-62, 209, 323, 333, 455, 459, 465; levies of,

147-48, 161-62, 176, 197-98, 209, 323-24, 333-34, 446, 450, 456, 475

foreign policy, Florentine, conceptions of, 107-11, 122-25, 129-30, 149-50, 154-55, 184-88, 198-202, 232, 237-40, 245-47, 294-300, 314-21, 344-51, 357-60, 366-67, 379-83, 386-94, 416-22, 429, 434-37, 455. *See also* war(s)

Forlì, 243, 246-47, 320, 446-52

Forlimpopoli, 452

Fortebraccio, Braccio, 237, 378, 385, 391-92, 393n, 418, 421-23, 436, 439-40, 442, 447, 451-52, 457, 460; Niccolò, 496; Oddo, 460, 462

Fortini, family, 256; Andrea, 403n; Benedetto, 285-86, 289; Ser Paolo, 290, 487n, 497, 498n; Ser Piero, 451n

Foscari, Francesco, 461

Fracassini, Piero, 502n

France, 102-03, 131, 144, 155n, 238, 402; Florentine relations with, 136, 152, 155-61, 205, 208, 225-27, 233-34, 347

Franceschi, Uguccione, 47n

Franceschini, Andrea, 90, 91n

Fregosi, family, 235, 341n

Frescobaldi, family, 31, 474; Baldo, 35n

Friuli, 419

Fronte, Antonio, 421n

Gabrielli, family, 122; Messer Cante, 71; Francesco, 112

Gaevia, castle of, 112n

Gaio, a Jew, 201n, 273n

Galilei, Bartolomeo, 24n; Galileo, 239, 305n, 414n, 436, 451n, 455, 458, 459n, 485n, 498

Gambacorta, family, 195, 207; Pietro, 120, 135, 149, 164, 166, 203, 207, 344n, 392

Genoa, 120, 136, 140, 153, 198, 201, 207, 210n, 332, 344, 346, 385, 430, 433-35, 436n, 437, 441, 447, 450, 452-53, 456; Florentine relations with, 135, 152, 155-56, 160n, 175, 189, 191, 194, 203-05, 208, 225-27, 235-36, 241-42, 244, 316-17, 340-42, 350-52, 410, 427-29. *See also* war, with Genoa

gente nuova, 33, 36, 47, 81, 88, 256-62, 336, 473-77, 489

Germany, 131, 144, 177, 179. *See also* Holy Roman Empire

Gherardi, Gherardo, 465; Nanni, 212n

Gherardini, Antonio, 279-80; Bartolomeo, 220; Ugolino, 66

Gherardini Giani, family, 271; Astorre, 434; Gherardino, 217n; Niccolò, 128n, 132n, 151

Ghibellinism, 41, 48, 50, 64, 66-68, 72-77, 95, 124, 126, 139, 222, 236, 314-15, 320, 428, 434. *See also* Guelfism

Giandonati, Lodovico, 34n

Gianfigliazzi, family, 256, 276, 277n; Antonio di Rinaldo, 25; Francesco di Messer Rinaldo, 473-74, 492; Giannozzo, 503n; Giovanni di Messer Rinaldo, 267n, 492, 497n, 505; Jacopo di Messer Rinaldo, 268, 412n, 444; Madelena, 276

Messer Rinaldo, 18, 28, 85n, 87n, 144, 162, 172n, 174, 178, 191n, 196n, 202, 205n, 208n, 209n, 245, 255, 260, 265, 267n, 268, 289, 291n, 293, 334, 336n, 344-45, 350, 381n, 396, 461n, 494n; assassination plots against, 97, 100, 249-50; political role of, 95-96, 137, 151, 248-50, 264, 268, 276-79, 314, 326, 361, 363n, 374, 386, 398-400, 507; political views of, 106, 121, 124n, 130, 153, 155-56, 170, 172, 179, 194n, 198, 200, 204, 208, 222, 226, 232, 238, 243, 246-47, 275, 285, 296, 308, 320, 330-31, 338, 340n, 342-43, 348, 349n, 353, 366, 368, 375n, 379, 380n, 383n, 387, 416, 418-19, 424, 458, 461

Ginori, family, 256; Giuliano, 445n; Simone, 400n; Zanobi, 196, 256

Giotto, 3

Giovanni, family, 37; Buonaccorso di Lapo, 84-85, 104, 106n, 108n, 113n, 141, 267n, 357; Francesco, 37; Giovanni di Tommaso, 482

Giovanni di Michele de Ser Parente, 463

Giovanni di Mone, Messer, 56

Giovanni di Ser Nigi, 393

Giraldi, Paolo, 172

Giugni, family, 486; Andrea di Niccolò,

492n; Domenico di Domenico, 25, 174n, 200, 282; Filippo, 267n, 268; Giovanni, 403n; Niccolò, 83n

Goldthwaite, Richard, 21

Gondi, family, 24; Antonio di Simone, 24n; Lionardo di Simone, 24n

gonfalone, 15, 255, 311, 463n, 485n, 500; of Black Ox, 257; of Chiave, 276n; of Curris, 336n; of Nichi, 87n; of Scala, 87n; of White Lion, 24, 88-89, 255

Gonzaga, Francesco, lord of Mantua, 148-49, 166, 411

Grandoni, Andrea, 47n

Grassolino, Giovanni, 157

Gregory X, pope, 297

Gregory XI, pope, 76, 102, 105, 115, 117, 291

Gregory XII, pope, 229, 295-96

Guadagni, Bernardo, 192, 225n, 230n, 268, 282, 307, 364n, 367, 368n, 392, 462n, 467n, 506; Vieri, 213, 242, 266, 268, 282, 317, 344n, 346, 358n, 385-86, 389, 391, 415, 425, 434-36, 447, 452-54, 460, 461n, 463-64, 470, 473

Guasconi, family, 27, 137, 268; Messer Biagio, 103n, 115, 117, 123-24, 126n, 130, 131, 273; Bernardo di Messer Biagio, 405; Filippo, 265n, 398n; Jacopo, 167, 170, 265n; Leonardo, 169; Niccolò, 151n, 154n, 162, 173-74, 178n, 194, 196n, 297; Ubaldino, 301, 332, 341n, 350

Guazza, Bernardo, 259n; Recco, 259n; Vieri di Recco, 258-59

Guazzalotri, family, 182

Gubbio, 113-14, 119, 122

Gucci, Alessandro, 56n; Benino, 154n; Dino, 272, 377, 381, 389, 436n, 439n, 445n, 448n, 450n, 461, 486n, 500; Giorgio, 128n; Guccio, 309n

Guelfism, 15, 17-18, 29, 33-34, 39, 41-42, 45, 48, 50, 51n, 60, 64-68, 72-77, 80-82, 84, 87-88, 93-94, 97, 102, 124, 126, 170, 229, 252, 258, 272, 314-15, 422-23, 429, 434

Guicciardini, family, 35, 268; Messer Giovanni di Messer Luigi, 268n, 404n, 429, 435, 437, 441n, 464, 469, 490n,

Guicciardini, family (*cont.*)
492, 497; Messer Luigi, 29, 35, 130-32, 191, 268n, 278n, 309n; Piero di Messer Luigi, 268n, 270n, 281, 292n, 312, 357, 368, 464, 495; Simone di Machirone, 35
Guichi, Bernardo di Rosso, 142
Guidalotti, Branca, 27, 59; Papi, 260n, 280
Guidetti, Guidetto, 233, 236, 296n, 305, 315n, 361-62, 380n, 382, 383n, 415, 417n, 420n, 425, 435, 467; Jacopo di Filippo, 404n; Tommaso, 51, 104-05, 106n, 124n
Guidi, counts, 90
Guido d'Asciano, 119
guild community, political role of, 11-13, 18, 39-70, 72-75, 82-84, 93-94, 106-09, 124-25, 132, 136-38, 145-46, 198-200, 260-62, 306-08, 400, 413-14, 437, 457-58, 468, 473-74, 491-92, 496n, 501-04, 506; values of, 7, 11-18, 30, 35-43, 46-48, 57, 65, 70-71, 87, 93-94, 106-10, 283, 484-85
guilds, lower (*arti minori*), 16-18, 38, 42-46, 54, 60-62, 75n, 81-83, 125n, 252, 411n, 465n, 473-76
Guinigi, Giovanni, 33; Paolo, lord of Lucca, 33, 196, 229, 267n, 296, 316, 423, 442, 494-96

Hawkwood, John, 61, 86, 103n, 119, 129, 130, 134-36, 148, 291n
Hay, Denys, 5
Henry VII, emperor, 48, 139, 382, 419
Herde, Peter, 10
Herlihy, David, 5, 403
historiography, Florentine, 3-13, 184-86, 300
history, in political debate, 290-94, 300-02, 304, 310, 451
Holmes, George, 6, 365
Holy Roman Empire, Florentine views of, 48, 177-79, 291, 298, 343, 376, 379-85, 419-21, 461
humanism, civic, 286, 289-94, 301-02
Hungary, 76, 102, 156, 322, 394, 402

Imola, 150, 446n, 455

imperialism, Florentine, *see* dominion, expansion of
Innocent VII, pope, 202n, 207
Isolani, Cardinal, 421

Jacomelli, Milano, 141
Jean II, count of Armagnac, 136, 156, 160, 163, 232, 291
Joanna, queen of Naples, 410
John of Gorlitz, 382
John XXIII (Baldassare Cossa), pope, 192-94, 205n, 229-30, 233, 237, 243-44, 246-47, 299, 321, 342, 358-60, 363-65, 370, 372-76, 378, 384-93, 399n, 417-18, 423
Jones, Philip, 5
justice, administration of, 34, 38-39, 49-51, 60, 216-22, 330

Kent, Dale, 256-57

Ladislaus, king of Naples, 114, 155n, 175, 183, 201, 207-08, 214-15, 227-32, 236-47, 260n, 263, 288-89, 293, 299, 301, 310, 342-43, 352, 357-59, 361, 363-64, 366-72, 374-76, 378-87, 389-94, 396, 406, 410, 413, 416-17, 420-21, 433, 442, 451. *See also* wars, Florentine, against Naples
Lamberteschi, Domenico, 482, 507n
Lamberti, family, 493
Lana guild, 44, 52, 60-62, 65, 89, 321
L'Aquila, 362, 451
Latino, Cardinal, 488n
Lazzari, Sinibaldo, 199
Lenzi, family, 19-20, 87, 256; Domenico, 27; Giovanni, 20, 27, 28n, 86n; Lorenzo, 435-36, 439, 444, 449, 454, 487n, 497n; Piero, 19, 84, 309n
Leonardo di Maestro Dino, Maestro, 95
Leonardo di Niccolò, 17
Leoni, Francesco, 271, 293, 322, 346, 347n, 350-52, 376-77, 385n
Leopold IV, duke of Austria, 163
Lerici, 320, 341, 352
Librafratta, 492
Libri Fabarum, 392, 474
Livorno, 204-05, 225-26, 229-36, 241, 320, 332-33, 340-42, 344, 346, 349-52, 426-30, 448, 450, 452

Livy, 293, 294
Lodi, 192, 376, 378
Lodovico di Ser Bartolo di Banco, 129n
Lombardy, 86, 119, 190-91, 195, 198,
    322, 433, 436, 457, 471
Louis of Anjou, claimant to the
    kingdom of Naples, 102-05, 118n,
    228, 232-42, 244, 246, 289, 299, 359
Luca del Melano, 65
Lucca, 114, 135, 140, 152, 153, 164, 179,
    198, 203n, 207, 214n, 215, 236, 316,
    392, 423n, 496; Florentine relations
    with, 61n, 122, 133, 151, 158, 164n,
    179n, 442. *See also* Guinigi, Paolo;
    war, Florentine, with Lucca
Lucignano, 107-11, 112n, 120-21, 128-29
Lunigiana, 195n, 434, 439, 441-42, 446,
    454, 460n, 491
Lycurgus, 293

Machiavelli, family, 35, 39; Buoninsegna,
    281; Chiovo, 38-39; Donnino, 140n;
    Filippo, 306; Messer Francesco, 312n,
    318n, 361-62, 373n, 386, 387n, 389,
    391-94, 420, 424-25, 428, 431, 441,
    444-46, 449, 454, 458, 461n, 464, 469n,
    472, 476, 478, 484-85; Lorenzo, 265n;
    Niccolò, 6, 11, 292, 294, 316, 484
Macinghi, family, 284n; Arrigo, 118n
Magalotti, family, 268; Bese di Guido,
    25, 62, 78n; Filippo, 78, 81n, 89n,
    168n, 170, 176, 184, 187n, 196n, 210,
    250n, 265n, 268n
magnates, 19-20, 31, 34-35, 39, 52, 56,
    64, 67n, 68n, 73, 93, 143, 302, 474
Malaspina, Margherita, 195n
Malatesta, family, lords of Rimini, 166,
    247, 391-92, 418, 421, 461n, 496;
    Carlo, 166, 190, 193, 195, 198, 205n,
    315n, 321, 378, 380, 399n, 495;
    Malatesta, 232n; Matteo, 29; Pandolfo,
    433, 448, 449n, 450-52
Malatesta da Dovadola, count, 202
Malavolti, Niccolò, 122-23, 125
Malefici, Paolo, 51, 57n
Malegonelle, family, 88; Jacopo, 242n,
    264, 268n, 297, 330, 335n, 342;
    Niccolò, 243
Mancini, Apollonio, 139n; Bardo, 81n,
    89, 214n, 265n; Duccio, 318n, 481, 497

Manetti, Bernardo, 445n
Manfredi, Amerigo, 197; Astorre, lord
    of Faenza, 90, 166, 174, 182-83, 315
Mangiadori, Benedetto, 165-173;
    Bernardo, 182
Mangioni, family, 88, 486; Antonio,
    188n, 192n, 238, 264n, 283n, 290,
    340-41, 351-52, 354n, 387, 421;
    Cionaccio, 237; Filippo, 311n, 456,
    472; Lippozzo, 226n, 239n, 350, 397n,
    412, 466n, 468-69, 486, 495n, 496, 497n
Mannelli, family, 79, 259; Francesco,
    327-29
Manni, Andrea di Bartolo, 405
Manni, Ser Giacomo, 61, 107-11, 112n,
    121, 124n, 126n
Mannini, Alamanno di Luigi, 444n,
    445n; Luigi, 224n
Manovelli, Giuliano, 455n
Mantua, 157, 379n, 421n, 482
Marches, 191, 241, 447, 451
Marchi, family, 220; Francesco, 70;
    Leonardo, 70; Tommaso, 135, 154n,
    167, 180n
Mariotto di Cristoforo, painter, 503
Marseille, 241
Marsili, Bernardo, 158; Sala, 371n, 378
Martelli, family, 507; Ugolino, 506
Martin V, pope, 260, 299, 417, 421-25,
    436, 439, 441, 447, 457-58, 460-61,
    469-71
Martines, Lauro, 6-10, 18, 295, 299
Martini, Francesco, 54n; Ser Martino,
    490n; Matteo, 385n; Nello, 42n, 313n,
    449, 484; Niccolò, 55n
Matteo di Guccio, 157-58
Matteo di Lorenzo, goldsmith, 260
Mazzei, Ser Lapo, 22n, 260-61, 278, 282
Medici, bank, 221, 429; family, 3, 6,
    19n, 27, 38, 40, 62, 81n, 97-98, 139,
    173, 255, 365, 403-04, 411n, 485n, 488n,
    492, 499, 506-07; Africhello, 34;
    Alamanno di Messer Salvestro, 98n;
    Antonio d'Albizzo, 165, 338; Antonio
    di Bartolomeo, 98n; Antonio di
    Giovanni di Cambio, 98n; Averardo
    di Francesco, 21, 258n, 311, 318, 390n,
    422n, 425, 431, 435, 437, 439-41, 445,
    462n, 464, 487, 490n, 496, 498-500;
    Bastardino, 100, 250, 256; Cosimo di

Medici, bank (cont.)
  Giovanni, 21, 267n, 486n, 487, 500, 503, 505-07; Francesco di Bicci, 96n; Foligno, 19; Messer Michele, 17; Nicola di Messer Vieri, 29, 472; Niccolò, 270; Salvestro di Messer Alamanno, 41-42, 46, 55; Messer Vieri, 17n, 37, 141n
  Giovanni di Bicci, 21, 324, 351, 355n, 356n, 398n, 403n, 421n, 428n, 441, 447, 448n, 457, 461, 466-67, 469n, 476, 486n; business activity of, 165-66, 177; diplomatic career of, 461; political role of, 266, 267n, 294, 475, 478, 480; political views of, 163n, 202n, 228, 231, 313, 343n, 350, 365-66, 399, 415, 429-30, 434, 440, 455, 458-60, 485
Menicluni, Antonio, 212n
mercenaries, Florentine, 119, 135, 140, 143n, 148, 154, 162, 202, 207, 209, 230-31, 243, 406-07, 409, 450. See also war(s)
Merchants' Court (Mercanzia), 10, 61n, 158, 243n, 270n, 297, 321, 373, 437n, 490
Michele di Lando, 46, 139n
Michele di Ser Parente, 314
Migliorati, Niccolò, 180n
Migliori, Migliore, 263, 362
Migliorotti, Antonio di Piero, 490
Milan, 4, 120, 136, 419, 439, 450, 457, 495; Florentine relations with, 78n, 85-86, 90, 125-35, 153, 188, 192-95, 230, 237, 427-35, 440-42, 449, 486. See also Visconti; wars, Florentine, with Milan
Minerbetti, Andrea, 120, 129n, 133, 148n; Giovanni, 211, 217, 309, 393n, 394n, 400n, 445, 463n, 476n, 486n, 497n, 499
Mocenigo, Tommaso, doge of Venice, 400, 402, 432
Modena, 443
Modigliano, Guido, count of, 273-74
Molho, Anthony, 408, 460
Monachi, Ser Niccolò, 53, 139n; Messer Ventura, 134, 260n
Monaldi, family, 258n, 464n; Giovanni, 45
monte, 53-54, 64, 65n, 74, 148, 210-12,

348, 353-54, 389, 396, 404, 406-09, 444, 465-66, 484, 498. See also fisc
Montebuoni, Gherardo, 153
Montefeltro, Guidantonio, 372n; Guido, count of, 112-13, 119, 125n, 247
Montegonzi, Messer Bartolomeo, 462n
Montepulciano, 120-23, 126, 128-31, 134-35, 173, 220-21, 224, 242, 429, 492
Montferrat, marquis of, 496
Morelli, family, 257; Giovanni di Jacopo, 468; Paolo, 23
  Giovanni di Paolo, 21n, 35-36, 234n, 317n, 424n, 487, 495, 498n; social attitudes of, 22-23, 30-31; political role of, 488n; political views of, 57, 126n, 177, 198-99, 203, 206-08, 245n, 261-62, 302, 312, 335, 417n, 497n
Morotta, Mariotta della, 354n, 367n
Mozzi, family, 271; Antonio, 327-29; Giovanni di Luigi, 259n
Mucini, Arrigo, 146n, 151n, 176n
Mutrone, 168, 179n, 196, 201

Naddi, Roberto, 258n
Naddo di Ser Nepo, Ser, 78n
Naples (city), 105, 174, 233, 239, 241, 372, 374
Naples, kingdom of (Regno), 114, 119, 234, 237, 242-43, 322, 378, 394, 402, 418, 430, 433, 457; Florentine relations with, 76-77, 97, 102-04, 124, 175, 207, 225-32, 238-41, 244-47, 319, 342-43, 357-64, 376-77, 386-91, 411, 451. See also Ladislaus, king of Naples; wars, Florentine, against Naples
Nardi, Bernardo, 281
Narni, 394
Nerini, Giuliano, 102n
Niccoli, Niccolò, 172, 302, 303n, 439n
Niccolini, family, 29; Biagio, 483-84; Filippo di Giovanni, 25; Giovanni, 289, 290n; Lapo di Giovanni, 24, 26, 36, 136n, 268, 355n, 461; Niccolò, 36n
Niccolò da Tolentino, 462
Niccolò di Chiaro, blacksmith, 134, 138, 158
Niccolò di Messer Leonardo, Ser, 249
Nigi, Ser Manno, 48n
Nobili, family, 21n; Guccio, 77n, 128, 134n, 167; Niccolò, 437

novina, 270-71, 438, 444n, 445-46, 463n

offices (officeholding), 28, 37-38, 51, 59, 67, 72, 75, 80-84, 92-93, 254-59, 335-37, 410, 443-44, 476-77, 503-04. *See also* scrutinies
Oltrarno, quarter of, 361
Ordelaffi, lords of Forlì, 166; Teobaldo, 446
Ordinances of Justice, 39-40, 303
Orlandi, Messer Rosso d'Andreozzo, 21, 101, 233, 311
Orlandini, Bartolomeo, 307, 440, 447, 458; Giovanni, 169, 178, 182, 235n, 237, 267, 270, 351
Orleans, duke of, 118n, 203, 225, 227n
Orsini, family, 421; Cardinal, 360; Paolo, 190n, 234, 237-38, 242, 323n, 373, 378, 381, 384-85; Rinaldo, 119, 122
Ottinelli, Giovanni, 17
Ottokar, Nicolai, 4

paciales, 63
Padua, 119-20, 128, 136, 139, 178-79, 292, 429; Florentine relations with, 127, 130, 148, 159, 192-93
Pagnini, family, 337, 468; Michele, 431, 436
Palermo, 321
Palmieri, Matteo, 408n
Panciatichi, family, 174; Gabriello, 271n; Giovanni, 459n
Pandolfini, family, 256; Filippo, 83n, 117n, 156n
    Agnolo di Filippo, 197n, 231, 238, 246, 256, 264n, 265, 270n, 293-94, 301n, 318n, 320, 328n, 332-33, 365n, 391n, 393, 441n, 445n, 448n, 470, 505; diplomatic career of, 388-89, 391, 470; political role of, 264, 271, 286, 381-82, 505; political views of, 183, 192n, 219, 290, 293n, 307, 317, 330, 332, 352, 370-71, 374, 376, 380, 383, 386-87, 428-29, 434, 437, 440, 451, 454, 467n
Paolo di Bartolo, 90-91
Paolo di Ser Guido, 105
papacy, Avignonese, Florentine relations with, 116-17, 156. *See also* Clement VII
papacy, of the council of Pisa, 358-60,

364-66, 370-75, 380-93, 417-18. *See also* Alexander V, John XXIII
papacy, Roman, Florentine relations with, 75, 97, 103-04, 114-19, 135, 153, 157n, 159, 175, 179, 183-84, 188-94, 207, 421-25, 441, 447, 460-61, 469-70; Florentine views of, 42, 45, 104, 114-18, 123, 295-301, 315-16, 358-61, 365-66, 371-75, 421-25. *See also* Boniface IX, Gregory XII, Martin V, Urban VI
Papal States, 102, 113, 118n, 122-23, 188, 207, 227-29, 233, 239, 244, 322, 352, 370, 373, 378-80, 387, 391, 406n, 416-19, 422, 433, 441-42, 449, 469
Paris, 170, 225n
parlamento, 62, 65-66, 91, 93, 231, 288, 392
Parma, 140, 433, 436n
Parte Guelfa, 14, 16, 18, 26, 32-33, 41-42, 43n, 44, 48, 50, 55-56, 60, 64, 66, 68, 70, 72-73, 75, 79, 92n, 224, 258-59, 314, 340n, 397, 489; captains of, 14-15, 360n. *See also* Guelfism
Pavia, 96, 131-33, 163
Pazzi, family, 403; Andrea, 34, 269n, 403n, 503; Piero, 313n; Poldo, 313n
Pazzini, Tommaso, 374n
peace sentiment, in Florence, 106-07, 130-33, 137-39, 157-58, 161-63, 188, 194, 197-200, 202, 237-46, 320, 343-46, 349-51, 359, 370-71, 384-87, 426, 454, 468-70
Pecori, family, 21n; Guidaccio, 467
Perrens, François, 6
Perugia, 135, 139, 148, 166, 177, 187-90, 192, 229, 239, 244, 316, 317n, 363, 384; Florentine relations with, 113, 115, 120n, 123, 133, 149, 169-70, 185, 418
Peruzzi, family, 24, 81n, 88n, 89, 137, 139, 199, 240, 257, 268-69, 277n, 279-80, 360-61, 363, 403, 487, 492, 497, 507; Andrea, 22, 219n, 420n; Messer Antonio, 38, 312; Bartolomeo di Giotto, 67n, 68, 444, 488n; Benedetto, 49, 130n, 154n, 159, 167n, 248; Bernardo di Andrea, 28n; Bindaccio, 245; Fruosino, 66; Giotto, 243, 247, 299, 335, 386, 411, 444, 472; Giovanni, 355, 390; Ridolfo di Bonifazio, 152,

Peruzzi, family (*cont.*)
  215, 217, 245, 267n, 313n, 373n, 375n,
  387, 403n, 436, 461n, 467, 469, 479,
  487, 497n; Rinieri, 106n, 134n, 143;
  Siepe, 205; Simone, 49, 62, 72-73, 103,
  124n; Verano, 24n
Pescia, 165n
Petriboni, family, 87; Matteo di Piero,
  258; Paolo, 405n, 421, 443n, 459n;
  Pietro, 482
Petrucci, Cambio, 260n
Philip of Macedon, 455
Piacenza, 433
Piccinino, Niccolò, 460, 462, 469
Piedmont, 227
Piero di Ser Grifo, Ser, 62, 257
Pierozzi, Ser Niccolò, 124
Pietrabuona, 173
Piombino, 189, 452
Pisa, 86, 133-35, 139-40, 158, 165, 175,
  179n, 184, 187-89, 194-95, 198, 217,
  220, 226-27, 230, 234n, 291n, 297, 301,
  304, 316, 321, 332, 340, 344, 382n, 411n,
  417, 427-29, 448, 452, 505n; Florentine
  administration of, 208-09, 212-15,
  218-19, 223-25, 434-35; Florentine
  conquest of, 202-08, 219n, 319, 413;
  Florentine relations with, 120, 132,
  149, 166-68, 185, 192-93, 196, 248
Pisa, council of, 228-29, 232, 298
Pistoia, 61n, 98, 173-74, 182, 221, 224,
  344, 491
Pitti, family, 20, 84, 240, 360, 363;
  Bartolomeo di Neri, 29n, 39, 362-63;
  Luca di Buonaccorso, 245, 360n;
  Luigi di Neri, 29n, 39, 357n, 360-63,
  397-99; Neri di Piero, 362; Piero di
  Cione, 35n, 36
  Buonaccorso di Neri, 29n, 39, 55n,
  156n, 159n, 163, 196, 203n, 206n, 214n,
  217n, 262, 264, 277n, 314, 322n, 401,
  432n; diplomatic career of, 157,
  176-77, 225n, 227n, 262, 432n; political
  role of, 262-63, 359-64; political views
  of, 245, 341n, 346, 359-60, 409, 441
Pius II, pope, 292n
plague, 319, 322; of 1399, 170; of 1417,
  414; of 1423, 452n
podestà, 67, 91, 216, 308, 323, 398,
  493-94

Popolani, Tommaso, 329n, 332
Popoleschi, family, 256; Aghinolfo,
  282; Bartolomeo, 180n, 225n, 265n,
  269, 294, 344n
popolo, see guild community
popolo minuto (Ciompi), 16, 33, 42-52,
  64-71, 259-60, 292, 325-30, 349, 401-03,
  408, 457
Poppi, counts of, 33, 166, 275
Porcellini, Giovanni, 63n, 260
Por San Maria, guild of, 63n, 260
Portinari, Bernardo, 492-93
Porto Pino, 352
Porto Pisano, 225-26, 230, 235, 321, 427,
  430
Portovenere, 331-32, 341, 345-47, 352
Portugal, king of, 321n
pratiche, 51-52, 106, 124, 137-38, 264-65,
  284-302, 310-12
Prato, 61n, 142, 182, 215n, 261, 443n
prestanze, see forced loans
Provence, 228, 233, 234n, 240, 447
provvisionati, 122, 125, 154, 190-91,
  197, 230, 439
Pucci, family, 21n; Puccio, 497n
Punic Wars, 293

Quaratesi (Da Quarata), family, 171,
  271, 397; Bernardo, 232, 378; Luigi,
  128n; Sandro, 41, 397-99, 443, 468;
  Simone, 176n, 390n

Raffacani, Lorenzo, 219n, 330; Nencio,
  206
ragionerii straordinarii, 147, 170, 465
Ragusa, 96
Ramini, Piero, 473
Rapallo, 467, 469
regime, of Ciompi, 6, 8, 43-46, 53-55,
  60, 67, 70-71, 292; of 1343-78, 40; of
  1378-82, 16-17, 46-60, 473; of Walter
  of Brienne, 39-40, 139n, 291, 292n,
  298, 304, 451
Regno, see Naples, kingdom of
republicanism, Florentine, see civic
  ideology
revolution, Ciompi, 6, 8, 11-12, 16-17,
  26, 32, 39-46, 52, 63-67, 70, 71n, 139n,
  292, 314, 397

rhetoric, in political debates, 285-93, 300-02, 311, 435, 480

Ricasoli, family, 32, 93, 245, 277n, 280, 360-61, 363, 487, 492; Bettino, 273; Pandolfo, 361

Ricchi, Donato, 51, 52n, 55n

Ricci, family, 40-41, 100, 139, 173, 255, 337, 365, 397; Antonio di Bernardo, 327, 339n; Ardingo di Gucciozzo, 157-58; Giovanni, 104, 106n, 113n, 117n, 129n, 131-32, 135, 154, 167; Gucciozzo, 128, 144, 158; Messer Lorenzo, 38; Maso di Salvestro, 250; Nanni, 399n; Salvestro, 174, 248; Sanminiato, 172, 250, 259n; Uguccione, 48, 51, 149

Ricoveri, family; 20n; Agnolo di Niccolò, 96-97, 99, 151n; Ricovero, 379n

Ridolfi, Jacopo di Luca, 491; Schiatta, 265n, 437
    Messer Lorenzo di Antonio, 194n, 197, 205n, 243n, 254, 265, 346, 352n, 373n, 385n, 388n, 412n, 441n, 444, 468, 473-74, 476, 498, 506; political role of, 264, 269, 286, 294, 367, 386, 488n, 505; political views of, 179, 236-37, 292-93, 297, 306-09, 311, 314, 329, 344n, 348n, 349, 367, 374n, 380, 390-91, 399, 409, 418, 435-37, 499

rimbotto, 412, 415-16, 476-77, 480, 487n

Rimini, 179n

Rinuccini, family, 28, 86-87, 255, 258, 271, 464n; Cino, 286n; Filippo, 401n, 420; Francesco, 50, 89, 257; Simone, 258

Rittafè, Bardo, 180, 309n, 479n, 497n

Riviera, Genoese, 191, 453, 462, 467

Robert, king of Naples, 291n, 297

Romagna, 114, 149-50, 156, 166, 179, 189, 191-93, 229, 446-47, 450, 454, 457, 467, 471; Florentine relations with, 125, 151, 153-54, 179n, 182, 195, 198, 202, 230, 243, 246-47, 418, 451-53, 495-96

Rome, 4, 183-84, 227-29, 233-39, 242, 244-45, 247, 296, 369, 372, 391, 394, 402, 424, 502. *See also* papacy, Roman

Rondinelli, Andrea, 41; Rinaldo, 244n, 247n, 271, 290n, 291n, 292n, 314, 329,

330n, 332n, 335, 377, 393n, 415, 448n; Veri, 172, 298n

Rossi, family, 31, 93, 473; Betto di Messer Pino, 141; Filippo, 56n; Giovanni, 56n; Jacopo, 191n; Piero, 197; Roberto, 286, 291n, 293, 315n, 320, 362, 381-83

Rossi, family, of Parma, 190, 192-93

Rosso di Piero, 242, 269n

Rothkrug, Lionel, 15

Rucellai, family, 20n, 25, 40, 88n, 240, 255, 268, 337; Giovanni, 39, 71, 400-01; Paolo, 363n, 438; Tommaso, 240, 282; Vanni, 282; Zanobi, 243n, 328n, 390

Rupert of Bavaria, emperor-elect, 176-79, 185, 232, 291, 298

Rustichi, Betto, 196n, 359, 390n, 429n

Sacchetti, family, 279-80; Andreuolo, 280n, 481; Filippo, 280n; Forese, 22, 214n, 221-22, 279-82, 315, 332, 356n, 364, 379, 413n, 428n, 434, 438, 440n, 480; Franco, 112n, 130, 138, 143, 217, 279; Giannozzo, 279; Jacopo, 279; Niccolò, 280n, 304, 354, 356, 453, 466; Tommaso, 178, 194, 197n, 200n, 201n, 265n, 279, 280n

Saguntum, 293

S. Ambrogio, district of, 70n

S. Antonio del Vescovo, monastery of, 372n, 375

S. Apollinare, piazza of, 506

S. Croce, quarter of, 24, 62, 88, 118, 256-57, 271, 361, 405n, 487

S. Frediano, district of, 44, 69, 70n; parish of, 327

S. Gimignano, 61n, 344

S. Giovanni, quarter of, 256, 487

S. John the Baptist, feast of, 15, 42, 482

S. Lorenzo, district of, 44, 69

S. Maria in Verzaia, parish of, 327

S. Maria Novella, church of, 44, 422; quarter of, 23, 88, 256, 258n

S. Miniato, 142, 165, 172-73, 182, 301, 344, 492

S. Niccolò, parish of, 68

S. Paolo fuori le Mura, church of, 394

S. Piero Gattolino, district of, 70n

S. Reparata, cathedral of, 37

S. Spirito, quarter of, 356n

S. Stefano, church of, 473-78, 489
Salimbeni, family, 190, 195; Niccolò, 173
Sallust, 293
Salterelli, family, 21n; Andrea, 35
Salutati, Ser Bonifazio di Messer Coluccio, 412n; Messer Coluccio, 27n, 64n, 69n, 122, 139n, 169, 195, 248, 250n, 265, 284-85, 289-90, 294, 301, 315
Salvemini, Gaetano, 4, 7
Salvetti, Ser Antonio, 462n, 491n; Messer Tommaso, 491
Salviati, family, 263, 279; Alamanno, 397n, 500; Bernardo di Filippo, 491, 492n; Cambio, 469n; Filippo, 410; Forese, 113n, 127n, 133n, 188n, 197; Giovanni di Messer Forese, 25, 445n; Jacopo, 184n, 220-21, 226, 230n, 244, 246, 263-64, 286, 297; Simone, 377n
Salvini, Andrea, 177n
Salvo di Nuto, 55n, 106-07
Sambuca, 173-75, 189
Sandro di Niccolò, 17
Sapori, Armando, 4
Sarzana, 195n, 197, 225-26, 236, 241-42, 320, 345-46, 439, 448, 452
Sarzanello, 320, 341, 352
Sassetti, family, 23-24; Bernardo d'Alessandro, 24; Federigo di Pierozzo, 24; Federigo di Pollaio, 23, Fiondina di Pollaio, 23; Lena di Bernardo, 24; Letta di Federigo di Pollaio, 23; Manente di Gino, 24n; Niccolò d'Alessandro, 24; Paolo d'Alessandro, 23-24; Piero di Sassetto, 24n
Sixteen (gonfalonieri delle compagnie), 14, 16, 59, 79, 84, 112, 151, 209n, 211, 234, 236, 295, 309, 323n, 457n
Soderini, family, 278; Francesco di Messer Tommaso, 404n; Giovanni, 312, 353, 393n; Niccolò, 42; Tommaso, 172, 273, 182, 493-94
Soldani, Soldo, 146n; Tommaso, 49
Soldanieri, Filippo, 28n
Solosmei, family, 256, 257n
Spalato, 170
speculum, 459
Spini, family, 25, 27, 88n, 365; Agnolo,

265n; Messer Cristofano, 129n, 154n, 158, 163n, 168n, 187n, 188, 196n, 201, 205n, 222, 228-29, 232, 256n, 264-66, 267n, 270, 280, 297-98, 300, 332n, 334n, 335, 348, 350, 356, 358n, 373; Doffo, 317n, 419; Guglielmo, 405, 459n; Scolaio, 155n
Spinola, Agostino, 321
standard-bearer of justice (gonfalonieri di giustizia), 78
Starmine di Amideo, 17
statism, concept of, 7-8, 11, 210-12, 305-10, 484, 501
Stefaneschi, Cardinal, 421
Stefani, family, 220; Marchionne, 41, 45-46, 48, 50, 52-53, 57-58, 60, 65, 76-77, 249
Stephen of Bavaria, duke, 135, 232, 291
Stoldo di Lorenzo, 139
Strada, Donato di Jacopo, 129n; Piero, 47n
Strozzi, family, 19-21, 24, 31n, 35n, 40, 68n, 84-85, 88, 171, 240, 255, 257, 268, 337, 403-04, 486; Bernardo di Giovanni, 27-28, 86n, 87n, 339n, 443n; Carlo, 273; Currado, 20; Filippo, 100n; Francesco di Giovanni, 35n; Giovanni di Marco, 259, 339n, 441; Leonardo, 20; Lorenzo di Messer Palla, 482; Marcello, 39, 174n, 459n, 486; Marco, 304, 311-12, 330, 335, 339n, 358, 378, 489n, 506; Marco di Francesco, 21; Marco di Goro, 268n, 355; Marco di Uberto, 258; Matteo, 181, 456n; Morello, 467n; Nanni, 454; Nofri, 19, 85n, 270, 271n, 324; Nofri di Pagno, 34; Nofri di Palla, 265n, 321, 408n; Pagnozzino, 19, 24n, 84-85; Palla di Messer Palla, 466n, 497n; Palla di Novello, 457, 467; Messer Pazzino di Messer Palla, 20-21, 130, 150n, 151n, 158, 406n; Piero, 456n; Rosso, 21; Salamone, 224, 233, 240n, 244, 286, 291n, 320, 332n, 350, 352n, 353n, 354-55, 367, 386, 427, 431n, 436, 441n, 442n, 454, 457-58, 460, 466n; Simone di Biagio, 56, 218n, 222, 403n, 436n, 446n; Strozza, 28, 238n, 292, 305n, 308n, 324, 336, 357n, 368, 386n, 389, 394-95, 402, 429, 434, 459, 465;

Strozza di Rinaldo, 268n; Strozza di Rosso, 224; Tommaso, 47, 51, 53, 57-60, 65, 69, 273-74; Messer Umberto di Geri, 21

Palla di Nofri, 222n, 306n, 311n, 396, 412n, 427-28, 436, 440n, 444n, 448n, 451-53, 458, 466n; diplomatic career of, 461; economic condition of, 503; political role of, 267n; political views of, 286-87, 307n, 434, 441, 450, 456, 460-61, 464, 483, 497

Switzerland, 452-53

Talamone, 167, 196, 201, 321
tamburazioni, 309
Tanagli, Guglielmo, 455n, 467, 483-84, 488n, 497n, 499
Tarlati di Pietramala, Carlo, 275, 416
Tecchini, Niccolò, 80
Tegne, Francino, 258n
Tenenti, Alberto, 6-9
Ten on War (*war balìa*; *Dieci di balìa*), 117n, 119, 131, 133, 151, 154-57, 160, 163, 173n, 176, 178-79, 190n, 192-93, 195-96, 198, 203, 205-06, 207n, 214-15, 219, 231, 234, 243-44, 448n, 450, 454, 456-57, 462, 472n, 473-74, 476-77, 499
Terzo, Ottobuono, 189, 230n
Testinella, wool-carder, 65
Teutonic knights, 274
Tinghi, Carlo, 381n; Matteo, 134n, 163, 178, 180n, 191n, 196n, 204, 206, 227n, 233-34, 236-37, 240-42, 243n, 264n, 265n, 282, 289n, 297, 311
Tinucci, Niccolò, 494n, 500n
Todi, 113
Tolosini, Lapo, 68; Marco, 68
Tommasino di Maestro Simone, Maestro, 124
Tommaso di Giovanni da Careggi, 47, 48n, 53
Torelli, Messer Torello, 388
Tornabuoni, family, 403; Filippo, 482; Francesco di Messer Simone, 269n, 270n, 367n, 429n, 439, 444, 448, 450, 464, 503n; Niccolò, 403n; Simone, 425
Tornaquinci, family, 31, 269n, 488n; Fagina, 56n; Niccolò, 502n
Torsellini, Giovanni, 497n
Tosinghi, family, 25

tre maggiori, 254, 487n
Trent, 177
Trinci, Ugolino, 372n
Turkey, 160
Twelve (*dodici buonuomini*), 16, 212n, 215, 306, 323n, 498
Tyrrhenian Sea, 321, 341, 429

Ubaldini, family, 172n, 175; Giovanni d'Azzo, 119
Ubertini, family, 33, 263; Ubaldo, 265n, 279
Ubriachi, Baldassare, 170
uditori, 266
Ugolini, Domenico, 216
Umbria, 113-14, 149, 169, 189, 191-92, 229, 241, 373, 378, 385, 422, 439, 447
Unghero, Giovanni, 238n, 335; Nanni, 379, 420n
Urban VI, pope, 77n, 102-04, 113-19, 123, 127n, 298n, 315
Urbino, 112-14
Uzzano, family, 403; Antonio, 55n; Bernardo d'Antonio, 493; Giovanni, 278
Niccolò, 145n, 180, 199n, 201n, 205n, 223n, 266, 270, 278, 282, 308n, 368n, 381n, 389n, 398-99, 403n, 416n, 427n, 442, 447n, 450, 455, 457, 473, 474n, 477, 488n, 497; assassination plot against, 493-94; business activities of, 270; diplomatic career of, 229, 278, 392; political role of, 250-51, 264-65, 267, 278-79, 286, 294, 361, 386, 505, 507; political views of, 168, 194n, 196n, 239, 241, 243, 246-47, 277n, 278, 292n, 298, 318, 329-30, 334, 357, 358n, 387, 414n, 429, 440-41, 442n, 458

Valdarno, 344
Valdilimona, 469
Valdinievole, 221, 344, 411n
Valerius, 293
Valliala, castle of, 112n
Valori, Bartolomeo, 28n, 144, 165n, 171n, 188, 192, 199n, 202, 205n, 224, 228n, 236-37, 265, 267n, 284n, 306, 333, 361, 366, 368, 394, 409, 412n, 417n, 418, 423n, 435, 441, 444, 448n,

Valori, Bartolomeo (*cont.*)
449, 472n, 478; Niccolò di
Bartolomeo, 500, 505
Valorini, Barna, 30; Valorino, 30, 95,
443n
Vecchietti, family, 88; Giovanni d'Ugo,
24n; Jacopo, 254, 311-12, 440n, 443;
Luigi, 486n; Marsilio, 217, 226, 243,
247, 299, 310, 318n, 380n, 382-83,
386-87, 389n, 391, 393-94, 411; Ugo,
111n, 130n
Velluti, family, 21n, 36; Bernardo, 51,
52n, 55-57, 69, 259; Donato, 308n,
464; Messer Donato, 22n, 35-36;
Filippo, 36n; Gherardino di Piero, 36
Venice, 4, 100, 120, 129-30, 133, 140, 148,
164, 171, 177, 218n, 320-22, 380, 385,
430, 442, 457, 461, 496n, 501;
Florentine relations with, 135, 159,
162-63, 172, 175, 178-79, 183-84, 188,
393, 419-21, 432, 435, 441, 469-72, 475,
481; Florentine vies of, 184, 317-18,
336, 381, 393-94, 419-20, 436n, 445-46,
464, 483
Ventura, Jacopo di Francesco, 27
Vercelli, 433
Vergil, 302
Verona, 119-20, 127, 136, 139, 292, 429
Verrazzano, Amerigo da, 373n;
Antonio, 375n; Banco, 320n, 329n,
338, 341n, 355, 373n, 381, 400n;
Fruosino, 443n, 498; Papi, 281
Vespucci, family, 87; Simone, 124
Vettori, family, 268; Andrea, 132n, 177,
265n, 268n; Giovanni, 314, 386, 436,
498n; Neri, 250, 281, 326
Vicenza, 429
Vico Pisano, 204, 207
Vignate, Giovanni de', 191n, 193n
Villani, Matteo, 41, 235n, 282
Visconti, family, 126, 133, 190-93, 195,
250, 436, 497; Bernabò, lord of Milan,
64, 126, 392; Filippo Maria, lord of
Milan, 387, 393, 419, 427, 428-29,

433-37, 439-42, 446-51, 454-55, 461,
469-70, 472, 482, 496; Gabriele Maria,
lord of Pisa, 187, 198, 203-06, 225;
Giangaleazzo, lord of Milan, 12n, 78n,
85-86, 96, 101, 113, 115n, 119, 123,
125-30, 132-35, 137-42, 144-45, 148-53,
155-61, 163-71, 173, 175, 178, 183,
185, 187-88, 190, 197, 200-02, 206,
237, 246, 274-75, 291-92, 298, 300-01,
316-17, 319, 373, 382, 394, 396, 400,
421, 428, 434-35, 442, 451, 462;
Giovanni Maria, lord of Milan, 187
Viviani, Messer Francesco, 266n, 440,
454, 472, 484, 486n, 496, 497n; Ser
Viviano di Neri, 265-66, 269n
Volognano, family, 31
Volterra, 146n, 173, 304, 494-95, 505

Waley, Daniel, 10
war, Florentine, against Genoa, 241-42,
319-20, 331-33, 340-52
war, Florentine, against Lucca, 491,
493n, 494-500, 504-05
war, Florentine, against the papacy
(war of the Eight Saints), 42, 76,
102, 119, 291-92, 315
war, Florentine, against Pisa, 204-08
war, Florentine, against Siena, 128,
133-35, 189, 195-96
war, Florentine, against Urbino, 112-13
wars, Florentine, against Milan, 9,
86-87, 101, 135-44, 152-65, 175-200,
203, 245-46, 250, 288, 420, 447-70,
480-81, 495-97, 500-04. *See also*
Visconti, Filippo Maria,
Giangaleazzo
wars, Florentine, against Naples, 231-47,
288-89, 368-95, 420, 447. *See also*
Ladislaus, king of Naples
Wenceslaus, emperor-elect, 135n,
176, 420n

Zagonara, 457-58, 460, 468

Library of Congress Cataloging in Publication Data

Brucker, Gene A.
    The civic world of early Renaissance Florence.

    Includes bibliographical references and index.
        1. Florence—History—To 1421.   2. Florence—
Politics and government.   3. Florence—Social conditions.
I. Title.
DG737.26.B69   945'.51   76-45891
ISBN 0-691-05244-1